REGULATION, ENFORCEMENT AND GOVERNANCE IN ENVIRONMENTAL LAW

Richard Macrory

·H A R T·
PUBLISHING

OXFORD AND PORTLAND, OREGON
2010

Published in North America (US and Canada) by
Hart Publishing
c/o International Specialized Book Services
920 NE 58th Avenue, Suite 300
Portland, OR 97213-3786
USA
Tel: +1 503 287 3093 or toll-free: (1) 800 944 6190
Fax: +1 503 280 8832
E-mail: orders@isbs.com
Website: http://www.isbs.com

© Richard Macrory 2010

First published 2008, in Hardback only, by Cameron May.
This edition published in paperback only by Hart Publishing, 2010.

Richard Macrory has asserted his right under the Copyright, Designs and Patents Act
1988, to be identified as the author of this work.

All rights reserved. No part of this publication may be reproduced, stored in a
retrieval system, or transmitted, in any form or by any means, without the prior
permission of Hart Publishing, or as expressly permitted by law or under the
terms agreed with the appropriate reprographic rights organisation. Enquiries
concerning reproduction which may not be covered by the above should be addressed to
Hart Publishing at the address below.

Hart Publishing Ltd, 16C Worcester Place, Oxford, OX1 2JW
Telephone: +44 (0)1865 517530 Fax: +44 (0)1865 510710
E-mail: mail@hartpub.co.uk
Website: http://www.hartpub.co.uk

British Library Cataloguing in Publication Data
Data Available

ISBN: 978-1-84946-035-4

Typeset by Hope Services, Abingdon
Printed and bound in Great Britain by
CPI Antony Rowe Ltd, Chippenham, Wiltshire

FOREWORD

I am delighted to be able to contribute a Foreword to this important collection. I have been lucky to have known and worked with Richard for many years, and have admired his intellect, his energy, and his fun (including his conjuring skills). He has had a distinguished and distinctive career, and has made a unique contribution to the development of environmental law in this country and abroad. He was the first editor of the *Journal of Environmental Law*, now recognized as one of the foremost scholarly Journals of its kind in the world. He has been specialist adviser to Parliamentary Select Committees in both the Lords and Commons, a long standing member of the Royal Commission on Environmental Pollution, and a board member of the Environment Agency, England and Wales. He was a founding member and first chairman of the UK Environmental Law Association which continues to thrive, and of which I am privileged to be the President. All this has been combined with practice at the Bar, and a brilliant academic career. He was the first Professor of Environmental Law in this country, and is now Director of the Centre for Law and the Environment at University College, London.

Regulation, Enforcement and Governance in Environmental Law is a selection of some of his most important writings and is focused on major themes concerning the nature of regulation, institutional arrangements, and enforcement. Richard's combination of serious scholarship and extensive experience in the world of environmental policy and regulation make this a particularly significant collection. It starts from his first article published in the *New Law Journal* some thirty years ago (a characteristic reflection on the law concerning bicycles – still relevant today), and brings the story right up to date, with the full text of his 2006 Cabinet Office Review on Regulatory Sanctions. His analysis and recommendations in this Review laid the basis for the core provisions in the Regulatory Enforcement and Sanctions Act 2008. They should have a profound effect on the way we think about regulatory sanctions in this country, far beyond the field of environmental law. The value of his work in this area is already being recognized in other countries.

This book should be essential reading for anyone concerned with the development of environmental law and policy. I hope also that it will be read by the next generation of environmental lawyers. They will be facing profound environmental challenges, which will undoubtedly require fresh legal solutions. The material in this collection will stand not only as a record of remarkable achievement, but as an inspiration for innovative thinking in the future.

Sir Robert Carnwath, Lord Justice of Appeal
and Senior Presidents of Tribunals
London
May 2009

TABLE OF CONTENTS

Foreword   7

Part I Regulatory Reform   9

1   Reforming Regulatory Sanctions   17
2   Regulatory Justice: Making Sanctions Effective   35
3   Regulating in a Risky Environment   155

Part II Institutional Reform and Change   181

4   The Environment and Constitutional Change   189
5   Modernising Environmental Justice: Regulation and the Role
    of an Environmental Tribunal   209
6   Trust and Transparency: Reshaping Environmental
    Governance in Northern Ireland   263

Part III The Dynamics of Environmental Law   349

7   Environmental Law: Shifting Discretions and the
    New Formalism   353
8   Loaded Guns and Monkeys: Responsible Environmental Law   367
9   Environmental Standards, Legitimacy, and Social Justice   393
10 Technology and Environmental Law Enforcement   403
11 The Scope of Environmental Law   421
12 Cycle Lore   433

Part IV The Courts and the Environment   439

13 European Court of Justice   441
14 House of Lords   477
15 Court of Appeal   503
16 High Court   519

Part V Europe and the Environment   545

17 The Amsterdam Treaty: An Environmental Perspective   553
18 The Legal Duty of Environmental Integration: Commitment
    and Obligation or Enforceable Right?   567
19 Environmental Citizenship and the Law – Repairing the
    European Road   585
20 Balancing Trade Freedom with the Requirements of
    Sustainable Development   607
21 Subsidiarity and European Community Environmental Law   649

22 Participatory Rights, Transboundary Environmental
    Governance and EC Law   661
23 Underlying Themes in the Policy Process   697

Part VI Supra-national enforcement of environmental law   711

24 Compliance Mechanisms in the European Community –
    A Global Model   713
25 The Enforcement of EU Environmental Law: Some Proposals
    for Reform   723
26 The Enforcement of Community Environmental Law: Some
    Critical Issues   735

Index   755
About the Author   766

PREFACE

Laws concerning environmental protection have a long history in the United Kingdom, but the last thirty years have seen an unprecedented development in both the substantive body of environmental legislation and in thinking about underlying principles and institutional arrangements. To the current generation of environmental lawyers it is almost unimaginable how rapid the change in profile of the subject has been in such a comparatively short time. My own exposure to environmental law began as a newly qualified barrister working for Friends of the Earth in London in the mid 1970s, then the only UK environmental group which employed a lawyer. Legal actions before the courts at that time seemed a fruitless and costly activity, and most of the legal effort was focused on pressuring Government for legislative reform and using public inquiries in the planning field as a forum for exposing the inadequacies and short-sightedness of government policy in addressing longer term environmental issues. Shortly afterwards I began my first academic appointment at Imperial College, London, consciously working with environmental scientists who then appeared to offer a more sympathetic intellectual environment than traditional law schools where the discipline of environmental law was scarcely acknowledged. I well remember meeting at this time a fairly intimidating Law Lord of the old school (and now long deceased) who asked me my field of specialism. I naturally replied environmental law, only to be faced with silence and an expression that somehow combined utter incomprehension and slight distaste.

The materials in this book should at least demonstrate what a long way we have come in less than a generation. In making a selection of my publications, I have largely avoided any analyses of detailed black letter law, but focused on material dealing with major themes concerning the nature of regulation, institutional arrangements, and enforcement which underlie the substantive detail of the law. Whilst acknowledging the growing importance of public international law relating to the environment, my concerns are mainly with UK and European Community law, though many of the core themes have much wider relevance.

Chapter I is concerned with major issues concerning regulatory reform, and in particular the debates on whether traditional British approaches towards constructing regulatory sanctions are best suited to contemporary needs. Chapter 2 considers challenges to current institutional arrangements, including the need for a specialised environmental court and tribunal, and the environmental implications of the major constitutional changes that have taken place in the United Kingdom in the last decade. Chapter 3 contains material that reflects on the shifting dynamics of environmental law as it copes with changing expectations of how we handle the development of new environmental standards, the opportunities of new technologies to assist enforcement, and the need to develop new notions of responsibility. Chapter 4 is a selection of reports of leading environmental cases over the last decade illustrating how both the European Court of Justice and the higher courts in the United Kingdom have grappled with the interpretation of environmental legislation and the development of legal principle. The final two chapters focus on European dimensions. Chapter 5 is largely concerned with key principles of European Community law such as environmental integration, free trade, and subsidiarity and how these influence and interact with the development of environmental law. The final chapter considers the enforcement of Community environmental law and the unique though by no means perfect mechanisms that have been developed under the Treaty to ensure that Member States comply with their obligations.

The scale and scope of environmental issues which face both this country and the world become ever more apparent. Law and legislation on their own cannot possibly resolve all these challenges, but will provide the bedrock for the decisions that will have to be made. As we move from handling more familiar environmental pressures to major questions of resource and energy use, the next generation of environmental lawyers will need to be even more imaginative in devising appropriate legal responses. I hope that some of the thoughts here will assist in stimulating these future debates.

I am grateful to Martin Hession, Sharon Turner, and Michael Woods who were co-authors on a number of the pieces reproduced here, and would like to thank Ned Westaway of the UCL Centre for Law and the Environment, Deborah Burns of the Law Faculty, Richard Hart and Rachel Turner of Hart Publishing for their assistance in the production of the book.

Richard Macrory
University College
May 2009

PART I
REGULATORY REFORM

PART I

REGULATORY REFORM

Contemporary environmental law is dominated by regulatory controls. Before the industrial revolution, legal protection for the environment in the United Kingdom largely rested on the availability of common law legal remedies such as the action in nuisance which could be employed by private landowners to protect their property from pollution and other forms of environmental degradation. Private legal remedies can still be of significance, but by the mid-nineteenth century Parliament and government had recognised the weaknesses of wholesale reliance on private legal action as a means of environmental protection. Individuals may not have the stamina or resources to engage in legal action. Private litigation requires the identification of a defendant who clearly caused the damage, and is ill suited where there are multiple potential contributors, or where pollution is diffuse. Where the environment concerned falls outside private ownership (such as wild animals, the atmosphere, public waters), the common law may simply provide no protection. Above all, such remedies are ill suited to ensuring preventative action or the gradual improvement of protective measures and behaviour.

The need for intervention by the State in the form of regulatory requirements concerning the environment therefore became apparent, and is now a familiar element of contemporary legal machinery.

Regulation in the environmental field can take many forms – from the imposition of fixed product standards such as vehicle emission requirements, the requirement of a licence or permit for particular activities, with detailed conditions set by the authorisation body, to various types of trading emission regimes. **Reforming Regulatory Sanctions** *(2007) and* **Regulatory Justice – Making Sanctions Effective** *(2006) are not dealing with evaluating the different types of regulatory regime as such, but instead are focused on the sanctions that are available where regulatory requirements are breached. Regulation of economic enterprises almost by definition is needed where the market cannot be relied upon by itself to achieve the policy goals desired by society, and an ineffective enforcement and sanctioning regime will undermine a regulatory system. It does not follow that a policy of no tolerance and excessive punishment is necessarily the most effective means to ensure compliance, and most modern regulators dealing with legitimate businesses sensibly adopt enforcement policies based on advice and persuasion in the first place, and* *preserving formal legal sanctions for more serious or repetitive breaches where persuasion has had little effect.*

One of the distinctive features of UK environmental law, present for over 100 years, has been the prevalence of the criminal law as the dominant formal legal sanction. In nearly every area of environmental regulation, breach of a regulation is made a criminal offence. Many environmental regulators have the power to serve a formal notice or enforcement order requiring compliance within a specified period, but breach of the notice is also sanctioned by a criminal offence. Mainstream criminal law generally requires evidence of intention or recklessness before an offence is committed, but in the regulatory field offences have commonly been drafted in terms such that the mere act of the breach is sufficient to secure conviction. Offences can be committed even where the immediate cause of the breach was the action of a trespasser or the event was caused by an unforeseen accident, as the 1998 decision of the House of Lords in Empress Cars demonstrates[1]. The so-called strict liability offence clearly reduces the evidential burden on the prosecutor and was developed in the nineteenth century when enforcement bodies were considered to lack the capability to investigate the internal complexities of business operations. An added advantage for the prosecutor is that a company can be readily convicted of such an offence where the breach was caused by the action or inaction of one of its employees, or failures of equipment or other systems. In contrast, where intention or recklessness is an ingredient of an offence, a company can generally only be convicted where a senior manager or director has shown such intention or recklessness.

The system is a tough one, though not unique to the United Kingdom[2]. In theory inappropriate application should be moderated by the discretion of the enforcement body in deciding whether or not to prosecute for a particular breach in the first place, and if a case reaches court in the sentencing practice of the courts that should reflect the perceived culpability of the defendant. Yet there remains intense academic debate on the justification and theory of strict liability offences.[3] But in the environmental field there was also increasing public debate in the 1990s in the United Kingdom as to the effectiveness of the ordinary criminal courts in handling such regulatory offences. Bodies such as the Environment Agency responsible for the enforcement of key areas of environmental law such as industrial pollution control, water management,

---

[1] *Environment Agency (formerly National Rivers Authority) v Empress Car Company (Abertillery) Ltd* [1998] 1 All ER 481 - see chapter 4

[2] See Faure and Heine (2005) *Criminal Enforcement of Environmental Law in the European Union* The Hague, Kluwer Law International. Within Europe, criminal liability of corporations is also familiar in Denmark, France, and the Netherlands and more recently Belgium and Finland. Concepts of criminal law do not allow for criminal liability of corporations in countries such as Austria, Germany, Italy, and Spain.

[3] For a recent study see Simester (ed) (2005) *Appraising Strict Liability*, Oxford University Press.

and waste controls, have criticised the apparent low level of fines handed down by magistrates' courts when cases reached them. Legitimate companies who complied with regulatory requirements had sometimes felt that competitors were making money from non-compliance or that where they had breached regulatory requirements through an oversight or accident they were being unfairly lumped together with the truly criminal. In a significant public lecture, 'Are the Judiciary Environmentally Myopic?'[4], the then Lord Chief Justice, Lord Woolf, called for the creation of a single specialist environmental court to handle criminal, civil, and administrative issues arising from breaches of environmental law. This gave rise to a number of studies and reports concerning the possible creation and functions of specialist environmental courts and tribunals, discussed further in part II.

Those considering reforms to the UK systems of environmental sanctions were well aware that many other jurisdictions, both in common law and continental countries, used a wider range of sanctions beyond simply criminal conviction. The US Environmental Protection Agency, for example, makes extensive use of administrative penalties, with the Department of Justice using criminal prosecutions for the most serious breaches.[5] German law has also long used administrative penalties as a core sanction for regulatory offences. Powerful critiques were made for the need for extending the range of sanctions available to British environmental regulators.[6] Regulators need enforcement measures that are both efficient in terms of using the minimum of scarce regulatory resources, and effective in terms of deterrence.[7] Yet one of the most difficult challenges for those in the environmental field seeking a change in traditional approaches was the question why should environmental regulation be treated so differently from other forms of regulation? With the exception of the regulation of the financial sector, the use of the criminal law as the core formal legal sanction permeates nearly every of regulation from trading standards to health and safety and food regulation. Arguments could be made that distinguish the environment from other fields of regulation,[8] but they were not wholly convincing, or at least sufficiently compelling to ensure political backing for a legislative change.

Enter the Hampton Review. The Review, led by Sir Philip Hampton, was commissioned by the Treasury to examine the relationship between regulators and the regulated community, and encompassed over 60 national regulators as

[4] Woolf (1991) 'Are the Judiciary Environmentally Myopic?' *Journal of Environmental Law*, Vol 4 No 1 pp 1-14.

[5] See Mushal (2007) 'Reflections upon American Environmental Enforcement Experience as it may Relate to Post-Hampton Developments in England and Wales' *Journal of Environmental Law* Vol 19 No 2 pp 201-226

[6] see, for example, Ogus and Abbott (2002) 'Sanctions for Pollution - Do We Have the Right Regime?' *Journal of Environmental Law* Vol 14 No 3 pp 283-300

[7] Gunningham (2002) 'Regulating Small and Medium Sized Enterprises' *Journal of Environmental Law* Vol 14 No 1 pp 3-32

[8] see *Modernising Environmental Justice* in part. II

well as local government. His final Report, published in 2005,[9] recognised the importance of regulation but identified unnecessary burdens on industry in terms of an excessive number of regulators, and overlapping inspections and data requirements. Hampton advocated that regulators should avoid a 'tick-box' mentality towards enforcement, and should adopt a stronger risk based approach that focused resources on where they would have greatest impact, and keeping the need for securing outcomes at the forefront of their enforcement strategy. To be fair, regulators such as the Environment Agency had already begun implementing such an approach, but Hampton found that generally there were inconsistencies in practice across the board. Hampton advocated advice and persuasion as the first approach towards securing compliance, but recognised the underlying importance of an effective sanction regime. He was concerned that over-reliance on the criminal law often appeared to lead to disproportionate results, and recommended that government initiate a special Review that focused on the issue of sanctions.

*I was commissioned by the Cabinet Office in 2005 to lead that Review, with the final Report published in 2006. **Reforming Regulatory Sanctions** (2007) is a revised version of the 2007 Brodies Environment Lecture, and contains a broad analysis of the context of my Review but with a particular focus on its implications for the enforcement of environmental law in this country. I noted that historically significant environmental reforms have often come about from what Lord Ashby, the first chairman of the Royal Commission on Environmental Pollution, described as an 'ignition' event – some well publicised environmental scandal or disaster. But major changes can also occur from what I describe in the paper as an unexpected alignment – in this case there were two such alignments: the Treasury-led Hampton Review driven out of concern of excessive regulatory burdens on industry, and, quite unconnected, a major reform taking place to the Tribunal system.*

***Regulatory Justice – Making Sanctions Effective** (2006) is the text of the final Report of the Review. The Review's remit, as was Hampton's, went well beyond the field of environmental regulation and covered some 61 national regulators as well as local government. The financial regulators and the economic regulators of privatised utilities were not within the scope of the Review, though we had extensive discussions with these regulators since generally they possessed sanctioning powers under modern legislation which were not so dependent on the criminal law. In examining such a wide range of laws and regulatory practice, it would have been all too easy to sink in a morass of detail, and it therefore seemed sensible to articulate a set of general penalty principles which should underline the design of a regulatory sanctions regime. These provide a basis for critiquing the adequacy of the present system, and for assessing any proposed reforms. Perhaps the two key principles were*

---

[9] *Reducing Administrative Burdens: Effective Inspection and Enforcement* H M Treasury, March 2005

that first a sanctioning regime should not be designed to punish per se (though sometimes punishment was necessary) but to ensure that the offending business was brought back into compliance, and second, that an effective regime should ensure that no economic gains are made from non-compliance.

Against those principles, the present system was found wanting. The Review did not deny the importance of the criminal law in dealing with certain types of regulatory offender, and made suggestions for improving the criminal system, including extending the range of sanctions available to criminal courts. But it concluded that essentially we were asking a criminal offence to do much work in this area. The single criminal sanction had to handle both the truly egregious 'rogue' trader as well as legitimate businesses who through oversight or carelessness breached regulations but in circumstances that required more than simply a warning or caution. There was a real danger that the stigma of the criminal law was being devalued by being overused. So it was necessary to propose that regulators had a far richer range of sanctions, including the use of administrative penalties without the necessary intervention of a criminal court, and the use of enforceable undertakers offered by the offending business.

During the Consultation, it became clear that while many recognised the attractiveness of this direction, there was equal concern that it would give even greater sanctioning discretion to regulators with a real danger that the powers could be abused, or used oppressively. As a consequence, governance issues concerning regulators assumed far greater importance during the development of the Review and form a major plank of the final Report. For example, the choice of sanction should always be determined by the core penalty principles rather than extraneous factors or perverse incentives such as internal targets. The revenue from many administrative penalties should never go directly to the regulator, even if ring-fenced for enforcement. Regulators need to act transparently as to the use of their sanctioning powers, and to provide regular reports of their use set against outcomes.

Gratifyingly, the Government accepted all the recommendations in the Report. The Regulatory Enforcement and Sanctions Act 2008 is intended to provide a core framework of administrative sanctions which can be drawn down by secondary legislation to specific areas of regulation. Other recommendations, such as those dealing with the criminal law and restorative justice, will be pursued separately. Many of the specific sanction proposals in the Review are not totally novel. They have been used in the financial sector in this country, and have been applied in countries such as Canada and Australia in regulatory fields such as the environment and health and safety at work. But the setting of the sanctions within a clear set of principles together with the emphasis on issues of regulatory governance does appear to be new, and the

Report is increasingly being well received in jurisdictions outside the United Kingdom.

Regulating in a Risky Environment *(2002), based on my inaugural lecture at University College in 2001, is focused on environmental regulation, but goes beyond the issue of enforcement and sanctions, and considers the nature and justification of environmental regulation as such. Over the last decade or so, direct regulation of the traditional type has been subjected to intense criticism as stifling innovation and being inefficient. There were powerful advocates of alternative, market based solutions, such as trading regimes and voluntary agreements. My analysis acknowledged that the varied and unpredictable nature of contemporary environmental challenges had of necessity seen the development of a whole new range of policy instruments in place of more conventional regulatory approaches. Yet, I was equally concerned that the division between so-called regulatory and non-regulatory approaches did not stand up to scrutiny. Fiscal taxes are equally a form of regulation. Emissions trading regimes need underpinning regulatory structures to ensure confidence in the market, albeit one of a different nature than those traditionally used. Even the term 'command and control' so often used to disparage traditional regulation was over-simplistic, and I advocated the more nuanced concept of 'determine and direct' to reflect contemporary regulatory challenges. Regulation comes in many forms, and new forms of regulatory instrument should be considered with an open mind. But it is important that their use is subjected to the same level of rigorous scrutiny for effectiveness and efficiency as would be applied to more traditional forms of regulation. Equally, it seemed to me – and still does – that their development should avoid sacrificing the qualities of transparency, accountability, and enforceability inherent in more formal legal structures.*

CHAPTER 1

REFORMING REGULATORY SANCTIONS[1]

Lord Ashby was a distinguished scientist and first chairman of the Royal Commission on Environmental Pollution in the early 1970s. One of his concerns was how major advances in environmental policy took place. The Royal Commission was and remains concerned with the rational and detached analysis of environmental issues and their policy solutions. But however convincing its approach, that was not necessarily sufficient to win political support for legislative change. Ashby considered that generally there had also to be what he described as an ignition event before such change would take place. An ignition event on its own was likely to lead to a knee jerk political reaction and often ill considered laws. It was only when this was combined with a pre-existing and well thought out analysis that truly effective changes in environmental law and policy took place.

Two examples in the development of British environmental law can be given that will illustrate his hypothesis. Smoke and the burning of coal was the curse of the British urban environment since the nineteenth century. The causes and the policy solutions were understood, and indeed draft legislation had been prepared since the early 1900s but nothing happened[2]. It was only with the ignition event of the Great London Smog of 1952 that saw the first Clean Air Act four years later. The second example concerns waste disposal. During the 1950 and 1960s there was no specialised law regulating the disposal of waste in Britain. Land use planning controls and reactive statutory nuisance controls provided the core legal controls, but their unsuitability for dealing with the complexities of modern waste management issues was well recognised by the late 1960s.[3] Experts committees had recommended what need to be done to fill the legislative gap, but again nothing happened. Again it needed the ignition event of the well publicised illegal dumping of waste contain cyanide near schools in the Midlands in the early 1970 to force the pace. Stop gap waste legislation[4] was passed

---

[1] A revised version of the 2007 Tercentenary Brodies Environmental Law Lecture, delivered at the University of Edinburgh, March 2007

[2] For a lucid history, see Ashby and Anderson (1981) *The Politics of Clean Air* Oxford University Press

[3] See, for example, 'Disposal of Solid Toxic Wastes' Report of the Technical Committee on the Disposal of Toxic Solid Wastes. Ministry of Housing & Local Government and Scottish Development Dept. London, HMSO

[4] Deposit of Poisonous Wastes Act 1972

within three days, and formed the foundation of the first bespoke waste management regulation system under Part I Control of Pollution Act 1974.

An ignition event might always suggest some sort of environmental catastrophe or major pollution scandal. But I think there is another sort of ignition that can take place and which can also provide the impetus for profound change. I would call this the *unexpected alignment*. By this I mean the quite fortuitous concurrence of a number of distinct drivers for policy and legislative change, each of which in themselves might be insufficient but which in combination provide a powerful impetus. I will use one of the Royal Commission's own reports to illustrate this. The Commission's Fifth report published in 1976[5] was initially concerned with the relationship of land use planning and air pollution control. The motivation for the study was some well documented *cause célèbres* involving poorly sited smelters causing local air pollution and where the then regulator, the central government Alkali Inspectorate, though technically highly competent, was failing to address contemporary concerns for greater transparency and public engagement. As often happens with a Commission study, detailed investigation of one issue throws up other problems. The Commission found itself examining how Britain regulated emissions from industrial processes generally, and was greatly concerned at the number of different regulatory agencies dealing with air emissions, water pollution and waste disposal under distinct legislation and with little coordination. As the Commission noted,

> Unless an industrial pollutant can be eliminated as opposed to being transformed, it must be disposed of elsewhere. It is sensible that the form and medium of disposal should be chosen to ensure the least environmental damage overall. This optimisation obviously calls for co-operation between the controlling authorities and we were surprised to find from our enquiries that there appears at present to be virtually none.[6]

The Commission called for the creation of single unified pollution inspectorate to regulate all emissions from key industrial processes. It would operate an integrated permit system and apply the criterion of the best practicable environmental option to determine to best solution. The Commission's recommendations are not binding, and the belated Government response was that the analysis was compelling but that it

---

[5] Royal Commission on Environmental Pollution (1976) 'Air Pollution Control – An Integrated Approach' Fifth Report Cmnd. 6371 London, HMSO.
[6] ibid, para 265

did not relish institutional reorganisation[7]. Instead, it advocated greater cooperation between the existing regulatory bodies, a solution the Commission had considered but rejected. That was in 1975 and nothing happened for a decade. In 1984, the Commission in its 10th Report[8] criticised the Government's advocacy of a pragmatic and cooperative approach – 'the danger, as we see it, is that such extreme open-mindedness and pragmatism may, in the absence of a more positive lead, generate much discussion but lead to little practical outcome'.[9] Essentially everyone knew the current arrangements were sub-optimal, but there was no ignition event in the sense of some environmental catastrophe, or major breakdown in the regulatory machinery, sufficient to ensure the issue was high on the political agenda.

But in 1986 an unexpected alignment occured. The Enterprise and Deregulation Unit of the Cabinet Office published a study concerning business regulation[10] and felt that the number of pollution permits and consents businesses had to obtain to operate from different regulators was inefficient and an excessive bureaucratic burden on industry. It called for a one stop consent system and a single inspectorate. The analysis and motives were not driven by environmental imperatives but purely on the need to reduce administrative burdens on business. But the unexpected alignment with the Royal Commission's previous analysis conducted from an environmental perspective was the push that was needed. Shortly afterwards the Government created a unified pollution inspectorate, and 1990 saw legislation creating the first integrated pollution control system with a single consent covering emissions into air and water and onto land from prescribed industrial processes,[11] with the best practicable environmental option as the core underlying concept for decision making. This is not the place for an exploration of the effectiveness of the new system, the struggle to find robust methodologies for determining BPEO, and indeed the missed opportunities. But it was undoubtedly an important step change in how we approach pollution regulation, and one that later heavily influenced the development of the EC Directive on Integrated Pollution and Prevention Control, which has now succeeded Integrated Pollution

---

[7] Department of the Environment (1982) 'Air Pollution Control' Pollution Paper No 18 London ,HMSO.

[8] Royal Commission on Environmental Pollution (1984) *Tackling Pollution – Experience and Prospects* Tenth Report Cmnd. 9149 London ,HMSO

[9] ibid, para 3.32

[10] Cabinet Office (1986) Efficiency Scrutiny Report. 'Inspecting Industry: Pollution and Safety' Cabinet Office London: HMSO. For a general background see see O'Riordan and Weale (1989) 'Administrative Reorganisation and Policy Change : The Case of Her Majesty's Inspectorate of Pollution' *Public Administration* Vol 67 Issue 3

[11] Part I Environmental Protection Act 1990. Her Majesty's Inspectorate of Pollution was later subsumed into the Environment Agency under the Environment Act 1995.

Control. In this context, the significant aspect of the environmental reforms that took place was that, as with the examples of clean air and waste, there was already a pre-existing powerful analysis of the policy problem before the unexpected alignment took place.

I am going to focus on the way that we have treated sanctions for breaches of environmental law in this country. For at least a decade there has been growing concern about the effectiveness of our existing sanctions and the legal and institutional arrangements within which they operate. Under-enforcement, low fines in the courts, and a judiciary that is often unfamiliar with the detailed complexities and dynamics of modern environmental regulation. Despite all the analyses and recommendations, nothing substantially changed. And it is difficult to locate an ignition event that would force a major policy shift. There are well publicised cases of apparently poor sanctions – for example, an Oxfordshire man fined £30,000 for dumping 184 drums of toxic waste. He had been paid £58,000 for doing so, and it cost the waste authorities £167,000 to incinerate them properly.[12] But these sparks were not sufficient to catch light.

But now through quite unexpected and fortuitous alignments of different concerns – and two strands in particular – which were quite unconnected with the environmental agenda we may be on a cusp on a sanctions revolution. One that in a decade hence might see the criminal courts focused on real environmental crimes, imaginative and effective sentencing techniques, the use of far more effective economic sanctions dealing with legitimate businesses who fail to comply with regulatory requirements, and a specialised environmental tribunal providing sophisticated and responsive judgments in environmental matters.

For the last 10 years there have been reports and articles written about the apparent low level of fines in the magistrates' courts dealing with environmental offences. The Court of Appeal has issued guidelines urging a tougher approach. Nevertheless, the Environment Agency and SEPA have continued to argue that sentencing is often insufficiently robust. Other methods of bringing pressure to bear have been developed – notably the publication of annual 'naming and shaming' league tables of fines, itself a controversial matter, and something incidentally that would be disallowed in Germany where stronger privacy laws protect the naming of companies even where they have been sanctioned for a regulatory breach.

---

[12] Quoted at para 2.6 in 'Regulatory Justice: Sanctioning in a Post-Hampton World' Consultation Document of the Macrory Review of Regulatory Sanctions May 2006 Better Regulation Executive, Cabinet Office

At the same time there have been calls for the development of a specialised environmental court system. 15 years ago Lord Justice Woolf in a notable lecture entitled 'Are the Judiciary Environmentally Myopic?'[13] called for the creation of a specialised court that would adopt an integrated approach to an environmental pollution incident, handling in one court criminal, civil, judicial review and regulatory matters. This was followed by a major study by Professor Malcolm Grant, then of Cambridge University, which was commissioned by the Department of the Environment.[14] He was asked to examine various environmental courts and tribunals in other parts of the world – notably Sweden, New South Wales, and New Zealand, and tasked with identifying various models that might be adopted in this country, but without firm recommendations. His report had all the virtues and weaknesses of an academic study – comprehensive, detached, and analytical, but immensely long and with too many options for politicians to make a clear choice. Although many environmental groups continued to argue for a 'big bang' solution to create an environmental court, it was clear that there was no political appetite for such a radical initiative – and as with any major institutional change, costs and benefits loomed large.

Enter the Royal Commission on Environmental Pollution again. In 2002 it presented its 23rd Report entitled 'Environmental Planning'.[15] In some way this was a throw-back to the 5th Report on air pollution in that it was concerned with the relationship of land use planning and environmental protection, but now dealing with a raft of new environmental policies and regulations, new institutional bodies, and a much wider perspective than simply pollution, covering all aspects of environmental protection from habitat protection to climate change. Tucked away in the chapter entitled 'Strengthening Public Confidence' was a section concerning environmental courts and tribunals[16]. The Commission noted the previous calls for single environmental courts, but felt that there was no compelling case for reforming judicial review arrangements. Equally, whilst it recognised the need to strengthen the criminal system, it did not feel it sensible to transfer environmental crimes to a new court. But where it did see a great deal of inconsistency at present were the arrangements for handling various administrative appeals under environmental regulations. Land use planning appeals have long been handled by a planning inspectorate, but when it came

---

[13] Woolf (1991) 'Are the Judiciary Environmentally Myopic?' *Journal of Environmental Law*, Vol 4 No 1 pp 1-14.

[14] Grant (2000) 'Environmental Court Project' Final Report Dept of Environment, Transport and the Regions.

[15] Royal Commission on Environmental Pollution (2002) *Environmental Planning* Twenty-third Report Cm 5459 , London, HMSO.

[16] paras 5.30-5.39, ibid.

to appeals under environmental regulations such as waste licensing, contaminated land, or packaging regulations there seemed a great deal of confusion. Some went to the planning inspectorate, some to the county court or magistrates' courts, some to the Secretary of State. The Commission recommended the establishment of an environmental tribunal to consolidate all these appeals, and bring greater expertise and consistency to the area. A recommendation that was less dramatic perhaps than a new environmental court but one that merited examination.

The Royal Commission was not able to investigate the subject, but a year later the Centre for Law and the Environment at UCL was commissioned by DEFRA to examine the case for such a tribunal in more detail.[17] We examined over 50 different appeal provisions in current legislation and confirmed the lack of apparent consistency.

We looked at possible ways of improving adapting existing appeal bodies but felt that the establishment of a dedicated tribunal was the best way forward, both for dealing with existing and future environmental laws. Setting up a new tribunal is a costly and complex business, and we tried to estimate the likely number of appeals there would and what this would cost, using the Lands Tribunal as a model – probably around £2m a year. Much more difficult was to determine whether this would bring economic benefits though one could quantify time saved from transfers from existing bodies.

There were two main challenges though. First, looking at the number of appeals on regulatory matters, it was quite difficult to be sure of the 500 or so appeals which seemed the sort of figure needed to warrant a new tribunal. We raised in the report the possibility of introducing civil penalties for environmental offences where appeals might also be routed to the proposed tribunal. This was not simply a way of boosting business for a new tribunal. For some years I have been interested in the question of environmental sanctions – how, for instance, the US Environmental Protection Agency largely relied on administrative penalties as a method of enforcement, avoiding the use of the courts and in this country similar methods used and available in fields such as competition law and economic regulation but never applied generally in the context of the environmental field.

The issue of civil penalties as a possible enforcement tool in for environmental regulations was examined in more detail in a further

---

[17] Macrory and Woods (2003) *Modernising Environmental Justice : Regulation and the Role of an Environmental Tribunal* Centre for Law and the Environment, University College, London. See Chapter 2 where the Report is reproduced.

study commissioned by DEFRA[18]. The second major intellectual challenge was to face the question if the environment, why not other areas of regulation? Was the environment so really different from say health and safety regulation, or trading standards, or food safety? As a good advocate I constructed what seemed to me a reasonably compelling case why environmental regulation did indeed have distinctive characteristics warranting special treatment.[19]

Seven features characterised much of contemporary environmental law – complex scientific and technical issues, often featuring underlying scientific uncertainties; a challenging and rapidly developing legislative and policy base; overlapping remedies in criminal, civil, and public law; a powerful and increasing body of European legislation, together with jurisprudence from the European Court of Justice; a substantial body of international environmental treaties; the development of fundamental environmental principles such as the precautionary principle and the polluters pay which need to be understood by courts or tribunals; the emergence of principles concerning public participation and access by the public to legal remedies, epitomised by the Aarhus Convention[20]; and finally, the emergence of the overarching principle of sustainable development which underpins contemporary policy approaches – a challenging concept with contestable interpretations but one which nevertheless a court or tribunal needs to be familiar with. Individually many of these features will be found in other areas of regulatory law, but it was their combination which appeared distinctive in the field of environmental law, and which posed particular challenges for conventional judicial bodies. The argument for distinctiveness and a specialist approach did not find favour in all quarters.[21], and at times it felt like special pleading.

Nevertheless, the report on environmental tribunals was well received by DEFRA and others, and provided valuable groundwork. But it was not as dramatic and therefore perhaps politically less exciting than

---

[18] Woods and Macrory (2004) 'Environmental Civil Penalties – A More Proportionate Response to Regulatory Breach' Centre for Law and the Environment, University College, London

[19] *Modernising Environmental Justice*, op.cit. paras 8.1-82

[20] Convention on Access to Information, Public Participation in Decision making and Access to Justice in Environmental Matters 1988

[21] see, for example the 2006 Consultation Document of the Scottish Government at para 2.99 : 'We acknowledge the special characteristics listed by Macrory and Woods and accept that they are features of environmental law. However, we are not persuaded that these features, or indeed this combination of features is unique to environmental law and it could be argued that similar statements could be made equally about other areas of law such as health, health & safety and employment none of which have specialist courts/jurisdiction ' *Strengthening And Streamlining: The Way Forward for the Enforcement of Environmental Law in Scotland* , Scottish Government, November 2006

proposals for a full-blown environmental court. And some months later, another study[22] which had also been commissioned by DEFRA rejected this model as insufficiently radical and called for a new environmental court. The Government, faced with apparent competing views even within the environmental law community felt justified in not proposing any significant institutional reform.

At this stage, I thought the political momentum for any reform had now passed, and there was unlikely to be a dramatic ignition event of the sort described by Ashby – such a series of scandalously poor decisions by the planning inspectorate. But enter the first of the two unexpected alignments. In 2004 the Treasury commissioned Philip Hampton, now chairman of Sainsburys, to conduct a review of administrative burdens on business in the regulatory field. The Hampton Report,[23] *Effective Inspection and Enforcement*, published in 2005 was not motivated by environmental concerns but more on how to regulate more sensibly, and reduce inappropriate burdens on legitimate business.

Hampton was particularly concerned at the large number of different regulatory bodies – at national level and outside the economic field over 60 different national regulators – and recommended the integration a large number of these bodies. But he was equally concerned at the extent to which many regulators appeared to following a rather tick-box approach to enforcement, and advocated a much stronger risk based approach. In essence this meant using limited resources more wisely, and focusing on the difficult and recalcitrant businesses rather than carrying out inspection for its own sake. Hampton certainly was not against regulation, nor did he want lighter sanctions. But he was concerned with evidence of the slow processes of criminal courts coupled with often apparently light fines which did not appear to reflect economic gains made from non-compliance and was unfair to legitimate businesses. He advocated quicker and tougher penalties. Nevertheless, he recognised that the whole issue of sanctions raised complex legal and institutional questions which he was unable to explore fully in his Review, and recommended that the Government initiated a further review focused on sanctions for regulatory offences.

This was when I was invited to conduct the sanctions review in 2005[24], a sort of son of Hampton. In terms of policy advance, one of the real benefits of the Hampton approach was the ability to stand back and

---

[22] 'Environmental Justice' Environmental Law Foundation, World Wildlife Fund, and Leigh Day and Co, March 2004

[23] P Hampton (2005) 'Reducing Administrative Burdens – Effective Inspection and Enforcement' HM Treasury, London

[24] Macrory (2006) 'Regulatory Justice : Making Sanctions Effective' Cabinet Office, London

look at the regulatory system as a whole, rather than seek special pleadings for particular fields of law. Regulation involves complex areas of different specialised law, some more technical that others, and some strongly influenced by European Community law, and others less so. There are a range of different types of enforcement agency, ranging from elected local authorities, government departments, specialised national agencies such as the Health and Safety Executive and the Environment Agency, and national bodies such as the Food Standards Agency that work in partnership with local government enforcement bodies. But despite all these complexities, there were common principles underlying the regulation of business that cut across all these specialised areas. My remit included some 61 national regulators ranging from the familiar Environment Agency, HSE, and the Food Standards Agency to more esoteric bodies such as the British Potato Council, as well as local authorities responsible for such areas as building regulations, local nuisances, and trading standards. But as with Hampton, it because clear that that when it came to the question of enforcement and sanctions, there were many similar legal techniques and approaches being adopted across the board, and many similar problems occurring with the current system.

In understanding my analysis and recommendations, it is worth emphasising what I was not doing, although it was clear from some of those submitting evidence that they hoped I would stray into these areas. It was not my task to propose any restructuring of the regulators, since this was an issue dealt with by Hampton. I did not intend to prescribe how regulators should exercise their enforcement discretion, since they were far better placed to do so. But I wished to give them more options as to the sanctions available, though this would imply acting in a rather more transparent way than was sometimes the case. Again, where cases reached the courts, it would have been inappropriate to interfere with the sentencing discretion of courts, though again I would propose giving them a richer range of more sanctioning options. I considered whether the existing legislation prescribing regulatory offences should be restructured, but rejected this as an unnecessary burdensome task – the existing offences could remain, but allow for a broader range of responses where breaches occurred. Finally, it was not my role to question the substance of the regulatory requirements – that is a matter for government.

Regulatory intervention in the business world exists because government cannot be certain that the market by itself will achieve the public policy goals it desires. Even if a substantial proportion of the market will head towards that direction, there exist a proportion who will not and thereby gain unfair competitive advantage. Like Hampton, I believe that advice and incentives are generally the first and preferable way to induce compliance. But regulatory sanctions remain essential to a regulatory system. At the very least, the existence of formal sanctions underpins regulator's authority to give advice. The availability of formal sanctions act as a deterrent, and where breaches occur they should ensure no economic gain from non-compliance, deter future breaches, and in appropriate cases impose a societal stigma on the person or company in breach.

Early on in the Review, it seemed helpful to articulate a set of principles that should underline the construction of any sanctions regime. These principles were not intended to be translated in the law or be used as the basis of a legal challenge to any particular enforcement action, but they were originally designed to help provide an underlying basis to assess our existing system and for making any proposed recommendations. Six principles were identified.[25] First, the core aim of a sanctioning system should not be to punish per se but to change behaviour. Changing behaviour does sometimes require punishment, but not always. Equally we need a system that should at a minimum ensure that any financial gain from non-compliance is eliminated. This is fair to those industries that do comply, and sends the right signals. Penalties systems need to be responsive to the particular circumstances and the character of the regulated body and allow for a proportionate response. Where there is actual harm caused by non-compliance whether to individuals or the environment, the system should, if at all possible, aim to restore harm caused. And ultimately the aim of a sanctioning system should be deter future non-compliance.

When one looks at the current system of regulatory sanctions in this country, be it environmental, trading standards or health and safety, it is remarkable how narrow the range of sanctions are. Essentially the threat of criminal sanctions. In many areas regulators possess the power to service various forms of enforcement or improvement notice, but ultimately these are backed up by the criminal law. Where a regime includes a licencing requirement – and not all do – there may be power to revoke a licence but this is rarely used. Regulators may also possess to power to seek injunctions, but again these are reserved for extreme cases.

As to the criminal law, nearly all the key offences are drafted in strict liability terms, implying that intention or recklessness is not an ingredient of the offence. The use of the criminal law in regulatory area can be traced back to first developments of regulatory systems

---

[25] Regulatory Justice, op. cit., para 2.11.

in the nineteenth century where essentially there were no specialised agencies or tribunals, and the local magistrates' courts were prepared to take on the role as the watchdogs and sanctioners.[26] The strict liability offence was introduced as a better deterrent and out of a recognition that probably only the industries themselves understood their internal workings and it would be near impossible for a prosecutor to prove intention or recklessness. For some offences there are defences available for due diligence or some similar wording, and on standard principles it is up to the defendant to prove his defence but on the balance of probabilities. As part of the Review, Professor Andrew Simester of Nottingham University was commissioned to analyse the availability of this defence across a range of regulatory offences to see if any principles emerged as to its usage. His analysis[27] revealed great inconsistency, both in the actual language of the defence used, and in the offences covered. Even within the same area of regulation, there appeared little in the way of rationale for the use of the defence. For example, the principal water pollution offences are truly strict[28], while the equivalent waste pollution offences contain a defence of due diligence.[29] As so often with law, these differences can probably only be explained by chance and historical development rather than a true underlying principle.

It was also clear from the evidence submitted to the Review that in almost every area of regulation there is a broad spectrum of offenders – from what one might describe as the truly criminal, the fly by night operators who know exactly what they are doing and are often making calculated estimates of the money to be made and the likelihood of being caught, to the poorly managed companies who have other overriding priorities, to legitimate companies who through carelessness or an oversight breach the regulations, but perhaps with serious consequences.

Against this background, the single criminal offence has to do an awful lot of work. The range of culpability is in part reflected in the enforcement discretion of the regulator, and also in the sentencing powers of the courts. But there was a real concern that we were over-using the criminal law. The criminal courts themselves are confused as to the type of law, which is being dealt with – strict liability offences are sometimes described as not criminal in the true sense. Personally, I view an intentional fly-tipper making money of illegal waste disposal

---

[26] see Sullivan (2005) 'Strict Liability and the European Convention on Human Rights' in Simester (ed) *Appraising Strict Liability* Oxford University Press, Oxford at p 201

[27] Strict Liability in UK Regulation Appendix E 'Regulatory Justice: Sanctioning in a post-Hampton World' Consultation Document, Macrory Review May 2006 Cabinet Office, London available on web only.

[28] s 85 Water Resources Act 1991.

[29] s 33 Environmental Protection Act 1990.

as being as criminal as a shop-lifter or burglar, but there was a danger that by over-relying on the criminal law as the core, formal regulatory sanction, we ended up devaluing the impact of the criminal law. And we had many examples of where magistrates' courts gave apparently low fines compared to economic gains. Equally a criminal prosecution is, rightly so, a time consuming process that is not to be undertaken lightly, and there was concerns that this could lead to under-enforcement.

The criminal processes could certainly be improved, and the Report contained a number of recommendations for so doing; for example, better training for court officials, and focusing regulatory offences on particular courts within a regional area so that both magistrates and the courts develop specialist knowledge. In England and Wales, there is heavy use of lay part-time magistrates, and it has been estimated than on average a magistrate might hear an environmental offence once every eight years. It is not surprising there that may be a lack of familiarity with the detail and nature of regulatory offences. Legal research had shown the extent to which defence counsel often make great play of the strict liability nature of the offences, and can confuse the court as to whether it is dealing with criminals or mere technical breaches.[30] But the Review also recommended sanctions that moved beyond the simple imposition of a fine. For example, where clearly defined profits had been made from the regulatory breach – such as the failure to pay a licence or registration fee – a profits order be imposed by the court. At present this may or may not be reflected in the overall fine but is sometimes difficult to tell. A profits order would simply remove the profits element of the offence in, as it were, a neutral manner, leaving the fine representing the degree of culpability the court considers to have been present.

Of current outcomes for regulatory offences 96% result in fines, and again the Review called for a more imaginative approach. When we deal with individual criminals, we have moved a long way from the courts being able to impose only fines or imprisonment, and there now exists a richer range of possibilities such as community service orders or probation designed to bring back offenders into compliance where a fine or imprisonment may be inappropriate. We should be thinking of a similar approach for businesses, and the Review recommended the development of what we described as corporate rehabilitation orders. The enforcement body would recommend to the court that the corporate rehabilitation order was appropriate, and supervision would no doubt rest with the regulator concerned. It might be especially suitable for smaller and medium sized enterprises where, say, managers are required

---

[30] See, for example, P. De Prez, (2000), 'Excuses, excuses: the ritual trivialisation of environmental prosecutions', *Journal of Environmental Law*, Vol. 12 No.1.

to undergo training or carrying out audits and so on. Some Australian states have developed a Publicity Order under which the court can order a company to take out publicity adverts in the papers.[31] A company, say, that causes a local pollution incident might be required to take out an advertisement in the local press explaining why the incident took place, what the company was doing to prevent it taking place again, that it apologised, and was donating £5,000 to a local community project. Companies do not necessarily relish the prospect of such publicity, but it may be something the affected local community would find more satisfactory that the simple imposition of a fine.

So we certainly can improve the criminal processes, but the analysis was that this was not sufficient in itself. There seemed many instances where criminal prosecution was still potentially inappropriate and heavy handed, but where a sanction was required. For instance, a company that had caused a significant water pollution incident through an act of carelessness, or a company that had failed to register under a regulatory requirement through an oversight rather than ill-intention. A formal warning might simply be an insufficient response in such circumstances, while a formal criminal prosecution might appear to be excessive. Here the concept of administrative penalties, familiar in areas of economic regulation and used in many other jurisdictions in the context of environmental regulation, seemed a positive addition to sanctioning powers.

The Review recommended that for certain minor breaches a fixed penalty system might be useful, but the key recommendation was for the use of variable penalties. A regulator would calculate the appropriate penalty using guidelines it had developed which would include negative factors such as the seriousness of the breach, its consequences, whether it was a repeat or not, but also credits to be given for cooperation, and any compensation given to victims if there were any. In the field of competition law, where such penalties can be imposed, there is an upper limit of 10% of the company's turnover[32]. That in itself can lead to complications, and I recommended no upper limit, but with a proviso that if the original offence was a summary only offence, the variable penalty should not exceed that amount. The purpose of this reform was not to introduce higher financial sanctions by the back door as it were, but a different form of penalty that did not involve a criminal prosecution.

[31] See Abbot (2005) 'The Regulatory Enforcement of Pollution Control Laws: The Australian Experience' *Journal of Environmental Law* Vol 17 No 2 pp 161-180.
[32] See s 36 Competition Act 1998.

It would be possible to redraft existing offences, distinguishing those offences which gave rise to criminal prosecution and those that gave rise to an administrative penalty. That might happen in the design of future legislation. But in my view it was simpler not to reframe existing offences, but to allow each to give rise to either a criminal prosecution or an administrative penalty. It would then up to the regulator having satisfied itself as to the existence of the offence and the need for a formal sanction to determine which was then the most appropriate sanction route. The choice of sanction would be influenced by the penalty principles, and it is vitally important that perverse incentives are not created which might determine the choice of sanction. For that reason I emphasised strongly that no revenue from administrative penalties should go directly to the regulator, even if it were to be ring-fenced and used only for enforcement purposes. It was clear from much of the evidence that the concept of administrative penalties has been corrupted for many through the direct experience or, perhaps, urban myths with parking enforcement and fixed penalties.[33] Many local authorities privatised enforcement with targets and incentives for the amount of penalties imposed, and some consciously introduced a no tolerance policy, balanced, they hoped, with a generous right of appeal after the event. That seems to me to be almost entirely contrary to the risk based approach towards enforcement. Regulators are tightly squeezed for resources and if ever there was a perception that the choice was being determined by the attraction of earning extra revenue, the system and the relationship between regulator and regulatee collapses.

That said, administrative penalties have considerable advantages. I do not believe that they will lighten the demands on investigation of potential breaches by regulators. Investigation will continue to be done by criminal standards, and only later will the choice of sanctioning route be taken. In the absence of any express legislative provision, the standard of proof for an administrative penalty will be on the balance of probabilities, though some regulators have indicated that they would be happy to have a criminal standard of proof. The Review received no evidence that that there was a pent up demand for prosecutions which failed on the standard of proof required. But what the new approach offered was the possibility of the regulator imposing a sanction reasonably swiftly, and should the offender not wish to appeal for the matter to be finalised equally quickly. Criminal prosecution is a lengthy and serious business, and there was a real concern that its implications can lead to under-enforcement. A good example might be where an enforcement or improvement notice is served on a business requiring compliance within a specified period. Breach of the notice is currently

---

[33] As one of the trade association responses to the Consultation Document noted, Administrative Penalties 'could become a nice little earner for the Council'.

a criminal offence but if the company complies, with four fifths of the requirements, it is unlikely that a regulator will consider it worthwhile prosecuting for the remaining parts still in non-compliance. Here the availability of an administrative penalty is likely to ensure 100% compliance.

An administrative penalty is nevertheless a serious sanction, and it is clear that businesses must have the right to appeal to an independent court or tribunal both as to the merits and as to the amount of the penalty. Some argued that the simplest method was to allow appeals back to the criminal courts. Magistrates in England and Wales do have some jurisdiction in some civil matters, and should be able to distinguish between whether they were dealing with civil or criminal matters. But the evidence we had – especially from Germany where appeals against administrative penalties go back to the criminal magistrates – was that this was not the optimum choice. The distinction between criminal and administrative penalties would become blurred, and the criminal stigma was bound to pervade. In fields such as competition or taxation law, appeals against administrative penalties go to a specialised tribunal established for the purpose. My preference was to keep the criminal and administrative routes entirely separate but by itself it was unlikely the government would relish establishing a new tribunal just for these purposes.

Enter here my unexpected alignment No 2. A few years before the Macrory Review, Sir Andrew Leggatt, a former Court of Appeal Judge, had been charged with reviewing our whole tribunal system in England and Wales. Rather than each and every tribunal being established under new primary legislation, he recommended[34] a much more flexible tribunal system where tribunals could be established as and when needed, share many facilities, and have a proper system of appeal first to an Upper Tribunal, and then to the Court of Appeal. His reforms are now being implemented under the framework of the Tribunals, Courts and Enforcement Act 2007.

The prospect of this new system made it much easier and more attractive to recommend that appeals from administrative penalties should, assuming the regulatory system in question did not contain a more appropriate specialised tribunal, go to a new regulatory tribunal within the new system. Government has accepted this recommendation. This is not yet quite the environmental tribunal that I originally envisaged, and it is likely that initially it will take the form of a regulatory tribunal handling appeals concerning administrative penalties in whatever

[34] Leggatt (2001) 'Tribunals for Users – One System, One Service' Report of the Review of Tribunals Department for Constitutional Affairs, London

area of law. But the system is flexible enough that it will give birth to a more specialised environmental tribunal or other specialised tribunals if the numbers of appeals warrants it. And as the system matures, it may be that government will realise that appeals concerning licences and enforcement notices and similar administrative elements of the regulatory machinery are best handled by this body.

The Report also recommended a number of other sanctioning responses which can provide appropriate approaches in certain cases. Undertakings in lieu of a formal sanction have been used in other jurisdictions notably Australia. In such a case the company concerned offers a formal undertaking laying out how it will respond to a particular breach, and the regulator may accept this rather than prosecuting or imposing a penalty. This is likely to be most suitable for a legitimate business that causes a breach through oversight or carelessness. The regulator would have to specify in its enforcement policy the sort of circumstances when it might consider an undertaking and the discretion whether or not to accept should rest with the regulator. But the advantage is that it gives an opportunity to the company itself to think out how best to deal with a breach. It is not necessarily a soft option and I was very clear that any undertaking would have to be a document on public record, rather than a private arrangement between the regulator and regulated.

Finally, I should mention restorative justice. The concept has many different connotations, but essentially reflects a need to involve victims of crimes in the process of sanctioning to a far greater extent that happens at present. It is currently being used extensively in England and Wales in the context of juvenile crime,[35] and results are generally positive.[36] The Review suggested that some of the concepts and approaches ideas might be transferred to the area of business regulation. There are examples in other jurisdictions where it has proved extremely effective. A well reported case in Australia involved the financial sector and the mis-selling of insurance policies. The company concerned could have been prosecuted, but as an alternative the regulator, the Trade Practices Commissioner, facilitated meetings with senior managers and the victims of those who has been pressurised by their salesmen. The victims were mostly poor aboriginals in remote communities, and apparently the meetings had a powerful effect on the CEO and top management who were based in Sydney. Some 80 employees were sacked, new

[35] see Home Office (2003) 'Restorative Justice : the Government's Strategy; Home Office, London

[36] for example, see, Hoyle et al (2002) 'Proceed with Caution : An Evaluation of the Thames Valley Police Initiative in Restorative Cautioning' Joseph Rowntree Foundation. More generally see Andrew von Hirsch et al (eds) (2003) *Restorative Justice and Criminal Justice: Competing or Reconcilable Paradigms?* Hart Publishing, Oxford.

training procedures introduced, a compensation package agreed, and new company policies designed to ensure it never happened again. It is certainly possible to think of cases where this might be valuable in the context of regulatory breaches, though with the environment it may of course be less easy to identify clear victims. The Review recommended that pilot schemes be undertaken and monitored.

The underlying thrust of the report is therefore to increase the range of sanctioning options available to a regulator. If and when regulators have access to these powers it is difficult to predict the pattern of sanctions that will be employed in the future. I would suspect that the number of criminal prosecutions will fall and be largely reserved for the truly egregious, where there is evidence of clear intent or recklessness, or the repeat offender. For legitimate businesses who breach through negligence or oversights but where the seriousness demands more than a warning letter, we will see much greater use of administrative penalties, and/or undertakings. But there will never be a clear divide. There may be circumstances where, say, a small illegal operator seems undeterred by criminal convictions and where the regulator judges that the rapid imposition of a large financial penalty will have a greater effect in changing behaviour. Alternatively, the results of an accident caused by a legitimate operator may be so serious that the public demand the stigma of a criminal prosecution rather than an administrative sanction, however large.

Nevertheless, given the greater discretionary powers being given to regulators, an important element of my report concerns issues of governance. The Cabinet Office has already indicated that regulators should not have access to these powers unless they can demonstrate that they are adopting a risk based approach to regulatory enforcement. My recommendations concerning governance echo and develop this approach. All regulators should have a published enforcement policy which gives signals as to how it will approach enforcement and the likely sanctions routes it will adopt – but not drafted in such absolute terms as to tie the regulator's hands in any particular case. Of the 61 national regulators within my review only 17 had such a published policy. New enforcement policies will have to reflect the new range of sanctions available, and indicate, say, the sort of circumstances in which the regulator is likely to impose an administrative penalty or consider an undertaking from the business concerned. Regulators should publish annual figures of the different types of enforcement actions they take, so that one can monitor trends as the use of the powers develop. That is the outputs. But equally important is the measurement of outcomes. If, say, the number of water pollution prosecutions drop and the number of administrative penalties rise, that does not greatly concern me provided that the number of serious water incidents has dropped during the same period or at least not increased. I appreciate that robust outcome measurements are easier in some areas of environmental protection than others, but nevertheless it is important they are developed.

As I mentioned one of the values of the original Hampton approach and the task I was given was that it required one to cut across different regulatory systems. During my Review, we had a large number of meetings where regulators from quite different fields including the financial sector were able to share experiences and it was clear this was a valuable forum for all concerned. I therefore recommended that the Cabinet Office continue to facilitate meetings which will be especially important as regulators begin to think about issues such as constructing enforcement policies to reflect new sanction options or developing penalty calculation schemes. On a similar cross-cutting theme, I recognised that departmental parliamentary select committees provide a useful accountability system for regulators falling within the particular departments accountable to each committee. But again it would be valuable if there were also a cross-cutting parliamentary committee concerned with regulators and regulatory techniques so that one could conduct robust comparative inquiries across different fields of regulations.

Government accepted all the recommendations in the Macrory Review and the Regulatory Enforcement and Sanctions Bill[37] will initially take forward the proposals for administrative penalties and undertakings. Regulators and Departments will not be forced to acquire these new sanctioning tools, and some are already indicating that they are satisfied with the effectiveness of their existing powers. I accept that this may be the case, but I think that in future the burden will be very much on regulators to demonstrate why a richer range of legal responses. as used by many other regulators both in this country and in other jurisdictions, should not be available in their field. Anyone involved in government reviews will know that there is many a slip between acceptance and implementation. But I am confident that we are at the foothills of what will eventually be a significant change in the way we approach the enforcement of environmental and other areas regulation – and in the environmental field at least one that will help to secure better environmental outcomes.

---

[37] Announced by the Prime Minister in his Legislative Programme Statement 11 July 2007

CHAPTER 2

REGULATORY JUSTICE - MAKING SANCTIONS EFFECTIVE*

Executive Summary

Introduction

E.1   I have looked at sanctioning regimes and penalty powers in detail over the last twelve months with the aim of identifying a set of fit for purpose sanctioning tools that can be used effectively, fairly and proportionately by regulators and those enforcing regulations in situations of regulatory non-compliance. I have considered the work of 56 national regulators and 468 local authorities.

E.2   I have published two previous reports as part of this review, a discussion paper, incorporating a call for evidence, which was published in December 2005 and a consultation document laying out options for reform in May 2006.[1] Both papers introduced many sanctioning options for consideration including administrative sanctions, venues for hearing regulatory cases, as well as alternative sanctions to be used by the judiciary such as reputation related sanctions or corporate rehabilitation, and the role for restorative justice. I present my final conclusions on these and other sanctioning tools in this report.

E.3   The regulators within the scope of the review (see paragraph 1.07) carry out more than 3.6m enforcement actions each year. These regulators carry out at least 2.8m inspections per year, hand out at least 400,000 warning letters, 3,400 formal cautions, 145,000 statutory notices and take forward at least 25,000 prosecutions.[2] These enforcement actions are taken across businesses of all sizes often with small businesses and legitimate businesses feeling more of a regulatory burden than larger companies, or those firms engaged in rogue trading activity. This strikes me as counterintuitive and repeat offenders as well as those that have

---

* R. Macrory, (2006) 'Regulatory Justice: Making Sanctions Effective (Final Report)', *Macrory Review,* Cabinet Office, London
[1] 'Regulatory Justice: Sanctioning in a Post-Hampton World', R. Macrory, May 2006 and December 2005.
[2] Data submitted to Macrory Review, September 2006.

an intentional disregard for the law should, under a risk based system, face tough sanctions.

E.4   I am therefore recommending that Government should consider:

- Examining the way in which it formulates criminal offences relating to regulatory non-compliance;

- Ensuring that regulators have regard to six Penalties Principles and seven characteristics when enforcing regulations;

- Ways in which to make sentencing in the criminal courts more effective;

- Introducing schemes of Fixed and Variable Monetary Administrative Penalties, available to those regulators who are Hampton compliant, with an appeal to an independent tribunal rather than the criminal courts;

- Strengthening the system of Statutory Notices;

- Introducing pilot schemes involving Restorative Justice techniques; and

- Introducing alternative sentencing options in the criminal courts for cases related to regulatory non-compliance.

E.5   The current regulatory sanctioning system, including both criminal sanctions and non-criminal sanctions, is a system that has developed over time and as such there are variations between the powers and practices among regulators. The reforms the review proposes are designed to bring consistency into the sanctioning toolkits across the system, reflecting the risk based approach to regulation and the broader regulatory reform agenda. These proposals will provide regulators and industry with greater flexibility whilst ensuring that regulatory outcomes, such as increased compliance, are not compromised.

E.6   The Hampton Review found that penalty regimes are cumbersome and ineffective.[3] I have taken forward Philip's findings and have considered options that could add to regulators' enforcement toolbox, broadening the flexibility available to both regulators

[3] *Reducing administrative burdens: Effective inspection and enforcement*, P. Hampton, HM Treasury March 2005.

and the judiciary to better meet regulatory objectives and improve compliance. These options would also benefit industry, by providing a transparent system with appropriate sanctions that would aim to get firms back into compliance, ensure future compliance, provide a level playing field for business and enable regulators to pursue offenders who flout the law in a more effective manner.

Problems With the Current System of Regulatory Sanctions

E.7 Regulatory sanctions are an essential feature of a regulatory enforcement toolkit and are central to achieving compliance by signalling the threat of a punishment for firms that have offended. Sanctions demonstrate that non-compliance will not be tolerated and that there will be a reprimand or consequence that will put the violator in a worse position than those entities that complied with their regulatory obligations on time.

E.8 It is important for Government to ensure that regulators have a flexible and proportionate sanctioning toolkit which also ensures the protection of workers, consumers and the environment. That toolkit should provide appropriate options to handle the regulatory needs of legitimate business as well as those businesses that intentionally and knowingly fail to comply with regulatory obligations on time.

E.9 Evidence submitted to the review suggests that many regulators are heavily reliant on one tool, namely criminal prosecution, as the main sanction should industry or individuals be unwilling or unable to follow advice and comply with legal obligations. Criminal prosecution may not be, in all circumstances, the most appropriate sanction to ensure that non-compliance is addressed, any damage caused is remedied or behaviour is changed. The availability of other more flexible and risk based tools may result in achieving better regulatory outcomes.

E.10 Many of the review's recommendations are a continuation of current Government proposals and reforms. The Home Office is exploring the role of restorative justice in areas such as corporate manslaughter and youth offending; whilst Defra is currently consulting on the introduction of administrative penalties in the area of fishing and marine activities.

E.11 Whilst the UK has a leading position in the area of regulatory reform and we have made advances in the development of sanctioning regimes in some areas of regulation, little has been done to evolve the sanctioning toolkit across all regulatory bodies. Across the board, we have failed to keep pace with the innovations being introduced in other leading OECD nations such as Australia and Canada, countries which share some of our legal tradition. The review believes that the UK must address this area in order to ensure that the Government's better regulation agenda, including the recommendations of the Hampton Review and the Better Regulation Task Force's report *Less is More*, is realised.[4]

My Recommendations

E.12   The review has considered a broad spectrum of sanctioning tools, ranging from persuasive methods, such as warning letters or the use of informal, pragmatic means like advice and persuasion, to criminal prosecution at the top end of the enforcement pyramid [see annex A]. The review has also considered the major motivations for non-compliance and I have recommended that suitable sanctioning options should be available to allow regulators to deal appropriately with each type of offender, including the rogue trading element present in some industries.

E.13   My recommendations are discussed throughout this document and summarised in chapter six. They include recommendations around the following areas:

- A list of Penalties Principles and a framework for regulatory sanctioning;

- The role of the criminal prosecution as a regulatory sanction;

- The role of Monetary Administrative Penalties;

- Statutory Notices and other innovations such as Enforceable Undertakings and Undertakings Plus;

- The role of Restorative Justice in regulatory non-compliance; and

- Alternative sentencing options that could be available in criminal courts.

---

[4] 'Less is More', Better Regulation Task Force, March 2005

E.14   Chapter one outlines the role of regulatory sanctions within the regulatory system setting out the context and scope of my review. Chapter two presents the underlying principles relating to regulatory sanctions, their purpose and function as well as the principles themselves. Chapters three and four set out the tools that I believe should be available in an expanded regulatory enforcement toolkit. This includes recommendations on Monetary Administrative Penalties, Statutory Notices, restorative justice and alternative sanctions within a criminal setting. I present some case studies to give examples of the way in which these tools could be used. Chapter five makes recommendations around issues of transparency and accountability for regulators and enforcers who use the enforcement toolkit. Finally, chapter six summarises all of my recommendations.

The Review's Work

E.15   The Penalties Review, as part of the implementation of the Hampton Report was commissioned by the Chancellor of the Duchy of Lancaster in September 2005, and its terms of reference are set out in 'Regulatory Justice: Sanctioning in a post-Hampton World', December 2005. Annex B contains more details.

Publications

E.16   The review published a discussion paper, 'Regulatory Justice: Sanctioning in a post-Hampton World', in December 2005 with a corresponding call for evidence.

E.17   The review published a consultation document, 'Regulatory Justice: Sanctioning in a post-Hampton World', with specific policy proposals for consideration in May 2006.

E.18   Following the publication of the interim report, the review team has been consulting extensively with key stakeholders and experts with a focus on the preparation of this final report.

Conclusion

E.19   The reforms suggested by this review are not intended to transform sanctioning systems overnight, but to bring into them the flexibility, efficiencies and responsiveness that can facilitate the full implementation of the Hampton agenda. This will result in better deterrence options for regulators, better compliance for business and better outcomes for the public.

Box E1 List of Recommendations

1. I recommend that the Government initiate a review of the drafting and formulation of criminal offences relating to regulatory non-compliance.

2. I recommend that in designing the appropriate sanctioning regimes for regulatory non-compliance, regulators should have regard to the following six Penalties Principles and seven characteristics.

Six Penalties Principles

A sanction should:

1. Aim to change the behaviour of the offender;

2. Aim to eliminate any financial gain or benefit from non-compliance;

3. Be responsive and consider what is appropriate for the particular offender and regulatory issue, which can include punishment and the public stigma that should be associated with a criminal conviction;

4. Be proportionate to the nature of the offence and the harm caused;

5. Aim to restore the harm caused by regulatory non-compliance, where appropriate; and

6. Aim to deter future non-compliance

Seven Characteristics

Regulators should:

1. Publish an enforcement policy;

2. Measure outcomes not just outputs;

---

3. Justify their choice of enforcement actions year on year to stakeholders, Ministers and Parliament;

4. Follow-up enforcement actions where appropriate;

5. Enforce in a transparent manner;

6. Be transparent in the way in which they apply and determine administrative penalties; and

7. Avoid perverse incentives that might influence the choice of sanctioning response.

3. I recommend that in order to increase the effectiveness of criminal courts for regulatory offences, the following actions should be implemented:

    - The Government should request the Sentencing Guidelines Council to prepare general sentencing guidelines for cases of regulatory non-compliance;

    - Prosecutors should always make clear to the court any financial benefits resulting from non-compliance as well as the policy significance of the relevant regulatory requirement;

    - Prosecutions in particular regulatory fields be heard in designated Magistrates' Courts within jurisdictional areas, where appropriate; and

    - Regulators provide specialist training for prosecutors and discuss with the Judicial Studies Board (JSB) contributing to the training of the judiciary and justices' clerks.

4. I recommend that with regards to Monetary Administrative Penalties:

    - Government should consider introducing schemes for Fixed and Variable Monetary Administrative Penalties, for regulators and enforcers of regulations, who are compliant with the Hampton and Macrory Principles and characteristics. This can include national regulators as well as local regulatory partners;

- Appeals concerning the imposition of an administrative penalty be heard by a Regulatory Tribunal, rather than the criminal courts;

- Fine maxima for Fixed Monetary Administrative Penalties (FMAP) schemes should be set out and not exceed level five on the standard scale; and

- There should be no fine maxima for Variable Monetary Administrative Penalties (VMAPs).

5. I recommend that for an improved system of Statutory Notices:

    - Government should consider using Statutory Notices as part of an expanded sanctioning toolkit to secure compliance beyond the regulatory areas in which they are currently in use;

    - Regulators should sytematically follow-up Statutory Notices using a risk based approach including an element of randomised follow-up;

    - In dealing with the offence of failing to comply with a Statutory Notice, regulators should have access to administrative financial penalties as an alternative to criminal prosecution. This power should be extended by legislative amendment to existing schemes of Statutory Notices; and

    - Government should consider whether appeals against Statutory Notices should be routed through the Regulatory Tribunal rather than the criminal courts.

6. I recommend that the Government should consider introducing Enforceable Undertakings and Undertakings Plus (a combination of an Enforceable Undertaking with an administrative financial penalty) as an alternative to a criminal prosecution or the imposition of VMAPs for regulators that are compliant with the Hampton and Macrory Principles and characteristics.

7. I recommend that Government should consider introducing pilot schemes involving the use of Restorative Justice (RJ) techniques in addressing cases of regulatory non-compliance. This might include RJ:

- as a pre-court diversion;

- instead of a Monetary Administrative Penalty; and

- within the criminal justice system – as both a pre or post sentencing option.

8. I recommend that the Government consider introducing the following alternative sentencing in criminal courts:

    - Profit Order – Where the profits made from regulatory non-compliance are clear, the criminal courts have access to Profit Orders, requiring the payment of such profits, distinct from any fine that the court may impose;

    - Corporate Rehabilitation Order – In sentencing a business for regulatory non-compliance, criminal courts have on application by the prosecutor, access to a Corporate Rehabilitation Orders (CRO) in addition to or in place of any fine that may be imposed; and

    - Publicity Order – In sentencing a business for regulatory non-compliance, criminal courts have the power to impose a Publicity Order, in addition to or in place of any other sentence.

9. I recommend that to ensure improved transparency and accountability:

    - The Better Regulation Executive should facilitate a working group of regulators and sponsoring departments to share best practice in enforcement approaches, the application of sanction options, development of outcome measures and transparency in reporting. Regulators and sponsoring departments should work with the Executive to include outcome measures as part of their overall framework of performance management; and

    - Publish Enforcement Activities – Each regulator should publish a list on a regular basis of its completed enforcement actions and against whom such actions have been taken.

I.   THE ROLE AND IMPORTANCE OF SANCTIONS WITHIN THE REGULATORY SYSTEM

This chapter sets out the importance of sanctions in a modern regulatory system and discusses the scope and context of my review as well as an assessment of the current sanctioning system.

This review was set up following recommendation eight of the Hampton Review. Hampton set out in his principles:

- No inspection should take place without a reason;

- Businesses should not have to give unnecessary information, nor give the same piece of information twice;

- Regulators should provide authoritative, accessible advice easily and cheaply; and

- The few businesses that persistently break regulations should be identified quickly and face proportionate and meaningful sanctions.

This review has considered the last of these principles with a view to ensuring that a level playing field is created for all businesses because there is no financial gain from failing to comply. In such a risk based system most breaches will face penalties that are quicker and easier to apply while there will be tougher penalties for rogue businesses which persistently break the rules.

Introduction

1.1   This review was established to consider appropriate sanctions that could become part of an extended enforcement toolkit available to regulators and Government departments. This would be in addition to the existing sanctions of criminal prosecution and Statutory Notices set out in the relevant regulatory legislation.

1.2   This chapter gives some background on the work of the review and the sanctioning regimes I have been investigating.

The Macrory Review is Integral to the Hampton Agenda

1.3   Philip Hampton in his report, 'Reducing Administrative Burdens: Effective Inspection and Enforcement', published in March 2005, recommended that the Government establish a comprehensive review of regulators' penalty regimes.[5] Following this recommendation, the Macrory Review was established under my leadership in September 2005.

1.4   The Hampton report identified the cumulative burden of regulation – multiple inspections and overlapping data requirements as well as inconsistent practice and decision making between and within regulators – as the main burden faced by the regulated community. Philip Hampton, in his recommendations, concluded that regulators should use risk assessment as an essential means of directing resources where they can have the maximum impact on outcomes. He went on to say that by eliminating unnecessary inspections, more resources should be directed at compliance advice to the regulated community. Lastly, he suggested Government develop better practice to reduce the administrative burden.

1.5   The Hampton Review also found that regulatory penalty regimes can be cumbersome and ineffective. The following features were identified as shortcomings:

*   Penalties handed down by courts are not seen as an adequate deterrent to regulatory non-compliance as the level of financial penalty can often fail to reflect the financial gain of non-compliance with regulatory obligations; and

*   The range of enforcement tools available to many regulators is limited, giving rise to disproportionate use of criminal sanctions, which can be a costly, time-consuming and slow process.

1.6   I have taken forward Philip's findings and I am recommending a suite of sanctions that could be added to the regulators' enforcement toolbox, broadening the flexibility available to regulators, the judiciary and business to better meet regulatory objectives, improve compliance and ensure a level playing-field for all.

---

[5] 'Reducing Administrative Burdens: Effective Inspection and Enforcement', P. Hampton, HM Treasury, March 2005, Recommendation 8.

Scope

1.7   In this report, references to 'the regulators' refer only to those regulators that are within the scope of this review as mentioned at the start of Annex C. This includes regulatory bodies at both national and local level. Over 60,000 people work for over 650 regulatory bodies within the scope of my review and have a combined budget of approximately £4 billion.[6]

1.8   The division of responsibility between national and local bodies varies. In certain areas, such as environmental regimes, responsibilities are split between national and local regulators; in the area of food standards, a national agency sets standards and Local Authorities enforce them; while in the area of health and safety, Local Authorities enforce regulation on some businesses and national regulators enforce the regulations on other businesses.

1.9   My review did not examine regulators that are the responsibility of the devolved administrations in Scotland, Wales and Northern Ireland, but did consider the operation of UK wide regulators there. Many of the underlying principles, though, are likely to be applicable within the devolved administrations. Where I have referred to penalties available to economic regulators, such as the Financial Services Authority, this is solely for the purposes of comparison. Specific terms of reference for the review are presented in more detail in Annex B.

1.10 In my review I have concentrated on the sanctioning tools available to regulators. The processes by which regulatory legislation is made and enforced is not strictly within the scope of the review and does not feature in my recommendations, although it has been commented on in various places in this report. Nor was it within my remit to consider the actual substance of the regulatory legislation, though it is evident that sensibly drafted and appropriate substantive law is vital to the effectiveness of any regulatory system.

The Role of Sanctions

1.11 The focus of my concern is with regulations that apply to businesses, whether individuals, partnerships, or companies,

---

[6] Ibid 5, pages 12-13.

rather than to individual householders or consumers. Almost by definition regulations are introduced where Government cannot be confident that the whole of the sector covered will voluntarily comply with the standards or achieve desired outcomes. I accept, as did the Hampton report, that advice and incentives should play a key role in ensuring regulatory compliance, and should normally be the first response of regulators. Nevertheless, an effective sanction regime plays an equally vital role in a successful regulatory regime. It underpins the regulator's advisory functions, and its very existence will often act as an inducement to compliance without the need to invoke the formal sanctions.

1.12 Where regulatory non-compliance occurs, sanctions can ensure that businesses that have saved costs by non-compliance do not gain an unfair advantage over businesses that are fully compliant. Where breaches result in damage or other costs to society, sanctions can assist in ensuring that those in breach provide proper recompense. Sanctions can equally represent a societal condemnation of the regulatory breach, acting as a deterrent to the sanctioned business against future breaches, and sending a wider message to the regulated sector.

My Assessment of the Current System

1.13 As part of my study to develop recommendations for an effective and proportionate sanctioning system, I have assessed the current regulatory sanctioning regimes in two prior publications.[7] Those documents highlight some of my findings in respect of the perceived shortcomings of the current system, which I summarise in the section below.

Heavy Reliance on Criminal Sanctions

1.14 Regulators have a range of responses to regulatory breaches, including issuing warning letters, giving advice, and serving various forms of Statutory Notices. But I found that ultimately there is heavy reliance on criminal sanctions as a formal response to regulatory non-compliance. I suggest that, although criminal sanctions are in some circumstances an effective tool, too heavy reliance on criminal sanctions in a regulatory system can be ineffective for the following reasons:

---

[7] 'Regulatory Justice: Sanctioning in a Post-Hampton World', R. Macrory, May 2006 and December 2005.

- Criminal sanctions currently are often an insufficient deterrent to the 'truly' criminal or rogue operators, since the financial sanctions imposed in some criminal cases are not considered to be a sufficient deterrent or punishment. Where businesses (as opposed to individuals) are prosecuted, criminal courts have a limited range of sanctioning options available beyond a fine, and must take into account the financial means of business concerned in setting a fine;

- In instances where there has been no intent or wilfulness relating to regulatory non-compliance a criminal prosecution may be a disproportionate response, although a formal sanction rather than simply advice or a warning, may still be appropriate and justified. However, regulators may not have any alternative available to them in their toolkit and so must prosecute, even where a different type of sanction may be more effective;

- Heavy reliance on criminal sanctions leads to some non-compliance not being addressed at all. Criminal sanctions are costly and time-consuming for both businesses and regulators. In many instances, although non-compliance has occurred, the cost or expense of bringing criminal proceedings deters regulators from using their limited resources to take action. This creates what has come to be known as a *compliance deficit*;

- Criminal convictions for regulatory non-compliance have lost their stigma, as in some industries, being prosecuted is regarded as part of the business cycle. This may be because both strict liability offences committed by legitimate business, and the deliberate flouting of the law by rogues is prosecuted in the same manner with little differentiation between these two types of offender; and

- Since the focus of criminal proceedings is on the offence and the offender, the wider impact of the offence on the victim may not be fully explored. There has been a limited evolution of the rights and needs of victims in the area of regulatory non-compliance which I have explored in more detail in my consultation paper.[8]

---

[8] Ibid, see chapter five of my interim report.

Table 1.1 Range of Sanctions Used by Some Regulators

	Inspections Carried Out	Warning Letters	Formal Cautions	Statutory Notices	Prose cutions	Fixed Penalties
Environmental Health[9]	2,029,793	232,023	*	105,681	*	
Trading Standards and related services[10]	203,697	40,806	2,486		4,692	
Environment Agency[11]	140,528		413	515	883	
Health and Safety Executive[12]	59,865			8,445	712	
Companies House[13]					7,570	190,945
Vehicle and Operator Services Agency[14]	134,164	1,078		16,666	10,642	
Meat Hygiene Service[15]		6,285	24	2,053	17	
Forestry Commission[16]	12,744	1,695		20	17	

Sources: CIPFA Trading Standards Statistics 2004, CIPFA Environmental Health Statistics 2003-04, Environment Agency, Health and Safety Executive, Companies House, Department for Transport, Rural Payments Agency, Meat Hygiene Service, and The Forestry Commission.

*Figures for Environmental Health Formal Cautions and Court summons for 2003/04 was 11,704 and is only available as an aggregate figure.

---

[9] 2003/04 figures, England and Wales only. Includes figures for Pest Control services.
[10] 2004 figures, apart from 'Inspections carried out' which is taken from 2003.
[11] 2005 figures.
[12] 2004/05 figures.
[13] 2004/05 figures.
[14] 2004/05 figures.
[15] 2004/05 figures apart from warning letters that relates to the calendar year 2004.
[16] 2005/06 figures.

Limited Range of Enforcement Tools

1.15 Over the course of my review, I have received evidence and submissions from many stakeholders including regulators, businesses, academics and many others that have supported my view that regulators have a limited range of enforcement sanctions within their toolkits.

'Defra supports the widely held view, espoused also in Hampton, that the current system is not sufficiently responsive, targeted and sensitive to ensure that appropriate penalties are applied in all cases. To this end, the department accepts that there is room for improvement but restates its basic tenet that a robust penalties framework should encompass different types and levels of sanctions depending on the nature, frequency and seriousness of non-compliance.' Defra

Source: Response from Defra to the Macrory Review, February 2006

1.16 Criminal prosecutions remain the primary formal sanction available to most regulators. While this sanction is appropriate in many cases, the time, expense, moral condemnation and criminal record involved may not be appropriate for all breaches of regulatory obligations and is burdensome to both the regulator and business. While the most serious offences merit criminal prosecution, it may not be an appropriate route in achieving a change in behaviour and improving outcomes for a large number of businesses where the non-compliance is not truly criminal in its intention.

Table 1.2 Mapping of Regulators' Enforcement tools

	Financial Services Authority[17]	Health Safety Exec.	Food Standards Agency	Enviro-nment Agency[18]	Comp. House[19]	Charity Comm.[20]	Defra Core dept. regulators[21]
Criminal prosecution	•	•	•	•	•	•	•
Licence revocation	•	•	•	•	N/A	N/A	•
Licence suspension		•	•	•	N/A	N/A	•
Admin financial penalty	•						
Fixed admin financial penalty				•	•		
Statutory Notices		•	•	•	•	•	•
Warning letter	•	•	•	•	•	•	•
Persuasion	•	•	•	•	•	•	•

Source: Responses from regulators to the Macrory Review, February 2006

1.17 Table 1.2 sets out the sanctions that regulators are currently able to access through their relevant legislation. The sanctions that the majority of regulators have access to are either a warning letter at the informal end of the spectrum or a criminal prosecution at the other. In some cases, they have access to civil injunctions. Most regulators have limited access to administrative penalties and other intermediate sanctions as a further step before escalating to prosecution or licence suspension or withdrawal as indicated in the table.

[17] Financial Services and Markets Act 2000, section 126, 127 for warning and decision notices and Part XXV, sections 380 and 382 for injunctions and restitution orders. The FSA does not provide for the use of Statutory Notices such as enforcement notices which require compliance on the part of a firm or a person, but the FSA does issue warning notices, decision notices and final notices. The FSA has access to other enforcement options, which are not in the table, and can for example seek injunctions, make restitution orders and make prohibition orders against persons who are not fit and proper.

[18] Many regulators including the Environment Agency can issue Cautions. These are formal written admissions of guilt which obviate the need for a prosecution.

[19] Companies House does not operate a licence regime. Therefore the licence suspension and licence revocation sanctions are not applicable.

[20] The Charity Commission does not operate a licence regime. Therefore the licence suspension and licence revocation sanctions are not applicable.

[21] DEFRA core departmental regulators include regulators operating in the areas of Environmental Impact Assessment (uncultivated land), Cattle Identification Scheme, Horticulture (classification of imported fruit and vegetables), Pesticides Safety, Waste Management, and Fisheries.

Financial Penalties Sending the Wrong Signal

1.18   Evidence presented to me over the course of the review has demonstrated that, in some instances, the fines handed down in court often do not reflect the financial gain a firm may have made by failing to comply with an obligation. This means that these penalties do not act as a deterrent and, in effect, give businesses an incentive to continue to fail to comply in return for a profit. In some cases fines do not fully reflect the harm done to society.

Box 1.1 Examples of fines that do not reflect the financial benefit or seriousness of the offence (environment regulation)

- An Oxfordshire man was fined £30,000 for abandoning 184 drums of toxic waste. The man received £58,000 for disposing of the material, and the Waste Authorities had costs of £167,000 to incinerate the waste properly.

- A fine of £25,000 was handed down to a small waste disposal company which was operating without a licence. The company saved £250,000 by operating illegally over a 2 year period.

Source: Examples submitted to the Macrory Review by the Environment Agency, March 2006

1.19   These apparently low financial penalties could be seen as an acceptable risk by businesses that have chosen to be deliberately non-compliant. In these instances it might be assumed that financial penalties in the current system are failing to achieve even the most basic objectives of an effective sanctioning regime.

1.20   If regulators are pursuing, as they should, a risk based compliance orientated enforcement strategy, prosecution will be a sanction applied for the most serious cases of regulatory non-compliance. When prosecutions do take place, it is reasonable to assume that they are for the most serious offences and offenders. Sentencing should also reflect this level of seriousness and be a strong deterrent signal for others in the regulated community.

1.21   This lack of an effective deterrent compromises the effectiveness of the regulatory relationship. Without credible and meaningful sanctions, regulators are forced to pursue a more burdensome and bureaucratic enforcement policy. Regulators are deterring non-compliance through their inspection activities. Effective sanctioning is an important signal in achieving deterrence. If criminal prosecutions sent out a strong signal of deterrence, then regulators would be able to impose less onerous burdens on legitimate business by conducting fewer inspections. However, currently legitimate businesses see their unscrupulous competitors cut corners, and gain competitive advantage, without facing serious financial or other consequences.

1.22 Information from my call for evidence suggests that the average fines handed down by magistrates are relatively low, when compared to the fine maxima available. As set out in Table 1.3 below, average fines for businesses ranged from as little as £488 to £6,855. In environmental and health and safety cases, the average fines are in the range of £5,000 to £7,000. This does indicate that the deterrent effect of fines is likely to be limited for all but the smallest businesses.

1.23 The level of fines seen in criminal courts tend to be small in relation to the size and financial position of large businesses. For example, the largest fine handed down to date for a health and safety offence is £15 million imposed against Transco (for breaches of regulations that resulted in the death of four members of the same family in a gas explosion). The financial penalty, while significant in absolute terms, represented five percent of after-tax profits and less than one percent of annual revenues for the company.[22] This shows that even large fines can be absorbed by companies and may not carry the necessary deterrent effect or motivate a change in a firm's behaviour although Transco began an accelerated programme of pipe replacement as an outcome of the incident and did change its behaviour.

---

[22] *Transco v HSE* August 2005, Edinburgh High Court.

Table 1.3 Level of Financial Penalties 2004/2005

	Prosecutions	Convictions	Average Financial Penalty
Health and Safety Executive[23]	1,267	999	£6,855[24]
Environment Agency[25]	887	876	£5,007
British Potato Council[26]	246	28	£488
Companies House	5,867	2,944	N/A
Financial Services Authority[27]	6	6	£75,500
Pesticide Safety Directorate	3	1	£1,800
Food Standards Agency	570	458	N/A

Source: Data submitted by regulators to the Macrory Review, Spring 2006

1.24   There is also evidence that for some offences the average fines are considerably below the maximum available fine. For example, the average fine for non-compliance with the Trade Descriptions Act 1968 was £1,524 against a maximum fine available in the legislation of £5,000. Offences under the Health and Safety at Work etc. Act 1974 led to fines of £6,014 on average, against a maximum fine up to £20,000 depending on the offence.[28] Finally, the maximum penalty available in a magistrates' court for non-compliance with controls on the transport of waste is currently £5,000, but the average fine is just £530.[29] These are only a few

[23] Figures for 2005.

[24] Sentencing handed down in courts reflects many factors including the ability to pay (JSB Adult Court Bench Book, pg 33). There is generally a band within which some fines will be small and others will be large. This figure excludes the convictions with fines of over £100,000. Of those excluded, there was one fine of £2,000,000; three fines at £300,000 or above; and thirteen fines of between £100,000 and £300,000. If these seventeen convictions were included, the average for 2004/05 rises to £12,642.

[25] Figures for 2005.

[26] Figures for 2003/2005. Of those businesses who receive a notification for summons, most decided to provide the requested information before the cases actually proceeded to Court. All cases that proceeded to court resulted in a successful conviction.

[27] Figures since 2000, under the Financial Services and Markets Act 2000.

[28] Data from the DCA, selected offences in magistrates' courts during 2004.

[29] Average fine awarded by the magistrates' courts in the 156 successful prosecutions taken in 2003

examples and are not meant to suggest that courts should always aim for the maximum penalty available. I do believe, though, that these examples are indicative of the level of fines currently handed down by the criminal courts for particular offences.

Previous Comments on Low Financial Penalties

1.25   I am not the first person to recognise that financial penalties handed down in the criminal courts may not be sending a strong deterrence signal.

1.26   The Government has previously recognised that in the area of health and safety, courts are in need of greater sentencing power and that there is scope for extending maximum fines available in the health and safety legislation.[30]

1.27   In 2004, the House of Commons Environmental Audit Committee found, in its sixth report, that the level of sentences given in courts for environmental crimes is too low and recommended the introduction of alternative sentencing powers such as adverse publicity orders and environmental service orders.[31] In its response, the Government noted the Committee's concerns and agreed that imaginative methods of dealing with offenders are necessary.[32] In addition to my report, new approaches have been considered by the Defra-led Review of Enforcement in Environmental Regulation, which was tasked with identifying obstacles to effective environmental enforcement and ways to overcome them. The report from the environmental review includes the suggestion that variable administrative penalties, financial and non-financial, would have the potential to create stronger incentives for compliance in a new balance with criminal prosecution. The report also sets out ideas for relating environmental penalties more transparently to the purposes of enforcement: removing financial gain from non-compliance; making damage good; making restitution to adversely affected communities; and exposing culpability where it exists.[33]

---

[30] 'Revitalising Health and Safety', Department for Environment Transport and Regions, June 2000, p.24.
[31] *Environmental Crime and the Court*, House of Commons Environmental Audit Committee Sixth Report, 2004. Reference Introduction paragraph 15, see www.publications. parliament.uk/pa/cm200304/cmselect/cmenvaud/126/12604.htm
[32] http://www.publications.parliament.uk/pa/cm200304/cmselect/cmenvaud/cmenvaud. htm
[33] http://www.defra.gov.uk/environment/enforcement/

1.28   The academic literature on penalties often reaches similar
        conclusions. For example, a study of penalties for environmental
        offences found that, with the exception of the Netherlands, fines
        were generally low in the European Union. Low judicial and
        public awareness of the harmful consequences of pollution were
        among the reasons for this, in addition to a lack of familiarity
        with environmental law on the part of the judiciary.[34]

1.29   I acknowledge that the financial circumstances of each firm and
        their ability or means to pay a fine must be taken into account
        by a court in determining the appropriate financial penalty.
        However, the low level of average financial penalties indicates
        that the deterrent effect of these penalties will be less meaningful
        for all but the smallest of businesses.

Resolution of Criminal Cases Takes Time and Money

1.30   Criminal prosecutions are time and resource intensive for
        business and for regulators. It may be that they are currently used
        in the absence of other formal sanctions, rather than because they
        are an appropriate response. For instance, the long and resource
        intensive process of taking a criminal prosecution through court
        may seem inappropriate for a company that is being prosecuted
        for a strict liability offence. The Environment Agency reported
        that, in its experience, cases take an average of seven months
        from discovery of non-compliance to when proceedings are
        commenced. The Health and Safety Executive (HSE) estimated
        that, from offence to approval of prosecution, about 20 per cent
        of cases are approved for prosecution within three months of the
        offence date, and by 12 months from the offence date four out of
        five cases will have been approved for prosecution.

1.31   For a business this means that, although the time spent preparing
        and investigating a case is necessary, a rectified regulatory non-
        compliance can still be an issue several months on. Industry and
        the regulator may prefer a timelier and less costly resolution to
        appropriate cases of regulatory non-compliance as the delay and
        uncertainty of prosecution is burdensome for both.

1.32   Furthermore, regulators may not choose to pursue cases for
        prosecution because of the low expected outcome. Enforcers may
        not pursue cases because the level of penalty is not seen to justify

---

[34] *Criminal Enforcement of Environmental Law in the European Union*, M. Faure& G. Heine,
IMPEL Working Group on Criminal Prosecution in Environmental Cases, 2000.

the time, effort and resources that will need to be deployed in order to bring a successful prosecution.

Is there a Compliance Deficit?

1.33   I believe that in many sectors compliance levels in the UK are generally high. However, it can be frustrating for both regulators and businesses when regulatory non-compliance is not addressed because the regulator lacks the appropriate enforcement mechanism. This problem creates what is known as a *compliance deficit*: where non-compliance exists and is identified but no enforcement action is taken because the appropriate tool is not available to the regulator.

1.34   It is difficult to assess the general level of compliance in the UK because not every firm is inspected and not every incidence of regulatory non-compliance is identified. Tangible data is absent in this area. However, I have attempted to get some indication from regulators on the overall effectiveness of enforcement strategies on compliance levels. This was a difficult process, as most regulators are able to comment on their outputs such as numbers of prosecutions or number of Statutory Notices imposed, but are unable to draw any conclusions on what impact this has on overall compliance. The results of this are discussed in my consultation document.[35]

Important Issues Beyond my Remit

1.35   It was clear from the responses to the consultation paper that there were certain subject areas that respondents wanted me to comment on, but which are outside of the remit of my review. I am constrained by the subject matter of regulatory legislation. It is outside the scope of this review to comment on the substance of regulatory requirements and I therefore have adopted the working assumption that regulations are sensible and necessary. Government should be regularly reviewing existing regulations to ensure this is the case.

1.36   In addition, it is not within my scope to comment on the structure of enforcement agencies. Philip Hampton recommended a change in regulatory structures with 35 regulators being merged into nine by April 2009.

---

[35] 'Regulatory Justice: Sanctioning in a Post-Hampton World', R. Macrory, , May 2006, p36.

1.37   At the conclusion of this review, I am not laying down prescriptive rules as to how regulators should respond to individual breaches of regulation, but I am suggesting that a more flexible range of sanctioning options is made available to them. I also suggest what safeguards should be present alongside an extended toolkit. Regulators will still retain the discretion as to how best to respond, and to choose the most appropriate sanction to ensure positive outcomes.

1.38   I do not wish to trespass on the sentencing discretion of the criminal courts. This report does not intend to make recommendations that will impinge on this discretion. I am, however, recommending options that enhance the sanctioning choices available to the criminal courts. I also make recommendations concerning specialisation and training which I believe will improve their effectiveness when dealing with criminal prosecutions for regulatory non-compliance.

1.39   Lastly, I am not prescribing changes to the legal framework or status of current offences relating to regulatory non-compliance. Offences relating to regulatory non-compliance come in many forms: some impose true strict liability, some allow for defences like taking reasonable precautions or similar wording, some require proof of knowledge or intent. The rationale for the differences is not always clear. This is a subject that I believe will merit further investigation in the future. Some interesting work relevant to this has been done in the course of my review. At Annex D and E of my interim report, I discuss the role of strict liability offences in the regulatory field. Some consultation responses have supported my view that there may be a case for decriminalising certain offences thereby reserving criminal sanctions for the most serious cases of regulatory non-compliance. It is however outside my terms of reference to consider this in great detail. My review has started a debate in this area and it may be something that the Government wishes to investigate further.

'We support the view that a distinction must be drawn between matters of regulation and criminal offending. There is a pressing need to avoid expensive court time being taken up with matters that are better suited to an administrative penalty'.

The Criminal Sub committee of the Council of HM Circuit Judges

Recommendation 1:

I recommend that the Government initiate a review of the drafting and formulation of criminal offences relating to regulatory non-compliance.

1.40 My recommendation above relates to exploring options for distinguishing whether some offences could now be better sanctioned administratively.

The Following Chapters

1.41 In the following chapters I recommend an extension to the range of sanctioning options available to enforcement agencies where formal sanctions are considered appropriate to deal with the regulatory non-compliance. This is a response to the findings of my review both from the analysis of original evidence presented to me and from further consultation with stakeholders.

1.42 I believe that the recommendations presented in this review constitute a blueprint of sanctioning tools that is fit for a risk based regulatory society. They present flexible and proportionate sanctions that will help to close the compliance deficit and do so in an effective and coherent manner.

1.43 In chapter two, I outline the underlying principles that my blueprint of sanctions should be based on. In chapters three and four, I recommend a suite of sanctions that I believe will be the blueprint and I describe how they will work. These are:

- Recommendations to improve the effectiveness of the criminal courts;

- Recommendations to introduce Fixed and Variable Monetary Administrative Penalties;

- Recommendations introducing an independent regulatory tribunal for the appeal of administrative sanctions;

- Recommendations for strengthening the system for Statutory Notices;

- Recommendations introducing Enforceable Undertakings and Undertakings Plus;

- Recommendations introducing Restorative Justice; and

- Recommendations introducing further sentencing options for the criminal courts.

1.44   I believe that these recommendations will bring a paradigm shift to the way in which regulatory sanctions are designed and used, making them more flexible and encouraging compliance.

Transparency and Accountability

1.45   The range of sanctions that are being recommended is wider than the current powers that are generally available. They would give many regulators sanctioning options that they will not have had before. This wide range of powers requires appropriate safeguards to prevent misuse of the system, as a disproportionate use of these powers could damage constructive relationships between regulators and legitimate business.

1.46   Consequently, in chapter five, I have set out my recommendations for making this a transparent system with appropriate frameworks for regulator accountability. I believe these proposals will be vital to the effectiveness and acceptability of the sanctioning system I am advocating.

1.47   Finally, chapter six sets out all of my recommendations for easy reference.

II.   UNDERLYING PRINCIPLES FOR REGULATORY SANCTIONS

This chapter sets out the 'Penalties Principles' that underpin my recommendations. I also describe the characteristics of the framework within which the principles must operate to ensure successful and consistent application across all regulators.

Introduction

2.1   My recommendations not only widen the range of regulatory sanctions, but deliberately shift some of this activity away from the criminal courts to regulatory bodies themselves. This means that regulators will have new and increased powers. Given this expanded role, I believe it is necessary to provide regulators and their sponsoring departments with guidance on the parameters within which an extended sanctioning toolkit should operate.

I have done this by identifying a series of principles and characteristics. These are consistent with the Hampton principles as well as the Five Principles of Good Regulation.[36]

2.2   I have also considered the Criminal Justice Act 2003 and the guidance it gives the criminal courts when considering a sentence.[37] It refers to five purposes of a sentence that the courts must have regard to when determining a sentence. I have attempted to mirror these five purposes in my own principles. These five purposes are summarised below:

   •   The punishment of offenders;

   •   The reduction of crime (including deterrence);

   •   The reform and rehabilitation of offenders;

   •   The protection of the public; and

   •   The making of reparation by the offenders to those persons affected by their offences.

The need for Principles

2.2   My vision of a contemporary sanctioning regime for regulatory non-compliance is underpinned by a set of Penalties Principles that I defined and invited comments on in my interim report. I believe offering regulators a new suite of sanctions brings with it a need to provide guidance on how these sanctions should be applied.

2.3   My principles are primarily intended to set out the underlying rationale for my analysis and detailed recommendations. They will help build a common understanding of what a sanctioning regime should achieve amongst regulators and the regulated community, and in turn will act as a framework for regulators when considering what sort of sanction or enforcement action to take. This will provide a safeguard that the new sanctions will be used fairly and consistently. This is particularly important during the transition phase, as my recommendations are introduced and

---

[36] *BRTF Principles of Good Regulation* – Proportionality, Accountability, Consistency, Transparency and Targeting, 2003
[37] Criminal Justice Act 2003, Part 12, section 142.

regulators develop capacity and understanding of a newer and wider toolkit.

2.4 Consultation responses were broadly supportive of the principles described in my interim report. However, some concern was expressed that the principles should be applied flexibly, taking in to account circumstances of individual cases, the relevant legislative frameworks within which regulators in the UK operate, and existing practice and policy of regulators.

2.5 A general concern amongst consultation respondents was that restrictive application of the principles may lead to adverse outcomes. I discuss an example in the box below.

Application of Penalties Principles

In relation to **Principle #5**: *sanctions should include an element of ensuring that the harm caused by regulatory non-compliance is put right.*

The Financial Services Authority (FSA) suggest that although the principle *is* a relevant consideration, not all cases can or should include a restorative element. For example, in some cases it may not always be possible to quantify the losses suffered by an identifiable person and in others individual losses as a result of regulatory breaches are more efficiently and effectively redressed through individuals directly pursuing claims with the firm concerned (through the Financial Ombudsman Services or through the Financial Services Compensation Scheme). The FSA suggest that Principle #5 be qualified to make it clear that regulators need only consider whether a sanction should include a restorative element.

Financial Services Authority (FSA)

2.6 I believe that the Financial Services Authority make a valid point and I want to emphasise that the principles should be taken into consideration only where appropriate. Following on the example in the box above, not all cases may have caused harm to a party. In these instances, restoration to a person or community may not be necessary or appropriate. In other instances, some of the other principles may not be relevant. It may not be appropriate for all of the principles to apply in every single case, but there is a need for a consistent approach in that the principles should always be considered when a regulator is taking an enforcement action, or designing a specific sanctioning scheme.

2.7   In addition, I wish to emphasise that the Penalties Principles should be regarded as the underlying basis of regulators' sanctioning regimes in order to achieve consistency, rather than legally binding objectives in themselves. To this end, I have qualified some of the original principles, expressing them as aims rather than absolutes.

Using the Principles

2.8   I envisage that the principles I have set out will be of particular value to:

- Government departments in the design of detailed regulatory structures should they accept the recommendations in my report;

- Enforcement agencies in the design and implementation of enforcement policies;

- Regulators when deciding what sanction to impose;

- The regulated community in that the principles provide clarity overlaying specific sanctioning policies and reassurance that non-compliance will be dealt with appropriately; and

- All stakeholders in the future assessment of sanctioning regimes.

2.9   Regulators need to have the flexibility to impose the sanction they believe is appropriate, and my principles aim to provide a framework for deciding what type of sanction is suitable in individual circumstances. The spirit of my recommendations around the Penalties Principles is that they are there for guidance and should not be a basis for specific legal challenges. I do not prescribe a particular priority with regard to the individual principles as I believe, regulators should have the discretion to when particular principles are more appropriate or relevant.

2.10   Fundamental to the Penalties Principles is the notion that the underlying regulation is fit for purpose and provides for a greater social objective such as correcting a market failure or the protection of consumers, workers, or the environment.

The Six Penalties Principles

2.11 Consultation responses generally supported the six principles I detailed in my interim report. The principles that I recommend are therefore as follows:

- Principle #1 – Changing behaviour

   A sanction should aim to change the behaviour of the offender. This means that a sanction is not focused solely on punishment but should also ensure that the offender changes its behaviour and moves back into compliance. Changing behaviour could involve culture change within an organisation or a change in the production or manufacturing process to ensure that regulatory non-compliance is minimised. When choosing between different sanctions, refulations should consider how best to achieve changes in behaviour.

- Principle #2 – No financial benefit

   A sanction should aim to eliminate any financial gain or benefit from non-compliance. Firms may calculate that by not complying with a regulation, they can make or save money. They may also take a chance and hope that they are not caught for failing to comply with their regulatory obligations or for deliberately breaking the law. Some firms may even believe that if they are caught, the financial penalties handed down by the courts will usually be relatively low and they will probably still retain some level of financial gain.

   If, however, firms know that making money by breaking the law will not be tolerated and sanctions can be imposed that specifically target the financial benefits gained through non-compliance, then this can reduce the financial incentive for firms to engage in this type of behaviour. For firms that persist in operating this way, removing financial benefits will ensure that, in future, the financial gains are not enough of an incentive to break the law. I accept that determining the financial benefit is a difficult process in some instances, and that there may be some areas of regulation where the notion of identifiable profits gained from non-compliance is not applicable. But I believe it is a challenge that can be met as demonstrated by the methodologies developed by several leading regulators in the UK and abroad including the Canadian Border Services Agency, the US Environmental Protection Agency and the Federal Office of Consumer Protection and Safety in Germany.

- Principle #3 – Responsive Sanctioning

A sanction should be responsive and consider what is appropriate for the particular offender and the regulatory issue, which can include punishment and the public stigma that should be associated with a criminal conviction. The regulator should have the ability to use its discretion and, if appropriate, base its decision on what sort of sanction would help bring the firm into compliance. It may be that some firms would respond better to a sanction such as an administrative penalty combined with advice regarding best practice, while other firms may need to be sanctioned by way of a criminal prosecution. It is important that among other factors, the regulator also considers the size of the individual firms when deciding which sort of sanction is most likely to bring about a change in a firms' behaviour.

Ultimately, a regulator is obliged to uphold the public interest and maintain a credible enforcement and sanctioning regime. It should have the flexibility to apply a sanction for punitive reasons even though a lesser sanction could be applied. This may be necessary for so-called 'repeat offenders' who have been given previous opportunities – alongside advice and guidance – to comply, but have deliberately and intentionally failed to do so. Similarly, a punitive sanction may be appropriate for a single contravention with very serious external consequences.

The regulator should also consider the needs of victims and the public when determining what enforcement action is necessary in any particular case. Responsiveness is a positive quality and I believe that as long as procedural fairness is maintained and regulators pursue consistent policy objectives, regulatory outcomes will be improved.

Punitive Sanctions

Postcomm (Postal Services Commission) commented that whilst it is in agreement with the six principles in my interim report, it suggested that some contraventions may be so serious that they deserve a serious public mark of disapproval through imposing a substantive financial penalty and that the principles need to recognise this.

- *Principle #4 – Proportionate sanctioning*

  A sanction should be proportionate to the nature of the offence and the harm caused. Whilst the previous principle is concerned with addressing the reasons for the failure to comply, this principle takes into account the nature of the non-compliance and its consequences. Inclusion of these factors will ensure that firms are held accountable for the impact of the actual or potential consequences of their actions and that these are properly reflected in any sanction imposed. The sanction should reflect the individual circumstances of the firm and the circumstances surrounding the non-compliance.

Overlap Between the Penalties Principles

In their consultation response the FSA (Financial Services Authority) commented that there was some overlap between Principles #3 and #4. Although I agree that, on a wide interpretation, some of the principles can be construed as overlapping, I nonetheless believe that there is a distinct element in each principle I have identified and a value in setting these out separately.

- *Principle #5 – Restore the harm caused*

  A sanction should aim to restore the harm caused by regulatory non-compliance, where appropriate. This principle encompasses the needs of victims as well as ensuring that business offenders take responsibility for their actions and its consequences.

- *Principle #6 – Deterrence*

  A sanction should aim to deter future non-compliance. Sanctions should signal to others within the regulatory community that non-compliance will not be tolerated and that there will be consequences. Whether this is by a criminal prosecution or some other sanction would remain at the discretion of the regulator, within the scope of the powers available to it in relevant legislation, but firms should never think that non-compliance will be ignored or that they will 'get away with it'.

Framework for Operation of the Penalties Principles: the Seven Characteristics

2.12   It is important, particularly from the perspective of the regulated community, that there is a consistent approach to sanctioning across all regulators. To help ensure this my interim report proposed a framework within which the Penalties Principles should operate. It would be for regulators themselves to establish this framework. Consultation responses were positive towards the seven characteristics of this framework I described in my interim report.

• *Characteristic # 1 – Enforcement policy*

   Regulators should publish an enforcement policy. This will improve transparency and accountability from regulators by signalling to business and society the kind of responses and standards they can expect from regulators in dealing with non-compliance. A public enforcement policy will also show that regulators will use their sanction powers in a proportionate and risk based way. The regulator would need to be able to justify any departure from its own enforcement policy. Research carried out for my review indicated that currently only 17 out of 56 national regulations have a published enforcement policy. Enforcement policies will need to incorporate the new range of sanction options that I recommend and should be consistent, where appropriate, with the Regulators' Compliance Code to be issued under Part Two of the Legislative and Regulatory Reform Act 2006.

• *Characteristic # 2 – Measure outcomes*

   Regulators should measure outcomes not just outputs. Regulatory outputs are quantitative measures such as the number of prosecutions, or the number of Statutory Notices imposed by a regulator, whereas a regulatory outcome seeks to measure what impact regulatory outputs may have had. Measuring outcomes will enable regulators and the public to know what impact the enforcement actions are having, whether these have improved compliance, or remedied the harm caused by regulatory non-compliance, and whether there needs to be any modification to the balance between different types of enforcement actions to get better results. I acknowledge this may not be an easy exercise and there may be difficulties in determining these measures, but I maintain that regulators and government departments should make every effort to identify and measure regulatory outcomes.

- *Characteristic # 3 – Justify choice of enforcement actions*

Regulators should justify their choice of enforcement actions year on year to stakeholders, Ministers and Parliament. I recommend that regulators should be required to justify overall what their general enforcement strategy is and why they have chosen the enforcement actions that make up their strategy in any given year. This will not just provide protection for legitimate business, but increase public and private sector confidence and understanding in the way regulatory non-compliance is dealt with. I consider this in more detail in chapter five when I discuss accountability and transparency.

- *Characteristic # 4 – Follow-up enforcement actions*

Regulators should follow up their enforcement actions where appropriate. This is of particular importance for low-level enforcement actions such as warning letters or enforcement/improvement notices, where I am concerned that lack of follow-up on the part of regulators means that they are not taken seriously and credibly by firms. However, I recognise that follow-up activity is dependent on the resources available to individual regulators and must be consistent with a risk based approach to regulation. I do take account of other priorities faced by regulatory bodies operating with finite resources, who may not want to dedicate any resource to following up minor enforcement actions. I suggest that in order to make these enforcement actions credible, some follow-up is necessary, even if this is done on a random selection basis. One outcome measure that might be adopted is whether enforcement action has been effectively brought a business into compliance – systematic follow-up by regulators would be one way of measuring the extent to which such an outcome measure has been achieved.

- *Characteristic # 5 – Be transparent in what enforcement actions have been taken*

  Regulators should enforce in a transparent manner. Regulators should disclose to key stakeholders and the wider public when and against whom enforcement action has been taken. This should not be isolated to criminal prosecutions, but should also be used for other enforcement action such as administrative penalties, enforcement or improvement notices or any other formal sanction, where appropriate. This information should be easily accessible and serves as a safeguard for firms, the regulator and the public interest. I talk more about the importance of transparency in chapter five.

- *Characteristic # 6 – Be transparent in the methodology for determining or calculating administrative financial penalties*

  Regulators should be transparent in the way in which they apply and determine administrative penalties. Regulators should disclose the methodology for calculating variable administrative fines including the relevant mitigating and aggravating factors firms should be aware of. Regulators should also publish a schedule of fixed administrative fines if operating an FMAP scheme. I discuss this further in chapter three.

- *Characteristic #7 – Avoid perverse incentives influencing the choice of sanctioning response*

  Regulators should avoid perverse incentives that might influence the choice of sanctioning response. Regulators should, for example, avoid any rise of perverse incentives when determining the appraisal and evaluation schemes of enforcement staff. It is important that regulators do not have targets for different types of enforcement actions or any correlation with salary bonuses or similar incentives. This might incentivise staff to pursue certain enforcement actions inappropriately. Secondly, while there is already Government guidance on revenue from administrative penalties, I would emphasise that regulators should not retain the revenue from Monetary Administrative Penalties, or exercise any control over how that revenue should be spent. I describe these arrangements more fully in chapter three.

Link with the Compliance Code

2.13   The Legislative and Regulatory Reform Act 2006, contains a power which will enable some of the Hampton principles of regulatory enforcement (see section 2.92 of the Hampton review 'Reducing administrative burdens: effective inspection and enforcement') to be placed on a statutory footing through a statutory Code of Practice (the 'Regulators' Compliance Code'). I would envisage, subject to consultation, that the section of the final version of the Code relating to proportionate and meaningful sanctions for businesses that consistently breach regulations will be consistent with the Macrory Penalties Principles. Regulators should be able to demonstrate transparency in process and procedures in order to comply with the Code and I would expect regulators' enforcement policies to be consistent with both the Code and the Penalties Principles.

Link with the 'Five Principles of Good Regulation'

2.14   The consultation response from the Better Regulation Commission (BRC) highlighted that we already have the Five Principles of Good Regulation and the ten Hampton principles of inspection and enforcement.[38] The Commission expressed concern that adding further principles and providing too much guidance risked confusing both regulators and those they regulate.

2.15   I should like to make it clear, if I have not previously done so, that the wider purpose behind my review is to further the better regulation agenda as a whole and build on the good work already completed or underway. To this end I share the BRC's concern that the regulatory regime remains light-touch and I acknowledge that so-called 'principles proliferation' risks duplication and dilution. However, I believe that my Penalties Principles, set in the context of regulatory sanctioning, are a natural extension of

---

[38] The Five Principles are proportionality, accountability, consistency, transparency and targeting http://www.brc.gov.uk/publications/principlesentry.asp

the Commission's own work. Although I agree that some of my Penalties Principles may be construed as an application of the existing Five Principles of Good Regulation, I believe that there is a need to set them out separately.

2.16 The radical changes I am proposing need to incorporate safeguards for industry and the public. By identifying a series of principles and characteristics, I have specified what I think regulators should have regard to when extending their toolkits. I have taken the concerns of stakeholders seriously, and have attempted to provide a workable framework within which regulators should operate when expanding their sanctioning toolkits and have sought to limit the scope for any inappropriate behaviour by regulators, such as over-zealous parking ticket writing, through the drafting and application of a series of common principles.

Recommendation 2:

I recommend that in designing the appropriate sanctioning regimes for regulatory non-compliance, regulators should have regard to the following six Penalties Principles and seven characteristics.

Six Penalties Principles

A sanction should:

1. Aim to change the behaviour of the offender;

2. Aim to eliminate any financial gain or benefit from non-compliance;

3. Be responsive and consider what is appropriate for the particular offender and regulatory issue, which can include punishment and the public stigma that should be associated with a criminal conviction;

4. Be proportionate to the nature of the offence and the harm caused;

5. Aim to restore the harm caused by regulatory non-compliance, where appropriate; and

6. Aim to deter future non-compliance.

Seven Characteristics

Regulators should:

1. Publish an enforcement policy;

2. Measure outcomes not just outputs;

3. Justify their choice of enforcement actions year on year to stakeholders, Ministers and Parliament;

4. Follow-up enforcement actions where appropriate;

5. Enforce in a transparent manner;

6. Be transparent in the way in which they apply and determine administrative penalties; and

7. Avoid perverse incentives that might influence the choice of sanctioning response.

2.17 I believe that only when regulators can demonstrate that they are compliant with a Hampton risk based approach to regulation, should they be allowed by Government to use the toolkit I propose later in this document.

III. MY VISION FOR CONTEMPORARY SANCTIONING REGIMES: FINANCIAL SANCTIONS

The previous chapter outlined my Penalties Principles and characteristics, which I believe provide the necessary framework and parameters for an expanded sanctioning toolkit. This chapter sets out my recommendations for what types of sanctions should become available to regulators and enforcers in order to be more flexible, effective and better meet the compliance needs of industry and the public with a specific focus on Monetary Administrative Penalties and improvements of financial penalties in the criminal courts.

Introduction

3.1 The reformed sanctioning system that I propose is designed to increase public confidence, give greater awareness of the needs of victims and ensure that business non-compliance is met with a proportionate response both by regulators and in the courts. It will do this by providing a transparent system with sanctions that encourage and assist firms to comply with their regulatory obligations while ensuring that the most serious acts of regulatory non-compliance are dealt with appropriately and effectively by the criminal justice system.

3.2   The reforms that I suggest are not intended to transform regulatory sanctioning regimes overnight. Rather, they are to bring into them the flexibility, efficiencies and responsiveness that can facilitate the full implementation of the Hampton agenda, resulting in better deterrence options for regulators, better compliance for business and better outcomes for society as a whole.

3.3   I consulted upon suggestions for reform that were outlined in my interim report and in this report I publish my final recommendations with regards to alternative sanctions for both regulators and the courts.

A Vision for the Future

3.4   I consulted upon a richer range of sanctioning tools to be made available to regulators which would permit a range of regulatory offences to be handled other than by means of criminal prosecution, leaving the most serious cases to be dealt with by the criminal courts. Making such options available would itself reinforce a more appropriate role for the criminal courts, where in turn I propose recommendations for improving effectiveness of criminal prosecution for regulatory non-compliance.

3.5   My vision of sanctioning options for a risk-based sanctioning system, based upon risk based enforcement is illustrated in Figure 3.1. Regulators would, against the background of their enforcement policy and the proposed Compliance Code and having regard to my principles, continue to exercise discretion as to when it is appropriate to apply a sanction, and the choice of the sanction would be determined by the nature and circumstance of the regulatory non-compliance. With the availability of additional administrative sanctions, I would expect to see some shift in the current use of sanctions.

Figure 3.1 An effective sanctioning system

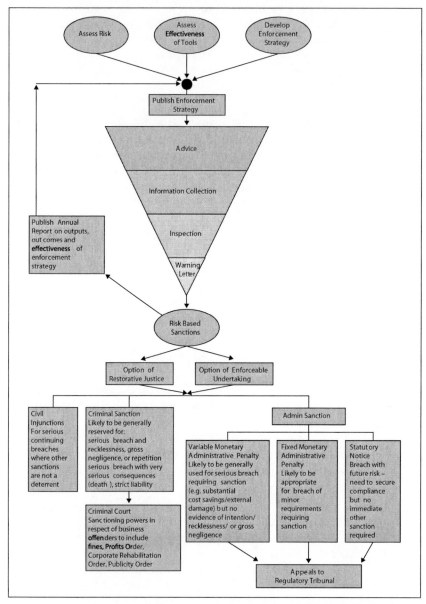

3.6   As part of this vision, the use of criminal prosecutions would remain appropriate for serious breaches where there was evidence of intentional or reckless or repeated flouting of the law. Regulators may decide within their discretion that criminal proceedings are justified where there is evidence of gross negligence and/or where the actual or potential consequences of the breach are so serious (such as a death or serious injury) that the public interest demands a criminal prosecution.

3.7   Some incidents of non-compliance with regulatory requirements would, I believe, be generally more effectively dealt with by the use of fixed or variable penalties (giving the offender an opportunity to have the case heard before an independent tribunal). Thus, breaches involving, for example, carelessness or negligence but still requiring a sanction (because, say, a substantial financial gain has been made or where there has been an external impact) are likely to be more appropriate for administrative sanctions rather than criminal proceedings.

3.8   Enforceable Undertakings may be introduced as an additional sanction for cases where the regulator has the necessary evidence to proceed to a criminal prosecution or the imposition of a Monetary Administrative Penalty, but where the business has committed to address the issues surrounding the regulatory non-compliance through an undertaking. These may offer business a less punitive sanction leading to a desirable change in behaviour and outcomes within the business.

3.9   I emphasise again, that I do not believe that all regulatory breaches require the imposition of a formal sanction. Warnings, advice and Statutory Notices will continue to play a key role in ensuring compliance. But where (in accordance with its enforcement policy) a regulator decides a formal sanction is justified, my proposals offer a richer range of appropriate response that is currently available.

3.10   I have given some views as to when each of the sanctioning options above might be appropriate. It is not possible to set out detailed factors for choosing between the options and it is ultimately up to regulators to decide what the appropriate response is in any particular case. The views I have expressed above may indicate a direction in which sanctioning regimes might develop. I accept, that there will be instances, for example, where a regulator feels that an offender who has been subjected to several prosecutions without changing their behaviour and may be more appropriately sanctioned with an administrative penalty. Conversely, there will be instances where a company has committed a strict liability offence giving rise to such serious consequences that a criminal prosecution is justified even though accidental circumstances or inadvertence was involved. Given this, any enforcement policy, while giving signals of a likely response, should allow for some degree of flexibility.

Specific Recommendations

3.11 Following the above discussion on my overall vision, I detail specific recommendations in several areas relating to penalties. These are presented as follows:

- Improving the effectiveness of criminal courts for cases of regulatory non-compliance;

- Introducing Fixed and Variable Monetary Administrative Penalties with appeals heard through an independent Regulatory Tribunal;

- Strengthening and extending the system of Statutory Notices in cases of regulatory non-compliance;

- Introducing Enforceable Undertakings and Undertakings Plus for cases of regulatory non-compliance;

- Introducing Restorative Justice for cases of regulatory non-compliance; and

- Introducing alternative sanctioning options for cases of regulatory non-compliance heard in the criminal courts.

Improving the Effectiveness of Criminal Courts for Cases of Regulatory non-Compliance

3.12 More than two million cases are heard annually in the Magistrates' Courts in England and Wales.[39] A small proportion of these relate to cases of regulatory non-compliance. I have some recommendations which should improve the effectiveness of the courts when working with cases of regulatory non-compliance.

Sentencing Guidelines

3.13 The Government should invite the Sentencing Guidelines Council to produce sentencing guidelines for cases of regulatory

---

[39] HM Court Service http://www.hmcourts-service.gov.uk/infoabout/magistrates/index.htm

non-compliance. These would be of great value to magistrates in the UK. The legal advisers in many of the local courts the review visited had prepared their own guidance documents and I think it would be beneficial for central guidance documents to exist. These guidelines could be high-level and focused on the principles that should be taken into consideration for sentencing cases of regulatory non-compliance.

Make the Financial Case Clear

3.14 Magistrates from around the UK commented to me that many prosecutors failed to provide adequate information to the court regarding the significance of the regulatory regime they are dealing with, the financial benefit gained through or financial circumstances surrounding cases of regulatory non-compliance. Prosecutors must make such matters clear to the court in order to better inform the courts so that the sanctions handed down can reflect more closely the financial and social impact of the case.

Focus Cases

3.15 Studying the existing practice of certain courts and regulatory areas, I believe it is sensible to consider consolidating certain types of regulatory non-compliance cases in a particular geographic area where possible. Focusing offences in this way gives greater opportunity for both magistrates and court officials to gain expertise and familiarity in the area of regulation concerned. This type of consolidation is already happening in certain areas of regulatory non-compliance. For example, in Greater London, health and safety prosecutions are initiated in the City of London Magistrates' Court. The British Potato Council, because of its location, concentrates prosecution in the Oxford Magistrates' Court and prosecutions for many regulatory offences under company law are heard before Cardiff Magistrates, reflecting the location of Companies House in Cardiff. It would appear sensible if further moves in this direction were taken. There must be limits – not least because of fairness implications for offenders who might be forced to travel long distances to a criminal court – to the extent this can be taken, but within the jurisdictional areas of magistrates, there may be further opportunities for particular magistrates' courts to take the lead in handling different types of regulatory offences. I believe the Government should consider this type of consolidation as part of the overall direction of Her Majesty's Court Service.

Training Legal Advisers

3.16   Almost all criminal prosecutions for cases of regulatory non-compliance against businesses are heard in the magistrates' courts.[40] There are over 28,000 magistrates at present in England and Wales, and I do not think it would be an effective use of time and resources to expect all Magistrates to have specialised training concerning cases of regulatory non-compliance. But I believe that there should be more systematic training made available which could be focused on district judges, prosecutors and justices' clerks who advise magistrates, and on those courts where it has been decided to focus particular regulatory prosecutions. The Judicial Studies Board (JSB) is responsible for judicial training. Regulators and sponsoring departments should discuss with the JSB the development of specialist training for district judges, justices' clerks and Magistrates where there is a sufficient volume of cases to merit this effort.

Recommendation 3:

I recommend that in order to increase the effectiveness of criminal courts for regulatory offences, the following actions should be implemented:

- The Government should request the Sentencing Guidelines Council to prepare general sentencing guidelines for cases of regulatory non-compliance;

- Prosecutors should always make clear to the court any financial benefits resulting from non-compliance as well as the policy significance of the relevant regulatory requirement;

- Prosecutions in particular regulatory fields be heard in designated magistrates' courts within jurisdictional areas, where appropriate; and

- Regulators provide specialist training for prosecutors and discuss with the Judicial Studies Board (JSB) contributing to the training of the judiciary and justices' clerks.

---

[40] 15,369 cases are heard in the magistrates' courts of a total of 15,445 cases of regulatory non-compliance committed by companies. HM Court Service.

Monetary Administrative Penalties (MAPs)

3.17   Monetary Administrative Penalties, in the context of my recommendations, are monetary penalties that are applied directly by a regulator, and I refer to them below as MAPs. Criminal courts do not play a part in the MAP process, and are generally not involved in issuing or enforcing such penalties. The recipient of a MAP has a right to appeal through an administrative appeals mechanism which usually takes the form of an administrative specialist tribunal. For example, a recipient of an administrative penalty under the Financial Services and Markets Act 2000 is entitled to a complete rehearing of their case before the Financial Services and Markets Tribunal.

Current use of Administrative Penalties

3.18   Administrative penalties are widely used in countries such as the US, Australia and Canada. In addition, many European countries, including Germany and Sweden, make extensive use of administrative penalties especially in areas of environmental regulation, health and safety, financial services and within other regulatory regimes, such as the regulation of utilities and water.

3.19   The UK experience with administrative penalties is largely limited to the financial regulators. The Financial Services and Markets Act 2000 gives the Financial Services Authority (FSA) a broad range of civil, administrative and criminal sanctioning powers, including the power to issue monetary administrative penalties. The majority of FSA cases are dealt with by using administrative routes. Since 2000 more than 70 cases have been concluded with an administrative penalty. Only six cases have been pursued through the criminal court system.

3.20   The Competition Commission can impose financial penalties under the Enterprise Act 2002 (set out in sections 109-111) in relation to its investigation powers. The penalties can either be a fixed amount, not exceeding £20,000 or calculated as a daily rate, not exceeding £5,000 per day.[41]

3.21   The Office of Fair Trading (OFT) has access to financial penalties for non-compliance with competition law. The OFT has discretion to impose financial penalties that can be severe, but may not

---

[41] As provided for in the Competition Commission (Penalties) Order 2003 [SI 2003/1371.]

exceed ten percent of turn over.[42] This power is set out in section 36 of the Competition Act 1998.

3.22 While the use of administrative penalties in the UK regulatory context is not unprecedented, they have tended to be used for cases of civil regulatory non-compliance rather than criminal regulatory non-compliance. The Hampton Review identified that out of the 60 regulators in scope only 15 were able to impose administrative penalties.[43] Of these 15, the majority only have access to fixed penalties which are for a low financial amount. I believe that the introduction of monetary administrative penalties, both fixed and variable, in more regulatory regimes, whether civil or criminal, would serve to help fill the gap that exists in the current enforcement toolkit of many UK regulators, where there is a lack of intermediate sanctions.[44]

The Effectiveness of Monetary Administrative Penalties

3.23 I have considered the academic literature, international experience and the responses provided to me through the consultation process and have found that administrative penalties are an effective way of ensuring regulatory compliance whilst reserving criminal prosecutions for the most serious of cases of regulatory non-compliance.

3.24 As discussed in my interim report, administrative penalties can provide an intermediate step between the formal, costly and stigmatising action of criminal prosecution and the more informal means of advice and persuasion to get firms back into compliance.[45] I believe that breaches of regulatory requirements can take in circumstances that require a formal sanction but not necessarily a criminal prosecution.

3.25 Well designed administrative schemes can also be flexible and take a more customised approach in dealing with regulatory non-compliance, especially in cases of variable penalties. For example, compliance history, the seriousness of the offence and its impact on the external environment or community can be taken into

---

[42] As defined in the Competition Act 1998 (Determination of Turnover for Penalties) (amendment) Order 2004 [SI 2004/1259]

[43] P. Hampton, *Reducing Administrative Burdens: Effective Inspection and Enforcement*, HM Treasury, March 2005, p.23

[44] See paragraphs 1.33- 1.34 on the compliance deficit

[45] *Regulatory Justice: Sanctioning in a post-Hampton World*, Consultation Document, R. Macrory, May 2006 p. 45 par 3.9

consideration. This flexibility can allow the regulator to ensure that the level of the MAP is appropriate to reflect the various aggravating and mitigating factors, encourage future compliance and be reflective and proportionate to the size of the business. Such a system could motivate offenders to take actions to move into compliance and provide a sanctioning option for those cases where it may not be appropriate to prosecute the offender and where previous advice or Statutory Notices have not been effective.

> Overall responses to my consultation document showed that over 70 percent of respondents believed regulators should have access to Monetary Administrative Penalties as part of their enforcement toolkits

Fixed & Variable Monetary Administrative Penalties

3.26 In my interim report *Regulatory Justice: Sanctioning in a Post Hampton World* I set out three models of Monetary Administrative Penalties. The majority of consultation responses supported my preferred option, in which regulators have access to Fixed and Variable Monetary Administrative Penalties with business being able to appeal to an independent Regulatory Tribunal.

Figure 3.2: Models of administrative penalties

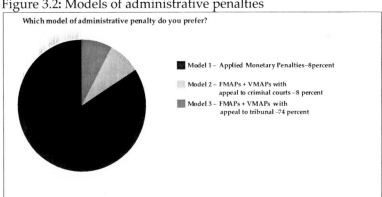

Which model of administrative penalty do you prefer?

■ Model 1 – Applied Monetary Penalties–8percent

Model 2 – FMAPs + VMAPs with appeal to criminal courts –8 percent

Model 3 – FMAPs + VMAPs with appeal to tribunal –74 percent

* These figures do not include individuals who responded in order to avoid undue distortion. I accept that because of the differences in size and expertise of the organisations involved these tables ate indicative only of the general thrust of the responses

Source: Macrory Review, Consultation August 2006.

3.27 This is the model that I have chosen to recommend because I believe that there are a number of advantages to this option which I mentioned in my interim report. I discuss the appeal mechanism for this system of fixed and variable penalties in the following section.

Fixed Monetary Administrative Penalties (FMAPs)

3.28   Fixed Monetary Administrative Penalties (FMAPs) are generally fines for a relatively low fixed amount that are applied in respect of low level, minor or high-volume instances of non-compliance. They can be applied directly by the regulator, where a business has been found to have failed to comply with regulations. Legislation specifies both the nature of the offence as well as the maximum amount of the fine. The regulator does not have discretion as to the level of the financial penalty, but does have discretion in whether or not to apply a penalty in the first instance.

> There are a number of offences for which a fixed monetary administrative penalty would be appropriate across the range of enforcement functions in local authorities, including Health and Safety, Food Safety and Trading Standards. This type of sanction may be particularly useful in tackling 'low-level, minor, high volume instances of non-compliance'.
>
> *Glasgow City Council*
>
> We believe FMAPs could be available in circumstances where the outcomes of the breach have little effect on consumer protection. Such examples might include late filing of accounts because the deadlines in one sense are 'arbitrary'.
>
> *Cattle PLC*

3.29   As FMAPs are for relatively minor amounts, they may not be appropriate for more serious or deliberate cases of regulatory non-compliance or where a firm has made significant financial gains or where the public interest would be best served by a criminal prosecution. However, international practice suggests that they can still be meaningful and significant as a sanctioning tool. As set out in the box below, in the area of health and safety in New South Wales, Australia, the on-the-spot fine scheme in operation by WorkCover, ranges in level of fine from A$80 to A$1,200 (£30-£500). The average fine is A$550 (£220). The schedule for the penalties is set out in the relevant legislation (Occupational Health and Safety Act 2002).

Box 3.1 Fixed Penalty Notices – A case study – WorkCover, New South Wales, Australia

The health and safety regulator, WorkCover, in New South Wales, Australia, uses fixed penalty notices as an enforcement tool against employers. The options include penalty notices, an on-the-spot-fine handed down to businesses where the inspector is of the opinion that advice or direction is not sufficient. WorkCover considers penalty notices are an effective method of dealing with less serious breaches of the legislation.

Inspectors will consider various factors when determining whether to issue a penalty notice.

These factors include:

- whether the breach can be remedied quickly

- whether the issuing of a penalty notice is likely to have the desired deterrent effect

- whether the breach is a one-off situation or part of an ongoing pattern of non-compliance

The Occupational Health and Safety Act 2002 identifies a range of offences and determines a corresponding penalty. Fines range from A$80 to A$1,200. (£30-£500) The average fine is A$550 (£220).

The schedule of breaches with corresponding fixed financial penalties secures that there is transparency when the decision is taken to impose an on-the-spot-fine on a business.

A person served with a penalty notice may elect not to pay the penalty and to have the matter dealt with by the court. The procedure for making an election is set out on the back of the penalty notice.

Source: WorkCover compliance policy and prosecution guidelines, WorkCover, New South Wales, March 2004

Scaling the FMAP

3.30   Small as well as large businesses could be liable for FMAPs but each type of business can have significantly different abilities to pay and absorb financial penalties. I believe it would be beneficial if the FMAP could reflect the size of the firm, relying on factors such as the number of employees or annual turnover, where small firms would get a fixed penalty and larger firms would get the same fixed penalty, but scaled up by a certain factor. This would ensure that regardless of the size of a business, an FMAP could still represent an effective deterrent.

Current use of Fixed Monetary Penalties

3.31   FMAPs already exist as an enforcement option in the UK for certain offences, for example Her Majesty's Revenue and Customs can issue fixed penalties of £100 for failure to deliver a self assessment tax return when required or if the delivered tax return is incorrect. They can also issue a fine of an amount up to a specified limit per day, for example up to £60 a day for continued failure to deliver a self assessment form.[46] The Clean Neighbourhoods and Environment Act 2005 enables authorised officers of a local authority to issue fixed penalty notices for failure to comply with some of the requirements of the Act, for example £100 for nuisance parking offences.[47] Companies House can also impose a penalty notice against a company because company accounts were not received on time. Companies House operates a scale of penalty that is dependent on how late the accounts are and whether the company is a private firm or a publicly listed company. These range from £100 to £5,000.[48]

> Companies House is a regulator with access to FMAPs under the Companies Act 1985. Companies House can levy a Late Filing Payment (LFP) for the late submission of company accounts. These were introduced in 1992. The Registrar of Companies House has discretion of not collecting a LFP in exceptional circumstances.

---

[46] The penalty is set out in s 93 of the Taxes Management Act 1970, as amended by s196 and paragraph 25 of Schedule 19 of the Finance Act 1994 (in relation to the year 1996/97 and subsequent years of assessment in accordance with s 199(2) of the 1994 Act).

[47] The Clean Neighbourhoods & Environment Act 2005, Part 2, S 6, (1). In 2004/5, Local Authorities issued 15,582 fines for litter, 2,296 for dog fouling, 19 for graffiti, 52 for fly-posing and 1 for noise.

[48] http://www.companieshouse.gov.uk/infoGuide/faq/lateFilingAppeal.shtml Companies Act 1985, s 242a

In 1991, the compliance rate for accounts was 86 percent. With the introduction of the late filing penalty regime in June 1992 the rate immediately increased to 92 percent and has continued to increase to a level of around 96 percent. There is no doubt, therefore that the penalty regime has achieved two major effects. Not only has it secured an initial significant increase in the level of compliance, but it has also maintained that level of compliance at that high percentage of companies.

Source: Companies House submission to Macrory call for evidence, February 2006.

Variable Monetary Administrative Penalties

3.32   Variable Monetary Administrative Penalties (VMAPs) are sanctions applied by the regulator where the amount is at the discretion of the regulator. Instead of being for a relatively small fixed amount whose maximum is pre-determined by legislation (as with FMAPs above), a variable penalty can, where appropriate and proportionate, be for a more significant amount initially determined at the discretion of the regulator in accordance with a published scheme. Relevant mitigating or aggravating factors, the specific circumstances of the offence and the means of the non-compliant business must be taken into consideration by the regulator when determining the amount of the penalty in any particular case. I discuss these factors in the following sections.

Yes, we agree that it would be a good idea for VMAPs to be made available to all regulators. The situations in which the FSA can impose VMAPs includes breaches of FSA rules by authorised firms, misconduct by FSA approved individuals, breaches of FSA listing rules by listed companies or certain other persons, and market abuse by any person whether regulated or not. We find our VMAP powers operate very effectively for us. They allow us a degree of flexibility with which to respond to different cases, and ensure that the penalty matches the misdemeanour.

Financial Services Authority

Yes, VMAPs should be available to regulators as part of a mixed system. A variable fine allows the regulator to operate flexibly and proportionately.

British Chamber of Commerce

It is important VMAPs are available. In high profitability areas, the costs of FMAPs could simply be built into business plans. This is certainly the case in the premium rate industry where even substantial fines (£100,000) can be simply written off as a business expense. Therefore VMAPs must be an option to ensure the principle of removing the benefit from the crime can be upheld. The consultation provides some good illustrations that can be used to good effect in preference to prosecution – it is a case of using the right tools for the right job.

South West England Coordination of Trading Standards

Relationship Between Criminal Offences and VMAPs – Parallel but Connected

3.33   As I have indicated in chapter one, I do not envisage a root and branch reform of existing offences relating to regulatory non-compliance. For those existing criminal offences where it is decided that a VMAP is an appropriate alternative sanction, the legislation would need to be amended to allow for the imposition of a Monetary Administrative Penalty. A regulator would then have the option, in line with its enforcement policy, and my suggested principles, to choose in appropriate cases the sanction of a VMAP rather than a criminal prosecution. A regulator would investigate a potential offence as usual and if satisfied that the evidence of a breach exists, then decide the most appropriate sanctioning route.

3.34   Criminal sanctions and VMAPs will be available as sanctions for the same regulatory non-compliance. The elements of the regulatory non-compliance would need to be proved to the requisite evidential standard. Where a criminal sanction is pursued, the regulator would need to meet the criminal standard of beyond reasonable doubt. Should the regulator choose to pursue a VMAP, the evidence should meet the civil standard of the balance of probabilities.

In the CBI's view, administrative fines may be viewed simply as a 'cost of doing business' for the deliberately non-compliant firm. There is also concern within the business community that introducing more administrative fines will foster a 'parking ticket' type mentality amongst inspectors, which will fundamentally change the existing relationship between inspectors and businesses – at a time when the aim should be to encourage more co-operation and flexibility and discussion between inspectors and businesses.

Confederation of British Industry

We reject the view that the application of penalties in such cases helps to secure compliance. Nothing could be more calculated to enhance tick a box inspections than the desire to levy such on the spot fines for instances that would almost certainly today be ignored or subject to advice. The plain fact is that compliant businesses would willingly act on such advice and introduce any necessary procedures to mitigate the chances of the offence recurring. On the other hand rogue traders would be more likely to be compliant with the threat of a court action than with an administrative fine that could be considered part of the costs of doing business.

British Retail Consortium

3.35   I recognise that there are concerns in some of the business community that this may unfairly encourage the use of VMAPs in place of current prosecutions and that smaller businesses may not have the financial resource to challenge a VMAP, but I do not believe these are sufficiently convincing to outweigh the advantages that the VMAP would bring as an alternative sanctioning route. I would note that the civil standard of proof does have adequate safeguards to protect the rights of the accused. The regulator would still need to ensure that the investigation process and the imposition of the VMAP protects the procedural rights of the recipient of the administrative penalty. These proposals are not about making it easier to penalise businesses but to create a system of sanctions that is more responsive and proportionate to the nature of the non-compliance.

3.36   The choice between criminal prosecution and the imposition of a VMAP should be based upon the principles I have set out in chapter two rather than on the applicable evidential standard. Regulators should consider which is the most appropriate sanctioning route relying on factors such as ability to change behaviour, ability to eliminate financial gain, and proportionality, I consider that VMAPs are a more responsive and appropriate sanction than criminal prosecution in a wide range of cases. Criminal prosecution should however be reserved for serious breaches of regulatory obligations such as cases of deliberate, reckless or repeated non-compliance.

3.37   It should be noted that these proposals are not about 'letting off' businesses for their regulatory non-compliance. While the imposition of an administrative fine such as VMAPs may not have the same stigma as a criminal conviction, the imposition of a VMAP can represent a significant sanction. One of the aims of VMAPs is to remove the financial gain made from the regulatory non-compliance – something a criminal conviction may not always achieve. This will help create a level playing field for compliant businesses and deter rogue businesses from non-compliance in the future.

Level of Financial Penalty

3.38   I have carefully considered the issue of the level of financial penalties for both FMAPs and VMAPs and there are advantages and disadvantages to setting a fine maxima in both instances.

FMAPs

3.39   In the case of FMAPs, I believe that these should have a statutory maximum level which should be set out in the relevant underlying legislation. By definition, FMAPs are for low level breaches and the financial penalty should be for a relatively low amount. I believe it makes sense for the maximum level of FMAPS to not exceed level five on the standard scale.[49] This is currently set at £5,000.

VMAPs

3.40   I have carefully considered the advantages and disadvantages of setting an upper limit to VMAPs in underlying legislation and in particular whether some cap such as a 10 percent turnover maximum should be provided in the legislation. I believe that to impose such an upper limit would pose undue legal complexity on the system, and could encourage regulators to set VMAPs at inappropriately high levels. I want to ensure that regulators have the flexibility and ability of capturing the financial benefit businesses may have acquired through a regulatory breach. I do not believe the legislation should specify an upper limit.

3.41   The business community clearly will need to be confident that such a scheme is not being used inappropriately or irresponsibly by a regulator. I have some recommendations that will seek to give business transparency into the way in which VMAPs are calculated.

[49] Criminal Justice Act 1982, S 37

Box 3.2 Aggravating and Mitigating Factors that should be Considered for VMAPs

In a system with Variable Monetary Administrative Penalties regulators would be required to develop and publicise a method for calculating the penalty for regulatory non-compliance. The following are examples of aggravating and mitigating factors which regulators could take into account when determining the appropriate level of Variable Monetary Administrative Penalty, although this list is not exhaustive and each decision will depend on the circumstances of the individual case:

Aggravating Factors

- Seriousness of the regulatory non-compliance, e.g. the harm or potential for harm to human health or the environment, the duration of non-compliance etc.;

- Evidence of intention (if any) behind the regulatory non-compliance;

- Disciplinary record or history of non-compliance of the business;

- Financial gain made by the business as a result of non-compliance with regulations;

- Size and financial resources of the firm that failed to comply with regulations;

- The conduct of the business after the regulatory non-compliance has come to the attention of the regulator; and

- Previous actions taken by the regulator, or other regulators, to help the business into compliance.

Mitigating Factors

- Actions taken to eliminate or reduce the risk of damage resulting from regulatory non-compliance;

- Actions taken to repair the harm done by regulatory non-compliance;

- Co-operation with the regulator in responding to regulatory non-compliance;

- Fast and accurate reporting of regulatory non-compliance;

- Size and financial resources of the firm that failed to comply with regulations;

- The conduct of the business after the regulatory non-compliance has come to the attention of the regulator; and

- Vicarious liability for failures by employees including the adequacy of management controls and the extent to which the employee was acting outside of his or her authority.

Who Makes the Decision to Impose the Sanction?

3.42   While Monetary Administrative Penalties could be a valuable addition to the enforcement toolkit, it is important that the regulatory relationship between business and the regulator is not compromised. I believe it is essential that I comment on what level of decision-maker should be involved in decisions of whether or not to impose a MAP so as to provide guidance to regulators. It is important that decision makers have sufficient experience and authority to impose MAPs. This would serve to maintain the current pragmatic relationship many within the regulated community have come to value with their enforcers.

3.43   FMAPs, because they are generally imposed for low-level, minor offences and for a low financial amount, could be issued by lower levels of staff within a regulator who have undergone the appropriate training. However, I want to assure the regulated community that such a regime should not bear resemblance to the 'parking-ticket' mentality mentioned to me by many respondents in my consultation. In order to avoid FMAP training becoming a tick-box exercise, I believe regulators should look to on-going monitoring in order to test that the FMAPs are being used appropriately and I make further suggestions concerning transparency and accountability in chapter five.

3.44   As VMAPs can be for more significant sums, decisions should be taken independently from field staff or inspectors. Regulators may also want to consider seeking representations from a business on the penalty proposed in advance of it being imposed. The field staff could make a recommendation on whether a VMAP should be imposed or not and recommend a level of penalty, but I believe the final decision should be taken by more senior officials within the regulator. This would serve to ensure that the relationship between the inspector and the business is not compromised. In addition, it would encourage consistent behaviour from the regulator since decisions on imposing VMAPs would be taken by the same group within a regulator. This would provide a good check on what VMAPS are being imposed, against whom and for how much.

Fines Would not be Accessed by the Regulator

3.45   Many of the concerns from the business community regarding MAPs is due to an uncertainty as to whether regulators will financially benefit from imposing administrative penalties. I have reflected this concern in my principles and characteristics. MAPs should not be viewed by regulators as a means to raise revenue from the businesses they regulate. I want to avoid creating any perverse financial incentives for regulators that might influence their choice of sanctioning tool. This view is already entrenched in relevant section of HM Treasury's Consolidated Budgeting Guide and I echo their views on the separation of revenue streams in order to eliminate perverse incentives.[50] I have also emphasised that regulators must avoid creating perverse incentives (such as staff appraisal criteria) that will encourage the use of financial penalties without regard to the regulatory outcomes to be achieved.

Recovery of Costs to the Regulator

3.46   I am aware that bringing any form of enforcement action generates costs for regulators. Regulators are able to recover some of their costs in pursuing the prosecution. I believe a similar system should exist for regulators that choose to use the MAP system. I do not think it is right that regulators should be incentivised to use the criminal system and I want to mention this so that cost recovery is a part of the consideration of any MAP scheme. Cost recovery should include the cost of collection of an administrative penalty, which I discuss in the next paragraph.

Enforcement of Monetary Administrative Penalties

3.47   In order for any administrative penalty regime to have credibility, businesses must know that when an administrative penalty is imposed, it will be enforced and that the regulator will pursue the collection of the penalty. If a business refuses to pay the penalty without initiating an appeal, then regulators should be able to pursue the payment of this penalty through ordinary civil debt recovery procedures.

---

[50] *Consolidated Budgeting Guidance for 2006/07*, HM Treasury, Chapter 3.

Administrative Penalties and Private Prosecutions

3.48   Some regulatory schemes permit private prosecutions. In theory, someone other than a regulator, who feels that the regulatory non-compliance justifies a criminal rather than an administrative sanction could also initiate a private prosecution for the same offence. This, of course, can happen under current arrangements where a regulator decides, in line with its enforcement policy, to issue, say, only a warning in response to an offence. A private prosecution could still be initiated in such circumstances. As a matter of general policy, I believe that the existence of the power of private prosecution can be a valuable check on regulator behaviour. There exist a number of mechanisms (such as the right of the Director of Public Prosecutions to take over a private prosecution) designed to prevent abuse or vexatiousness of private prosecutions.

3.49   I recognise that where a VMAP has been imposed on a business, it needs to be insulated from the risk of double jeopardy which a private prosecution might impose, and additional procedural checks (such as leave of a court before a private prosecution can be initiated in such circumstances) may be required. I have received very little evidence on this issue, and do not think it appropriate for me to make detailed suggestions as to the most appropriate mechanisms needed. But I recommend that when designing the legislative scheme of VMAPs, the Government needs to consider whether existing mechanisms are sufficient to prevent this form of double jeopardy, and if not, what would be the best way of handling the issue.

Recommendation 4:

I recommend that with regards to Monetary Administrative Penalties:

- Government should, introduce schemes for Fixed and Variable Monetary Administrative Penalties, for regulators and enforcers of regulations, that are compliant with the Hampton and Macrory Principles and characteristics. This can include national regulators as well as local regulatory partners;

- Appeals concerning the imposition of an administrative penalty be heard by a Regulatory Tribunal, rather than the criminal courts;

- Fine maxima for Fixed Monetary Administrative Penalties (FMAP) schemes should be set out and not exceed level five on the standard scale. FMAPs should also be scaled to differentiate between small and large firms; and

- There should be no fine maxima for Variable Monetary Administrative Penalties (VMAPs).

3.50 In order for these administrative penalties to be effective, it is important that prior to regulators expanding their toolkits, regulators should be compliant with the Hampton Principles and demonstrate an ability to comply with the Macrory Principles and characteristics. Compliance with the principles and characteristics will be considered for regulators who want to gain access to these sanctions prior to the new sanctions being awarded, including both national and local regulators. This role will likely fall to the Better Regulation Executive and some national regulators (who use local regulatory partners) to ensure that regulators gaining access to the expanded sanctioning toolkit are compliant and operate in a risk based manner.

3.51 Regulators who want to use administrative penalties should ensure the following:

- Clearly identify the persons within their organisation who are authorised to impose a Fixed and Variable MAP;

- Publish the way in which VMAPs will be calculated; and

- Regulators should not make any financial gains from the imposition of Monetary Administrative Penalties, but they should be entitled to some cost recovery.

3.52 In addition, the Government should consider whether additional provisions are needed to prevent the risk of double jeopardy from a private prosecution initiated for an offence that has been sanctioned by a VMAP.

Appeal Mechanisms and an Independent Regulatory Tribunal

3.53 In my consultation document, I set out three models for the application of Administrative Monetary Penalties. The key differences in these models related to the mechanism for access to a fair and timely appeal.[51]

An Independent Tribunal as a Route to Appeal

3.54   It is important that any administrative penalty system where decisions are taken by public officials, acting as part of a Government department or agency, carries with it the necessary protections for any person or business served with a penalty notice. Having access to an effective and quick appeal route is an absolute necessity when referring to administrative financial penalties. The Department for Constitutional Affairs' White Paper on *Complaints Redress and Tribunals* states that 'where mistakes occur we are entitled to complain and to have the mistake put right with the minimum of difficulty; where there is uncertainty we are entitled to expect a quick resolution of the issue'.[52]

3.55   The tribunal I recommend could serve as an appeals mechanism for all administrative sanctions including MAPs as well as other administrative sanctions. The Regulatory Tribunal would provide the regulated community with a chance to have its say before an independent body in cases where there is disagreement over the imposition or conditions of an administrative sanction. It would also hold regulators accountable for the imposition of an administrative sanction and ensure that regulators follow their own enforcement policies and procedures when imposing sanctions. I detail further accountability mechanisms in chapter five.

3.56   For those regulators who already operate schemes of Fixed and Variable Monetary Administrative Penalties with appeals being heard with an existing tribunal, I believe that these appeals can continue to be heard in the existing tribunal. There is no need to shift any of these cases to the Regulatory Tribunal, unless a sponsoring department and regulator agree that the Regulatory Tribunal would be more appropriate.

---

[51] *Regulatory Justice: Sanctioning in a Post-Hampton World*, n 1 above.
[52] *Transforming Public Services: Complaints, Redress and Tribunals*, DCA White Paper, July 2004, p3.

> We believe that an independent specialist tribunal composed of members with specialist expertise is a good idea and would minimise the burden on the magistrates' court.
>
> *Trading Standards Institute*
>
> A tribunal would have the specialist skills and experience to deal with a new evidential test and procedure that would be required to make the MAP option work efficiently. MAPs should be viewed as an entirely separate sanction to prosecutions and the distinction could be blurred if appeals were to progress through the criminal courts.
>
> *Office of Rail Regulation*

Why Did I Choose to Create Another Tribunal?

3.57   The evidence presented to me consistently commented that there was a need to separate out those cases of regulatory non-compliance that would be better sanctioned outside of the criminal setting. It follows that if administrative sanctions are to be most effective, then it is necessary to remove appeals relating to these cases from the criminal courts. This would also avoid creating a hybrid system with no distinct separation between administrative and criminal sanctions.

3.58   Operating a hybrid system with appeals of both administrative and criminal sanctions going to a criminal court would raise some of the same issues that I have previously highlighted in my interim report when considering cases of regulatory non-compliance within a criminal setting.[53] These include:

- Low deterrence can sometimes be the outcome of a criminal prosecution as levels of fines can fail to remove the financial benefit arising from non-compliance.

- Appeals of administrative sanctions would be heard alongside mainstream violent and anti-social crime cases.

- Cases of regulatory non-compliance make up less than one percent of all cases head in magistrates' courts making it difficult to provide specific training to magistrates and legal advisers.[54]

---

[53] *Regulatory Justice: Sanctioning in a post-Hampton World*, n 1 above.
[54] Ibid p 89.

3.59 I recognise that magistrates' courts in some areas already handle both criminal and civil matters, and as a matter of administrative simplicity it would be tempting to refer all appeals concerning MAPs back to the magistrates' courts. Given the proposed creation of the new unified tribunal system (see paragraph 3.67 below), I believe it would be a wasted opportunity not to incorporate a dedicated Regulatory Tribunal which would be better suited to handling these issues, and would clearly separate criminal and administrative processes. In my consultation report I suggested that there would be two advantages to a separate tribunal for appealing administrative sanctions. First, that the tribunal could be composed of members with both legal and specialist expertise in the subject matter, providing the tribunal with a fuller understanding of the issues. Second, a tribunal would not consider regulatory cases alongside cases of conventional crime which constitute the main workload of the criminal courts. A Regulatory Tribunal would also be a flexible and accessible appeal mechanism.

3.60 Overall, in cases of administrative sanctions, I believe that a tribunal would continue to provide sufficient procedural safeguards necessary to protect the needs of the regulated community and regulators. An independent tribunal would also allow for the differentiation and sanctioning of some cases of regulatory non-compliance outside of the criminal setting.

Appeal Route for an Administrative Sanction

3.61 Ultimately, it is for a regulator and sponsoring department to determine what the best appeal arrangements would be for its particular area of regulation provided that the minimum standards which I outline in this section are met. However, I would encourage all regulators who have an administrative sanctioning scheme to consider using the Regulatory Tribunal because it can be designed to be flexible enough to address regulatory issues in more than one particular regulatory field. I discuss this more in detail in the following section.

> This would allow for such appeals to be heard in a timely manner and will help consistency, as the criminal and civil courts are already 'over-burdened'. The tribunals should be given adequate sentencing powers, in order that they are seen by regulators, consumers and legitimate business as being a worthwhile and punitive measure.
>
> *Yorkshire and Humberside Trading Standards*

Overall Appeal Process for FMAPs

3.62   The first stage of any appeal process in relation to FMAPs should be an internal review of the case carried out by the regulator. This would not involve the tribunal. Having access to an internal review process would give the regulated industry the opportunity to question the regulator's decision and present any information that the regulator may not have had access to at the time the sanction was originally imposed. Following an internal review, the regulator could either affirm its decision and uphold the sanction, or cancel and impose a lesser sanction if appropriate.

3.63   If the member of the regulated community is not satisfied with the outcome of the internal review, an appeal of that decision could be taken forward to the Regulatory Tribunal. The appeal could either be for a complete re-hearing of the issue where the member of the regulated community believes no sanction should have been applied in the first instance because the circumstances of the breach have not been made out (including any defences available for the offence in question) or that the regulator has acted unreasonably in imposing the FMAP. The appropriate grounds for appeal will be determined in legislation. A tribunal case could be conducted on the basis of papers alone if this was agreed to by both parties, or by an oral hearing. As the tribunal will be reviewing the application of administrative sanctions, it will apply the civil standard of proof.

Overall Appeal Process for VMAPs

3.64   As VMAPs would be for more significant financial amounts, I believe that the regulator should give notice to a business that it intends to propose a VMAP, providing the business with an opportunity to make representations to the regulator for consideration. Following this process, a regulator may impose a VMAP by issuing a penalty notice.

3.65   If a business is not satisfied with the level of the VMAP or believes the VMAP should not have been imposed, it has the right of taking this matter to the Regulatory Tribunal for consideration. The appeal could either be a complete re-hearing, or pertain to a specific point of law and should take the form of an oral hearing. The appropriate grounds for appeal will be determined in legislation. Similar to the process outlined above for FMAPs, the tribunal would work on the civil standard of proof, as it is reviewing the application of an administrative sanction.

3.66   It would be up to the regulator and sponsoring department to consider what would constitute an appropriate panel and there are many models that exist. In general, I believe that the Regulatory Tribunal for VMAPs should consist of a panel of three made up of a legal expert, which could include members of the judiciary or lawyers, a relevant expert in the area of regulation before the tribunal, and a member from a relevant stakeholder group such as the industry or another relevant stakeholder.

3.67   Depending on the timing of legislation, the Regulatory Tribunal would either be a new, bespoke tribunal or would form part of the new First-tier Tribunal, proposed in the draft Tribunals, Courts and Enforcement Bill, which was published on 25 July 2006. The Bill sets out a new statutory framework for a unified tribunal system. The tribunal system will have two new, generic tribunals, the First-tier Tribunal and the Upper Tribunal. They are intended to be adaptable institutions, able to take on any existing or new jurisdictions. For those parties that are not satisfied with the outcome of an appeal to the Regulatory Tribunal, there would be a right of appeal on a point of law (and with permission) to the Upper Tribunal. The Tribunals Service, a new Department for Constitutional Affairs agency launched in April 2006, will provide common administrative support to the unified tribunal system.[55] The flexibility of the new unified tribunal system will ensure that the relevant panel of experts need only sit when there is a case to be heard in a particular regulatory area. It will also ensure a good geographical distribution so that cases can be heard in appropriate locations.

Funding

3.68   Funding and set up costs for the Regulatory Tribunal should be provided by the sponsoring departments whose regulators are using the tribunal as part of their appeal for administrative sanctions including MAPs. It is important that any tribunal fees that might be introduced in no way inhibit the right of appeal against Monetary Administrative Penalty which I believe is inherent to a fair system.

---

[55] http://www.tribunals.gov.uk/

IV. MY VISION FOR CONTEMPORARY SANCTIONING REGIMES – NON-FINANCIAL SANCTIONS AND ALTERNATIVES FOR THE CRIMINAL COURTS

The previous chapter presented my recommendations for improving the effectiveness of criminal courts in addressing cases of regulatory non-compliance. It also presented my recommendations on the introduction of both Fixed and Variable Monetary Administrative Penalties. This chapter looks at non-financial sanctions such as Statutory Notices, Enforceable Undertakings and Undertakings Plus. It also presents recommendations for alternative sentencing in the criminal courts.

Introduction

4.1   I am aware that monetary penalties may not be effective in every instance and I want to ensure that regulators have access to a broad range of tools. This chapter sets out some reasons why financial penalties alone may not always achieve the best regulatory outcomes and presents some recommendations for sanctions that are less reliant on financial censure and include broader considerations such as rehabilitation.

Why Monetary Penalties alone are not always Sufficient

4.2   In my interim report, I showed that 96 percent of the sentences handed down against corporations in Magistrates' Courts were financial penalties.[56] Financial penalties, whether imposed as a result of a criminal prosecution or through an administrative system, may not always be the most appropriate sanction to bring a business into compliance. In some instances, the regulator need only 'persuade' the firm through advice or an informal warning letter, and move it into compliance by explaining the merits of the regulation or explaining what it is the firm would need to do in order to comply. In other instances, where the provision of advice and guidance has failed and where a prosecution or a financial penalty is not appropriate, the regulator may need access to other types of sanctions.

---

[56] The focus in this chapter is on the sentencing of businesses for regulatory non-compliance. Sentences for individual offenders not pertaining to regulatory non-compliance are not considered.

Box 4.1 Some Limitations of Financial Penalties

A body of research has developed over the past two decades that has raised some of the limitations of relying on fines alone to change business behaviour.[57] I highlight some of the shortcomings that a strategy of enforcing by fines alone could include:

Deterrence: I have previously mentioned that unless the financial penalty is of the optimal amount, it may be the case that small financial penalties can be easily absorbed by a large company and become a part of doing business, for example, treating them like overhead costs, with limited impact on the day-to-day decision making on compliance made within a business. On the other hand, smaller firms, may not have the means to pay a fine that would be large enough to deter future lawbreaking.[58]

Getting the level of the fine right is essential to their effectiveness and I believe this will continue to be a challenge for both the courts and regulators. I believe regulators may be better placed, through administrative sanctions to determine the most effective level of financial penalty, which can be subject to review by the Regulatory Tribunal. The regulator can have access to information and consider all of the relevant details when determining the level of a VMAP. Courts may have a more difficult time as the judiciary is often reliant on the prosecution for providing the relevant information. I have heard evidence which suggests that in many instances, prosecutors fail to impart this information to the court.

Spill over: Fining a corporation may also fail to change business behaviour because the company can pass on the financial cost to third parties such as shareholders, employees, creditors and customers, and deferring responsibility away from company management. Shareholders experience losses resulting from fines through falls in the value of shares and reduced future dividends. The cost of a fine also spills over to consumers through increases in the prices for the firm's goods and services, and to employees through adverse effects on wages and staffing.[59]

---

[57] See for example – Sentencing options against corporations, B. Fisse, *Criminal Law Forum* 211, 1990; 'Sanctions Against Corporations: Economic Efficiency or Legal Efficacy?' Sydney University Transnational Corporations Research Project Occasional Paper No 13, 1986; 'Sentencing: Corporate offenders', *New South Wales Law Reform Commission*, 2003; 'Principled Regulation: Federal, Civil and Administrative Penalties in Australia', *Australian Law Reform Commission*, 2002

[58] 'No Soul to Damn: No Body to Kill: an Unscandalised Inquiry into the Problem of Corporate Punishment', J. Coffee, 79 *Michigan Law Review* 386 refers to this as the 'Deterrence Trap' – where the fine necessary to render future compliance the 'rational' choice for amorally calculating businesses is beyond the means of the business being punished.

[59] *Sanctions Against Corporations: Economic Efficiency or Legal Efficacy*, B. Fisse, n 57 above.

Discrimination/Unequal impact: Fines tend to impact more upon small businesses whose operations are generally more vulnerable to monetary penalties.[60] The reliance on fining in the sanctioning of a business could also be perceived as representing discriminatory and unfair practice against individual offenders who arguably face far more serious sentences (such as imprisonment).[61]

Reflecting the Harm Caused: The reliance on financial sanctions alone also suggests that the harm caused by corporate criminal regulatory breaches is financial. However, harm might also include physical, psychological or environmental damage and, financial sanctions alone, may not always result in the best outcomes.

Lack of Rehabilitation: Lastly, financial penalties alone may not incentivise businesses to take appropriate measures to address procedures within the business that gave rise to the offence. Instead of taking the necessary steps to build long-term compliance corporate managers may decide to treat fines as recurrent business losses. This can be reinforced if non-compliance results in large financial gains and fines that are imposed do not adequately withdraw the financial benefit.

4.3   Non-financial administrative penalties could be used to deal with firms that want to comply but may have some gaps in their management system or are small firms with limited resources. They could also be appropriate for offenders who may be in severe economic difficulties and may not be able to pay even small fines. In some cases the offending business or individual might be able to, and have a desire to, undertake activities which aim to restore the harm that has been done.

4.4   For these reasons I have considered sanctions that look beyond the imposition of monetary penalties.

Statutory Notices

4.5   In some instances of regulatory non-compliance, regulators will decide to issue a Statutory Notice. An example could be in instances where a company has failed to carry out, prepare, record and implement a suitable and sufficient risk-assessment addressing the risks that could arise from the use of workplace transport.

---

[60] Small businesses find it more difficult than large businesses to absorb a fine due to the constraints on their finances and credit. These constraints make it difficult for a small business to stay afloat through the payment period of a substantial fine.
[61] 'Sentencing: Penalties', Discussion Paper 30, Australian Law Reform Commission, 1987.

4.6   These notices require the recipient to do or refrain from a particular behaviour. They specify the steps a business must take in order to be compliant and the timescale for these changes. Depending on the statutory provision, a Statutory Notice may also include remediation provisions relating to the damage caused by the failure to comply with regulations. Failure to carry out the actions laid out in the notice may also be a criminal offence.

4.7   Although many regulators may have recourse to this sanction, the precise forms of Statutory Notices and their conditions of use vary between regulatory areas. My report *Regulatory Justice: Sanctioning in a post-Hampton World*, published in December 2005, identified examples of different types of Statutory Notices that businesses can be subjected to by the regulator.

Box 4.2 Types of Statutory Notices

- Improvement Notices – demanding certain improvements to work practices while allowing time for the recipient to comply;

- Prohibition/Suspension Notices – prohibits an activity until remedial action has been taken in order to prevent serious harm from occurring;

- Work Notices – to prevent or remedy water pollution; and

- Enforcement Notices – served where it is believed that a breach of regulatory consent or licence has occurred. The notice specifies the steps to rectify the breach and the timescale for these changes, and, depending on the statutory provisions, may include remediation provisions relating to the damage caused by the breach.

Source: *Regulatory Justice: Sanctioning in a Post-Hampton World*, Macrory, R., December 2005.

4.8   In the majority of cases, failure to comply with the terms of a Statutory Notice is an offence in its own right, punishable either by a fine or imprisonment. For example, if the terms of an Improvement/Prohibition Notice imposed by the Health and Safety Executive are not met, this is an offence that may be prosecuted. This demonstrates the seriousness of a notice, but may also deter a regulator from pursuing action against businesses that fail to comply with a notice. A regulator may view the stigma and potential imprisonment as a disproportionate response to the underlying breach.

> An enforcement notice should be the preferred form of action over penalties. The enforcement notice system works well for business because there is an emphasis on prevention of injury or harm rather than on prosecution.
>
> *Confederation of British Industry.*

Scope for Strengthening the Statutory Notices System

4.9   In my consultation report, I presented several ideas for strengthening the system of Statutory Notices. I elaborate on these in the following discussion. My recommendations could apply to both new and existing notices. Such a strengthened system of Statutory Notices should be used in a wider range of regulatory non-compliance.

Notices That are Fit for Purpose

4.10   A number of regulators already have access to some kind of Statutory Notice, but there has been some innovation and development of the design of notices over time. New types of notices have been created and some regulators may benefit from updating their system of Statutory Notices to ensure that their system of notices is up to date and appropriate for a risk based approach to regulation. For example, in the area of consumer protection, Part Eight of the Enterprise Act 2002 gives Local Authority regulators access to Enforcement Orders, which are a type of Statutory Notice. Enforcement Orders are injunctions granted by the court to restrain breaches of specified law, but enforcers can accept agreed undertakings as an alternative to being taken to court. These replace and expand the scope of what were called 'Stop Now Orders' and are used in many areas of consumer protection such as in cases of giving customers written notification for cancelling contracts. This represents an example of an appropriate and effective Statutory Notice.

Box 4.3 Statutory Notices

Statutory Notices need to be improved in the following ways:

- Statutory Notices should be made available as a tool for all regulators to use, in order to ensure consistency.

- Regulators should follow up Statutory Notices through a risk based approach, in order to ensure that Statutory Notices are complied with.

- An appeal mechanism should be made available through independent review and the tribunal system.

- Breaches of notices should be able to be sanctioned by the regulator through Monetary Administrative Penalties, in order to give them strength as a sanction.

Failure to Comply with a Notice

4.11   Failure to follow up notices to check that compliance has been reached can undermine Statutory Notices as a sanctioning tool, and could encourage reluctant businesses not to take them seriously. Furthermore, without follow-up, regulators are not in a position to evaluate the outcomes obtained by using notices. I believe it would be good practice for regulators, as part of evaluating their enforcement activities and outcome measurement to include some assessment of their notice system beyond just reporting on the number of notices issued. I also believe it is important for regulators to follow-up notices on a risk-adjusted basis.

> If business gains the impression that such notices are not enforced, it will damage the credibility of the enforcement regime. Failure to do so would penalise the vast majority of business who have taken action and incurred expense to ensure they have complied.
>
> *Small Business Service.*

4.12   Non-compliance with a Statutory Notice is usually a criminal offence, but as with other cases of regulatory non-compliance, I believe it would be helpful if regulators had greater flexibility in how to sanction the non-compliance with a Statutory Notice, such as applying a MAP rather than solely relying on criminal prosecution for non-compliance. It should remain at the discretion of the regulator whether it would be more appropriate to sanction the failure to comply with a Statutory Notice, in the particular circumstances of a case, with a MAP or a criminal prosecution, and their enforcement policy should indicate the factors that will guide their discretion.

4.13   Regulators may decide that non-compliance with a Statutory Notice always justifies prosecution because an intentional act is implied, or that this should be reserved, say, for repeated non-compliance. But I believe there will be circumstances where the use of a MAP will be a more appropriate and effective sanctioning tool to ensure compliance with a statutory notice. For example, where a business has clearly saved money by delaying compliance but the behaviour does not justify a criminal prosecution. Or where a business has complied with most of the requirements of a notice, with the knowledge that a regulator is unlikely to consider that the costs and time of a prosecution is justified to deal with a small proportion of outstanding issues.

4.14 Lastly, I suggest that regulators ensure that the notice itself is clear in its language and make those who receive such notices aware of the legal status of each notice and the consequences of not complying with the terms of the notice.

Appeals of Statutory Notices

4.15 Most statutory provisions concerning Statutory Notices allow for the right of appeal against the service of the notice (including its requirements). As research undertaken for my review demonstrates the current appeals routes are varied – many provide for appeals to the magistrates' courts, but Health and Safety legislation, for example, provides for appeals to an Employment Tribunal.[62] Where a regulator decides to impose a VMAP in response to a breach of a Statutory Notice, any appeal of the VMAP would, in accordance with my recommendations, be to the Regulatory Tribunal rather than the criminal courts or other fora.

4.16 Strictly my terms of reference are concerned with sanctions, but I would recommend that government consider whether any existing appeals against Statutory Notices would be more effectively and speedily handled by the Regulatory Tribunal rather than magistrates' courts. This may not be appropriate in all areas of regulation (it has been argued, for example, that the local knowledge possessed by local magistrates may be especially valuable for dealing with statutory noise nuisance appeals), but appeals against notices are essentially administrative in nature, and may raise complex technical issues where the more specialist make-up of the tribunal would provide a more effective forum.

---

[62] Parker, C. 'Health and Safety at Work Act 1974, s 24(2), restorative Justice in Business Regulation? The Australian Competition and Consumer Commission's Use of Enforceable Undertakings', , *Modern Law Review*, Vol. 67, No. 2, 2004.

Recommendation 5:

I recommend that for an improved system of Statutory Notices:

- Government should consider using Statutory Notices as part of an expanded sanctioning toolkit to secure future compliance beyond the areas in which they are currently in use;

- Regulators should systematically follow up Statutory Notices using a risk based approach including an element of randomised follow up;

- In dealing with the offence of failing to comply with a Statutory Notice, regulators should have access to administrative financial penalties as an alternative to criminal prosecution. This power should be extended by legislative amendment to existing schemes of Statutory Notices; and

- Government should consider whether appeals against Statutory Notices should be routed through the Regulatory Tribunal rather than the criminal courts.

Enforceable Undertakings

4.17   I have previously commented that the current system of regulatory sanctions lacks both financial and non-financial intermediate sanctions. Regulators have access to informal sanctioning through advice or warning letters, or extremely serious sanctions such as criminal proceedings, but there is a gap relating to intermediate sanctions. Regulators have limited sanctions for cases that are not serious enough to be prosecuted and too serious to just receive an informal warning. For this reason, I am suggesting the addition of some sanctions to fill this gap. As well as MAPs and, where appropriate, Statutory Notices, a further sanction, which I have called Enforceable Undertakings, should be introduced into the enforcement toolkit, for those instances where a non-financial intermediate sanction may be more suitable. I also make recommendations to combine both non-financial and financial administrative elements of a sanction, which I refer to as Undertakings Plus.

4.18   Enforceable Undertakings and Undertakings Plus introduce an intermediate sanction with elements of restoration into the enforcement process. If adopted in the UK, they could facilitate negotiations between regulator, business and, in appropriate cases, the victims of regulatory non-compliance. They represent a powerful alternative to traditional coercive, regulatory enforcement action, and have the potential of imposing fit-for-purpose sanctions which are more satisfying for both offender and the victims of non-compliance.

What are Enforceable Undertakings?

4.19   Enforceable Undertakings (EUs) are a flexible sanction that enable regulators to tailor their enforcement response to individual circumstances taking industry considerations and resources, such as management capacity and willingness to restore harm, into account. They represent a valuable alternative to traditional regulatory enforcement action because they can address the needs of several parties involved in, or affected by, the wrongdoing as well as correcting and preventing breaches and their underlying causes.

4.20   EUs, in the form in which I am recommending them, are a sanction not currently available in the UK. Although some elements of EUs do exist in other contexts, their application across the regulatory landscape would be an extension of regulators' existing enforcement toolkits.[63]

4.21   EUs have proven successful abroad and I have discussed these experiences in more detail in chapter four of my interim report.[64] A report for the Australian Competition and Consumer Commission – cited by the Australian Law Reform Commission in its review of regulatory penalty schemes – concluded that Enforceable Undertakings provide a quicker and more cost-effective mechanism for resolution of regulatory non-compliance than court proceedings. The Commission also quoted businesses which observed that undertakings are a 'nice way' of warning and giving the regulated business 'another chance'. Businesses also stated that Enforceable Undertakings can encourage greater candour and promote compliance.[65]

---

[63] The Competition Act 1998 s 31A and the Enterprise Act 2002 s 73 and s 82
[64] *Regulatory Justice: Sanctioning in a post-Hampton World*, Consultation Document, R. Macrory, May 2006, p70
[65] 'Principled Regulation: Federal, Civil and Administrative Penalties in Australia', *Australian Law Reform Commission*, 2002 , Chapter 16

Box 4.4 Undertakings in lieu of Enforcement Orders

1. Under Part Eight of the Enterprise Act 2002, the power is given to certain regulators to apply for Enforcement Orders from the court. Enforcement Orders are final orders given by a court to require the cessation of, or otherwise prohibit the infringement of certain legislation, where the infringement harms the collective interests of consumers.

2. The regulators that can use this power are General Enforcers (OFT, local weights and measures authorities, DETI), Designated Enforcers (bodies designated in a Statutory Instrument by the Secretary of State) and Community Enforcers (only enforcers from other EEA states).[66]

3. A business is usually given a period of at least 14 days consultation regarding such an action and may seek to make undertakings to the regulator during that time. These may be to rectify any infringement made by the business.

4. The regulator may accept or reject the undertakings made. If rejected, then the application for an Enforcement Order proceeds. If accepted, then the steps that the business makes to comply with the undertakings are monitored. If they are complied with then no further action will be taken.

5. If undertakings are not complied with then the regulator may apply to court for it to issue an Enforcement Order. The court may choose instead to accept the undertaking from the business. If the undertakings accepted by the court are breached after this then it is deemed to be a contempt of court. The process is outlined in Figure 4.1.

---

[66] DETI – Department of Enterprise, Trade and Investment in Northern Ireland

Figure 4.1 Enforcement Orders in the UK

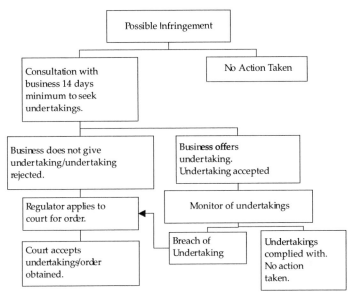

Source: Enforcement of Consumer Protection Legislation Guide on Part 8 of The Enterprise A ct, OFT, March 2005.

4.22   EUs are legally binding agreements between the regulator and business, under which the business agrees to carry out specific activities to rectify its non-compliance. An EU could include a commitment to future regulatory outcomes, including steps to ensure that a specific type of incident does not re-occur. EUs would be most effective when monitored closely by the regulator and where non-compliance with an EU is not tolerated.

4.23   EUs could be more effective in cases where a financial penalty or criminal conviction is likely to be absorbed by the business with a limited impact on the culture or management of the firm. They are also likely to be more effective in securing a change in businesses' behaviour when compared to warning letters or other means of persuasion currently available to the regulator. This is due to the way in which an EU is designed. Warning letters and advice are imposed by a regulator and specify what actions need to be taken by a business. The business may not have bought into the actions required. With EUs, it is the businesses who would apply for an EU and come up with their own list of conditions, and take ownership of the regulatory solution presented. Conditions that form part of the EU would be proportionate to the underlying breach and would hold business to account for their non-compliance.

4.24   Business responses to my call for evidence and consultation strongly supported the notion that there is a need for more flexible sanctions. EUs would allow for regulators to use a more flexible and individually tailored approach, which takes business considerations into account when determining how best to deal with cases of regulatory non-compliance. My recommendations here are very much in line with the Hampton ideas focusing on improving behaviour and moving firms into compliance through advice and persuasion.

> Enforceable Undertakings focus strongly on behaviour change and damage restitution. The IoD has also been impressed by the Australian experience of using EUs.
> *Institute of Directors*
>
> EUs may work well not only as an alternative sanction but also as an additional sanction to our current regulatory tools. We particularly see the benefit of Enforceable Undertakings in larger organisations or major outbreaks of food borne disease or major food incidents. An Enforceable Undertaking Agreement would allow proportionality with the breach and the defendant's resources. Small duty holders may also be encouraged by the principal of agreeing a strategy that is clear, objective and measured. Enforceable Undertakings could provide scope and benefit to agree restorative and community elements. Enforceable Undertakings could also be a powerful tool to deliver sustained compliance. The Enforceable Undertaking option promotes openness of organisations and transparency of the enforcement process and fits well with the Agency's developing enforcement strategy.
> *Food Standards Agency*

How Enforceable Undertakings could work in the UK

4.25   Enforceable Undertakings should be available to regulators as an alternative to imposing a VMAP, or taking court action and prosecuting a business for regulatory non-compliance. It will be for individual regulators or their sponsoring departments, to determine which of the offences set out in their regulatory legislation, and in what circumstances an EU might be an appropriate sanctioning response. A key benefit of EUs is that the system offers the industry concerned the opportunity to demonstrate how it proposes to respond to a regulatory breach and to make open and binding commitments accordingly.

4.26   I believe that EUs should be a sanction that the regulator could consider in cases where they have the necessary evidence to bring an enforcement action. Regulators may prefer to accept an application for an EU in cases where they believe the EU will better deliver:

   •   the best regulatory outcomes which could include redressing the harm caused by the breach; and/or

   •   the motivation for the necessary change in behaviour that could be brought about through an EU.

4.27   The specific actions required of a company that could be set out in Enforceable Undertakings include provisions for compensation, reimbursement or redress to affected parties. Actions may also include requirements that the offender does a service to the community, such as funding or implementing a compliance education program, and can also include a restorative element. I believe that once an Enforceable Undertaking has been agreed, there must be a consequence for the failure to comply with it.

4.28   If regulators have EUs as part of their toolkit, it will be important to make businesses aware that it is a sanctioning option. It would be helpful for regulators to provide guidance as to what might constitute an acceptable EU in order to avoid businesses offering too little. This could be included as part of a regulator's enforcement policy.

4.29   I do not intend to set out, in this report, the detail of exactly how Enforceable Undertakings would operate, as the details would be best left with by those responsible within government for the implementation of such a sanction. However, I do believe there are some key features, based on the experience of this sanction in other jurisdictions that are necessary to ensure the effective operation of this new regime, which I outline in the section below.

Enforceable Undertakings in Practice

Application

- A regulator's enforcement policy should indicate the type of circumstances in which it would consider accepting an EU rather than pursuing another sanction. In cases where a business has received notification that it is being prosecuted for an alleged breach of regulation, the business may decide to apply for an Enforceable Undertaking. When the regulator receives an application for an EU, legal proceedings connected with the alleged breach are put on hold. If the application for an EU is not accepted, prosecution will proceed.

- Where the regulator has decided to impose a VMAP on a business, and where the business may not have the financial resources to pay the administrative penalty, the business may decide to apply for an EU. When the regulator receives an application for an EU, proceedings connected with the breach and the imposition of the VMAP are put on hold. If the application for the EU is not accepted, the imposition of the VMAP will proceed.

- I suggest that business is not guaranteed a right to an Enforceable Undertaking; it would be granted at the discretion of the regulator.

Content

- Enforceable Undertakings could take the form of a written agreement between the regulator and the business. This would clearly set out the specific action(s) for the business.

- The actions set out in the EU should be proportionate to and bear a clear relationship with the underlying breach. The time period within which compliance with actions is required should be defined.

- Regulators could also consider the impact on and, in some cases, consult third parties that have been affected by the regulatory non-compliance when deciding whether to accept the Undertaking.

- One of the conditions of an EU could include a financial element through a Monetary Administrative Penalty ('Undertaking Plus') *see s 4.30 below.*

Process

- Enforceable Undertakings would require an increased monitoring role for the regulator, as it will be involved in following up EUs to ensure that the conditions are carried through.

- Where a regulator has accepted an EU, the Undertaking should be made available publicly. This is important to secure public confidence in the regulatory enforcement system, but businesses who have agreed undertakings will also benefit since it will demonstrate that it is taking responsible action in relation to a breach.

Non-compliance

- There should be consequences for the business if it fails to comply with the EU. Having agreed and accepted the Undertaking as an appropriate response to specific regulatory non-compliance, if a business fails to comply with the conditions of an EU, the regulator could apply for a court order directing compliance with the undertaking or directing the payment of a fine.

'Undertakings Plus'

4.30   A regulator may consider that while an undertaking offered by the business may be appropriate, the circumstances of the breach also require the payment of a financial penalty, and I think the system of EUs should be sufficiently flexible to incorporate this. This might be appropriate where, for example, the business has made a clear financial gain from non-compliance. The financial element of an Undertaking Plus would be based on the same principles as I described earlier in this chapter when discussing Fixed and Variable Monetary Administrative Penalties, and any revenue from the penalty would not go direct to the regulator. The Undertaking Plus would also be a voluntary but legally binding agreement. Both the financial element and the conditions of the EU would need to be agreed upon by both the company and the regulator. If a company did not agree with the level of the financial penalty, then it would choose not to enter into the EU and the regulator would decide what, if any enforcement action should be taken.

Guidance in the Enforcement Policy

4.31 Regulators would need to prepare guidance on when and under what circumstances EUs and Undertakings Plus might be considered and this should be reflected in and be part of the regulators' enforcement policy. This policy, in turn, will be subject to the statutory Compliance Code.

Recommendation 6:

I recommend that the Government should introduce Enforceable Undertakings and Undertakings Plus (a combination of an Enforceable Undertaking with an administrative financial penalty) as an alternative to a criminal prosecution or the imposition of VMAPs for regulators that are compliant with the Hampton and Macrory Principles and characteristics.

Box 4.5 Case study of EUs in Australia and USA

Australia

In 2006, Black & Decker admitted a potential contravention of Australian law by selling a product with packaging which represented that it was made in Australia when it was, in fact, imported. After negotiation with the Australian Competition and Consumer Commission (ACCC) the company provided a court enforceable undertaking that it would (1) refrain from making misleading and false representations in regards to its products, (2) take remedial action in relation to stock held by retailers, and (3) implement a compliance programme to ensure future conduct did not contravene Australia law.

Source – ACCC Public Undertakings Register

USA

In June 2005, the Environmental Protection Agency reached an agreement with Saint-Gobain Containers Inc. to resolve Clean Air Act allegations. The agreement required Saint-Gobain to install state-of-the-art pollution control and monitoring equipment at a cost of approximately $6.6 million. Saint-Gobain was also

> required to pay a civil penalty of $929,000 and spend $1.2 million
> for an environmental project to operate and maintain the new
> equipment. In addition, Saint-Gobain agreed to immediately
> comply with interim air pollution limits, obtain proper air permits,
> install pollution control equipment on its furnaces, and donate
> approximately $1 million worth of emission credits generated by
> the emission reductions.
>
> *Source – Compliance and Enforcement Annual Results 2005, Environmental Protection*
> *Agency, Office of Enforcement and Compliance Assurance, November 2005*

Restorative Justice

4.32   Restorative Justice (RJ) is a philosophy that views harm and crime
        as violations of people and relationships. It is a holistic process
        that addresses the repercussions and obligations created by harm
        with a view to putting things right. When compared with current
        models of punishment, RJ requires a paradigm shift in thinking
        about responses to harm. RJ is different from retributive justice.
        It is justice that puts energy into the future, not into what is past.
        It focuses on what needs to be restored or repaid and what needs
        to be learned and strengthened in order for the harm not to re-
        occur.[67]

4.33   The basic principles of RJ are focused around harm and
        relationships such as the harm caused to individuals by injury
        at a workplace or a financial loss to a consumer because of mis-
        selling. Harms to the environment could include industrial spills
        or emissions into the environment. There are several definitions of
        RJ that I have come across although none is universally accepted.
        A frequently used and common definition of RJ which I have
        adopted in this Review is:

        Restorative Justice is a process whereby those most directly
        affected by a wrongdoing come together to determine what needs
        to be done to repair the harm and prevent a reoccurrence.[68]

---

[67] 'Introduction to Restorative Justice', The Centre for Restorative Justice, Simon Fraser
University, Vancouver, Canada –http://www.sfu.ca/crj/introrj.html
[68] 'Restorative Justice and Practices' – presented at 'Restorative Justice in Action...into
the Mainstream', The 3rd International Winchester Restorative Justice Group Conference,
29th and 30th March 2006, London

Benefits of an RJ Approach

4.34 **Outcomes** – The use of RJ has the potential to give good long-term outcomes for both victims and offenders. Victims show consistently greater levels of satisfaction in systems using Restorative Justice when compared to those relying on court-based justice, and many studies have strongly suggested that the re-offending rate of offenders is lower if they have undergone an RJ process.[69]

4.35 **Flexible response** – An RJ process is also flexible, as there is no pre-conceived notion of what 'restoration' is. It is a dynamic process reflecting the needs and capabilities of the stakeholders involved.

4.36 **RJ is focused on restoring the harm** – A restorative style approach will have a slightly different focus than the criminal justice system, which is more concerned with fault and punishment. In contrast, RJ is focused on the harm caused and on what can be done to make things right.

These positive aspects of RJ are reflected in the experience of its use in the UK within non-regulatory areas of the UK justice system. This has included work in areas such as Youth Justice and prisons.

RJ in Regulators' Sanctioning Toolkits:

4.37 In my interim report I outlined the case for using RJ in regulators' sanctioning toolkits as a further alternative to criminal prosecution, administrative fines or statutory notices. This case relied on evidence from Australia of the successful application of RJ to regulatory matters, discussed the use of RJ in the UK justice system, and put forward options for consultation.

4.38 Respondents to the consultation document on this review shared my positive outlook on the potential for Restorative Justice in this area.

---

[69] *The Effectiveness of Restorative Practices: A meta-analysis*, Latimer, J., Dowden, C. Muise, D. Canadian Department of Justice, 2005; *The positive effect of Restorative Justice on Re-offending*, Restorative Justice Consortium, January 2006

RJ used in conjunction with other enforcement tools may provide a good framework to proportionately match the breach, and involve and meet the needs of victims e.g. rehabilitation, workers retraining, reassurance and support, closure and public support. RJ would enable an organisation to do the right thing quickly. RJ may well result in improvements in health and safety outcomes in businesses as well as educate the organisation and managers.

Health and Safety Commission

There are many areas of regulatory non-compliance where restorative justice may well be appropriate. These will include Financial malfeasance, environmental damage and injury or risk to members of the public.

Trades Union Congress

We consider Restorative Justice (RJ) to be an innovative means of imposing sanctions on a particular business. RJ has the potential to educate where a strict financial penalty would not. It would also ensure a satisfactory outcome for the victims of regulatory non-compliance.

British Chamber of Commerce

4.39   Overall, 74 percent of respondents believed that RJ could be applied to the area of regulation, 24 percent believed that it could not be applied to this area. Furthermore the responses were favourable on the potential use of RJ in all three potential options for its use raised in the consultation document.

Figure 4.2 Consultation Response to RJ proposals

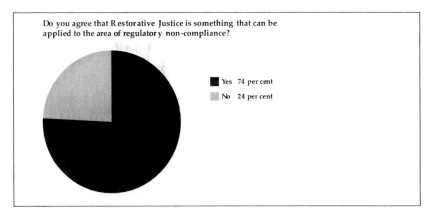

Recommendation 7: I recommend that Government introduce pilot schemes involving the use of Restorative Justice techniques in addressing cases of regulatory non-compliance. This might include RJ:

- as a pre-court diversion;

- instead of a Monetary Administrative Penalty; and

- within the criminal justice system – as both a pre or post sentencing option.

Some Considerations to make RJ Effective as a Regulatory Sanction

RJ Practitioners

4.40 RJ events can have very serious consequences for all stakeholders involved. Victims will often be very raw and sensitive about the physical, emotional, or financial harm that has been inflicted upon them. Offenders, on the other hand, will often be very nervous about facing those who they have harmed. Furthermore, the result of an RJ event will be an agreed remedy for the harm that has been caused. This agreement could amount to a significant burden on the offender, for example, financial compensation or a commitment to undertake unpaid work.

4.41 Given the importance of these potential consequences, and the sensitivities on both sides that need to be respected, RJ must be carried out by trained experts. I understand that Skills for Justice, the standards setting body for the justice sector, will be publishing Occupational Standards by the end of this year and these will form the basis of any professional qualifications for such experts.

RJ Best Practice

4.42 There is a good body of work on the use of RJ in the UK that provides many good points of learning that will provide safeguards for participants and give RJ the best chance of success. Any schemes introduced to implement RJ in the area of regulation should use this Best Practice guidance as the basis for designing RJ procedures.[70]

---

[70] *Restorative Justice Guidance: Best practice for practitioners, their case supervisors, and line managers,* Home Office, December 2004.

Piloting RJ

4.43   Pilots could help capture for the regulatory system, the positive experience of RJ in other non-regulatory areas. Building on the Government's evidence-based approach to RJ policymaking I believe the best way to take forward the use of RJ in the area of regulation is through the use of pilots. The evidence from the use of RJ in the UK in non-regulatory areas, and the positive experience from Australia of the use of RJ in regulation show that there could be a use for RJ in regulatory sanctioning in the UK. I believe it would be good practice for a few pilot schemes to be undertaken to better develop RJ in the context of regulatory sanctioning.

Alternative Sanctions in the Criminal Courts

4.44   Throughout this chapter, I have recommended a number of non-financial administrative sanctioning options to supplement the regulators' enforcement toolkit. Finally, in this last section, I look at expanding the sanctioning options available to the judiciary in cases of criminal prosecution.

Introduction

4.45   In recent years, the criminal justice system in England and Wales has seen innovations in sentencing options for individual offenders beyond the traditional options of financial penalties or imprisonment. This is evident in the range of community sentencing options made available to judges in the Criminal Justice Act (CJA) 2003. Amongst these options are Unpaid Work Requirements, Curfew Requirements, Supervision Requirements, and Electronic Monitoring.[71] While these examples are not directly applicable to regulatory legislation, I mention them to demonstrate the flexibility in sanctioning of individuals.

4.46   There has been very little development in relation to the sanctioning of businesses for cases of regulatory non-compliance as the options I mentioned under the CJA 2003 are only available for individuals. I believe that there are existing tools that could be developed to effectively sanction the regulated community in cases that lead to a criminal conviction.

---

[71] As defined in s 199, 204, 213 and 215 of the Criminal Justice Act 2003.

My Recommendations for Alternative Sentencing in Criminal Courts

4.47 I believe criminal courts should have more flexibility in the sanctions available to them in cases of regulatory non-compliance. I discuss several options that could be adopted in legislation by regulators and departments to better achieve increased compliance when sanctioning through a criminal prosecution in the section below.

Box 4.6 Holistic use of Alternate Sanctioning in Australia

In November 2004, Vilo Assets Management was convicted by the Environmental Protection Agency (EPA) of the explosive discharge of over 6,500 litres of partially reacted bio-diesel. A number of people were injured and property on other sites damaged due to the incident. The company was ordered to pay $20,000 towards an indigenous planting project within 30 days of the court order and to provide the EPA with proof of the payment within 45 days of that order. The business was prohibited from referring to the payment without also referring to the fact that they were ordered to do so by the court as a result of their regulatory non-compliance. The order also required Vilo to publish in the local and metropolitan media a notice about the offence and its impact in a manner specified by the court.

Source – EPA media release November 2004 – Vilo Assets Management Pty Limited v EPA (Victoria) 2004

Profit Orders

4.48 Evidence has been presented in the course of both the Hampton Review and this review that clearly demonstrates that current levels of fines do not appear to reflect the gains from non-compliance with regulatory requirements in most cases.[72] As I discuss with regard to VMAPs and setting of the fines in Box 3.2, I believe that there are many factors that should determine the level of a financial penalty. These factors include whether the business has gained a financial benefit as a result of the non-compliance.

4.49 Fine levels imposed by the criminal courts should take into account any savings made by non-compliance, but in cases where the savings are clear (such as the failure to pay licence fees for a number of years) I believe that it would be preferable if the criminal courts had the power to impose a Profit Order that is separate from any fine imposed. The Profit Order would be a non-

---

[72] Hampton P., *Reducing administrative burdens: Effective inspection and enforcement*, HM Treasury, March 2005, paragraph 17, page 6

judgmental sanction in that it reflected solely the profits made from non-compliance, while the fine imposed would reflect the court's assessment of the seriousness with which they regard the breach. Thus it would be perfectly possible for a court to impose a substantial Profit Order where the savings were large, but impose a small fine because it considered the business had acted carelessly rather than with intent or recklessness. Identifying and removing the financial benefit from a regulatory breach is something I believe would strengthen enforcement and send a clearer signal to industry that it is not acceptable to make financial gain from non-compliance. It also seeks to provide a more level playing field for business and provides a deterrent for non-compliant businesses. Adding this level of differentiation and transparency and separating out financial benefits from punitive fines would ensure that businesses did not feel subject to large punitive sanctions unnecessarily and would guard against those types of accusations.

Box 4.7 A New Sanctioning Tool: Profit Orders

Profit Orders would aim to ensure that the criminal offender should not gain from committing an offence and would seek to remove any financial gain that arose as a result of the non-compliance.

In effect, the Profit Order would seperate the financial gain from the fine (the punitive sanction representing social and moral condemnation). Financial gains can include direct financial benefits as a result of non-compliance as well as deferred costs.

The Profit Order should reflect the actual gain made and should not be subject to any statutory limit. Nevertheless, in assessing both the fine and Profit Order imposed, the courts would be required to take into account the financial means of the offender.

4.50   To my knowledge, there is no similar scheme in operation in the UK at present, but there have been some attempts to remove the financial gains from wrongdoing. Most often, this takes the form of Confiscation Orders, which are made after conviction to deprive the defendant of the benefit that has been obtained from crime as set out in the Proceeds of Crime Act 2002. The Assets Recovery Agency uses the Proceeds of Crime Act 2002 to disrupt organised criminal enterprises and recover criminal assets.[73] It appears that Confiscation Orders have generally been used

---

[73] Proceeds of Crime Act 2002 – that Act deals with Confiscation Orders in Part 2 in relation to England and Wales, Part 3 for Scotland and Part 4 for NI.

against individuals. Magistrates do not currently have access to Confiscation Orders and must refer cases up to the Crown Court to have access to this sanction. In addition, Confiscation Orders are strict in that they can only be used to capture acquisitive benefits such as profits that result from an offence. This benefit does not currently include provision for costs avoided, deferred or saved, which is a substantial part of the financial benefit obtained as a result of regulatory non-compliance.

Box 4.8 Criminal Convictions and Confiscation Orders

When deciding how to sanction a business who has not complied with regulatory requirements, the regulatory authority should also consider the power of the court to make a Confiscation Order under the Proceeds of Crime Act 2002 in the event of a conviction. For offences committed up to 24 March 2003, the relevant legislation is the Criminal Justice Act 1988 (as amended).

When a defendant (including a corporate body) has benefited from an offence and the prosecution asks the court to proceed, the court must make an Order for the offender to pay the amount by which they have benefited from the criminal conduct, or the available amount, whichever is the lesser.

In cases of offending by a corporate body, the starting point for calculating the defendant's benefit may be the gross turnover of the business during the period of the offence, i.e. deductions are not made for legitimate expenditure and so the amount of the Confiscation Order may be considerably greater than the net profit during the relevant period.

In deciding whether to prosecute an offender, the likelihood of a Confiscation Order being made in the event of a conviction is a public interest factor in favour of prosecution in the Code for Crown Prosecutors.

Box 4.9 Use of POCA in the Regulatory Context by UK Local Authorities

Evidence from UK Local Authorities shows that POCA (Proceeds of Crime Act 2002) has been successfully used to remove illegal profits from rogue traders such as counterfeiters. Three examples that have been submitted to the review are:

- Counterfeit Goods – The London Asset Recovery Team (RART) secured a confiscation order of £1,077,700 against an offender from Leyton working with Hackney Trading Standards Authority. The offender was also sentenced to 18 months' imprisonment after he was convicted of selling counterfeit goods, including well known brands to various retail outlets across London. (see http://cms.met.police.uk/met/news/convictions/forgery/1million_confiscation_order)

- Counterfeit Goods – Brent and Harrow Councils Trading Standards Departments secured the first confiscation order against a limited company. Trading Standards, with the Police and the London Regional Asset Recovery Team raided the premises of the offending company (a handbag wholesalers) and found over 1,700 counterfeit items which breached trademarks belonging to Louis Vuitton, Celine and Versace. The company's business records, accounts and computer hard drives were searched to determine the extent of the financial benefit from selling counterfeit goods. Following a successful prosecution, the company was ordered to pay £400,000 in August, this year.

- Clocking Cars – Northamptonshire County Council – A financial investigation by Northamptonshire Police established that the defendant had benefited to an amount of £180,507 and identified realisable assets amounting to at least £123,472. A confiscation order in the sum of £25,611 was made, together with an order for costs in the sum of £15,000 and compensation orders totalling £10,404. The Crown Court judge accepted the prosecutor's submission that in calculating the benefit he should make a confiscation order in respect of all 33 cars. The judge also accepted that method of calculating the benefit submitted by the prosecution (i.e. the *Glass's Guide* true mileage price for the vehicle less the Guide's lower mileage price) was appropriate. Two alternative methods were suggested by the defendant but application for leave to appeal was dismissed. The Court of Appeal found that the method adopted by the prosecutor was not unjust and indicated that the benefit may even have been aptly assessed by reference to the gross proceeds of the sale of the 'clocked' cars.

  Source: LACORS response to Macrory Review consultation

4.51 It would be up to the prosecution to apply for a Profit Order. They will not be appropriate in all cases of regulatory non-compliance, but suitable where the profits or financial gains made are clear. It would be at the discretion of the court whether or not to impose such an order.

Corporate Rehabilitation Orders (CROs)

4.52 Financial penalties represent the main sanction available to criminal courts in dealing with businesses who have not complied with regulatory obligations. Even where courts have access to a Profit Order as recommended above, the level of any financial penalty imposed will always take account of ability to pay which may account for some of the apparent low level of fines imposed on smaller businesses. In dealing with individual offenders, criminal courts now have access to a wide range of sanctions beyond fines and imprisonment, designed to bring home to the offender the consequences of the breach or secure rehabilitation. I believe that in dealing with regulatory breaches by businesses, the criminal courts should also have access to a more flexible range of sanctioning tools beyond the simple imposition of a financial penalty.

4.53 Corporate Rehabilitation Orders, as they are currently used in Australia, contain provisions to enable a court to require a company to undertake specific actions or activities during a specified period, such as one or two years. Corporate Rehabilitation Orders, as implied by their title, aim to rehabilitate the offender by ensuring tangible steps are taken that will address a company's poor practices and prevent future non-compliance. They involve a period of monitoring of the activities, policies and procedures of a business, with a view to organisational reform.[74]

4.54 Activities specified in the order could include training of personnel in regulatory related matters, the adoption and implementation of action plans to address regulatory non-compliance or taking steps to remedy the harm caused by regulatory non-compliance.

4.55 I believe a similar model could be introduced in the UK. Although I do not want to be too prescriptive in the models set out because different regulatory areas will have different needs, I do outline the way in which these could work in practice here in the UK.[75] CROs give criminal courts access to a sanction similar to Enforceable Undertakings.

---

[74] *Sentencing: Corporate Offenders*, New South Wales Law Reform Commission, 2003.
[75] M. Jefferson 'Corporate Criminal Liability: The Problem of Sanctions', *Journal of Criminal Law* 65, 2001.

- On conviction the company would be invited to put forward to the court a plan of action to remedy the matter which caused the harm. This could include a community project or a compliance audit;

- The court, in consultation with the regulator would either approve that scheme or appoint its own experts (who would be paid by the company) to design a more robust plan;

- The court would make its order;

- The relevant regulator would monitor compliance with this order; and

- Failure to comply with the order would lead to the company being brought back to court and sentenced in an alternative way, with the court taking into consideration, failure to comply with the CRO.

4.56   Corporate rehabilitation is an effective means of rehabilitating an offending firm and reducing the likelihood of future harm. The imposition of this sanction goes beyond what a fine can achieve in this respect by identifying tangible steps that a company must take and binding that company to their implementation. In taking steps to solve a company's compliance problems (as opposed to simply fining) there is also a greater chance that the individuals responsible will be identified and be held to account for their offences. A CRO will often replace a fine imposed, but in appropriate cases courts should retain the discretion to impose a fine in addition to the order.

Box 4.10 Case study for Corporate Rehabilitation Orders

US v World Air Conditioning Inc

On October 30, 1997, US Federal Court found World Air Conditioning Inc. guilty of failing to report income in federal tax returns, obstruction of justice and mail fraud. The defendant was ordered to pay $1.5 million in fines and several conditions of corporate probation, including co-operation with the IRS (Internal Revenue Service) and periodic reports of financial condition and periodic investigations of the company's records by independent experts were imposed on it.

Source – US Department of Justice press release October 1997

US v Royal Caribbean Cruises Ltd

On September 17, 1998, Royal Caribbean Cruises Limited was sentenced to a $1 million criminal fine for dumping oil and lying to the US Coast Guard. In addition the court imposed a period of corporate rehabilitation of five years, during which the conduct of the company will be closely monitored, with periodic reports to the court and the Government, detailing the company's environmental compliance and including the results of independent audits.

Source – US Department of Justice press release September 17, 1998

Community Projects

4.57   The range of requirements that could form the elements of Corporate Rehabilitation Orders should be flexible, reflecting both the circumstances of the regulatory breach and the nature of the defendant. It could, for example, include a requirement for the business to complete an appropriate community improvement project within a specified period and for a specified value related to the underlying harm or benefit that has been caused or obtained by the offender. Community projects would enable the business community to take responsibility for its actions within a local community and restore the harm it may have caused to the community or individuals. The project symbolises the restitution of the loss to the community that corporate crime involves, and could be appropriate where the business does not have the ability to pay a large financial penalty.

4.58   Examples of community projects include funding and delivering an education campaign in a specific subject or funding and delivering a project in the built environment, such as a park or a garden, or making some donations to the local community of time or resource as our examples in Box 4.11. More generally, the projects should be:

- Carried out in addition to something the company is already legally obliged to do;

- The firm should not be allowed to use the project for its own public relations purposes; and

- The community project could be used where the defendant is not in a position to pay a high financial penalty.

4.59　International experience with such community requirements has been positive. Australian environmental and health and safety legislation provides broad powers to judges to order businesses to carry out specified projects to either restore the environment or improve health and safety respectively. Not only do the projects deliver tangible benefits to the local community where the offence was committed, but it has also engaged the business more so than a financial penalty would, for example, to ensure that future compliance is secured. This engagement would enhance the rehabilitative element of the sentence as the offender recognises the serious harm that has been caused.

Box 4.11 Examples of Community Projects

Six bakeries convicted of price fixing in the US were excused from paying substantial portions of the fines imposed on condition that they provided baked goods to various organisations assisting the needy for one year. The court identified several reasons for making the order:[76]

Avoidance of 'spill over' – Imposing fines commensurate with the gravity of the offence would have bankrupted the bakeries. This would have caused a large spill over effect through creating widespread unemployment amongst the bakeries' production-line employees.

Reflecting non-financial aspect of the crime – The community project required the firm to make symbolic restitution for their offences by doing something more onerous and thought-provoking than merely paying fines.

Publicity – The community project brought the offences to the attention of the public, thereby increasing deterrence without harming the needs of employees, consumers or communities that would otherwise be affected by a fine.

This example illustrates some of the added value that a community project can deliver in comparison to a simple fining approach.

In February 2002, Rosedale Leather pleaded guilty to one charge of air pollution after offensive odours from its tannery affected local residents. As part of the sentence handed down by the magistrates' court the company was ordered to pay $20,000 to a local community project to aid in the implementation of streetscape beautification works in the town of Rosedale.

Source: EPA media release February 2002 (Rosedale Leather v EPA (Victoria) 2002)

---

[76] *United States v Danilow Pastry Co* (1983) 563 F Supp 1159 at 1166-1167.

Mandatory Compliance Audits

4.60   The power to compel companies to undertake an 'audit' is common in Australian states, especially in the area of environmental regulation.[77] This type of sanction is designed to remedy deficiencies in the business's management and may be appropriate where systemic organisational change would help to better achieve future compliance. Bringing in external expertise could get the business the help it needs to identify how to improve its operations and meet its regulatory objectives.

4.61   A Mandatory Compliance Audit, by an accredited third party, ordered by the court, would identify the necessary changes to a business, to protect the public and also provide a framework to ensure that the changes would be made.[78] Audits by third parties would be systematic, documented and objective reviews of a business' facilities, operations and product lines.[79] The outcome of such a review would be an action plan of what corrective actions would be necessary to bring the business back into compliance.[80] The court could then direct the regulator to monitor the business to ensure it takes all of the necessary corrective action.

4.62   Mandatory audits have the potential to be wide ranging in their operation; in Australia they can be sought not only in relation to the premises and operation where the original offence was committed or brought to the regulator's attention, but to all sites and operations carried out by the defendant.[81] The scope of audits can also include an examination of both physical and managerial activities.[82]

4.63   I believe that as part of a Corporate Rehabilitation Order, the court should have discretion on whether such an audit is appropriate, seeking guidance from the regulator and its prosecutors on whether it is appropriate. The regulator could keep a list of accredited agents who could carry out the audit, with the costs of this met by the non-compliant business. If a business contested

---

[77] *Regulatory Justice: Sanctioning in a Post-Hampton World*, see n 1 above.

[78] Berlin, M., 'Environmental Auditing: Entering the Eco-information highway', *New York University Law Journal*, p 2 1998.

[79] O'Reilly, J.T., 'Environmental Audit Privileges: The Need for Legislative Recognition', 19 *Seton Hall Legis.* J 119 – 120 1994.

[80] Berlin, M., 'Environmental Auditing: Entering the Eco-information highway', see n 78 above.

[81] *Guidelines for Seeking Environmental Court Orders*, NSW Environmental Protection Agency.

[82] *Environmental Audit Privileges: The Need for Legislative Recognition*, see n 79 above.

and a court agreed that the business did not have the means to pay, then such a sanction would not be appropriate.

Box 4.12 International Use of Mandatory Compliance Audits

In August 2002, the Environmental Protection Agency fined Shell Refining Australia Limited for three separate incidents of oil discharges to Corio Bay beach. After a number of other cases of pollution were taken into consideration the EPA issued a clean up order and after discussion with the company initiated a number of independent environmental audits to identify and fix problems at the refinery.

Source – EPA media release 2 August 2002 [Shell Refining (Australia) Pty Limited v EPA Victoria 2002]

On 10 May, 2006, the US Environmental Protection Agency (EPA) brought a civil action for injunctive relief and civil penalties against AgriProcessors Inc. for numerous violations of federal environmental laws. The consent decree required the company to pay an administrative fine as well as undergo a Compliance Audit, carried out according to provisions set out in the consent decree, by an independent auditing firm. The purpose of the audit was to determine and achieve the firm's compliance with federal environmental legislation and was at the expense of the defendant. Provisions of the Compliance Audit included stipulations for a audit work plan, what the audit report should contain and the timing of when the audit report has to be submitted to the EPA.

Source US Department of Justice – www.usdoj.gov

Publicity Orders

4.64   Reputation is an important asset to many businesses. When thinking about how to motivate firms to change their behaviour, reputational sanctions can have more of an impact than even the largest financial penalties. The use of reputational sanctions is already in practice in some areas of UK regulation as I outline in Box 4.14.

4.65   Publicity Orders are an effective means of deterring regulatory non-compliance as it can impact the public reputation of a business. A company's reputation and prestige is an important and valuable asset. The consequences of damaging a firm's reputation can potentially exceed the effect of a maximum fine that a court could impose.[83] A company that loses its reputation

---

[83] A. Cowen, 'Scarlet letters for corporations? Punishment by publicity under the new sentencing guidelines' (1992) *Southern California Law Review* 2387.

even for a short time can suffer significant damages to consumer confidence, market share and equity value.[84]

4.66   Publicity Orders can also make a business's behaviour more public and really hold it to account for its regulatory failures. The threat of this type of sanction may encourage firms contemplating not complying with regulatory objectives to re-consider, even if the non-compliance would generate significant financial benefit.

4.67   Adverse publicity could also trigger other non financial consequences such as interest from other regulatory agencies as well as consumers and they can be applied without limitations of a business' ability to pay.[85] Small and large firms with regard to their reputation could be sanctioned without the constraints that a financial sanction would impose which could be effective in some instances of regulatory non-compliance.

Box 4.13 Example of Publicity Orders in the US

Under Federal sentencing guidelines a judge may order a convicted company to publicise, at its own expense, its conviction and what steps it is putting in place to avoid future non-compliance. For example, the American Caster Corporation was found guilty of the illegal dumping of 250 deteriorating drums of solvents. The company's officers pleaded guilty to the charges and were ordered to take out a full page advertisement in the *Los Angeles Times* at a cost of $15,000. In addition, the company also had to pay $20,000 for the cleaning of the site and the president and vice president received a six month custodial sentence.

Source: As reported in New York Times, *February 17 1985 (Polluter Purchases Ad To Tell Of Its Illegal Toxic Dumping)*

Box 4.14 Reputation as a Motivation for Regulatory Compliance

UK regulators already recognise and utilise policies of 'naming, faming and shaming' both good and bad practice. The Health and Safety Executive currently discloses details of its enforcement actions on its Web site which the CBI has said 'puts peer pressure on those firms that have issues to address and threatens adverse impact on their reputation'.[86]

---

[84] C. Harvard, *Reputation*, Formbrum, (1996) Business School Press.
[85] C Abbot, 'The Regulatory Enforcement of Pollution Control Laws: the Australian Experience', *Journal of Environmental Law* (2005) Vol 17 No2 161-180.
[86] Evidence submitted to the Macrory Review, Spring 2006.

In addition, the Financial Services Authority accompanies a penalty with a press release giving details of the non-compliance and the size of penalty as does the Environment Agency who issues press releases for successful prosecutions to local and national media.

Recommendation 8:

I recommend that the Government consider introducing the following alternative sentencing in criminal courts:

- Profit Order – Where the profits made from regulatory non-compliance are clear, the criminal courts have access to Profit Orders, requiring the payment of such profits, distinct from any fine that the court may impose;

- Corporate Rehabilitation Order – In sentencing a business for regulatory non-compliance, criminal courts have on application by the prosecutor, access to a Corporate Rehabilitation Order (CRO) in addition to or in place of any fine that may be imposed; and

- Publicity Order – In sentencing a business for regulatory non-compliance, criminal courts have the power to impose a Publicity Order, in addition to or in place of any other sentence.

4.68 I believe that the requirements of a CRO should be flexible, reflecting both the circumstances of the offence and the nature of the business and could include mandatory audits and the carrying out of community projects. The regulator would, under appropriate guidance from the court, be responsible for supervising the carrying out of the CRO.

4.69 For Publicity Orders, I believe that this type of order would enable a court, to order that a notice (with wording agreed by the regulator and the business) to be placed in an appropriate publication, such as a local or national newspaper, a trade publication or another appropriate media outlet such as radio or television, or in a company's annual report within a specified period. The notice would state the background to the offence, the steps taken by the offender to prevent repetition and any remedial or compensatory measures taken by the offender. While some regulators have a strategy for 'naming and shaming', the recommendation on Publicity Orders differs in that they would be imposed by the court, an independent third party, and not by the regulator. This would ensure that the business has a received a fair and objective assessment of the offence.

Conclusion

4.70 Chapters three and four have gone through my main recommendations regarding the types of sanctions that I think should be available to regulators. These represent additional tools and are not meant to replace criminal prosecution as a regulatory sanction. The additional sanctions may be more appropriate in some cases that are currently prosecuted. They provide a range of administrative financial and non-financial options where criminal prosecution is not appropriate. Furthermore, I have also made recommendations for more flexible sanctions for cases of regulatory non-compliance that are sentenced within the criminal courts. The addition of these sanctioning tools to a regulator's and courts' toolkit will make them more effective when it comes to enforcement and this will strengthen the entire regulatory regime of advice, inspection and enforcement.

4.71 The next chapter focuses on transparency and accountability mechanisms that I believe are necessary for a well functioning and effective sanctioning system that includes financial and non-financial sanctions.

V.   TRANSPARENCY AND ACCOUNTABILITY

The previous two chapters presented a blueprint for an effective sanctioning system that reinforces and is consistent with a risk based approach to regulation. This chapter discusses the transparency and accountability frameworks that are necessary to support this blueprint.

Introduction

5.1 Regulators wield power over the regulated community and have been entrusted to act on behalf of the public to maintain and safeguard certain obligations or requirements. There is a strong culture of good governance within the UK regulatory system that acts as a check on these powers.

5.2   Some of my recommendations in the previous two chapters involve extending regulators' enforcement options, thereby giving some of them access to powers they have not previously held. Both regulators and industry have expressed some concern on how new powers of enforcement will be introduced and used in the coming years. However, some UK regulators, most notably the economic regulators, already use most of the sanctions that I have suggested should be part of an extended toolkit.[87] There is much good practice already in existence here, in particular strengthened transparency and accountability frameworks such as open board meetings.

5.3   Although standards of accountability and transparency amongst UK regulators in general are already high, I believe these systems must be developed further in order for a more flexible sanctioning system to be effective and credible. I detail some recommendations for these areas in the following discussion.

Transparency

5.4   Transparency is something that the regulator must provide to external stakeholders, including both industry and the public, so they have an opportunity to be informed of their rights and responsibilities and of enforcement activity. However, it is also important for the regulator itself, to help ensure it uses their sanctioning powers in a proportionate and risk based way.

5.5   I have set out recommendations relating to an increased level of transparency for regulators through:

- The publication of an enforcement policy;

- Publicly disclosing who enforcement actions have been taken against; and

- Publishing information on the outcomes of enforcement action.

Accountability

5.6   Regulators see their primary accountability to Ministers and elected officials whether in Parliament or at local level and this

---

[87] These regulators include Financial Services Authority, OFGEM, OFT and Competition Commission

relationship is already strong. In addition, regulators are making some good progress on increasing their accountability to those who they regulate and those on whose behalf they are regulating. Some of my recommendations will strengthen the answerability of regulators to stakeholders further. I also propose that Ministers and Parliament should also look more closely at the enforcement and sanctioning activities of regulators, rather than focus mainly on financial accountability in order to provide a complete overview of a regulator's activities including enforcement.

What do I Mean by Transparency?

5.7   Being transparent is necessary to ensure that business knows what consequences it could face for failure to comply with regulatory requirements. Transparency can be achieved in several different areas, for example transparency in procedural decision making also ensures high standards when the regulator makes its enforcement decisions. Broadly speaking, regulators should be able to outline the process by which decisions are arrived at, the types of factors that may influence a regulator's enforcement decisions, and what types of enforcement action could be taken in what circumstances.

5.8   The culture of transparency is strong in those national regulators who have published enforcement policies available to the public and regulated communities. At present, however, the use of enforcement policies is patchy amongst UK regulators. Internal research I commissioned for my review showed that only 17 of the 60 national regulators surveyed had a publicly accessible enforcement policy.

5.9   Other agencies may have policies available for internal reference, but these are not easily available publicly. For local authority regulators, 96 percent have signed up to the Enforcement Concordat, which articulates general 'Principles of Good Enforcement'.[88] Although this is a good starting point, more specific guidance on its enforcement practice in particular regulatory areas should be produced beyond the Concordat by those local regulators who want to use an expanded sanctioning toolkit. Businesses should have a clear idea what they need to do in order to comply with regulations. In addition, where local authority regulators are enforcing on behalf of a national regulator, they should do so following the national regulators' policy guidelines.

[88] http://www.cabinetoffice.gov.uk/regulation/documents/pst/pdf/concord.pdf#search=%22enforcement%20concordat%22

Transparency through Enforcement Policies

What are enforcement policies?

5.10   An enforcement policy is a public document setting out what action the public, and the regulated community, can expect from a regulator when a regulatory breach has been identified. This will specify the range of enforcement options available to the regulator, when enforcement action is likely to be taken and in what circumstances. It should also talk about the regulator's policies for risk based enforcement, enforcement action in cases of conflicting regulations, the provision of advice and information it requests from business.

Characteristics of a good enforcement policy

5.11   Enforcement policies must always retain a degree of flexibility, since I believe the choice of sanctioning response can never be a purely mechanical exercise. But if they are to be of real value to the regulated community, it is important that they are drafted with reference to the specific area of regulation to which they relate, rather than expressed in over-generalised terms, although I expect there would be some over-arching principles which would apply to all areas.

5.12   The language in an enforcement policy should not however be over-specific on what a business should expect when found in each and every potential type of breach. This would be arduous and bureaucratic and would bind a regulator's discretion too tightly leading to an overly rigid enforcement system that would not be beneficial for the regulator, the regulated community, or the public. Flexibility remains a cornerstone of a good enforcement system.

Positive influence of published enforcement policies

5.13   **Consistent decision making** – public enforcement policies both facilitate and incentivise regulators to make decisions on a fair and consistent basis. They facilitate consistency by giving enforcers a reference point – applicable to all their enforcement activity – for how they should react to different circumstances. This delivers consistent decisions as regulators act in the knowledge that when formal enforcement proceedings are pursued this should happen in a manner consistent with the public policy. It would also require the regulator to explain and justify any significant departure from its public policy.

5.14 **Safeguards for stakeholders** – public enforcement policies provide a valuable safeguard for businesses against the misuse of regulators' powers. Likewise they provide reassurance for the public that decisions on enforcement are made consistent with public policy.

5.15 Given that some regulators already have experience in publishing enforcement policies I suggest the sharing of best practice here which could be co-ordinated by the Better Regulation Executive.

Each policy should:

- Have regard to the Principles of Good Regulation, the Enforcement Concordat, the Compliance Code (when established) and the Macrory Penalties Principles;

- Set out what a regulator may do to bring businesses into compliance without the need for taking punitive action;

- Explain the range of enforcement options available to the regulator;

- Explain the criteria upon which decisions are made when choosing what specific enforcement action to take in each case of non-compliance, including any aggravating or mitigating factors the regulator might take into account before applying a particular sanction;

- Where a regulator has FMAP powers – outline the scheme for imposing these sanctions detailing, for example, relevant time limits, the scale of charges, and methods of paying FMAPs, and complaints and appeals procedures;

- Where a regulator has VMAP powers – outline the calculation mechanism for deciding the appropriate fine including aggravating and mitigating factors that will impact on the level of VMAP, and give relevant details relating to payment of the VMAP;

- Where a regulator has FMAP and/or VMAP powers – outline complaints and appeals procedures;

- Where a regulator has access to Statutory Notices – outline the circumstances under which these might be appropriate and the consequences of non-compliance; and

- Where a regulator has access to Enforceable Undertakings or Undertakings Plus – outline the scheme for entering into these agreements, for example, the relevant time limits, application process, types of conditions and consequences for non-compliance.

5.16 Enforcement policies should be clearly identified and readily accessible on the regulator's own website. They may take the form of separate documents addressing each sanction individually provided that there is overall transparency about the regulator's sanctioning options.

5.17 Enforcement policies once published should not be subject to constant change, but regulators should ensure that they are subject to periodic review, to ensure that in the light of experience they are fit-for-purpose and up-to-date. While I do not propose any formal assessment of regulators' enforcement policies, actions taken by the regulator will be held against the policies when it reports on outputs and outcomes, which I discuss in the next section.

Transparency Through Reporting Outcomes

5.18 As I discussed in my interim report, I have found that most regulators, when reporting on enforcement activity or compliance, focus on the outputs of this activity, for example, the number of prosecutions or the number of Statutory Notices that have been issued. This information is important, but there is very little evidence on what the actual result, or outcomes, of these enforcement actions are. I think that regulators should be encouraged to measure and communicate their regulatory outcomes and objectives in addition to the outputs.

5.19 Reporting on these measures through existing reports to stakeholders or Parliament, would let the regulated community and the public know what activities the regulator is engaged in. It also is an indication of the effectiveness of the regulator in discharging its statutory duties, thereby holding it to account.

Measuring outcomes

5.20   Appropriate outcome measures will vary in different areas of regulatory activity, but are essentially concerned with the expected consequences and goals of the regulator's enforcement activity rather than an account of the amount and type of enforcement activity it undertakes. In some cases, the regulatory requirements themselves may clearly identify a policy goal. In other cases, it may be appropriate to formulate an outcome that can be measured, such as the quantifiable reduction of pollution incidents or reduction in deaths and serious injuries. Evaluating the extent to which non-compliant businesses become compliant could also form an outcome measure. Determining the appropriate outcome measures and the methodology by which they should be measured are challenging tasks. However, it is only by measuring outcomes that regulators, the regulated community, and the public will begin to know what impact enforcement actions are having on regulatory outcomes and whether these have improved compliance. It will also highlight for the regulator if there needs to be any modification to its choice of enforcement actions in order to better meet regulatory objectives.

5.21   During the course of the review, it became apparent how little information is available on the effectiveness of sanctioning regimes. If government accepts my recommendation, I would suggest that sponsoring departments and/or regulators use the opportunity of introducing new sanctioning tools to study and develop information, including commissioning independent research, relating to the sanctions and their effectiveness especially during the transition period. This will be very helpful to many within the regulatory sector.

> The Office of Fair Trading has established an evaluation programme into how effective enforcement (and non enforcement) methods, such as information campaigns, are at changing business and consumer behaviour. It is also planning work on establishing appropriate performance measures in consumer regulation enforcement and market studies work. It will be working with academics and other competition authorities internationally to set baseline and success criteria that will enable a robust evaluation of performance and impact.
>
> Source: http://www.oft.gov.uk/NR/rdonlyres/F704C245-D32B-4E17-854D-715C23073A6D/0/AnnualPlan07.pdf

5.22   Alongside providing the regulatory community with greater information, a focus on outcomes will also ensure that industry is better served. Regulators will need to demonstrate that their enforcement actions are having a measured impact. Simply publishing the number of enforcement actions, will no longer suffice as a demonstration of the effectiveness of a regulator in meeting its regulatory objectives. Business should be reassured because the regulator will need to go one step further in supporting its enforcement strategy. It will, for example, need to demonstrate that imposing administrative sanctions is improving regulatory outcomes compared with sanctioning by criminal prosecutions alone.

5.23   I do recognise that regulation is not an exact science and that regulatory outcomes are not the only measure of a regulator's success. Nonetheless I believe that measuring outcomes has been a neglected area of reporting within the regulatory community that is essential to the credible functioning of a modern regulatory system and I would like to see regulators strive towards achieving this.

5.24   Regulators and sponsoring departments should in their annual reports:

- Summarise the relevant regulatory output measures for the relevant period;

- Summarise the relevant regulatory outcome measures during the relevant period; and

- Comment on the relationship between the outcomes and the outputs.

Transparency Through Publishing Enforcement Actions

5.25   When regulators make a decision to enforce and impose a formal sanction, I believe that this should be a matter of public record. This will:

- Ensure that the public knows that the regulator is taking action in cases where regulatory non-compliance has occurred;

- Demonstrates to industry that the regulator will take action and is doing so against firms that do not comply; and

- Publicly hold industry to account for its behaviour.

5.26   A number of regulators have made this part of their current practice and I think this is something that others should also adopt. For example, the HSE has a database of enforcement actions available on its website for prosecutions that the agency has taken forward and where Statutory Notices have been applied. I believe that disclosure of when and against whom enforcement action has been taken should not be isolated to criminal prosecutions but should also be used for other enforcement action such as administrative penalties, enforcement or improvement notices or any other formal sanction in order to be consistent and transparent in the approach to enforcement and publishing sanctions.

5.27   I believe that making public outcome measures, success in achieving them, and information concerning the number and types of enforcement sanction pursued provides one source of performance accountability of regulators. But I also believe that more formal channels of accountability should be strengthened and I discuss this in the section below.

Accountability

5.28   A previous study of independent regulators found that, when asked to whom they are accountable, most national regulators suggested that it is to ministers and parliament.[89] This is an important mechanism of accountability, especially where the regulator is funded either in full or in part, by public money. Rigorous financial accountability mechanisms are a crucial part of a well-functioning, effective and credible regulatory system. There are currently a number of good accountability mechanisms in place including:

- All regulators have an accounting officer;

- They have to produce annual accounts – available to everyone;

- They can be audited by the National Audit Office or the Audit Commission;

- They can be subject to value for money examinations by the National Audit Office; or

[89] *Independent Regulators*, Better Regulation Task Force, October 2003, page 22,

- They can be called to appear before the relevant House of Commons or Lords select committee to answer for their actions.

5.29 Local Authority regulators are accountable through their management structures to the chief executive and ultimately to the elected councillors. All authorities will have a corporate complaints procedure to deal with complaints about the service and local authorities are also governed by the Local Government Ombudsman. All local authorities also have their own independent auditors plus a range of government inspectors and reporting requirements to central government.

5.30 Whilst accountability to Parliament and Ministers is important, it is equally important that regulators are clearly answerable to those that they regulate, and those on whose behalf they are regulating. Such accountability would assist in reassuring the regulated community that non-compliance is dealt with effectively. My recommendations on improved transparency will serve to strengthen regulators' accountability to the public and the regulated community through the publication of their enforcement policies and outcomes of their enforcement actions.

5.31 Many regulators are making real progress in their efforts to become more answerable to their stakeholders. Some examples of these include:

- Corporate plans (sets out priorities and details of how these will be achieved);

- Open meetings;

- Accessible and affordable appeal mechanisms;

- Open consultation exercises and feedback;

- Publication of board agendas, papers and minutes where appropriate;

- Regulatory impact assessments presented alongside proposed legislation; and

- Comprehensive and easy to use websites.

The Better Regulation Executive (BRE)

5.32   Many of my recommendations may pose a challenge to regulators and I believe the BRE is the right body to facilitate the introduction of many of my recommendations, given its oversight of the better regulation agenda.

5.33   The Better Regulation Executive is the central government body that promotes delivery of the government's regulatory reform agenda. As such, it plays a key role in working with government departments and regulators to improve performance on better regulation, embedding the principles of better regulation and identifying areas of best practice. This work should continue and be extended to include the implementation of the extended sanctioning toolkit.

5.34   The Better Regulation Executive should facilitate a working group of regulators and sponsoring departments to share best practice in enforcement approaches, the application of sanction options, development of outcome measures and transparency in reporting. Regulators and sponsoring departments should work with the Executive to include outcome measures as part of their overall framework of performance management.

5.35   This working group would consist of regulators, departments, industry representatives where appropriate, and BRE staff with an interest and expertise in enforcement related issues. Its aims could be to share best practice on many issues relating to enforcement including risk assessment, designing appropriate sanctioning schemes and providing support and guidance to enforcers more generally on the better regulation agenda. It could also assist regulators and departments in the development of regulatory outcome measures and enforcement policies.

5.36   The working group would exist to facilitate the exchange of best practice and assist regulators and sponsoring departments in developing expertise and competence in the extended range of sanctions. It could work alongside other expert groups such as the Whitehall Prosecutors Group and the Joint Regulators Group.

Accountability for Specific Enforcement Decisions

5.37   My proposals envisage that regulators will have a wider range of sanctioning responses to particular instances of regulatory breach, but that their enforcement discretion is exercised in the context of strengthened overall transparency and accountability. However, it is also important to consider what protective mechanisms exist to deal with allegations of abuse or poor practice in individual cases.

5.38   Where a regulator imposes an administrative penalty, I have proposed a right of appeal to a regulatory tribunal in order to provide a speedy and cost-effective protection for those who feel that the imposition of a sanction is unjustified, or the circumstances do not amount to a breach. The tribunal could also censure the regulator where there had been abuse or poor practice thereby also holding the regulator to account.

Third Parties Can Improve Accountability

5.39   Third parties such as non-governmental organisations, victims or consumers can provide an important challenge and accountability function. They act to ensure that regulators are carrying out their public duties with due care. If a regulator is not seen to be carrying out its public duties, then third parties can challenge the regulator and hold the regulator to account for its actions. I outline some of these mechanisms below.

5.40   Judicial review is a check on the lawfulness of actions and decisions of public bodies, examining the way in which a decision has been made.

5.41   The expanded toolkit I recommend in this review will not change recourse to judicial review for third parties. However, given that my recommendations will improve the transparency of regulators' enforcement procedures and policies, I envisage this in turn will reduce the need for regulatory cases to be referred to the Administrative Court.

5.42   Finally there is the option of bringing a private criminal prosecution, which individuals may do in most areas of regulation even where the regulator has decided not to commence prosecution. Although the powers are rarely exercised in the regulatory field, I believe the right of private prosecution represents a valuable public safeguard. Mechanisms already exist to prevent abuse and vexatiousness, but I have recommended that in the design of any scheme for VMAPs the Government ensure that businesses are protected from double jeopardy.

A Further Role for Parliament

5.43   As I mention above, regulators are currently accountable to Ministers and Parliament. However, I have some specific suggestions I believe will strengthen these relationships. Many of my recommendations in this area have been previously mentioned by other reports or reviewers and I want to add my endorsement for these. I fully recognise that these recommendations will be for Parliament rather than government to consider, and I have therefore not formulated them as formal recommendations. Nevertheless, I hope that they will be addressed by Parliament in the context of my other proposals.

Departmental Select Committees

5.44   Departmental Select Committees are the parliamentary bodies responsible for scrutiny of each Government department. Their role is to examine 'the expenditure, administration and policy' of the relevant department and its 'associated public bodies' and they are the leading bodies assessing the work of independent regulators with sponsoring departments. They serve to challenge and consider annual reports and specific ad hoc issues which are deemed of importance. Departmental Select Committees are widely perceived amongst the regulatory community to be the most important body holding regulators to account.

5.45   However, as highlighted in a report by the House of Lords Select Committee on the Constitution, this scrutiny function could be improved further.[90] In the first instance, I would hope that Departmental Select Committees could systematically review the enforcement performance of regulators sponsored by the departments which they scrutinize. My recommendation that regulators publish outcome measures should facilitate this process. To facilitate the scrutiny process by Select Committees, the Better Regulation Executive could, through the Enforcement Working Group I have recommended, work with regulators to create some models of good practice on reporting regulatory outcome measures and enforcement activity, which may make the material more intelligible and user-friendly.

---

[90] *The Regulatory State: Ensuring its Accountability*, House of Lords Select Committee, May 2004.

Select Committee on the Regulatory System

5.46   Departmental Select Committees work on issues relevant to their specific government department. While this sector specific scrutiny is appropriate in many instances, the cumulative impact of regulatory issues is difficult to capture under such governance arrangements. Both the Hampton Review and my own review have demonstrated that, despite very different legislative structures and institutional arrangements, there are many common issues and challenges in the regulatory field that cut across sectoral boundaries. I support the view of the House of Lords Select Committee in recommending that a joint Parliamentary Select Committee be created to focus on overarching regulatory issues. This recommendation was also endorsed by the Hampton Review.[91]

5.47   Such a committee could make a substantial contribution on the evaluation of the extended sanctioning toolkit, and issues pertaining to the regulatory system as a whole. It would not duplicate the work of Departmental Select Committees in examining individual regulators, but would assist in investigating both good and bad practice across the regulatory spectrum, and, in the context of my report, help assess the effectiveness of different sanctioning approaches.

5.48   The Parliamentary Select Committee should preferably be a joint committee of both Houses. The functions of this committee could include the right to be consulted over proposals to confer statutory powers and enforcement powers on a new or existing regulator with enough time for its comments to be taken into account during pre-legislative scrutiny.

5.49   This committee could also take on additional functions, which fall outside of my remit, but I suggest some options for Parliament to consider.

- Having regard to issues such as the potential duplication or overlap of regulatory activities, the clarity of the hierarchy of regulatory objectives with specific attention to the development of a 'whole of Government' view of regulation;

---

[91] P. Hampton, *Reducing Administrative Burdens: Effective Inspection and Enforcement*, HM Treasury, March 2005. p77 at 4.119.

- Identify and promote good practice in its role as the Parliamentary counterpart of the Better Regulation Executive within the Cabinet Office;

- Monitor the consistency and effectiveness of regulators in complying with the Principles of Good Regulation, the Compliance Code (when established) and my Penalties Principles; and

- Focus on annual reports of regulatory bodies with a view to maintaining the consistency and co-ordination of Parliamentary scrutiny.

5.50   I believe it is important for such an over-arching committee to exist in order to institutionalise this scrutiny function over regulators and sponsoring departments across a wide number of regulatory fields. The business community usually interacts with several regulators. At present, the accountability mechanisms that exist are often narrow and sectoral in scope, and therefore have difficulty in assessing the wider consequences of regulatory requirements and their enforcement, both for those that are regulated and society as a whole.

Recommendation 9:

I recommend that to ensure improved transparency and accountability:

- The Better Regulation Executive should facilitate a working group of regulators and sponsoring departments to share best practice in enforcement approaches, the application of sanction options, development of outcome measures and transparency in reporting. Regulators and sponsoring departments should work with the Executive to include outcome measures as part of their overall framework of performance management.

- Publish Enforcement Activities – Each regulator should publish a list on a regular basis of its completed enforcement actions and against whom such actions have been taken.

5.51   To further emphasise the importance of transparency and accountability I refer readers back to chapter two where I reinforce two of the characteristics I mentioned. Regulators should:

- Publish an enforcement policy – this policy should be drafted in consultation with both the regulated community and wider stakeholder groups where appropriate.

- Outcome measures – regulators alongside sponsoring departments should work, in consultation with stakeholders, to determine meaningful outcome measurements which can assist in the achievement of regulatory objectives. These outcome measures and the extent to which they have been achieved should be reported in the regulator's annual report.

5.52 Where I suggest publishing enforcement activities, this can be in the form of a database on a website, through a press release, or other appropriate means for the dissemination of such information, in accordance with the relevant data protection rules. This can further promote the risk based approach to regulation as there would be more information on compliant and non-compliant businesses and this would better inform risk assessment frameworks. The increased information on compliant and non-compliant businesses will further promote transparency, by providing regulators with more information to take targeted enforcement actions on business that break the rules and allowing good businesses a light touch.

VI. SUMMARY OF RECOMMENDATIONS

This chapter is a summary of my recommendations.

Introduction

6.1 This chapter summarises my recommendations that have appeared in the previous five chapters of this report. I want to highlight that reforms to the sanctioning regimes are an essential feature of a risk based approach to regulation envisaged by Philip Hampton in his report. Having an effective and credible sanctioning system should result in the need for fewer routine inspections on compliant businesses and allow regulators to focus attention on those businesses who fail to comply with the law. Most breaches identified in a risk based system, should face penalties that are quicker and more proportionate to the offence, while there will continue to be tough criminal sanctions for those offenders who persist in rogue trading activity.

6.2   The recommendations in this report suggest that regulators should have access to a more flexible sanctioning toolkit. It is important that only regulators who are following the risk based approach should gain access to these sanctions. That is why I have qualified many of my recommendations with a need for regulators to demonstrate that they are compliant with both the Hampton and Macrory Principles. The Regulators' Compliance Code takes Hampton's seven principles, which support a risk based approach to regulation (such as inspections being risk based, regulators sharing data between them, sanctions being proportionate and meaningful) and puts them on a statutory footing under Part Two of the Legislative and Regulatory Reform Act 2006). Regulators will have a statutory duty to have regard to the Compliance Code as it relates to their enforcement activity. The government intends to issue the Code and accompanying guidance after further consultation with regulators and the regulated community and after necessary Parliamentary scrutiny (as laid out in the Act).

6.3   The Better Regulation Commission have recently published a report on risk, entitled *Risk, Responsibility and Regulation – Whose risk is it anyway?* Recommendation Four of this report has commented on the need to identify what are the principal risks regulators are protecting against and what regulatory outcomes regulators are trying to achieve. This is very much in line with my own thinking and I have also recommended that regulators look beyond outputs to also consider measuring outcomes. Outcome measures will represent a challenge for regulators to identify and determine, but I believe that this is something that government should strive towards.

Summary of recommendations

I.   THE ROLE AND IMPORTANCE OF SANCTIONS WITHIN THE REGULATORY SYSTEM

1.   I recommend that the Government initiate a review of the drafting and formulation of criminal offences relating to regulatory non-compliance.

II.   UNDERLYING PRINCIPLES FOR REGULATORY SANCTIONS

2.   I recommend that in designing the appropriate sanctioning regimes for regulatory non-compliance, regulators should have regard to the following six Penalties Principles and seven characteristics.

Six Penalties Principles

A sanction should:

1.   Aim to change the behaviour of the offender;

2.   Aim to eliminate any financial gain or benefit from a non-compliance;

3.   Be responsive and consider what is appropriate for the particular offender and regulatory issue, which can include punishment and the public stigma that should be associated with a criminal conviction;

4.   Be proportionate to the nature of the offence and the harm caused;

5.   Aim to restore the harm caused by regulatory non-compliance, where appropriate; and

6.   Aim to deter future non-compliance

Seven Characteristics

Regulators should:

1.   Publish an enforcement policy;

2.   Measure outcomes not just outputs;

3.   Justify their choice of enforcement actions year on year to stakeholders, Ministers and Parliament;

4.   Follow-up enforcement actions where appropriate;

5.   Enforce in a transparent manner;

6.   Be transparent in the way in which they apply and determine administrative penalties; and

7.   Avoid perverse incentives that might influence the choice of sanctioning response.

III.   MY VISION FOR CONTEMPORARY SANCTIONING REGIMES: FINANCIAL SANCTIONS

3.   I recommend that in order to increase the effectiveness of criminal courts for regulatory offences, the following actions should be implemented:

- The Government should request the Sentencing Guidelines Council to prepare general sentencing guidelines for cases of regulatory non-compliance;

- Prosecutors should always make clear to the court any financial benefits resulting from non-compliance as well as the policy significance of the relevant regulatory requirement;

- Prosecutions in particular regulatory fields be heard in designated magistrates' courts within jurisdictional areas, where appropriate; and

- Regulators provide specialist training for prosecutors and discuss with the Judicial Studies Board (JSB) contributing to the training of the judiciary and justices' clerks.

4.   I recommend that with regard to Monetary Administrative Penalties:

- Government should, consider introducing schemes for Fixed and Variable Monetary Administrative Penalties, for regulators and enforcers of regulations, that are compliant with the Hampton and Macrory Principles and characteristics. This can include national regulators as well as local regulatory partners;

- Appeals concerning the imposition of an administrative penalty be heard by a Regulatory Tribunal, rather than the criminal courts;

- Fine maxima for Fixed Monetary Administrative Penalties (FMAP) schemes should be set out and not exceed level five on the standard scale. FMAPs should also be scaled to differentiate between small and large firms; and

- There should be no fine maxima for Variable Monetary Administrative Penalties (VMAPs).

IV. MY VISION FOR CONTEMPORARY SANCTIONING REGIMES – NON-FINANCIAL SANCTIONS AND ALTERN-ATIVES FOR THE CRIMINAL COURTS

5. I recommend that for an improved system of Statutory Notices:

- Government should consider using Statutory Notices as part of an expanded sanctioning toolkit to secure future compliance beyond the areas in which they are currently in use;

- Regulators should follow-up Statutory Notices using a risk based approach including an element of randomised follow-up;

- In dealing with the offence of failing to comply with a Statutory Notice, regulators should have access to administrative financial penalties as an alternative to criminal prosecution. This power should be extended by legislative amendment to existing schemes of Statutory Notices; and

- Government should consider whether appeals against Statutory Notices should be routed through the Regulatory Tribunal rather than the criminal courts.

6. I recommend that the Government should consider introducing Enforceable Undertakings and Undertakings Plus (a combination of an Enforceable Undertaking with an administrative financial penalty) as an alternative to a criminal prosecution or the imposition of VMAPs for regulators that are compliant with the Hampton and Macrory Principles and characteristics.

7. I recommend that Government introduce pilot schemes involving the use of Restorative Justice techniques in addressing cases of regulatory non-compliance. This might include RJ:

- as a pre-court diversion;

- instead of a Monetary Administrative Penalty; and

- within the criminal justice system – as both a pre or post sentencing option.

8.   I recommend that the Government consider introducing the following alternative sentencing in criminal courts:

- Profit Order – Where the profits made from regulatory non-compliance are clear, the criminal courts have access to Profit Orders, requiring the payment of such profits, distinct from any fine that the court may impose;

- Corporate Rehabilitation Order – In sentencing a business for regulatory non-compliance, criminal courts have on application by the prosecutor, access to a Corporate Rehabilitation Order (CRO) in addition to or in place of any fine that may be imposed; and

- Publicity Order – In sentencing a business for regulatory non-compliance, criminal courts have the power to impose a Publicity Order, in addition to or in place of any other sentence.

V.   TRANSPARENCY AND ACCOUNTABILITY

9.   I recommend that to ensure improved transparency and accountability:

- The Better Regulation Executive should facilitate a working group of regulators and sponsoring departments to share best practice in enforcement approaches, the application of sanction options, development of outcome measures and transparency in reporting. Regulators and sponsoring departments should work with the Executive to include outcome measures as part of their overall framework of performance management.

- Publish Enforcement Activities – Each regulator should publish a list on a regular basis of its completed enforcement actions and against whom such actions have been taken.

Annex A

Sample Enforcement Pyramid

A.1 The sample 'enforcement pyramid' below, illustrates the range of sanctioning and penalty powers exercised by regulators. The sample enforcement pyramid does not correspond to the sanctioning powers of any particular regulator, but is a generalised model. Individual regulators have specific and different sanctioning options, depending on the powers provided by the underlying legislation.

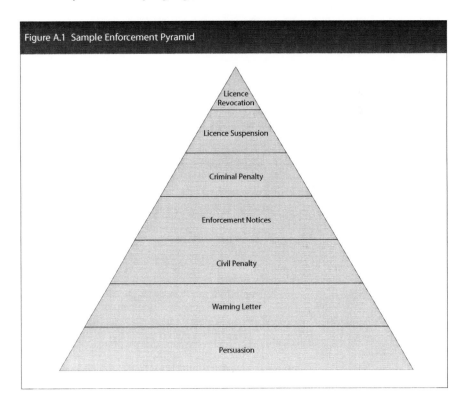

Figure A.1 Sample Enforcement Pyramid

A.2 The enforcement pyramid indicates a range of sanctioning options starting at the least severe at the base of the pyramid. As one moves towards the apex, the enforcement actions increase in severity. Regulators usually choose which level of the pyramid to commence their enforcement action depending on the nature of the offence, the seriousness of the consequences, and the level of intent of the offender.

CHAPTER 3

REGULATING IN A RISKY ENVIRONMENT*

In October 2000 the Prime Minister delivered a major speech on the environment.[1] For those concerned with environmental policy, it was a politically significant occasion in that it was his first speech on the subject as prime minister. But for British lawyers who over the past two decades or so have studied and contributed to an extraordinary development of what is now known as environmental law there was an equally intriguing aspect: regulation as a policy tool received just one scant mention in the whole speech.[2]

Regulation is a notoriously difficult concept to define with precision. One commonly used definition refers to the 'sustained and focused control exercised by a public agency over activities that are socially valued',[3] though as Hilson notes[4] this does not necessarily capture all those undesirable activities which one could also expect to be controlled by environmental regulation. For the purposed of my analysis, a further key essential is that regulation is clearly enforceable by a legal sanction,[5] distinguishing it from many forms of economic intervention by government. What is clear is that there is a number of challenges facing contemporary environmental regulation and my underlying concern is with the extent to which governments have lost confidence in regulation as an instrument of environmental policy. We need to understand the reasons for this, whether they are sound, and, I would argue, explore mechanisms for revitalizing its role. For a country such as the United Kingdom where traditionally one might have expected the clear location of responsibility for designing environmental regulation to rest with central government, in part any present discomfort with

---

* Macrory R (2002) 'Regulating in a Risky Environment' in Freeman M (ed), *Current Legal Problems 2001*, Oxford University Press, Oxford 619-648
[1] Prime Minister, 'Richer and Greener', speech to the CBI/Green Alliance Conference on the Environment (London, 24 October 2000).
[2] The one reference to regulation in the speech is 'On regulation, our aim must be to raise environmental standards without imposing unnecessary burdens on business'.
[3] G. Majone, 'The rise of the regulatory state in Europe' (1994) 17 *West European Politics* 77, 81; P. Selznick, 'Focusing Organisational Research on Regulation' in R. Noll (ed.), *Regulatory Policy and the Social Sciences* (Berkeley, 1985).
[4] C. Hilson, *Regulating Pollution: A UK and EC Perspective* (Oxford, 2000), ch. 1.
[5] For the purposes of the present analysis, whether sanctions take the form of criminal penalties, civil penalties as extensively used in the United States, or administrative sanctions such as the withdrawal of a licence is a second-order question, which is not further explored here, though clearly significant in the design of effective regulation.

regulation can be attributed to the uncertainties brought about by a general realignment of formal powers away from central government, with supra-national 'pressures' for 'concerted' International action competing with continuing and sometimes contradictory pressures for increased decentralisation. The environment is a particularly complex policy field, and poses especially difficult challenges for the allocation of government responsibilities. Traditional models of federal or quasi-federal constitutions which attempt to articulate a clear separation of powers in the environmental field are unlikely to reflect the physical and political, dynamics of the issue.[6] Such questions concern what might be described as the vertical allocation of powers, but as Peter Hain has forcefully argued in a recent study[7] the realities of global capitalism and an increasingly articulate citizenship create new challenges for the traditional authority of national governments:

> power is also moving outwards into new configurations that have little to do with governments at any level, or with the physical boundaries that define where they hold sway.[8]

These considerations form a background to the exercise of regulatory power in any policy field by contemporary government at whatever level. But environmental regulation has been subject to a distinctive and sustained intellectual challenge in recent years, and it is on a number of those themes that I intend to focus. In doing so, I will test the validity of theory against a number of case studies in recent United Kingdom policy, and draw on my personal experience as a member of the Royal Commission on Environmental Pollution[9] and a board member of the Environment Agency.[10]

[6] R. Macrory, 'The Environment and Constitutional Change', in R. Hazell (ed.), *Constitutional Futures: A History of the Next Ten Years* (Oxford, 1999) where I discuss some of the difficulties in the context of current constitutional reform in the United Kingdom.. For a recent study of the challenges of locating power in the context of federal systems and particularly that of the United States, see R. Ravesz, 'Environmental Regulation in Federal Systems', in H. Somsen (ed.), *Yearbook of European Environmental Law* (Oxford, 2000) 1.

[7] P. Hain, *The End of Foreign Policy? British Interests, Global Linkages and Natural Limits* (London, 2001) ch. 5.

[8] At the time of writing the author was Minister of State at the UK Foreign and Commonwealth Office, but the concerns of a practising politician clearly reflect themes of the authority of government explored by contemporary political sociologists such as Ulrich Beck and Anthony Giddens; see in particular U. Beck, *Risk Society: Towards a New Modernity* (London, 1992) and A. Giddens, *The Consequences of Modernity* (Cambridge, 1990). For insightful British accounts see P. Macnaughten and J. Urry, *Contested Natures* '(London, 1992) and D. Goldblatt, *Social Theory and the Environment* (London, 1997) especially chapter 5 where the author questions the applicability of some of Beck's analysis to a number of British environmental issues.

[9] The Royal Commission on Environment Pollution was established in 1970 'to advise on matters, both national and international, concerning pollution of the environment; on the

Continued

Market Failure and Regulatory Prescription

There are two important underlying presumptions concerning environmental regulation, both of which can be challenged. The first is that the justification for environmental regulation is solely based on the concept of market failures in a free economy: The dominant economic theory is that the sum of individual consumer choices in a free market will maximise collective welfare, and the role of areas of law such as property, contract, and tort is to define the rights and responsibilities of these economic actors. In certain areas, through – and the environment is an obvious example – there will be market failure in that costs can be externalised and imposed on others than the actor concerned, and hence the need for government intervention, traditionally in the form of regulation. The analysis of course has a powerful logic. Furthermore, it provides a driver and justification for seeking methods other than legal regulation to perform functions equivalent to interventionist regulation. The redefinition of property rights provides one example, while current proposals to develop tort principles concerning civil liability for environmental damage as a tool of public policy provide another example.[11]

Yet there are deficiencies in the argument. For a start the model consciously avoids attributing any moral dimension to regulation. Yet few would attempt to argue that many areas of criminal law are based solely on market failure, nor would the various legal principles concerning, say, rights and obligations that have been developed in the area of family law be described as a response to market failure. As well as economic considerations, environmental issues do raise important moral and value questions of our relationship with the environment,[12]

...adequacy of research in the field; and the future possibilities of danger to the environment'. It is the only remaining standing Royal Commission in the United Kingdom, and produces major reports around every 28 months.

[10] The Environment Agency was established in 1995 under Part I Environment Act 1995 as a non-departmental public body with extensive responsibilities in England and Wales for the regulation of waste, water pollution and water resources, fisheries, radioactive wastes, and key industrial processes. In addition the Agency has operational functions concerning land drainage and flood management. The views expressed in this article are personal, and do not necessarily represent the collective views of the Royal Commission or the Agency.

[11] At European Community level see in particular European Commission (2000) *White Paper on Environmental Liability*, COM (2000) 66 final. For a recent legal analysis see M. Wild, 'The EC Commission's White Paper on Environmental Liability: Issues and Implications' 13 *Journal of Environmental Law* 21. In the same issue Peter Cane provides a powerful critique of the use of civil liability mechanisms as an instrument of public policy goals: P. Cane, 'Are Environmental Harms Special?' (2001) 13 *Journal of Environmental Law* 3.

[12] A valuable collection of recent material written on the subject of ethical value and the environment is contained in R. Elliot (ed.), *Environmental Ethics* (Oxford, 1993).

or our relationships with each other and with future generations. In this context, environmental regulation reflects questions of value as well as market failure, and merely adjusting notions of private property or internalizing external costs are unlikely to satisfy those aspirations.

Even within its own terms, the theory has serious problems. In its pure form it provides a justification for seeking to determine and to quantify in financial terms the economic costs imposed by environmental externalities. But it seems unlikely that we will ever succeed in measuring environmental costs with such a degree of precision that they can be imposed on relevant economic actors in a way that will allow us to rely upon market forces alone. Two recent examples illustrate the difficulties involved. In 1997 Andrew Stirling of Sussex University collated over thirty studies published between 1979 and 1995 estimating in monetary terms the environmental externalities of modern coal-fired power stations.[13] The results of individual studies were often expressed in extremely precise terms and with considerable confidence, but when presented collectively the variations were so immense as to throw doubt on their validity as a policy tool: values on the lowest estimates were less than 4/100 of a cent per kilowatt hour with the highest around $20 per kilowatt hour, a factor of more than fifty thousand. Deriving a workable and acceptable set of fiscal instruments to internalise such an uncertain range of costs would have proved near impossible, or have involved so many political choices as to undermine the intellectual grounding of the exercise.

The second example concerns transport. In its 18th Report on Transport the Royal Commission on Environmental Pollution attempted to estimate the external costs imposed by transport in the United Kingdom[14] Some costs, as property. costs, were quantifiable with a reasonable degree of certainty. Others, such as global warming, are based on arguable assumptions, and in any event contain an enormous range of uncertainty. When considering damage from transport in the form of, say, visual intrusion, loss of habitats, and severance of communities, the Commission, rightly in my view, eventually concluded that the methodologies were so suspect that any numerical figures would not produce useful results. Instead, it was felt preferable to start with a judgment of the environmental goals one wished to secure, and then to consider the most cost-effective ways of achieving them. This does not mean that an exercise in estimating external costs in general terms is without value. In that case it provided a broad-scale picture of the extent of external damage imposed by transport, and highlighted substantial

---

[13] A. Stirling, 'Limits to the Value of External Costs' (1997) 25 *Energy Policy* 517.
[14] Royal Commission on Environmental Pollution, *Transport and the Environment*, 18th Report, Cm. 2674 (London, 1994) ch. 7.

discrepancies between the costs paid by private motorists and heavy goods vehicles. But it also revealed the enormous difficulties facing those who wished to internalise external costs. The problem of the logic was underlined by the fact that in relation to private motorists, at least, it was not easy to show that their external environmental costs in fact exceeded the actual costs paid in the form of both direct and indirect taxes. If motorists were prepared to pay such costs, did it then follow that all was well with the market-based approach and that society should accept that consequential environmental damage was being paid for?

The second prevailing presumption concerns so-called command and control regulation. The term is often used rather loosely and as a pejorative to attack all traditional forms of environmental regulation, particularly in the field of pollution control. As Gunningham and Grabosky have observed, the term 'command and control' has now largely replaced the more traditional term of direct regulation.[15] Much of the sustained criticism of command and control has come from the legal and economic literature in the United States over the past decade or so,[16] and a central concern is that by prescribing the details of technical solutions, such command and control regulation stifles innovative solutions and leads to inefficient outcomes.

Yet an analysis of the form of regulation that has developed in practice reveals a considerably richer picture. In the field of pollution control, where much of the criticism has been focused, one can identify three broad approaches in the design of regulation: true technical standards which prescribe particular forms of technical solutions; emission- or performance-based standards which are outcome-focused and are concerned with prescribing levels of pollutants which may be discharged; and finally, ambient-based controls which relate to the quality of the receiving medium and may be set either on a single medium basis (air, water, etc.) or on a more integrated multi-media basis. In relation to the first, type. technical standards, as the distinguished US environmental lawyer, Turner T. Smith Jr, has noted, even in the United States:

> other than (1) management standards for transportation, storage and disposal of hazardous waste and (2) limited case of US work practice rules, virtually all of the technology

---

[15] N. Gunningham and P. Grabosky, *Smart Regulation: Designing Environmental Policy* (Oxford, 1998) 39.

[16] Examples include B. Ackerman and R. Stewart, 'Reforming Environmental Law: The democratic case for market incentives', (1988) 13 *Columbia Journal of Environmental Law* 171; R. Stewart, 'Models for environmental regulation: Central planning versus market based approaches' (1992) *Boston College Environmental Affairs Review* 547; S. Breyer, *Regulation and its Reform* (Cambridge, M., 1992).

based air and water standards and some off the hazardous
waste treatment standards are not command and control
in the sense of expressly requiring use of a specific type of
technology[17]

Such standards are clearly related to technological solutions, but
industry is free to choose its most effective method of achieving them,
whether by process management or alternative technologies. The
same analysis can be made of much of the environmental legislation
in Europe, where at European Community level there have been long
standard philosophical disputes between the merits and weaknesses
of emission and quality orientated standards.[18] Yet true technological
standards which prescribe particular forms of technology remain rare.
It is true that recent European Community legislation such as the IPPC
Directive makes reference to the 'Best Available Technology', yet even
here it is clear that the legislative intent is to focus on the production of
emission standards rather than particular forms of technology.[19]. See,
for example, para. 4 of Article 9 which states that:

emission limit values and the equivalent parameters and
technical measures referred to in paragraph 3 shall be
based on the best available techniques without prescribing
the use of any technique or specific technology.

The attack on command and control regulation as a form of law that
prescribes forms of technical solution is therefore somewhat misplaced,
and has sometimes been promoted by those who fail to appreciate the
flexibilities that even apparently tough environmental regimes can
provide.[20] Nor should one ignore the very real achievements of direct
regulation in the last twenty years or so. In its recent report on the state
of the environment in England and Wales,[21] the Environment Agency
notes significant progress in the improvement of air and water quality
over the last decade, but a decline in the quality of soil, an area where in
comparison with water and air there has been a signal lack of dedicated
environmental regulation. Despite this background, direct regulation

---

[17] Turner T. Smith Jr and R. Macrory, 'Legal and Political Considerations', in P. Douben
(ed.), *Pollution Risk Assessment and Management* (Chichester, 1998) 406.
[18] N. Haigh, *EEC Environmental Policy and Britain* 2nd edn. (London, 1987) 20-3.
[19] G. Lübbe-Wolff, 'Efficient Environmental Legislation: On Different Philosophies of
Pollution Control in Europe' (2001) 13 *journal of Environmental Law* 79.
[20] See, for example, N. Hanley, J. Shogren, and B. White, *Environmental Economics in Theory
and Practice* (Basingstoke, 1992) quoted in Lübbe-Wolff, n. 19 above. At 58 the authors
appear to characterise command and control regulation as imposing 'technological
restrictions such as mandated abatement methods'.
[21] Environment Agency, *Environment 2000 and Beyond* (Bristol, 2001).

remains a politically vulnerable instrument of policy, and over the last decade or so two key forms of policy tool have been promoted as alternatives to regulation: economic instruments and voluntary agreements.

Economic Instruments and their Weaknesses

The use of economic instruments has a powerful theoretical basis if one believes that the root cause of environmental problems is market failure. As the 1996 Government Annual Report on the UK's Sustainable Strategy put it:

> Economic instruments use the efficiency properties of markets to attain environmental objectives in the most cost-effective way. Moreover this cost-effective solution is achieved through the operation of market mechanisms themselves, dispensing with the need for a regulator.[22]

Economic instruments in the form of taxes or charges appear to be consistent with the 'polluter pays' principle. and to provide a mechanism for government to influence the direction of behaviour without determining solutions. But where the aim is to achieve articulated policy goals, their effectiveness is less certain, and we are entitled to test their seductive theory against practical experience. Three recent examples from the United Kingdom suggest a need for some degree of scepticism.

The differential taxes on leaded and unleaded petrol were for many years promoted as a prime example of an effective economic instrument. Yet as the table from the second assessment of the European Environmental Agency indicates,[23] a comparison of the United Kingdom reduction rates with other European countries hardly inspires unqualified confidence in the ability of the instrument to achieve policy goals. Comparing reductions of lead emissions from petrol between 1990 and 1996 Britain's reduction is half that of Scandinavian countries and comes between Georgia and Lithuania.

The next example relates to the landfill tax, introduced in the United Kingdom in October 1996, initially applying a tax of £7 per tonne of waste, with various reductions and exemptions.[24] To anyone who is critical of

---

[22] United Kingdom, 'This Common Inheritance', Cm. 3188 (London, 1996) para. 147.

[23] European Environment Agency, *Europe's Environment: A Second Assessment* (Copenhagen, 1998) 27.

[24] Landfill Tax Regulations, SI 1996 No. 1527; Landfill Tax (Qualifying Material) Order, SI 1996 No. 1528; Landfill Tax (Contaminated Land) Order, SI 1996 No. 1529.

direct regulation because it can consist of complex, legally binding rules, the lengthy regulations required to implement the landfill tax clearly illustrate that economic instruments equally require mandatory rules, and often of similar density. The policy intention behind the landfill tax, namely to increase the cost of landfill so that other waste disposal methods including minimisation, recycling, and incineration became more economically attractive options, is environmentally persuasive. Yet markets behave in unpredictable ways. The cost of landfill did indeed rise considerably, but also led to a substantial diversion of waste to other destinations which were not included in the preferred options: increased fly-tipping, and more seriously the substantial diversion to, and possible abuse of various form of disposal exempted under current regulations. As the (ENDS) report noted:

> Within months of the landfill tax taking effect in 1996, reports came rolling in that golf courses and farms had become prime destinations for the disposal of construction and demolition waste.[25]

A government-commissioned report suggested that land filling of inert wastes had fallen from around 66 million tonnes before the introduction of the tax to about 30 million tonnes in 2000.[26] The Environment Agency itself was hampered in effective supervision, partly because its revenue streams in relation to waste derived from charges on licensed landfills, and it is only recently that the government is seriously addressing the need to tighten up the exempted routes. A key lesson from the saga was the danger of assuming that a market instrument by itself could achieve desired policy goals. Without a powerful and adequately enforced regulatory framework, unexpected consequences can arise. This of course is particularly the case when dealing with an issue such as waste which generally has negative economic value for producers, and where the cheapest diversion route will have a powerful attraction. In that context economic instruments need to be supportive rather than substitutive of regulation.

Whether the landfill tax by itself, even against a background of strengthened regulation against undesired diversion, would have had the desired outcome of reducing landfill is difficult to judge. What is now clearly going to have a far more substantial impact on shifting the hierarchy of waste management options is the European Community Landfill Directive,[27] which came into force in July 2001, and which imposes

---

[25] ENDS Report, 'Inertia over inert waste embarrasses Ministers and Agency' (2000) 303 ENDS Report 22.
[26] Ecotec, *Effects of the Landfill Tax* (London, 2001).
[27] EC Directive on the Landfill of Waste 99/31/EC OJL 182 17.7.99.

direct bans on overall quantities of waste going into landfill over the next decade or so.[28] The Landfill Directive represents a form of command and control instrument, albeit one at supranational level. Again, far from prescribing in detail forms of technological choice, it leaves considerable discretion to choose the most effective means; to achieve the prescribed goals. Government may well choose a form of market instrument, permits tradeable between local authorities,[29] as a method of achieving the requirements, but against the backdrop of a regulatory instrument. Now that the European Court of Justice possesses the power to impose sanctions in the forms of penalties or fines for member states who fail to comply with its judgments, directives have come to resemble classical legal forms of regulation, though developed at supranational level and directed at national governments. The power of the court to impose direct sanctions[30] – a unique ability among international courts – was introduced under the Maastricht amendments with the strong support of the UK government. At the time it was being proposed, the House of Lords Select Committee on the European Communities investigated the whole issue of the implementation of Community environmental law[31] and, as one of the specialist advisers to the Committee, I admit entertaining misgivings about the prospective power of the European Court. At its crudest, it appeared to denigrate the rule of law to accept that governments need to be threatened with financial sanctions to ensure compliance with judgments of a court. Despite the Committee's reservations at the time, the power was introduced, and we have since seen the first case in which the Court of Justice imposed a fine,[32] at the same time endorsing the Commission's policy documents explaining its approach towards establishing the level of appropriate penalty.[33] Evidence to date suggests that even the threat of the sanction has had a considerable effect in concentrating the minds of governments to ensure proper implementation.[34]

---

[28] Amongst other requirements, biodegradable municipal wastes must be reduced to 75% of 1995 levels by 2010, 50% by 2013, and 35% by 2020.

[29] Department of the Environment, Transport, and the Regions, 'Consultation Paper on Tradeable Landfill Permits' (London, 2001).

[30] Art. 228, European Community Treaty.

[31] House of Lords Select Committee on the European Communities, *Implementation and Enforcement of Environmental Legislation*, 9th Report Session 1991-2 HL Paper 53 (London, 1992). In its subsequent report, *Community Environmental Law: Making It Work*, 2nd Report Session 1997-8 HL Paper 12 (London, 1997) the Committee held a more positive view towards the sanction powers of the court: para. 98.

[32] *Commission v Greece* (C-387/97) ECJ 4 July 2000. For a discussion see R. Macrory, 'Greece gets first fine for breach of EC environmental laws' (2000) 306 ENDS Report 47.

[33] EC Commission Communications of 1996 and 1997: [1996] OJ C242/6 and [1997] OJ C63/2.

[34] See L. Kramer, *EC Environmental Law*, 4th edn. (London, 2000) 291-2.

My third example again concerns transport. A key concern of the Royal Commission's 18th Report on Transport was the continuing contribution of carbon dioxide emissions from road transport. Carbon dioxide (CO_2) is the main greenhouse gas affected by human activity, and UK emissions from transport have been rising over the past quarter century. Twenty-five per cent of UK CO_2 emissions are attributable to transport, with the vast proportion coming from road transport.[35] With CO_2 emissions likely to reduce from other major sources such as heavy industry, transport's contribution is likely to rise in future years. In contrast to many other forms of pollutant emissions, it is not practicable to remove carbon dioxide from individual motor vehicles, and since the amount of carbon dioxide is broadly proportional to the amount of fuel used, a reduction of total fuel consumption is an obvious route towards achieving policy goals. Yet it was clear in 1994 that very large improvements in fuel efficiency could be achieved using known technology, and evidence from government indicated that it was technically possible to improve the weighted average fuel efficiency of new cars by 40 per cent over the next ten to fifteen years.[36] It was equally clear, however, that there was a trend for cars to become heavier and more powerful, more than compensating for any trends in improved efficiency. The average fuel consumption of new cars registered in the United Kingdom fell by about 20 per cent between 1978 and 1987.[37]

Faced with such a challenge, what is the most appropriate policy response? As the Commission noted, without policy intervention, improved design of the scale required would not come by itself:

> It is unlikely to be applied in practice unless government provides appropriate signals to influence decisions by manufacturers and the behaviour of the general public as purchasers and drivers.[38]

Regulatory instrument in the form of mandatory efficiency standards represents one form of policy mechanism. Corporate Average Fleet Economy Standards have been mandatory in the United States since 1976, and though starting from a higher point than European averages produced a 25 per cent reduction in fuel consumption between 1970 and 1990.[39]

---

[35] Royal Commission on Environmental Pollution, 'Transport and the Environment', 18th Report, Cm. 3752 (London, 1997) para. 2.34.

[36] Royal Commission on Environmental Pollution, 'Transport and the Environment', para. 8.39.

[37] Ibid., para. 8.36.

[38] Ibid., para. 8.59.

[39] Ibid., para. 8.50.

The Commission, however, was eventually persuaded that the use of economic instruments, in the form of an annual fuel escalator, might achieve the same effect, sending a sustained signal to car manufacturers to introduce greatly increased efficiencies. Such an escalator was introduced by the government, but when the Commission revisited the subject of transport in 1997[40] and again in its 2000 report on Energy[41] it was apparent that while there had been some reductions of CO_2 emissions from the average new car, there had been no reduction in overall fuel consumption. Improvements in engine efficiency had been more than offset by increased sales of larger vehicles (including four-wheel-drive vehicles) and increases in vehicle weights. At the same time the intended price signals of the fuel escalator tax had been weakened by fluctuations in the price of crude oil, with prices at the pump failing to match increases in the tax. The sudden escalation in crude oil prices revealed the political vulnerability of the escalator, and the Chancellor of the Exchequer announced its abandonment in November 1999 stating that any future fuel duty increases would be determined on a budget-by-budget basis. A striking feature of the initial political response to fuel demonstrations was the failure to justify the fuel escalator as a policy instrument for improving efficiency. Instead it was presented as an important source of government income for sectors such as education or health which would otherwise have to be raised from other forms of taxation.

In a 1996 study on European political responses to climate change[42] Professor Tim O' Riordan, described the then emerging fuel price escalator as 'a real piece of policy innovation'. Yet he was also sufficiently perspicacious to note that:

> The test will come in the political determination to continue the increase, year in and year out, and the manner in which the additional revenue is spent.[43]

The demise of the fuel escalator demonstrates the potential vulnerability of relying solely on an economic instrument as a means of securing policy goals, whatever the underlying theory. Its intended effect lacked precision, its impact was subject to many external economic forces outside the control of government, and its original purpose could be easily forgotten and overtaken by the attractions of its value to

---

[40] Royal Commission on Environmental Pollution, *Transport and the Environment: Developments since 1994*, Cm. 3752 (London, 1997) para. 2.35.
[41] Royal Commission on Environmental Pollution, *Energy:. The Changing Climate*, Cm. 4749 (London, 2000) para. 6.110.
[42] T. O'Riordan and J. Jager (eds,), *Politics of Climate Change* (London, 1996).
[43] Ibid., 249.

government as a revenue stream. In comparison to the sorry saga of the fuel escalator, one may conclude that direct regulation in the form of mandatory efficiency standards with sufficient advance notice to manufacturers would have had a greater effect on achieving key policy goals.[44]

Indeed, in its Energy Report last year the Royal Commission came very close to endorsing the need for such standards.[45] That they did not do so was because in the meantime another form of policy instrument had been employed. In 1998 the European Commission and the European Automobile Manufacturers Association reached an agreement under which the average fuel consumption of new cars within the European Union would reduce by 25 per cent between 1995 and 2008.[46] The agreement was presented as a political breakthrough, but as with economic instruments, while voluntary agreements offer considerable attractions to government, their use raises a number of significant concerns.

Voluntary Agreements

The automobile agreement was by no means unique, and the past decade has seen the increasing use in both Europe and the United States of voluntary agreements between governments and industry as a means of handling environmental challenges, and as an alternative to direct regulation. According to a study in 1997 by the European Environment Agency, by 1996 more than 300 environmental agreements had been concluded at the national level within the European Union, with the Netherlands leading the way.[47] The underpinning of such approaches in the United States can again be traced to trenchant criticisms by lawyers such as Richard Stewart of the perceived failures and shortcomings of traditional regulatory approaches.[48] Continental lawyers have developed

---

[44] Efficiency standards, of course, deal with only one aspect of the transport issue, and increased efficiencies in individual vehicle performance may be offset by overall increased usage. Government projections published in 2000 suggest that overall road traffic volumes will increase by 16-29% between 1996 and 2010, but on the assumption that voluntary agreements between the European Commission and vehicle manufacturers are complied with projected decreases in overall CO_2 emissions of between 1% and 10% in the same period: Department of the Environment, Transport, and the Regions, *Tackling Congestion and Pollution: The government's first report under the Road Traffic (National Targets) Act 1998* (London, 2000).

[45] Royal Commission on Environmental Pollution, n. 40 above, para. 6.123.

[46] Similar agreements between the Commission and Japanese and Korean car manufacturers were reached at the same time.

[47] European Environment Agency, 'Environment Agreements, Environmental Issues' Series No. 3 (Copenhagen, 1997).

[48] See, for example, B. Ackerman and R. Stewart, 'Reforming Environmental Law' (1985) 37 *Stanford Law Review* 1333.

a deeper underlying theory of reflexive Jaw according to which the perceived inadequacies of goal-orientated and instrumental public law is replaced by an emphasis on using law to encourage actors to assess critically -and to determine their own environmental performance.[49]

Voluntary agreements clearly represent one form of such reflexive law. They come in many forms, including agreements made between private parties, such as industries and non-governmental organisations. My concern, though, is with agreements with government and sectors of industry or of a particular industry, since these more starkly reflect a conscious decision by government to develop an alternative to direct regulation. Even within this class we can distinguish several different forms of voluntary agreement currently being employed. Some forms of voluntary agreement are heavily encased within a public law framework: in this country agreements with landowners under the Wildlife and Countryside Act 1981 are a strong example. Other agreements may be made after a clear threat by government to use existing powers of enforcement or to introduce legislation if agreements are not forthcoming. Some appear to have no enforcement mechanism attached to them.

In the same year as the publication of the report by the European Environment Agency, the distinguished German environmental lawyer, Ekhard Rehbinder, described environmental agreements as a 'new instrument of environmental policy'.[50] It is true that in continental Europe various forms of environmental agreements were first employed in France and Germany in the early 1970s,[51] but for British environmental lawyers the idea of agreements being novel is somewhat surprising. While the post-War development of British environmental law lacked the more sophisticated theoretical underpinning of continental law,, voluntary agreements were a clear feature of government environmental, policy until the 1980s – so much so that in 1983 the then Chief Scientist of the Department of the Environment could describe as one of the key features of British environmental policy before joining the European Community the 'acceptance, where possible, of a voluntary approach

[49] See in particular G. Teubner, 'Substantive and Reflexive Elements in Modern Law' (1983) 17 *Law and Society Review* 239, and in the context of environmental law; G. Teubner, L. Farmer, and D. Murphy (eds.), *Environmental Law and Ecological Responsibility: The Concept and Practice of Ecological Self-Organization* (Chichester, 1994).
[50] E. Rehbinder, 'Environmental Agreements: A New Instrument of Environmental Policy', Jean Monet Chair Paper RSC 97/45 (Florence, 1997).
[51] E. Orts and K. Deketelaere (eds.), *Environmental Contracts* (London, 2001) 22. The volume as a whole provides some excellent studies of contemporary practice in the United States and Europe.

where Government relies on a polluting industry to impose its own measures'.[52]

Some reflection on that experience suggests that concern about the current use of environmental agreements is justified. A key example relates to pesticide control, where from 1954 until 1983 the regulation of the marketing and use of pesticides in the United Kingdom was largely achieved under a voluntary arrangement between government, manufacturers, and distributors: the Pesticide Safety Precaution Scheme.[53] Essentially the parties agreed to ensure that new pesticides were subject to risk assessments initiated under the scheme and to withdraw from the market pesticides that had raised environmental or health concerns. In many ways the scheme illustrated the attractions of voluntary arrangements: it was reasonably efficient, could act speedily where needed, and industry was fully engaged in the process. But it also underlined real structural weaknesses which eventually led to its replacement by a statutory scheme under the Food and Environment Act 1985. Participation in the scheme was limited to government and industry, and wider public interests, especially those of agricultural workers and environmental bodies, were excluded from the process. There was a lack of transparency in the information and assumptions being used to justify decisions, and the role of the independent scientists and government officials involved was unclear. Finally, and most crucially, the scheme depended on the complete involvement of all manufacturers and wholesalers; voluntary agreements cannot tolerate nor are they compatible with free riders. Britain's accession to the European Community in 1973 meant that this voluntary-scheme was unlikely to be compatible with the right of free movement of goods by foreign pesticide manufacturers and distributors:[54] hence its transformation in 1985 into a statutory regulatory scheme.

The Pesticide Safety Precaution Scheme was perhaps the most comprehensive and long-lasting example of a voluntary arrangement between government and industry in British environmental policy. Yet the development of post-War British environmental law exhibited a similar tendency towards a consensual system and a largely closed system of regulation. Even where a legal framework existed, such as that under the old Alkali Act 1863 dealing with atmospheric emissions from certain industrial processes, it tended to be expressed in broad terms,

---

[52] M. Holdgate, 'Environmental policies in Britain and Mainland Europe', in R. Macrory (ed.), *Britain, Europe and the Environment* (London, 1983).

[53] For a history of the scheme see R. Macrory and D. Gilbert, *Pesticide Related Law* (Farnham, 1989).

[54] The issue was never tested in the courts, though there were threats of legal challenges.

leaving the details of licensing standards to be negotiated between those responsible for regulation and those whom they regulated. The heart of the protection system for Sites of Special Scientific Interest under the Wildlife and Countryside Act 1982 was based on the negotiation $ of agreements between landowners and bodies responsible for nature protection, a system later memorably summarised by Lord Mustill in the first decision of the House of Lords on the legislation:

> It needs only a moment to see that the regime is toothless for it demands no more from the owner or occupier of a Site of Special Scientific Interest than a little patience.[55]

The courts were rarely involved-in interpreting legislation To take one example, the key legal criterion for industrial air pollution – employing the 'best practicable means' to prevent or minimise emissions – which existed for almost one hundred and fifty years until the introduction of the new system of integrated pollution control under Part I of the Environmental Protection Act 1990 – never once received authoritative interpretation from the courts, despite each word in that phrase being rich in ambiguity. Outside the Town and Country Planning legislation, opportunities for public consultation and public access to information were minimal or non-existent.

The development during the 1970s and 1980s of what I have described as the 'new formalism' in British environmental law[56] led to a transformation of legal structures in the United Kingdom: more comprehensive rights of public consultation, public registers of information, greater use of explicit environmental standards, and the applications of procedural safeguards developed in public law. The causes are diverse and include: sustained criticisms by bodies such as the Royal Commission on Environmental Pollution and by individuals such as Nigel Haigh of the Institute of European Environmental Policy, the privatisation of key public utilities such as the water and electricity industries, and the need to transpose European Community obligations into national legislation consistent with doctrines developed by the European Court of Justice.[57]

---

[55] *Southern Water Authority v Nature Conservancy Council* [1993] 5 *Journal of Environmental Law* 109.

[56] R. Macrory, 'Environmental Law: Shifting discretions and the new formalism', in O. Lomas (ed.), *Frontiers of Environmental Law* (London, 1991).

[57] As Derrick Wyatt QC noted, before the development of the ECJ's doctrines on formal transposition the early phase of the. UK's implementation of Directives 'was characterised by a tendency towards regarding EEC Directives as helpful if eccentric recommendations to be gently eased into the United Kingdom scheme of things, ideally by government circular rather than legislation and ideally without cost': D. Wyatt, .'Litigating Community-Environmental Law' (1998) 10 *Journal of Environmental Law* 1-9.

There is a certain degree of irony in the fact that the United Kingdom has transformed its legal structure of environmental law in this way at a time when other countries in Europe are discovering and promoting voluntary arrangements as an instrument of environmental policy. Yet many of the concerns which led to changes in the nature of British environmental law still dog the development of contemporary voluntary agreements. There is no guarantee that wider public interests will be engaged in the process, nor any legally guaranteed rights in that respect. It is true that some countries, such as the Netherlands and Belgium, have developed more systematic procedures of consultation leading to agreements which are binding under private contractual law.[58] Dutch practice, and in particular the intervention of the Dutch Supreme Court, has attempted to elaborate in far more detail than has happened to date in this country the relationship between public law and the appropriate use of environmental agreements.[59] But this structured approach begins to resemble regulation, albeit a system where standards and goals are subject to intense negotiation prior to their legal enactment. And it is an approach which is still the exception. Danish legislation in 1991 established the possibility of voluntary agreements encased in law, but industry and government. appear still to prefer non-legal agreements.[60] This is hardly surprising since the more that voluntary agreements are encased in legal frameworks, the more they lose the very qualities of flexibility and consensuality which were their initial attraction. In contrast to the details of regulatory requirements or individual licences or consents, there is no guarantee that the terms of voluntary agreements will be publicly available, nor is there systematic monitoring of their success. The 1997 study by the European Environment Agency reported that in most of the sample agreements studied it was impossible to make a quantitative assessment of their effectiveness due to the lack of reliable monitoring data and consistent reporting.[61] In 1996 the UK government concluded agreements with five industrial sectors concerning the reduction of certain products containing greenhouse

---

[58] But as Seerden notes, in relation to collective environmental agreements in the Netherlands between industry sectors and government there appears to be no example of court actions concerning their enforcement: 'This paucity of litigation may be due in part to the fact that many agreements, though formally written as private law contracts, function also as an expression of internalised behaviour': R. Seerden, 'Legal Aspects of Environmental Agreements in the Netherlands', in E. Orts and K. Deketelaere, *Environmental Contracts* 193 (London, 2001).

[59] See the discussion of the 1990 *Windmill* decision of the Dutch Supreme Civil Court and subsequent case law in R. Seerden, n. 58 above, 180.

[60] G. Calster and K. Deketelaere, 'The Use of Voluntary Agreements in the European Community's Environmental Policy', in E. Orts and K.Deketelaere (eds.), n. 51 above, 239, where the authors report that only one such agreement under the legislation has been made to date.

[61] European Environment Agency, n. 47 above, 9.

gases, but according to ENDS Report in 1998 nothing was known about their success or otherwise.[62]

It is nevertheless clear that the use of voluntary agreements still holds attractions for policy-makers both in this country[63] and at European level.[64] At their extreme, the use of voluntary agreements represents a new form of corporatism under which governments bargain with key interest groups, avoiding the use of formal legal powers. Yet it is equally clear that their use may threaten important qualities inherent in contemporary regulatory approaches: transparency, enforceability, monitoring, and public involvement in the form of both participation and accountability.[65] A similar structural criticism can be made of the use of economic instruments.[66] The dilemma is that it is the very avoidance of these legal and procedural complexities which may be seen as a benefit to the parties involved and to the efficiency of the instrument. The more they are incorporated into the negotiation and implementation of agreements, the less the apparent advantages of agreements over regulation. Indeed, in a recent review by Professor Gaines of Houston University and Cliona Kimber,[67] the authors, who treat voluntary agreements as one example of reflexive law, go so far as to conclude that policy makers have over the last decade or so misdirected their efforts on self-regulation in areas of industrial pollution control as a substitute for regulatory machinery. In their view, voluntary approaches are certainly not without validity, but would be better directed towards areas where there has traditionally been a lack of regulatory machinery

---

[62] ENDS Report 281 (1998) 39

[63] Department of Environment, Transport, and the Regions, 'Sustainable Business', Consultation Paper (London, 1998). See also UK government, 'A Better Quality of Life: A Strategy for Sustainable Development for the United Kingdom', Cm. 4345 (London, 1999), though the endorsement seems rather more muted at para. 5.11: 'The Government will continue to consider the scope for voluntary agreements with industry'. In the context of climate change, by April 2001 more than 40 negotiated agreements had been concluded between government and industry: see ENDS Report, 'Looking to the future with negotiated agreements', 315 (2001) 6.

[64] European Commission, *Communication on Voluntary Agreements*, COM (96) 561 final (Brussels, 1996). For further discussion of the development of Commission policy in this area see J. Verschuuren, 'EC Environmental Law and Self-Regulation in the Member States: In search of a Legislative Framework', in H. Somsen (ed.), *Yearbook of European Law* (Oxford, 2000) 103,.

[65] For a recent review of UK experience see Green Alliance, *Signed, Sealed and Delivered? The Role of Negotiated Agreements in the UK* (London, 2001).

[66] In the context of New Zealand, see B, Richardson, 'Economic Instruments and Sustainable Management in New Zealand' (1998) 10 *Journal of Environmental Law* 21. The author concludes at 38 'Economic instruments cannot be applied without regulatory frameworks, and the choice of mechanisms and situations in which they are applied must be governed by public consultation processes to ensure that equity and ethical issues are not inappropriately excluded from management decisions'.

[67] S. Gaines and C. Kimber, 'Redirecting Self-Regulation' (2001) 13 *journal of Environmental Law* 167.

and where reorientation of environmental behaviour is desirable even
though precise goals are difficult to determine: the activities of private
households and public service organisations are given as examples.
The argument has attractions; if nothing else, it forces a re-evaluation,
from an environmental perspective, of potentially important uses of
agreements which do not threaten or devalue the positive aspects of
existing regulatory structures.

Scientific Risks

The political attractions of alternative mechanisms to direct regulation
cannot however, simply be attributed to advocates of a free or less
regulated market. In the environmental field one of the prime unsettling
influences for governments in recent years has been a reassessment of
the contribution by science to government policy underlying regulatory
systems. Where difficult decisions of judgment are involved, one
approach for government is to divest responsibility to other bodies.
Contemporary areas of environmental law such as private and public
nuisance, of course, do just that, leaving individual judges to determine
the environmental standards to be applied in particular instances,
against a background of general principles. Despite the recent decision
of the House of Lords in the *Alconbury*[68] case, calls will continue for the
setting up of an independent planning or environmental tribunal to
act as the final decision maker on individual decisions, and no doubt,
whatever the stated public position, there will be some in government
who would welcome decisions on, say, the more intractable and
sensitive planning cases being handled by a body other than themselves.
An alternative approach, which is in line with the theories of reflexive
law, is to focus the attention of environmental legislation on procedural
requirements rather than outcomes, leaving the goals of the regulation
to be determined through a guided process of decision making.[69]

We are likely to continue to see initiatives along those lines but, for very
good reasons, the tendency in the last thirty years has been to elaborate
detailed environmental standards or goals in the body of legislation

[68] R. *v Secretary of State for the Environment, Transport, and the. Regions ex parte Hilding &
Barnes, ex parte Alconbury, ex parte Legal and General Assurance* (conjoined appeals) House
of Lords May 2001 [2001] UKHL 23. If the House of Lords had agreed with the High
Court that the Secretary of State could not be both a policy maker and a decision maker
in planning cases in order to comply with the Human Rights Act, the argument for a new
independent body, or at least for complete delegation of all planning decisions to the
planning inspectorate, would have been overwhelming.
[69] Reflecting Mashaw's 'accommodatory' rather than 'determinate' model of decision
making. See J. Mashaw, 'An overview: Two models of regulatory decision', in J. Nyhart
and M. Carrow (eds.), *Law and Science in Collaboration: Resolving Regulatory Issues of Science
and Technology* (Lexington, 1983).

itself. Courts tend to be uncomfortable with handling preventative issues; industry requires a degree of certainty in advance for forward investment; there is greater public demand for legal certainty in the environmental standards they can expect to enjoy; in a European Community context, the goal of a free and competitive market provides a key driver for explicit standards in the field of products, and more controversially for processes. At the same time as these developments were being made one of the key underlying principles consistently advocated by governments was that environmental policy must be based on 'sound science'.[70] To the extent that science was perceived by policy makers and the public to provide certainty and undeniable objective truth, legal standards based on science could be said to derive an authority over and above that of the law itself. We are now of course aware that this is a very simplistic and misleading picture, particularly in the field of the environment. As concerns move from acute problems of human health to more chronic and less direct effects, from individual to synergistic effects, and increasingly to impacts on the natural environment, the uncertainties of contemporary scientific knowledge have become increasingly apparent. Even within different scientific disciplines relevant to environmental issues there may be distinct biases and assumptions which can be obscured in more simplistic scientific evaluations.[71]

For the policy maker, and indeed the lawyer, not trained in science, the growing appreciation of certain inherent uncertainties in science is uncomfortable. Yet as the Royal Commission tried to demonstrate in its study of Environmental Standards,[72] science is not a matter of certainties but of hypothesis and experimentation. 'Sound' science possesses qualities of transparency, scepticism, and peer review.[73] It can and should lead to greater understanding, but not necessarily to the certainty for

---

[70] See, for example, the 1990 White Paper on environmental policy: 'United Kingdom, This Common Inheritance: Britain's Environmental Strategy', Cm. 1200 (London, 1990) HMSO, where it is stated 'We must base our policies on fact not fantasy and use the best evidence and analysis available'; 'United Kingdom, This Common Inheritance: UK Annual Report', Cm. 3188 (London, 1996): 'It is) however fundamental to achievement of sustainable development that decisions should proceed from the basis of sound science, with an assessment of the likely costs and benefits (environmental and economic alike)' (para. 176).

[71] D. Fisk, 'Environmental Science and Environmental Law' (1998) 10 *Journal of Environmental Law* 3.

[72] Royal Commission on Environmental Pollution, 'Setting Environmental Standards', 21st Report, Cm. 4053 (London, 1998). See also R. Macrory, 'Environmental Standards: New Procedures for New Paradigms' (1999) 56 *Science in Parliament* 6.

[73] See A. Stirling, *On Science and Precaution in the Management of Technological Risk* vol. 1, European Commission Institute for Prospective Technological Studies, EUR 19056 EN Spain (Seville, 1998). In addition to the qualities of sound science listed above, the author includes systematic methodologies, independence, accountability, and learning in the

Continued

which a policy-maker may wish. What is equally clear is that a decision concerning a particular environmental standard is a political choice: in stark terms the role of scientific assessment is to describe a dose-effect curve but not to determine a legally defined standard of acceptability. This will be informed by other considerations including-economic and technological appraisal and ultimately value judgments, and it follows that scientific committees should ideally present to a decision-maker options rather than solutions.[74]

In the field of environmental policy-making there have been two important institutional and policy responses to this growing understanding of the nature and extent of scientific uncertainty. First, and still far more apparent at international level, the development of the type of elaborate exercise in scientific assessment epitomised by the Intergovernmental Panel on Climate Change.[75] The extent to which such .an exercise can be replicated with the same degree of legitimacy and general public confidence in other fields of environmental controversy, such as genetically manipulated organisms, remains to be seen.[76] The second key development has been the emergence of the precautionary principle as an underlying norm in decision-making, explicitly recognised in the 1992 Rio Declaration on Environment and Development,[77] increasingly

---

...sense that understanding is open to continuous change and challenge. See also. Office of Science and Technology, *The Use of Scientific Advice in Policy Making* (London, 1997) where the then Chief Scientific Advisor to the Government, Sir Robert (now Lord) May notes at para. 11 'Scientific advice will often involve an aggregation of a range of scientific opinion and judgment as distinct from statements of assured certainty'. The advice of government departments was updated in 2000: Office of Science and Technology, *Guidelines 2000: Scientific Advice and Policy Making* (London, 2000).

[74] In this respect I probably go somewhat further than the conclusions of the Phillips report on BSE which appears to concede that it may be appropriate for *I* government to ask scientific advisory committees, to advise on a policy option, though it is noted at 14.1290 that 'Where a policy decision involves the balancing of considerations which fall outside the expertise of the committee, it will normally not be appropriate to ask the committee to advise which policy option-to follow': *Report of the Inquiry into the emergence and identification of Bovine Spongiform Encephalopathy (BSE) and variant Creutzfeldt-Jakob' Disease (vCJD) and the action taken in response to it up to.20 March 1996* (London, 2000). My view is that, at least where a decision on environmental standards is involved, there will be considerations which will *always* be outside a scientific committee's expertise.

[75] The Intergovernmental Panel on Climate Change (IPCC) was established by the World Meteorological Organization and the United Nations Environment Programme in 1988. The role of the IPCC is to assess the scientific, technical, and socio-economic information relating to the understanding of the risk of human-induced climate change, and the Panel has produced three assessments to date.

[76] See ENDS Report, 'Government proposal for global GM panel runs into fire' 305 (2000) 6, where some leading UK environmental observers are strongly critical of any analogy between the IPCC model and the government's proposal for a similar exercise in the field of GMOs.

[77] Principle 15 of the Rio Declaration: 'Where there are threats of serious irreversible damage, lack of full scientific certainty shall not he used as a reason for postponing cost-effective measures to prevent environmental degradation'.

articulated in international environmental treaties, and a principle of European Community environmental policy.[78] Far from being a political or anti-scientific approach, the Royal Commission on Environmental Pollution endorsed it as a perfectly rational principle which was consistent with the inherent qualities of science.[79] It is, though, hardly surprising that operationalising the principle is far less straightforward and more open to contention than simply stating it.

Yet for the development of environmental law these important shifts in process and understanding raise significant challenges for legal process. The procedures of scientific assessment and open peer review developed by the Inter-governmental Panel on Climate Change have yet to be adopted at national or regional level. This is particularly so in the case of European Community legislation where many decisions on environmental standards are effectively made by management and regulatory committees under rules of comitology,[80] processes which are frequently obscure and little understood by the wider public and where the line between scientific and political decision making is often opaque. The precautionary principle raises issues concerning the development of appropriate standards of legal review. If one of the main functions of public law is to restrain inappropriate or irrational behaviour by government, how should principles be applied in a situation where the application of the precautionary principle implies a lack of substantive scientific evidence supporting a decision?[81] As the House of Lords acknowledged in the recent *Alconbury* decision, basing a decision on no evidence or on a wrong factual basis, can now be considered a ground for judicial review in British law.[82] At the level of international trade disputes we have already noted the unease of the GATT panel in handling issues of scientific uncertainty in trade and environment

[78] Art. 174.2, Treaty Establishing the European Community.

[79] See Royal Commission on Environmental Pollution, n. 72 above, paras. 4.41-4.48. The European Commission's *Communication on the Precautionary Principle* 2 February 2000 (Com. (2000)1) echoes much of the analysis of the Royal Commission on Environmental Pollution. According to the accompanying explanatory text (IP/00/96), 'The Communication makes it clear that the precautionary principle is neither a politicisation of science nor the acceptance of zero-risk but that it provides a basis for action when science is unable to give a clear answer'.

[80] See J. Falke and G. Winter, 'Management and regulatory committees in executive rule making', in G. Winter (ed.), *Sources and Categories of European Union Law* (Baden-Baden, 1996) ch. C.ll. The authors note at 542 that in 1996 the Council of Ministers adopted 468 legislative acts, while in the same period the Commission, acting under delegated powers, adopted 7034 acts. The number of Committees listed in the Community budget increased four times between 1975 and 1995.

[81] As. David Fisk notes, n. 71 above, 'it is a fallacy to assume, that the absence of evidence to support a proposition can be taken as equivalent to [the presence] of evidence that refutes it'.

[82] *Per* Lord Slynn in *Alconbury*, n. 68 above, para. 55. See also *Smith, Woolf, and Jowell's, Judicial Review of Administrative Action* (London, 1995) 288.

disputes, and where the invocation of the precautionary principle by a national government can clearly more readily disguise less legitimate motivations for restricting trade. Recent decisions of the Appellate Body, though, are beginning to display greater sensitivity to the problem of scientific uncertainty.[83]

Yet until we have developed more consistent and transparent procedures for the appropriate application of the precautionary approach by government to any given situation,[84] there is the danger that the function of judicial review as a restraint on irrational behaviour by government is inhibited. From that perspective, the precautionary principle may be beneficial to the environment but is not necessarily so to the rule of law. Above all, the appreciation that in many environmental areas the old model of scientific certainty will no longer provide the policy maker with an underlying legitimacy for his decisions raises issues concerning the authority of law itself: As Raz has argued,[85] this in part rests on the authority of the institutions responsible for developing and making law. In contemporary environmental politics, governments, faced with difficult and complex policy decisions, can now less easily hide behind a cloak of science, and will constantly need to develop new approaches and procedures to reestablish their legitimacy.

Handling Enforcement Risks

If direct regulation is to maintain its key role in many areas of environmental protection, inadequate enforcement will clearly undermine its effectiveness as an instrument for motivating behaviour. Inconsistent enforcement will give rise to cynicism and distrust. Indeed, one of the attractions of both economic instrument and voluntary agreements is that they are perceived to be largely self-enforcing, while enforcement by regulatory bodies can be portrayed as expensive, never adequately funded, arbitrary, and never complete. At the European

---

[83] See the decision of the Appellate Body in the *Beef Hormones* case, EC *Measures against Meat and Meat Products* AB-1997-4 16 January 1998. At para. 194 the Appellate Body note that 'In most cases, responsible and representative governments may act in good faith on the basis of what, at a given time, may be divergent opinion coming from qualified and respected sources'.

[84] For a recent review of the development and application of the principle see O. MacIntyre and T. Mosedale, 'The Precautionary Principle as a Norm of Customary International Law', (1997) 9 *Journal of Environmental Law* 221. The authors discuss emerging practices including precautionary assessment, though not in the context of my own concern here which is the alignment of the principle with those concerning the rule of law and appropriate judicial restraint against its. misuse.

[85] See J. Raz, *Authority of Law* (Oxford, 1993) where he argues that one of the origins of the autonomous authority of law is the authority of the institution with the power to make laws. My argument here is that in the context of environmental law institutional authority based on old models of scientific certainly has been substantially weakened.

level, recognition has been growing of the significance of implementation and enforcement, and in 1996 the European Commission promoted the concept of the 'chain of regulation' which correctly acknowledges that effective implementation of legislation depends as much on the quality of legislative drafting, appropriate training, adequate funding, and feed-back mechanisms as on the actual enforcement of legal rules.[86] The analysis is sound, and is applicable at the national as well as the European level, though we remain some way from the ideal picture presented.

At national level we have progressed considerably from the period in the 1970s when environmental regulators possessed a wholly unfettered and largely untransparent discretion towards enforcement. It was only the efforts of legal scholars such as Keith Hawkins and Genevra Richardson,[87] whose research, particularly in the water industry, revealed to the wider public some of the motivations behind the decisions as to whether or not to prosecute for non-compliance. As with any bureaucracy, motivations for non-prosecution were not always driven by sound environmental policy reasons. But in 1998 the Environment Agency made its first public statement on enforcement and prosecution policy, though recent internal audits reveal considerable regional variations in its interpretation and application.[88] Nevertheless, despite the self-imposed difficulties of ensuring consistent enforcement practices, the publication of such a statement is an important advance in providing greater accountability and improved signals to those who are required to comply with regulation.

But much remains to be improved. Legislators could take a more systematic interest in the successes and failures of implementation. Risk management techniques, properly applied, can play an important role in using limited regulatory resources to target inspection and enforcement.[89] Regulation could be more outcome-orientated, and where this involves the adoption of ambient environmental

[86] European Commission, *Implementing Community Environmental Law*, 22 October 1996 COM(96) 500 (Brussels, 1996). A similar expression of the 'chain of regulation' is the concept of 'compliance-orientated regulation' as defined in a recent OECD study of regulatory compliance generally: 'An outcome-orientated approach to promulgating and revising regulation where regulatory drafting, implementation, monitoring and enforcement are all designed to maximise the potential for compliance with substantive regulatory goals'. C. Parker, *The State of Regulatory Compliance: Issues, Trends and Challenges*, Report prepared for the Public Management Service of OECD, para. 7 (Paris, 1999).

[87] G. Richardson, A. Ogus, and A. Burrows, *Policing Pollution – A Study of Regulation and Enforcement* (Oxford, 1982);. K. Hawkins, *Environment and Enforcement: Regulation and the Social Definition of Pollution* (Oxford, 1984).

[88] ENDS Report, 'Agency flounders on prosecution policy', 315 (1991) 3.

[89] In 1997 the Environment Agency introduced an Operator and .Pollution Risk

Continued

standards, regulators need to be more transparent in the assessment of methodologies used to calculate and assign load responsibilities of individual contributors.[90] Modern technology can be harnessed to provide extensive warnings of regulatory noncompliance. Continuous monitoring equipment providing an automatic alert of non-compliance is already extensively used in the field of water pollution control[91] and can be extended in the future. In the field of land use, satellite imaging is already used by government departments to monitor compliance by farmers with set-aside requirements, and has been used in the fields of marine oil pollution and fisheries control. The use of such techniques is not appropriate for all forms of environmental regulation, and they raise significant legal questions, notably about their consistency with principles of privacy.[92] Yet their contribution towards establishing a more secure and consistent compliance regime has scarcely yet been tapped, especially given the rapidly developing higher resolutions of the most recent satellites.[93] A major recent European research project[94] has suggested that such imaging could be employed in the enforcement of a broad range of environmental legislation, including damage to habitats, breaches of planning law, and illegal waste disposal.

In a democratic society it is important that the information concerning the results of regulation are made as accessible as possible, and that imaginative uses of modern information technology are employed to the fullest extent to achieve these goals. To take one example, we are still a long way from making publicly available in a systematic way the results of prosecutions for breaches of environmental law. The position has improved from a decade or so ago when information in areas such as waste was scattered among local authorities, and Home Office statistics

...Appraisal (OPRA) in relation to industrial processes falling under the Integrated Pollution Control regime: ENDS Report (1997) 271, 32. A similar scheme is being discussed in relation to waste management sites: Department of the Environment, Transport, and the Regions, 'Waste Management Licensing Risk Assessment Inspection Frequencies' (London, 1999).

[90] T. Smith Jr and R. Macrory, 'Legal and Political Considerations', in P. Douben (ed.), *Pollution Risk Assessment and Management*(Chichester, 1998) 402.

[91] A. Mumma, 'Use of Compliance Monitoring Data in Water Pollution Prosecutions' (1993) 5 *Journal of Environmental Law* 191.

[92] R. Purdy, 'Legal and Privacy Issues of Spy in the Sky Satellites' (1999) 3 *Mountbatten Journal of Legal Studies* 33. It is likely, though, that their most useful value will be as a warning to regulators of potential non-compliance rather than as direct evidence in court proceedings.

[93] To date the most widely used satellites have been SPOT and LANDSAT, with resolutions of 20m and 30m respectively, and repeating coverage of most areas of the world every two to three weeks. More recent satellites such as IKONOS II have far greater resolution and can be programmed to obtain images at predetermined locations. More high-resolution satellites were launched in 2002, some with resolutions of as little as 0.5m.

[94] APERTURE Project (1998-2000) (Environmental Typological Space Mapping Facilitating the Implementation of European Legislation) http://www.iis. gr/aperture/.

were insufficiently detailed.[95] Bodies such as the Environment Agency have produced reports summarising the results of key prosecutions, though not without controversy,[96] and any such exercise inevitably involves difficult judgements concerning the appropriate benchmarking criteria to be adopted by the regulator. But it is technically feasible to develop a far more open system where the results of all environmental cases heard before the courts are systematically collated, and retrievable from a database by free-form searches. Such a system would allow any individual to obtain information on regulatory enforcement concerning, say, an individual company, a region, or a particular substance.[97] It would not obviate the need for interpretation by official bodies, but would 'democratize' core data to wider and potentially richer critiques

'Direct and Determine': a New Regulatory Paradigm?

These technological possibilities are to some extent operational issues, though of immense importance to the future design and application of environmental regulation. They hint at future possibilities of remedying some of the key deficiencies in regulatory implementation. But there remain what at times seem utterly irreconcilable views of the role of direct regulation. Traditional forms of regulation can be presented as stifling of innovation, over-bureaucratic, and incapable of handling more than the most direct impacts of human intervention on the environment. The environmental challenges facing society are immense, varied, and often unpredictable, and it is hardly surprising that the last, decade has seen experimentation with a whole range of new forms of policy instruments in place of the more conventional approaches founded on old paradigms. Yet it remains equally important to ensure that the qualities of transparency, accountability, and enforceability inherent in the more formal legal structures are not lost in the process. Similarly, however pressing the environmental concerns, it would be a backward step if new instruments allowed governments to side-step the discipline both on themselves and on agencies of government of contemporary principles of the rule of law.

[95] For an early attempt to review information in one field of environmental law see R. Macrory and S. Withers, *Application of Administrative and Criminal Punishments with regard to Hazardous Wastes in England,* Report to the European Commission (London, 1985). The report was a contribution to a comparative European study for the European Commission. With the exception of Italy, the other countries within the study, including France and Germany, revealed equal difficulties in obtaining comprehensive data.

[96] House of Commons Select Committee on Environment, Transport, and Regional Affairs, *The Environment Agency* HC 289 (London, 1999).

[97] To my knowledge, the only country in Europe which has attempted to develop such a comprehensive database is Italy at the Center Ellettronico, Corte Suprema di Cassazione. See A. Postiglione, *La Giurisprudenza Ambientale Europea a la Hanca Dati Enlex Della* (Milan, 1987).

Lawyers need to be innovative and forward-looking, but perhaps the time has also come to be less defensive about the positive qualities of environmental regulation. Continuous critical evaluation of the existing effectiveness of regulation remains vital, but we are equally entitled to impose the same level of scrutiny on the true environmental effects of non-regulatory initiatives. It may well be that the term 'command and control' is now burdened with so much critical baggage that new terminology should be developed to provide the space for a more detached appreciation and relocation of the appropriate role and development of future environmental regulation. My own preference would be 'determine and direct'. 'Direction' (rather than 'control'), reflects the need to ensure that as far as possible regulation is designed which is outcome-focused and which harnesses the inventive power of industry and the market to determine solutions but within clearly defined boundaries endorsed by legal sanction. 'Determination' implies that it remains the ultimate responsibility of government, rather than of science or economic theory, to decide the goals of environmental policy. In the contemporary political climate, it may well be that governments or agencies can no longer simply 'command' but need to develop new procedures and more sensitive processes for securing legitimacy and understanding of the policy choices that are made, but that does not detract from the requirement to make those choices. It is true that instruments such as fiscal measures and voluntary agreements can and should equally involve the articulation of policy choices, but crucially, in my view, not necessarily with the same degree of precision, and nearly always involving no legal compulsion or accountability. We are in a process of social transition which is making ever more apparent the political nature of the decisions involved in designing and applying environmental regulation; in that context, avoiding hard policy choices by diminishing the role of regulation or transferring those decisions to other spheres is clearly an attractive option, but it is ultimately a derogation of political responsibility.

INSTITUTIONAL REFORM AND CHANGE

PART 2

INSTITUTIONAL REFORM AND CHANGE

It is all too easy for politicians to initiate change to the structures of government as a substitute for the delivery of effective policy. Yet there are times when it becomes necessary to acknowledge that the existing shape of institutions inhibits the achievement of contemporary environmental goals, and change is needed. Equally, major reforms occurring for other reasons may have a significant impact on the way that environmental policies are determined and delivered, and need to be evaluated.

The Environmental and Constitutional Change (1999) arose out of an ambitious project of the UCL Constitutional Unit conducted at a time of profound constitutional change taking place in the United Kingdom. The new Labour Government had introduced no less than twelve constitutional reform bills in its first session, described by the then prime minister as the 'biggest programme of change to democracy every proposed.'[1] The aim of the UCL project was a first attempt to consider the implications and interactions of the reform programme as a whole, and to predict what it might imply for the citizen in the future. Other contributions to the book that resulted[2] largely focussed on particular areas of constitutional change such as devolution, the machinery of government, and the Human Rights Act. My task was to take a particular policy area and consider how the changes taking place might impact on it. My underlying assumption was that environmental policy had moved well beyond a traditional model of public administration where problems could be clearly identified, were amenable to conventional scientific or technical analysis, and were likely to be resolved by classical regulatory approaches. The nebulous concept of sustainable development now pervaded the environmental agenda, reflecting competing visions of what might be implied by a sustainable let alone an environmental sound society. The path towards sustainability has been described as a journey whose destination is unknown[3] - a parallel in many ways to constitutional change which seemed equally to imply new directions where no one can predict the outcome with any degree of certainty.

---

[1] Tony Blair, Speech to the Labour Party Conference, 4 October 1994.
[2] Hazell (ed) (1999) Constitutional Futures - A History of the Next Ten Years Oxford University Press.
[3] see O'Riordan and Voisey (1998) *Sustainable Development in Western Europe: Coming to Terms with Agenda 21* Frank Cass, London, and quoted below.

Many of the themes identified in **The Environment and Constitutional Change** *remain of significance nearly a decade later. Devolution in Scotland and Wales has seen the gradual development of diverging approaches in environmental policy, despite what is often a common legal framework derived from European Community environmental legislation.[4] Yet we have yet to see major legal disputes concerning the division of environmental responsibilities, of the sort seen in Federal structures such as Canada and Australia, which have had to be resolved by the judiciary – and that despite obvious potential ambiguities in the allocation of powers under devolution legislation. This may be a tribute to the common sense and co-operative approach of civil servants dealing with potential conflicts, though the situation could change where different political parties are in power in London, Edinburgh, or Cardiff. The language of Human Rights has now entered the handling of environmental cases before the British Courts as witnessed by decisions such as Alconbury[5] and Marcic[6], yet perhaps has not had such a dramatic impact as some environmental lawyers would have predicted. The European Court of Human of Rights has also developed its jurisprudence in environmental cases, notably with the Hatton case[7] concerning aircraft noise where the Court signalled the large margin of discretion that still rested with governments to determine where the public interest might override individual human rights. The tensions between central government direction and local authority decision-making powers still remain in the land use planning field, as witnessed by current proposals to reform the planning system.[8] At European Community level, the principle of subsidiarity[9] has not inhibited the development of new Community environmental legislation, but is nevertheless reflected in the content of legislation such as the Water Framework Directive and the Integrated Pollution Prevention and Control Directive which give considerable discretion to Member States in their implementation. Much greater emphasis is now being given to rights of access of information and rights of participation in decision making.*

Constitutional change may have affected the workings of the courts, but had little to say about their actual structure. In the United Kingdom, environmental cases, be they concerned with criminal law, civil disputes, or public law, have been handled by the ordinary courts dealing with areas of law. Yet for nearly 20 years there has been discussion and reviews on whether there is the need for some form of specialised court dealing with environmental cases. In 1989

---

[4] See, for example, Jenkins (2005) 'Environmental Law in Wales', *Journal of Environmental Law* Vol 15 pp 207-227.

[5] *R. (Alconbury) v. Secretary of State for the Environment, Transport* (House of Lords [2001] 2 All ER 929) - see part 4.

[6] *Marcic v. Thames Water Utilities Ltd* (House of Lords [2004] 2 AC 42) - see part 4.

[7] Hatton and others v. United Kingdom ECHR, 8 July 2003, no. 36022/97.

[8] White Paper *Planning for a Sustainable Future*, 21 May 2007 and proposed Planning Reform Bill 2007/8.

[9] See *Subsidiarity and European Community Environmental Law* in part 5.

Robert (now Lord Justice) Carnwath proposed the idea of combining various courts and tribunals dealing with land use planning and environmental protection into a single jurisdiction[10] Two years later the then Lord Chief Justice, Lord Woolf, put forward the idea of a single environmental court than might handle all the legal issues, be they criminal, civil, or public, that could arise from an environmental dispute or incident.[11] Professor Malcolm Grant was subsequently commissioned by government to examine the workings of specialist environmental courts in other jurisdictions such as New South Wales and Sweden, and to propose possible models for this country.[12] Six alternative models were identified, ranging for a new planning appeals tribunal to a new division of the High Court. At the time. however, Government was not convinced that the costs of significant institutional upheaval would be outweighed by any benefits resulting, and in any event any proposals would be premature prior to the outcome of major reviews of the criminal and tribunal system then being undertaken.

*Three years later, I was commissioned by the Department of the Environment, Food and Rural Affair to re-examine the case for an environmental tribunal in England and Wales, resulting in the report **Modernizing Environmental Justice** (2003), co-authored with my researcher, Michael Woods. The focus of the research was concerned with administrative appeals under environmental legislation. Under planning legislation, developers have long had the right to appeal against a decision of local government to central government, with appeals now conducted and largely decided by an agency of government, the Planning Inspectorate. Similar rights of appeal now pervaded environmental legislation where licences and similar permits were sought, but it became clear that there was little coherence in the choice of bodies for determining such appeals – some went to the planning inspectorate, some to the Secretary of State, some to local courts, with apparently little rationale for the choice of forums.*

Our proposal for a single environmental tribunal to handle such appeals was certainly more modest than some of the earlier ideas for a full-blown division of the High Court handling all environmental legal issues. Although there was clearly a case for improving the way that existing criminal courts handled environmental cases, I felt that criminal environmental prosecutions should remain in the criminal courts rather than being given special treatment. Again, I was not convinced that the civil litigation in the environmental field such as

[10] Carnwath (1989) *Enforcing Planning Controls* Department of the Environment, April 1989.

[11] Woolf (1991) *Are the Judiciary Environmentally Myopic?* Journal of Environmental Law, Vol 4 No 1 pp 1-14.

[12] Grant (2000) *Environmental Court Project* Final Report Dept of Environment, Transport and the Regions.

nuisance cases raised such distinct issues as warranting a special court, nor that judges in the Administrative Court were incapable of handling environmental public law issues effectively, though undoubtedly issues concerning costs and the expense of judicial review needed to be tackled. In this context, the 1998 Aarhus Convention to which both the United Kingdom and the European Community are now parties, is highly significant. Under the Convention, members of the public and non-governmental organization are given the right to challenge the legality of environmental decisions of government and public bodies before an independent court or tribunal which are 'equitable, timely, and not prohibitively expensive.' To be fair, the courts themselves have proved sensitive to the implications of Aarhus, and have, within their limits of their own powers, signalled new approaches to costs provisions, such as a more generous application of Protective Costs Orders which can limit in advance a party's exposure to costs should they lose. Government at present remains convinced that our current system satisfies the Aarhus requirements, but this remains questionable, and may yet be subject to European Community infringement procedures with a final decision being by the European Court of Justice.

Intellectually, then, it seemed justifiable in **Modernizing Environmental Justice** *to focus on a more modest reform to the judicial system. But it was also clear at the time that government did not have the appetite for a major institutional upheaval, and my study was equally influenced by a realistic assessment of the politics of the possible. The drafting of the report deliberately avoided an overly academic approach, and was written in a style that would be accessible and intelligible to Ministers and civil servants. We consciously examined the implications of different options including 'do nothing' or adapting existing bodies, and in the contemporary style of policy analysis considered the cost implications and possible financial savings that would result from the recommendations. The report was well received. But its proposal for a fairly focused new tribunal handling administrative appeals under environmental legislation did not sit well with the aspirations of those looking for a more radical institutional change. Another study, commissioned by DEFRA,[13] and published the next year rejected the modest approach and called for a specialist environmental court. Faced with such divergent views even from within the environmental law community, government was able to refrain from taking positive action.*

Transparency and Trust *(2004) examines in detail the case for institutional reform for handling environmental policy and regulation in Northern Ireland, and in doing so contains comparative analysis of arrangements in other parts of the United Kingdom and Europe. The report was commissioned by a coalition of environmental non-governmental organisations in Northern Ireland, but it*

---

[13] *Environmental Justice* Environmental Law Foundation, World Wildlife Fund, and Leigh Day and Co, March 2004.

*was agreed that the study should be entirely independent, and the analysis my own. The commission did not allow for extensive public consultation, and in any event it seemed to me fairly presumptuous for a single academic to decide how Northern Ireland should organise its affairs. Instead, a preferable approach was to make a clear analysis of current governmental structures, and to set out the pros and cons of the various institutional options that might be realistically chosen. In this context, **Transparency and Trust** was designed to provide the core information for a political debate that was clearly emerging.*

The subject area was important to me both intellectually and on a personal level. Five generations of Macrorys had been millers in Northern Ireland, and I had spent most of my childhood holidays on my grandfather's farm in County Derry. I had been a specialist adviser to the House of Commons Select Committee on the Environment in 1990 when it produced the first Committee report examining Northern Ireland and the environment. During my membership of the Royal Commission on Environmental Pollution, I persuaded the Commission to visit Northern Ireland, the first time it had done so in over 25 years. I was clear that Northern Ireland should not necessarily slavishly copy arrangements in other parts of the United Kingdom, yet there was clearly an opportunity to learn from developments that had taken place elsewhere, and to create a distinctive structure of environmental governance that would serve the region well as it emerged from decades on internal conflict.

A particular concern of the non-governmental organizations was the legal status of the core environmental regulator in Northern Ireland, the Environment and Heritage Service. The equivalent regulators in other parts of the United Kingdom were non-departmental public bodies, implying that they were legally independent entities from government. In contrast, the Environment and Heritage Service was an agency within the Northern Ireland Department of the Environment, giving it a degree of managerial freedom but still part of the Department. It was argued that this arrangement unduly compromised its ability to act independently from the political process, though those in favour of the existing arrangement considered that being part of the Department gave it more internal policy influence, and that a small jurisdiction such as Northern Ireland could ill afford the luxury of a `legally distinct Agency. Those commissioning the report initially thought that Northern Ireland was the only part of Europe which did not have a legally independent environmental regulator, but the study revealed that this was not in fact the case. The United Kingdom has a strong tradition of establishing legally independent national bodies to regulate and deliver policy, but this is not replicated in other parts of Europe, with the exception of Sweden. Nevertheless, within the United Kingdom constitutional practice, the attractions of an independent agency were considerable.

Trust and Transparency did not simply deal with the question of environmental regulators. It considered questions of arrangements for political accountability through Assembly select committees and the role of audit bodies in dealing with environmental policy. Advisory bodies such as the Royal Commission on Environmental Pollution and the Sustainable Development Commission played a significant role in the development of policy in the United Kingdom, and the report considered the potential role of such bodies in Northern Ireland. The Report also mapped out the environmental responsibilities of the different government departments in Northern Ireland, demonstrating clearly the extent to which the modern environmental and sustainability agenda cuts across conventional organisational lines. But it is almost certainly a fruitless exercise to conceive of the environmental challenge as simply one of the finding the correct organisational structures in government: '...the most successful way of resolving the dilemma, the solution adopted in the Netherlands, depends on recasting the problem not as one about administrative organisation, raising as it does all the issues about turf disputes between different departments, but as one about policy process.'[14] Nevertheless, the rationale for some of the divisions of responsibility in Northern Ireland were perplexing to say the least, though they were clearly as much a product of the demands of political balance in Northern Ireland as of any more rational choice.

The report formed the basis of a public consultation exercise initiated by the Northern Ireland environmental organisations, and led to the Northern Ireland Government in 2006 establishing an independent review of environmental governance in Northern Ireland, under the chairmanship of Tom Burke, CBE. The Burke Review's final report, **Foundations for the Future**[15] *was published in May 2007, and came out firmly in favour of the setting up of a legally independent Environmental Protection Agency. The Review, which had conducted extensive public consultation and hearings, felt able to go further than* **Trust and Transparency***, and recommended, inter alia, that the responsibility for strategic land use planning be transferred completely to the Department of the Environment, and that the existing Planning and Waters Appeal Commissions be combined to create a new environmental tribunal for Northern Ireland.* **Trust and Transparency** *had been written at a time when the devolved administration in Northern Ireland had been suspended. The Burke Review was produced after the Northern Ireland Assembly has been reinstated, with the implication that decisions on the future structure of environmental governance in the region now rest squarely on locally elected politicians.*

---

[14] See Weale et al (2000) *Environmental Governance in Europe,* p 228.
[15] 'Foundations for the Future', The Review of Environmental Governance, Final Report, May 2007.

CHAPTER 4

THE ENVIRONMENT AND CONSTITUTIONAL CHANGE*

This chapter considers one sector of policy, the environment, and its relationship to constitutional change in this country. The last twenty-five years have seen an extraordinary development in the politics of the environment. Major international environmental treaties have been negotiated, the national legal framework has changed beyond recognition, and there have been significant developments to the structures of UK administration responsible for the regulation and delivery of environmental policy. Membership of environmental organisations in the early 1990s exceeded the total membership of political parties. A number of the themes discussed in previous chapters, such as the development of legal rights to information and participation, and the principle of subsidiarity, were first played out on the environmental stage. Elements of constitutional changes now under way, including devolution, an enlarged European Union, and the incorporation of the European Convention on Human Rights can be expected to influence profoundly the context in which environmental policies are negotiated and developed in the future. Paradoxically, however, the environment appears to have played little part in providing the rationale for constitutional change or in shaping the proposals now being implemented. Two broad questions therefore need addressing. To what extent are the major proposals consistent with the administrative and policy developments that have already taken place in the environmental field? Second, will the constitutional changes provide a framework that will assist in the effective development and delivery of environmental policies appropriate for the beginning of the next century?

The environment is a dynamic and complex policy field. This chapter will not attempt a comprehensive analysis of substantive aspects of environmental policy in all its guises. Instead, it will focus on four themes of constitutional change and how they are likely to impact on environmental policy: structures of national administration; the European Community; legal rights concerning the environment; and the role of Westminster and Whitehall. Nevertheless, there are a number of important general themes concerning the nature of the

* R Macrory (1999) The Environment and Constitutional Change in Hazell R. (ed) *Constitutional Futures - A History of the Next Ten Years* Oxford University Press, Oxford, pp178-195

contemporary environmental policies which pose significant challenges for constitutional reform, and form a necessary backdrop to any discussion.

'Think Globally – Act Locally', which became a pervasive mantra in environmental politics after the Rio Earth Summit of 1992, hardly forms a firm basis for determining the allocation of environmental responsibility between different levels of government. Yet it reflects the pervasive nature of many environment issues and how the cumulative effect of local human impacts can affect the overall condition of the environment, on a national, regional or even global scale. Models of federal or quasi-federal government which attempt to identify a clear separation of powers in the environmental field are unlikely to reflect the physical and political realities of the issue. If the environment is not readily susceptible to a vertical disaggregation of functions, still less is it amenable to what might be described as horizontal compartmentalisation of responsibilities, the traditional model of administrative structures. Differing perceptions of what constitutes the sphere of environmental concern have been a major source of tension between government and non-governmental organisations over the last two decades, with key issues of concern, such as agriculture, energy, and transport often falling outside the direct responsibility of more narrowly focused environment departments. The need to integrate an environmental dimension into nearly all aspects of the machinery of government is now widely acknowledged, and indeed given legal expression in the European Treaty.[1] Tentative experiments in new forms of co-ordinating and consultative mechanisms have been initiated, though progress remains slow.

The concept of sustainable development now pervades the environmental agenda, and introduces a new set of intellectual and political challenges. Previous chapters have identified minimalist and maximalist concepts of constitutional change. The implications of sustainable development are equally subject to competing visions, with the narrowest concerned with ensuring that contemporary decision makers take a longer-term view of the environmental impacts of existing trends than has been usual practice.[2] Others envisage a far more complex and politically unsettling picture incorporating notions of greater economic and social justice both within and between generations, and a revitalisation of local and

---

[1] Under Art. 130r of the Maastricht Version of the Treaty, 'Environmental protection requirements must be integrated into the definition and implementation of other Community policies.' The Amsterdam Treaty strengthened the status of the integration principle by putting it at the head of the Treaty in a new Article 6, and including an express reference to sustainable development.

[2] Encapsulated in the phrase of John Gummer, former Secretary of State for the Environment of the previous Government 'We must not cheat on our children.' Reported in Hansard HC Col 994, 4/12/96.

community identities.[3] There are inevitable tensions and contradictions involved – one criterion of success for constitutional change will be its ability to provide a political and legal framework for accommodating and resolving these concepts in the future. Yet, significant perhaps of a lack of coherent vision, the most recent government consultation paper on sustainable development, 'Opportunities for Change',[4] contains one reference to the constitutional changes now taking place.[5]

A final important element of the current debate concerns increasing public unease with the ability of governmental bodies to reach acceptable decisions especially in areas of scientific uncertainty, epitomised by the BSE crisis and contemporary arguments over genetically modified organisms. Expert judgment is no longer treated with the same unquestioning respect it might have been a generation ago. Understanding the mechanisms for improving trust in regulatory decision-makers, and appreciating the nature and role of public values will be a major challenge for those involved in public administration.[6]

Structures of National Administration

The Centralisation of Environmental Control

Within the United Kingdom the trend of environmental administration has been to shift power away from local government towards Westminster or specialised public agencies. This was not due to some grand design or overarching theory about central-local government relations, but occurred incrementally over a lengthy period, with each shift being justified by the logic of the particular type of environmental problem at hand. The first major re-allocation of powers to a central authority took place well before more recent attacks on local government, with the establishment in the 1860s of a centralised government inspectorate to regulate emissions into the air from certain industrial processes. The political justification was that local authorities and local courts lacked both the technical competence and the political determination to ensure effective control. This initial concept of a largely technocratic and functional agency, not directly accountable to local political direction, has remained a powerful model which has continued to influence the

[3] For a recent review see T. O'Riordan, and H. Voisey, *Sustainable Development in Western Europe: Coming to Terms with Agenda 21* (London: Frank Cass, 1998).
[4] Department of the Environment, Transport and Regions, 'Sustainable Development: Opportunities for Change. Consultation Paper on a Revised UK Strategy' (1988).
[5] The one reference is to the proposals that the Welsh Assembly and the Regional Development Agencies should have explicit responsibilities for developing policies on sustainable development.
[6] An underlying theme of much of the most recent report of the Royal Commission on Environmental Pollution, 'Setting Environmental Standards' (1998).

shape of contemporary administrative structures. A similar but much more gradual pattern of the concentration of powers developed in the field of water management, where the traditional geographical jurisdictional boundaries of local government were seen as failing to reflect the physical realities of the water cycle and river systems. The pattern of centralisation continued in 1995 when the powers to regulate waste management and disposal were removed from local authorities in England and Wales to a newly established body, the Environment Agency.[7] The immediate cause of the loss of power was a series of critical reports questioning the commitment and competence of many local authorities in regulating what had become a highly technically complex industry. At the same time there was an increasing awareness that a medium-by-medium (air, water, land) approach to regulation which had characterised the development of administrative structures did not reflect the need to treat the environment as a whole. Waste, water, and many air pollution functions were therefore subsumed into the new Agency. This pattern of centralisation of functions was reflected in Scotland with the creation of a Scottish Environment Protection Agency, though with a slightly different range of powers. An added pressure in recent years for centralisation of responsibility has been the need for central government to demonstrate that it can ensure compliance with European Community obligations in the environmental field. As Nigel Haigh demonstrated over ten years ago this required central government both to preserve and threaten the exercise of reserve powers where local authorities were failing to achieve Community obligations.[8] More recently the model has been to translate Community environmental policies into binding national legislation as a mechanism for ensuring compliance.[9]

Local Authority Responsibility

Yet the allocation of environmental powers away from local authorities to specialised agencies of various types is not in reality as straightforward or inevitable as it might first appear. The environment is not amenable to clear boundaries of responsibility. Not every environmental regulation has been transferred to centralised authorities – local noise control, the control of site-specific statutory nuisances and air pollution from certain

[7] Part I Environment Act 19 5.'

[8] N. Haigh,, 'Devolved Responsibility and Centralisation the Effects of EEC Environmental Policy', *Public Administration* 4(1986), 197-207.

[9] In a more recent study, Vanice Morphet, Chief Executive of an English County Council, questions the extent to which Haigh's thesis now holds true and suggests that the contemporary nature of European Community environmental policies with greater emphasis on local and regional involvement has shifted the balance of influence in favour local authorities. P. Lowe and S. Ward, *British Environmental Policy and Europe* (London: Routledge, 1988).

industries remain with local authorities, with the issue of contaminated land split between local authorities and the agencies.

Above all, land-use planning controls have remained largely with local authorities, though with strong overall policy and appeal functions resting with central government. Land-use planning controls have never been exclusively concerned with environmental protection, but their importance as a mechanism for anticipating and preventing environmental problems has been increasingly recognised. This linkage was legally strengthened in 1988 with the introduction of requirements for environmental assessment procedures into the planning system as a result of European Community legislation on the subject. Nevertheless the role of local authority powers in the planning field, where they are dealing with a project which is also subject to specialised regulation by the Environment Agency, has proved a source of tension, especially where politically sensitive processes such as waste incinerators have been involved. Litigation has followed, with the courts attempting to devise principles which essentially recognise that while the environmental impact of a new project is a legitimate concern of local planning authorities they should not try to duplicate the regulatory functions of specialised agencies. But as the lengthy judgments, indicate these are principles which are simple to state but less easy to apply in practice.[10]

Other major areas of contemporary environmental concern clearly do not fall within the remit of site-specific industrial control which historically dominated the development of regulatory structures. Transport, in particular, is now the most important source of most main pollutants in this country, with the exception of sulphur dioxide, with road transport predominating. Future projections, including those about carbon dioxide levels (the key contributor to global warming) indicate that the proportion attributable to road transport will rise considerably. Analysing the longer-term effect of land use planning on transport patterns and the concomitant effect of transport infrastructure on the location and shape of development is complex, but it is clear that local authority influence on one of the most significant environmental challenges could be considerable.

But there remain a number of problematic challenges in existing structures. Leaving local authorities to make the difficult decisions may satisfy problems of local accountability but in the absence of clear rational policies render authorities vulnerable to unruly competitive pressures where local authorities are in effect played off against each other by

---

[10] See *Gateshead Metropolitan District Council v. Secretary of State for the Environment* [1995] Env.LR 37. *R v. Bolton Metropolitan District Council*, Court of Appeal. 5 May 1988.

larger economic interests – the development of out-of-town shopping centres in the 1980s being a clear example.[11] At the same time, the functional, and more technocratic model which underlies the specialised agencies sits unhappily with notions of political accountability, and may obscure the more ambiguous value and economic judgments inherent in environmental regulation. Moreover, the emerging policy objectives concerning sustainability call for decision-making structures that can encompass a broader mix of interests from environmental protection, economic consumption and development, to issues of equity. The enthusiasm with which many local authorities have seized upon developing sustainable development policies can in part be attributed to the desire of a sector of government which lost so many powers in recent years to be associated with new policy areas which resonated positively with many sectors of the public. The significant role of local authorities is also recognised at international level with the launch of the Local Agenda 21 initiative at the 1992 Earth Summit and, according to the Secretary-General of the International Council for Local Environment Initiatives, it 'has engendered one of the most extensive follow-up programmes' to the agenda established at Rio.[12] The recent White Paper on local government[13] acknowledges the potential of local authorities to integrate concerns, and proposes a new legal duty to promote economic, social, and environmental well-being within their jurisdictions: this 'will put sustainable development at the heart of council decision making and will provide an overall framework within which councils must perform all their existing functions'.[14]

The Impact of Devolution

How will these patterns of administrative structure be shaped by constitutional change? There already exist asymmetrical patterns of responsibility between the specialised environmental agencies in England and Wales, Scotland, and Northern Ireland. To take one example, in England nature protection and the preservation of the countryside for amenity and recreational purposes have fallen to separate bodies, English Nature and the Countryside Commission, while in Scotland and Wales single bodies have carried out both areas of

[11] Sec the 18th Report of the Royal Commission on Environmental Pollution. *Transport and the Environment* (London: HMSO. 1984).

[12] J. Brugman, 'Local Authorities and Agenda 21' in F. Fodds, (ed.) *The Way Toward – Beyond Agenda 21* (London: Earthscan, 1997), 101-13. According to Tim O'Riordan and Heather Voisey (note 3 above). 'With slow progress so far at national level it is local government which is proving to be the most active and innovative in implementing sustainable development in the United Kingdom...' (p.46).

[13] Department of the Environment Transport and Regions, *Modern Local Government – In Touch with the People* (1988).

[14] Ibid., para. 8 10.

responsibility since 1990. Northern Ireland has frequently lagged behind in the development of environmental legislation, but the creation of the Environment and Agency Service in 1996 as an executive agency within the Northern Ireland Department of the Environment could provide a more radical integrating model. The Agency combines powers for countryside protection, nature preservation and pollution control in a way unseen in the rest of the United Kingdom. With pollution regulation increasingly concerned with effects on the natural environment as well as human health, the model has attractions. A minimalist view of the effects of devolution would see these distinctive patterns of administration being preserved and the asymmetry even perhaps growing over time. Alternatively, the opportunity for experimentation may provide pressure for successful examples to be adopted elsewhere. Precedent remains a powerful factor, and it is less easy for governments to resist changes which are already operating effectively in other parts of the country. Combining countryside and nature-protection functions in England along the lines in Wales and Scotland can be predicted. The more ambitious Northern Ireland model is unlikely to be adopted in Great Britain for some years but its very existence means that it cannot be readily dismissed as a concept. Asymmetric development also appears to underline the Government's recent proposals for local government reform with opportunities for experimentation and example – 'The Government is clear that councils which perform consistently well will be able to acquire additional powers and freedoms that over time will be significantly wider than those available to councils which are performing less effectively.'[15]

Other effects of devolution on the current structure of environmental administration can be predicted. The devolved assemblies in Scotland, Wales, and Northern Ireland are likely to increase the political accountability of the specialised environmental agencies in those regions. In England, the minimalist approach to devolution is less likely to do so. Regional Development Agencies will hardly provide the appropriate forum for doing so. Similarly, if regional assemblies in England develop on an asymmetric model, it will be complex to develop lines of accountability for a body such as the Environment Agency with countrywide jurisdiction. The most radical model of devolution in England would eventually see regional assemblies in all areas of the country – that in turn could lead to pressure for a remodelling of existing structures, with the establishment of regional environmental agencies, perhaps on the Northern Irish model, more closely politically accountable on a regional basis.

[15] *Modern Local Government—In Touch With the People,* Note 13 above para. 8.29.

The other significant area will be the development of mechanisms for discussion and co-operation on environmental policies between the different regions of the United Kingdom. In 1990 the Nature Conservation Council which has responsibility in Great Britain for nature protection matters was abolished in favour of separate agencies in England, Wales, and Scotland. A Joint Nature Consultative Committee which was established to retain a degree of co-ordination between the regional bodies has been criticised as lacking sufficient influence. The devolution model for Scotland proposes essentially that Westminster and Whitehall retain control over environmental policies which fall within the remit of international or European Community agreement with other aspects fully devolved.[16] This will not be an easy line to draw as the subsequent discussion demonstrates. But any re-emergence of agencies with environmental responsibility across the whole of the United Kingdom now seems unlikely. Yet experience of countries such as Australia indicates that there will be the need to develop new institutional mechanisms to discuss and co-ordinate the development of environmental policies and standards in the different regions.[17] Here the proposed Council of the Island may offer an appropriate forum for handling discussion of environmental policies, and for allowing the further development of cross-border environmental initiatives that have already been developed between Northern Ireland and Eire.

The European Community

European Community Legislation in the 1970s and 1980s

Whatever the future distribution of environmental responsibilities, the United Kingdom no longer has a free hand in developing environmental policies whether at a national or strengthened devolved level. Only thirty years ago the national inspectorate responsible for regulating emissions from power stations could publicly doubt whether it had any jurisdictional responsibilities to consider the transboundary effects of atmospheric emissions from the industries they were controlling. Such an attitude could not be sustained today either politically or legally. The European Community in particular has provided the base for developing a substantial body of legally binding environmental instruments over the last twenty-five years. For a country such as the United Kingdom where nationally binding environmental standards were resisted in favour of giving extensive discretion to regulators, the incorporation of Community legal requirements into the existing body of UK environmental law has been profound. Environmental emission and quality standards are now an accepted part of the legal landscape.

---

[16] See Scotland Act 1998, Schedule 5.
[17] See Ch. 9.

The obligation to produce plans concerning various environmental objectives, and procedural rights including that of public access to environmental information are now enshrined in national law.

The 1970s and 1980s saw the rapid development of a range of environmental legislation at Community level encompassing such matters as water quality, air emissions, chemicals control, and environmental assessment. The first flush of enthusiasm has, however, now given way to a rather less confident and more measured approach, despite the European Parliament's continued promotion of green issues and increasing influence over the legislative process. There has been a growing appreciation that the early model of rigorously expressed environmental standards, often based on a confusing mixture of politics and science, is insufficient and too inflexible to deal with the range and breadth of environmental issues facing the European Community.

Until 1987 the Treaty contained no explicit legal powers concerning the environment, creating the need to look to other provisions in the Treaty as a legitimate basis for environmental legislation. Article 100, which permits harmonisation to remove distortions of trade, was the preferred basis for many environmental directives, and in the case of product standards such as vehicle emissions standards and industrial pollution standards such use could be justified. The economic case for the need to harmonise, say, drinking water or bathing water standards on the grounds of potential trade distortion was intellectually far more dubious yet did not deter Member States from agreeing to such legislation.

With the Single European Act introducing explicit environmental provisions into the Treaty[18] this intellectual sleight of hand was no longer required. Nevertheless, the Treaty contained significant procedural differences for legislation based on trade-related Treaty provisions or environmental provisions, leading to a series of inter-institutional legal disputes between the Council, the Commission and the European Parliament. The Amsterdam Treaty has now largely removed such differences, with co-decision procedures applying equally to trade-related and the majority of environmental legislation. Fine legal arguments concerning the dividing line between environmental protection and trade harmonisation are likely to disappear. But at the same time the legislative influence of the European Parliament will be substantially increased, requiring both Member States and the Commission to be more attuned to its approach to environmental issues. Non-governmental environmental organisations and other lobby

---

[18] Art. 130r EC Treaty, now Art. 174 under the Amsterdam version.

interests are likely to pay increasing attention to securing influence with Parliamentarians at European level.

Subsidiarity

The environmental provisions of the 1987 Treaty were also significant in that they contained the first legal expression of the subsidiarity principle. The Treaty has never contained a clear division of competencies between the Community and Member States, not least in the environmental field where Laurence Brinkhorst, a former Director-General of DG XI, described the system as 'not so much a separation of powers but rather an intermingling of powers'. The subsidiarity principle contained in the Single European Act 1987 required the Community to act only if environmental objectives can be attained 'better' at Community level rather than at the level of individual Member States. As such it could be seen as suggestive rather than a formal expression of competencies, and appeared to have had little real influence. Many argued that it said little more than had already been expressed in the Community's First Action Programme on the Environment some fourteen years earlier, where it was clearly stated that the level of action, be it local, regional, national. Community or international, must be best suited to the type of pollution issue at hand.

The Maastricht Treaty saw the transformation of the principle into one of general application which was positioned at the head of the Treaty,[19] signifying at the very least its political significance. Lawyers have argued over whether the principle is truly justiciable in the courts,[20] but one of the few cases where the principle has been raised before the European Court of Justice, the United Kingdom's challenge to the Working Time Directive in 1996, suggests that the judiciary will be reluctant to intervene on those grounds alone: 'The Council [of Ministers] must be allowed a wide discretion in an area which as here involves the legislature in making social policy choices and requires it to carry out complex assessment.'[21]

---

[19] Art. 3b EC Treaty now contained in Art. 5 of the Amsterdam version.

[20] In one key collection of papers, three distinguished lawyers come to differing conclusions on this point—see D. O'Keefe, and P. Twomey, (eds.). *Legal Issues of the Maastricht Treaty* (London: Chancery Law Publishing, 1994).

[21] *United Kingdom v. EC Council* C-84/94 [1996] ECR 1-5755. More recently, Advocate General Leger considered that in view of the importance of the principle of subsidiarity in allocating powers between Member States and the Community, it did not seem excessive for Community institutions 'in the future systematically to state reasons for their decisions in view of the principle of subsidiarity'. The European Court, however, did not consider that an express reference to subsidiarity need be made in justifying Community action: *Germany v. European Parliament and EU Council* [1997] 3 CMLR 1379.

Even if legal challenges on the grounds of breach of subsidiarity are likely to remain a rarity in the future, this does not mean that the principle is devoid of political effect. At the time of Maastricht, some Member States appeared to foster extravagant expectations with talk of rolling back the frontiers of Community environmental legislation. Certainly the introduction of the principle and its heightened significance since Maastricht resulted in both Member States and the Commission in setting out in more detail a set of principles and procedures concerned with ensuring that measures were tested against the concept of subsidiarity.[22] But there has been no major withdrawal from a substantive area of policy.[23]

The Division Between Community and National Interests

The nature of environmental problems, people's perceptions of their relationship with the environment, and the capacity for cumulative localised impacts to have significant regional or even global effects make it extraordinarily difficult to draw hard lines of substantive competence between the Community and national interests. A minimalist approach would confine Community interest to environmental issues where there was a clear transboundary physical impact (such as the movements of waste, or transfrontier air emissions) or a clear transnational economic impact. But this ignores concepts of a European environmental heritage, or what has been described as transboundary cultural interests where a citizen of, say, France could be said to have a legitimate interest in the protection of natural habitats in Spain, or vice versa.[24] The notion of European citizenship, and the increasing reference to certain environmental rights (discussed further below) adds further to the complexity of drawing substantive boundaries.

Nevertheless, even if there are few issues which can be definitively described as no-go areas, the concept of subsidiarity is likely to have continuing influence on the content of Community environmental policies. The notion of 'shared responsibility' has been pursued in the environment field under the Fifth Action Programme on the Environment, and the detailed provisions of Community environmental legislation are likely to contain a greater role for Member States. Already there are important signals. Recent environmental proposals are making more use

[22] Inter-Institutional Agreement on procedures for implementing the principle of Subsidiarity [1993] 10 EC Bull.
[23] The only clear example being the Commission's decision in 1994 to substitute its proposal for a Directive concerning zoos with a Recommendation. Even this change caused concern in the European Parliament.
[24] W. Wils, 'Subsidiarily and EC Environmental Policy – Taking People's Concert Seriously. *Journal of Environmental Law*, Vol. 6 (1994), 85-92.

of framework directives, and there is likely to be less use of Community-wide environmental standards expressed in numerate form. For example, Commission proposals to amend EC legislation concerning drinking water standards would mean that standards concerning aesthetics or smell would no longer be determined at Community level. Member States will be given more discretion in the designation of areas subject to Community environmental policies, or the determination of decisions, say, concerning the award of eco-labels, without the need for a further, hierarchy of decision making at Community level. These developments could imply a greater role for new devolved administrations within the United Kingdom, but it could also lead to tension. Will, say, aesthetic standards for Scottish drinking water in future be determined by the Scottish Parliament on the grounds that the relevant EC law permits a Member State to determine such standards? Or since it falls within the ambit of EC law, does the responsibility remain with Westminster as a reserved matter?

Such trends away from Community-wide environmental standards are likely to be strengthened with the likely expansion of the Community. Given the difficulty of many of the accession states in securing compliance with current Community environmental standards in fields such as air or water quality, sensitive political decisions will have to be taken concerning the possibility of time-limited derogations (as happened with East Germany) or substantial financial assistance to ensure compliance. And the moves towards greater degrees of discretion at Member State level, more variegated standards, and the reciprocal recognition of decisions taken within Member States (such as approval to market a new chemical substance) implies a considerable degree of trust in the capabilities of institutions within other countries. Even where existing environmental directives (such as those concerning bathing waters or shell-fish waters permitted a degree of discretion in designation, there have been well known examples of Member States abusing the process. The concept of shared responsibility is therefore not necessarily a panacea but one fraught with the possibility of misuse. But if, as seems likely, it is a trend that will continue, it follows that it will be all the more important to develop procedural principles such as the public right to information concerning the environment and the right of action before national courts which can go some way to check that governmental powers are exercised legitimately. At the same time, there will be a pressure to create more sophisticated Community-wide monitoring and reporting systems, using comparable databases, a task being led by the new European Environment Agency and one that will require increased co-operation and co-ordination amongst the devolved players. Yet such a task of identifying objective criteria of measurement is far from mechanical and value-free, and can reveal subtle and often deep-seated differences between local and centralised perceptions of the environment.[25]

Procedural Rights

European Law

For the United Kingdom at any rate the environmental field provided an early example of broad based legislative rights to information. The need to implement the EC Directive on Access to Environment Information in 1990 required the Government to introduce in 1992 regulations granting any member of the public legal rights to an extensive range of information concerning the environment held by public bodies. Both the Community and national legislation contained a wide range of exemptions which can be expected to continue to be subject to legal dispute, although case law to date indicates that the courts will interpret these restrictively, on the assumption that the general right to information is the grounding principle.[26] The effectiveness of the national regulations has, however, been weakened by the failure to establish a dedicated appeals tribunal, relying instead on judicial review as a remedy against refusal to supply information or the imposition of excessive financial charges for supply. New institutional mechanisms such as a specialised appeals tribunal for appeals, perhaps in the context of wider freedom of information legislation, can be predicted.

The concept of general legal rights to a 'healthy environment' or some similar phrase is one that is found in some written constitutions, both within Europe and elsewhere, the most recent being the 1996 Constitution of South Africa. In case law before the European Court of Justice Advocates General have promoted the idea of EC environmental legislation concerning, say, air quality or water quality, as granting public rights to a clean environment, though beyond justifying the requirement for Member States to transpose such Community standards into national binding legislation rather than by administrative guidelines, the implications of such concepts have yet to fully realised.[27]

---

[25] 'Since rationalization and standardisation are among the most prominent tasks of the [European Environment Agency] these issues of local variability and the question of how to respect legitimate cultural differenced while maintaining enough consistency across cultures to provide a comprehensive review are among the most difficult challenges facing this new institution.' B. Wynne, and C. Wintenon, 'Public Information and the Environment' in P. Lowe. and S. Ward, *British Environmental Policy and Europe* (London: Routledge, 1988).

[26] Sec the decision of the High Court in *R v. British Coal Board ex parte Ibstock* (21 October 1994) and the first decision of the European Court of Justice on the Directive, *Mecklenburg v. Kreis Pinneberg – Der Landrat* (C-321/96. 17 June 1988).

[27] R. Macrory, (1996) 'Environmental Citizenship and the Law: Repairing the European Road, *Journal of Environmental Law*. Vol. 8, No. 2 (1996) 219-36. Reproduced in chap. 19 of this volume.

Certainly, in the absence of any implementing standards, the concept of a general right to a clean or healthy environment is extremely nebulous and so imbued with complex scientific and political choices as to make it almost devoid of substantive legal meaning in terms of the actual environmental quality to which individuals are entitled.[28] Moves to insert such a general right into the European Treaty have been resisted to date and are likely to continue to be so.

The European Convention on Human Rights

Moves to insert explicit environmental rights into the European Convention on Human Rights have similarly been resisted. But accession to the Convention is likely to require national courts to handle disputes raising Convention rights in the context of environmental disputes. The Convention contains no express individual or collective rights concerning the environment, but other articles in the Convention have been invoked as implicitly relating to the environment, though more often with lack of success to date. The Article 2 protection of right to life has been restrictively interpreted to mean physical life rather than quality of life – in contrast, say, to the Indian High Court which has built up extensive environmental case law from a similarly worded constitutional provision.

Similarly, environmental claims concerning the right to the peaceful enjoyment of property under Article I of Protocol 1 have been unsuccessful. But in 1994 the European Court of Human Rights found against Spain in a case concerning the authorisation and building of waste treatment plants near the applicant's home on the grounds of breach of Article 8 giving a right to respect for private and family life: 'severe environmental pollution may affect individuals' well-being and prevent them from enjoying their homes in such a way as to affect their private and family life adversely without, however, seriously endangering their health.'[29] A large award of compensatory damages was made. Though the facts of the case were extreme, it is predictable that the principles may be invoked in environmental disputes before UK national courts in the future. As Paul Craig has indicated[30] the most likely source of litigation is likely to be in the context of judicial review actions against bodies such as the Environment Agency or local planning authorities relying upon Section 6 of the Human Rights Act. Human rights, though, even if interpreted with an environmental

---

[28] For a valuable comparative survey see B. Brandl and E. Bungert, (1992) 'Constitutional Entrenchment of Environmental Protection. *Harvard Environmental Law Review,* Vol. 16. No. 1. (1992).

[29] *Lopez Ostra v. Spain* App. No. 16798/90. 9 December 1994

[30] Paul Craig, Constitutionalism, Regulation & Review (p67-85)

gloss, are inherently anthropocentric, and cannot satisfactorily protect all environmental interests – the requirement under Section 6 of the Human Rights Act that a litigant be a 'victim' of an unlawful act means that non-government environmental organisations are unlikely to have standing.

Other Sources of Procedural Rights

Other procedural rights concerning participation in decision making may be further developed in the future. Both existing national laws and EC Directives such as that concerning environmental assessment grant considerable rights of public participation. The European Convention on Access to Information. Public Participation in Decision Making and Access to Justice in Environmental Matters, proposed by the United Nations Economic Commission for Europe, can be expected to come into effect in around five years, and it seems unlikely that the United Kingdom would find it politically acceptable not to ratify. Many of the provisions build upon or reflect existing rights, but detailed changes to certain current national provisions may be required to secure compliance.

Recent years have seen a proliferation of judicial review actions in the environmental field, often brought by non-governmental organisations. Liberal interpretation of standing rules now appears to mean that there is little real difficulty in bringing such actions, but other procedural issues are likely to require far greater attention in the future. Examples include strict time-limits which often fail to reflect the reality of the complexities involved for organisations in deciding whether to proceed with a legal action; the problems in securing interlocutory injunctions where sites of high environmental value arc threatened; and the whole question of costs. These are all the more important in the context of Community environmental obligations where the Commission has recently emphasised the importance of the role of national courts as the first line of defence in securing compliance.[31] The Commission has acknowledged the significance of these types of procedural differences within Member States but is equally aware of the political sensitivities in proposing Community measures to address them. As other chapters indicate, the current developments in constitutional change in this country imply a greater role for the courts, yet they have failed to address critical procedural issues concerning environmental litigation. The pressure to do so will increase.

---

[31] Communication from the European Commission, Com (96) 500 final, 22 October 1996, *Implementing Community Environmental Law.*

Westminster and Whitehall

The Role of Committees

The 15 per cent vote to the UK Green Party in the 1989 European Parliamentary elections hugely sensitised mainstream political parties to public dissatisfaction with the effectiveness of existing environmental policies. But although electoral reform may increase the chances of some Green Party representation at national or regional level, it seems unlikely that the mainstream parties will allow themselves again to be marginalised on environmental policies. Within Parliament the House of Commons Select Committee on the Environment performed a critical role in the 1980s and early 1990s in exposing inadequacies in environmental policies. But the departmental basis of the Committee was ill-suited to handling the cross-departmental nature of key contemporary environmental problems, with substantial issues such as transport and agriculture falling outside its remit. The 1997 restructuring of the Department of the Environment to re-incorporate Transport permitted the Committee to expand its terms of reference, but there will be increasing pressure to sensitise other Committees to the environmental aspects of their work. Further development of Joint Committees inquiries may be expected.[32] The new Environment Audit Select Committee established by the government clearly reflected the peculiarly horizontal nature of environmental policies, but it has yet to define fully a distinctive role which does not create turf-battles with others. Initially, the government proposed that this Committee be called a Sustainable Development Audit Committee but it was renamed in order to be more understandable to the public. Whether this change of name will encourage the Committee to avoid the more radical implications of the sustainable development agenda remains to be seen but it will be a lost opportunity if it does. The House of Lords Select Committees have provided a consistent focus for inquiry into proposed European Community environmental legislation at a time when its significance was little recognised in the House of Commons, and its body of reports has generally commanded respect both in this country and other parts of the Community, including the European Commission. Furthermore, since it lacks the department structures of the Commons Committees, it has shown more flexibility in establishing particular select committees on issues such as sustainable development.[33] Similarly, the Science and

[32] Reflecting the experiments made at European Community level with Joint Council of Ministers on issues such as energy/environment and transport/environment, and a particular feature of the recent British Presidency. The Committee structure of the European Parliament remains heavily sectorally based, and pressure for new initiatives can be expected.

[33] *Report from the Select Committee on Sustainable Development.* HL Paper 72. Session 1994-5 (London: HMSO. 1995).

Technology Committee has addressed a number of critical areas of environmental concern. The role of such committees into a reformed House of Lords, and their effective co-ordination with the functions of their counterparts in the Commons appears to have been little addressed as yet.

Devolution, Westminster and Whitehall

The relationship between the new devolved administrations and Westminster and Whitehall will be crucially influenced by the nature of Community and international environmental obligations. A division of powers which preserves international and Community affairs for Westminster sits uneasily with the nature of contemporary environmental politics, where there is a dynamic linkage between international, regional, national and local action. International environmental treaties continue to develop in importance. The relationship between environmental protection and the liberalisation of world trade underpinned by the General Agreement on Trade and Tariffs and new initiatives such as the proposed Multi-lateral Investment Agreement is of equal significance, and potentially inhibits the capacity of nation states, let alone regional administrations, to promote unilateral environmental policies. Despite the development of an environmental division of the International Court of Justice, in the past many international environmental treaties have probably been more honoured in their breach than obeyance. But more recent environmental treaties have paid far more attention to developing more sophisticated administrative mechanisms for monitoring compliance, increasing the pressure on signatory states to demonstrate good faith. Furthermore, contemporary international obligations such as those under the Climate Change Convention and its Protocols potentially have immense significance for the internal policies of countries, and achieving, say, carbon dioxide reduction obligations can involve a range of sectoral areas such as transport, energy production, building standards, and domestic energy conservation. Potential areas of conflict between Westminster and the regions can be predicted. Suppose the Welsh Assembly fails to introduce policies restricting business parking. Could a Secretary of State invoke his powers under the Government of Wales Act to direct the Assembly to take action in order to give effect to Climate Change obligations?[34] Or, as Paul Craig notes, the demarcation of reserved functions under the Scotland Act bristles with potential ambiguities. Could the Scottish Parliament legislate to prohibit the disposal of radioactive waste or the field testing of genetically modified

---

[34] Under s. 108 of the Government of Wales Act the Secretary of State may direct the Welsh Assembly to take action required for giving effect to international obligations or require it not to take action incompatible with such obligations.

foodstuffs in Scotland on environmental grounds, or does this clearly fall within one of the areas reserved for Westminster?[35]

Conclusions

Environmental policy has moved well beyond a model of public administration where problems were clearly identifiable as discretely environmental, amenable to scientific or technical analysis, and soluble by classical regulatory intervention. Uncertainty and risk pervade many areas of the environmental challenge, and competing visions of what is implied by an environmentally sound, let alone a sustainable, society abound. Some important institutional changes have been initiated, yet, as other chapters indicate in relation to constitutional change, no one really knows the outcome. As O'Riordan and Voisey have noted in a recent study, 'Sustainable development is a socially motivating force where we are not at all sure where we will end up but we keep on trying because we perceive our long term survival is at stake.'[36]

Constitutional change is about altering the relationships of citizens with government and parliament, and of levels of government with each other. Some impacts of the current changes under way can be predicted. The courts will be more involved in environmental litigation, both in boundary disputes between levels of government and in developing principles of environmental and human rights. Devolution will lead to potentially variegated environmental standards in different parts of the United Kingdom, but with the concomitant need to develop new institutional mechanisms for co-operation and co-ordination. Other aspects of contemporary debate concerning the environment and sustainability appear to be scarcely addressed by the current proposals. The precise role and powers of local authorities in securing policy goals still remain uncertain despite the commitment to put sustainable development at the heart of their functions.[37] The degree to which current models of devolution will satisfy environmental demands, for local empowerment set against the apparently contradictory internationalisation of many economic and environmental issues is equally unclear. Other aspects of the current constitutional changes would appear to many involved in environmental and sustainability

---

[35] Environmental policies are essentially devolved to the Scottish Parliament, but Schedule 5 of the Scotland Act, 'nuclear energy and nuclear installations', are reserved matters for Westminster; but this reservation does not include the subject matter of the Radioactive Substances Act 1993, which regulates the disposal of radioactive waste. Product standards and requirements in relation to Community obligations and product labelling are reserved matters, but food and agricultural produce are exempted from the reservation.

[36] T. O'Riordan, and H. Voisey, *Sustainable Development in Western Europe: Coming to Terms with Agenda 21* (London: Fank Cass, 1998).

[37] *Modern Local Government – In Touch with the People*, para. 8.10.

politics to be based on overly conventional models of divisions of power and representative democracy which will do little to progress the more radical agenda. Openness of decision making, new mechanisms for exploring and articulating public values, and imaginative means of securing cross-departmental co-operation are all likely to be important elements of future debates. It is perhaps asking too much of the current proposals to address them all. Constitutional change will undoubtedly shift conventional patterns of decision making in profound ways and with consequences that are uncertain. What is rather more predictable is that those involved in the current environmental and sustainability debate will fully exploit the new opportunities provided by the changes under way as a means for influencing the future direction of policy.

CHAPTER 5

MODERNISING ENVIRONMENTAL JUSTICE – REGULATION AND THE ROLE OF AN ENVIRONMENTAL TRIBUNAL*

Procedures have grown up haphazardly with no apparent underlying principle, and we consider they fail to provide a system appropriate for contemporary needs. We recommend the establishment of Environmental Tribunals to handle appeals under environmental legislation other than the town and country planning system.

Royal Commission on Environmental Pollution
23rd Report 'Environmental Planning' 2002

We express our conviction that the deficiency in the knowledge, relevant skills and information in regard to environmental law is one of the principal causes that contribute to the lack of effective implementation, development and enforcement of environmental law.

Johannesburg Global Judges Symposium 2002

In order to contribute to the protection of the right of every person of present and future generations to live in an environment adequate to his or her health and well-being, each Party shall guarantee the rights of access to information, public participation in decision making, and access to justice in environmental matters in accordance with the provisions of this Convention.

Aarhus Convention 1998

Key Messages of the Study

1.   This study is concerned with modernising the ways in which we handle environmental regulation. It stems from a recent recommendation of the Royal Commission on Environmental Pollution that a specialist environmental tribunal system be set up to consolidate and rationalise a range of environmental appeal mechanisms which are currently distributed amongst an array of different courts and other bodies.

---

*Macrory R (2003) with Woods M_Modernising Environmental Justice: Regulation and the Role of an Environmental Tribunal   Centre for Law and the Environment, University College, London.

2   The right of applicants for planning permission to appeal to the
       Secretary of State is a familiar and developed feature of our land-
       use planning system. Land-use planning appeals are handled
       (and most cases now decided by) the Planning Inspectorate.
       Similar rights of appeal have been built into many existing
       environmental laws, ranging from waste management licensing
       to the service of statutory nuisance abatement notices. But the
       institutions that determine such appeals are many and varied.
       This study has examined over 50 different appeal provisions in
       contemporary environmental legislation, with appeal bodies
       ranging from the Secretary of State and the Planning Inspectorate
       under delegated powers, to the magistrates' courts, county courts
       and the High Court. There are also examples where the applicant
       has no right to question regulatory decision other than by way of
       judicial review.

3.   The system that has developed is complex, and not one easily
       intelligible to direct users, let alone the general public. It lacks
       any underlying coherence, and fails to reflect contemporary
       developments in environmental law. The system's haphazard
       nature can only be explained by the fact that as new environmental
       regulatory requirements have been introduced, decisions as to
       the choice of appeal route have been made on a pragmatic basis
       from a diversity of existing bodies which were not originally
       established for such purposes.

4.   Pragmatism can often be a virtue. But evidence from existing
       users of the system (including regulatory bodies) suggests
       unease with the current arrangements. It is questionable
       whether local magistrates' courts are the best fora for handling
       technically complex appeals brought by trade and industry
       under statutory nuisance provisions, and even more so, appeals
       under the emerging contaminated land regime. The Planning
       Inspectorate appears to be coping effectively with the relatively
       small number of environmental appeals that it now handles,
       but there are concerns about how it deals with difficult legal
       issues, the accessibility of its decision letters, and the fact that it
       is not a suitable forum for providing authoritative decisions on
       environmental appeals which can then be used as more general
       guidance for the better application of environmental regulation.
       There are also glaring gaps in the existing legislation where no
       appeal route is provided.

5.   The study has also considered pressures on existing judicial review
       procedures. An examination of over 50 case files over the past three

years has indicated that judicial review applications concerning environmental decisions are brought as much by industry as by members of the public or environmental organisations, and are frequently merits driven rather than concerned with purely legal grounds. Failure to tackle the existing weaknesses and gaps in appeal mechanisms will only increase the pressure on judicial review as a default appeal route to which it is not best suited.

6   One way forward is based on the adaptation of current arrangements, and the study identifies a number of possible improvements which could be made to existing institutions. This includes the transfer of contaminated land remediation notice appeals to the Lands Tribunal, and the strengthening of legal and environmental expertise within the Planning Inspectorate.

7.   However, this is likely to be very much a second-best solution. A key concern is whether such a 'pick and match' approach can be sustained in the light of future demands. On the horizon there is a range of new and challenging sets of environmental requirements, often involving smarter regulatory concepts than more traditional approaches – examples include end of life vehicles, carbon dioxide emissions trading, agricultural waste and environmental liability to name but a few. An appeals system based on a specialised tribunal, bringing heightened legal authority and coherence to the system, would significantly improve confidence in future environmental regulation for direct users, the regulatory authorities, and the general public.

8.   The need for a specialised jurisdiction is reflected in the distinctive characteristics of contemporary environmental law, and it is possible to identify a core environmental jurisdiction that could fall within a new Environmental Tribunal system. Estimates of the current numbers of environmental regulatory appeals being made indicate that that they could be transferred to a single Environmental Tribunal operating along similar lines to the current Lands Tribunal, with establishment costs of under £2m. This would provide a secure basis for any extension of jurisdiction to meet future requirements. Such a tribunal would fall within the new unified Tribunals Service, and benefit from being associated with the Government's reform programme for tribunals.

9.   The need for a new institutional framework is all the more pressing given the changing context of the role of environmental regulatory appeals. The Aarhus Convention, in particular, promotes the

concept of a more active environmental citizenship, and introduces a new concept of environmental justice. This includes the right to legal review mechanisms for members of the public and non-governmental organisations that are fair, equitable, timely and not prohibitively expensive. An Environmental Tribunal is likely to provide a more appropriate basis for meeting the aspirations of Aarhus than relying on current procedures.

10   The model of the Environmental Tribunal considered in this study is more modest than earlier proposals for a 'one-stop' environmental court or a land and environment tribunal. Yet it is also one that offers a manageable and viable solution, with a core structure that could be established without undue cost or administrative upheaval. Regulatory appeal mechanisms are only one element of our system for delivering and implementing environmental law, but they play a vital role, and their potential benefits have been largely ignored to date. A new appeal body in the form of such an Environmental Tribunal would bring greater coherence and authority to the development of the legal and policy dimensions of environmental regulation, and would make a significant contribution to our justice system.

The Report

1.   The Context

1.1   Environmental law has grown rapidly in its scope and content in this country over the last two decades. It is a subject that is being continually developed to face new environmental challenges. Much effort is currently being focused on ensuring that the design of modern environmental regulation is proportionate, intelligible for the user, and effective in achieving beneficial outcomes. This study, though, is not concerned with the substantive content of regulation – it is equally important that we have in place the most appropriate legal machinery to resolve environmental disputes in a way that is fair, attracts public confidence, and provides an authoritative and coherent approach to environmental law and policy. This led us to concentrate on certain key aspects of the current arrangements for administering and implementing environmental regulation.

1.2   This challenge of institutional design is not unique to the United Kingdom. Other countries have developed or are thinking about new legal machinery for handling the interpretation and application of environmental law. In this country, various models for change have been proposed during the last decade or so. The 1989 Carnwath Report on Enforcing Planning Control argued the need to review the jurisdictions of the various courts and tribunals dealing with different aspects of what might be called 'environmental protection' (including planning), and saw merit in combining them in a single jurisdiction.[1] In his 1991 Garner Lecture 'Are the Judiciary Environmentally Myopic?', Lord Woolf spoke of the benefits of a specialist tribunal with a general responsibility for overseeing and enforcing safeguards provided for the protection of the environment.[2] Professor Malcolm Grant's major study on Environmental Courts, commissioned by the government and published in 2000[3], identified six alternative models, ranging from a planning appeals tribunal to an environmental court as a new division of the High Court. But at the time, the government was not convinced of the need for change, and were particularly concerned about the institutional upheaval involved in introducing such models. In the Parliamentary debate on the issue, the government minister noted the apparent lack of consensus on the types of environmental issues that might be included in a new jurisdiction, as well as the diversity of courts that could currently deal with what might be described as environmental disputes[4]. Any significant institutional change was also considered premature prior to the outcome of major reviews of the criminal and tribunal systems then being undertaken.

1.3   More recently, there has been much increased international discussion and co-operation amongst the judiciary in the search for new approaches to environmental law and the mechanisms for delivering effective results. In August 2002, senior members of the judiciary from sixty countries met at the Global Judges Symposium as part of the Johannesburg World Summit. They affirmed the Johannesburg Principles on the Role of Law and Sustainable Development[5], stressing the vital role of the judiciary and environmental law in the enhancement of the public interest in a healthy and secure environment. This has been followed by meetings of the judiciary in London last year, and most recently in Rome in May 2003, where the establishment of a European

---

[1] Robert Carnwath QC, *Enforcing Planning Control*, published by the Department of the Environment, April 1989

[2] Woolf LCJ, Garner Lecture, 'Are the Judiciary Environmentally Myopic', *Journal of Environmental Law*, Vol 4, No 1, p.1

[3] M.Grant, Department of the Environment Transport and the Regions (UK), Environmental Court Project FinalReport (2000)

[4] House of Lords Hansard 9th October 2000

[5] The full text of the Johannesburg Principles is reproduced in *Journal of Environmental Law* (2003) Vol 15, No. 1

Judicial Forum was confirmed. Key substantial issues identified at the Rome meeting for further work included:

- the pros and cons of establishing specialist environmental courts or tribunals.

- the ability of citizens to obtain access to the courts to further enhance the effective implementation, compliance with, and enforcement of environmental laws.

- consideration of environmental scientific evidence and the fashioning of appropriate remedies, including restoration of the environment.

2.   The Report of the Royal Commission on Environmental Pollution

2.1   The most recent significant UK study dealing with these issues, and which provides the context for this report, was the 23rd Report of the Royal Commission on Environmental Pollution (RCEP), entitled *Environmental Planning* and published in 2002[6]. Much of the RCEP's study was concerned with improving strategic planning for the environment, but it also included recommendations dealing with current institutional arrangements for handling planning and environmental disputes.

2.2   Following the recent establishment of the Administrative Court, the RCEP did not consider that there now exists a compelling case for creating a specialist environmental division of the High Court to handle environmental judicial reviews. It was of the view that criminal environmental offences were probably still best handled by ordinary criminal courts, though it recommended improved training for magistrates. The RCEP also recognised that in respect of applicants for planning permission, we have a well developed system of appeal procedures under the town and country planning legislation as handled by the Planning Inspectorate.

2.3   But when the RCEP examined current arrangements for dealing with environmental appeals outside the planning system, such as appeals against the refusal of a waste management licence, or the service of a statutory nuisance abatement notice, it concluded that the present system lacked consistency and coherence, both

---

[6] Royal Commission on Environmental Pollution 23rd Report *Environmental Planning* Cm 5459, 2002, Stationery Office, London

as to whether there are any rights of appeal on merits, and as to which forum decides such appeals. It therefore recommended the establishment of a new environmental tribunal system to consolidate and rationalise the handling of such appeals. Although the RCEP recognised that there might be merit in bringing all environmental appeals under the jurisdiction of the Planning Inspectorate, it considered that it would be preferable to establish a specialist environmental tribunal system in order to provide a more visible focus for the development and application of environmental law and policy, and to avoid environmental appeals being treated as a sub-set of the much greater number of planning appeals.

3.   The Purpose of This Study

3.1   The aim of this project has been to test the merits of the RCEP proposal in greater detail, and to provide more extensive underlying data to allow a rigorous analysis of some of the important questions that need to be addressed if the proposal is to be taken forward:

- How coherent is the present system for appeals?

- Are there concerns with how current arrangements operate in practice, and could these be met by incremental adaptation rather than a new tribunal system?

- Will the current arrangements be able to handle the new environmental legislation on the horizon?

- Would there be a viable jurisdiction for an Environmental Tribunal?

- What would be the likely workload, and what are the costs and benefits involved?

- What are the current pressures on judicial review procedures, and to what extent could these be addressed by a new Environmental Tribunal?

- Would a specialist Environmental Tribunal improve confidence in the application and enforcement of environmental law?

- Would such a Tribunal contribute towards meeting the aspirations of active environmental citizenship underlying the Aarhus Convention?

3.2 The research also needs to be seen in the context of wider concerns about the current effectiveness of environmental law, including the adequacy of criminal penalties and enforcement mechanisms. The RCEP model did not envisage an environmental tribunal system directly handling criminal cases, which would remain as now with the criminal courts. We will argue that a coherent regulatory appeals system is in any event an important element for the more effective enforcement of environmental regulation, but we also consider later in the report the extent to which an Environmental Tribunal system might take on more overt enforcement functions.

3.3 The current regulatory arrangements now need to be tested against the provisions of the 1998 Aarhus Convention on Access to Information, Public Participation in Decision-Making and Access to Justice in Environmental Matters. The Convention (which is in the process of implementation within the European Community) promotes the concept of an active environmental citizenship to ensure sustainable and environmentally sound development, including public participation, transparency, and accessible and effective judicial mechanisms. Governments are required to establish and maintain 'a clear, transparent and consistent framework' to implement the Convention's requirements. We have to consider the extent to which a new Environmental Tribunal system might contribute to fulfilling both the letter and spirit of Aarhus.

3.4 Our study should also be viewed in the context of the government's current reform programme for tribunals, following the 2001 Leggatt Report, *Tribunals for Users*[7]. The government has recently announced its intention to create a unified Tribunals Service responsible to the Lord Chancellor as part of its wider agenda for reforming the country's legal systems and public services. Current plans envisage the establishment of such a service in incremental stages, and a White Paper should be published later this year. The Leggatt Report was largely concerned with existing tribunals rather than the creation of new jurisdictions, but contains a valuable set of principles against which changes

---

[7] *Tribunals for Users – One System, One Service – Report of the Review of Tribunals* by Sir Andrew Leggatt, March 2001,Stationery Office, London

to the current system of environmental appeal procedures can be judged. It is clearly important that any proposals for change are consistent with the proposed reforms of the tribunals system as a whole.

3.5   This report is focused on the legislation and appeals procedures in England and Wales only. Nevertheless, we suspect that many of the underlying concerns and the arguments for change will be of relevance to Scotland and Northern Ireland as well.

4.   Environmental Appeals Under Existing Legislation

4.1   A key part of the research has been to establish in more detail the range of what might legitimately be described as environmental appeals provided for in existing legislation, as well as the current numbers of such appeals taking place. The types of appeals that we have considered fall into two broad categories:

(i)   appeals against the refusal of a licence/permit (or against conditions imposed in a licence/permit) required under environmental legislation

(ii)   appeals against some form of notice served under environmental legislation requiring remedial action or the cessation of activities

4.2   We describe these as 'regulatory appeals' in part to distinguish them from judicial review applications. The appeals are distinct from legal actions between private parties such as private nuisance actions, but are concerned with resolving disputes between the citizen (whether an individual or a company) and the state (in the form of central government, a specialised agency, or local government). This is described in the Leggatt Report as the typical jurisdiction of most tribunals. One distinction, though, from the range of work carried out by many existing tribunals is that the majority of regulatory decisions in environmental law that might be subject to appeal are likely to involve companies and businesses rather than private individuals. Statutory nuisances are an exception where many appeals, such as those relating to noise nuisance or housing conditions, involve domestic premises. Importantly, where such rights of 'regulatory appeal' exist, they currently rest with the person or business immediately affected (i.e. the licence applicant or the person served with the notice), and other members of the public have no general right of appeal other than by way of judicial review, and subject to normal standing requirements. The question of whether third party rights of appeal should be introduced within an Environmental Tribunal system is considered more fully later in this study.

4.3　Where grounds of appeal are provided in the legislation, they are typically very broad, covering both the factual merits of the original decision, procedural questions, and questions of law. In other cases, appeals are effectively based on the right to a *de novo* decision. Regulatory appeals are therefore in effect full merits appeals, often involving questions of fact and law, and should be treated as distinct from judicial review applications where more restricted grounds of review apply – though we consider later in the study the extent to which judicial review procedures in environmental matters are in practice being used a default merits appeal route.

4.4　The regulatory appeals that we have described are concerned with resolving disputes concerning the validity of the action of a governmental body rather than the prosecution of environmental offences. We discuss further on in the report whether any Environmental Tribunal system could usefully incorporate enforcement functions in addition to determining regulatory appeals, but in any event there is an intimate connection between a regulatory appeals system and environmental enforcement. Non-compliance with an environmental licence or permit, or with notices such as those served under statutory nuisance or contaminated land legislation, is generally deemed to be a criminal offence, and under contemporary environmental legislation there are now few 'stand-alone' environmental criminal offences, i.e. nearly all such offences are at least indirectly connected with the type of licence or notice handled by the environmental regulators as described above. A regulatory appeals system which can deliver effective, consistent, and authoritative rulings on the interpretation and application of regulatory requirements can therefore be seen as an essential building block – though not the only one – in ensuring improved compliance with, and the enforcement of environmental legislation.

4.5　The government's agenda for the reform of public services emphasises the need for modern, user-focused services, and any critique of the current arrangements for handling environmental appeals should be seen from the perspective of the user. The direct users of the current appeal system are the individuals or companies who are subject to environmental regulation and would legitimately expect the opportunity to question the factual and legal basis of administrative decisions directly affecting them. But in the environmental field there are also other interests involved whose perspectives need to be taken into account, and might best be described as 'indirect' users. They include:

- Bodies responsible for implementing environmental regulation who should be able to rely on an appeals system that delivers decisions with consistency and authority, even where individual decisions are made against them (e.g. the Environment Agency and English Nature).

- Members of the public who are indirectly affected by environmental decisions taken by regulatory bodies (e.g. owner/occupiers in the vicinity of a proposed landfill site). Whilst the main impact of administrative decisions in fields such as social security entitlement or immigration is likely to be on the individual seeking entitlement, the environmental field is distinctive in that decisions taken by regulatory bodies may also have real or perceived impacts on the health and physical environment enjoyed by a wide group of third parties.

- Companies seeking to comply with regulatory requirements who do not necessarily wish to exercise rights of appeal, but need to be assured that where competitors do appeal, decisions are made fairly and consistently.

- The general public, who have a stake in a system that delivers effective environmental outcomes in a manner in which they can have confidence.

5.   Legislative Analysis

5.1   We have conducted a systematic analysis of legislation to determine the extent of current appeal provisions and their decision forums. Determining the boundaries of 'environmental' legislation with precision is always a question of judgment, but we have excluded from the analysis at one end of the spectrum, town and country planning and transport legislation, legislation broadly concerned with amenity questions (such as tree preservation orders or hedgerow appeals), valuation appeals and the type of land dispute that falls within the jurisdiction of the Lands Tribunal; and at the other end, we exclude health and safety, and similar workplace controls.

5.2   We do not claim this to be a complete exercise, nor that all such appeals should necessarily be handled by a single Tribunal system. Nevertheless, Appendix A lists over 50 different appeal routes under specialised environmental legislation that fall within these parameters. Broadly, we can categorise the different routes of appeal under the following headings:

(a)   Appeals to local magistrates' courts (mainly in respect of notices served by local authorities under statutory nuisance and contaminated land provisions).

(b)   Appeals to the Secretary of State but formally delegated to the Planning Inspectorate (mainly Integrated Pollution and Prevention Control (IPPC) consents, waste management licences, and water discharge consents, plus contaminated land notices for 'special' sites designated by the Environment Agency).

(c)   Appeals to the Secretary of State which are handled by the Planning Inspectorate but with the final decision resting with the Secretary of State.

(d)   Appeals to the Secretary of State where no specific procedure may yet have been identified.

(e)   Appeals to the High Court on merits grounds (a rag-bag set of provisions, often dealing with off-shore activities).

(f)   Miscellaneous appeals to a variety of other courts and tribunals (including, for instance, the County Court in respect of charging notices served under the contaminated land regime)

(g)   Cases where no right of merits appeal is provided under the legislation (typically where the initial decision is made by the Secretary of State such as on GMO licences; in some cases the procedures allow for further representations to be made on proposed decisions, but otherwise it is necessary to use judicial review as a default means of appeal)

(h)   The use of arbitration (as introduced in respect of decisions by the Secretary of State under recent voluntary agreements concerning carbon emission reductions to avoid the likelihood of judicial review)

5.3   The only existing appeal route against the refusal by a public body to release environmental information under the Environmental

Information Regulations has to date been by way of judicial review. A Consultation Paper was issued by government in November 2002, proposing an appeal route in respect of environmental information to the new Information Commissioner with a further right of appeal to the Information Tribunal established under the Freedom of Information Act 2000. Against this background, we do not consider this area of law further in the report.

5.4   The pattern of appeal routes clearly presents a complex picture and one not easily intelligible to the expert, let alone the ordinary citizen. Even within some discrete regimes, such as contaminated land, there is more than one appeal body involved. It is not easy to discern any underlying principles that determine the choice of appeal forum, though some rationale can be identified in particular cases. Statutory nuisance provisions, for example, were based on structures originating in nineteenth century public health legislation and were already locked into the magistrates' courts system before appeal provisions against notices were introduced (first for noise nuisances in 1974 and then for other statutory nuisances in 1990). Statutory nuisance abatement notice appeals may be argued to involve the need for local knowledge where magistrates are considered to have expertise. The new contaminated land provisions were modelled on the statutory nuisance provisions, justifying the choice of magistrates' courts rather than any other forum for dealing with appeals in respect of local authority sites. IPPC and waste management consents are usually associated with land based projects which perhaps explains the choice of the Planning Inspectorate as the body for handling appeals. Three examples of key legislative appeal mechanisms are provided in Box 1.

BOX 1 – Examples of Key Legislative Appeal Mechanisms		
WASTE	**CONTAMINATED LAND**	**GENETICALLY MODIFIED ORGANISMS**
Waste management on land in the UK is regulated under Part II of the Environmental Protection Act 90 and related regulations, on order to comply with the EC Waste Framework Directive.	The new contaminated land regime is covered by Section 78A of the Environmental Protection Act 1990 (introduced by the Environment Act 1995) and related regulations.	The deliberate release and contained use of Genetically Modified Organisms (GMOs) are controlled under separate legislation designed to implement relevant EC requirements.

This legislation set up a waste management licensing system to cover the keeping, treatment and disposal of controlled waste, under the supervision of the Environment Agency.

There is a right of appeal to the Secretary of State in relation to decisions by the Environment Agency on licence applications, including their tran sfer or surrender. This right of appeal is available to the applicant, the holder or a proposed transferee of a licence. The appeals can take the form of a hearing or written representations, and are delegated to the Planning Inspectorate. Such delegation is normally carried out as the need arises, by way of a formal letter with legally binding effect.

The Government is currently consulting on the proposed End of Life Vehicles (Storage and Treatm- ent) (England and Wales)

Local authorities are under a duty to inspect their areas in order to identify contaminated sites so that remediation can be addressed. The local authority is then to serve a remediation notice on those parties it considers should be responsible for carrying out the remediation. This will mainly be the person who 'caused or knowingly permitted' the contamination to take place, but if such a person cannot be found, then liability may rest with the current owner or occupier. The local authority will need to allocate liability where a number of parties have contributed to the contamination. Local authorities also have default powers to carry out remediation work and then recover their costs. If a site is more seriously contaminated, then it will be designated a 'special' site, in which case, the Environment Agency takes responsibility for addressing the remediation process.

Under the new Genetically Modified Organisms (Deliberate Release) Regulations 2002, the Secretary of State can authorise the release of GMOs into the environment. Applications for commercial releases need a collective decision by all the EC Member States, but decisions on releases for certain research purposes can be taken by the Secretary of State without the same level of EC involvement. Such decisions are handled by Defra officials in practice, based on EC consultations, expert advice and any public representations. However, no formal right of appeal is provided in the Regulations, and applicants would have to use judicial review to challenge the decision

The Genetically Modified Organisms (Contained Use) Regulations 2000 cover the use of GMOs in laboratory and similar conditions where there is a

Regulations 2003, which will implement (in part) the EC End of Life Vehicles Directive. These Regulations will require some operators of sites who currently comply with the waste management licensing system, to obtain a permit if they wish to continue to undertake recovery activities on end of life vehicles before existing pollutants have been removed. A right of appeal would be available against decisions taken by the Environment Agency to the Secretary of State, or her appointee.	Parties served with a remediation notice have a right of appeal. If the notice was served by a local authority the appeal will be heard by the local magistrates' court. If the notice was served by the Environment Agency then the appeal is to the Secretary of State. Such appeals can take the form of a hearing or written representations, and are currently delegated to the Planning Inspectorate.

In addition, there is a right of appeal to the county court in respect of a charging notice served by a local authority in order to recover its costs in carrying out remediation work itself. There is also a right of appeal to the Secretary of State regarding a determination by an authority to hold confidential information relating to the affairs of an individual or business on a public register for contaminated sites. | barrier to contact with the public. Applications for authorisations are processed by the Health and Safety Executive, and decisions are made by the Secretary of State and the Health and Safety Executive acting jointly. There is a right of appeal available to the Secretary of State. |

5.5   Nevertheless, one must suspect that as new environmental
       requirements have been introduced, choices as to appeal
       routes have been made on a pragmatic basis from the array of
       existing fora, leading to the haphazard nature of the present
       arrangements. A senior judge told us: 'Some environmental
       legislation is extraordinarily deficient in terms of the sufficiency
       or availability of appeal mechanisms...but pressures from the
       Human Rights Act and for third parties' rights will change
       this...' Complexity in itself is not necessarily a justification for
       change, but a drawback of the current disparate structure is that
       it may inhibit consistent approaches to resolving environmental
       appeals, and the development of environmental decision-making
       that will attract both business and public confidence. An effective
       appeals system is equally important for the confidence of those
       public bodies charged with the responsibility for delivering
       environmental regulation, and as we have noted, is closely linked
       to more effective criminal enforcement.

5.6   In addition, we need a system that will meet future environmental
       regulatory requirements. This need is particularly driven by
       developments in the European Community (EC), and Box 2
       provides a selective list of anticipated EC legislation, requiring
       transposition into UK law, much of which will require new appeal
       procedures. Looking to the future, a key policy choice has to be
       taken as to whether it is preferable to continue to make pragmatic
       choices as to appeal routes on an ad hoc basis by loading the
       variety of existing institutions with new responsibilities, or if it
       would be better to establish a more specialised Environmental
       Tribunal system with the expertise and capability to handle both
       current and future requirements.

BOX 2 – Selected New And Anticipated EC Legislation			
STATUS	ISSUE	TYPE OF MEASURE	PURPOSE
Adopted	Emissions Ceilings	Directive	Sets national emissions ceilings for SO_2, NO_x, VOCs and NH3 to be reached by 2010, requiring the extension of air pollution controls through IPPC to ammonia emissions from agriculture and in particular the dairy sector
Adopted	Waste Electrical & Electronic Equipment (WEEE)	Directive	Requires that producers (manufacturers, sellers, distributors) will be responsible for financing the collection, treatment, recovery and disposal of WEEE from private households which are deposited at collection facilities (and from non-households from 2005)
Adopted	Restriction of Hazardous Substances in Electrical and Electronic Equipment (ROHS)	Directive	Restricts the use of certain hazardous substances in the manufacturing of new electrical and electronic equipment
Adopted	End of Life Vehicles (ELVs)	Directive	Requires that producers reduce the use of hazardous substances and increase the quantity of recycled materials in the manufacture of vehicles and (from 2007) pay the costs of free take-back of zero or negative value vehicles to authorised treatment facilities
Adopted	Water	Framework Directive	Requires that all inland and coastal waters reach 'good status' by 2015 by establishing a river basin district structure within which environmental objectives will be set, including ecological targets for surface waters

Pending	IPPC	Possible amending Directive	Possible general review and revision of IPPC to expand its scope by applying the Directive to industrial activities not currently subject to IPPC; may also amend the energy efficiency provisions in light of the proposed Directive on emissions trading
Pending	Emissions Trading	Directive	To prepare for a single EC greenhouse gas emissions trading regime by 2005
Pending	EU Chemicals Policy	Proposed Regulation	To create a single regulatory system for existing and new chemical substances
Pending	Environmental Liability	Directive	Proposes a harmonised European civil liability regime
Pending	Traceability of Genetically Modified Organisms (GMOs) & Products Derived from GMOs, & Labelling of GMOs	Amending Directive	To provide a framework for the traceability of GMOs & food & feed produce from GMOs, with the objective of facilitating accurate labelling, environmental monitoring and the withdrawal of products
Pending	Packaging Waste Targets	Amending Directive	To fix new targets for recovering and recycling packaging waste to be achieved by 2006
Pending	Mining Waste	Measure to be proposed	To regulate the handling and storage of hazardous waste arising from mining
Pending	Battery & Accumulator Waste	Amending Directive	To cover the disposal, recycling & collection of batteries as well as the the banning of nickel/cadmium in certain types of batteries

n.b. this list is indicative only

6. Current Numbers of Environmental Appeals

6.1 Our research has also explored the numbers of environmental appeals currently taking place under the environmental legislation identified above. There are no comprehensive statistics maintained by government, which is perhaps not surprising given the variety of routes that exist. We would recommend at the very least that government pays greater attention in the future to monitoring the number of environmental appeals being made on a more systematic and complete basis than is currently the case. Details of the figures we have been able to acquire are contained in Appendices B and C, and are focused on statutory nuisance appeals heard in magistrates' courts and those environmental appeals handled by the Planning Inspectorate. For other appeals such as those to the county court or the more specialised routes to the High Court, we suspect that the numbers are small, or that in some instances appeal rights have not yet been exercised.

6.2 For statistical purposes, the Planning Inspectorate includes hedgerow appeals under its category of 'environmental appeals', but as indicated we have excluded them from our list of environmental regulatory appeals as being more akin to land-use planning and amenity issues. In the twelve month period between April 2002 and March 2003, the number of environmental appeals as we have defined them received by the Planning Inspectorate was 233, with the vast majority (211) relating to water discharge consents. Other categories of appeals included: waste management regulation (8); Integrated Pollution Control and Air Pollution Control under Part I of the Environmental Protection Act 1990 (8); water abstraction (3); and anti-pollution works in respect of water (3)[8]. During this twelve month period, 68 appeals were withdrawn or turned away as invalid or out of time, and there were 8 decisions issued. There is also a very large backlog of appeals relating to water discharge consents (755), and our understanding is that these are either still the subject of negotiation between the parties and the regulatory authority, or have been held up pending policy advice being provided by the Department for Environment, Food and Rural Affairs (Defra).

6.3 For contaminated land, the procedures are insufficiently mature to predict the typical numbers of appeals that might be made. For 'special' sites handled by the Environment Agency, 13 sites had

---

[8] Source, Planning Inspectorate

been designated by the end of 2002 with a target set of 80 sites by 2007. To date 47 sites have been designated by local authorities, but information on predicted numbers is still difficult to obtain. One leading expert on the subject whom we interviewed, predicted a growing number of appeals, rising to around 100 a year in ten year's time, mainly in respect of local authority notices.

6.4   For statutory nuisance appeals, there are no current comprehensive statistics available on a national basis. With the assistance of the Chartered Institute of Environmental Health, we have therefore surveyed all local authorities in England and Wales, and the response rate has been sufficient to form a general picture of overall numbers. Details of the survey are provided in Appendix B. There is clearly a variable picture across the country with some local authorities having no appeals, whilst others experience considerable numbers. From the returns we estimate that around 14,700 statutory nuisance notices are issued each year, with about 3,000 being served on trade and industry. There appear to be around 1,000 appeals made each year to magistrates' courts. Many of these are likely to involve domestic noise nuisances or housing repairs, but we estimate that around 135 are made by trade and industry.

6.5   Compared to land-use planning appeals (running at around 14,000 per year) the total number of environmental regulatory appeals currently being made is therefore not large. Such a workload is clearly much less than that undertaken by the first tier tribunals such as the Appeals Service or the Immigration Appellate Authorities, but is comparable to some of the smaller, specialised tribunals. The Lands Tribunal, for example, which acts both as a first tier and appellate body, disposes of around 600 cases a year. Assuming at least the inclusion of the environmental appeals currently handled by the Planning Inspectorate, contaminated land remediation notice appeals and those statutory nuisance abatement notice appeals involving trade and industry, we estimate that under current legislation an Environmental Tribunal system could be handling a comparable figure to the Lands Tribunal, at around 500 appeals a year. This does not take into account future legislative requirements or the possible incorporation of some form of third party right of appeal. These numbers do not undermine the case for an Environmental Tribunal, but instead can be seen as a positive advantage when considering the costs and benefits of establishing a new discrete Tribunal. We would also note that:

- small numbers of appeals may indicate unease with or under-use of current procedures; for example, we were informed by one expert on the new contaminated land procedures that there was likely to be a reluctance amongst local authorities to make full use of the remediation notice powers because of unease with the capacity of local magistrates to handle such appeals.

- there remain significant 'gaps' under present environmental legislation where there are no rights of regulatory appeal other than by way of judicial review. We discuss the pressures on judicial review in section 9 below, and the extent to which this has become a surrogate means of merits appeal.

- the need for an effective and efficient appeal procedure is likely to increase as environmental requirements assume more public significance.

- those regulatory appeals which do take place are very often technically complex and therefore more time consuming.

- there is also a clear advantage in anticipating the future climate of environmental law resulting from European and international requirements. This is particularly significant in the context of the implementation of the Aarhus Convention which introduces the concept of 'equitable, timely, and not prohibitively expensive' appeal procedures for members of the public and environmental organisations in respect to specified licensing procedures (as discussed further in section 10 below). Scale as well as substance is also significant. For example, IPPC licensing requirements are being extended to around 1,600 pig and poultry operations; new permitting will be required for around 2,500 sites as a result of the End of Life Vehicles Directive; and the extension of waste legislation to cover agricultural waste is likely to require around 8,500 new licences, together with waste exemptions extending to 170,000 farms[9].

6.6 A concern with previous proposals for combined planning and environmental courts or tribunals was that the major institutional upheaval involved would outweigh the advantages

[9] Source: Environment Agency

that might flow from the proposals. The more focused model of an Environmental Tribunal system being considered here would require the transfer of appeal functions from the existing bodies identified above, but given the numbers involved, this should not cause significant disruption to those institutions. The size and costs involved are likely to be comparable to those for the Lands Tribunal. We consider in more detail, in section 15 below, a possible model and the likely costs involved. Even though there will be cost savings from reducing the pressure on existing appeal bodies, establishing a new Tribunal system is unlikely to be wholly cost neutral. However, it is clear from the existing numbers of appeals that we are talking of a manageable institution and one that can develop focus and coherence in a key area of public policy. It would also provide greater confidence in anticipating future environmental regulatory requirements. The policy gains from such a discrete initiative may be hard to quantify but could be very large.

7.   Concerns About Existing Appeal Procedures

7.1   Within the project time-scale, research on the quality of existing procedures has been necessarily limited, and largely confined to interviews with a number of senior members of the judiciary, experienced environmental law practitioners representing users of the system, and policy makers and officers in regulatory bodies with experience of the current system. Our survey of local authorities also invited comments on the quality of the present arrangements. These reflections are therefore bound to be somewhat impressionistic, but valuable insights have nevertheless emerged.

7.2   There does appear to be concern at the ability of lay magistrates to handle highly technical issues such as the definition of 'Best Practicable Means' (BPM) in statutory nuisance appeals involving trade and industry. Again, in relation to statutory nuisances, there are worries that appeal procedures are often used by trade and industry as a delaying tactic, and that appeals take too long to come to court (nine months was quoted as a typical figure). Appeals appear to be given a lower priority by court administrators by being reserved for infrequent 'local authority' days. A senior environmental health officer also commented that, 'cases take a long time because appeals are treated no differently by the courts to prosecutions.' Many environmental health officers do appear to favour the improved decision making which an Environmental Tribunal might bring, but would not wish to see the loss of local knowledge in such decision making. There is clearly a tension in environmental adjudication between the need for local fact finding and the need for expertise in handling technical issues. It may be possible to distinguish between more technically complex issues (such as BPM) and more straightforward environmental issues (such as neighbourhood noise nuisance) when considering whether there would be benefit in transferring jurisdiction for statutory nuisances appeals to a specialised tribunal.

7.3   Our interviews have also indicated a real concern as to whether current arrangements will deliver an effective appeals system in respect of remediation notices served under the contaminated land regime introduced by the Environment Act 1995. As detailed in Box 1, appeals for local authority sites will be made to local magistrates' courts, and current regulations specify 19 separate grounds of appeal, often involving highly complex issues of both a technical and economic nature. Appeals for the smaller number of 'special' sites identified by the Environment Agency are made to the Secretary of State and will be handled by the Planning Inspectorate. As mentioned above, this system was largely based on the model for statutory nuisance procedures, which justified the use of the magistrates' courts for appeals in respect of local authority sites, but as the writers of the leading guide to the legislation have noted: 'It must be questioned whether the magistrates' court is a suitable forum for resolving such appeals, and whether the civil procedures in the magistrates' court are adequate for the purpose. It also seems strange that there should be two entirely different modes and forms of appeal for ordinary remediation notices and for those relating to special sites.'[10]. A key objective in introducing the new contaminated regime was to increase the consistency of approach taken by different authorities, and there is understandable concern that the current appeal routes will undermine that goal. As one of the leading experts in the area told us: 'Consistency in judgement is the key to transparency in the contaminated land regime.'

7.4   We should stress that our analysis of environmental appeals currently heard in Magistrates' Courts is not intended to detract from the integrity or commitment of individual magistrates, or to question their concern to ensure the effective application of environmental law. Rather, it raises questions as to whether it is the best use of their time and the qualities they can bring to the justice system, if they are required to handle the sorts of issues involved in these types of environmental appeals.

[10] Tromans and Turrall-Clarke *Contaminated Land – The New Regime*, 2000 Sweet and Maxwell, London

7.5   We have noted that in addition to the more familiar land-use planning appeals, the Planning Inspectorate now handle a range of environmental appeals on behalf of the Secretary of State. These are mainly concerned with pollution related licences dealt with by the Environmental Agency. The Planning Inspectorate will also be responsible for appeals under the contaminated land regime relating to 'special' sites. A leading barrister with experience of environmental appeals handled by the Planning Inspectorate commented favourably on their approach and expertise: 'The strengths of the Planning Inspectorate are individual technical expertise, good legal awareness, good procedures, and flexibility'. However, he noted that difficult points of law could be a problem, and that greater use of legal expertise within the Planning Inspectorate would be valuable if the current system were continued, but also appreciated the wider advantages of bringing environmental matters into one forum by way of rationalisation. At present, our understanding is that where necessary, the Planning Inspectorate seeks legal advice on environmental law issues from the Government. Another leading environmental solicitor noted that the Planning Inspectorate 'does seem to be a default appeal forum for environmental matters but it is not the right place as the Inspectors are not generally legally trained'. He also questioned whether the Planning Inspectorate was the right forum for environmental appeals because of the distinctive nature of the legal and technical issues often involved: 'Environmental regulation is different from planning control as the former often focuses on whether active harm is being caused.'

7.6   Officials from regulatory bodies who had experienced environmental appeals handled by the Planning Inspectorate were reasonably favourable about the procedures, though there was concern that Inspectors may have problems in understanding specialist areas of the law, for example IPPC/PPC or concepts such as 'Best Available Techniques'. As one noted: 'In an ideal world, I would like there to be a specialist appeal body, but one could also improve the panel of environmentally trained Inspectors'. There was also concern at the difficulty in accessing decision letters from the Planning Inspectorate: 'PINS is opaque or worse when it comes to accessing decision letters, though my experience of appeal hearings is relatively favourable.' Regret was also expressed that individual decisions of the Planning Inspectorate do not have sufficient gravitas to be used as general guidance in the application of regulation: 'Proper reporting of cases is needed and PINS decisions don't carry the proper weight.'

7.7   Even if within their individual jurisdictions, the current arrangements for appeals were considered satisfactory by existing users – and the comments we have received suggest some distinct unease in certain areas - this fails to meet what are probably the more important deficiencies. There are significant gaps in the system where no appeal routes lie other than by way of judicial review, and there is a need to ensure an adequate and coherent basis for appeal mechanisms under future environmental regulation. The Aarhus Convention will require a framework that is clear, transparent and consistent, and review mechanisms for citizens that are fair, equitable, timely, and not prohibitively expensive. The current haphazard structure is based on a piecemeal and old fashioned approach towards the application of legislation concerning the environment, and fails to reflect the need for greater expertise and consistency brought about by the special characteristics of environmental law which are now emerging. As one leading solicitor commented: 'Trade and industry want consistency of approach even if the decision-makers are therefore tougher on them.' We consider the nature of these special features of environmental law in the following section.

8.   Does Environmental Law Warrant A Special Jurisdiction?

8.1   We have identified a broad range of appeals which can be described as environmental, but to warrant the establishment of a single form of tribunal to handle most or all of them, we need to establish whether there are sufficiently special features of environmental law which would justify such an approach. We feel it is possible to identify a number of distinctive elements:

(a)   Evidential and judgmental issues involving complex technical/ scientific questions, usually of a quite different sort to those found in planning/amenity type decisions. The nature of the science involved in many environmental and public health questions (such as pathways of exposure to pollutants, or effects of chemicals on human health) is often characterised by inherent uncertainties distinct from those found in disciplines such as engineering or surveying. As the RCEP pointed out in its 21st Report, Setting *Environmental Standards:* 'In a scientific assessment of an environmental issue there are bound to be limitations and uncertainties associated with the data at each stage.'[11]

---

[11] Royal Commission on Environmental Pollution, 21st Report *Setting Environmental Standards* Cm 4053, 1998, Stationery Office, London

(b)   A challenging legislative and policy base, which as demonstrated above, is rapidly developing.

(c)   The overlapping of remedies (civil and criminal) as well as interests (public and private). We have pointed out how the validity of licences and regulatory notices in environmental law are critically connected with the subsequent enforcement of environmental standards under criminal law. In relation to the interests involved, one environmental lawyer told us: 'Environmental law is qualitatively different from other areas of the law in terms of the values and interests that are engaged - many of which are not properly represented.'

(d)   A powerful and increasing body of EC legislation and a growing number of interpretative judgments of the European Court of Justice (notably in areas such as IPPC, waste management, water pollution, genetically modified organisms and habitats protection). The density of the European Community policy and legislative background in the environmental field is far greater than, say, in town and country planning (with the exception of environmental assessment requirements) or health and safety. Not all regulatory appeals in the environmental field will explicitly raise issues of EC law, but those charged with the responsibility of determining such appeals are likely to need to be fully familiar with this dimension and the underlying policy objectives of the legislation.

(e)   A substantial body of international environmental treaties and law covering issues such as trade in endangered species, pollution of marine waters, transnational shipments of hazardous waste and climate change. The intensity of this international dimension, which influences the content and interpretation of both EC and national environmental law, is again of a quite different scale to that found in planning or health and safety law.

(f)   The development of certain fundamental environmental principles such as the precautionary approach, polluter-pays, prevention at source, and procedural transparency. The extent to which these are yet binding legal principles and how they are to be put into practice is still being developed, but they have now entered the common language of environmental law and policy.

(g)   The emergence of principles concerning third party access to environmental justice, and the requirement under the Aarhus Convention for review procedures that are timely and not prohibitively expensive. These aspects are discussed further in section 10 below, but are now a significant backdrop to thinking about structures that will meet future public expectations.

(h)   The emergence of the overarching principle of sustainable development which underpins contemporary policy approaches. This is not a straightforward concept and is subject to differing interpretations, but it is a policy dimension that increasingly requires appreciation by those handling environmental law disputes.

8.2   Technical and legal complexity is not in itself a compelling reason for a special jurisdiction, and can be found in other areas of the law. Some of the above features will be more apparent in certain applications of environmental law than others, and they may not be of equal significance in any particular decision. But it is the combination of all these factors which is of particular importance.

9.   Judicial Reviews and Stated Cases

9.1   One of the arguments made by the RCEP was that in the absence of a specialised tribunal, there was likely to be increased pressure on the judicial review system as a surrogate means of undertaking merits appeals, both by third parties and those directly affected. Conversely, the creation of a more specialised and comprehensive tribunal appeal system could reduce the pressure on the higher courts handling such judicial review cases.

9.2   To test this argument in more detail, we have examined the judicial review applications and stated cases heard by the High Court involving environmental legislation over the past 3 years. We excluded town and country planning cases, and in particular those involving environmental assessment. There is inevitably some difficulty in categorising cases, but the overall numbers were in the order of 60-70 environmental judicial review applications and 25 stated cases arising over the 3 year period. The number of judicial reviews in 2001 was slightly higher than 2002, but we believe this was caused by a 'spike' of cases concerning foot and mouth controls, and overall the trend does appear to be upwards. It can therefore be predicted that under current legislation an average of some 25-30 environmental judicial review applications per year will arise. Further details of these figures are provided in Appendix D.

9.3.   We examined in detail some 55 case files from the last three years, and it is apparent that, despite the publicity given to a number of high profile cases brought by environmental groups, the current system is as much driven by companies and industry. The applicants were companies or industries in 28 cases, while in 22 cases the applicants were individuals and environmental or similar associations. For related reasons, only in a minority of cases was legal aid involved, with reference being made to the Legal Services Commission in the files for only four cases. The decision-makers being challenged included government departments in 27 cases and the Environment Agency in 16 cases. The average time for cases to reach a full hearing in court was six months from the date of lodgement to a final court order, and the average duration of the main hearing before court was 1.3 days. This does not take into account the time spent in pre-hearing procedures, nor judicial time spent in making decisions solely on written material and affidavits.

9.4   Only 4 out of the 55 environmental judicial reviews examined were successful. Otherwise 18 cases were dismissed, 13 withdrawn, and leave for judicial review refused in 12 cases. The remaining cases were still outstanding at the time of examination. This seems to be consistent with the views of the RCEP, as well as the judges and lawyers whom we interviewed, who indicated that judicial review applications in environmental cases frequently appear to be merits driven, with a tendency to build cases on the permitted but restrictive grounds for judicial review. Our own examination of the files suggested that around two thirds were essentially merits-driven i.e. seeking a substantial rehearing of the facts. It also appears clear from the figures that only a small minority of judicial reviews followed a previous merits appeal. In 36 out of the 55 files examined, there had been no previous appeal, mainly because there was no merits appeal route available (as will have been the case for most of the 22 actions brought by third parties), or in a small number of exceptional cases, where leave was granted despite the non-exercise of an appeal right.

9.5   The overall picture of current judicial reviews in the environmental field suggests that a considerable amount of judicial time in the High Court is being spent on handling applications which are largely merits-driven; the numbers of environmental judicial reviews are increasing steadily (though not dramatically); and that the users are as much regulated businesses as individuals and other third parties.

9.6   The picture is a little different for the stated cases from magistrates' courts, in relation to which we examined 22 case files from the past three years. Sixteen of these cases followed on a criminal prosecution, and the remaining six related to the service of notices. Companies brought half of the cases, with the other half brought by individuals or local authorities. Just over half the cases related to statutory nuisance provisions. The average length of time to complete the proceedings was around the same as for judicial review (five months), but the average length of the hearing in open court considerably less, at around two and a half hours. However, the 'success' rate was considerably higher with the applicant succeeding in half the cases. This may support the comments in section 7 regarding the suitability of magistrates' courts for handling more complicated environmental issues.

9.7   It is less straightforward to predict the extent to which improvements to the current regulatory appeals system might reduce the number of applications for judicial review. Unless third parties have some access to a merits appeal route, third party judicial reviews will continue, though these do not represent the majority of current environmental judicial review applications. On the other hand, should a first-tier appeal body in the form of an Environmental Tribunal have both specialised environmental legal and technical expertise, then the decisions it takes should be manifestly more legally and technically sound, thereby reducing the likelihood of applications for judicial review. In a recent case concerning a Social Security appeal[12], the Court of Appeal noted that where a tribunal structure is sufficiently expert to be able to take an independent and robust view, the Court could afford to be circumspect in entertaining further appeals. This case concerned statutory appeal rights rather that judicial review, but a similar approach is likely to be taken.

9.8   For similar reasons, if regulatory appeal rights to an Environmental Tribunal were provided where none exist at present other than by way of judicial review, this must also be predicted to reduce the pressure on the judicial system. There is the example of environmental information rights where the only current appeal route against the refusal by public bodies to disclose information is by way of judicial review. The proposal for the Information Commissioner/Tribunal to handle such disputes would fill a significant gap in the availability of an appropriate appeal mechanism. Furthermore, if an effective first-tier appeals

---

[12] *Cooke v Secretary of State for Social Security* [2001] EWCA Civ 734

structure were created, it would become more legitimate to build in stronger filter procedures whereby leave for judicial review against the decision of a regulating body would not be granted unless the right of appeal to the first-tier appeal body had already been exercised. This is consistent with the views of the Law Commission and the Leggatt Report[13], and from the judicial review files we examined, it was rare for leave to be granted unless an available appeal right had previously been exercised.

9.9 For stated cases from the Magistrates' Courts, the majority related to criminal matters, and unless this jurisdiction were changed, the current numbers are likely to continue. It could be suggested that provision be made in relation to these cases for obtaining advisory opinions from a specialist Environmental Tribunal, this being in effect what the High Court does at present in many cases. We could also expect that the decisions of a specialised Environmental Tribunal dealing with a novel policy point or a set of new environmental regulations, would contain sufficiently authoritative guidance and be sufficiently publicised to be of value to fora such as the Magistrates' Courts and the County Courts, so reducing the number of stated cases where the substantive meaning of the legislation is at issue.

9.10 One of the attractions of creating a specialised first-tier Environmental Tribunal is that it could now be integrated into the Government's proposals for modernising the tribunal system following on the Leggatt Report. One of the recommendations of the Leggatt Report was for a unified tribunal appeal system, which would replace judicial review to the High Court as a route of appeal against tribunal decisions. Our understanding is that the Government intends to create such a unified appellate body, possibly on a divisional basis. As noted in the Leggatt report, 'The aim of the new Appellate Division will be to develop by its general expertise and the selective identification of binding precedents, a coherent approach to the law. In this, although operating with greater procedural flexibility and informality than may be found in the High Court, as well as being considerably cheaper to approach, it will be comparable in authority to the High Court so far as tribunals are concerned.'[14]

9.11 The Leggatt report also recognised that it would be valuable if the proposed Appellate Division had first-tier jurisdiction in

---

[13] Leggatt Report, para 6.29
[14] Leggatt Report , para 6.32

particularly complex cases, in much the same way that the Lands Tribunal has a mixture of first instance and appellate cases. We could see this model working well for environmental appeals. Where, for example, an appeal concerned the interpretation of provisions of new environmental regulations or the application of a novel or controversial policy, a rapid decision of the Appellate Division would be of value to all users of the system.

10. Access to Justice and the Aarhus Convention

10.1 The Aarhus Convention has been signed by the United Kingdom and is currently awaiting ratification by the European Community. It contains important principles concerning public participation and access to justice. The key provisions on access to justice are detailed in Box 3. In relation to rights of access to environmental information (which largely reflect the provisions of the existing EC Directive on the subject), the Convention guarantees that members of the public who claim to have been refused information by a public authority should have access both to court review procedures, and a free or inexpensive expeditious procedure for reconsideration of the matter by a public authority or review by an independent and impartial body other than a court of law. As we have noted in paragraph 5.3 above, under existing legislation concerning environmental information, review procedures have previously only been possible by judicial review, but if introduced, the proposals by the Government to integrate environmental information appeals procedures into those provided under the Freedom of Information Act should now meet these concerns.

BOX 3 – The Aarhus Convention on Access to Information, Public Participation in Decision Making and Access to Justice in Environmental Matters

The Aarhus Convention was adopted on 25 June 1998 in the Danish city of Aarhus (Århus) by the UN Economic Commission for Europe, and entered into force on 30 October 2001 following its ratification by sufficient member state Parties.

Considered to be the most forward thinking international treaty on public participation yet completed, it places obligations on the member state Parties to ensure the availability in their national law of procedural rights for the public based on the three 'pillars' described in the Convention's title.

Key provisions of the Convention relating to access to justice are as follows:

Article 1 Objective

In order to contribute to the protection of the right of every person of present and future generations to live in an environment adequate to his or her health and well-being, each Party shall guarantee the rights of access to information, public participation in decision making, and access to justice in environmental matters in accordance with the provisions of this Convention.

Article 3 General Provisions

1. Each Party shall take the necessary legislative, regulatory and other measures...to establish and maintain a clear, transparent and consistent framework to implement the provisions of this Convention.

Article 9 Access to Justice

1. Each Party shall, within the framework of its national legislation, ensure that any person who considers that his or her request for information under Article 4 [dealing with Access to Information] has been ignored, wrongly refused...or otherwise not dealt with in accordance with...that Article, has access to a review procedure before a court of law or other independent and impartial body established by law.

2. Each Party shall, within the framework of its national legislation, ensure that members of the public concerned: (a) having a sufficient interest...have access to a review procedure before a court of law and/or another independent and impartial body established by law, to challenge the substantive and procedural legality of any decision, act or omission subject to the provisions of Article 6 [dealing with Public Participation in Decisions on Specific Activities] and, where so provided for under national law...of other relevant provisions of the Convention.

3. In addition...each Party shall ensure that, where they meet the criteria, if any, laid down in its national law, members of the public have access to administrative or judicial procedures to challenge acts and omissions by private persons and public authorities which contravene provisions of its national law relating to the environment.

4. In addition...the procedures referred to in paras 1, 2 and 3 above shall provide adequate and effective remedies, including injunctive relief as appropriate, and be fair, equitable, timely and not prohibitively expensive.

In order for the European Community (and therefore the UK) to be able to ratify the Convention, amending legislation has been and will be adopted to ensure the consistency of the EC environmental regulatory framework with the provisions of the Convention. The Government will also have to amend existing UK legislation in various respects.

A replacement Directive on public access to information has been adopted and a new Directive has been proposed on public participation in respect of the drawing up of certain plans and programmes. A consultation process has also been commenced by the European Commission for a Directive on access to justice.

10.2   The Aarhus Convention also guarantees the right of public participation in a range of consent procedures for projects specified in the Convention, which largely follow those currently the subject of mandatory environmental assessment under EC legislation. Article 9 of the Convention also requires that members of the public 'with sufficient interest' should have access to a review procedure before a court of law or other independent body 'to challenge the substantive and procedural legality' of the consent related decisions covered by the Convention. What constitutes sufficient interest is to be determined with the objective of giving the public concerned wide access to justice. Non-governmental organisations promoting environmental protection and meeting any requirements under national law are deemed to have such an interest.

10.3   The grounds for such rights of appeal are confined to 'the substantive and procedural legality' of the decision in question, and the drafting is clearly rather narrower than the full review procedure required under the Convention for environmental information. The present view of Government is that this phrase is consistent with the grounds for review currently provided in this country by judicial review. There are, though, other views that while the Aarhus Convention may not provide third parties with a full merits appeal, the phrase 'substantive and procedural illegality' implies a rather more intense scrutiny than that traditionally provided for by judicial review. Whatever the answer on this point, the Convention also provides that the review procedures provided must be 'fair, equitable, timely, and not prohibitively expensive', and there have to be concerns whether existing judicial review procedures can meet all these criteria. One experienced environmental lawyer told us that the potential costs of judicial review and the risk of uncapped adverse cost orders appeared to prevent many cases being commenced. Under the Convention, Governments must also provide public information on access to administrative and review procedures, and consider appropriate assistance mechanisms to remove or reduce financial and other barriers to access to justice. The European Community is itself a party to the Convention and a proposed Directive on access to justice will implement the Convention with respect to areas covered by EC environmental legislation. The draft Directive would require such review procedures to be 'expeditious' and 'not prohibitively expensive'.

10.4   The longer-term significance of the Aarhus Convention is that it explicitly introduces new concepts of access to justice in environmental decision making, and the need for inexpensive review procedures to be made available to members of the public and environmental organisations. As one environmental lawyer suggested to us, the Convention is based on establishing a system 'rooted in broad and deep citizen participation and access to justice'. As such it is quite different from the more familiar regulatory appeal models which have been largely developed to provide protection to the interests of applicants or those directly subject to regulation. Governments are required to publicise the legal remedies that are available, and without any change to current structures, existing pressures on judicial review procedures are therefore only likely to grow. There may also be benefit in making regulatory changes in order to enhance compliance with the spirit of Aarhus rather than allow the United Kingdom to rest on what was characterised to us as 'the lowest common denominator interpretation' of the strict letter of the Convention.

10.5   In the past, members of the public or environmental organisations unable to afford the costs involved in legal challenges have often made use of the complaint procedure to the European Commission when possible breaches of EC law are raised. This quasi-administrative procedure can lead to investigations by the Commission, and possible enforcement action by the Commission before the European Court of Justice. There is a heavy administrative burden involved and a backlog of cases, especially where the non-application of Community law is raised (rather than claims that formal transposition into national law is defective). The Commission may in future require that all national legal remedies are exhausted before considering such a complaint, this being more in line with the practice of the European Commission on Human Rights, and arguably consistent with the principle of subsidiarity. The number of environmental complaints received by the Commission varies tremendously from Member State to Member State, though the United Kingdom has consistently produced some of the highest numbers. The comparative figures probably reveal less about the extent of compliance than they do about the accessibility of national dispute mechanisms and the strength of non-governmental organisations[15]. But any introduction of a principle of exhaustion of national remedies within Commission procedures, suggests that there be will be even greater pressure on existing national procedures (especially those of judicial review), and therefore strengthens the case for developing new approaches. Against this background, we consider in the next section, whether there is case for introducing some form of third party right of appeal within the current environmental regulatory system.

11.   Third Party Rights of Appeal

11.1   The RCEP considered that there was a strong case for a specialised environmental tribunal system, whatever the position on third party rights of appeal. Nonetheless, it went on to recommend that in the interests of public confidence, the concept of third party rights of appeal should be introduced in both planning and environmental decision-making. The government has to date rejected the implementation of third party rights of appeal within the land-use planning system, and it is not the purpose of the study to revisit this particular issue.

11.2   However, the question of third party appeals in the context of environmental rather than planning regulation has received rather less examination. Whatever the position in town and country planning legislation, there are a number of distinctive special features in the environmental field which suggest that the issue should be addressed seriously:

•   A key argument of the government in rejecting third party rights of appeal in planning matters is that the public have the opportunity to participate in the land-use plan-making process, and that community based involvement should be revitalised and encouraged in that arena. In relation to the sort of environmental decision-making to which third party rights of appeal might be applied (such as GMO or IPPC

[15] Macrory and Purdy *'The Enforcement of EC environmental law against Member States'* in Holder (ed) The Impact of EC Environmental Law in the United Kingdom, 1997, Wiley, Chichester

licensing) there is generally no equivalent and developed plan-making context involving the public. The selective introduction of such third party rights into environmental decision-making would therefore not undermine the Government's preferred approach to land-use planning.

- A second important argument against the introduction of third party rights of appeal within the planning system is that the majority of decisions are made by elected local authority members who are directly accountable to the local electorate. But in contrast to land-use planning, many of the key decisions in contemporary environmental regulation are made by the specialist agencies of government, such as the Environment Agency or English Nature. In relation to decisions made by such bodies, the arguments concerning the direct local political accountability of the decision-maker are less compelling.

- As noted in section 10 above, in relation to permitting decisions for a large number of specified projects, the Aarhus Convention and the EC implementing legislation will require review procedures for members of the public and non-governmental bodies that are fair, equitable, timely, and not prohibitively expensive. As we will discuss below, the Convention may provide a workable basis for a 'filtered' appeals system.

11.3 These factors suggest that the question of third party rights of appeal should be seriously addressed in the context of environmental regulation and a possible Environment Tribunal system. As one senior environmental lawyer commented to us: 'The Rubicon has been crossed in relation to third party rights of appeal but standing still needs to be addressed.'

11.4 The RCEP acknowledged that, even with the use of strict time-limits for making appeals, the introduction of third party rights of appeal could increase the time and cost of procedures, but concluded this was a price worth paying for improved public confidence and ensuring that environmental considerations are given their proper weight. We would also expect that a specialist Environmental Tribunal would have the ability to act speedily and effectively to handle such appeals, including the use of flexible procedures and mediation techniques where appropriate.

11.5 The RCEP also recognised that the introduction of wholly unrestricted merits based rights of third party appeal was unlikely to be practicable, and that filtering mechanisms should be developed. In relation to town and country planning, the Government considered these would be difficult to devise with any precision, but for environmental regulation, the provisions of the Aarhus Convention may now provide an effective basis. Third party appeals could be restricted to members of the public and non-governmental organisations as defined in the Convention; confined to licensing procedures relating to projects defined in the Convention; and made only on grounds of substantive or procedural illegality as prescribed in the Convention. These grounds, as we noted in section 10 above, may require rather closer scrutiny than those traditionally applied in judicial review, but certainly should not raise the spectre of a full merits review by third parties across the board.

12. The Human Rights Act And Access to an Independent Tribunal

12.1 Following the entry into force of the Human Rights Act 1998, many commentators considered that the introduction of a more comprehensive system of independent tribunals deciding merits appeals would be a legal precondition for both planning and environmental regulation in order to satisfy the requirements of Article 6 of the European Convention on Human Rights. This requires that that in the determination of civil rights, 'everyone is entitled to a fair and public hearing within a reasonable time by an independent and impartial tribunal established by law.'

12.2 There has now been a fair amount of case law, both nationally and before the European Court of Human Rights, testing the application of Article 6 in the context of the type of regulatory procedures considered in this report. See for example *R (Alconbury Developments Ltd) v Secretary of State for the Environment, Transport and the Regions* [2001] 2 WLR 1389 (on the role of the Secretary of State in planning decisions); *R (Aggregate Industries UK Ltd) v English Nature* [2002] EWHC 908 (regarding the designation of Sites of Special Scientific Interest by English Nature); *R v Rhondda Cynon Taff CBC* [2002] Env. LR 15 and *Bryan v United Kingdom* [1995] 21 EHRR 342 (considering the function of Planning Inspectors and judicial review).

12.3 The generous interpretation of what is meant by 'civil rights' developed by the European Court of Human Rights (and now adopted by the British courts) implies that in most of the areas of environmental regulation considered in this report, civil rights (within the meaning of the Convention) will be engaged in respect of applicants for licences or permits, or those served with enforcement notices or similar requirements. Rather less clear as yet, is the extent to which third parties indirectly affected by such decisions can be said to have their civil rights determined by such decisions.

12.4   The legislative analysis in Appendix A indicates that in certain areas of environmental law, full rights of merits appeal against a decision of a governmental body are available to what is clearly an independent court such as a magistrates' court. It is also clear from the case law that an appellate body such as the Planning Inspectorate or the Secretary of State does not in itself represent the independent court or tribunal required by Article 6. However, the courts have established that, even where any appeal to a court is restricted to legal grounds or judicial review, this can still be sufficient to satisfy Article 6 by looking at the procedures as a whole (the composite approach) and by considering the nature of the decision at hand. Essentially, the more that an administrative decision involves the exercise of discretion against a policy background, the less it is necessary that appellate procedures before a court or tribunal are required to stray beyond judicial review grounds to incorporate a full merits review. As Lord Hoffmann noted recently in *Begum v London Borough of Tower Hamlets* [2003] UKHL 5: 'The question is whether, consistently with the rule of law and constitutional propriety, the relevant decision-making powers may be entrusted to administrators.'

12.5   We cannot be sure that all of the existing environmental appeal routes outlined in Appendix A satisfy Article 6 requirements, and certainly the establishment of an Environmental Tribunal handling merits appeals would guarantee a better degree of certainty of compliance. But it does now seem reasonably clear from the case law that in many areas, a fully independent review tribunal is not absolutely essential to ensure compliance with Article 6. The need to introduce an Environmental Tribunal has therefore to be justified by reasons other than securing compliance with the European Convention.

12.6   We should note, however, that the approach being taken in the current case law, which essentially preserves the remedy of judicial review, may put greater pressures on those procedures. Some of the recent human rights case law hints that where judicial review is the only independent appellate remedy, courts may be justified in exercising a rather more intense scrutiny than has traditionally been the approach in judicial review. Our study of recent environmental judicial review cases indicates the extent to which the process is already being driven by the desire to achieve merits reviews. In this context, an Environmental Tribunal may provide a more appropriate forum for handling such issues.

13. Separating Land Use Planning and Environmental Appeals?

13.1 The model of the environmental tribunals proposed by the RCEP envisaged that (initially at any rate) the proposed tribunals should handle only environmental regulatory appeals, whilst town and country planning appeals would remain within the well-established jurisdiction of the Planning Inspectorate. On the surface this appears to run counter to much of the thrust of the RCEP critique, which was about ensuring a greater connection between land-use and environmental planning. However, the main concerns in this respect were addressed more at the strategic planning level than the handling of individual permissions and licences.

13.2 At present, a number of appeal procedures mainly in the field of pollution control (IPCC, water discharge consents, etc.) are in practice handled by the Planning Inspectorate, and transferring that jurisdiction to a separate Environmental Tribunal might inhibit a closer integration of land-use planning and environment regulation. For some years, there have been calls for the 'twin tracking' of planning application and environmental licence procedures, but in practice this has proved very difficult to achieve. The political accountability and the application of political policy in decision making inherent in the planning system is also seen by some as a positive factor which might be lost in a more independent tribunal structure. We also recognise that, especially since the introduction of environmental assessment procedures within the town and country planning system, environmental factors are now an integral element of many land-use planning decisions.

13.3 Based on this recognition of the close connection between land-use planning and environmental protection, a combined planning and environmental tribunal (one of the models in the original Grant report) may still be an attractive option. Alternatively, more environmental appeals could be transferred to the Planning Inspectorate (as has happened with IPPC and other pollution related consents) in effect transforming the body into a Planning and Environmental Inspectorate. But there remain compelling arguments in favour of a specialist Environmental Tribunal dealing solely with the type of environmental appeals identified in Appendix A:

- As indicated in section 5 above, there are a number of distinctive features in environmental law, the combination of which calls for special treatment; these features are not so apparent in land-use planning.

- Although the Planning Inspectorate at present handles a number of environmental appeals, the total number and range of environmental regulatory appeals that currently exist and are likely to arise under environmental legislation in the future will be much greater; a full-scale transfer of jurisdiction to the Planning Inspectorate would therefore require the development of additional legal and new types of specialist technical expertise. Given other current pressures on the Planning Inspectorate and its focus on land development issues, the extension of their jurisdiction to cover all such appeals may not be attractive.

- Whilst the Planning Inspectorate may handle discrete environmental appeals effectively at present, it is less suited than a specialised tribunal to provide authoritative decisions which can serve as guidance on the meaning and application of regulatory requirements. A specialised tribunal could assist the development of environmental law and policy in a way that is beneficial to both business and public interests.

- As the RCEP report indicated, the most significant challenge for securing improved integration in land-use planning and environmental policy lies not in the area of individual planning or regulatory decisions but in the area of strategic plan and policy making which provides the context for discrete decisions.

- Environmental considerations are so pervasive that drawing a line for jurisdictional purposes is never perfect, but for practical purposes the core land-use planning remit of the Planning Inspectorate does provide a useful and practical line of demarcation.

- The major administrative upheaval which would be involved in setting up a new Planning and Environmental

Tribunal might simply outweigh any policy advantages to be gained; conversely, we have identified a number of real gains which could be achieved by establishing a dedicated Environmental Tribunal system operating within the proposed new Tribunals Service.

14. Options for the Way Forward

14.1 Our research has identified the complex and haphazard array of appeal routes that exist in contemporary environmental legislation; particular problem areas; and the possible advantages to be gained from a more coherent approach. Based on our research and findings, there appear to be a number of key options:

14.2 Carry on with the current system

Undertaking no change at all would not meet some of the specific problems with current arrangements identified in this report. Pressures on judicial review as a default appeal route will continue. As a senior judge noted to us: 'Unless something is done now the pressures will manifest themselves through third party claims especially in the High Court'. Magistrates' Courts will have to contend with the complex contaminated land regime. The Planning Inspectorate will have to accommodate an increasingly complicated environmental jurisdiction driven by new legislation at the EC and international levels. Difficulties will be faced in adapting to new requirements for access to environmental justice, leading to increased public discontent with the system.

14.3 Incrementally adapt and improve existing structures

Improvements could certainly be made to the current arrangements to meet some of the problems identified in our research. We can identify a number of steps that might be appropriate, though this is by no means a complete list:

- The Planning Inspectorate could ensure the availability of greater legal and specialist technical expertise for handling its existing environmental appeals.

- The Planning Inspectorate could do more to ensure that key environmental appeal decisions are readily accessible and given wider publicity.

- Existing 'gaps' in the range of appeal mechanisms could be filled, so reducing the dependence on judicial review as a 'surrogate' means of appeal.

- Contaminated land appeals could be transferred from the Magistrates' Courts and the Planning Inspectorate to the Lands Tribunal, which might be considered a more appropriate body to develop the particular expertise necessary to handle these issues.

- The greater use of District Judges in Magistrates' Courts for handling the more complex statutory nuisance appeals could be formalised; where there is no District Judge in an area, clerks to the justices could be encouraged to apply for one.

- Further specialised training and advice for magistrates in the application of environmental law could be provided, perhaps along the lines of the 'Costing the Earth' toolkit recently produced by the Magistrates' Association and the Environmental Law Foundation to assist sentencing practice in environmental cases.

- Ways of reducing the costs involved in judicial review procedures could be considered.

14.4 Nevertheless, there remain drawbacks to this incremental approach. Whilst it might improve arrangements for existing appeals, it fails to provide a secure basis to properly meet future demands. This more limited and ad hoc approach would sacrifice the opportunity to develop more coherent approaches towards the interpretation and application of environmental law and policy in what is a rapidly developing field. As new environmental requirements were implemented, decisions would still be needed each time as to the most appropriate forum for handling new appeals, by choosing from the existing array of bodies. The development of new and more flexible procedures for handling access to justice issues would also be more difficult to achieve within existing structures.

14.5 Establish a specialised Environmental Tribunal within the proposed unified Tribunals System

As the Leggatt report has noted, tribunals combining both legal and specialist expertise and an understanding of underlying policy issues, can be particularly effective in dealing with the mixture of fact and law which is often required to review decisions taken by administrative or regulatory authorities.

14.6   Although the RCEP envisaged a system of part-time tribunals operating on a regional basis, our research indicates that in order to meet the current levels of environmental appeals being made, it would be more feasible to establish a single Environmental Tribunal, operating in a similar way to the Lands Tribunal. The Lands Tribunal has a single President, three expert members and a legally qualified member, and disposes of nearly 600 cases a year, this being equivalent in number to the environmental regulatory appeals currently being made. Although based in London, the Lands Tribunal sits outside London where this is more convenient to the parties, and we understand that in practice almost half its cases are heard in this way, normally sitting in local courts.[16] We would expect a single Environmental Tribunal to have a similar flexibility of approach, hearing cases out of London where appropriate. Interlocutory matters or appeals raising more straightforward technical issues might be dealt with by the non-lawyer specialist members, leaving appeals raising more complex legal issues or new regulatory requirements to be heard by the full Tribunal. Again this is in line with the practice of the Lands Tribunal, where we understand about half of the cases are handled in this way[17]. Operating within the proposed new unified Tribunal Service, appeals from such an Environmental Tribunal would be made to the Tribunals Appellate Division rather than by way of judicial review.

14.7   Unlike the Lands Tribunal, though, an Environmental Tribunal would not need to be a court of record with a status equivalent to the High Court. It would not handle private party disputes, nor would we envisage it handling appeals from other tribunals or judicial bodies

14.8   Through its incorporation within the Government's proposed unified Tribunal Service, the new Environmental Tribunal would benefit from being associated with the general modernisation programme now under way. We would expect the Tribunal to develop procedures that are fair, economic, proportionate and speedy, and to make the fullest use of modern case management systems and information technology. The use of alternative dispute resolution procedures, including mediation and arbitration, would be encouraged and adopted within its procedures where appropriate.

[16] Source; Lands Tribunal
[17] Source; Lands Tribunal

14.9 This new way of handling environmental appeals would also benefit from being grounded in the Government's key objectives for delivering an improved tribunal system:

- To provide the user with a focused modern service in line with the Government's agenda for the reform of public services.

- To ensure better information for and support to users.

- To encourage common standards of service and deliver all the efficiencies and economies to be gained from bringing services together.

- To allow the findings of tribunals to be a positive voice in the reviewing and shaping of policy and standards of administrative decision-making.

15. A new Environmental Tribunal in Practice

15.1 If the model of a single Environmental Tribunal were adopted, its precise jurisdiction must ultimately be a matter for Government. The core initial jurisdiction could involve the transfer of appeal functions from existing bodies covering the majority of regulatory environmental appeals currently being made, and might consist of:

- Appeals relating to decisions of specialised environmental agencies, such as the Environment Agency and English Nature.

- Appeals in respect of industrial processes regulated by local authorities.

- Appeals in respect of the contaminated land regime.

- Appeals in respect of statutory nuisance abatement notices involving trade and industry.

15.2 We see attractions in appeals relating to abatement notices served in respect of domestic premises (such as noise nuisances) remaining with local Magistrates' Courts, but perhaps with the greater use of District Judges where appeals raise difficult technical or evidential issues. Current legislation provides for special grounds of appeal in respect of notices served on trade and industry and includes the use of 'Best Practicable Means', a concept involving expert technical judgment. We feel that statutory nuisance appeals involving trade and industry would be a sensible part of the jurisdiction for the Environmental Tribunal. Criminal offences for non-compliance with such notices would remain with the magistrates' courts. We note that the current legislation also provides trade and industry with a special defence of 'Best Practicable Means' to such criminal prosecution. Given that an appeal on these grounds can already be made against a notice, we feel that the opportunity should be taken to remove what appears to be anomalous duplication. Magistrates dealing with non-compliance with a valid notice would then able to focus on the determination of fact.

15.3   As the Environmental Tribunal developed experience and reputation, the opportunity could then be taken to transfer further existing appeals in order to clear up anomalies under existing legislation, and reduce the pressure on judicial review. The Tribunal would also provide the natural forum for appeals arising under future environmental legislation. Examples include proposed EC legislation concerning environmental liability and emissions trading. Where there is discretion as to whether to establish appeal mechanisms for such new legislation, the principles contained in the Leggatt Report are valuable: 'Where any legislation establishes a statutory scheme involving decisions by an arm of Government, the responsible minister should explicitly consider whether a right of appeal is required, on the basis that there should be strong specific arguments if an appeal route is not to be created, and that a tribunal route, rather than redress to the courts, should be the normal option in the interests of accessibility.'[18]

15.4   Our model for the Environmental Tribunal envisages that the Planning Inspectorate would continue to handle appeals under planning legislation, and we recognise that there would need to be close liaison between the two institutions. Under current procedures, a considerable number of planning judicial reviews are concerned with the interpretation and application of environmental assessment requirements in relation to development projects, a subject underpinned by the EC legislation and case-law. The opportunity could be taken to transfer jurisdiction relating to the legal challenges concerning environmental assessment to the new Environmental Tribunal.

---

[18] Leggatt Report, 1.13

15.5   Environmental appeals often raise both legal and policy issues, and as with many other existing tribunals, we would expect the Environmental Tribunal to be fully conversant with relevant policy dimensions and to apply them in their decisions. We would hope that Government would have sufficient confidence in the Tribunal to allow it to determine the vast majority of individual appeals, including those of a controversial nature. Nevertheless, there may be cases of such significance that the Government would wish to retain the right of final decision along the lines of recovered jurisdiction in planning appeals. We see it as perfectly feasible that such a mechanism could be applied to the Environmental Tribunal, provided suitable guidelines were issued and cases kept to a minimum. In such cases, the Environmental Tribunal would in effect be making a recommendation to Government rather than exercising the final decision.

15.6   We also recognise that the operation of an Environmental Tribunal may encourage Government to publish more developed statements on environmental policy objectives, to provide a more explicit policy context for the decision-making role of the Tribunal, as has happened in the town and country planning field. We feel this would be a positive development, and is in line with recommendations of the RCEP in its 23rd Report on this subject. We would also anticipate that the Environmental Tribunal would be allowed to make direct references to the European Court of Justice under Art 234 (formerly Art 177) in appropriate cases.

15.7   We have argued that serious attention should be paid to the question of introducing some form of third party right in relation to environmental appeals, both as a matter of principle, and in order to be more consistent with the concept of environmental citizenship and access to justice implied by the Aarhus Convention. Such appeals would fall within the jurisdiction of the Environment Tribunal. But we would emphasise that there is a good case for such a Tribunal even within the confines of current procedures, and we would be reluctant to see any initiative become stalled or delayed because of the issue of third party rights. In any event, we would expect the Tribunal to adopt sufficiently flexible rules of procedure and approach to incorporate the views of third parties where appropriate.

15.8   Appendix E provides more details of the possible costs and benefits involved in establishing such an Environmental Tribunal. As to the direct costs of establishment, based on the initial lines we have suggested, the costs of the Lands Tribunal are calculated in the background papers to the Leggatt Report at £1.25 M a year, and this provides a useful benchmark given that we are thinking of a comparable case-load and size. If the Environmental Tribunal's jurisdiction were extended with the introduction of appeals under new environmental legislation, the costs would be likely to be neutral since they would otherwise have to be borne by other appeal bodies.

15.9   We have listed in Appendix E some of the direct cost-savings that are likely to result, though we leave it to others to quantify these in detailed financial terms if that is possible or indeed necessary. In respect of Governmental costs, these include, for example, a reduction of the current work-load of the Planning Inspectorate and Magistrates' Courts; reduced pressure on High Court and Court of Appeal time in handling judicial reviews; and the freeing up of Governmental time currently taken up in advising the Planning Inspectorate on environmental law and policy issues. We would also expect that the coherence and authority the Tribunal would bring to the current system would be of direct benefit to the regulatory bodies concerned with the implementation and enforcement of environmental law. As we have indicated, the overall public policy gains from this proposal, in terms of increased public confidence and improved environmental outcomes, are likely to be considerable, though difficult to quantify in straightforward financial terms.

15.10   Two case-studies may give a better idea of how the Tribunal might operate in practice:

A Ltd operate a foundry works in an urban area. Following complaints of noise and dust pollution from local residents, the local authority serve a statutory nuisance notice under Part III of the Environmental Protection Act 1990. A Ltd appeal against the notice on the grounds that they are operating the 'Best Practicable Means' in respect of the noise and dust. The appeal is made to the Environmental Tribunal rather than the local magistrates' court. The Tribunal operates an up-to-date case management system, and the local authority request that because of a history of poor compliance, and a suspicion that this is a holding appeal to allow operations to continue, the matter is dealt with expeditiously. The case papers indicate that the issues are largely technical rather than legal, and the case is assigned to a specialist member of the Tribunal rather than the full Tribunal. The appeal is heard in the local area, and with the co-operation of the parties, informal procedures are adopted. The validity of the notice is upheld by the Tribunal. A Ltd later fail to comply with the notice, and the prosecution for non-compliance is heard before the local magistrates' court. The defence of 'Best Practicable

Means' is no longer available, and the court is concerned only with the assessing the factual evidence of non-compliance.

B Ltd operate an industrial site requiring a licence from the Environment Agency under new Pollution Prevention and Control Regulations recently introduced under an EC amending Directive. B Ltd appeal against licence conditions imposed by the Agency, and the appeal is heard by the Environmental Tribunal (rather than the Planning Inspectorate as now). The case raises new legal and policy issues, and is one of the first of its kind under the new Regulations. The case is therefore heard in London before the full Tribunal. Because of the distinctive features of the case, the Tribunal permits an intervener representation by a non-governmental organisation with a track record of interest in the area. In making its decision in favour of the Agency, the Tribunal takes the opportunity of providing more general guidance on the interpretation and application of the regulations against the policy background. The analysis in the Tribunal's determination is sufficiently legally watertight and convincing to deter any judicial review application or appeal to the Appeals Division of the Tribunal Service. The decision of the Tribunal is immediately posted on the Tribunal's website, which is regularly accessed by the regulatory bodies, trade associations, non-governmental bodies and interested members of the public. As a result of the decision, a number of similar pending appeals by other industries are withdrawn.

15.11 The position in which the Environmental Tribunal might fit into the existing court structure is shown in Box 4.

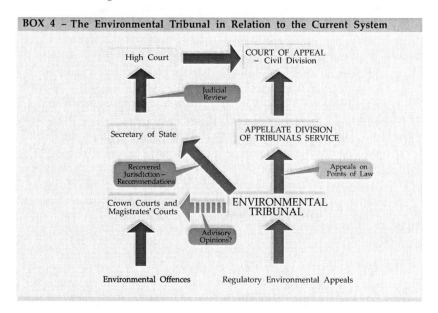

BOX 4 – The Environmental Tribunal in Relation to the Current System

16.   A More Direct Enforcement Role for an Environmental Tribunal?

16.1   This report has largely been confined to considering the role of an Environmental Tribunal system in handling environmental regulatory appeals. On this model, the hearing of criminal environmental cases and the application of penalties to ensure compliance with environmental law would remain with the ordinary criminal courts. We are aware of current concerns over the effectiveness of current environmental enforcement regimes, and various initiatives have already been made to improve training and sentencing practice in the criminal courts. Specific research projects have recently been commissioned by Defra on enforcement and sentencing in the criminal courts in relation to environmental offences, and it would be inappropriate to anticipate their outcomes.

16.2   We need to recognise, however, that the model of an Environmental Tribunal handling regulatory appeals, though perhaps not as ambitious as earlier conceptions of a 'one-stop' specialist environmental court, is still likely to have a beneficial impact on ensuring the more effective application and enforcement of environmental regulation. Licences and enforcement notices of the type identified in this report form the core basis of contemporary environmental law. We would expect the specialist Environmental Tribunal to develop the capacity to issue authoritative interpretations and rulings on environmental law, especially where new, complex regulations are involved, and this will again assist the application of environmental regulation in the context of criminal law.

16.3   Nevertheless, there are arguments that were an Environmental Tribunal system established, its remit could be extended to include some form of criminal enforcement function. It is beyond the scope of this research to explore this issue in detail, but we raise three areas for future consideration.

16.4   Administrative or civil penalties: There is growing interest in the possible value of the imposition of civil financial penalties as an additional enforcement tool to criminal prosecution. In this country civil penalties have not previously been used in the field of environmental law, and instead the traditional use of strict liability criminal offences as the final sanction prevails. In British law, the use of civil penalties is more familiar in areas of fiscal regulation such as competition and tax. For example under

Section 36 of the Competition Act 1998, the Director General of Competition may impose a penalty on an undertaking which has intentionally or negligently infringed key competition provisions, up to a maximum of 10% of the undertaking's turnover, this being recoverable as a civil debt. Appeals may be made to a specialist tribunal with a further appeal to the Court of Appeal.

16.5   More recently, some of the policy advantages of civil penalties were spelt out in Parliament when the Occupational Pensions Regulatory Authority (OPRA) was given power to impose civil penalties under the Occupational Pension Schemes (Penalties) Regulations 2000. According to the Minister of State (Mr Jeff Rooker): 'OPRA could operate more quickly and effectively if it had power to impose civil penalties, as it would not always have to resort to criminal penalties which are extremely onerous as they must be enforced under the Police and Criminal Evidence Act... Criminal sanctions should be used only in open-and-shut cases of fraudulent activity.'[19]

16.6   Criminal sanctions could remain for the most serious environmental cases, but greater use of civil penalties might be a method for unravelling concerns about the low level of criminal fines currently imposed for many environmental offences, since the level of a civil penalty can be more directly related to economic advantages gained by non-compliance. The system could be uncoupled from the constraints clearly still felt in criminal courts (despite efforts being made to increase the level of fines), where magistrates and judges are conscious of the need to ensure that levels of fines are not totally out of step with those imposed for other criminal offences. Magistrates and judges may also sense that punitive sanctions are less appropriate for strict liability offences where no intention or recklessness is involved.

16.7   Civil penalties are familiar as a modern enforcement tool for environmental law in other countries. In the United States, for example, most Federal environmental statutes authorise the Environmental Protection Agency to apply civil administrative penalties against industries that fail to comply with legal requirements, and these are assessed against published rules of practice. Appeals against such penalties can be made to the courts, while criminal offences are reserved for the most serious violators. In 1999, the US Environmental Protection Agency recovered $166.7 million in civil penalties, compared to $61.6

[19] House of Commons, Standing Committee on Delegated Legislation, 8 March 2000

million in criminal fines. Germany has a developed system of administrative offences (*Ordnungswidrigkeiten*) where financial sanctions are considered distinct from criminal fines, and where appeals against such sanctions are made to administrative tribunals rather than criminal courts[20]. To take one example in the environmental field, the German Federal Emission Control Act dealing with industrial air emissions provides for an administrative offence leading to a fine for failure to comply with operator requirements under the Act, while criminal offences are provided under the Criminal Code for more serious failures which are likely to injure human health, animals, plants or other objects of value.

16.8   The question of the introduction of civil penalties in the context of environmental enforcement was beyond the precise terms of reference of this study, and we have therefore not considered, for example, whether it would be appropriate to confine their use to certain specialist authorities such as the Environment Agency. We recognise that in Europe, the requirements of the Human Rights Act on potential criminal liability may also need to be incorporated into their application, reducing some of the procedural flexibility. However, there do appear to be attractions in using civil penalties, and we hope that the government will consider the issue further. If the power to impose civil penalties was introduced, the Environmental Tribunal could play a central role in their development and consistent application. The standard model of a penalty system enables the enforcement agency to impose a penalty for non-compliance with regulatory requirements, and allows a right of appeal against the assessment. In other fields of law, where civil penalties are used, tribunals operate as the first-tier appellate body, and the Environmental Tribunal rather than a conventional criminal or civil court, would be the more appropriate body for hearing appeals against the imposition of such penalties.

16.9   Criminal enforcement: In addition to its powers to determine environmental appeals, the jurisdiction of the Environmental Tribunal could be extended to handling designated criminal environmental offences. The Tribunal might, for example, deal with environmental offences currently considered in magistrates' courts, leaving the Crown courts, as now, to handle the most serious cases. This is a more radical approach, and would require

---

[20] A. Ogus and C. Abbot 'Sanctions for Pollution: Do We Have the Right Regime?', *Journal of Environmental Law*, Vol 14, Issue 3, pages 283-298

a more elaborate system than the single Tribunal we have proposed. Again it is an issue that was beyond the particular terms of reference of this report, but we considered it should at least be raised.

16.10 A combined civil and criminal jurisdiction would acknowledge that many of the distinctive characteristics of environmental law identified in this report are arguably also relevant to the application and interpretation of criminal environmental offences. The specialist Tribunal would bring a deeper appreciation of the environmental policy background and the significance of regulatory compliance than is often possible in ordinary criminal courts. It could also command greater confidence from those charged with enforcement responsibilities, as well as providing greater assurance to the majority of industries and individuals who comply with environmental requirements, that transgressors are being treated in an effective and consistent manner.

16.11 Some models of environmental court in other countries include a criminal jurisdiction. The New South Wales Land and Environment Court, for example, hears certain criminal cases, though this aspect of their work has not been without controversy. The drawback of including a criminal jurisdiction is that criminal law of necessity involves greater procedural formality, different evidential requirements and the incorporation of specific safeguards for the defendant. It is less clear whether the model of Environmental Tribunal, which we are recommending, could readily handle these distinctive requirements of the criminal process.

16.12 Other judicial enforcement powers: If a more direct enforcement role were considered appropriate for the Environmental Tribunal, it would be necessary to address the assignment of powers such as the award of injunctions, interlocutory relief, and other similar judicial remedies. In this context, the Aarhus Convention requires that procedures concerning the rights of appeal by the public and non-governmental organisations shall provide 'adequate and effective remedies, including injunctive relief as appropriate.' We also note that the Stop Now Orders (EC Directive) Regulations 2001 have introduced new powers for enforcement bodies to apply to the courts for a 'Stop Now' orders to speed up action against businesses which breach a number of existing consumer protection laws. If such powers were extended to environmental regulation, the Environmental Tribunal might provide the most appropriate forum for handling them.

17. Conclusions

17.1 The current system of environmental appeals is haphazard and lacks coherence. It reflects an outmoded approach to environmental law, and is unlikely to provide a sound basis for handling future regulatory demands in a convincing manner. Existing structures could continue to be adapted as has been done in the past, but we see considerable benefits in establishing a new system based initially on a single Environmental Tribunal. The costs and administrative changes involved in setting up such a Tribunal to handle the majority of existing appeals would be modest compared to the policy gains to be made. Such a Tribunal would bring a greater consistency of approach to the application and interpretation of environmental law and policy. The improvements in authority and specialist knowledge would also foster increased confidence in those subject to environmental regulation, the regulatory authorities, and the general public. For these reasons, even without any direct enforcement functions, the Environmental Tribunal would substantially improve the application of environmental regulation.

17.2 Operating within the proposed Tribunals System, the Environmental Tribunal would have the flexibility to develop innovative and cost-effective approaches in the resolution of disputes, as well as greater inherent capacity to adapt to the developing principles on access to environmental justice. Incorporating rights of appeal for concerned members of the public or non-governmental organisations, based on grounds of substantive and procedural illegality as defined in the Aarhus Convention, would be consistent with the vision of the Convention, and provide a more cost-effective appeal route than judicial review procedures. Both in Europe and internationally, it would mark the United Kingdom as a leader in the design and practice of modern environmental governance.

17.3 The functions and jurisdiction of the Environmental Tribunal considered in this study are rather more modest than some of the earlier proposals for environmental courts or land use and environmental tribunals. We do not claim its introduction would resolve all the challenges involved in delivering effective and modern environmental regulation, but it does appear to offer an attractive and viable model which fits well with the current reform agenda for public services. The Environmental Tribunal would lead to the better application of current environmental law and policy, a more secure basis for addressing future challenges, increased public confidence in how we handle environmental regulation, and the improved environmental outcomes which should follow.

CHAPTER 6

TRUST AND TRANSPARENCY – RESHAPING ENVIRONMENTAL GOVERNANCE IN NORTHERN IRELAND*

EXECUTIVE SUMMARY

Background to the Report

1. This Report is concerned with developing and strengthening ways in which Northern Ireland deals with environmental policy. It was commissioned and funded by a coalition of non-governmental organisations, but the analysis and recommendations reflect the independent judgement of the author. The Report deliberately avoids making overly prescriptive recommendations – the intention is that the analysis will provide the basis for a serious debate on how existing structures could be improved. It was written at a time when devolution was suspended, but assumes that at some point the process of devolution will be re-continued – in the meantime suspension should not inhibit discussion on improving current arrangements.

The Environmental Challenge for Northern Ireland

2. Environmental policy and law have developed rapidly in the last decade. On the horizon is a range of challenging new environmental requirements, many deriving from European Community legislation, which will need to be implemented fully in Northern Ireland. The report considers ways of improving governmental arrangements in Northern Ireland in order to ensure more effective development and implementation of environmental policy. Useful lessons can be learnt from structures that have been set up in other parts of the United Kingdom and in other European countries, but this does not mean that Northern Ireland should slavishly copy arrangements in other jurisdictions. Equally there is a danger it could find itself left behind in developing the best of contemporary practice.

3. Current governmental structures in Northern Ireland for handling environmental policy are complex. This is hardly surprising. Contemporary environmental concerns do not readily

*Macrory R (2004) *Trust and Transparency: Reshaping Environmental Governance in Northern Ireland* Centre for Law and the Environment, University College, London.

fall into discrete categories, which can easily be handled by a single government department or body. They can legitimately encompass local issues such as noise, waste disposal or river pollution, which may have immediate impacts on individuals and local communities. But they also raise wider, longer-term challenges such as biodiversity, transport patterns, resource use and, in the global context, climate change, that are bound to cut across the interests of many departments. The diagram on Environmental Governance (fig. 1, p 279) provides a snap-shot of the key government departments and their associated bodies in Northern Ireland with a direct interest in environmental policy. Government departments have responsibility for the development of policy, but in order to ensure better implementation of policy, many have also established bodies such as Executive Agencies (which are part of their departments but act with a degree of managerial independence) or non-departmental public bodies (which are legally independent from their sponsoring department). In addition, many departments have also set up bodies which have no executive function but whose role is to provide advice on specific areas of policy.

4.   In 1990 the House of Commons Environment Select Committee described the quality of the environment as one of Northern Ireland's greatest assets. Since then there have been improvements in the way that government handles the environment, but there have also been a number of recent official reports in areas such as water pollution and nature conservation which have highlighted problems of poor resourcing, inadequate management systems and poor enforcement. Northern Ireland has also gained a reputation for late transposition of European Community Directives concerning the environment, and as a result the United Kingdom is currently facing a number of infraction actions brought by the European Commission. In recent years much effort has been made to ensure that the formal legislation transposing EC obligations into Northern Ireland law is up to date and comprehensive. The challenge in the future will be to ensure proper implementation in practice. Failure to do so can lead to infringement proceedings before the European Court of Justice and the possibility of severe financial penalties that will fall on Northern Ireland.

The Three Core Themes of the Report

5.   Against that background, the report is based around three core themes:

(i)   *Delivery arrangements* – the nature of the governmental bodies responsible for delivering core environmental policy and for ensuring that the requirements of environmental law are fully implemented in practice,

(ii)   *Accountability mechanisms* – the methods by which government departments and their executive bodies are held accountable to the public for what they do, and

(iii) *Provision of policy advice* – the arrangements by which government secures independent policy advice on environmental matters.

These are all important issues which are common to many areas of government, but the cross-cutting nature of the modern environmental agenda poses particular challenges in developing effective arrangements. Under each of these three themes the report suggests a number of key options for Northern Ireland, together with their main benefits and disadvantages. The themes are clearly connected with each other, but they are not necessarily mutually dependent. For instance, it might be decided to retain the existing structure of the Environment and Heritage Service in Northern Ireland (Theme 1), but this would not avoid the need to consider both ways to improve accountability (Theme 2) and provide for cross-departmental sources of independent policy advice to government (Theme 3).

Theme 1: Delivery Arrangements

Environment and Heritage Service

6.1   As the diagram on Environmental Governance shows, a number of different government departments have a direct responsibility for various environmental issues. This report does not reexamine the present allocation of different environmental policy responsibilities between individual departments, though some of the divisions may appear somewhat perplexing. At the core, though, lies the Department of the Environment together with its key body for implementing environmental policy and law within its responsibility, Environment and Heritage Service (EHS). Environment and Heritage Service is currently an executive agency, meaning that it has no independent legal status distinct from the Department, although it operates with a degree of financial and managerial freedom.

6.2 When it comes to comparisons with environmental agencies now operating in other parts of the United Kingdom, two features of EHS are striking. First, it is the only environmental regulator structured on the executive agency model rather than as a non-departmental public body and therefore lacks formal independence from the Department of the Environment. As a consequence, it has not developed the transparency of decision-making now seen in equivalent environmental regulatory bodies in other parts of the United Kingdom, nor has it been able to develop a distinctive, authoritative, and more independent voice in policy debate in Northern Ireland. The second distinctive feature of EHS is the broad sweep of its environmental responsibilities, which encompass pollution control, nature conservation and heritage protection. These are much wider in scope than those available to other environmental agencies in the United Kingdom, and could be seen as providing a sound basis for a truly integrated approach to the delivery of environmental policy and regulation.

Options for the future

6.3 Against that background, and in the light of future demands on environmental regulation, there are a number of key options concerning the future structure of Environment and Heritage Service.

Option 1.No change in the current status of the Agency. This is the least costly option, both in terms of institutional disruption and financial costs. It would allow EHS to improve services within its existing structure, but will fail to satisfy the demands for a more independent regulator, and for a governmental body that can engage more openly in debate and policy development. The opportunities for providing the Government with a distinctive, and more independent, source of environmental policy advice based on operational experience and technical expertise would be lost.

Option 2. Remove the executive agency status of EHS and fully incorporate it within the Department of the Environment. This would ensure a closer connection between policy development and policy delivery, and avoid the extra costs of establishing a more independent environment agency. It would acknowledge that the Executive Agency model, while suited for some types of public service delivery, is less appropriate for a body with extensive regulatory functions, and may indeed give a misleading impression to the general public that it is more independent than is the reality. Political accountability would rest more clearly with the Minister. The disadvantages are that this would reduce the mechanisms for performance accountability associated with Executive Agencies and, as with Option 1, would fail to meet concerns for a more independent regulatory body. It is likely to inhibit moves towards standards of greater transparency in decision-making now being seen in environmental agencies in other parts of the United Kingdom.

Option 3. Transform EHS into an environmental protection authority with separate legal status based on the structure of a non-department public body. This would be consistent with structures now familiar in other parts of the United Kingdom, and satisfy desires for an environmental regulator with more independence from government departments. Its focus on the delivery of regulatory outcomes is likely to assist Northern Ireland in meeting the requirements of both existing and future European Community environmental legislation. Assuming that all or many of the existing responsibilities of EHS were transferred to the new body, its combination of functions across the environment would give Northern Ireland a distinctive new authority that could become one of the leading integrated environmental authorities in Europe. Such a body would provide a valuable independent source of policy expertise to government and, in line with practices adopted by environmental authorities in the rest of the United Kingdom, would find itself acting in a far more transparent way than is possible with government departments or Executive Agencies.

However, there are disadvantages with such a route. Legislation would be required for the establishment of such a body. There would be real extra costs involved following the loss of common services currently supplied by the Department, such as legal, personnel and finance. By its very nature, such an authority would be less directly politically accountable than the Department or an executive agency, though accountability can to some extent be met by greater transparency in its procedures. Once such a body is established, flexibility in changing its functions is reduced, and such bodies can become institutionalised and over-defensive of existing structures rather than responsive to public policy needs.

Option 4. Transform EHS into a new non-ministerial government department. This follows the model of a body such as the Food Standards Agency, which in formal terms is a government department but headed by an appointed Board rather than a Minister. It would give the authority even more independent legal status than a non-departmental public body but, as with Option 3, would require legislation for its establishment and would involve real extra costs. Such an authority would no longer be financially dependent on the Department of the Environment. A key disadvantage of such a model is greater lack of political accountability (there being no Minister directly responsible for the Agency) and a much greater detachment from the Department of the Environment. A non-ministerial government department may be considered problematic in constitutional terms, and one that should be reserved for rare cases or where there has been a dramatic loss of public confidence in a policy issue, such as that preceding the establishment of the Food Standards Agency.

Option 5. Revert the delivery of major areas of environmental regulation back to existing elected Local Authorities or new forms of local regional government if developed. This has the advantages of ensuring greater local political accountability and may be seen to be consistent with the principle of subsidiarity and the local delivery of services. EHS (or its replacement body) could exercise a supervisory role. This approach, however, does not meet the perceived advantages of an independent regulator which can deliver a consistent approach divorced from direct political interference. It would reverse the trend seen in other parts of the United Kingdom, where local authorities lacked sufficient resources and technical expertise needed to deliver many areas of contemporary environmental regulation. It would make it more difficult to ensure the consistency of approach now required by European Community legislation and could increase the risk of infraction proceedings. There would be considerable disruption during the years in which local authorities acquired the skills and staffing needed to perform new functions.

Theme 2: Improving Accountability

7.1   There already exist a number of mechanisms designed to hold executive agencies such as Environment and Heritage Service accountable for their actions. As part of the Department of the Environment, the Minister is ultimately politically answerable for its performance and, through the Department, it can be subject to judicial review where its actions might be illegal. The accountability of governmental bodies can also be substantially strengthened by the creation of institutions with a specific role and sufficient resources to investigate the performance of Government agencies and bodies. Already a number of bodies can perform this role: the Ombudsman (on reference from an

Assembly member), Assembly Committees, and the Northern Ireland Audit Office, which has already produced a number of detailed reports on particular aspects of EHS performance. Nevertheless, the opportunity should be taken to consider to what extent these mechanisms could be strengthened. It is clear that the challenge of effectively implementing environmental regulation and policy will grow in Northern Ireland over the next decade. Non-governmental environmental organisations are growing in sophistication and the public needs to have confidence that there is effective government machinery to hold the performance of departments and their associated agencies to account where there are failings, and to identify lessons for the future.

A new cross-departmental Assembly Committee on Sustainable Development

7.2   The Assembly Environment Committee can perform an important role in monitoring the performance of the Department of the Environment and its associated agencies, but many contemporary environmental issues do not readily fall within discrete boundaries which can easily be handled by a single government department or agency. It is sometimes still all too easy for officials and others to view the environment in a narrow way and assume it falls outside their sphere of interest. Within Northern Ireland many policy issues with profound environmental implications – such as transport, energy, housing and agriculture – either fall within the prime responsibility of departments other than the Department of the Environment or require a co-ordinated approach between a number of departments. These types of issues often fall within current concepts of sustainable development.

It would therefore be valuable for the Assembly to establish a new cross-departmental Committee on Sustainable Development, following the model of the Westminster Environmental Audit Committee. It would not replace the Assembly Committee on the Environment. Its primary role would be to focus on cross-cutting environmental issues which involve a number of departmental interests other than those of the Department of the Environment, and which might otherwise escape sufficient scrutiny from Assembly committees.

Options for New Environmental Audit Bodies

7.3   The current machinery for carrying out independent auditing of departments and public bodies with environmental responsibilities could also be strengthened.

Option 1. Create an Environmental Audit Commissioner. This would be a new, independent position with specific responsibility to investigate and report on the performance of governmental bodies in their exercise of environmental responsibilities. The Commissioner would develop the specialist environmental knowledge and expertise needed for investigations and, unlike the more general accountability bodies, would avoid being distracted by other responsibilities. Creating such a Commissioner would be a clear signal by Government that it is now taking the environment seriously. However, it would be necessary to establish that the environment is sufficiently distinctive from other areas of government policy to warrant a dedicated new body. There are real costs involved in establishing such a body, and it could lead to unnecessary duplication with the functions of other bodies such as the Northern Ireland Audit Office.

Option 2. Strengthen the capacity of the Northern Ireland Audit Office in the environmental field. This option has the advantage of building on an existing institution with the necessary powers and experience in investigating the performance of governmental bodies, and one that has already developed an interest in the environment with its two reports on the performance of Environment and Heritage Service. It would recognise that the environmental challenge is sufficiently broad to require greater resources and more specialised expertise that is presently available. This model has considerable attractions, though there remains a danger that the environment would still be lost within the wider responsibilities of the NI Audit Office. Furthermore, the rationale for the Audit Office's decisions to choose particular areas of investigation is not especially clear. There are, for example, no developed mechanisms for investigating complaints by members of the public.

Option 3. Create a dedicated Environment Audit body and/or Environment Commissioner within the existing Northern Ireland Audit Office. This is a variation of the second option, but one which gives a more visible significance to the environment and acknowledges the distinctive challenges it raises. This model in many ways would mirror the Canadian Commissioner of the

Environment and Sustainable Development, established in 1996 within the Office of the Auditor General. This option, though also involving costs, has the advantage of building on the strengths of an existing institution and avoiding unnecessary overlap of functions between institutions but creates a visible, distinctive entity within the Audit Office.

Theme 3: Provision of Independent Policy Advice on the Environment

8.1   The Department of the Environment has already established a number of official bodies with a responsibility to provide it with independent advice on various aspects of environmental policy. This report does not examine the effectiveness of these existing arrangements, nor does it question the need for their continued existence. Independently structured environment agencies can also provide government with a valuable source of policy advice, based both on their experience in actually operating on the ground and their technical expertise.

8.2   However, experience in Europe shows that, in addition to these types of bodies, there are considerable gains to be made in setting up an independent environmental advisory body that can provide government with a longer-term examination of environmental issues that do not necessarily fall within existing departmental boundaries. Broadly two forms of bodies have developed. Bodies such as the UK Royal Commission on Environmental Pollution or the German Council of Environmental Advisers are composed of individual experts from different disciplines or with particular experience. One of their key roles is to provide an independent, authoritative and in-depth analysis of key environmental challenges. The second type of body, which includes many of the more recent sustainable development commissions that have been established in other European countries, is more in the way of a stakeholder body, with its members tending to represent particular sectors of society with an interest in the environment. These two types of bodies are not mutually exclusive, though an expert rather than a stakeholder body has particular attractions, provided it adopts a multi-disciplinary approach, and operates with an open mind. It is important to recognise that the existence of such a body does not replace the need for more specialised departmental advisory bodies. It is essential to the effectiveness of such a body that, in addition to the appointment of members of distinction and expertise, it is given the freedom to choose its own areas for study and has a sufficiently resourced secretariat support to ensure depth and authority in its reports.

8.3 Both the Royal Commission on Environmental Pollution and the UK Sustainable Development Commission are UK-wide bodies that take an interest in Northern Ireland. However, Northern Ireland currently lacks any dedicated arrangement that provides for an authoritative and independent analysis of longer-term environmental challenges for the region, and one that is detached from existing departmental boundaries. If the model of the multi-disciplinary expert body were adopted, there are a number of options:

Option 1. Strengthen links with the Royal Commission on Environmental Pollution. The Royal Commission is a United Kingdom wide body and, although in recent years it has engaged more fully with the devolved administrations, more might be done to ensure that the interests and concerns of Northern Ireland are fully reflected in its inquiries. This would require departments to be more fully engaged with the development of the Commission's reports. Ideally, there should be at least one member appointed with a Northern Ireland background, though this may not always be possible since, in the final analysis, members should be appointed for their individual expertise and experience rather than as representing any particular region or sector of society.

Option 2. Establish a new Northern Ireland Commission on the Environment. This would be along similar lines to the RCEP, and would reflect the fact that, as a UK wide body, the RCEP is unlikely to have the time and resources to examine in depth environmental issues relating specifically to Northern Ireland. It would not replace the RCEP, but its establishment could lead to difficult issues of overlap of functions, and might lead to a detachment of RCEP concern with Northern Ireland in its consideration of environmental issues facing the United Kingdom. It might also lead to demands from other devolved administrations to create their own Commissions, diminishing the distinctive authority of the Royal Commission. It may also be that the costs of establishing such a body solely concerned with Northern Ireland are not justified against the benefits that would result.

Option 3. Establish a Commission on the Environment in Ireland. This is a more challenging proposal and envisages an expert advisory body established jointly by both the Northern Ireland

Government and the Irish Government under the auspices of the British-Irish Council, and reporting to both governments. It would be based on the premise that there are environmental issues where in-depth, independent studies on the longer-term implications of current trends and policies as they affect the whole of the island would be a valuable input to policy thinking to both Governments. Transport patterns, water management, and waste management might be good examples. Environmental issues were already identified in the Good Friday Agreement as a suitable area for cooperation, and there already exist examples of cross-border cooperation in fields such as water pollution and fisheries. However these arrangements develop, it should be stressed that the proposed Commission would have no executive functions or powers to bind governments, but would be a source of independent expert advice to both governments from a distinct perspective. The advantages of this option are that it would be less likely to create problems of overlap with a UK body such as the Royal Commission on Environmental Pollution. The establishment and running costs would be shared between the two governments.

1. Delivery Mechanisms Surrounding Environment And Heritage Service (EHS)

Option 1   No change of existing status as an executive agency within the Department of the Environment

Option 2   Abandon executive agency status and incorporate functions of EHS fully within Department of the Environment

Option 3   Create a new Environment Authority structured as a non-departmental public body

Option 4   Create a new Environment Authority structured as a non-ministerial government department

Option 5   Give Local Authorities prime responsibility for implementing environment regulation with EHS (or its replacement body) having enhanced supervisory powers

2. Improving Accountability

Assembly Committee

Create a new cross-departmental Sustainable Development Assembly Committee

Options for Auditing Mechanisms

Option 1   Establish a new independent Environment Audit Commissioner

Option 2   Strengthen environmental capacity within the NI Audit Office

Option 3   Create a dedicated Environmental Unit/Commissioner within the NI Audit Office

3.   Cross-Departmental Independent Policy Advice On The Environment

Option 1   Strengthen links with the Royal Commission on Environmental Pollution

Option 2   Establish a Northern Ireland Commission on the Environment

Option 3   Establish a Commission on the Environment for the island of Ireland reporting to both governments

1.   THE CONTEXT

1.1   This report is concerned with ways of developing and improving environmental governance in Northern Ireland. Environmental law and policy have developed rapidly in the last decade, and on the horizon there is a range of new environmental requirements, many deriving from European Community legislation, which will need to be implemented effectively. But the detailed substance of existing and future environmental law is not the prime concern of this report; rather, it considers how existing institutional arrangements in Northern Ireland could be developed to secure more effective policy and practical outcomes for the future.

1.2   The report is based on three key themes:

(i)   Delivery Arrangements – the nature of the governmental bodies responsible for delivering core environmental policy and ensuring that the requirements of environmental law are fully implemented in practice,

(ii)   Accountability Mechanisms – the methods by which such bodies are held accountable to the public for what they do and

(iii)   Provision of Policy Advice – the arrangements by which government secures independent policy advice on environmental matters.

These are all important issues that are common to many areas of government, but the cross-cutting nature of the modern environmental agenda poses particular challenges in developing effective arrangements to handle each of them. Under each of these three themes the report suggests a number of options for Northern Ireland, together with their main benefits and disadvantages. The themes are clearly connected with each other, but they are not necessarily mutually dependent. For instance, it might be decided to retain the existing structure of the Environment and Heritage Service in Northern Ireland (Theme 1), but this would not invalidate the need to consider both ways to improve accountability (Theme 2) or provide for better sources of independent cross-departmental policy advice to Government (Theme 3). The Report deliberately avoids making prescriptive recommendations – the intention is that the analysis will provide the basis for a serious debate on how existing structures could be improved. The Report was written at a time when devolution was suspended, and assumes that at some point the process of devolution will be resumed – the suspension should not in the meantime inhibit discussion on improving current arrangements.

The Report also considers institutional structures in other parts of the United Kingdom and other European countries since these may provide useful lessons and pointers for the future. This does not mean that Northern Ireland should slavishly duplicate arrangements in other jurisdictions, but equally it should not allow itself to be left behind in the development of structures for contemporary environmental governance.

The Review of Public Administration

1.3   Any such study has to been seen in the context of the wider Review of Public Administration that was established by the Northern Ireland Executive in 2002 as the first major review in 30 years of how public services in Northern Ireland are organized and delivered. The Review identified over 140 organisations operating within the public sector , and in 2003 issued a consultation document, 'The Review of Public Administration in Northern Ireland'[1] which identified a number of key themes and issues which are likely to shape future models of governance. This study is not intended to pre-empt the outcome of the Review, and some of the principles already being highlighted by the Review, such as efficient and effective delivery and arrangements for accountability, also feature strongly in this Report. The Review is not examining the detailed operation of all the governmental organisations falling within its terms of reference, and bodies concerned with environmental protection have not been a focus for its study to date.

1.4   As section 2 indicates, the current governmental structures in Northern Ireland for handling environmental policy are complex and diffuse. This is hardly surprising. Contemporary environmental concerns do not readily fall within discrete boundaries which can be handled by a single government department or agency. They can legitimately encompass local issues such as noise, waste disposal or river pollution, which may have immediate impact on individuals and localities; but they also raise wider, longer-term challenges such as biodiversity, transport patterns, resource use and climate change – policy issues which are bound to cut across many departmental interests. In fact, under current arrangements in Northern Ireland, the majority of departments can be said to have a direct interest in environmental policy issues, but it is sometimes still all too easy for officials and others to view the environment in a narrow way and as mainly the responsibility of specialised departments or bodies. This would be a mistake in the light of contemporary debates on longer-term sustainability issues, and a particular challenge for Northern Ireland is how to devise suitable arrangements for tackling these cross-departmental aspects of environmental policy.

2.   MAPPING CURRENT ARRANGEMENTS IN NORTHERN IRELAND

Departmental Responsibilities

2.1   Nearly all areas of government policy have implications for the environment, and the existing policy responsibilities currently

[1] The Review of Public Administration in Northern Ireland' (2003) Discussion Document

assigned to different departments within the NI Executive underline the complexities involved, and the need for effective interlinkages and co-operation. Excluding the Office of the First Minister and Deputy First Minister, all of the 10 departments have policy responsibilities with significant environmental content.

Some of the divisions may appear somewhat perplexing, both to the general public and to individuals or companies subject to environmental regulation who can find themselves dealing with a confusing range of departments and their agencies. In the future there may well be opportunities for rationalisation and simplification, although this study is not primarily concerned with re-evaluating the responsibilities of differing government departments. Instead, it focuses on the key aspects of the institutional structures for the delivery of environmental policy requirements.

Department of the Environment	Land use planning control, pollution control, countryside protection, nature conservation and biodiversity, local government, road licencing, marine environment, climate change, promotion of sustainable development across NI Executive
Department for Regional Development	Strategic land use planning, transport planning, roads, provision of water and sewerage services, ports and harbours, energy efficiency in private sector
Department for Social Development	Urban regeneration and housing, energy efficiency in domestic housing
Department of Agriculture and Rural Development	Flood defence, agriculture, agri-environment, inshore fisheries regulation
Department of Culture, Arts and Leisure	Fishery protection
Department of Education	Education curriculum, teaching of environmental education in schools

Department of Enterprise, Trade and Investment	Energy, tourism, mineral development, health and safety at work
Dept of Finance and Personnel	Building regulations, public sector energy efficiency, purchasing policy including green purchasing
Department of Employment and Learning	Education in colleges and university, professional training
Department of Health, Social Services and Public Safety	Public health including effects of air pollution and noise

The Delivery Of Environmental Policy

2.2   Over the years, government departments have established various arrangements for the delivery of environmental policy in Northern Ireland. These include different forms of public bodies, such as executive agencies and more independently structured bodies, which operate with various degrees of managerial and financial freedom from their core departments. They also include a number of advisory bodies which have no operational functions as such, but have been established to provide expert advice to departments on various aspects of environmental policy. Figure 1 provides an overall picture of the key arrangements currently in place, and identifies governmental bodies whose responsibilities and functions are most likely to have environmental implications.[2] The Department of the Environment has, of course, a central interest in the environment, but if one took, for example, the policy implications of climate change the number of additional departments and bodies potentially involved becomes considerable; to take some examples, the NI Authority for Energy Regulation, the Home Energy Conservation Authority, the Building Regulations Advisory Committee (for energy efficient building standards), and the Rivers Agency (for flood risk management). The figure does not claim to be comprehensive and, while it deliberately places bodies in concentric circles reflecting in broad terms degrees of operational independence

---

[2] The Review of Public Administration has recently produced a comprehensive set of organisational charts of public sector bodies operating in Northern Ireland. In contrast to Figure 1, the core information is structured on vertical lines under each Department, though the report also includes analysis based on various policy themes relating to service to the citizen and the public organisations involved.

from departments, the precise arrangements and relationships with departments will often vary considerably, both as a matter of law and in practice. Section 5 of this Report considers the implications of the distinctions between the various forms of arrangements that government can adopt.

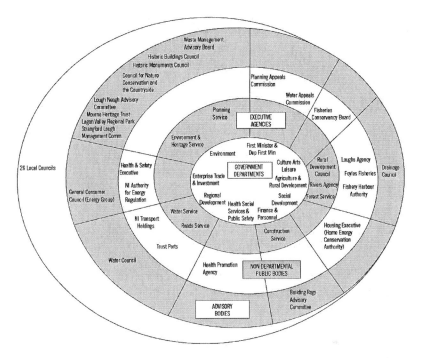

Figure 1 Environmental Governance in Northern Ireland.
The diagram focuses on Northern Ireland departments and bodies and does not include certain UK wide bodies such as the Food Standards Agency, and Crown Estates which will also have an interest in certain NI environmental issues.

Implementing Modern Environmental Regulation

2.3   In thinking about current governmental arrangements it is important to stress that the implementation and enforcement of contemporary environmental regulation is not a straightforward, mechanistic exercise. Regulation based on the licensing or permitting of processes or discrete activities (such as discharges into waters) has long formed the key element of environmental protection. This type of direct regulation can achieve much in improving environmental quality and will continue to do so, though many environmental regulators are now looking for smarter ways of implementing this form of regulation – avoiding, for example, a 'tick-box' mentality towards implementation, and focussing on ensuring positive environmental outcomes, using risk based approaches to concentrate resources on activities most likely to give rise to problems. At the same time, the nature of many contemporary environmental challenges will also require new approaches towards designing and enforcing regulation which involve the use of mechanisms such as environmental taxes, trading schemes and negotiated agreements.

Appendix 1 provides an indicative list of key environmental legislation currently in force in Northern Ireland, together with the government departments and public bodies charged with its implementation. Although the Department of the Environment and its executive agency, Environment and Heritage Service, have major responsibilities in many areas, it will be seen that significant powers rest with other departments and bodies that they sponsor, reflecting the division of core policy responsibilities.

2.4   It is also important to recognise that many of those bodies or individuals who are subject to existing or new regulatory requirements are likely to need authoritative and consistent advice on how to meet their legal requirements. This will especially be the case for smaller and medium sized enterprises, or where sectors are faced with new sets of environmental obligations. It is clear that in some sectors such as agriculture those subject to regulation will, under current arrangements, find themselves dealing with a potentially confusing number of departments and governmental bodies with a legitimate interest in their activities. One ideal model would have those subject to environmental regulation dealing with a single regulatory body while technical advice and appropriate financial assistance would be sought from a parallel but similarly focussed government body. In practice it is not easy to make such a sharp distinction of functions, nor, given the range of modern environmental requirements, is consolidation easy to achieve. However, it is important to acknowledge the confusion that the present picture must present to many who are seeking to comply with environmental requirements

2.5   The Better Regulation Task Force, an advisory body to the UK Government, has established five key principles for modern regulatory regimes: transparency, accountability, consistency, proportionality, and the need to assess performance against actual outcomes. Regulatory bodies can also provide government with an important source of policy advice, based on their distinctive practical experience. In the environmental field it is therefore clear that, when we talk of a regulatory body or agency, it would be wrong to view such a body as one that is simply concerned with enforcing regulation in a mechanistic way. The functions are much richer and rather more subtle. It is equally clear that demands on bodies in Northern Ireland with the responsibility for implementing environmental regulation will grow, both in complexity and substance. The next section therefore focuses on the Department of the Environment and its core agency for delivering much of Northern Ireland's environmental policy, Environment and Heritage Service. These are the bodies with the core environmental responsibilities in Northern Ireland.

3. DEPARTMENT OF THE ENVIRONMENT AND ENVIRONMENT AND HERITAGE SERVICE

Department Of The Environment And Its Current Structure

3.1   The Department of the Environment is currently structured on the basis of a number of central policy divisions together with four Executive Agencies: Environment and Heritage Service, the Planning Service, Driver and Vehicle Licensing (Northern Ireland) and the Driving and Vehicle Testing Agency. In addition, there are three statutory advisory bodies, the Council for Nature Conservation and the Countryside, the Historic Buildings Council, and the Historic Monuments Council; and more recently a non-statutory Waste Management Advisory Board. Co-ordinating and monitoring of the work of the Department is carried out by a Departmental Board, consisting of the Permanent Secretary, the Deputy Secretary (Planning and Local Government Group), the Deputy Secretary (Environment and Road Safety Group) and the Director of Corporate Services.

Environment And Heritage Service

3.2   Environment and Heritage Service (EHS) was established in 1996 as an executive agency of DoE(NI) following a decade or so of discussion concerning possible new structures in governmental arrangements for the environment. In the context of nature conservation, the 1984 Balfour Review had recommended against following the practice in the rest of the United Kingdom of establishing a separate agency for nature and countryside protection.[3] Instead, the review recommended that these functions

---

[3] J Balfour (1984) *A New Look at the Northern Ireland Countryside* Belfast HMSO. See also K Milton (1990) *Our Countryside Our Concern* Report for Northern Ireland Environment Link

remain within the government department, mainly on the grounds that the distribution of central and local government functions (especially in land use planning) was distinct in Northern Ireland. It was felt that more influence would be achieved by working 'on the inside' of government rather than from a more independent position.

In its 1990 report on Environmental Issues in Northern Ireland (the Rossi report) the House of Commons Select Committee on the Environment (HC 39 Session 1990-91) recommended that an independent regulatory environmental agency should be established in Northern Ireland. It did not want Northern Ireland to lose out on developments in effective, independent environment agencies that had taken place in other parts of the United Kingdom, and envisaged an agency that would develop its own character and be a focus for local pride in the environment. At the time of the Rossi report, the Department of the Environment NI was responsible both for the enforcement of environmental controls and the provision of water and sewerage services, and the Committee was particularly concerned that the Department's 'poacher-gamekeeper' role inevitably compromised its effectiveness as a regulator and undermined public confidence. In 1994 a 'prior options' study carried out by government considered the model of an independent environment agency, but rejected it in favour of establishing the Environment and Heritage Service as an executive agency within the Department. According to the 1998 Report of the Comptroller and Auditor General for Northern Ireland, the main reasons given were that (i) an agency model would be more effective in regulating other government agencies such as the Water Service and (ii) it would be inappropriate for an independent agency to regulate agencies falling within government departments.

Structure and Responsibility of EHS

3.3 As an executive agency EHS has no legal status independent from the Department of the Environment, but operates with a degree of managerial and financial independence against specified performance targets established by the Department. In the area of environmental regulation, the Department has delegated the main responsibility for implementation and enforcement to EHS, including key areas such as industrial process control, water pollution, nature conservation and, most recently, waste management licensing. The main aims of EHS, according to its Corporate Plan, are 'to protect and conserve the natural environment and built heritage and to promote its appreciation for the benefit of present and future generations'. In support of these aims, its key objectives are to implement the Department's responsibilities for:

- protecting and improving the quality of air, land and water (including marine protection);

- conserving biodiversity and the countryside and protecting species;

- protecting, recording and conserving historic monuments and buildings;

- promoting awareness and appreciation of the environment and heritage.

Environment & Heritage Service	2002-3[4]
Staffing	521
Main income sources	
Government grant	£34.8m
Environmental charges	£1.6m
Other income sources including admission charges	£0.9m

EHS is similar in size, both in staff numbers and resource costs, to the Scottish Environment Protection Agency, though with a different range of responsibilities. According to the Corporate and Business Plan of the Department of the Environment NI,[5] it is planned to recruit an additional 162 staff to EHS in 2003/4 with an increased cost allocation to total £54.7m; thereafter, until 2006, the figures are planned to remain roughly level.

Concerns about Environment and Heritage Service

3.4 This study is not designed to provide a fresh evaluation of the effectiveness of EHS in achieving all its objectives, and in recent years it has been subject to scrutiny by official bodies in certain fields of its operations. In a 1998 report, *The Control of Water*

---

[4] EHS Annual Report and Agency Accounts 2002/2003. Figures are rounded.
[5] Dept of the Environment (NI) (2003) Corporate Plan 2003-06, Business Plan 2003-04

Pollution in Northern Ireland, the Northern Ireland Audit Office[6] was concerned that EHS failed to have effective systems in place to measure data against its policy objectives for water pollution control. It recommended that a formal target for compliance with water discharge consents be introduced. The report welcomed steps that had been taken to provide better controls of discharges by the Water Service but concluded that much remained to be done. It identified weaknesses in dealing with pollution incidents and the enforcement of discharge consents by industry and urged the introduction of detailed and unambiguous policy guidance to ensure effective enforcement in a consistent and equitable manner.

3.5   In 2001 the report of the Public Accounts Committee of the Assembly, *The Control of River Pollution in Northern Ireland*[7], welcomed new increases in EHS staff resources and the reduction in numbers of pollution incidents reported, but expected EHS to set a firm target for bringing Northern Ireland into line with the standard of response service provided elsewhere in the United Kingdom. It considered that EHS must take more robust action against all who cause pollution incidents and demonstrate that the action it takes against the Water Service is as rigorous as possible, given the constraints imposed by the latter's Crown immunity. The Public Accounts Committee was pleased that EHS had increased dramatically the length of rivers being monitored but was concerned that almost 50% of consented discharges were not subject to systematic monitoring. The PAC noted improvements in the development of an enforcement policy but was generally extremely concerned at the slow progress being made by DoE – described as *'slow to the point of lethargic'* – in implementing recommendations of the 1998 Audit Office Report. It accepted that resources had previously been a problem, but this was symptomatic of the *'deplorably low priority'* that had been given to environmental issues in the past.

3.6   In 2003 the Northern Ireland Audit Office reported on Areas of Special Scientific Interest.[8] It noted that, in the continuing absence of sufficient resources, EHS had not yet produced a long-term strategy for completing designation of the ASSI network in Northern Ireland, which had fallen behind the rest of the United

[6] Northern Ireland Audit Office (1998) *Control of River Pollution in Northern Ireland* HC 693 Session 1997/8

[7] Public Accounts Committee (2001) 3rd Report *Control of River Pollution in Northern Ireland*

[8] Northern Ireland Audit Office (2003) *Areas of Special Scientific Interest* NIA 103/02 HC499

Kingdom. There was no comprehensive database on candidate sites, and it was not possible to estimate the extent of damage occurring due to delays in designation. The report recommended that EHS draw up a more challenging timetable for completion and establish a formal ASSI management information system. The report noted that EHS had no comprehensive, up-to-date picture of the condition of ASSIs similar to that available in other parts of the United Kingdom. In relation to enforcement, the report acknowledged weaknesses in the existing Northern Ireland legislation which are intended to be met by what is now the Environment Order 2002, but it criticised the continuing failure of EHS to produce fully documented and consistently applied enforcement policies and procedures as representing 'poor management practice.'

Calls for EHS to become a More Independent Environmental Regulator

3.7   The original Rossi report had called for the establishment of an independent environmental regulator comparable to those then being developed in the rest of the United Kingdom. One of the main reasons then given by government for preferring the model of an agency within the Department was the fact that key functions concerning water and sewerage services in Northern Ireland remained fully within the public sector, and it was considered that an executive agency within a department would be in a better position than a more independent body to influence and regulate part of government services. Whatever the merits of the argument at the time, the current consultations taking place on new models for the delivery of water and sewerage services, even if not resulting in full privatisation,[9] clearly provide an opportunity to re-evaluate the current regulatory arrangements.

3.8   Other bodies have continued to make the case for a more independent environment regulator. The Public Accounts Committee, in its 2001 report, noted that 'Despite all the promises of progress, we remain deeply concerned about a situation where NI is the only part of the United Kingdom without an independent environmental protection body. The totally unsatisfactory nature of the watchdog role within government up until now strongly suggests that real independence is essential for building up long-term public confidence that our environment is being properly safeguarded.'[10]

[9] Department of Regional Development (2003) *Reform of Water and Sewerage Services in Northern Ireland Public Consultation Report* and see *Ministerial Press Release* 7 Oct 2003
[10] PAC Report supra, para 42

3.9   In October 2002, EHS was directed by the Minister of the Environment to cease its practice of formally objecting to planning applications for new housing where existing sewerage infrastructure would fail to meet legal standards, although the Minister stated that EHS would continue to 'alert the Planning Service to the environmental issues'. The European Commission is now investigating a complaint concerning 22 sewerage treatment works which are claimed to fail to comply with European Community law. Against this background, Friends of the Earth is campaigning for an independent Environment Protection Agency.[11]

3.10   In its 2003 report 'Worth the Paper',[12] Northern Ireland Environment Link, whose members include 41 environmental and conservation organisations in Northern Ireland, also called for the establishment of an independent environmental protection authority for Northern Ireland.

4.   THE SIGNIFICANCE OF THE EUROPEAN COMMUNITY DIMENSION

4.1   Establishing new institutions can be costly, both in real financial terms and in the distraction and administrative upheaval inevitably caused. But in weighing up the costs and benefits of change, the significance of the European Community dimension and the very real financial risks facing Northern Ireland should it fail to comply with the requirements of existing and future Community environmental law are significant factors that now need to be taken into account.

4.2   Community environmental legislation now represents a dominant influence in many areas of environmental regulation. Once a Community law is agreed, Member States are obliged to implement it within the time-scales prescribed (normally two or three years), and under the European Treaty the European Commission has a supervisory duty to ensure that Member States comply with their obligations. This can lead to enforcement action by the Commission against the Member State concerned and eventually to a case before the European Court of Justice. In 1997 the Treaty was amended, largely at the initiative of the UK government, to allow the European Court of Justice to impose financial penalties on a Member State which failed to comply

[11] Friends of the Earth, (2003) *Northern Ireland Newsletter* Issue 7 August 2003
[12] Northern Ireland Environment Link (2003) *Worth the Paper* NIEL, Belfast

with a judgement of the Court. Penalties are suggested by the Commission based on a Commission policy document. The first such penalty imposed by the Court concerned an illegal landfill site in Greece and resulted in a daily penalty of Euro 20,000 on Greece for as long as the relevant EC law was breached. In giving its judgment in *Commission v Greece*[13], the Court endorsed the approach to penalties being taken by the Commission.

4.3   Most EC environmental legislation takes the form of Directives, and the initial obligation of Member States is to formally transpose the obligations of Directives into their national legal systems. In 1990, the Rossi report noted that, compared to the rest of the United Kingdom, Northern Ireland was failing to give sufficient priority to the issue of timely transposition of EC environmental law into Northern Ireland legislation. One excuse given was the distinct and more time-consuming procedures for introducing Northern Ireland legislation, but the European Court of Justice has consistently held that internal constitutional difficulties in national lawmaking is not a good legal defence for a Member State which fails to transpose in time.[14] Despite the recommendations in the Rossi report, there have continued to be significant delays in transposition in Northern Ireland, though the Department of the Environment is now making strenuous efforts to ensure that all necessary legislation is in place and the legislative backlog is shortly to be cleared.

4.4   Ensuring formal transposition of EC law is the responsibility of the Department's Environmental Policy Division rather than EHS. But the European Commission has long insisted that even where national legislation is in place, failure to ensure compliance with EC laws *in practice* is equally a breach of Community law by the Member State, and this approach has been fully endorsed by the European Court of Justice.[15] In the environmental field, the Commission possesses no direct power of inspection within Member States to determine the extent to which Community obligations are complied with in practice. Instead, it has sometimes commissioned reports from consultants on actual practice, and has also encouraged individuals and environmental organisations to alert it to potential areas of non-compliance through a citizen's complaint procedure. If such complaints

---

[13] Case C-387/97 ECR I-369
[14] see, for example, *Commission v Belgium* [1970] ECR 237, *Commission v Italy* [1984] ECR 2361
[15] *Commission v Germany* [1995] ECR I-2189

reveal a *prima facie* case of non-compliance, they are followed up by inquiries to the Member State concerned which may then result in formal enforcement procedures.

4.5   Ensuring compliance in practice is a key responsibility for the body charged with implementing environmental regulation. Although in 1996 the Commission indicated that its first priority would be to ensure that national legislation was in place, it is clear from the table below that the number of enforcement actions in the environmental field concerning non-compliance in practice is still growing.

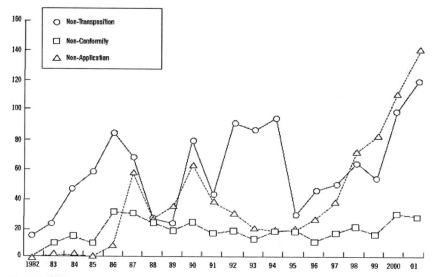

Figure 2. Numbers and types of infraction proceedings initiated by the European Commission in environmental cases 1982-2001.
'Non-transposition' means that the Member State has not sent the Commission any national legislation implementing EC Directives within time-limits;'Non-conformity' means that legislation sent is considered to be defective;'Non-application' refers to examples in practice where, whatever the state of the national law, EC requirements are not actually being met. Note that these now represent the largest number of environmental actions brought by the Commission. Source: Hattan (2003).[16]

4.6   The European Court of Justice has held that, in the absence of express provisions concerning derogation in a particular EC law, financial or practical difficulties offer no defence to non-compliance in practice[17]. The UK government has agreed that, where the failure is the responsibility of a regional administration, the financial costs of any penalty imposed by the European Court

[16] Hatton (2003) 'The Implementation of EC Environmental Law' *Journal of Environmental Law* Vol 15 No 3 273-288
[17] *Commission v Belgium* [1990] ECR I-2821

on the UK will fall to that administration. These sums can be considerable. In the landfill case against Greece, Greece ended up paying a fine of around EUR5m before the landfill site in question was closed. A recent study[18] has listed 11 other cases where the Commission has sought penalty payments in the environmental field for non-compliance with a judgment of the Court, although these were all settled before reaching court. The sums sought were considerable, including, for example, daily penalty payments of EUR106,800 (United Kingdom) and EUR105,500 (France). In November 2003 in *Commission v Spain*[19] the European Court of Justice considered its second case concerning penalties. The case resulted from Spain's continuing failure to comply in practice with the Bathing Water Directive following a decision of the Court in 1998. Although Spain had secured an improvement of compliance of bathing waters from 54.5% in 1992 to around 80% in 2000, the Court imposed a penalty payment of EUR 624,150 per year for non-compliance and the same figure per percentage of bathing waters not in compliance, amounting to over EUR9m.

4.7   According to the European Commission, in April last year there were 16 environmental cases against the United Kingdom involving Northern Ireland, either on its own or as part of a case against the United Kingdom as a whole, that had reached Reasoned Opinion stage or beyond[20]. It is thought that about half of these involve non-implementation in practice as opposed to formal transposition issues. It is clear from the current case law referred to in the previous paragraph that the exposure of Northern Ireland to large penalty payments is now considerable. This is a factor that now needs to be taken into account in weighing up the financial costs of new arrangements, and underlines the need to have in place the most effective institutional machinery for ensuring that EC environmental obligations are met *in practice*. The implementation challenge does not concern simply existing EC environmental law, concerning such areas as habitat protection and sewerage treatment. On the horizon is a range of new EC laws, often involving challenging new targets and mechanisms, and these will also require full implementation both in law and in practice (see Figure 3).

---

[18] Kramer (2003) *EC Environmental Law* Fifth Edition p 390 Sweet and Maxwell, London

[19] *Commission v Spain* C-278/01 25 November 2003

[20] Correspondence, European Commission to Friends of the Earth, February 2003.The 'Reasoned Opinion' stage of European infringement proceedings is the last stage before a country is taken before the European Court of Justice and implies that the Member State must implement in accordance with the Commission's view to avoid action before the Court.

Selected new and anticipated EC environmental legislation

Strategic environmental assessment

Emissions trading for greenhouse gases

Emissions ceilings for key air pollutants

Producer responsibility for waste and electrical equipment

Restrictions on hazardous substances in electrical and electronic equipment

Water framework

New chemicals regulation

Civil liability for environmental damage

End of life vehicles

Traceability of genetically modified organisms and GMO products

Expansion and amendment of Integrated Pollution and Prevention Control Directive

Hazardous waste from mining

Amendment of packaging waste targets

Battery and accumulator waste

Figure 3. Selected new and anticipated EC environmental legislation.

5.   ORGANISATIONAL STRUCTURES FOR THE DELIVERY OF POLICY

5.1   Governments employ various different arrangements for delivering policy objectives, and in many areas there is now an increasing recognition of the need for working in partnership with the voluntary and private sector. Government departments may exercise powers directly but, where it is thought helpful to separate departmental policy making from the actual implementation of policy on the ground, there are four main types of body currently employed in the United Kingdom:

- Executive agencies (e. g. Environment and Heritage Service, Water Service);

- Executive non-departmental public bodies, (e.g. NI Authority for Energy Regulation, Health and Safety Executive for Northern Ireland);

- Non-ministerial government departments (e.g. UK Food Standards Agency); and

- Elected local authorities.

This section considers in more general terms the nature of these bodies, and in doing so reflects a number of significant recent government studies on the issue. This is an important backdrop to evaluating possible options for change in the structures of existing bodies such as Environment and Heritage Service, which are responsible for delivering environmental policy in Northern Ireland.

Executive Agencies

5.2 Executive agencies were launched in the United Kingdom by the 1988 Ibbs Report[21], and used to be more commonly known as 'Next Steps Agencies'. Ibbs advocated the use of agencies within government departments to carry out executive functions of government within a policy and resources framework set by government departments, and with an underlying aim to improve managerial efficiency and re-orientate systems towards the delivery of services. In legal terms, executive agencies remain part of their department but operate with a degree of independence. In its 1998 *Next Steps Report*,[22] the government acknowledged that executive agencies were not the complete answer to the delivery of better services but that the principles they embodied were a step in the right direction. Executive agencies have been the subject of a number of recent high-level reviews in the United Kingdom. In July 2002 the Cabinet Office and HM Treasury published *Better Government Services – Executive Agencies in the 21st Century.*[23] Its main conclusions were that the agencies had provided a flexible and responsive structure for the delivery of executive functions of central government, but there were concerns that in some cases

---

[21] Sir Robin Ibbs (1988) *Improving Management in Government*
[22] Cabinet Office (1998) *Next Steps Report*
[23] HM Treasury and the Prime Minister's Office of Public Services Reform (2002) *Better Government Services – Executive Agencies in the 21st Century* Cabinet Office, London

departments had allowed their agencies to become too divorced from their own strategic thinking.[24]

5.3 The National Audit Office 2003 report, 'Improving Service Delivery – The Role of Executive Agencies'[25] highlighted the central role that executive agencies now play in the delivery of public services. It analysed the role of targets in improving service delivery in 30 executive agencies and, although the study found the majority of existing targets applying to the agencies studied were being met, it made a number of key recommendations to improve performance standards.[26]

Non-Departmental Public Bodies

5.4 Non-departmental public bodies (NDPB) remain the most common alternative form of governmental executive body. The key distinction from an executive agency is that an NDPB is given

---

[24] Key recommendations for Departments to strengthen department – agency relationships include:
(i) Departments should carry out a high-level review to ensure that delivery mechanisms were appropriate to contemporary requirements,
(ii) Department should consider outcome mechanisms as well as policy,
(iii) Departments should maintain simple and clear frameworks at strategic levels with agencies,
(iv) Departments should improve the integration and agency and departmental business planning, and that agency targets should been kept down and focus on areas relating to departmental objectives,
(v) In place of five yearly reviews of individual agencies and non-departmental public bodies, there should be a rolling programme of 'end to end' reviews to examine the delivery of particular policy objectives or Public Service Agreement Targets,
(vi) To provide greater management flexibility, agencies should be given three-year funding agreements to support three year business plans.
[25] National Audit Office (2003) *Improving Service Delivery :The Role of Executive Agencies* HC525 Session 2002-2003
[26] Including :
(i) Agencies need to be more proactive to ensure that targets are sufficiently strengthened in the light of changing public expectations and opportunities offered by new technologies and partnerships,
(ii) Agencies need to have more comprehensive and up-to-date systems in place to assess their customer needs and preferences,
(iii) Agencies need to give more attention to consistent measurement and reporting of performance over time,
(iv) Agencies need to target their actions on improving service delivery on key drivers which have the most potential for sustained improvements which are likely to have real value for users and
(v) Agencies need more sophisticated approaches to measuring their costs and productivity, including benchmarking their processes and costs with other organisations.

a legal entity separate from its sponsoring department with its core structure and functions defined by legislation. Generally, overall management of the body is entrusted to a board appointed by government. This lack of direct accountability through an elected representative was one of the reasons why the 1970 Review Body on Local Government in Northern Ireland[27] concluded that what it then described as 'autonomous boards' were not suitable except for a very limited range of technical or operational functions. While the concern about accountability remains real, it is noteworthy that in recent years bodies such as the Environment Agency in England and Wales have made great efforts to conduct their affairs as transparently as possible, as is illustrated in section 6.

5.5   The degree of independence is, in legal terms, determined by the Statute establishing the NDPB and may vary subtly from body to body. Ministers are generally given the power to issue formal directions, sometimes only on general matters, but in other cases on any specific issue. Such formal directions generally must be published. Income may be derived solely from grant-in-aid from the sponsoring department, but may also include sources of revenue from service functions such as granting licences.

5.6   The recent UK government reviews of executive agencies and non-departmental public bodies have tended to focus on the issue of improving service delivery, and there has been less in the way of agreed principles concerning the choice of the models available and their suitability for particular types of function or activity. Policy development, especially in the environmental field, is a complex process and it is clear that the concept that a government department makes policy while an executive body (whether such a body is in formal terms an executive agency or a non-departmental public body) merely implements policy on the ground is too simplistic. Ideally, final policy-making should remain the responsibility of politically accountable Ministers and government departments, but an implementing agency can also provide a significant source of policy influence and advice based on its specialised expertise and operational experience. When it comes to the implementation of regulation, the recent report on Independent Regulators[28] from the UK Better Regulation Task Force noted that nearly all consultees who were subject

[27] Review Body in Local Government in Northern Ireland (1970) Cmd. 546 HMSO, Belfast
[28] Better Regulation Task Force (2003) *Independent Regulators*, BRTF, London

to regulation[29] agreed that being regulated by an independent regulator was preferable to being regulated by a government department.[30]

5.7   More recently, the Haskins review[31] on the delivery of government policies in rural England, published in October 2003, recommended the establishment of a new body, the Land Management Agency, to incorporate the function of various existing bodies including English Nature. In considering the status of such a body, Lord Haskins recommended a non-departmental public body: 'I believe that incorporating it in DEFRA (for example, as a 'next steps' agency) would not provide the level of independence that is necessary for such a body to work in the decentralized and devolved delivery landscapes to which government is committed.' In February 2004, The Government agreed that the status of the new agency should be a non-departmental public body.[32]

5.8   In considering a choice between an executive agency and a non-departmental public body the main advantages and disadvantages can be summarised as follows:

Executive Agency

Benefits

- Flexible to establish, no legislation needed, and functions easily changed

- Economical since common support services (such as finance, personnel, legal) are provided by the department

- Managerial and resource efficiencies through defined service agreements

- Focus on delivery of services

---

[29] The taskforce defined an independent regulator as 'A body which has been established by Act of Parliament but which operates at arm's length from Government and which has one or more of the following powers : inspection; referral; advice to a third party; licensing; accreditation; or enforcement.' para 2.1, ibid

[30] The benefits noted included: more consistency of decision making, long-term decisions rather than short-term decisions, more transparency, better accountability, more trust between the regulated and the regulator and freedom from political interference.

[31] DEFRA (2003) *Rural Delivery Review* Report by Lord Haskins October 2003

[32] 'It is important to me that the Integrated Agency should have a strong and authoritative voice commanding respect both within and outside Government. It is equally important that the advice I receive from the Integrated Agency is not only independent but is seen to be independent. 'Written Statement, House of Commons, Environment Secretary of State 24/2/04

Disbenefits

- No separate legal status from department

- Form and structure implies greater independence that is the reality

- Form less suitable for a body with regulatory functions

- Role in providing policy advice to the department is often unclear and not properly resourced or accounted for in service agreements with department

- Difficult for agency management to establish fully transparent working practices

Executive Non-Departmental Body

Benefits

- Separate legal status from department

- Greater trust as a regulator in operating consistently, fairly and free from political interference

- Ability to develop longer-term perspectives

- Role in providing independent policy advice to government and greater freedom to engage in public debate

- Able to develop transparent working practices (open board meetings etc.)

- Powers and responsibilities clearly defined

Disbenefits

- Legislation needed to establish body, and to change functions at later date

- Costly to operate – no common services provided by department

- Distanced from direct political accountability with board members appointed rather than elected

- Can become too detached from policy making, and lead to over-separation of policy development and policy delivery.

- Can become over-institutionalised and unresponsive to structural changes

- Funding streams can be complex and too short-term

Non-Ministerial Government Department

5.9 A further variation of organisation, but one found rarely, is a non-ministerial government department. Unlike a non-departmental public body, such an organisation has no formal sponsoring department and funding is sought directly from the government treasury or financial department. Ministers have no power to give directions to such bodies, though clearly they can establish the policy and legal framework within which they operate. Examples of regulatory bodies with this status include the Inland Revenue in England and Wales, where it is considered that impartial decision making without the possibility of any Ministerial interference is essential. A more recent example of a non-ministerial government department operating in a policy sensitive field is the Food Standards Agency, established under the Food Standards Act 1999, where the need for even sharper independence was considered necessary following a loss in public confidence in the wake of the BSE crisis. Non-ministerial government departments are accountable to Select Committees, the National Audit Office and the Ombudsman, but the need for such a department to develop open and consultative procedures to counteract its lack of direct political accountability is even stronger than in the case of non-departmental public bodies. The National Audit Office in England and Wales recently singled out the Food Standards Agency as demonstrating a range of good practice initiatives in an area where public trust and confidence were essential.[33]

Local Government

5.10 An alternative model to establishing various forms of independent agencies is to give more power to elected local government. The

---

[33] National Audit Office (2003) supra, p10

question of whether major public services in Northern Ireland should be provided by enhanced local government bodies, perhaps operating on a regional basis, is one of the models now being considered by the Review of Public Administration in Northern Ireland. In other parts of the United Kingdom local government retains a number of important environmental regulatory functions such as noise control, public nuisances, and contaminated land. Unlike current arrangements in Northern Ireland, land use planning control is primarily the responsibility of local government with central government exercising an appeal function.

5.11   The advantages of a greater role for local government include the more direct political accountability through locally elected representatives and the fact that local government may be more sensitive to local needs and issues. Nevertheless, the trend in many core areas of environmental regulation such as water pollution, waste management licensing, habitat protection, chemical controls and the regulation of industrial processes has been to assign these functions to specialised agencies rather than local government. This is due in part to the high level of specialised technical and scientific expertise required for implementation, and the need for consistency in approach, especially where the implementation of European Community legal requirements is involved. Whatever the future shape and responsibilities of local government in Northern Ireland, it is probably unlikely that these types of more specialised environmental functions are appropriate to revert back to local government, even if it were structured along more regional lines. Nevertheless, it will be important for an environmental agency (whatever model is adopted) to develop cooperative relationships with local government, both at a strategic level (such as the *'Working Better Together'* plan agreed in England and Wales between the Environment Agency and the Local Government Association) and at local level.

	Environment and Heritage Service	Environment Agency (England and Wales	English Nature	Scottish Environment Protection Agency	Irish Environmental Protection Agency
Status	Executive agency of Dept of the Environment (NI)	Non-departmental public body	Non-departmental public body	Non-departmental public body	Non-departmental public body
Management	Chief Executive plus senior management team	Chair, Chief Executive, and Non-executive Members appointed by Ministers	Chair, Chief Executive, and Non-executive Members appointed by Ministers	Chair, Chief Executive, Non-executive Members appointed by Minister	Director-General plus 4 directors appointed by Government plus Advisory Committee appointed by Minister from list
Board Meetings	Not open to the public	Open to the public and papers on web-site	Open to the public and papers on web-site	Open to the public and papers on web-site	Not open to the public
Key Executive Functions	Regulation of pollution, nature conservation, and protection of built heritage	Pollution and waste regulation, fisheries and navigation, flood management	Nature conservation and regulation	Pollution and waste regulation, water management in sensitive areas	Industrial pollution and waste regulation; supervision of local authority environmental functions
Staffing	520	10,000	900	900	250
Income Sources	Government grant 93% Regulatory charges 4.3% Misc. Sources 2.7%	Government grant 18% Flood levies/ grants 47% Regulatory charges 35%	Government grant 84% Other sources 16%	Government grant 58% Regulatory charges 42%	Government grant 69% Regulatory charges 23% Other 8%
Independent Policy Adviser to Government?	No	Yes, established in 2002 government statutory to government guidance	Yes, established in legislation	Yes, role as policy adviser acknowledged in management statement from Scottish Executive	Yes, role established in legislation

Figure 4 Summary comparison of main environment agencies in the United Kingdom and Ireland.
(note: staffing levels and income sources are rounded)

6. EXPERIENCE OF OTHER MODELS OF ENVIRONMENT AGENCIES

6.1 This section considers a number of different environment agencies with a focus on the key agencies currently operating in other parts of the United Kingdom and Ireland. Given the European dimension to so much of contemporary environmental policy and law, the section also includes an overview of some environmental agencies operating in other European Community Member States, together with more detailed analysis of the Swedish Environment

Protection Agency. It is not the purpose of this section to advocate that any particular model must be slavishly followed in Northern Ireland and, as the Review of Public Administration stated in its 2003 consultation document, 'Northern Ireland is a society with distinctive characteristics and needs, and it may therefore continue to require arrangements which are different, in various ways, from those found elsewhere.'[34] Equally, however, Northern Ireland should not remain in a backwater in the design of modern environmental governance and the intention is to provide food for thought. As the summary table indicates, Northern Ireland now remains unique within the United Kingdom and Ireland in that its key environmental regulatory body is an executive agency rather than a non-departmental public body. The more detailed analysis of the bodies operating indicate that there are important and often subtle differences in structure and style which also need to be taken into consideration in any detailed evaluation of possible future models.

Environment Agency (England And Wales)

Structure and functions

6.2   The Environment Agency was created under the Environment Act 1995 as a non-departmental public body. The background to its creation was an increasing policy concern for a more coherent and integrated approach towards pollution control and a series of official reports highly critical of the inconsistent approach to the regulation of waste, which was then the responsibility of local authorities. Following water privatisation in England and Wales in 1989, a National Rivers Authority (NRA) was created which was responsible for both flood defence and the protection of surface and groundwater, including fisheries and navigation. One model considered at the time of the Agency's creation was to hive off solely the regulatory aspects of the NRA's responsibilities to the new Agency, leaving water operational functions to the NRA, but this was eventually considered too destructive of the cohesive approach towards water management that had been developed. The result is that, in contrast with most other examples of environmental agencies, the Environment Agency has extensive operational responsibilities in the field of water management in addition to its broad environmental regulatory responsibilities. This is reflected in both staffing numbers and finance. The creation of the Agency was complex in organisational

---

[34] Review of Public Administration, supra, para 5.2

terms since establishing its core involved bringing together into one organisation three groupings with distinct cultures and expertise – the National Rivers Authority, Her Majesty's Inspectorate of Pollution (a small central government inspectorate regulating emissions from certain industrial processes), and waste management staff from over 80 local authorities.

The Agency's core current responsibilities encompass:

- waste management regulation;

- radioactive waste regulation;

- regulation of industrial processes under IPPC and PPC regimes;

- contaminated land on special sites;

- water pollution and water abstraction control;

- fisheries and navigation; and

- flood defence and management.

Environment Agency [35]	2001/02
Staffing	10569
Income	
Government grant (DEFRA)	£107.7m
Government grant (Welsh Assembly)	£13.7m
Capital Grants (flood defence)	£56.8m
Flood defence levies and precepts	£258m
Fee income from charges	£230m

The Agency's budget is based on three main sources: flood defence based mainly on levies, grant in aid from both DEFRA and the Welsh Assembly, and charges and fees from licences. These used to be in roughly equal proportions but, with continual financial pressures on DEFRA's own resources, government grant is reducing while the proportion of income from environmental charging schemes is increasing.

[35] Environment Agency (2003) *Corporate Plan 2003-06*. Figures have been rounded

6.3   Under the Environment Act 1995 the Agency was structured as a non-departmental public body under a board of between 8 and 15 members appointed by the government, and as such has separate legal identity from government departments, with its staff being employees of the Agency rather than civil servants. The Act gives a reserve power to the Secretary of State to give the Agency binding directions on both general and specific matters relating to its functions. Directions have to be published, and while a number of directions concerning general policy issues have been made (concerning implementation of EC targets, for example) there appears to have been no direction yet made on a specific matter.

6.4   The Act states that in discharging its functions the Agency's principal aim, subject to other statutory responsibilities, is to make a contribution towards attaining the objective of sustainable development. Statutory guidance must be given by government on how it should fulfil those objectives and this must be taken into account by the Agency in the exercise of its functions. The Guidance was last revised in 2002 and is intended to provide a new framework of accountability and context for the Agency

Regulatory enforcement

6.5   In its regulatory functions the Agency possesses a range of enforcement tools such as the service of warning letters and enforcement notices but, unlike the Northern Ireland EHS or the Scottish Environment Protection Agency, the Agency may undertake its own prosecutions. It was one of the first environmental agencies to publish an explicit Enforcement and Prosecution Policy,[36] supplemented by Functional Guidelines which are also published. The policy states that, assuming there is sufficient evidence, the Agency will normally prosecute for (a) incidents or breaches with significant consequences for the environment (b) carrying out an operation without a licence and (c) excessive or persistent breaches of regulatory requirements. In 2002 there were 1387 events leading to prosecution by the Agency, leading to 1712 successful charges.[37]

6.6   As with many environmental agencies, the Environment Agency has a continuing concern about the low level of average fines imposed by the courts, especially at magistrates' court level, and in 1998 for the first time published a report which named convicted

---

[36] Environment Agency (1998) *Enforcement and Prosecution Policy*
[37] Environment Agency (2003) *Spotlight of Business Performance*

companies sector by sector and in league tables based on levels of fine. This gave rise to extensive national and local press coverage, but there was also criticism both from parliament and industries that the 'name and shame' approach was too crude and negative. Since then the Agency has published an annual report, 'Spotlight on Business Environmental Performance', which continues to include 'naming and shaming' sections on prosecutions but also includes information on regulated industries that have significantly improved their performance.

Environment Agency's role as an independent voice

6.7   The Environment Agency is a government body that is nevertheless independent from governmental departments, and it is here that some of the most telling comparisons with Environment and Heritage Service lie. The most damning official evaluation of the Agency's performance to date was the 2000 Report of the House of Commons Select Committee on the Environment, Transport and Regional Affairs[38] which touched on this issue. The Committee urged the Agency to be more of a 'champion of the environment' than simply a regulatory arm of Government, and as the chairman of the Committee noted in the Parliamentary debate on the Report, 'I would like the Environment Agency to take a much stronger role in giving the government advice...I think the Agency should be pushing harder than the government, whereas my impression is that the government are pushing hardest and the Environment Agency is following behind.'[39]

6.8   The 2000 Parliamentary report probably represented the low point in the Agency's reputation, and since then there have been considerable improvements. A Financial Management and Performance Review carried out by the government confirmed the continuation of the Agency,[40] while Stage 2 of the Report[41] published in 2002 was more concerned with improving efficiency and accountability for its performance which the review stated was important in maintaining public confidence in the Agency as an independent regulator. The Agency followed SEPA's lead and initiated open meetings of its board (bar some categories

---

[38] House of Commons Select Committee on Environment, Transport and Regional Affairs (2000) *The Environment Agency* 6th Report Session 1999-2000, HC 34
[39] Hansard 24 November 2000 col 554
[40] DEFRA (2001) *Environment Agency Financial Management and Performance Review Stage 1*, DEFRA London
[41] DEFRA (2002) *Environment Agency Financial Management and Performance Review Stage 2 Report*, DEFRA, London

of confidentiality such as those relating to personnel or judicial proceedings), where journalists and members of the public could watch the board discussions and decisions being made. Full board papers are now available on the internet before the meetings. Management was reorganised to ensure greater consistency in operations, and a new chairman and chief executive gave a stronger public profile to the Agency. The Board initiated a new 'corporate scorecard' system to provide it with greater high-level information on the Agency's performance achievements against its corporate targets, and a risk based approach to regulating activities has been developed with the aim of ensuring that resources are better employed.

6.9   The Agency acknowledged that it should be more focused on achieving outcomes in its regulatory and operational roles and, in 2001, following extensive stakeholder consultation, published 'An Environmental Vision – the Environment Agency's contribution towards sustainable development' based on nine key themes and identifying the long term goals which it wished to see happen. It might be argued that such a vision document should have been produced by government rather than the Agency, but the assessment at the time was that the government's own material, including its Sustainable Development Strategy, failed to provide a long-term vision for the environment. The document has had two main effects. It has set a framework for both the Agency's own accountability, but also identified clearly that many of the outcomes could not be achieved by the Agency alone using conventional regulatory instruments. There was a much greater need in many areas for partnerships with industry, local government and the public. The Agency is committed to measuring trends and assessing environmental information against the longer-term vision and targets. As it states in its latest Corporate Plan 'We will put this information in the public domain where it will act as a catalyst for environmental change.'[42]

6.10   The 2002 Government Statutory Guidance to the Agency marked an important stage in recognising the Agency's value as an independent source of policy advice. For the first time in a document with legal force it defined that one of the key roles of the Environment Agency was to be an 'independent adviser' on environmental matters affecting policy making both within government and more widely. The Guidance notes that the Agency will be one of the government's main sources of expert

---

[42] Environment Agency (2002) *Making It Happen* Corporate Strategy 2002-07.

advice on environmental matters, and is also well placed to influence the actions of others in relation to environmental matters. It recognises that it is legitimate for the Agency to play a role beyond its core regulatory and flood defence functions and refers, for example, to the Agency's role in land use planning, both in advising on regional planning guidance and development plans, and on individual planning applications. In this context, the Agency regularly objects to planning applications where, for instance, they relate to development on flood plains. All this type of activity, however, has to be funded from government grant imposing internal demands on prioritisation. In its recent report on Environmental Planning,[43] the Royal Commission on Environmental Pollution expressed concern that the Agency was not playing a fully effective role in influencing local and regional authorities at the strategic level of land use planning, and more effort is likely to be devoted to these tasks in the future. In 1999 the Agency and the Local Government Association signed an agreement[44] which stated ten commitments to improving working relations and to act as a framework for more specific local agreements.

6.11   In its open board meetings, which are regularly reported by the specialist press, the nature of the discussion often underlines the Agency's distinctive and independent voice. For example, in its December 2000 board meeting it discussed openly funding problems posed by the imposition of new regulatory duties mainly under EC legislation, with the Chairman stating it was a 'complete fantasy' to believe the Agency could deliver its new duties within current resources, while the Director of Environmental Protection criticised the Government Department's legal capacity for transposing Directives – 'there is not sufficient lawyer capacity within DEFRA to take these things through at a pace we would like.'[45] Another example of an independent perspective being presented by the Agency occurred at the 2001 waste summit organized by the Secretary of State for the Environment and attended by over 60 representatives from stakeholder interests. In presenting the Agency's proposals to strengthen the government's waste strategy, the Chairman of the Agency observed that the Government's strategy "fails to inject sufficient urgency about

---

[43] Royal Commission on Environmental Pollution (2002) *Environmental Planning* 23rd Report Cm 5459 HMSO, London
[44] Environment Agency and Local Government Association (1999) *Working Better Together in England.* An equivalent agreement was signed in 2001 between the Environment Agency Wales and the Welsh Local Government Association.
[45] ENDS Report 323 pp15-16

the pace and scale of the change that will be necessary to turn the problem around.'[46] Clearly, at the end of the day, it is important that these examples of the Agency visibly acting as an independent arm of the government rather than a constituent part of a government department represent a constructive tension that assists the development of improved policy and leads to greater public understanding of the difficult choices that are often involved. The Agency's own opinion survey work indicates that trust in the Agency as a body is increasing, and the Board has decided that this is one of the key attributes for the Agency to seek. Although sometimes uncomfortable for government departments, these more open discussions are usually accompanied by a great deal of co-operative working between Agency officers and government officials, and by regular Ministerial meetings. It is unlikely that these sorts of changes towards more open policy development could take place in Northern Ireland as long as Environment and Heritage Service remains a constituent part of the Department of the Environment.

English Nature

Structure and functions

6.12   English Nature (formally the Nature Conservancy Council for England) was established under the Environmental Protection Act 1990, following a politically controversial decision of the government to split the original Nature Conservancy Council which covered the whole of Great Britain into three separate organisations covering England, Wales, and Scotland. English Nature is a non-departmental public body with members appointed by the Secretary of State, though in formal legal terms it is rather more independent than the Environment Agency. For example, while the Secretary of State may give general or specific directions to English Nature, these powers do not extend to its regulatory functions. The Environmental Protection Act 1990 also expressly states that one of the functions of English Nature is to provide advice to the Secretary of State on the development and implementation of nature conservation policies, while in the case of the Environment Agency this role is now stated in statutory guidance rather than in the body of the primary legislation.

---

[46] ENDS Report 322 p 16 'Beckett announces Whitehall rethink on waste'

2002/2003[47]	
Staffing	906
Income	
Grant in aid	£63.1m
Aggregates Levy	£2.7m
Shared conservation income	£3.4m
Activities and other income	£5.9m

6.13   English Nature's functions in the field of nature conservation encompass regulatory activity, advice to government at national, regional and local level, and operational activities. It plays a key role in advising government on the selection of protected sites under European and international legislation, and is responsible for notification and protection of Sites of Special Scientific Interest. Its regulatory powers in this context have been considerably strengthened by the Countryside and Rights of Way Act 2000 and, according to its current Corporate Plan, it aims to ensure that 72 per cent of the over 4,000 SSSIs in England are in a favourable condition by 2006 (from a figure of 57 per cent in 2003). English Nature is the lead organisation for achieving the government's goals in its Biodiversity Strategy for England[48], and has agreed concordants with other bodies such as the Environment Agency where they have more direct means of protecting particular species and habitats. In addition to its regulatory functions, English Nature is responsible for the management of national nature reserves, including marine nature reserves, and provides grants under a Biodiversity Grant Scheme.

Role as independent policy adviser

6.14   English Nature has a statutory function of providing advice to the government on nature conservation and, though largely funded by government grant-in-aid, it has established a reputation as being fearlessly independent of government. Compared to the Environment Agency it has tended to be more overtly critical of government policy – due in part to its tighter environmental remit, and the personalities of lead officers. English Nature was one of the first statutory bodies to express concern over the potential damage to biodiversity from GM crops which led to extensive farm scale evaluations by the government, and is the lead agency for British

---

[47] English Nature (2003) *Annual Report* . Figures have been rounded.
[48] DEFRA (2002) *Working with the Grain: a Biodiversity Strategy for England*

statutory conservation agencies on biotechnology. It regularly responds to government consultations and provides evidence to Parliamentary Select Committees,[49] and has not refrained from being robust in its criticism of government policy. For example, in evidence before a 1999 House of Lords inquiry on GM crops, it told the inquiry,'There has been little, if any, direction given by Government on the development of GMOs, giving rise to an "anything goes" attitude within the biotechnology industry.'[50] Its responses often raise concerns about the impact of Government proposals on nature conservation. For example, its 2002 evidence to the Parliamentary Select Committee on the proposals of the Office of the Deputy Prime Minister for an extra 200,000 homes in southeast England highlighted their impact on water supply and waste/sewage disposal. Similarly, it has recently expressed concern about the effect on wildlife that might arise from the Department of Transport's consultation proposals on airport expansion.

6.15   English Nature now faces a major challenge following the publication in October 2003 of the Haskins review on the delivery of government policies in rural England.[51] The review was mainly concerned with making more effective the delivery of the government's rural policies, and raised concerns at both excessive centralisation and the complex nature and number of organisations now involved which caused confusion to customers and stakeholders. One of the institutional recommendations made by Lord Haskins was for the creation of a new Land Management Agency as a non-departmental public body that would incorporate English Nature, some functions of the Countryside Agency, and the Government Department's own Rural Development Service. The government has in principle endorsed the recommendation (though is less convinced about the case for abolishing the Countryside Agency). The extent to which English Nature is perceived as an independent body was reflected in much of the initial press coverage. The director of Friends of the Earth, for example, was quoted as stating 'English Nature was becoming an increasingly effective independent wildlife protection agency, and no matter what arrangements results from the review, that must remain'[52], while the Opposition environment spokesperson noted, 'It is no surprise that the government seeks to abolish

---

[49] According to its 2003 Annual Report, supra, in 2002 it responded to 125 Government consultation documents and 18 Parliamentary Select Committees.

[50] ENDS Report 291, p 34

[51] DEFRA (2003) *Rural Delivery Review* Report by Lord Haskins October 2003

[52] Guardian November 12 2003

an agency that openly criticises and hinders them.'[53] In truth, muzzling English Nature does not appear to be the rationale for either Lord Haskin's recommendations or the government's response,[54] but some of the immediate response was a compelling example of the distinctive reputation that the organisation has established in the public eye.

Scottish Environment Protection Agency

Structure and functions

6.17   The Scottish Environment Protection Agency (SEPA) was established under the Environment Act 1995 as a non-departmental public body, with a board of between 8 and 12 members appointed by Scottish Ministers. It is, though, a much smaller body than the Environment Agency with around 900 staff at present. This reflects not simply a smaller jurisdiction, but a tighter range of functions that are more focussed on pollution control and prevention. Unlike the Environment Agency, SEPA is not directly responsible for flood defence and management, which rest with local authorities, though it is responsible for flood warnings.

6.18   SEPA's principal regulatory responsibilities include:

- Control of discharges to surface and groundwater, and tidal waters to the 3 mile limit. This is mainly achieved through the setting of consents, with around 30,000 consents currently in place.

- Regulation of water abstraction in sensitive areas.

- Regulation of industrial processes under integrated pollution control. There are around 200 permits currently in operation.

- Regulation of 'Part B' industrial processes for air emissions. There are around 1000 authorizations currently in force.

- Licensing of waste management sites, regulation of waste shipments, special waste transfers, registration of waste carriers, regulation of packaging producers. There are

[53] ibid
[54] See Burke (2003) *The Nature of the Game* Guardian November 12 2003

currently around 1,000 licensed waste activities. Regulation of radioactive waste.

• Preparation of National Waste Strategy for Scotland.

• Regulation of 'special sites' under the contaminated land regime.

2001/2002[54a]	
Staffing	879
Operations	79%
Finance and corporate	10%
Strategic planning	7%
Public affairs	3%
Chairman/Chief Executive	1%
Income	
Grant in aid	23.5m
Fee income from charges	17.5m

6.19 Unlike the Environment Agency in England and Wales, SEPA has no general aim relating to sustainable development specified in its constituent legislation, the difference being explained by the government during the Parliamentary passage of the Environment Act as due to the fact that the narrower functions of SEPA made such a statement of legislative aims unnecessary. Under Section 31 EPA 1995 the Scottish Executive must give SEPA guidance from time to time with respect to aims and objectives, and in performing its functions SEPA must have regard to the guidance. There are also equivalent powers to those available to government with respect to the Environment Agency for the Scottish Executive to give directions of both a general and specific character with respect to carrying out of any of its functions.

6.20 The overall goal of SEPA, as set down by the Scottish Executive, is to provide 'an efficient and integrated environmental protection system for Scotland that will improve the environment and contribute to the Scottish Minister's goal of sustainable development.' A management statement, last issued in July 2002, sets out the formal relationship of SEPA with the Scottish Executive. It acknowledges that, in addition to its regulatory

[54a] 2001-2002 (figures rounded) SEPA Annual Report 2001-2002

functions, SEPA functions include the collation of data to provide an overview of the state of the environment in Scotland, and the provision of advice during the development of policy at Scottish, UK, European and international level.

6.21   In terms of regulatory enforcement, SEPA has a range of responses equivalent to those of EHS, such as the service of warning notices and enforcement notices. Unlike the Environment Agency, it has no independent power of prosecution but must refer reports to the Procurator Fiscal, and in this respect it is in a similar position to EHS. On average SEPA submits around 65 such reports a year, with around 68% going on to court, a rather higher success rate compared to the average ratio of reports handled by the Procurator Fiscal.

Government evaluation of SEPA

6.22   The most recent comprehensive evaluation of SEPA's performance was the 2002 Financial Performance and Management Review conducted by the Scottish Executive.[55] One of the underlying themes of the Review is to recognise and indeed strengthen SEPA's independent role in environmental policy development and delivery. As part of a public awareness survey conducted by the Review, it was found that SEPA had achieved a high level of recognition among the Scottish public and that, in terms of effectiveness in protecting the environment, SEPA was ranked higher than the Scottish Executive and local authorities. The Review called for more regular high-level meetings between SEPA and the Scottish Executive and stated that if environmental policy and legislation was to be well founded and workable the Scottish Executive should continue to draw extensively on SEPA's *"wealth of experience in implementing existing legislation and on its expertise in the field of the environment."*

6.23   The Review also recognised that SEPA's role should not be confined solely to implementing environmental regulation. If it were to achieve its longer-term environmental corporate targets, *"It must play a wider, complementary role as an environmental champion"*. This included forging of strategic partnerships and acting as an advocate for best environmental practice in pursuit of its agreed corporate targets. The Review acknowledged that the Board of SEPA was crucial to its accountability. SEPA was the first environmental non-departmental public body to

---

[55] Scottish Executive (2002) *Financial Management and Performance Review: Scottish Environment Protection Agency*

initiate board meetings that were open to the general public. The Environment Act 1995 also required SEPA to establish regional boards, but did not specify their function. The Review felt that the regional boards that had been set up were essentially too inward looking, and that their core function should change from one of monitoring SEPA's local performance to that of engaging directly and proactively with local communities and other stakeholders.

6.24   SEPA has two main sources of income: grant in aid and fees from charges for licences and consents. The proportion of its income from charges has risen substantially from around 22 per cent in its first year of operation to around 42 per cent in 2002-2003 and, although the Review recommended that SEPA needs to improve the transparency of its charging schemes, it endorsed the general approach of recovering all costs of its work performed in support of its regulatory activity (including, for example, the development of internal guidance and electronic licence management systems) as well as direct costs. This was in line with the polluter pays principle. Grant in aid should be a quite separate source of income given to fund those non-regulatory activities that SEPA is legally obliged to carry out, or in response to ministerial policy or requests.

6.25   The Review welcomed the increased consistency in the approach to regulation being achieved by SEPA. Consultation suggested that SEPA was too focused on regulatory activity, and needed to develop a more outcome driven approach, and one that was more risk based. As one local authority noted 'Reliance on regulation by role rather than being based on objective measures of risk appears to be the main modus operandi'. However, the Review acknowledged that these goals were not easy to achieve. SEPA has legal duties concerning regulation and monitoring, and rigorous and consistent regulation necessarily involved a measure of repetitive activity if its credibility with the public and operators was to be maintained.

Irish Environmental Protection Agency

Functions

6.26   The Irish Environmental Protection Agency was established as a non-departmental public body under the Environmental Protection Agency Act 1992. The background to the legislation was a commitment by the then government to overhaul the regime for environmental regulation in Ireland in the light of public concern over the effectiveness of planning and local authorities in regulating industry, and against the need for a more integrated approach towards pollution control.

2001/2[56]	
Staffing	237
Income	
Government Grants	EUR17m
Licence charges	EUR5.6m
Regional laboratories	EUR1.6m
Other income sources	EUR0.3m

6.27   The mission statement of the EPA is'to promote and implement the highest practicable standards of environmental protection and management which embrace the principles of sustainable and balanced development.'

Its core regulatory activities include:

- licensing and regulation of industries under Integrated Pollution Control with just over 500 licences issued since 1994. The legislation has recently been strengthened under the Protection of the Environment Act 2003 which is intended to fully reflect the provisions of the EC IPPC Directive.

- licensing and regulation of waste management facilities under the Waste Management Act 1996.

- GMO regulation for contained use and release.

6.28   These regulatory functions are clearly narrower than those of Environment and Heritage Service in Northern Ireland. For example, the protection of natural and man-made heritage falls to Duchas, the heritage service of the Department of the Environment, Heritage, and Local Government. Nor does the Irish EPA have extensive direct regulatory powers over water and sewerage pollution which mainly fall to local authorities, as do land use planning powers. But the legislation gives the Agency a supervisory role to oversee the performance by local

---

[56] Environment Protection Agency (2002) *Annual Reports and Accounts*. Figures have been rounded.

authorities of their environmental protection functions, and this supervisory role is more akin to the role of the Swedish Environment Protection Agency in relation to municipal and regional government. This supervisory role is exercised in part by the publication of assessment reports on subjects such as the quality of bathing waters and drinking water, and the Agency has recently developed a management system for better identifying and assessing the performance of local authorities. Its supervisory powers have recently been strengthened as discussed in paragraph 6.30.

Distinctive management structure

6.29   The structure of the Irish EPA presents some distinctive features. In contrast to the more usual model of non-departmental public bodies led by a board of members appointed by government, the EPA is managed by a small executive board composed of senior officials and chaired by its Director General. The main reasons for choosing this model appear to have been to ensure greater independence of the new authority by avoiding undue political interference in the choice of individual members, coupled with the fact that in its licensing activities the board was seen to be acting in a quasi-judicial function where the need for independence was even more important. External input is provided by an Advisory Committee of 12 members, also chaired by the Director General. Members are appointed by the Minister for the Environment and Local Government and mainly selected from nominees proposed by organisations with an interest in environmental and development matters. It can therefore be seen more as a stakeholder advisory body, and in 2002 it met three times. Under the EPA Act, the Advisory Committee has a duty to make recommendations relating to the functions of the Agency, though it cannot bind the Agency in any way. It is difficult to judge the effectiveness of the Advisory Committee though it may be that it would establish a clearer, more independent voice if it were not chaired by the Director General but by a separate chairman.

Enforcement and supervisory role

6.30   The EPA has both direct enforcement powers and a supervisory role in respect of local authorities. In 2003 it established a new office within the Agency, the Office of Environmental Enforcement, designed to provide more focus and expertise for both these roles within a dedicated unit and with extra government funding from revenue raised from the plastic bags tax. Its powers have been strengthened under provisions of the Protection of the Environment Act 2003 both in relation to its direct regulatory role (including, for example, increased maximum fines and improved powers concerning obtaining of evidence) and its supervisory role of local authorities. In the case of the latter, it may request information from local authorities in both general and specific cases, and provide advice and recommendations. It may issue a binding direction to a local authority which fails to follow its recommendation, or where significant environmental pollution has resulted or may result from a failure of the local authority to carry out its statutory functions. Under the original legislation directions could only be given if the local authority had the funds to carry out the required actions, and there was no sanction for non-compliance other than the Agency doing the work itself and recovering the costs from the local authority. The 2003 legislation has considerably strengthened these powers by removing the reference to funds being available to the local authority as an excuse for non-compliance, and making it a criminal offence for an authority to fail to comply with a direction. Directions to local authorities have been given in the past, but no criminal prosecution for non-compliance has yet been issued. Given the large areas of environmental regulation which remain with local authorities in Ireland, these are potentially significant powers and can be seen as a more cost-effective and efficient route than judicial review. The Agency has a published prosecution policy which reflects those developed in the United Kingdom, and is based on the five key principles of proportionality, consistency, transparency, targeting, and that the polluter pays..

6.31   The EPA suffered somewhat of a baptism of fire in that shortly after it was established it was charged with investigating a major industrial fire at the Hickson Pharmaceutical chemical plant in Cork. Its subsequent report identified the unauthorised discharges of chemicals, but no significant environmental damage, and in some quarters its approach was criticised as unduly technocratic and cautious.[57] Since then the EPA has tended to be criticised by industry for being over-prescriptive in its approach to IPC licensing,[58] while at the same time it has been condemned by environmental groups for a failure to implement effective

---

[57] Pearce (1994) *Chemicals, Conflicts and the Irish Protection Agency* Cork Environmental Alliance News Spring 1994. See also McCarthy and Yearly ((1995) 'The Irish Environmental Protection Agency:The Early Years', *Environmental Politics* Vol 4 No 4 pp 258-264

[58] see for example, IBEC (1997) *Striking the Balance: An Environmental Policy for Economic Growth*

environmental standards, especially in relation to EC legislation.[59] In relation to IPC licensed activities, the EPA issued nearly 300 notices of non-compliance in 2001 and took 13 prosecutions, 12 of which resulted in convictions. Its annual report on IPC Licensing includes a degree of 'naming and shaming,' including names and details of prosecutions and lists of the IPC facilities that received the highest number of complaints.[60] Currently, the new Office of Environmental Enforcement has set illegal dumping of waste as a key priority, which is recognised as a major problem against a background of declining legal sites and growing costs.[61] Its effectiveness in dealing with this issue, together with the use of its enhanced powers of supervision over local authorities, is likely to be a key test for the EPA's reputation over the next few years.

Independent status of the EPA

6.32   Compared to bodies such as English Nature and the Environment Agency in England and Wales, the legislation establishing the Irish Environmental Protection Agency contains many more express provisions establishing its independent status. The appointment of the Director General, for example, is not solely within the discretion of the Secretary but is made from nominees proposed by a committee of different interests. The Minister has powers to give directions but these may only be general directions relating to policy concerning environmental protection. The Act gives express authority to the Agency, both of its volition and at the request of a Minister, to give advice, information, or recommendations concerning the progress of environmental protection, and Ministers must have regard to such advice. There is a specific offence to attempt to influence the Agency in an improper manner. The Agency assiduously promotes its status as an independent body, with its documentation stating that 'Independence is assured through the selection procedures for the Director General and Directors, and the freedom, as provided in the legislation, to act on its own initiative.'[62]

6.33   The EPA publishes an extensive range of policy and technical material, and has regular meetings with sectoral groups, including non-governmental organisations. It has, however, not yet developed the sorts of transparent decision making now seen in agencies such as English Nature and the Environment Agency.

[59] See, for example, Friends of Irish Environment (2002) 'Report on the decision of the EPA to grant a landfill licence at Kilbarry in October 2001'.
[60] EPA (2001) *Report on IPC Licensing and Control* 2001
[61] *Irish Times* (2003) 'Watchdog in need of sharper teeth' 23 October 2003
[62] EPA (2002) *Annual Report and Accounts*, supra

Neither the meetings of its management board nor its advisory committee are held in public, nor are full papers available on the Internet. Some have considered that the EPA should be more openly vociferous in its engagement in issues of controversial public policy, though when the current Director General recently spoke in favour of waste incineration this led to a degree of local uproar, and it was subsequently made clear this was a personal opinion rather than EPA policy.[63] The EPA has recently undergone a substantial internal restructuring which includes the creation of a small strategic planning unit, and greater delegation of formal licensing powers from the management board to its officers. As a result the Agency is likely in the future to play a more visible role in contributing towards policy development in addition to carrying out its regulatory functions.

Models Of Environment Agencies In Other European Countries

6.34   Figure 5 provides an overview of the key environmental agencies operating in other European countries. European models are of interest in part because Member States are under common obligations in respect of the implementation of Community environmental legislation. But there is also increasing contact and cooperation between such agencies, through informal networks such as the EU Network for the Implementation and Enforcement of Environmental Law (IMPEL), and under the auspices of the European Environment Agency.[64] As can be seen, many such agencies are mainly concerned with the provision of technical advice to Ministries and the assessment of environmental information rather than direct regulation which often remains the responsibility of local or regional authorities. In some cases, and rather similar to the position of the Irish Environmental Protection Agency, the Agencies have a supervisory role in respect of local authorities. In this context, the following sections look more closely at the Swedish Environment Protection Agency, which is similar in size to Environment and Heritage Service and is one of the longest established environment agencies in Europe.

Swedish Environment Protection Agency

6.35   The Swedish Environment Protection Agency was established in 1967 and claims to be the first national agency in the world

---

[63] *Irish Times* (2003) 'Meath anti-incineration activists angered by comments of EPA head' 26 August 2003
[64] The EEA held a first meeting of European environment agencies in November 2003

with overall responsibility for environmental issues. It is headed by a Director General who also chairs the Board of the Agency, and is advised by a number of Advisory Councils, including an Enforcement and Regulations Council, Council for Recreation Issues, Scientific Council for Biological Diversity, and the Council for Predator Issues. It currently has around 550 staff.

6.36   The Agency's activities encompass a large range of environmental issues including nature protection, pollution control and resource management, and many of its activities are concerned with providing advice and keeping abreast of new policy developments in accordance with guidelines from the Swedish Parliament and Government. It has little direct regulatory role, and in this capacity mainly acts to supervise the activities of regional and municipal authorities. In 1999 a new Swedish Environment Code came into force which consolidated some 15 previously separate environmental laws and included general principles of environmental protection. Under Chapter 26 of the Code the Swedish Environment Protection Agency is given a central supervisory role to ensure that the provisions of the Code and rules made under it are implemented. This can include the Agency taking direct legal action before the Swedish environment courts, reporting breaches to the relevant public authority, or providing local authorities with guidelines and technical advice to assist them in fulfilling their functions.

Country	Name of Agency	Relevant Ministry	Main functions	Added observations
Austria	Federal Environment Agency	Environment Ministry	Specialist advice to Ministry; holding data bases and environmental analyses; evaluation of chemicals and contaminated land	Implementation and enforcement of environmental law largely responsibility of provincial government and municipalities
Belgium	Federal Service for Environmental Affairs	Ministry of Social Affairs, Public Health and Environment	Co-ordination of policy, product standards, waste transport, risk management, chemicals	Implementation of many environmental policies and laws conducted at regional level through variety of administrative bodies

Denmark	Environmental Protection Agency	Environment Ministry	Advice to Ministry, evaluation of structures of environmental protection, pollution control of air, soil, and water	Implementation and enforcement largely responsibility of local government; EPA handles complaints on their activities
Denmark	National Forest and Nature Agency	Environment Ministry	Implementation of legislation concerning nature protection, forestry, ancient monuments and mineral extraction	Agency also manages state forests
France	Agences de l'Eau	Ministry of Environment	Implementation of water policies based on main watersheds	Public sector state bodies, independently financed by water charges
France	ADEME	Ministry of Environment	Research on renewable energy, waste, pollution, clean technologies	
France	ANDRA	Ministry of Environment	Research and management of radioactive wastes	
Germany	Federal Environment Agency (UBA)	Federal Ministry of Environment, Nature Conservation and Nuclear Safety	Scientific and technical support to Ministry, including assistance in preparation of environmental regulations	
Germany	Federal Agency for Nature Conservation (BfN)	Federal Ministry of the Environment, Nature Conservation and Nuclear Safety	Specialist advice to Ministry on nature conservation and landscape management; research	BfN approves imports and exports for protected animal and plant species
Germany	Federal Office of Radiation Protection (BfS)	Federal Ministry of the Environment, Nature Conservation and Nuclear Safety	Assistance to Federal Ministry in Ministry's supervisory functions under Federal Nuclear Safety	BfS has some enforcement tasks under Federal Nuclear legislation

Greece	No distinct national agencies	Ministry of Environment, Physical Planning and Public Work		Most responsibilities for implementation of environmental law and policy delegated to regional and local authorities
Italy	Agency for Protection of the Environment and for Technical Services (APAT)	Ministry for the Environment and Land Protection	Technical and scientific support to the Ministry, and advice of development of legislation; collection and evaluation of environmental data	
Italy	Regional Environment Protection Agencies	Regional governments	Organisation of information, education, development of pollution control measures	Regional agencies have some responsibilities for inspection and regulation of processes
Luxembourg	No distinct national agency			Private consultancies acting under government authorisation carry out number of functions including EIA and eco-audit
Netherlands	Inspectorate of Housing, Spatial Planning & the Environment	Ministry of Housing, Spatial Planning & Environment	Part of Ministry but 'relatively independent'; responsibility for enforcement of laws falling within Ministry competence, and supervision of local government implementation	Implementation, permitting etc largely responsibility of local government (Provinces and Municipalities); water management and flood protection carried out by Water Boards
Portugal	No distinct national agency			

Spain	No distinct national agency			Implementation and enforcement largely responsibility of strongly decentralized government (Autonomous Communities and Local Authorities)
Sweden	Environment Protection Agency	Ministry of Environment	Propose targets, measures etc, collate data on environment, supervision of implementation of Government and Parliamentary decisions on the environment	Licensing and Permitting largely responsibility of environmental courts and regional and local government; Environment Protection Agency exercises supervisory functions
Sweden	National Chemicals Inspectorate (KemI)	Ministry of Environment	Competent authority for many aspects of EU chemicals laws	Priority areas for Inspectorate laid down by Ministry
Sweden	Nuclear Power Inspectorate (SKI)	Ministry of Environment	Regulation of nuclear activities	

Figure 5 Overview of key European Environment Agencies.

6.37   The Agency is a legal entity in its own right and separate from government departments in the same respect as other Swedish Agencies. The status of the Agency as a distinct entity from government departments operates within a well developed constitutional framework and general understanding of the role of agencies in the Swedish political system which applies to all agencies, and is coupled with the specific role and responsibilities given to the Agency by legislation. Government annually prescribes the political priorities for the Agency, which may include the publication of reports and similar tasks, but it is not entitled to interfere directly in any individual case.

6.38   The Agency's core relationship is with the Ministry of the Environment, and where contacts are made directly with other departments the Ministry is kept informed. The annual budget is also negotiated with the Ministry of the Environment, and is largely directly financed by government, with a very small amount of extra income derived from the administration of an industry tax and a battery fund. Much of the Agency's research and policy priorities are determined by government, though it sometimes initiates work that strays beyond existing government policy and which has subsequently proved beneficial for later policy development. In practice, it would be rare for the Agency to be openly critical of government policy but, according to public opinion surveys, there is considerable public trust in the Agency. The Agency's relationship with government is currently rather more complex in the context of European Union policy development. Following Sweden's accession to the European Union, the Agency's main role was to handle relations with Community technical committees, leaving the Ministry to handle policy negotiations at European level. However, in recent years it has increasingly been drawn into supporting the Environment Ministry in negotiations at European Council and Parliament level.

7. OPTIONS FOR CHANGE TO ENVIRONMENT AND HERITAGE SERVICE IN NORTHERN IRELAND

7.1 The previous section has examined various different models of environmental agencies currently operating in Europe. This report does not argue that one type of Agency will always work better than another since so much depends both on the political, historical, and legal context in which they operate, and on the policy priority given to the environment by the governments in office. Equally it is clear that if it is decided to give an environmental public body certain types of functions, some structures will allow it to perform these more effectively than others. For example, where an environment agency is given direct powers to regulate, all the recent studies in other parts of the United Kingdom suggest that the more the body is structured independently from government departments, the more it will be trusted to carry out its functions fairly and impartially, both by those who are subject to regulation and by the general public. On the other hand, where regulation and enforcement of environmental controls still largely rest with regional/local government (as is the case in many European countries) the advantages of an agency having independent legal status from central government are less obvious. The exception (as the Swedish and Irish examples show) is where the agency is given a supervisory/enforcement function in respect of local government, and where the detachment from undue political interference which more independent legal status affords is important to preserve the impartial exercise of powers.

7.2   All environmental agencies can provide a valuable source
        of technical and specialist expertise to government in the
        development of environmental policies and controls. Clearly,
        where the agency has regulatory responsibilities, its expertise
        will be supplemented by experience of operating controls on the
        ground. But a crucial question for government is whether the
        development of effective environmental policies and confidence
        in government will be assisted by the existence of a government
        environment agency which is sufficiently independent from the
        relevant government department to be able to raise politically
        difficult issues, engage with the public and provoke policy
        discussion. This role – which may be summarised as the agency
        being described as a 'champion for the environment' as well as
        an agent for government – is one that is now firmly established
        for environment agencies operating in other parts of the United
        Kingdom, and the value of independence in this context has been
        endorsed by recent government reviews of bodies such as the
        Scottish Environment Protection Agency and the Environment
        Agency in England and Wales. At present, whatever its internal
        influence on policy, Environment and Heritage Service is unable to
        play an equivalent role because it remains part of the Department.
        Nor, given its current status as an Executive Agency, is it in a
        position to develop the sorts of transparent decision-making
        procedures now seen with environment agencies operating in
        other parts of the United Kingdom.

7.3   As to the range of responsibilities given to environmental
        agencies, these clearly vary widely and are often the result of
        historical and political developments rather than any 'rational'
        choice based on environmental reasons. However, it should be
        stressed that, compared to other agencies operating in the United
        Kingdom, Ireland and most other European countries, the
        Environment and Heritage Service now has the greatest sweep of
        environmental powers, encompassing pollution control, nature
        conservation, and heritage protection. This potentially allows it
        to take a truly integrated approach to the issue. Moreover, EHS
        is unencumbered by heavy operational responsibilities such as
        those relating to flood management, which account for a large
        proportion of the staff and budget of the Environment Agency
        in England and Wales. This might well be considered a positive
        basis on which to think about future structures of environmental
        governance in Northern Ireland.

Key Options for Change

7.4   Against that background, and in light of future demands on environmental regulation, there are a number of key options concerning the structure of Environment and Heritage Service. Under each option some of the most significant advantages and disadvantages are highlighted.

Option 1. No change in the current status of the Agency, but the development of improved accountability mechanisms such as those outlined in Section 8.

Pros

• Least cost option

• No new legislation needed

• No staff disruption

• EHS can seek improvements without the distraction of major reorganisation

Cons

• Fails to meet demands for a more independent regulator

• Opportunity for 'champion of the environment' role is lost

• Government loses out on a source of independent policy advice

• Northern Ireland structure is out of step with rest of the United Kingdom

• Transparent decision-making is difficult to achieve

Option 2. Remove the Executive Agency status of the EHS and fully incorporate it within the Department of the Environment.

Pros

• Ensures closer connection between policy development and policy delivery

- Less costly than establishing a more independent authority

- Accepts that Executive Agency structure, while suited for some types of public service delivery, is less appropriate for a body with extensive regulatory functions

- Political accountability rests more clearly with the Minister

- Public is no longer misled into thinking the 'Agency' is more independent from Government Department that it is in reality

Cons

- Mechanisms for performance accountability associated with executive agencies are lost

- Advantages of a more independent regulatory body and more independent source of policy advice are lost

- Likely to make moves towards greater transparency of decision-making more difficult

- Would be seen as a backwards step compared with developments elsewhere

Option 3. Transform EHS into an environmental protection authority with separate legal status based on the structure of a non-department public body.

Pros

- Consistent with structures now familiar in other parts of the United Kingdom

- Satisfies concerns for an environmental regulator with more independence from government departments

- Provides government with a source of independent policy advice on environment, and a body able to stimulate and provoke public debate on environmental issues

- Focus on regulatory outcomes is likely to assist Northern Ireland in meeting obligations under both existing and future European Community environmental legislation, and thereby better controls the UK's exposure to infraction fines due to regulatory failure in Northern Ireland.

- Stimulates development of transparent decision making

- Using the basis of current EHS responsibilities, Northern Ireland could create one of the leading integrated environment agencies in Europe

- Requirements for new legislation could provide an opportunity to rationalise some of the existing division of responsibilities

Cons

- Legislation is needed to establish a new body and therefore interim disruption

- Extra costs through loss of common departmental services etc.

- Less direct political accountability via Minister

- Delivery of policy can become over-separated from its design

- Loss of flexibility to change structures once established

- Body can become over defensive of its existing structures and less responsive to change

Option 4. Transform the EHS into a new non-ministerial government department.

Pros

- Advantages in independent regulator and source of independent advice as with Option 3

- Operates with greater independence than a non-departmental public body and may gain greater public trust as a consequence

- More readily able to provide advice and influence policies of government departments other than Department of the Environment (NI) since no longer seen as an agency of that Department

- Able to negotiate for government funding directly rather than via departmental bids and allocations

Cons

- Legislation and disruption as with setting up non-departmental public body (Option 3)

- Greater operating costs involved than at present through loss of common services provided by department

- Greater detachment from Department of the Environment

- Less political accountability

- Constitutionally an anomaly which should be reserved for the rarest of cases

Option 5. Revert the delivery of major areas of environmental regulation back to elected local authorities or forms of regional government if developed.

Pros

- Ensures greater local political accountability

- Consistent with the principle of subsidiarity and the local delivery of services

- Supervisory role could be exercised by EHS

Cons

- Loss of opportunity to establish independent environment regulator and source of independent policy advice to government

- Local authorities lack technical expertise needed for many contemporary environmental policies and will need extra resourcing

- Disruption while local authorities acquire new skills and staffing

- Could lead to lack of consistency in application of controls and policies across Northern Ireland

- Northern Ireland would be more vulnerable to infraction proceedings under European Community law

Lessons to be Learned

7.5   If the decision were taken to create a more independently structured regulator out of EHS, there are some further lessons that can usefully be taken on board. These derive in part from the recent government overview studies on independent regulators and executive agencies, as well as from experience with existing bodies in other parts of the United Kingdom.

(a)   It is essential that a new authority acts as transparently as possible, not least to act as a counterbalance to the lack of direct political accountability. The best practices currently adopted by bodies such as the Food Standards Agency and the Environment Agencies in other parts of the United Kingdom should be followed. The public and press should be able to observe board meetings, and all papers before the board should be available on the Internet.

(b)   The authority would have a key role in the implementation and enforcement of environmental regulations, but needs to adopt an outcome focused approach, and one that recognises the need to develop a range of regulatory approaches and partnerships in addition to traditional approaches.

(c)   In addition to its regulatory functions, the authority's role as an independent adviser to government on environmental policy needs to be formally acknowledged, ideally in the legislation that establishes it. Government needs to appreciate that at times this role will prove uncomfortable, even where practice is based on a 'no surprises' principle (i.e. government is given advance warning before the authority goes public on a potentially embarrassing issue). In the long run, though, public confidence is likely to improve and more effective policy may be developed.

(d)   Three year settlements for departmental funding should be established to provide a degree of continuity and a more secure base for forward planning. Inflation should be automatically included, and there should be the minimum amount of ring fencing.

(e)   The principle of full cost-recovery from holders of licences and consents should be adopted across the board, reflecting both the polluter pays principle and the need for income sources not wholly dependent on department funding in order to reinforce the authority's independence. Charge schemes should be sufficiently flexible to include an element of cost-reflectivity based on risk scores relating to the particular process or activity. It is important that government recognises that, before an authority can charge for a licensing scheme under new legislation, it will incur considerable costs in developing its capacity to handle a new regulatory regime. These development costs have to be reflected either in direct departmental grant or in future charge schemes.

(f)   Good lines of communication between the authority and its sponsoring department need to be established, both at high level (with regular meetings between the Minister and the board) and at policy level, in order to ensure that the authority's expertise and experience are taken on board in the development of policy. This is likely to be especially important in the drafting of new regulations where the authority's operational knowledge of what works and what does not work can be critical to effectiveness.

(g)   A clear and transparent enforcement policy should be developed and publicised. Consideration should be given to allowing the environmental regulatory body to undertake its own prosecutions within such a framework.

(h)   Investment in good information and IT systems needs to be made early, and management structures kept as straightforward as possible. Matrix management systems where lines of accountability can easily become obscured are best avoided.

8.   ACCOUNTABILITY MECHANISMS

8.1   This section considers a number of issues relating to accountability. As the Review of Public Administration put it, 'Regardless of the way in which services are delivered, whether by central or local government or by public bodies, there is a common concern that there should be enhanced and transparent accountability.'[65] The question of accountability is one that runs parallel to the issue of delivery structures considered in the previous section, and there are proposals here concerning the Assembly Committees and audit mechanisms which need be addressed independently of decisions concerning the future structure of Environment and Heritage Service.

Accountability Of Environment And Heritage Service

8.2   Before considering these issues, it is important to recognise that the five options for structures considered in para 7.4 affect issues of the accountability of EHS or its successor body in slightly different ways. Accountability is a concept that has many different facets, and the Review has also published a valuable briefing paper on what accountability can involve.[66] As the Briefing Paper notes, accountability derives from a desire of the public 'to receive an account from those to whom power and resources are delegated and also hold them to account'. Or, in the present context, the question can be more simply put: 'Who regulates the regulator?'

8.3   Environment and Heritage Service in its present form as an executive agency is already subject to a number of accountability mechanisms. Through the Department of the Environment it can be subject to judicial review where its actions may be illegal, and is subject to investigation by the Northern Ireland Ombudsman for maladministration. Also, EHS can be subject to investigation by the Northern Ireland Audit Office, the Public Accounts Committee, and the Assembly Environment Committee. Since EHS is part of the Department, the Minister is ultimately politically answerable to the Assembly for its actions, although this direct line of accountability is rather less clear in the case of executive agencies. Ensuring clearer accountability through an elected representative might be considered an advantage of

---

[65] Review of Public Administration in Northern Ireland (2003) supra, para 4.1
[66] Review of Public Administration (2002) *Briefing Paper : Accountability* Independent report by Watt, Richards and Skelcher

Option 2 (re-merging EHS fully within the Department), or of Option 5 (reverting delivery to local government bodies).

8.4 Establishing EHS as a non-departmental public body along the lines suggested in Option 3 would loosen its direct political accountability through an elected representative. Indeed, one of the perceived benefits of a more independent status is a detachment from short-term political interference. Such an authority, though, would remain subject to external scrutiny by the Northern Ireland Audit Office, the Public Accounts Committee and the Assembly Environment Committee. It would also be subject to judicial review in its own capacity. The requirement on non-departmental public bodies to publish separate corporate plans and annual reports is another important mechanism by which performance can be judged.

8.5 It is equally clear from the experience of the environmental regulators in other parts of the United Kingdom that considerable efforts have been made to develop openness and transparency as a way of compensating for the lack of conventional political accountability. Open board meetings and access to board papers are clear examples. In theory an executive agency could adopt similar standards of transparency, but the pressures for doing so are much greater in the case of a non-departmental public body. It is equally important that effective internal scrutiny machinery is developed, and here again board members have a critical role to play. Mechanisms can be established for 'lessons learnt' reviews to be conducted by the board, if necessary with the input of independent advice, which do not undermine the operational authority of staff but ensure that lessons for the future are taken on board.

Assembly Committees

8.6 Prior to suspension, the majority of the Assembly Committees were essentially organized along departmental lines, and could clearly perform a valuable function in holding departments (including their agencies) to account. To date, the major reports of the Environment Committee have been largely concerned with scrutinising new environmental legislation rather than picking up broad environmental issues along the lines of Westminster Select Committees. This in part reflects the fact that Assembly Committees were given express responsibilities for legislative scrutiny, more akin to Westminster Standing Committees. The four reports published by the Committee in 2001-2002 covered the *Local Air Quality Bill, the Planning (Amendment) Bill, the Local Government (Misc. Provisions) Bill* and the *Pollution, Prevention and Control Bill.* These can be contrasted with reports published by their Westminster counterpart in the same period which included *Developments affecting Floodplains, Delivering Sustainable Waste Management, Inland Waterways* and *Rail Investment.* To be fair to the Northern Ireland Environment Committee, it did also pick up a number of discrete issues, though these were not subject to full reports. For instance, in a Press Notice issued in 2001, the committee expressed concern, following representations from the Woodland Trust, about the effectiveness of tree preservation legislation in Northern Ireland and called for DoE officials to come before the committee to explain 'why it has taken 28 years to recognise weaknesses that have been obvious to so many for so long.'[67] On the resumption of devolution, it would be valuable if the Environment Committee were to investigate substantial environmental issues as well as the details of new legislation.

8.7   Consideration might also be given to establishing a cross-departmental Sustainable Development Committee. This would mirror the Westminster model where, in addition to the departmental Select Committees, there now exists an Environment Audit Committee. The intention is not to duplicate the work of the departmental committee, but to allow issues to be investigated which not do necessarily fall within conventional departmental lines and which might otherwise escape effective political scrutiny. This is one of the distinctive features of the environment as a policy issue, and one of the reasons that many governments have established broadly based advisory commissions as discussed in section 9.

8.8   Close co-ordination between a new Sustainable Development Committee and the existing Environment Committee would be needed to ensure no unnecessary duplication. A flavour of the types of issues that might be examined is reflected in the subject areas of some of the recent reports of the Westminster Environment Audit Committee: *Greening Government, The Sustainable Development Headline Indicators, Learning the Sustainability Lesson, Energy White Paper – Empowering Change, Timber Trade and Public Procurement,* and *Waste – An Audit.* It would not have been possible for a departmental Select Committee to examine such

---

[67] Environment Committee (2001) Press Notice 'Environment Committee Calls for Tough Action against Developers Destroying Trees'. 12 April 2001

issues from a cross-departmental perspective, yet a mechanism for doing so is an important element of ensuring improved political accountability.

Independent Auditing

8.9 The accountability of governmental bodies can also be substantially strengthened by the creation of institutions with a specific role and sufficient resources to investigate the performance of agencies. Although a number of existing bodies perform this role, the opportunity should be taken to consider to what extent these mechanisms could be strengthened. It is clear that the challenges of effectively implementing environmental regulation and policy will grow in Northern Ireland over the next decade. Non-governmental environmental organisations are growing in sophistication, and the public needs to have confidence that there is sufficient government machinery to hold the performance of official bodies to account where there are failings and to identify lessons for the future. This is especially important if there is a move to create more independent bodies with substantial environmental responsibilities. Bodies such as the Audit Office perform a distinct and complementary audit role to that of Assembly Committees in that their main function is to examine the effectiveness and efficiency of departments and public bodies in the performance of their functions, holding them to account for the public money which they spend.

Options for Improving Accountability Mechanisms

8.10 In this context there are three main options that should be considered:

Option 1. Create an Environmental Audit Commissioner. This would be a new, independent post with specific responsibility to investigate and report on the performance of governmental bodies in the exercise of their environmental responsibilities. The Commissioner's precise jurisdiction and powers would be a matter for government. The advantages are that the Commissioner could develop the specialist environmental knowledge and expertise needed for investigations and, unlike the more general accountability bodies, would avoid being distracted by other responsibilities. The establishment of such a post would be a clear signal by the government of the seriousness with which it is now taking the environment and of the need to ensure public trust in the performance of its bodies and agencies. Nevertheless, it would be necessary to establish that the environment is sufficiently distinctive from other areas of government policy to warrant a dedicated new position. There are real establishment costs involved, and it could lead to unnecessary duplication with the functions of other bodies such as the Northern Ireland Audit Office.

Option 2. Strengthen the capacity of the Northern Ireland Audit Office in the environmental field. This option has the advantage of building on an existing institution with the necessary powers and experience in investigating the performance of governmental bodies, and one that has already developed an interest in the environment with its two reports on the performance of Environment and Heritage Service. It would recognise that the environmental challenge is sufficiently broad to require greater resources and more specialised expertise that is presently available. It would, for example, reflect the concerns of the Northern Ireland Authority for Energy Regulation in a discussion paper in 2003 of the need for improved accountability mechanisms of government departments in the context of energy efficiency: 'The role of the Northern Ireland Audit Office should be expanded to require Departments to explicitly report on their energy efficiency performance and to demonstrate that they are purchasing their energy services economically.'[68] This model has considerable attractions, though there remains a danger that the environment would still be lost within the wider responsibilities of the NI Audit Office. Furthermore, the rationale for the Audit Office's decisions to choose particular areas of investigation is not especially transparent, and there are no developed mechanisms for investigating complaints by members of the public.

Option 3. Create a dedicated environment audit body and/or Environment Commissioner within the existing Northern Ireland Audit Office. This is a variation of the second option, but one that gives a more visible significance to the environment and acknowledges the distinctive challenges it raises. It reflects a recommendation of the Westminster Environmental Audit Committee which, in 2001, called for the creation of a distinct environmental unit within the National Audit Office,[69] noting that the Audit Office lacked sufficient expertise to carry out effective environmental audits and had failed to take on board sufficiently the implications of the sustainable development agenda. This model in many ways would mirror the Canadian Commissioner of the Environment

[68] NI Authority for Energy Regulation (2003) Discussion Paper on DETI Energy Policy
[69] House of Commons Environment Audit Committee (2001) First Report : *Environmental Audit* Session 200-2001

and Sustainable Development, established in 1996 as a specialised unit within the Office of the Auditor General. The Commissioner monitors the implementation of the sustainable development strategies by 25 federal departments, produces an annual report to Parliament, undertakes special investigations, and monitors the handling by government departments of environmental petitions made to them by members of the public.[70] This option, though also involving costs, has the advantage of building on the strengths of an existing institution and avoiding unnecessary overlap of functions between institutions but creates a visible, distinctive entity within the Audit Office. Government should also consider the possibility of strengthening public influence and connection with such bodies by instituting a petition system, under the auspices of the Audit body, along the lines of the Canadian model.

9. INDEPENDENT ENVIRONMENTAL ADVISORY BODIES

9.1   This section considers a number of issues relating to the provision of policy advice on the environment to the Northern Ireland administration. As a policy issue, the environment is one that can be especially complex for decision-makers, often involving considerable scientific and technical uncertainties and contested public values. Governments in most countries have established various mechanisms to provide authoritative advice to assist in policy development on the environment. As with issues of accountability in Section 8, this is an issue which can largely be considered independently from questions concerning the future structure of Environment and Heritage Service.

Role of Environment Agencies as Sources of Independent Policy Advice

9.2   The view that government departments make policy and agencies merely deliver is now recognised as being far too simplistic a picture. It is clear from the experience in other parts of the United Kingdom that environment agencies can be a valuable source of information and advice to government, and their role as an independent source of influence on the development of policy is increasingly recognised. No doubt Environment and Heritage

---

[70] Under the 1995 amendments to the Canadian Auditor General Act, members of the public may, via the Auditor General, ask Federal Departments questions about environmental standards and sustainable development issues. Departments must respond within 120 days.

Service currently provides policy advice within the Department of the Environment, but, as an Executive Agency which is a constituent part of the Department, it is less easy to characterise it as an independent and detached source of advice. Certainly where the structure of a non-department public body is adopted the role of such a body in providing independent policy advice to government can more readily and more transparently be defined, either in the legislation establishing the body or in statutory guidance.

Departmental Advisory Committees

9.3   As noted in Paragraph 3.1, the Department of the Environment has a number of statutory and non-statutory advisory committees providing independent advice in certain areas. Environment ministries in most jurisdictions make use of various forms of advisory committee, some highly scientific and others with a broader input, but generally with a clearly defined remit. It is not the purpose of this report to evaluate the role and effectiveness of the current DoE advisory bodies, nor to suggest whether they should be restructured. Some may criticise them as not being perceived to be sufficiently independent and too close to the government machinery. The Department must decide to what extent such bodies should develop a more independent voice, and this will be reflected in decisions on matters such as the provision of independent secretariat and research support.

Cross-Departmental Environmental Advisory Bodies

9.4   The need for the Department of the Environment to have sources of advice from specialised advisory committees is likely to continue. One of the developments in Europe over the past 20 years has been the establishment of official advisory bodies which can take a much broader and longer-term look at environmental issues, often across departmental boundaries, reporting to government as a whole. Broadly two forms of bodies have developed. Bodies such as the UK Royal Commission on Environmental Pollution or the German Council on Environmental Advisers are composed of individual experts from different disciplines or with particular experience. One of their key roles is to provide an independent, authoritative and in-depth analysis of key environmental challenges. The second type of body, which includes many of the more recent sustainable development commissions in other European countries, is more in the way of a stakeholder body with its members tending to represent particular sectors of society with an interest in the environment. A variation of this latter model is a body such as the UK Sustainable Development Commission composed of individuals with expertise, but with a role to promote sustainability and to seek consensus in the wider world. Expert and stakeholder type bodies are not mutually exclusive in that they often perform complementary functions. Given the complexity of many environmental issues an expert rather than a stakeholder body has particular attractions, provided it adopts a multi-disciplinary approach and operates with an open mind. It is important to recognise that the existence of such a body does not replace the need for more specialised departmental advisory bodies. Equally, it is essential to the effectiveness of such a body that, in addition to the appointment of members of distinction and expertise, it is given the freedom to choose its own areas for study and has a sufficiently resourced secretariat support to ensure depth and authority in its reports.

Figure 6 provides a snap shot of the main environmental and/or sustainable development councils currently operating in Europe. This section looks in more detail at two such expert bodies, and then considers how the approach might be further developed in Northern Ireland.

Country	Name of Body	Type of Body
Austria	Clean Air Commission of the Academy of Sciences (1962)	Expert body originally concerned with research but increasingly now with policy issues
	Council for Sustainable Development (1991)	Stakeholder body; secretariat provided by Ministry for Environment
Belgium	Walloon Environmental Council for Sustainable Development (1985)	Stakeholder body
	Environment and Nature Council of Flanders (1991)	Stakeholder body
	Federal Council for Sustainable Development (1993)	Stakeholder body; own secretariat; reports to President

Finland	Council for Natural Resources (1977)	Expert body
	National Commission on Sustainable Development (1993)	Stakeholder body; secretariat provided by Environment Ministry; chaired by Prime Minister
France	Commission on Sustainable Development (1995)	Stakeholder body; secretariat provided by Ministry for Environment
Germany	Council of Environmental Advisers (1971)	Expert body reporting to Government as a whole
	Advisory Council on Global Change (1992)	Expert body
	Council for Sustainable Development (2001)	Stakeholder body; independent secretariat; reports to Chancellor
Greece	Council for Physical Planning and Sustainable Development (2001)	Stakeholder body
Ireland	National Sustainable Development Partnership (1998)	Stakeholder body
Netherlands	Council for the Housing, Spatial Planning and the Environment (1997)	Expert body
Portugal	National Council on Environment and Sustainable Development (1998)	Expert body
Spain	Environmental Advisory Council (1994)	Originally an expert body but changed to stakeholder in 1997
Sweden	Environmental Advisory Council	Expert body
	National Committee on Agenda 21 and Habitat (2000)	Stakeholder body

| United Kingdom | Royal Commission on Environmental Pollution (1970) | Expert body; own secretariat; budget from Dept of Environment, Food and Rural Affairs (DEFRA); reports to Queen and Parliament |
| | Sustainable Development Commission (1998) | Expert/stakeholder body with promotional role; secretariat provided by DEFRA |

Figure 6. Main environmental and sustainable development advisory bodies in Europe
adapted from Macrory and Niestroy (2004) 'Emerging Transnational Policy Networks' in Vig and Faure (eds) Green Giants MIT Press, Mass

Royal Commission On Environmental Pollution

Structure

9.5   The Royal Commission on Environmental Pollution was created in 1970 as part of series of UK institutional reforms in response to the Stockholm international conference. It now remains the only standing Royal Commission in the UK, and this status is important in that it is clearly seen as much more than a departmental advisory committee. Its reports are formally addressed to the Queen and this has allowed it to address, from an environmental perspective, issues such as transport or energy that cut across departmental responsibilities. The Commission has extremely broad terms of reference that have remained unchanged since its formation: 'to advise on matters, both national and international, concerning pollution of the environment; on the adequacy of research in this field, and the future possibilities of danger to the environment.' The term 'pollution' has never inhibited the Commission from taking a broad interpretation of its remit and, although a few years ago there were suggestions from the Government that its title might be changed to reflect more accurately its stance (such as Royal Commission on the Environment), the Commission resisted any change on the grounds that it already had a well established brand image.

9.6   The RCEP is by definition an advisory body with no executive functions. The Commission is sometimes described as a scientific body, and to date it has always been chaired by a distinguished scientist. However, its membership has been drawn from a wide range of disciplines (including economics, law, social science, and moral philosophy) and has included individuals with particular knowledge or experience such as in agriculture or utility industries. Unlike stakeholder bodies, members are appointed for their individual expertise rather than as representative of any particular group. In that sense it can be described as a body of experts rather than an expert body, and one whose legitimacy largely depends on the quality of its reports and analysis and on its choice of subject matter to study. Observers have consistently said that a key quality of members, in addition to expertise and experience, is an openness of mind and a willingness to learn. Following the implementation of Nolan rules, membership of the Commission is now advertised, and candidates formally interviewed with recommendations eventually put to the Prime Minister. Again following Nolan, membership is normally for three years with the possibility of one further period of extension. Members of the Commission are expected to attend a monthly meeting lasting between 1.5 and 2 days, and are paid travel expenses and a small daily rate for attendance, though not for reading and preparation time. Members are supported by a small, permanent secretariat of around 11 members.

9.7   A Framework Document laying out the basic formal relationships between the RCEP and the government was published in February 2001 and sets out that the primary aim of the RCEP 'is to contribute to policy development in the longer term by providing an authoritative factual basis for policy-making and debate, and setting new policy agendas and priorities. In reaching its conclusions, the Commission seeks to take account of the wider implications for society for any measures proposed. This involves consideration of the economic, social and ethical aspects of issues as well as the scientific and technological aspects.' The Foreword to the document expressly establishes that the RCEP 'is independent of the government of the day.' The RCEP now publishes an annual corporate plan defining its strategic direction and priorities over a three year period, including financial management and information necessary for budget allocation. The costs of the Commission in 2001/2 were just over £1m, including staff costs, rental of premises, consultancy reports and members' fees.

Relationship with Devolved Administrations

9.8   The RCEP is essentially a UK-wide body but, with the development of devolved administrations that are responsible for environmental policy within their respective competences, new relationships are being developed. Under the Scotland Act 1998 the Royal Commission is specified as a Cross Border Public Authority, and Scottish Ministers have the right to refer matters to the RCEP for suggested study, but unlike UK Ministers there is no requirement on the RCEP to inquire into such matters. No such formal status has been established in relation to Northern Ireland and Wales, though it has been agreed that the RCEP will consider requests for areas to study on the same basis as Scotland. RCEP reports will be now presented to the Scottish Parliament, the National Assembly of Wales and the Northern Ireland Assembly (when sitting) at the same time as they are presented to the UK Parliament. Ministers in the devolved administrations are consulted on potential candidates for membership of the Commission.

9.9   With the advent of devolution the RCEP has paid more regular visits to the devolved administrations than was previously the practice, and recent reports (such as the 2002 study on Environmental Planning which singled out the Northern Ireland Regional Development Strategy as a sensible approach to the type of spatial planning being advocated by the Commission) have contained more extensive analysis of regional differences in policy and practice where relevant. Nevertheless, none of the reports to date has focused on environmental issues specific to a UK region and, given current resources, it is unlikely that the Commission could, or indeed is best suited, to take on much more in the way of discrete studies for the devolved administrations.

Choice of studies

9.10   The main output of the RCEP has been detailed studies published as Command Papers which normally take around 18 months to two years to complete. Twenty four reports have been published to date, including subjects such as transport, energy, soil, GMOs, and agriculture and pollution. According to the original Royal Warrant, the Commission may either itself determine the subject areas it wishes to investigate or must inquire into matters referred to it by Secretaries of State or Ministers. In practice, the choice has in almost all cases been left to the Commission. In 1993 for the first time the Commission published a list of five criteria which would guide it in choosing a suitable topic for inquiry: a) issues that require detailed and rigorous analysis before satisfactory policies can be adopted, b) topics that raised wide issues both intellectually in the sense of spanning several disciplines and organisationally in the sense of not falling within the terms of reference of any single body, c) topics that are likely to involve general issues of principle, d) topics that did not normally duplicate other studies already in progress or planned in the near future and e) topics where there would be a reasonable prospect of producing worthwhile conclusions within two years and within the resources available to the Commission.

9.11   In practice, the Commission consults informally with DEFRA on possible subjects for study, and against its own criteria for choice of study the Commission develops a short list of potential topics with the expected focus of each, which is published and subject to wide consultation. In 2003, for example, the Commission published a short list of four potential candidates to follow their current study on marine fisheries: environmental effects of food production, tourism and the environment, the urban environment, and waste recycling and recovery policy.

9.12   Both the choice and timing of a study are critically important for the continuing impact of the Commission's work though, particularly with regard to timing, predictions are not always easy. Certainly many observers felt that the publication of the 1992 *Water* Report, for example, came too late after significant legislative and policy changes had been set in place following the privatisation of water in England and Wales. In recent years the Commission has been more aware of the significance of the European dimension to policy making; for example, following the publication of its recent Report on *Chemicals in Products* (where European legislation dominates many areas), the Commission made special presentations to both the European Commission and Members of the European Parliament at what turned out to be a critical stage in the development of thinking on the direction of European policy. In this context, the Commission has been an active member of the network of European Environmental Advisory Councils, a loose organisation of equivalent official but independent policy advisory bodies across Europe, and one of its Members was recently chair of the EEAC's Steering Board for two years.

Value of RCEP Reports

9.13   There is no formal requirement (as there is for reports of Westminster Select Committees) for government to respond to RCEP reports. In practice, with the exception of the first Transport report published in 1994, government has always published a formal response, normally with DEFRA taking the lead in coordinating responses, though with a report such as Environmental Planning the task of coordination fell to the Office of the Deputy Prime Minister as the department with lead responsibility for planning. The Commission now carries out formal evaluations of the impact and success of its reports, generally commissioning an independent consultant to carry out the initial study. Nevertheless, this is not a straightforward task, and simply judging by the number of recommendations accepted in the first response by government is misleading. Recommendations in some reports have been accepted almost immediately (the record is three days in the case of the 1983 *Lead in the Environment* Report), but others, such as Integrated Pollution Control recommended in the 1974 Fifth Report, took almost 16 years before they were reflected in legislation.

9.14   A more sophisticated approach recognises the extent to which RCEP reports have changed the framework for debate and policy analysis both within and outside government. Despite the very different subject matters chosen for inquiry, and its changing membership, the permanent nature of the Commission has given it significant institutional 'memory' and allowed it to develop certain core principles (such as transparency, public participation, precaution) that consistently find their way into different reports. In terms of policy influence, it is equally important to appreciate that, according to the subject matter and the prevailing policy and political climate, different reports may well have different functions, even if at the time of the inquiry this is not a conscious decision by the Commission. Five key functions can be identified,[71] some of which will be more apparent in some studies than others:

-   •   resolving disputes between government and interest groups through its independent and dispassionate analysis (e.g. the Lead in the Environment report),

---

[71] adapted from Owens and Rayner (1999) *When Knowledge Matters :The Role and Influence of the Royal Commission on Environmental Pollution* Journal of Environmental Policy and Planning 1 7-24

- acting as a knowledge broker between original researchers and policy makers (e.g. the Soil report),

- being a policy 'entrepreneur' where the Commission itself develops original approaches, or tackles a novel subject not subjected to previous policy analysis (e.g. the Report on *Genetically Modified Organisms*),

- making radical ideas more respectable (e.g. the first Report on *Transport and the Environment*) and

- having an 'enlightenment function' where the Commission is able to change the framework of debate and advocate different ways of examining issues (e.g. the *Energy Report*).

German Council of Environmental Advisors

9.15   The German Council of Environment Advisors was established in 1971 and currently consists of seven independent members appointed by the Federal Government but with the Environment Ministry making formal proposals. The Council is supported by a secretariat (currently ten), together with scientific researchers, and has a generous budget which includes providing members with research and secretarial support, and substantially higher fees than those paid to members of the Royal Commission on Environmental Pollution.

9.16   As with the Royal Commission on Environmental Pollution, the German Council is not an advisory body to the Environment Ministry but reports to the government as a whole, allowing it an unconstrained analysis of environmental issues. There are regular consultations with the Environment Ministry but the Council has established contacts with other ministries, and before submitting its reports is obliged to consult with other ministries which might be affected by its proposals. The choice of subject matter for study is determined by the Council, though it has not yet developed the public consultation procedures on possible topics that the Royal Commission has in recent years. The main constraint is that in 1992 the government established another broad ranging independent advisory committee, the German Advisory Council on Global Change, whose tasks include analysing and reporting on global environmental and development problems, assessing national and international research in the field of global change, and developing and recommending strategic responses for policy makers and the public. The Global Change Council is partly financed by the Ministry of Research and Technology, and one consequence of the establishment of this new body is that the Council of Environmental Advisers now tends to focus more on national and EC environmental matters. There are some concerns whether the analysis of environmental issues can be so readily divided along international, European and national lines.

9.17 In contrast to the Royal Commission on Environment Pollution, which is mainly concerned with the production of a report on a single topic every 18 months or so, the Council of Environmental Advisers has tended to produce a general report on the environment every two years that examines a broad range of environmental issues. These have been supplemented by special reports on issues such as energy and the environment, agriculture, waste, and forestry which have often been primarily directed at ministries other than the Environment Ministry.

9.18 Extracts from recent reports indicate clearly the independent perspective taken by the Council. In Environment 2002,[72] discussing the German Government's approach to the Aarhus Convention, the Council notes: 'The obligations embodied in the Aarhus Convention to allow public participation in plans, programmes, and policies are formulated in weak language. The Council advocates that the current German policy, pursued at home and at the EU level, of interpreting and implementing these provisions such that participation is avoided to the greatest possible extent be abandoned.' The Report also discusses the German draft Sustainable Development Strategy and, while welcoming many aspects of it, warns 'The eight priority areas of action in the draft are largely a reflection of current Government policy. Whereas the strategy formulates concrete and detailed objectives and measures for problems already dealt with in this legislative period, it is very vague as regards long-term planning. This runs counter to the basic function of sustainable development, namely to provide society's actors with a means of orientating themselves for more than one legislative period.'

9.19 Unlike the Royal Commission on Environmental Pollution, the Council has not yet begun a systematic evaluation of the effectiveness and impact of its published reports. Certainly some reports, such as the 1990 special report on waste, had a major influence on pushing national waste policy towards

---

[72] German Advisory Council on the Environment (2002) *Environment 2002 – Towards a New Leading Role*

waste avoidance and producer responsibility. A number of its reports in the 1970s clearly had significant impact. The report on contaminated sites, for example, paved the way for new federal soil pollution legislation, while its report on environmental standards led to the establishment of a new inter-agency commission which followed the direction the Council proposed. As with the Royal Commission, there are other reports that do not so much break new ground as assist policy makers by providing an authoritative and sound factual understanding of the issue at hand. In its recent reports, the Council has given greater emphasis to the European dimension of environmental policy, but has tended to date to be rather reactive, being concerned mainly with the EU impact on national law and policy. A challenge facing the Council, as with many other national councils, is the extent to which it should try to directly influence the development of European policy-making and how to do this in a timely fashion.

Options for Northern Ireland

9.20   The experience in Europe shows that there are considerable gains to be made from the existence of an independent advisory environmental body that can provide a longer-term and in-depth examination of environmental issues that do not necessarily fall within existing departmental boundaries. An expert rather than a stakeholder body has particular attractions, provided it adopts a multi-disciplinary approach and operates with an open mind. As discussed in paragraph 9.4, this would not replace the need for specialised departmental advisory bodies and it would need to have the freedom to choose its own areas for study and be sufficiently resourced.

9.21   If the model of an expert body were adopted, there are a number of options:

Option 1. Strengthen links with the Royal Commission on Environmental Pollution. This would require departments to be fully engaged with the development of the Commission's reports. Ideally, there should be at least one member appointed with a Northern Ireland background, though this may not always be possible since in the final analysis members should be appointed for their individual expertise and experience rather than as representing any particular region or sector of society.

Option 2. Establish a new Northern Ireland Commission on the Environment. This would be along similar lines to the RCEP and, while not replacing the RCEP, would reflect the fact that a UK -wide body such as RCEP is unlikely to have the time and resources to examine in depth environmental issues relating to Northern Ireland. However, it could lead to difficult issues of overlap of functions, and might lead to a detachment of RCEP concerns with Northern Ireland in its consideration of environmental issues facing the United Kingdom. It might also lead to demands from other devolved administrations to create their own Commissions, diminishing the distinctive authority of the Royal Commission. It may also be that the costs of establishing such a body solely concerned with Northern Ireland are not justified against the benefits that would result.

Option 3. Establish a Commission on the Environment in Ireland. This is a more challenging proposal and envisages an expert advisory body established jointly by both Northern Ireland and the Republic of Ireland, possibly under the auspices of the British-Irish Council, and reporting to both governments. It would be based on the premise that there are environmental issues where in-depth, independent studies on the longer-term implications of current trends and policies as they affect the whole of the island would be a valuable input to policy thinking for both governments. Transport patterns, water management and waste management might be good examples. Environmental issues are already identified in the Good Friday Agreement as a suitable area for co-operation, and there already exist examples of cross-border co-operation in fields such as water pollution and fisheries. However these arrangements develop, it should be stressed that the proposed Commission would have no executive functions or powers to bind governments, but would be a source of independent expert advice to both governments from a distinct perspective. An advantage of this option is that it would be less likely to create problems of overlap with a UK body such as the Royal Commission on Environmental Pollution. The establishment and running costs would be shared between the two governments.

Transparency and Trust: Reshaping Environmental Governance in Northern Ireland Summary of Key Options

1.   Delivery Mechanisms Surrounding Environment and Heritage Service (EHS)

Option 1   No change of existing status as an Executive Agency within the Department of the Environment

Option 2   Abandon Executive Agency status and incorporate functions of EHS fully within the Department of the Environment

Option 3   Create a new Environment Authority structured as a non-departmental public body

Option 4   Create a new Environment Authority structured as a non-ministerial government department

Option 5   Give local authorities prime responsibility for implementing environmental regulation with EHS (or its replacement body) having enhanced supervisory powers

2.   Improving Accountability

Assembly Committee

Create a new cross-departmental Sustainable Development Assembly Committee

Options for Auditing Mechanisms

Option 1   Establish a new independent Environment Audit Commissioner

Option 2   Strengthen environmental capacity within the NI Audit Office

Option 3   Create a dedicated Environmental Unit/Commissioner within the NI Audit Office

3. Cross-Departmental Independent Policy Advice On The Environment

Option 1   Strengthen links with the Royal Commission on Environmental Pollution

Option 2   Establish a Northern Ireland Commission on the Environment

Option 3   Establish a Commission on the Environment for the island of Ireland reporting to both governments

PART 3

THE DYNAMICS OF ENVIRONMENTAL LAW

The substantive content of environmental law is constantly changing, as policy makers and legislators attempt to deal with fresh environmental challenges. Yet beneath the detail of particular legal provisions it is possible to detect underlying patterns which reflect more substantial changes in the way that society is organized, and the role of law in that process.

Environmental Law: Shifting Directions and the New Formalism *(1991) was an early attempt to assess profound ways in which the style of British environmental legislation was changing, and to consider the impact of this on the practice of environmental law. Environmental regulation, especially of pollution from industrial processes, had been well established in the United Kingdom for over 100 years. A core feature of the legislative structures was the large degree of discretion given to regulators, with the legislative provisions largely focusing on process and procedures rather than prescribing detailed environmental standards. The law on industrial air emissions, for example, imposed a duty to use the 'best practicable means' to control emissions; water companies had a duty to supply 'wholesome' water. Occasionally, the courts would be asked to provide greater interpretation of these open-ended phrases, but to a large degree it was left to regulators and government to convert them into practical reality as they thought best. Courts and lawyers were largely excluded from the regulatory process, a feature that caused endless bewilderment to US environmental lawyers. By the 1980s, however, it was clear that significant changes to the structure of environmental law and regulations was taking place, with far more detail in the way of the substantive environmental standards, usually expressed in precise scientific terms, being contained in the body of the law. The influence of European Community environmental legislation, the recent privatisation of key utilities, and greater public distrust of regulatory discretion were all important factors. As **Shifting Discretion and the New Formalism** predicted, environmental regulators would soon be acting within the constraints of legal process and judicial oversight to an extent unheard of even a generation before, though perhaps it remains an open question whether this necessarily leads to improved environmental outcomes.*

Loaded Guns and Monkeys: Responsible Environmental Law *(1994) built on these themes but focussed on the concept of 'responsibility' as an underlying feature of liability under law. The House of Lords had recently given judgment* *in the seminal* Cambridge Water Company *case exploring the extent to which polluters should be liable for damage they had caused even where it was not predictable at the time, or whether some degree of negligence or reasonable foreseeability was an essential ingredient of liability. I was particularly intrigued that one of the cases quoted in argument before the House of Lords was an 1846 decision of the High Court concerning a pet monkey which had escaped through no fault of its owner, and attacked a passer-by. For the first time, the court espoused a general principle of strict liability on the owner on the grounds that animal was known to be potentially dangerous. The analogy with the operator of a potentially hazardous installation is obvious. The notion of responsibility seemed particularly interesting in the environmental field – should designers of poorly insulated flats be responsible for noise nuisances that inevitably resulted? did consumers of cheap flights bear any responsibility for damaging emissions from aircraft? Four years after the lecture, Lord Hoffmann discussed the notion of causation in* Empress Cars *decision[1], where liability under the relevant water pollution legislation rested on the term 'causes'. Lord Hoffmann argued persuasively that the notion of causation was not, as previous courts had often treated it, a matter of common sense fact but one of legal construct:'one cannot give a common sense answer to a question of causation for the purpose of attributing responsibility under some rule without knowing the purpose and scope of the rule.'*

Environmental Standards, Legitimacy and Social Justice *(1999), a revised version of a lecture given at the 1998 Environmental Justice and the Legal Process Conference in the University of Cape Town, is a further reflection on the implications of the increasing use of formalised, scientific standards in environmental law, which had become so apparent at both British and European Community level. Although such standards provided a comforting sense of certainty, closer examination of the underlying science revealed the degree of uncertainty involved and the value judgments that were necessarily being made in deciding on a particular standard. One legal response has been to introduce greater rights of public participation and access to information, but this tends to be most effective at a local level, while increasingly in reality standards are being determined at European Community or international level, often in fairly obscure committees and other forums. Nor, did it seem to me, that a rejection of the simplistic notion that standards were derived from sound science could be replaced by an equally simplistic invocation of the precautionary approach. At the time, I was a member of the Royal Commission on Environmental pollution which was discussing many of these themes during its study on environmental standards. The Commission's Report, published later that year,[2] argued for a far more nuanced process for establishing standards, and one that involved new*

---

[1] *Environment Agency (formerly National Rivers Authority) v Empress Car Company (Abertillery) Ltd* [1998] 1 All ER 481 see part 4

[2] Royal Commission on Environmental Pollution (1998) *Setting Environmental Standards* 21st Report Cm 4053 HMSO London

forms of public engagement. Yet the dilemmas and contradictions involved, and the challenges of devising fresh approaches remain with us today.

Effective enforcement of environmental law is essential to achieve the environmental outcomes implicit in the legal requirements and to ensure public confidence in the legal system. The work on sanctions presented in Chapter 1 concern is extending the range of options available to enforcement bodies where regulatory breaches occur. **Technology and Environmental Law Enforcement (2003)** *is concerned more with methods of supervising the implementation of regulatory requirements and the detection of breaches, another key element in the chain of enforcement. The last 15 years have seen a significant extension of the range of environmental laws for which enforcement bodies are responsible, but coupled with a constant squeeze on resources. One response to the new challenges has been to develop so-called risk-based approaches to enforcement – rather than carrying out inspections and supervision to the same level of intensity on all the activities falling within the scope of control, calculated assessments are made to focus enforcement attention on where the most risk is likely. The Environment Agency, for example, has developed a scoring tool for appraising the likely compliance risks of waste facilities and IPPC processes, based both on the operator's performance history and the site's environmental risks.[3] Targeting resources in this way is a sensible approach, though as with any prior assessment techniques not without its own risks should the unexpected occur.* **Technologies and Environmental Law Enforcement** *considers rapid developments in technologies such as automatic monitoring devices and the use of satellites, which provide complementary aids to supervision, and are likely to prove of increasing importance.*

Defining the scope of environmental law with any precision is extraordinarily difficult. The environment affects and is affected by so many distinct policy areas that it becomes almost a fruitless, and indeed potentially pernicious to draw precise boundaries, whether for the purposes of administrative organisation or legal discipline. The distinguished German environmental lawyer, Gerd Winter, has argued that the contemporary challenge is not to treat environmental law as a distinct field of law which restrains or mediates the excesses of market based law such as free trade or company law but to ensure that all such law becomes 'inoculated with ecological solutions.'[4] We are still a long way from that goal, but the term 'integration' has increasingly entered the language of environmental law, as for example, in the EC Directive on Integrated Pollution and Prevention Control, and the duty under Article 6 concerning integration

---

[3] Environment Agency *Operator and Pollution Risk Appraisal Scheme,* Version 3.2,April 2007

[4] Winter (1989) 'Perspectives on Environmental Law - Entering the Fourth Phase' *Journal of Environmental Law* Vol I No I pp38-47 at 45

of an environmental dimension in all Community policies areas.[5] Yet what is implied by the concept of integration is by no means obvious. **The Scope of Environmental Law** *(1996) is a reflection on the range of interpretations than can be given to the term, ranging from modest administrative co-operation between different bodies to more fundamental rethinking of legal structures and principles.*

Finally, **Cycle Lore** *(1979) is included in part out of sentiment as my first published legal article, but it also illustrates a number of themes echoed in later writings. The lawyer concerned with the environment should not necessarily be constrained by conventional boundaries of environmental law, but be prepared to examine areas of law such as transport or planning. It also demonstrates how the promotion of policies – here the greater encouragement of cycling – may be unwittingly inhibited by the details of existing and long-established legal frameworks. To take one example, prior to 1978 local authorities possessed extensive powers to construct 'street furniture' such as horse troughs, public lavatories, lamps stands, and bus shelters but no equivalent explicit powers to erect cycle racks. Some authorities ignored the constraint, but it was nevertheless a detail of law not without legal consequence. Street furniture erected without statutory authority would be an illegal obstruction of the highway, and someone, such as a blind person, who was injured by walking into an illegally erected stand would have the right to sue the authority concerned. As part of a transport campaign, I and my then colleagues at Friends of the Earth successfully lobbied government to change the law in 1978.[6] The delightful Victorian case law testing at what point a bicycle ceased to be a vehicle in law resonated over 100 years later in 2006 when a commuter successfully evaded a private rail operator's restrictions on the carriage of bicycles on trains by wrapping his cycle in brown paper and turning it legally into a parcel.[7]*

---

[5] For a legal analysis of the integration duty, see chapter 18 (1998) in this volume.
[6] See s 12 Transport Act 1978 which extends the power of authorities to provide parking places 'to providing, in roads or elsewhere, stands and racks for bicycles.'
[7] Macrory (2006) 'Cycling Mad' *The Times Letters* Page, 21/4/06

CHAPTER 7

ENVIRONMENTAL LAW: SHIFTING DISCRETIONS AND THE NEW FORMALISM*

Introduction

Public concern and governmental interest in environmental issues has reached new peaks in the last few years. Many of the most serious problems have international or transboundary implications, and will not necessarily be receptive to conventional legal solutions. My concern here, though, is with the domestic response as it is reflected in the structure and style of new legislation, and the ensuing implications for future regulatory approaches in this country. The sheer volume of legislative material that has been produced in the United Kingdom, particularly in the field of pollution control, in the space of a little over two years is itself quite remarkable – even more so when set against underlying government policies promoting industrial deregulation. When one comes to examine in more detail the substantive content of this new body of law, it is clear that fundamental shifts of principle have taken place; from a legal perspective, at least, long-standing characteristics of British practice of environmental management no longer hold true.

Pollution and the Legislative Framework

Legislative development often takes place in a rather haphazard and unco-ordinated fashion. Laws concerning pollution control provide a compelling example. We may talk of 'pollution' as a single all-embracing idea but from a legal perspective it is perhaps only the common law concept of 'nuisance' which comes closest to reflecting this generalised notion of environmental damage. The classic general definition of common law nuisance is that provided by the text-book writer Winfield and subsequently adopted with approval by courts: 'an unlawful interference with a person's use or enjoyment of land, or with some right over or in connection with it.' In contrast, statutory controls, since their substantive emergence in the nineteenth century, have sliced up the subject into specialised fields, generally on a basis of the receiving medium, such as air or water or land – even in the latter case the emphasis has been on waste disposal rather than the broader approach of land contamination as such. The fields have been treated

* R Macrory (1991) Environmental Law: Shifting Discretions and the New Formalism in: O Lomas, (ed.) *Frontiers of Environmental Law*, Chancery Law, London. pp 8-23

distinctly, with different laws emerging at different times (examples include Alkali etc Works Regulation Act 1906, Public Health Act 1936, Rivers (Prevention of Pollution) Acts 1951 and 1961, Clean Air Acts 1956 and 1968, and Deposit of Poisonous Wastes Act 1972). Given the often complex technical questions intimately involved in this field of law, the approach is understandable. But it has been at the expense of developing underlying and consistent legal principles. While it is true that some preferred and common regulatory approaches emerge, detailed examination of significant provisions – such as those relating to public registers or statutory defences – indicate just how uncoordinated the design of legislation has been.[1] Even the apparently reassuring title, the Control of Pollution Act 1974, cannot disguise the fact that it contained essentially three separate codes of law concerning waste, water, and land, with little overlap or cross-referencing between them.

This predeliction for disaggregated treatment in the law is mirrored and in part explained by the structure of the relevant government departments developing and promoting the legislation, and the manner of their internal administrative divisions. It is not of course a phenomenon that has been confined to Britain. The Environmental Protection Agency in the United States has long been heavily split into separate air and water quality divisions with little real overlap between the two[2]; Federal US air and water legislation has been based on fundamentally different approaches, the former heavily dominated by environmental quality objectives concerning the receiving environment, the latter by emission standards based on what is technically feasible – incidentally, almost the exact reverse of key British legislation in this field. The control of air emissions from major industrial premises has been based on general operator duties under s 5 Health and Safety at Work etc Act 1974 and annual registration with a central government inspectorate, formerly the Alkali Inspectorate, and now part of Her Majesty's Pollution Inspectorate. Although the legislation did not generally provide for statutory emission limits, the Inspectorate developed emission limits as an administrative tool for enforcement: see 'Best Practicable Means: General Principles and Practice' BPM Notes 1/88, Department of the Environment, London 1988. The control of discharges into waters has largely been based on a statutory consent system administered by specialist public bodies since 1951, and more recently under the Control of Pollution Act 1974. In a mirror image to the air pollution controls, the legislation made no provision for statutory water quality objectives

---

[1] See Macrory (1988) *Legislation, Enforcement, and the Courts* (National Society of Clean Air, Spring Workshop Proceedings, Brighton, Sussex), and Macrory (1989) 'UK Pollution Controls' in *Environmental Regulation in the European Community*, Legal Studies and Services Conference Proceedings, London.

[2] For a recent critique see Davies (1990) 'The United States: Experiment and Fragmentation' in Haigh and Irwin (eds) *Integrated Pollution Control*, Conservation Foundation, Washington DC.

or standards, though authorities tended to adopted a quality objective approach as an aid to setting standards. There remains controversy as to whether this approach was always explicit or conscious as Government would sometimes have it believed: Haigh (1984) *EEC Environmental Policy and Britain – An Essay and a Handbook,* Environmental Data Services and Renshaw (1980) 'Water Quality Objectives and Standards' in *Water Quality in Catchment Ecosystems* (ed Gower), John Wiley & Sons, Chichester. The most recent pollution control provisions under the Water Act 1989 and more particularly Part I Environmental Protection Act 1990 have rendered this long-standing dichotomy almost obsolete, at least in formal legal terms. Even the European Commission with its much smaller Directorate-General for the Environment shows similar signs of disaggregation in its internal organisation leading to inconsistencies in principle and even differences in fundamental terminology used in Community legislation. Just to take one example, the term 'limit value' has been used in water pollution Directives to imply minimum standards applicable to discharge emissions, and in strong and pointed contrast to the term, 'quality objective', which indicates the standard of the receiving environment.[3] In those Directives relating to air quality, however, the term 'limit value' is also used but in exactly the opposite sense, and is equivalent to a quality objective.[4] Other examples abound, and are again no doubt in part caused by the internal administrative divisions. It is only at the beginning of this year that the Directorate-Gerneral has been reorganised to reflect the need for a rather more co-ordinated approach towards industrial emissions. The internal administrative units of DG XI (Environment, Nuclear Safety, and Civil Protection) were reorganised in early 1990 to reflect new priorities. Previous arrangements contained explicit divisions between technical units for water and air pollution; under the new system, one unit is dealing wholly with 'industrial installations'.

The Environmental Protection Act 1990

Despite its title, the Environmental Protection Act 1990 encompasses only a relatively discrete area of the law relating to the environment. Nevertheless, Part I of the Bill introduces the concept of integrated pollution control, and for a specified and limited number of industrial processes will provide a common set of legal controls over physical emissions of whatever type, be they to land, air, or water. This itself

---

[3] Directive on Pollution caused by certain Dangerous Substances discharged into the Aquatic Environment Dir 76/464/EEC.

[4] See, for example, Directive on Air Quality Limit Values and Guide Values for Sulphur Dioxide and Suspended Particulates 80/779/EEC, plus those for Nitrogen Dioxide 85/203/EEC and Lead 82/884/EEC. In these Directives the term 'Limit Value' is used in contrast with the term 'Guide Values' to indicate a mandatory as opposed to a discretionary standard.

represents a major legal advance, and a conscious attempt to produce a single, co-ordinated set of regulatory rules, albeit within a limited sector of industry.[5] If one goes on to take a broader view to encompass the most recent legislative items in the field of pollution control generally, certain common policy themes do now emerge. Formerly divergent legal approaches are being brought into line with each other. I am not convinced that, until the most recent provisions concerning integrated pollution control, these developments took place under the direction of clearly articulated and co-ordinated policies. Nevertheless, the results represent, for the first time in this country, the gradual formulation of a number of consistent legal principles in this field. I will argue that these will have profound and often unpredictable implications to those responsible for enforcement of the resulting controls and the public concerned with their implementation.

Much of the focus of pollution control has been on the direct discharges or deposits from industrial sources. A key legal control mechanism has long been the licencing or authorisation of potential sources, coupled with the establishment of specialist regulatory bodies responsible for the setting of licences and their enforcement. This basic approach will continue to underly much of pollution law. But while the licence mechanism is, of course, familiar in many jurisdictions, it is worth emphasising a number of points of British practice which have long played a critical role in shaping the context of this type of regulation.

Legal sanctions for non-compliance for licence conditions or the avoidance of a licence has been based on a combination of criminal penalties and administrative sanctions, such as the revocation of a licence. The concept of civil penalties, well developed in United States environmental laws, is not to be found in equivalent British legislation. Indeed, outside the field of taxation, civil penalties have been little favoured by policy makers - though the emergence of automatic customer payments or credits for failure to comply with performance standards under the Water Act 1989 perhaps represent a cautious and modest shift of approach.[6] Administrative procedures and criminal enforcement have to a large extent been intertwined. The same public bodies have tended to be responsible for both licensing and the enforcement of criminal sanctions, and in many instances have an option as to which route to employ – *e.g.* whether to threaten a criminal prosecution to

---

[5] For background policy discussion, see *Integrated Pollution Control* A Consultation Paper, Department of the Environment/Welsh Office, July 1988.

[6] See Water Supply and Sewerage Services (Customer Services Standards) Regulations 1989 SI 1989/1147, as amended. Under these regulations, made under Water Act 1989, the failure by an undertaker to conform to certain standards (such as keeping a domestic appointment) can result in a £5 daily payment or credit to the customer affected.

revoke a licence. (In practice local or regional authorities may adopt different approaches, some finding the use or threat of administrative sanctions more effective that criminal proceedings, and vice versa: see Macrory and Withers (1985) *Application of Administrative and Criminal Punishments concerning Hazardous Waste in England*, Report for European Commission, Imperial College Centre for Environmental Technology, London.)

The Use of the Criminal Law

The structures of the legal controls similarly overlap criminal and administrative provisions. Typically, one finds a criminal offence concerning pollution coupled with a statutory defence of acting in accordance with a licence.

From a perspective of administrative management, this type of legal structure is efficient. Social-legal studies of pollution control authorities, though, have shown the extent to which the emphasis on smooth environmental administration rather than law enforcement as such has encouraged a non-confrontational relationship between regulators and those they regulate.[7] Reinforcing what has been effectively a large measure of leeway by the enforcement authority to determine what level of emissions or discharge should be licenced or not has been the general principle that gives a discretion to enforcement authorities to decide whether or not to take legal action in respect of suspected or even admitted offences. In other fields of criminal law, this discretion has been held to be one that is essentially a matter of operational judgement by authorities and one that is virtually unreviewable by the courts.[8] Even this picture, though, is not entirely consistent. The provisions of Part III of the Water Act 1989 concerning water pollution contain no obligations on the National Rivers Authority as to how it should exercise its powers in respect of suspected offences. (The key pollution offence is s 107 Water Act 1989. Significantly, there is no restriction on who may bring prosecutions.) Part III of the Control of Pollution Act, though, concerning noise pollution, required local authorities to service a statutory notice once they are satisfied of the existence of a noise nuisance – an obligation clearly more honoured in its breach in practice, as annual statistics reveal.[9] Section 14 of the Environmental Protection Act, relating to

---

[7] The best recent UK accounts in the environmental field are K Hawkins (1984) *Environment and Enforcement: Regulation and the Social Definition of Pollution*, Clarendon Press, Oxford and J Richardson et al (1982) *Policing Pollution: A Study of Regulation and Enforcement*, Clarendon Press, Oxford.

[8] See *R y Metropolitan Police Commissioner ex p Blackburn* (1968) 2 QB 118, and *R v Metropolitan Police Commissioner ex p Blackburn*, (no 3) (1973) QB 24.

[9] See s 58 Control of Pollution Act 1974. The provisions have now been replaced by Part III Environmental Protection Act 1990.

integrated pollution control and air pollution, will oblige enforcement authorities to serve a prohibition notice once they are satisfied that a process within their jurisdiction is carried on 'with a severe risk to the environment'. A similar position on enforcement exists in the United States where the Environmental Protection Agency has resisted legal interpretations that would compel its exercise of enforcement powers.[10] The US courts, too, have supported the presumption of discretion in the absence of explicit statutory provisions, and in at least one case have gone as far as to interpret the statutory obligation that the EPA 'shall' take enforcement action in respect of violations still to imply a discretion.[11]

In England and Wales, at least, an authority's discretion is tempered by the general principle that prosecution is not an exclusive function of public agencies – a position that can be contrasted with that in countries such as West Germany or the Netherlands. Subject to express statutory restrictions, any individual, whether or not they have a legal interest in the matter, may initiate private prosecutions – the closest that British law has come to developing the concept of citizen's suits. The power to impose restrictions on the right to prosecute in any particular statute in turn demands a policy response by government on the issue, and the differing positions that have existed in British pollution demonstrate some degree of unease with the subject. Until 1974 restrictions existed in the field of water pollution, but were removed under Part II of the Control of Pollution Act, and were not reintroduced in replacement provisions under the Water Act 1989. Part I of that Act contained no restrictions in the field of waste disposal, but Part II of the Environmental Protection Act, which will replace these provisions, originally provided that proceedings in respect of offences for uncontrolled deposit could not be initiated without the consent of the Director of Public Prosecutions of a waste regulation authority.[12] This restriction no longer appeared in the Bill when it was presented to the House of Lords. Legislation concerning emissions into the air from scheduled processes restricted private prosecution, but these will no longer apply in the new provisions governing integrated pollution control and air pollution under Part I of the Environmental Protection Act. We are therefore reaching a position where the principle of the availability of private prosecution in the field of most areas of pollution control (radioactive waste disposal being the main exception) has been accepted – its use in practice by environmental groups and other members of the public, and the effect of its availability

---

[10] See Reich and Shea (1990) *A Survey of US Environmental Enforcement Authorities, Tools and Remedies* in International Enforcement Workshop Proceedings, Ministry of Housing, Physical Planning and Environment, the Netherlands.

[11] See *State Water Control Board* v *Train* 559 F 2d 921 (4th Circuit 1977).

[12] Cl 25(10) of Bill as published.

on the behaviour of regulatory agencies will be an increasingly fruitful area for research.

The legal provisions and principles concerning enforcement might be described as the micro-end of the process. At the macro-end, one of the most distinctive characteristics of British pollution laws has been the extent to which the legal provisions have been largely absent of statutory policy goals or precise standards, whether they relate to the content of emissions or the quality of the receiving environment. Where standards have appeared, they have classically been expressed in open-textured language, providing general guidance on performance (such as 'best practical means') or the quality of the product released or emitted ('wholesome' water[13]). The tendency has in part been encouraged by prevailing scientific approaches which emphasised the need to examine the particular receiving environment before determining its capacity to handle potential pollution loads, a principle which was considered would be compromised by the setting of statutory standards which by their nature have a generic effect. Foreign observers, particularly from the United States, have emphasised the peculiar constitutional characteristics of law-making in this country which give the Executive near unfettered power to determine the detailed content of both primary and secondary legislation.[14] In the absence of powerful political pressure, whether domestic or international, the inclination of an executive will be to strive for legislative flexibility and at the very least to avoid placing uncomfortable legal obligations on itself.

Policy and Pollution Control

Pollution control authorities have not, of course, denied themselves the use of technical standards nor have they shrunk from formulating explicit policy goals – but from a legal perspective the significant feature is that these developments have taken place administratively. The use of such broad language as 'best practicable means' in legislative provisions, rich as it is in ambiguity, would at first sight – and especially in a common law jurisdiction – have appeared to have offered a significant opportunity for extensive judicial interpretation. But the enforcement discretion available to regulatory authorities and the prevailing administrative culture which resisted making use of the courts as a testing ground has resulted in a remarkably low level of high-level case law in the field. The fact that the key criterion of industrial air pollution legislation for over

---

[13] See s 38 Health and Safety at Work etc Act 1974. See Macrory (1986) 'Science Legislation and the Courts' in Conway (ed) *The Assessment of Environmental Problems,* Imperial College, London.

[14] For a general comparison see Vogel (1986) *National Styles of Regulation: Environmental Policy in Great Britain and the United States* Cornell University Press, Ithaca.

100 years, 'the best practical means', has never been the subject of case-law in the higher courts provides the starkest example of this distinctive feature of the law in this field. (For over 100 years, the general legal duty for operators of many industrial premises was 'to use the best practicable means' to prevent or render harmless emmissions into the atmosphere: see s 5(1) Health and Safety at Work etc Act 1974. The phrase has been considered in the context of these controls in at least one case, before an Industrial Tribunal, and another before a Crown Court, but there is no reported decision of the higher courts on the points. Nor is there ever likely to be since the controls have now been replaced by new statutory provisions under Part I Environmental Protection Act 1990.)

Fundamental legal changes concerning this question of policy expression are now taking place. Statutory environmental quality standards have recently made their first appearance. The 1989 Air Quality Standards[15] introduce into British pollution legislation the concept of legal air quality standards and represent a clear reversal of the preferred policy approach, established by the Royal Commission on Environmental Pollution in 1976.[16] Statutory water quality-objectives have begun to be introduced under the Water Act 1989,[17] brought about in part by the initial plans for water privatisation where the government accepted the logic that were the whole water industry placed in the private sector only legal standards would ensure that a non-public body pursued public policy aims.[18] The revised plans for creating the National Rivers Authority invalidated that argument from a purely domestic and administrative perspective, but by then the political advantages of such mechanisms, coupled with pressure from the European Community, ensured the policy shift was maintained.[19] These mechanisms provide visible and binding policy goals on government and public authorities, and will provide a new critical base for judging their individual administrative decisions. The change is not confined to environmental quality objectives. The quality standard for drinking water for human consumption under the Water Act 1989 retains the familiar criterion, 'wholesome' but detailed regulations now provided the technical

---

[15] Air Quality Standards Regulations 1989 SI 1989/31 7.

[16] Royal Commission on Environmental Pollution (1976) Fifth Report, HMSO London.

[17] For example, see Surface Water (Classification) Regulations 1989 SI 1989/1148, Surface Water (Dangerous Substances) (Classification) Regulations 1989 SI 1989/2286. Statutory classification under s 104 Water Act 1989 is the first step towards the making of statutory water quality objectives under s 105 of the same Act.

[18] *The Water Environment - the Next Steps*, Department of the Environment/Welsh Office Consultation Paper, April 1986.

[19] See *The National Rivers Authority: the Government's Proposals for a Public Regulatory Body in a Privatised Water Industry* Department of Environment, Ministry of Agriculture Fisheries and Food, and Welsh Office,July.i987. For analysis of the Water Act see Macrory R (1990) *The Water Act 1989: Text and Commentary*, Sweet and Maxwell, London.

criteria for interpreting the concept of wholesomeness.[20] Standards for emissions from industrial sources such as large combustion plants and municipal incinerators have been agreed at Community law level in recent years, and will undoubtedly be transposed into national law.[21] The Environmental Protection Act 1990 goes much further, and in relation to integrated pollution and air pollution provides the most extensive power to the Secretary of State to set a range of various types of standards by regulation including, in relation to emissions of specified substances limits on 'the concentration, the amount or the amount in any period of that substance which may be so released'[22] and the establishment of quality objectives or standards for any environmental medium.[23] These developments have mainly been in the field of air and water pollution and one can see a distinct convergence of policy approach in these two fields. Statutory standards in relation to waste disposal on land and soil contamination have yet to be seen in this country, though they must be on the horizon. Following a request from the Council of Ministers, the European Commission is in the process of producing a draft Directive on standards for landfill, and its eventual adoption would require national legislation on the subject. As to soil quality, the House of Commons Select Committee in a report on land contamination earlier this year called for the introduction of a range of legally binding soil quality objectives – not as rigid as those implemented in a country such as the Netherlands but legal innovation in this country.[24]

We are therefore entering a new era of legal formalism in relation to pollution standards and objectives. The long-familiar preferred approach of a legal framework concentrating on administrative structure and procedures, leaving policy content to the realm of shadow mechanisms such as circulars or technical notes no longer holds true.

European Community Influences

Doctrines of European law have undoubtedly provided an underlying dynamic for change. Most Community environmental legislation has been made by means of Directives which according to Article 189 of the Treaty are binding on the Member States as to the result to be achieved but leaves a discretion as to the form and methods for

---

[20] Water Supply (Water Quality) Regulations 1989 SI 1989/1147, as amended.

[21] EC Directive of 24 November 1988 on the Limitation of Emissions of Certain Pollutants into the Air from Large Combustion Plants (88/609/EEC); EC Directive of 8 June 1989 on the Prevention of Air Pollution from New Municipal Waste Incineration Plants (89/369/EEC).

[22] S 3(2) (a) Environmental Protection Act 1990.

[23] S 3(4) *ibid.*.

[24] House of Commons Environment, Committee (1990) *Contaminated Land* First Report, Session 1989-90, HMSO, London.

implementing those aims. Case law of the European Court of Justice has elaborated on the extent to which this is an open discretion, and a series of decisions has held that, at least where the Directive concerns matters of harmonisation or affects the rights of individuals they must be transposed in a manner that is clear and certain. (Key cases are *EC v Belgium* (1982) 2 CMLR 622, *EC v Netherlands* (1982) ECR 171. For a discussion of the case-law, see Macrory (1988) 'Industrial Air Pollution Legislation: Implementing the European Framework', Proceedings of 55th Annual Conference, National Society of Clean Air, Brighton, Sussex.) Administrative practices and circulars which can be changed at the whim of national authorities have therefore been held as insufficient means of transposition. But there remains grey areas in the current state of case law on the subject, and at least one of the leading textbooks on Community law suggests that where a Member State's previous rules had been in the form of circulars, implementation of a subsequent Directive by circular should be sufficient.[25] Nevertheless the Commission has rejected such an interpretation, and pushed hard for implementation by legal means, probably going further than the present state of case law warrants. After initial resistance, the United Kingdom appears to have largely accepted the Commission's approach

Conclusions

Two other policy themes are reflected in the emerging legislation. The 1974 Control of Pollution Act introduced new public rights to information concerning the detailed workings of the licencing system by means of public registers. These were restricted to waste disposal and surface water pollution control, but are now to be extended generally to the field of integrated pollution control and air pollution under the Environmental Protection Act.[26] The Water Act 1989 made the trade effluent consents to sewers available to public scrutiny for the first time.[27] Again here we see the emergence of a general principle which will now make it hard to resist the presumption of open registers. The European Community's Directive on Freedom of Access to Environmental Information goes a good deal further than simply making available registers of consents. Under the Directive[28] public authorities would be required to make available any information relating to the environment in their possession. This will include, according to the definitions in the Directive, information on the state of water, air, soil, fauna, land or

[25] Kapteyn and van Themaat (1989) *Introduction to the Law of the European Communities* 2nd ed (L Gormley ed), Kluwer, Deventer, NL.
[26] S 20 Environmental Protection Act .1990.
[27] S 7A Public Health (Drainage of Premises) Act 1937, as inserted by Water Act 1989, Sched 8.
[28] EC Directive of 7 June 1990 on the Freedom of Access to Informatiron on the Environment (90/31/EEC).

natural sites and on activities or measures likely to adversely affect them and on measures designed to protect them.[29] Derogations are provided where matters relate to judicial proceedings, for example, or trade and industrial secrecy, and where the request is 'manifestly unreasonable'.[30] Nevertheless, the Directive is likely to major advance in principle in this area.

These provisions concerning registers and associated information can be characterised as passive environmental legal rights. Obligations to involve members of the public in participating in the actual decision making on individual consent applications represent a more active form of right. In the United Kingdom, the town and country planning system has long provided the most extensive possibilities of participation, while pollution control has largely been a closed system. As with registers, Part II of the Control of Pollution Act marked a first shift in principle in this country, by providing for participation and consultation where consents for discharges into waters were concerned.[31] Again, one can now detect an extension of the principle to other areas of pollution control, though perhaps with a greater degree of caution than for registers. The Environmental Protection Act now provides for the possibility of public consultation and public inquiries where applications of licences under the integrated and air pollution provisions are made.[32] Public consultation for waste disposal is still largely subsumed under development control procedures. In this context, it should be stressed that the requirements for environmental assessment for certain types of development, introduced in 1988 as a result of the Community Directive on the subject,[33] ensure that pollution implications and control strategies are intimately linked into the planning procedures.

Public registers, participation procedures, statutory environmental policy goals and standards, together with rights of private prosecution form a potent mixture unfamiliar to British practice. The rapid process of legal change produces its own institutional dynamic evidenced by the sudden increase of major law firms now offering specialist advice on the interpretation and implications of the new law. (One indicator of the growth in interest is the rapid increase of membership of the UK Environmental Law Association, founded in 1986 with an initial membership of around 40. There are now over 1,000 members.) For the

---

[29] Art 2(a) *ibid.*

[30] Art 3.3 *ibid.*

[31] S 41 Control of Pollution Act 1974. For a critical analysis of their use in practice see Burton (1989) 'Access to Environmental Information: the UK Experience of Water Registers' *Journal of Environmental Law* 1989 vol 1 no 2 192-208.

[32] Environmental Protection Act 1990, s 6 and Sched 1.

[33] EC Directive of 27 June 1985 on the Assessment of the Effects of Certain Public and Private Projects on the Environment (85/337/EEC).

public authorities charged with day to day application of the controls, we may not yet have reached what Richard Stewart described as 'transmission belt justice'[34], but undoubtedly they will be operating in a more constrained framework, and will be obliged to develop a more formal and detached relationship with those that they regulate.

To those who argue that legal obligations should be transparent and should be obeyed the developments will be welcome. But some dangers should be noted. Legal standards by their inherent nature lack flexibility and are slow to change, even when transmitted by secondary legislation. Technical standards that are clothed in legal form assume a quasi-moral justification which may obscure scientific unsoundness. At a Community level, where so many standards are now first developed, securing agreement to change is as complex and time-consuming a process as agreeing a Directive in the first place. Even moves towards establishing procedures for rapid adaptation and upgrading by technical committees can be subject to the charge of constitutional impropriety as witnessed by the difficulties in securing unanimous agreement to proposed new powers for technical committees in the field of water pollution.[35]

In some respects, formalised policy goals and standards enshrined in the law simplify the operation of a consent system. But they also add a new form of complexity. The opportunities to raise legal challenges to the validity of an individual licence or consent on the grounds of incompatibility with legal standards or quality objectives are enhanced even taking on board the somewhat cautious language of some of the legal provisions that now make the formal connection between legal policy and operational decisions (for example, under the Air Quality Standards Regulations 1989, the Secretary of State 'shall take any appropriate measures to ensure' that the prescribed air quality standards are not exceeded. If he granted a planning permission that would be likely to result in local breaches, would his decision be challengeable on the basis of this duty?). The possibility of legal challenge has immediate implications for the regulator but it may in the future raise the type of complex jurisprudential questions on the relationship between criminal administrative law already well developed in West German environmental law (the concept of *'Verwaltungsakzessorietat'* (roughly, the subordination of criminal law to administrative law) is discussed in Ensenbach (1989) *Die Probleme der Verwaltungsakzessorielat im Umweltstrafrecht*, Frankfurt). Suppose a company raises a statutory defence to a charge of discharging effluent into waters on the grounds that it acted in accordance with consent. The consent is then proved to be invalid on the

---

[34] R B Stewart (1975) 'The Reformation of American Administrative Law' 88 *Harvard Law Review*.

[35] See ENDS Report 168 January 1989, p 27.

grounds that the authority was acting contrary to statutory objectives or policies, or even simply Community obligations. No criminal intent is required for this sort of offence, but can the defence be raised? The solution, to avoid the prospect of retrospective liability, may be to find the consent voidable rather than void, but it is no doubt the type of question that will be required to be explored before too long.

Finally it is important to recognise the possible contradiction between policy formalism of the type I have described and participation procedures of the sort being developed. The expectations aroused by increased legal rights concerning public comment and participation in individual consent procedures will be frustrated the more that fundamental policy questions and applicable standards have been predetermined in the applicable legislation. As a matter of law, it may be that public involvement will have to be confined to the application of nationally prescribed policies to particular local situations, areas still untouched by the relevant law, or for a call for stricter environmental standards to the case in hand to the extent that the legal framework allows for this. It remains to be seen whether these opportunities will prove sufficient to satisfied public needs. However, the trend towards policy formalism is now, I believe, a committed policy approach in this field, and one that is now irreversible. As a result, the exercise of discretion in determining contemporary environmental standards has shifted from the immediate regulators to other forums, reducing the significance of local participation procedures. More than ever it therefore becomes important to examine critically the procedures surrounding policy development both at central government and Community level. These are constitutional questions that go beyond the immediate subject of pollution control or environmental regulation but they are legitimate issues of great importance all the same.

CHAPTER 8

LOADED GUNS AND MONKEYS – RESPONSIBLE ENVIRONMENTAL LAW*

One hundred and fifty years ago a pet monkey escaped and then attacked and bit a Mrs Sophia May who in the words of the law report consequently became 'sick, sore, lame and disordered'[1]. With her husband she sought compensatory damages from the owner. There was no allegation of actual negligence or fault in the way that he had secured or looked after the animal, but he was nevertheless held liable. For the first time, the Queen's Bench articulated a general principle that if someone keeps an animal known to be potentially dangerous they should be liable for damage caused by it however careful they had been in its control: the gist of liability lay in keeping the potentially dangerous animal in the first place.

Lawyers and non-lawyers will see immediately the potential for extending such a liability principle from a pet monkey to the storage of chemicals or other potential sources of environmental damage. And the 1846 decision of *May v Burdett*[2] re-emerged in argument at the end of last year before the House of Lords in the *Cambridge Water Company* case[3]. That decision has been described by some as the most important environmental case this century and is one to which I return.

At the heart of both the *May v Burdett* and *Cambridge Water Company* cases lie notions of responsibility, and I want to use the theme of responsibility as a basis for considering various strands of contemporary environmental law. It is critical in the development of the more conventional types of legal liability seen in both those cases, but I will also place it in a wider context of what might broadly be described as institutional behaviour. Some of the underlying questions are not, of course, peculiar to environmental law. Jurists have long wrestled with the relationship between moral responsibility and legal liability. In this country the alignment between actual intention and criminal liability has been broken in many areas of social regulation with the introduction of strict liability offences. These are especially prevalent in the environmental field.

* R Macrory (1994) *Loaded Guns and Monkeys – Responsible Environmental Law*, Imperial College, pp 1-31
[1] May v Burdett (1846) 9 QB 1213 at p.1214.
[2] ibid, at pp.1217-8.
[3] *Cambridge Water Co. Ltd v Eastern Counties Leather pic* (1994) 1 All ER 53.

In the last century, Oliver Holmes, in his essays on the Common Law, developed the notion of 'objective liability', a theory designed to impute knowledge and hence liability on individuals who did not actually possess it[4]. The doctrine of vicarious responsibility under which employers can be held liable for actions of their employees can, at least in the field of civil liability, be hardly justified other than on grounds of efficient loss apportionment. In criminal law, companies can face what has been described by Glanville Williams as 'the tyrannous combination'[5] of strict and vicarious liability – criminal liability being imposed even where those in charge of company policy knew nothing of the act concerned or even prohibited it. The doctrine, which incidentally is unknown in Germany where only individuals can be convicted of criminal offences, was reconfirmed earlier this year in the Divisional Court in its application to water pollution offences[6]. According to the Court the magnitude of environmental pollution justified the approach[7]. Over thirty years ago, the British jurist Herbert Hart in his exploration of Punishment and Responsibility quoted a character from Dostoevsky's *'Crime and Punishment'* concerned at the way in which Western utilitarian concepts were threatening notions of individual responsibility:'... in this age the sentiment of passion is actually prohibited by science, and that is how they order things in England where they have political economy'[8].

But I would argue that the environmental field introduces a particular sense of urgency and dimension to the universality of these issues. There is an increasing awareness of the scale and dimension of some of the environmental problems that may face us. Environmental science has an apparently limitless capacity to reveal threats to environmental systems and suggest new causative links, while principles of precaution indicate that what may be unpalatable action should sometimes be taken without any real proof of damage[9]. There has been an extraordinary rise in interest in environmental law by academics and practitioners in this country, both for opportunistic as well as idealistic reasons; taking just one marker, membership of the UK Environmental Law Association has risen from about 40 members to over 1200 since its formation in 1986. Equally one can point to the sheer number of regulations made

---

[4] Holmes, O.W., The Common Law (1881), Lecture II, The Criminal Law.

[5] Quoted by Lord Justice Simon Brown in *National Rivers Authority v Alfred McAlpine Homes East Ltd*, QBD (Divisional Court), 26 January 1994 (copy of case report on file with author).

[6] National Rivers Authority v Alfred McAlpine Homes East Ltd, ibid.

[7] see judgement of Mr. Justice Morland, ibid, at pp.22-23.

[8] Hart, H.L.A., *Punishment and Responsibility: Essays in the Philosophy of Law* (1968), Clarendon Press, Oxford, at p. 158.

[9] See for example, Art. 130r of the European Community Treaty which post-Maastricht now, requires that Community environmental policy'... shall be based on the precautionary principle and on the principles that preventive action be taken ...'.

in the environmental field over the equivalent period, or the number of European Community laws agreed in recent years. This is set against a backdrop of what are often divergent and powerfully held moral philosophies of right and wrong concerning the environment. The description by the House of Lords in the 1970s of strict liability pollution offences as not being crimes in a true sense[10] is one that would not be shared by many environmentalists. The German philosopher, Niklas Lumann, concludes rather depressingly, 'The scope and opacity of the causal connections imparted by the environment makes every value consensus trivial'[11].

At the same time there is a crisis of confidence in the ability of conventional environmental regulation to deliver. We look at the worst examples of environmental legalism in the States and like not what we see. Solutions are offered by the economist rather than the lawyer. Yet legal notions of responsibility both reflect and inject an ethical dimension which is inherent in many environmental perspectives and which is either unattainable or lost in the language of welfare economic analysis. Or to put it another way, legal concepts of responsibility may need to fill the spaces left unoccupied by the economist.

Even where environmental legislation expresses liabilities in the strictest of terms, socio-legal research has demonstrated the extent to which enforcement authorities resist acting like automatons. In the early 1980s Keith Hawkins, Genevra Richardson and others explored the actual practice of regulation in the field of water pollution and trade effluent control, and revealed how individual enforcement officers' own notions of justice and responsibility influenced their discretion to prosecute, whatever the actual wording of the law[12].

My own, more modest contribution to this type of research was in the field of hazardous waste law, when in the mid-1980s the European Commission was concerned at apparent wide discrepancies in the level of sentences imposed for waste disposal offences by national courts in different Member States. A systematic comparative evaluation was commissioned, with academic experts in each country being asked to compile reports examining the results of criminal prosecutions. Sonia

---

[10] per Viscount Dilhorne in *Alphacell v Woodward* (1972) 2 All ER 475 at p.483.
[11] Lumann, N., (1989) *Ecological Communication*, Polity Press, Cambridge.
[12] Hawkins, K., (1984) *Environmental and Enforcement Regulation and the Social Definition of Pollution*, Clarendon Press, Oxford; Richardson, G., Ogus, A., and Burrows, P., (1982) *Policing Pollution - A Study of Self-Regulation and Enforcement*, Clarendon Press, Oxford; Hutter, B.M., (1988) *The Reasonable Arm of the Law?: The Law Enforcement Procedures of Environmental Health Officers*, Clarendon Press, Oxford.

Withers, then of Loughborough University, and I were assigned the United Kingdom[13].

Perhaps somewhat naively, Commission officials initially thought that this would be a fairly straightforward exercise on the assumption that detailed records of criminal convictions were compiled at some central location. In the UK this was not the case. National judicial statistics did not have nearly the level of detail needed, while individual courts did not record offences by subject matter. To provide even some basic information, in part we had to look at newspaper cuttings – on the way availing ourselves of the extensive personal collection collated by Richard Hawkins, then company lawyer for one of the main private waste disposal firms. This was followed by interviews with selected waste disposal authorities.

Even this did not always help. Disposal authorities did not necessarily keep accessible records of prosecutions – as one remarked, 'We don't mark up prosecutions'. Waste disposal regulation was then largely the responsibility of County Councils and here our research demonstrated the importance of the institutional location of waste disposal regulators within a Council's organisational structure, a matter which had been left to the discretion of each authority following implementation of the relevant provisions of Part I of the Control of Pollution Act 1974. To take two extreme examples, in one authority they were located within the Highways Department which had little experience of prosecution work but was operationally geared up for effective practical clean-ups of spilt or dumped loads of waste. In another, they were located within the Trading Standards Department which traditionally adopts a fairly aggressive approach to enforcement. In a third authority, they were essentially self-standing rather than incorporated within an existing administrative unit. Equally revealing was the often poor relationship between the enforcement officers who were technically qualified but had no formal legal training, and local authority legal staff who were frequently located in the County Solicitor's Department many miles away. These institutional factors had a powerful influence on the approach that each body took towards the law and its enforcement.

A policy-maker trying to rationalise the system that then operated would have argued that such flexible arrangements were appropriate given differing characteristics of local waste issues and, in time-honoured

---

[13] R Macrory and S Withers, (1985) 'Application of Administrative and Criminal Punishments concerning Hazardous Wastes in England'. Report for Directorate General XI, European Commission (copy on file with author).

British fashion, the heterogeneous nature of the receiving environment. Even accepting the argument for variety as convincing, our research indicated that in reality important institutional differences that occurred were often explained by historical accident or administrative tradition rather than environmental problems at hand. None of these features were apparent or addressed in the black letter of the relevant statutory provisions, and underlined the importance of this form of socio-legal research in illuminating how legal systems work in practice.

While we conducted this research within the United Kingdom, I thought that this lack of hard information on prosecutions was perhaps a peculiarly British weakness. But not so when it came to comparative discussion with our counterparts. The German researcher, for example, found herself in almost exactly the same position as we did, and similarly had to resort to newspaper cuttings and interviews. Counter-intuitively perhaps, it was the Italians who had the most sophisticated database under which the results of every court decision including magistrates' are logged on a central computer for ready access[14].

More fundamentally, the research revealed the difficulties of comparing performance of the effectiveness of environmental law even within a comparatively small number of countries, all with developed legal systems and operating under a reasonably common framework of policy and law. Certainly, we argued that comparing numbers of prosecutions and levels of fines was but a crude indicator. A nil or small level of prosecutions might indicate an utterly effective law that was being fully complied with, or it might equally suggest exactly the opposite. Furthermore, unless one knew a lot more about the cultural and political context in which fines and criminal convictions are received, comparing levels per se made little sense. More systematic information concerning environmental quality or the ability of the legal system to secure environmental improvement goals was needed but in the waste disposal field at that time no such data was developed, and even now it remains elusive. The example of the Italian computer system confirmed that comprehensive data collection by itself does not guarantee effective implementation, but nevertheless without it one is swimming in the dark, buffeted by anecdotal prejudice concerning foreign practices. In this context the recent establishment of the so-called Chester informal network of European environmental enforcement authorities can only

---

[14] Il Centro Elletronico di Documentazione (CED), Rome. See also 'La Giurisprudenza Ambientale Europea a la Banca Dati ENLEX della CEE' (1987) (ed. Postiglione) Dott. A. Giuffre, Milan, p. 137.

be to the good[15]. So too after so much wrangling concerning its location should be the setting-up of the European Environment Agency[16].

The need to understand the attitude of environmental regulators towards the implementation and enforcement of law is, of course, made all the more important by the large degree of discretion they possess over how they approach prosecution policy. Strict liability offences which permeate much of British environmental legislation clearly heighten the significance of that enforcement discretion, and the extent to which knowledge and legal responsibility, whether in the criminal or civil field, should be linked remains a critical theme in contemporary environmental law.

On the facts of the case Mr Burdett actually knew that his monkey enjoyed biting people. But later case law developed the idea that what were essentially strict liability principles would apply to certain classes of wild animals, whether or not the particular animal was known to be dangerous or not.

As a law student, the first case which really excited my intellectual curiosity and made me realise that no amount of imaginative thinking could compete with what could occur in real life concerned this principle. Johannes and Emmie Behrens were midgets, Mr Behrens claiming at 30 inches to be the smallest man in the world. In 1954, Bertram Mills' Circus held their Christmas season at Olympia, and the Behrens were exhibited in a booth near the circus ring. One of the acts involved six Burmese elephants who were led to the ring for each performance, but one afternoon as the elephants were being led past the midgets' booth, a dog belonging to their manager and tied up began barking. The third elephant in the procession panicked, chased after the dog, knocked down part of the booth and caused serious injuries to Mrs Behrens.

In an action for damages against the circus owners, it was recognised that these particular animals were not in fact wild but highly trained circus elephants. As Mr Justice Devlin put it, 'The elephant Bullu is in fact no more dangerous than a cow; she reacted in the same way as a cow would do to the irritation of a small dog; if perhaps her bulk made

[15] See section on 'Institutional Process in EC Developments' in *Review of European Community and International Environmental Law*, Vol. 3, No. 1,1994, p.49.
[16] Council Regulation 1210/90 of 7 May 1990 on the Establishment of the European Environment Agency and the European Environment Information and Observation Network, OJ L 120/1. In October 1993 it was agreed that the location of the Agency would be Denmark: Decision taken by Common Agreement between the Representatives of the Governments of the Member States, Meeting at Head of State and Government Level of 29 October 1993 on the location of the seats of certain bodies and departments of the European Communities and of Europol, OJ 1993 C323/01, Article 1 (a).

her capable of doing more damage, her higher training enabled her to be more swiftly checked'[17].

Nevertheless, the principles of liability for animals had already classified all elephants, like monkeys, as potentially dangerous, and the owner was consequently held liable whatever the special characteristics of the particular beast. A tough rule of liability, and one which offended against my own adolescent notions of fairness, whatever my sympathies for the plaintiffs.

Last year's *Cambridge Water* case displayed similarly stark competing models of liability. During the 1960s and 1970s, drums of solvents were regularly delivered to the defendants' tanning company and transferred to a large storage tank. According to the findings of fact, spillages occurred during the transfer process, but at the time anyone would have thought that these would have simply evaporated in the air.

What in fact appears to have occurred was that the spillages seeped through a concrete floor, into the ground below, and eventually entered a chalk aquifer. A groundwater source owned by the Cambridge Water Company over a mile away was found to be contaminated, proved unusable, and the company sued the tanning company for the cost of developing a new source of supply, over £1m.

The distinctive feature of this pollution case was that the trial judge made a clear finding of no negligence in the sense that at the time of the spillages the defendants did not fall below then accepted standards of precaution and care.[18] But the Court of Appeal rediscovered an old Victorian case concerning natural rights and water and decided that despite no negligence the defendants could still be liable for all the damage that naturally flowed from the spillages whether or not it could have been foreseen at the time.[19]

Whatever one thought of the result, I criticised the way in which the Court of Appeal had argued their principle of liability.[20] Last December, the House of Lords reversed the Court of Appeal decision, holding the company not liable.[21] The judgment is intellectually more sustained,

---

[17] *Behrens v Bertram Mills Circus Ltd* [1957] 2 QB 1 at p. 14.

[18] *Cambridge Water Co. Ltd v Eastern Counties Leather pic,* Queen's Bench Division, *Journal of Environmental Law* (1992) Vol. 4, No.1, p.81.

[19] *Cambridge Water Co. Ltd v Eastern Counties Leather pic,* Court of Appeal, (1994) 1 All ER53.

[20] R. Macrory, (1992) '£1 million award in historic aquifer pollution case', ENDS Report. 214, November 1992, p.41; R. Macrory, (1993) 'European Initiatives in the Field of Pollution Control: Civil Liability for Environmental Damage', Advocates for Change, 1993 Bar Conference, London.

[21] op.cit., n 3 above.

elaborating general principles of environmental liability, and, to condense 22 pages in a few lines, in essence their Lordships held that under the so-called rule in *Rylands v Fletcher* there were certain types of industry and activity for which liability would apply even in the absence of negligence. But even then where the pathway of the pollution was not reasonably foreseeable no liability should arise. In this case, at the time of the spillages no-one could have reasonably foreseen that the escape of the solvents would have travelled the route it did, and therefore there was no liability.

The line between negligence-based liability for all the damage that is reasonably foreseeable and strict liability for damage unless the pathway of the pollutant was not reasonably foreseeable is clearly fine. But it is real, and the practical distinctions must now be addressed by professionals. Their Lordships point out, for example, that the taking of reasonable precautions (say, the construction of a protective bund) would generally suggest the absence of negligence but would not be a defence in itself where *Rylands v Fletcher* applied.

Given the findings of fact – though there remain arguments over exactly what did happen – I personally find the decision a fair result. The House of Lords has accepted that mere control of certain activities is sufficient to impose liability but in determining what the controller is liable for, has rejected the notion, pursued by the Court of Appeal, that responsibility and natural causation are equivalent. Responsibility here incorporates an ethical dimension by asking what were the reasonable standards of predictive knowledge at the time. What the decision does mean is that environmental scientists will now play a significant role in defining the legal boundaries of responsibility which will shift with the passage of time. Changing knowledge, advances in research, and publication of results will be of critical importance in determining what pathways of pollution are or are not reasonably foreseeable at any particular time.

But the decision does contain anomalies. The House of Lords held that in general it is better for Parliament and legislation rather than the courts to impose strict liability on activities of high risk – since this will lead to much clearer definitions and, to quote, 'Those concerned can know where they stand'[22]. Yet the common law principles of strict liability which the case endorsed and revived applies to an ill-defined group of so-called 'non-natural' users of land. The House of Lords indicated that the storage of substantial quantities of chemicals on industrial premises should be regarded as almost a classic case of non-natural use,[23] a clearly

---

[22] per Lord Goff, ibid, at p.76.
[23] per Lord Goff, ibid, at p.79.

more generous approach than applied in previous case law in Britain.[24] In essence, one is revisiting the old *scienter* rule for animals. Or to put it another way, is, say, the disposal of municipal landfill by waste more akin to a familiar grazing cow or a ferocious wild elephant?

A further twist to the *Cambridge Water* case was the fact that initially and certainly at the time of the spillages the amount of contamination was minuscule. It satisfied the then prevailing British legal standards of 'wholesomeness' for drinking water, there was no evidence of human health risk, and the Cambridge Water Company could have carried on using the bore-hole for water supply.

But in 1980 the EC Drinking Water Directive[25] was agreed, containing a large number of standards for various parameters. Britain adopted the strict values in the Directive relating to organochlorines, and it was only then that testing for the particular solvent was carried out, and the supply found to fail in this respect.

Yet the actual spillages from the solvent deliveries had ceased several years before the Directive was agreed. To that extent it is arguable the damage to the plaintiff's resource was as much due to the introduction of new legislative standards as the previous actions of the company. Or using distinctions drawn by the Royal Commission on Environmental Pollution,[26] contamination – that is the introduction of the substance in question – of the water source may have already occurred but there was no pollution – or damage – until the new standards were applied.

This in itself was not sufficient to excuse the defendants on the grounds that *Rylands v Fletcher* is a type of tort which is completed only when damage occurs. It may be that their Lordships' insistence on introducing a foreseeability test for damage was at least influenced by this factor,

---

[24] In the High Court, following the spirit of such earlier cases, Mr Justice Kennedy had rejected liability in Rylands v Fletcher on the grounds that in a modern society this sort of activity could not be regarded as 'non-natural' or out of the ordinary. (Cambridge Water Co Ltd case, op.cit. note 18atp.96).

[25] Council Directive of 15 July 1980 relating to the quality of water intended for human con sumption (80/778/EEC) OJ 1980 L 229/11.

[26] Royal Commission on Environmental Pollution, Tenth Report, 'Tackling Pollution -Experience and Prospects', Cmnd. 9149, February 1984, especially 1.9-1.[12] At the time, some, including the Chemical Industries Association, argued that 'contamination' should be used to describe situations where the presence of substances was believed or positively asserted to be harmless, while 'pollution' implied actual damage. The Royal Commission rejected such a clear-cut distinction and preferred to use the term contamination to imply the presence of alien substances or energy in the environment without passing judgment on whether they cause or are liable to cause damage. In that sense, contamination can be seen as a necessary but not a sufficient condition for pollution.

though it is little explored in an explicit fashion[27]. But the relationship between liability for present actions and environmental standards that may arise in the future is an issue that is likely to assume more significance, especially in areas of gradual as opposed to acute pollution. In *Cambridge Water* neither contamination nor pollution was predictable. But suppose that the manner in which a substance is introduced into part of the receiving environment is reasonably predictable. In the absence of any new legislative standards, the environmental scientist would say that contamination was foreseeable, but not pollution. The lawyer might respond that this foreseeability test is not confined to the actual damage that is foreseeable but encompasses the total extent of the kind of damage that is foreseeable.[28] Once the process of contamination is foreseeable, the concept of 'kind of damage' is sufficient to include the effect of future environmental standards, even if it is not possible to predict precisely what these will be.

The complex policy background in the case raises more fundamental questions concerning the overlay between science and legislation. A key feature in the development of British environmental law in the last ten years is the extent to which precise standards of various types have been incorporated in the structure of environmental legislation. This is particularly so in the field of pollution control.[29] As *Cambridge Water* showed, legislative standards such as 'wholesome' water whose practicable meaning used to be largely left to technical administrators to determine have been superseded by elaborate lists of parameters and concentration levels specified in legislation.

The pressures for such changes have been powerful. The style of Community environmental legislation, doctrines developed by the European Court of Justice concerning the transposition of Community obligations into national law,[30] and the institutional distancing of major utilities from government following privatisation all contribute to the

---

[27] See case-note on the *Cambridge Water* case by Ogus, A., (1994) in *Journal of Environmental Law. Vol. 6 No. 1, p. 137.*

[28] The approach taken in the remoteness for damage test applied to negligence and nuisance cases in determining what extent of damage a defendant will be liable for (see *The Wagon Mound (No. 1)* (1961) AC 388; *The Wagon Mound (No. 2)* (1967) 1 AC 617; *Barnett v Chelsea Hospital Management Committee* (1969) 1 QB 478). Their Lordships' judgement in *Cambridge Water* seems to come close to applying a remoteness test but is not expressed in this way.

[29] See for example, Water Supply (Water Quality) Regulations 1989 (SI 1989/1147); Air Quality Standards Regulations 1989; Surface Water (Classification) Regulations 1989 (SI 1989/1148).

[30] Especially the almost wholesale rejection of the use of national administrative methods such as circulars as opposed to legislation to transpose obligations. *Commission v Netherlands Case* 238/85, (1987) ECR 3989, *Commission v Germany Case* C-131/88, (1991) 1 ECR 825. See also R Macrory, (1988) 'Industrial Air Pollution – Implementing the European Framework', 55th Annual Conference Proceedings, National Society for Clean Air, Brighton.

process.[31] The introduction of what I have described as specificity[32] into environmental legislation has been encouraged by other factors at play which are sometimes less clearly articulated: a demand for consistency in the interpretation and application of legal controls; administrative simplicity in application; developments in techniques of measurement and recording; a public lack of confidence in over-extensive discretion being given to environmental regulators; and, at least in the field of criminal law, a need for certainty and clarity. In effect, scientific terminology is being employed to define legal levels of responsibility. Examples can be given where the extent of the scientific language employed in legislation renders it unworkable. As my former Ph.D. student Pat Lucas will recall, until recently, the noise standards for motor vehicles in use on the road contained such complex measurement requirements that they were near unusable in practice.[33] No doubt justifiable and correct from the perspective of an acoustic scientist but paying little respect for day-to-day realities. Similarly the choice of language employed in the legislation may itself constrain or provide opportunities for day-to-day technical solutions. Nicola Atkinson in our Environmental Law Group, along with scientific colleagues in the Waste Management Centre, is currently leading a research study on the relationship between law and the choice of remedy selection for dealing with land contamination.[34]

More importantly, the incorporation of a standard expressed in scientific terminology into the body of law provides it with both respectability and a degree of moral imperative. My colleagues here know only too well some of the contradictions at work. For example, the persuasive concept of critical loads has entered into the language of international agreements following the 1988 Sofia Protocol on Transboundary Movements of NOx.[35] Yet Professor Nigel Bell in his own inaugural explained, to a layman at any rate, some of the fundamental scientific uncertainties

---

[31] Government can ensure that its policy goals are carried out by public sector bodies through less formal means such as directions. Once these bodies are in the private sector, legislative standards must be employed. See R Macrory, (1990) 'The Privatisation and Regulation of the Water Industry', *Modern Law Review*. Vol. 53, pp.78-87.

[32] See R Macrory, (1991) 'Environmental Law: Shifting Discretions and the New Formalism' in *Frontiers of Environmental Law* (ed. O Lomas,) Chancery Law Publishing, London, chap.2. See also chap. 7 above

[33] See R Macrory, (1986) 'Science, Legislation and the Courts' in *The Assessment of Environmental Problems* (ed. G.R. Conway,), Imperial College Centre for Environmental Technology, London; and P Lucas, (1989) 'Science in Legislation and its Enforcement: A Study of Neighbourhood Noise', Ph.D. Thesis, University of London.

[34] The research is concerned with legal process and technical remedies for cleaning up contaminated land as opposed to principles of law for dealing with civil liability for contamination.

[35] Protocol to the 1979 Convention on Long-Range Transboundary Air Pollution Concerning the Control of Emissions of Nitrogen Oxides or their Transboundary Fluxes, (Sofia, 1988) *International Legal Materials*, (1989) Vol. 28, 214.

inherent in the concept.[36] Attempting to move from the effect of one pollutant on a single plant strain under controlled conditions to a cocktail of mixes in real life conditions is riddled with difficulty. Others can tell of the spurious science involved in coming up with some of the figures for the ICRCL (Inter-Departmental Committee on the Redevelopment of Contaminated Land) guidelines for land contamination currently in use, and maybe yet to enter the legal language.

Let me make it clear that I am not calling for the wholesale return to halcyon days of open-textured legal terminology in environmental legislation. As much as anyone I have been an advocate of a more formalised and transparent structure than used to be the norm in this country. But my concern is where the development can send wrong signals of when there are or are not transcientific judgements involved. To take the Drinking Water Directive again,[37] the changing retrospective justification for the infamous standard of 1 microgram per litre of individual pesticides[38] provides a dramatic example. Some years ago this was frequently justified as a scientific decision taken by Member States at the time. It now tends to be characterised as a political judgment made by Ministers in 1980 that drinking water should contain no pesticides. The truth, as one of our M.Sc. students discovered in research, was no-one now seems quite certain of its origin, though the most likely explanation is that the standard was adopted from then World Health Organisation Guidelines.[39] But as with the nitrate standard appearing in the Directive, heavy qualifications appearing in the WHO documentation were consciously or mistakenly lost in the process of translation from a discursive guideline into a legal instrument.[40] And according to one senior Commission official the figure of 5 micrograms per litre for total pesticides was justified by simply pointing the number of fingers on his hand.[41]

Greater understanding of processes at work in the development of such standards, both at national and international level, and their eventual

---

[36] N. Bell 'Clearing the Air: Revealing the Hidden Effects of Air Pollution on Plants', Inaugural Lecture delivered in October 1990 at Imperial College of Science, Technology and Medicine, London (copy on file with author).

[37] Council Directive, op.cit, n 25.

[38] ibid., Article 3 and Annex 1, Table D, para 55.

[39] G Wood (1989) 'A Critical Review of the Drinking Water Directive (870/778/EEC) with respect to Parameter 55 (Pesticides and Related Products)', unpublished M.Sc. Thesis, ICCET, London.

[40] The WHO 1970 Guidelines, 'European Standards for Drinking Water' (2nd Edition, WHO, Geneva), proposed that the contamination of water by pesticides 'should be prevented so far as possible', but stated that, 'it should be stressed that the proposals set out in this report are intended to be for guidance only; they are recommendations and in no sense mandatory'.

[41] Wood, op.cit. note 39 at p. 135.

seepage into law is needed. In my own research group, Steve Hollins is exploring the complex and little understood world of chemical regulation. Rosalind Twum-Barima and John Stonehouse are preparing papers for the United Nations Trade and Environment Programme on international trade issues and environmental science concepts.[42]

This change in legislative style goes on to raise deeper questions concerning the nature and location of decision making. In 1986, Gordon Conway organised a conference here on the assessment of environmental problems, where I contributed a paper on science, legislation and the courts.[43] I touched upon the changing style of UK environmental laws which were beginning to emerge, and suggested that this was throwing into sharp relief differing styles of administrative and regulatory management.

Developing from an approach of Professor Mashaw of Yale University,[44] I characterised two competing models of administrative decision-making as a 'determinate' and an 'accommodatory' model. Both are persuasive but are largely incompatible with each other. In the determinate model the goal of the regulator is to implement a programme of which the goals have been previously prescribed in legislation. Value and political judgements inherent in the establishment of such a goal are removed from the regulator charged with implementation, leaving him with the responsibility of devising effective mechanisms to achieve the goals. The success of their activities is measured by the efficiency and accuracy with which such goals are achieved.

The accommodatory model of decision making does not aim to achieve such a clearly predetermined goal. Instead it requires the administrator to achieve as harmonious accommodation as possible of competing interests involved in a particular issue or problem before him. The means and procedures for doing so may or may not be defined by law. The critical distinction from the determinate model is that the legal framework does not attempt to define in advance the programme to be achieved - the process of accommodation itself is used to identify and determine appropriate values to be assigned during decision making.

---

[42] R Twum-Barima, (1994) 'Protecting the Ozone Layer Through Trade Measures: Reconciling the Trade Provisions of the Montreal Protocol and the Rules of the GATT', Environment and Trade, UNEP, Geneva (to be published); J.M. Stonehouse, and J.D. Mumford (1994) Science, Risk Analysis and Environmental Policy Decisions, Environment and Trade, UNEP, Geneva (to be published).

[43] op.cit. note 33.

[44] J. Mashaw (1983) 'An overview - two models of regulatory decision-making' in *Law and Science in Collaboration: Resolving Regulatory Issues of Science and Technology*, (eds J.D. Nyhart, and M.M. Carrow), Lexington Books, Lexington, M, USA.

Models of this sort are of course heuristic devices used to illuminate characteristics by artificial exaggeration. In reality many aspects of environmental regulation will not fall completely within one or the other model though dominant strands may be apparent. Common law nuisance concepts often fall within the accommodatory model; likewise, perhaps, local public inquiries over controversial planning developments.

British pollution legislation used to provide the barest indication of precise policy goals or standards. Regulators were given extensive discretion to determine the content of individual discharge consents and standards – a structure endorsed, it should be admitted, by British environmental scientists pushing what is now a less convincing case for the local resilience of the natural environment. And it was an approach which was often misunderstood or subject to suspicion by other countries. Patrick Marnham in his travel book *So Far From God* records meeting an Italian girl in South America who considered that 'the English had been driven to reconcile morality and reality. What they called pragmatic others called immoral'[45].

That sort of structure only reflected an accommodatory style of regulation, even if in the case, say, of the old Alkali Inspectorate there was criticism that the accommodation process was confined to too narrow a band of interests.[46]

These characteristics no longer prevail.[47] Emission standards and various environmental quality objectives expressed in the language of science increasingly enter the body of legislation.[48] Yet there are contradictions at work. At the same time as we have seen a move towards a more determinate model of decision making, we have also seen the introduction of greater rights of public participation and access to information being introduced into many areas of environmental regulation. For example, licence procedures in the field of water pollution discharges,[49] and Integrated Pollution Control under the Environmental Protection Act 1990.[50] Yet if many of the goals and environmental standards which

---

[45] P Marnham (1985) *So Far From God*, London Jonathan Cape.
[46] See especially, Royal Commission on Environmental Pollution, Fifth Report, 'Air Pollution Control: An Integrated Approach', Cmnd. 6371, 1976, HMSO, London.
[47] See R Macrory, (1986) 'Environmental Policy in Britain: Reaffirmation or Reform?', Discussion Paper 86/4, International Institute for Environment and Society, Berlin, and R Macrory, (1990) 'The United Kingdom' in *Understanding US and European Environmental Law* (eds. T Smith Jr., and P Kromarak,) Kluwer Academic, Amsterdam.
[48] For some examples see n 29 above.
[49] See Water Resources Act 1991 and Control of Pollution (Registers) Regulations 1989 (SI 1989/1160).
[50] See Environmental Protection Act 1990, s 20 and Environmental Protection (Applications, Appeals and Registers) Regulations 1991 (SI 1991 No. 507).

the regulator must achieve have already been largely predetermined at another level, expectations of what can be achieved in a local participation process may well be frustrated or considered nugatory. Indeed, there are signals that it is just some aspects of these procedures which may first be sacrificed on the altar of deregulation.[51] In effect, new provisions concerning access to information, public registers and the like become a means of checking the performance of regulators rather than a mechanism for influencing or participating in the determination of policy.

There is no easy answer. But at the very least one needs to recognise how frustrations may boil to the surface where the procedures are ill-aligned. This situation is all the more challenging with the growing interplay of local, national, and supranational procedures at work. My own experience two years ago as Specialist Adviser to the House of Commons Select Committee on the Environment provided a particular vivid example. The Committee had long been interested in the subject of waste disposal, and were aware of proposals by the European Commission for a landfill Directive which would clearly be of key policy significance in this area. They wished to make the proposal a subject of an inquiry, and consciously decided to investigate at a stage when draft versions of the Directive were readily accessible but before a final version had been issued by the Commission. Just as any professional non-governmental organisation knows only too well, it is important to make one's mark at an early stage in policy formulation before viewpoints become too fixed.

The Committee invited two Commission officials behind the draft to provide evidence on their thinking and an explanation of their approach. I went to Brussels to encourage them to appear, even explaining the nature of such a Committee – an emanation of the State maybe but certainly not part of the executive government. They agreed to do so enthusiastically.

Unbeknown to me, what we had done was to set in train a mini-constitutional row. A few days before they were due to appear, the officials were forbidden to do so by the Commissioner on the grounds that the European Parliament had not yet formally commented on the proposal, and that to allow them to appear would not be 'constitutional'. Yet to rub salt in the wounds of the national Members of Parliament, the officials could and did visit Britain at the same time to talk with representatives of the British waste industry, and these same representatives were

---

[51] See Department of the Environment Consultation Paper, 'Proposed Amendments to the Water Resources Act 1991 and the Reservoirs Act 1975', October 1993.

then able to provide a second-hand account to the Committee of the Commission's current thinking on the proposed Directive.

Beneath the hurt egos and furious letters that were written at the time,[52] the experience raised serious questions concerning the process of policy-making at national and Community levels. In particular, how does the role of a national Parliamentary body such as the Commons Select Committee relate to its equivalent body in the European Parliament? And what, if any, should be the responsibilities of those initiating policy at supra-national level towards members of national legislatures? Are such members excluded from the accommodatory process at that level? The Maastricht Treaty makes explicit new institutional arrangements for involving local authorities and other regional interests in the process of policy influence via the new Committee of the Regions,[53] but new formal mechanisms for involvement by national Parliaments have not been created, other than an acknowledgement of the need to do something in one of the Treaty's Protocols.[54] I could describe that saga as one of institutional accommodation. Let me take now an example of what I would call the problem of conceptual accommodation. The 1992 Community Eco-Labelling Regulation[55] reflected a new trend in European environmental law – what was at heart a voluntary scheme relying upon market and consumer forces but encased in a regulatory framework. In essence, the scheme provides for production of environmental standards for categories of consumer products, aimed at reducing confusion over misleading and unintelligible environmental claims in the market place. Industries whose products meet the approved standards may, if they wish, apply at national level for the award of an eco-label.

The process of devising eco-labelling criteria is one that takes place at Community level, while the awards of labels to individual products take place at national level. The regulation as originally proposed introduced a degree of public consultation but it seemed to me to be utterly ill-aligned to the real questions of interest.

[52] The correspondence between the Environment Commissioner and the Chairman of the Environment Select Committee is published in the Committee's report: House of Commons Environment Committee, Eighth Report: 'The EC Directive on Landfill Waste', Volumes I & II, HC263-1 and HC263-2, HMSO, London. I should stress that I attach no personal blame to the individuals involved, though for a witty but scathing account of the process see the review of the Committee's report by Richard Hawkins in *Journal of Environmental Law* Vol. 4 No. 2, p.307.

[53] Article 198(a)-(c).

[54] Protocol on the Economic and Social Committee and the Committee of the Regions.

[55] Council Regulation (880/92/EEC) of 23 March 1992 on a Community Eco-Label Award Scheme OJ 1992 L 99 [1]See also R Macrory, (1991) 'Administering the Eco-Label Scheme' in *Eco-Labelling of Durable Goods*, MR Industrial Conferences, and Macrory, R. (1991) 'Eco-Labelling: Some Legal Considerations', Green Consumerism Conference, Lancaster University.

Applications for the awards of individual labels at national level were to be advertised and a period allowed for representation. The development of approved eco-labelling criteria on the other hand were to be in the hands of closed technical committees at Community level. Yet the application stage seemed to fall within the determinate model – products either meet the preset criteria or they did not. But the really crucial questions of value judgement occur at a different level. For example, the decision to choose a particular product category for development of eco-labelling criteria. Would a motor car ever be eligible as a potential product? Equally significant would be the decision as to the boundaries of that particular product category; or in more legal language, products with the same equivalence of utility. If, say, one was developing eco-labelling criteria for nappies, should one be confining the investigation to the relative environmental merits of disposable nappies, or including in the relative analysis non-disposables? Or should criteria for dishwashers include washing by hand?

These questions are not technical issues, but raise significant ethical questions and value judgements. And they of course echo similar questions over the boundaries for analysis of the best practicable environmental option[56] or the treatment of alternatives in environmental impact analysis.[57] Yet the original mechanisms in the draft Eco-Label Regulation provided no legal requirements for genuine external critique or accommodation at this stage, or even an acknowledgement that this was a live issue. The process was to be largely lost in a world of expert committees and consultants.[58]

The experience of the Canadian eco-labelling board which went to extensive efforts to hold consultation exercises, including formal hearings, on just these sorts of questions, provided one possible model. These concerns were raised by the UK Eco-Labelling Advisory Board and to be fair to the UK government were communicated to Commission officials during the process of negotiation, only to be initially met by the response from Commission officials that they could not see how such

---

[56] See Royal Commission on Environmental Pollution, Twelfth Report, Best Practicable Environmental Option, Cmnd. 310, February 1988, HMSO, London.

[57] The European Directive on Environmental Assessment Directive 85/337 of June 27, 1985 on the assessment of the effects of certain public and private projects on the environment, (OJ 1985 L 175/40) is deliberately coy on the question of considering alternatives in contrast to US legislation on environmental impact statements where 'alternatives' must be considered, and where courts have been involved in determining just how far such considerations should go. See the US National Environmental Policy Act 1970, s.102, 42 USC 4341(a).

[58].1 expressed some of these concerns in R Macrory, (1991) 'Administering the Eco-Labelling Scheme', Eco-Labelling of Durable Goods, op.cit. n 55; and R Macrory, (1991) 'Eco-Labelling: Some Legal Considerations', op.cit, n 55.1 also served on the UK National Advisory Committee on Eco-Labelling, 1990-91.

a procedure could be incorporated at Community level with so many national Member States involved. We do now, however, at least see in the final version of the Regulation as agreed the introduction of a small Consultation forum where draft criteria are discussed.[59] But even then I am not convinced that the non-technical nature of many of the issues involved has been fully appreciated or the procedures for their effective consideration effectively devised.

It is already apparent how difficult it is to disentangle developments in environmental law at national, Community and international level. Community law in particular as a working laboratory of a unique supra-national legal system provides endless lessons both of what can or cannot be achieved and sometimes how not to go about issues. The status and impact of the Community on the international environmental stage itself raises legal questions of considerable difficulty, and will assume growing importance in future years. It is a subject matter which Martin Hession within our Law Group is exploring both in relation to Climate Change and in the near future sustainable development issues.[60]

I have already mentioned concerns with the process of Community law policy-making. For the environmental lawyer one of the most distinctive features of the Community is the enforcement mechanism built into the governing Treaty. The responsibility of the European Commission for ensuring that Community obligations are implemented, together with the quasi-legal procedures it may invoke, eventually bringing a Member State before the European Court of Justice, distinguish the system from most other areas of international law. The new powers of the European Court, post-Maastricht, to fine or penalise a Member State which fails to respect its judgment is unparalleled in international law. According to the Commission in its tenth report on Implementation, some 90 judgments, including 27 in the environmental field, have not yet been complied with by Member States.[61] It is perhaps a sad reflection on the moral authority of the law that fiscal sanctions may have to be threatened to ensure governmental compliance.

I have written elsewhere about the Article 169 procedures and the Commission's own development of the complaint procedure as a means of involving the public in the process of law enforcement.[62] I have also

---

[59] Council Regulation, op.cit n 55, Article 6.
[60] M Hession, (1993), 'The Role of the EC in the Implementation of International Environmental Law', *Review of European Community and International Environmental Law*. Vol. 2 No. 4, FIELD, (eds) Blackwell Publishers, Oxford, pp.341-347.
[61] Tenth Annual Report to the European Parliament 'Monitoring of the Application of Community Law', 30 August 1993, OJ 93/C233/01.
[62] R Macrory, (1992) 'The Enforcement of Community Environmental Law: Some Critical Issues', *Common Market Law Review*. Vol. 29, pp.347-369. See also chap. 26 below.

suggested both legal and administrative changes to improve the very real concerns about current practice. But in pursuing my theme of responsibility let me take two issues which are beginning to emerge.

The first arose in both the recent environmental cases brought by the Commission against the United Kingdom, the bathing water and drinking water cases. In the drinking water case,[63] the United Kingdom argued strongly that their duty under the Directive was to do the best they could but not to achieve absolute standards. Not surprisingly, the Court rejected that argument on interpretation of the Directive. But a more subtle argument was raised in respect of nitrates. The United Kingdom argued that the government had done what it could, but in essence any failure to meet the standards was due to matters beyond their control, notably technical limitations of denitrification processes and disparate agricultural practices. In effect, they were questioning to what extent they should be held responsible for breach of the Directive. Again, the Court rejected the argument with little discussion.

It was, perhaps, not the best of cases on which to base such a submission. But it does raise the question as to what we really mean by saying that the Member State has failed to implement Community law. Are we talking of just governments and are there areas genuinely outside their responsibility for which different considerations applied? In the *Bathing Water* case[64], an analogous argument was raised, and again rejected. But the Court did hint that absolute physical impossibility to comply with obligations (whatever that means) might justify non-compliance but this was not proved here. How far the new power to fine Member States will change the perception of the Court or allow these sorts of issues to be more fully developed as a mitigation rather than an absolute defence remains to be seen.

In practice, it is central government which appears before the Court representing the Member State. Many areas of British environmental law used to be largely the preserve of local or regional bodies. Nigel Haigh of the Institute for European Environmental Policy some years ago first pointed out how in some fields such as air pollution the need to comply with Community law was forcing the Department of the Environment to assume or threaten to exercise more reserve powers over local authorities than had hitherto usually been the practice.[65] In the United Kingdom we of course live in what is constitutionally a

---

[63] *Commission v United Kingdom* C-337/89 (1992).
[64] *Commission v United Kingdom*, Case C-56/90 (1993).
[65] Haigh, N., 'Devolved Responsibility on Centralisation: Effects of EEC Environmental Policy' (1986) 64 *Public Administration* 197.

highly centralised system. Parliament has given Ministers extensive powers to implement Community obligations by regulations even if these must amend primary legislation to do so.[66] Many other Member States possess more clearly federated structures.

What is the position where a Member State is failing to implement a provision of Community environmental law because of the inaction of a local or regional administration over which the national government has no internal national power? Can the central government claim it has then no responsibility - on the grounds of constitutional rather than physical impossibility? The simplistic approach adopted by the Court is to turn a blind eye to internal problems of administration and say that is not a matter of Community law. The State still fails.[67] More subtly, Art. 5 of the Treaty requires Member States to abstain from any measures which could jeopardise the attainment of the objectives of the Treaty. In a case before the Court in 1988,[68] Belgium was accused of failing to transpose waste directives into national law, and the Belgian government argued that its recent constitutional reforms involving heavy decentralisation made this impossible for them. Advocate General Mancini raised the question whether such constitutional legislation which prevented the central government from implementing Community obligations was not a failure to comply with the general duties of Art. 5. Perhaps wisely, the ECJ did not address this point recognising that it was, in the words of the Advocate General, a 'delicate' question.

Yet it is a question that should be tackled. One response is simply to ensure that a Central Government possesses necessary powers – yet this flies in the face of concepts of federalism that invoke genuine decentralised powers as well as centralising forces. Or invoking the doctrine of subsidiarity,[69] one can suggest that areas where local or regional administrations possess exclusive powers are just those where the Community should not be acting. Yet this assumes that areas of Community interest are to be determined by the internal allocation of powers within Member States. Furthermore, there are likely to be issues where it is arguable that both the Community and local administrations have a real interest. The practice of sustainable development is one such example.

The new Post-Maastricht Committee of the Regions[70] provides some political recognition of these needs. But from a more formalistic

---

[66] European Communities Act 1972 section 2(2).
[67] see *Commission v Netherlands*, Case 96/81, (1982) ECR 1791.
[68] *Commission v Belgium*, Case 227-230/85, (1988) ECR 1.
[69] EC Treaty (as amended at Maastricht), Article 3b.
[70] EC Treaty (as amended at Maastricht), Article 198(a)-(c).

perspective, part of the problem again results from exactly what we mean by the Member State. Maybe we need to recognise that the current assumption that it is always central government which is responsible or represents the Member State needs reconsideration. It is derived from customs of international diplomacy and external relationships which may no longer be appropriate for the European Union post-Maastricht. Could we move to a situation where the Commission can bring Art. 169 enforcement proceedings directly against a local administration where it possesses under national laws exclusive competence to implement a Directive? And it would be the local administration which would be responsible for paying any fines if it failed to respect the Court's judgement. Certainly, this might better reflect the realities of responsibility. And if the alternatives are either greater centralisation or a minimal role for the Community it might be preferable.

International environmental agreements still largely lack the formal enforcement mechanism developed with the Community system. Here it is necessary to rely upon elaborate reporting and review mechanisms of the sort seen in the Climate Change Convention, which ultimately rely upon peer pressure and a degree of trust. For some time there used to be a rather sterile debate as to whether this absence of effective enforcement procedures meant that such agreements, though part of international law, were not law in any real sense. Yet even at a national level the role of legally expressed duties which are non-enforceable in a strict legal sense should not be too readily dismissed. As Ross Cranston has noted, legislation can give 'legitimacy to aspirations ... and can provide a backdrop against which specific decisions with legal consequence can be made'[71].

In 1986, Robin Grove-White was a research fellow at ICCET and leading an ESRC contract with me concerning the integration of an environmental dimension into policy areas hitherto almost unaffected by such considerations. A principle that now finds expression in the European Treaty,[72] but as Robin Grove-White demonstrated, one that is riddled with uncertainties not least because of fundamental differing perspectives of what is meant by the environment. Part of our research concerned the role and significance of general environmental duties expressed in legislation. The most long-standing and general being the familiar s 11 of the Countryside Act 1968:

---

[71] R Cranston, (1987) *Law Government and Public Policy*, Oxford University Press, Melbourne.
[72] Art 130R(2)'... Environmental protection requirements must be integrated into the definition and implementation of other Community policies.'

> In the exercise of their functions relating to land under any
> enactment every Minister, government department and public
> body shall have regard to the desirability of conserving the
> natural beauty and amenity of the countryside.

For such a blandly expressed duty the Parliamentary debates during the
passage of the Bill revealed a surprising degree of passion and conflict.[73]
One Bishop noted the long gap between the broad generality and any
actual legal compulsion while an opposing view described it as the focal
point of the whole Bill.[74]

Certainly it provided a symbolic marker of a new acknowledgement.
Other such general duties have generated more intense debate. In 1985,
I drafted a clause for the Council for the Protection of Rural England
(CPRE) which would have imposed a general conservation function on
the Minister of Agriculture, Fisheries and Food.[75] This was at a height of
concern over the environmental effects of that Ministry's activities at the
time. The clause was supported by the National Farmers Union and the
Country Landowners Association but lost in Standing Committee by
one vote with William Waldegrave for the Government ridiculing the
idea of such specific duties laid on specific departments on the grounds
of collective responsibility.[76]

Yet a little less than a year later, the Minister for Agriculture, Fisheries
and Food with remarkably little shame introduced under the
Agriculture Act 1986 a clause imposing upon himself a general duty
of balancing conservation and other interests.[77] Measuring in any

---

[73] The origin of the clause can be found from the recommendations of a Legal Study Group
adopted at 'The Countryside in 1970', a major conference organised by the Council for
Nature, the Royal Society of Arts and the Nature Conservancy and held in London, 10-12
November 1965. Significantly, perhaps, the original proposal was for the amenity clause
to be confined to functions under the town and country planning legislation which would
have given it consider ably more focus.

[74] 2nd Reading, House of Lords, Hansard, Vol. 53, 10 November 1967, HMSO, London.

[75] 'In the exercise of such of his functions as relate to agriculture and forestry, the Minister
of Agriculture, Fisheries and Food shall, in so far as it is consistent with his statutory duties,
further the conservation and enhancement of the natural beauty and the conservation of
flora, fauna and geological or physiological features of special interest'. (Proposed clause
in Wildlife & Countryside Amendment Bill 1985 drafted by Richard Macrory).

[76] 'We end up with the ridiculous situation that everybody has duties laid upon them
that cancel out all the duties laid upon everybody else. It is almost a logical absurdity.'
(William Waldegrave, House of Commons Standing Committee E, Hansard, 6 March
1985, HMSO, London).

[77] Agriculture Act 1986, s.13: 'In discharging any functions connected with agriculture in
rela tion to any land the minister shall, so far as it is consistent with the proper and efficient
dis charge of those functions, have regard to and endeavour to achieve a reasonable
balance between the following considerations:
(a) the promotion and maintenance of a stable and efficient agricultural industry;
(b) the economic and social interests of rural areas;   *Continued*

quantifiable way the effect of such a duty is near impossible. Would MAFF have acted differently in subsequent years in the absence of such a duty? Direct discussions with senior officials suggested the answer were not so straightforward. For the institution, such duties could be seen as providing a set of underlying principles, and their expression in legal forms provides a permanence and detachment from government policy-making it quite distinct from a White Paper. It legitimised internal sources of pressures for changes and affected the securement of priorities within limited resources.

Such duties par excellence attempt to express environmental responsibilities in aspirational tones which are nonetheless important for that. Yet securing the right balance of specificity and generality is a challenge. The Countryside Act duty was probably expressed too broadly and across too many parties to have real purchase. From 1957 until privatisation in 1990, the Central Electricity Generating Board was under a general duty to take into account environmental considerations in formulating or considering any proposals relating to its functions[78]. The Board had tended to interpret that duty as applying to specific projects, but at the Sizewell inquiry the CPRE argued with some success that it applied at higher levels of decision making and in particular to the formation of general strategies.[79] Now since privatisation the so-called amenity duty has been recast in its application to utility companies - on the one hand in more specific and demanding terms, but on the other no longer applicable at a strategic level but confined to proposals for individual power stations and similar projects.[80] In the long run this shift will, I suspect, be detrimental.

I have argued one role of law is to define and redefine boundaries of environmental responsibility. I started with case law concerning the content of responsibility. Let me conclude with examples of two cases where the location of responsibility was pushed to new limits.

...(c) the conservation and enhancement of the natural beauty and amenity of the countryside, including its flora and fauna and geological and physiographical features; and

(d) the promotion and the enjoyment of the countryside by the public.'

[78] 'In formulating or considering any proposals relating to the functions of the Generating Board or of any of the area Boards (including any such general programme as it is mentioned in subsection (4) of section 8 of this Act), the Board in question, the Electricity Council and the Minister, having regard to the desirability of preserving natural beauty, of conserving flora, fauna and geological or physiographical features of special interest, and of protecting buildings and other objects of architectural or historic interests, shall each take into account any effect which the proposals would have on naturaf beauty of the countryside or on any such flora, fauna, fea tures or objects.'

[79] See Sizewell B Public Inquiry Report by Sir Frank Layfield. 5th December 1986, HMSO, London.

[80] s 38 and Sched. 9 Electricity Act 1989.

First, a statutory noise nuisance in 1985. A Miss Rossall who lived in the basement flat of a Southwark Council block of flats suffered intensely from the noise of the occupants of the flat above her. The main ground of complaint concerned the loud sound of persistent love-making. The relevant legislation states that the person primarily liable for a noise nuisance is the person 'responsible' for the nuisance, and only if they cannot be identified, can the owner of the premises be taken to court.[81] Rather than taking her neighbours to court, Miss Rossall took her landlords, Southwark Council, on the grounds that by failing to provide effective sound insulation they were in fact the party responsible for the nuisance. It appears to have been the first time a landlord in such circumstances had been taken to court, and Miss Rossall won her case, with the Court ordering the installation of effective insulation. A preventative environmental policy could be introduced by reinterpretating and relocating legal responsibility.

My second example was the 1980 lead in petrol case, *Budden v BP Oil and others*[82], which in retrospect raised a number of legal issues concerning responsibility well ahead of its time. This was at a time when leaded petrol was available and legal, but the first campaigns and concerns about its effects on children were being raised. Three families living near the Westway section of the A40 in London, concerned at possible lead poisoning of their children, decided to avoid standard political campaigning but sued in the civil courts four parties they identified as being responsible for the situation: Associated Octel, Shell and BP Oil as two major petrol producers, and the Ford Motor Company on the grounds that a large number of the cars passing by were manufactured by them.

The critical causes of action were in nuisance and negligence, but fundamentally much of the argument as the case worked its way up from a Registrar to the Court of Appeal concerned the location of responsibility. The plaintiffs argued that the companies were putting a product on the market which would inevitably cause damage to children near urban motorways. Individual drivers had no option but to use motorcars with leaded petrol. The analogy was a supplier of a gun and bullets which he knew was to be used in a murder – he would be liable and in this case the car manufacturer was equivalent to a gun supplier. Octel, Shell and BP were equivalent to the companies who make the bullets, and provided innocent drivers with loaded guns.

---

[81] see now s.80 Environmental Protection Act 1990. *Rossall v London Borough of Southwark* (November 1985, unreported) and see Bettle, J. (1988) 'Noise: The Problem of Overlapping Controls', *Journal of Planning Law*.

[82] *Albery & Budden v BP Oil Ltd & Shell UK Ltd*. See also R Macrory,(1981) 'Lead in Petrol' (1981) *Journal of Planning and Environment Law* 258.

Or to use another analogy put forward in oral argument by one of the plaintiffs – it was like someone sending out robots who spray aerosol cans into strapped prams.

The defendants raised counter-views of responsibility. Ford Motor Company dropped out at an early stage after showing that their cars could run on both leaded and lead-free petrol. The others argued that they were not the equivalent of gun manufacturers and in any event you could not make the manufacturer of a dangerous as opposed to a defective product liable for all the consequences. Furthermore, if one accepted that there might be a problem it was confined to heavily trafficked urban roads. If anyone was responsible it was the highway authorities – the alleged harmful effects were equally well known to them and they could have taken steps to do something about the situation.

In the event the plaintiffs' case came unstuck in the Appeal Court. All along the defendants had been complying with the then statutory limits for lead in petrol prescribed by the Secretary of State. This in itself was not a good defence for those were matters of criminal rather than civil law. But the Court of Appeal argued that since one had to assume that the Secretary of State had acted reasonably when he set those limits, any reasonable manufacturer would have come to the same decision. Hence no case in negligence could ever be proved.

That particular logic can be questioned.[83] But the arguments concerning the nature of responsibility raised by the case are still very much with us today. Lead in petrol may now be of marginal significance. But I am acutely conscious during the Royal Commission on Environmental Pollution's present study into transport and the environment of the nature of our own personal responsibilities with respect to motor cars (and I exclude those present who rely solely on bicycles, walking or public transport).

The trail between Mr Burdett's monkey and the loaded gun of contemporary transport issues has been fairly lengthy, but raises a consistent question of the role of law in ensuring that both collective and individual choices are exercised with environmental sensitivity. 5th-century Irish law developed remarkably extended notions of those to whom legal responsibility were owed and who were entitled to compensation in the event of a wrong being committed. Thus, according to the book of Aicill, in the event of a theft from a house eleven persons

---

[83] ibid.

were affected and entitled to a compensation-fine from the wrong-doer: namely, the owner of the house, the owner of the object stolen, the owner of the bed in which the person slept who suffered the injury, the person who slept in that bed and the seven noblest chiefs who were in the habit of visiting the house.[84] Even coming from someone with a surname such as mine, that may seem like a peculiarly Irish approach to the definition of standing. But perhaps we should now turn this legal notion of extended rights to compensation on its head. We may all be potential noble chiefs, but in relation to the environment, what matters now is extended notions of responsibility rather than entitlement.

---

[84] Quoted by John A. Costello in (1913) *Leading Principles of the Brehon Laws*, p.415.

CHAPTER 9

ENVIRONMENTAL STANDARDS, LEGITIMACY AND SOCIAL JUSTICE*

I want to raise concerns about environmental standards in the context of the current and likely future developments in environmental law. Standards of various sorts have a critical role in many areas of environmental law yet the procedures and processes at work are revealing disturbing tensions. Inevitably my perspectives will be shaped and possibly distorted from my involvement in United Kingdom and European Community law, but many of the issues raised have more general application.

For someone who has worked in British and European environmental law for a number of years, one of the most striking features during the last decade or so has been the enormous proliferation of legally binding environmental standards of different types. British environmental law, in particular, used to be permeated by flexible legal frame-works, especially in the field of pollution regulation. These gave considerable interpretative discretion to those bodies responsible for enforcement – with the occasional nudge by the courts where litigation occurred. To take two examples, for many years the legal standard for drinking water was simply expressed as 'wholesome water'. The key criterion for air pollution control of emissions from industries was the 'best practicable means' to prevent or minimise or render harmless emissions. The formal law gave no further guidance of the meaning of those terms. Yet for operational purposes, regulatory bodies had to convert these qualitative criteria into something more precise, expressed in scientific and technological language often drawing on the work of international bodies such as the World Heath Organization.

Discretion has now given way to a large degree to legally binding environmental standards. We now see a vast array of environmental standards covering areas such as air quality, emissions from particular types of processes, water quality, chemical regulation and the like. Coupled with this has been the development of an enormously complex range of institutional machinery, for the development and making of such standards.

* R Macrory (1999) Environmental Standards, Legitimacy, and Social Justice, *Acta Juridica* (University of Cape Town) pp 257-265

The underlying reasons and indeed attractions of such a development are not hard to find. Environmental standards in this context represent a rule of some general application which reflect a public judgment about the acceptability of human activities on the environment. By conversion into specific terms, they provide an apparent transparency of that judgement, and assist in ensuring consistency in application. For industry or those affected by such standards they provide a benchmark for investment and performance. They remove from the realm of the courts the need for the judiciary to make complex economic and policy judgements which many would argue is not their legitimate role. In parenthesis I might add that at the height of deregulatory policies in the previous Conservative government there was rumoured to be a paper circulating cabinet sub-committees arguing that the protection of the environment should be left to private interests relying on common law remedies such as the law of nuisance, and leaving it to individual courts to determine appropriate levels of protection on a case by case basis. The complex regulatory machinery of public law could then be safely filleted. This was in retrospect one privatisation too far and was never seriously pursued.[1]

At the same time advances in scientific understanding, the development of toxicology and ecotoxicology as distinct disciplines, developments in reliable instrumentation and measurement techniques have helped develop the concept of rigorous standards expressed in quantifiable form.

Above all the impact of globalised markets has driven the development of environmental standards. Within the European Community in particular environmental policy was originally justified by the demands of market harmonisation and concerns about the distorting effects of differing standards. We are now in an era where the principle of subsidiarity potentially modifies excessive enthusiasm for complete harmonisation. At the same time explicit provisions in the Europe Treaty concerning environmental protection remove the need for what were sometimes intellectually spurious justification for environmental intervention on purely market harmonisation grounds.[2] Yet the standardisation process remains powerful. One attribute of subsidiarity is the idea of national mutual recognition and reciprocity. Under such

---

[1] Standards, whether legally binding or not, may of course assist the judiciary when determining tests for common law nuisance, though they will only be one factor. See, for example, *Murdoch v Glacier Metal Co* 19 January 1998 *Times Law Reports* where in a noise nuisance case the Court made reference to World Health Organization guidelines but held that noise just above the levels did not amount to a nuisance in law.

[2] See Title XVI of the European Community Treaty, Articles 130r and following which give express authority for Community environmental measures. The provisions were originally inserted under the 1987 amendments to the Treaty.

legal frameworks, authorisation by a national regulatory body in one Member State is automatically recognised and accepted by others – this principle, originally encouraged by the European Court of Justice in its famous judgments in the 1970s such as *Cassis de Dijon*[3], is increasingly reflected in many areas of the law such as chemical regulation. Yet it demands either considerable trust by national bodies on the capacity and ability of others, or a degree of standardisation of procedures such as risk assessment. These developments can already be seen in the latest proposals for revising EC legislation concerning genetically modified organisms where greater authority will be given to national authorities to grant authorisation but against a clearer framework of approach.

This does not imply that standardisation necessarily implies uniformity of approach nor removes significant elements of discretion turning regulators into blind automatons. Many standards may be expressed as minimum rather than uniform standards giving discretion to public authorities to determine tighter standards according to particular local circumstances. Standards expressed in the form of environmental quality standards leave discretion to regulators how to ensure they are met, often involving complex distributional judgements in dealing with individual emitters – to take one example, if an environmental quality standard for a particular stretch of water is established, should all existing dischargers will treated equally in order to ensure that the quality standard is not breached; should a safety allowance be made for potential future development and new dischargers who might arrive?

At a national level, supranational trade systems still permit a degree of discretion in developing distinct national environmental standards. Within the context of the common market, the European Treaty rules make allowance for individual Member States to determine national environmental protection standards in the absence of harmonised rules.[4] These provisions, reflected in GATT rules,[5] are constrained by rules of proportionality, necessity, and equal application to national and imported goods.

It is an area where the European Court has frequently been obliged to intervene. The court has to a large degree accepted that even in the context of human health standards among apparently homogenous and neighbouring countries, differing cultural and social contexts may

---

[3] Case 120178 *Rewe Zentral AG v Bundesmonopolverwaltung fur Branntwein (Cassis de Dijon)* [19791 ECR 6497.

[4] Art 36 EC Treaty and *Commission v Denmark* Case 302/86 [1988] ECR 4607.

[5] See Art XX(b) GATT. For the connection between Art XX(b) GATT and Art. 36 EC Treaty see Petersmann (1993) Freie Warenverkehr und nationale Umweltschultz in EWG und EWR *Aussenwirtschaft* 95.

justify differing standards.[6] Even where environmental standards have been promulgated at European level, Treaty rules permit national derogations though again bounded by considerable restrictions.[7] The recent Amsterdam amendments to the Treaty governing directives harmonising standards based on the operation of the market in fact represent a move in favour of European standardisation and against national discretion. The national discretion to impose tighter standards remain but, if the Treaty amendments are approved, constrain that discretion considerably. Where after a harmonisation measure has been adopted at Community level, a Member State may still introduce national measures relating to the protection of the environment provided these are not a means of arbitrary discrimination or disguised restriction of trade. But they may only do so on the basis of new scientific information on the grounds of a problem specific to that Member State. So a Member State, say, concerned at the inadequacies of an EC law concerning endocrine disrupters and wishing to introduce tighter standards would be unable to introduce national laws unless there was evidence relating to specific problems in their country.

These complexities are worthy of a conference in themselves. But if we accept that in certain countries and regions at any rate the proliferation of environmental standards as I have described them has been an inherent feature in the development of contemporary environmental law I want to highlight particular concerns.

There are a number of distinct trends which, in conjunction, are producing what might be described as an intellectual crisis in the conventional approaches towards environmental standard setting. Science is inherently built upon uncertainties, but the nature of contemporary environmental science is particularly complex. Moving away from pollutants affecting acute human heath to more chronic, and invidious, issues raises difficult questions of causation and correlation. Many human health standards have been based on toxicology and derived assumptions from the effects on animals to humans. But closer analysis suggests real problems. To take one well-known example, concerning the effects of dioxins on human health. Toxic tests on hamsters and guinea pigs have indicated extraordinarily different results, with guinea pigs being some 5 000 times more vulnerable than hamsters.[8] There was no convincing explanation nor, more importantly, any principles which could suggest whether humans were more similar to guinea pigs or hamsters. The

---

[6] See eg Case 272/80 *Fumicot* [1981] ECR 3277.
[7] See, especially, EC Treaty Art 100a(4). Case 41/93 *France v Commission* [1994] ECR 1-1829. See A Zieglar *Trade and Environmental Law in the European Community* (1996), 161-7.
[8] See Royal Commission on Environmental Pollution *17th Report Incineration of Waste* Cm 2181 (1993) HMSO London.

classic analysis by Filov and others[9] trying to determine the effective dose of LSD that would give a trip to an elephant illustrates differing calculations depending on comparative body weight, metabolism rates, or brain weights of cats and humans reveals a correct answer that varies by a factor of 1,000. Current scientific research concerning the effects of vehicle pollution on respiratory diseases, including asthma, again shows tremendous uncertainties, whatever one's intuitive experience.[10] Standards relating to the protection of the natural environment as opposed to humans used to be largely calculated by crudely applying a safety factor but again this is increasingly recognised as far too simplistic an approach. The sheer volume of activity required under some regimes is also daunting. Under European Community legislation dealing with existing chemicals on the market since 1981[11] it was estimated that over 100,000 chemicals substances exist on the market. A number of priority lists were compiled between 1994 and 1997 numbering 109, but to date only four assessments have been submitted and agreed for submission to the relevant Commission directorate generals. At this rate we are talking of 100 years to deal with just the priority list.

Finally despite the importance of scientific underpinning where appropriate, scientific committees have sometimes been misused. In simple terms it is an appropriate use of science to determine a dose-effect curve, but it cannot be a purely scientific judgment to determine at what point on that curve a standard should be set. David Fisk, Chief Scientist at the United Kingdom Department of the Environment Transport and Regions has recently argued[12] for the need to separate scientific assessment to test our current state of knowledge with all its inherent uncertainties from the process of risk assessment whose purpose is to lead to a conclusion or decision based on the assessment. Yet we have clear examples where the process is confused. More subtly, much of the contemporary scientific process involves risk assessment which in itself can reflect cultural and social perspectives often obscured. Josef Falke and Gerd Winter have provided a fascinating study of the workings of various technical committees at European Community level dealing with the regulation of dangerous substances.[13] Examining the issue of asbestos, French and German delegates came to diametrically opposed views, mainly because the French approach to risk assessment includes in the equation a benefit comparison of the current use and need of the

[9] V A Filov *et al Quantitative Toxicology* (1973).
[10] Royal Commission on Environmental Pollution 18th Report Transport and the Environment Cmnd 2674 (1994), HMSO, London.
[11] See EC Council Directive 79/831 and EC Council Regulation No 293/93.
[12] D Fisk 'Environmental Science and Environmental Law' (1998) 10(1) *Journal of Environmental Law*.
[13] J Falk and G Winter 'Management and regulatory committees in executive rule making' in G Winter (ed) *Sources and Categories of European Union Law* (1996).

product while the Germans adopted the approach of considering solely the health and environmental risks.

It is hardly surprising that faith in the concept of scientific certainty is less sure than it was. Regulators and those responsible for devising environmental standards now operate in a political and social climate where professional judgments are not accepted unquestioningly. The so called 'nanny knows best' syndrome which operated in the United Kingdom for many years no longer holds true. One political and legal response has to be to open up decision making, and to allow members of the public and other interests to participate to some extent in decision making. We have seen at national level extensive new rights under environmental laws of consent applications being publicised, rights of the public to inspect public registers, and to comment on proposed decision making. Yet here we see a conundrum. During the same period as these rights were being extended at local level, many areas of the standard setting processes were moving up at a regional or international level. The pressures of the free market, the moves toward reciprocal recognition or standardisation of product standards, and in the European context at least the harmonising of many process standards in an effort to remove competition distortions has removed much of the discretionary powers and authority of national or local regulatory bodies. Public participation at a local level may still have a function but is heavily reduced, and may indeed be counterproductive in that it can raise expectations which cannot be fulfilled. Yet certainly in the European context we have scarcely begun to develop mechanisms of real transparency and participation. Much of the detail of European law making is delegated in various forms to sub-committees with a total of nearly 400 currently operating, quadrupling between 1975 and 1995.[14] Even at what might be described as primary law making, much of the procedures are still clouded in traditions of international diplomacy.

A further challenge to the concept of standard setting derives from their legal context. In the field of pollution control in particular, the setting of standards has been associated with classical forms of interventionist regulation. The last decade has seen a sustained critique of so called command and control regulation as being excessively costly, inefficient, and stifling of innovation. Other methods of environmental management,[15] from economic instruments, self-regulation, various forms of contractual arrangements,[16] and voluntary initiatives are being advocated and experimented with. For my part, I resist the simple

---

[14] The figures are derived from the annual General Budget of the European Union.

[15] O'Riordan (ed) *Eco-Taxation Earthscan* (1997); J Bowers *Sustainabilty and Environmental Economics - An Alternative Text* (1997).

[16] European Environment Agency *Environmental Agreements EEA* (1997).

division between legal and non-legal methods, and the over-simple characterisation of command and control. Furthermore while the use of economic instruments in particular can provide a means of achieving policy aims, I am not convinced that they can define those aims in themselves. Environmental standards will still have a key role in goal-setting even if the means of achieving those goals are varied.

This is particularly important where one is dealing with issues that move beyond the control of identifiable fixed sources. A good example is the recently introduced British national air quality standards and a legal framework requiring local authorities to devise strategies of achieving those standards, using a variety of instruments from land use planning controls, traffic regulation, control of industrial emitters and the like.[17]

The final challenge to the environmental standard setting process is the shift of policy goals from that of environmental protection to one of sustainable development. I have already described the difficulties of moving from human health protection to the protection of the natural environment. Sustainable development, which is already working its way into legal expression, brings in a range of other factors including social equity and economic consumption making the identification of standards all the more challenging. The shift reflects the move away from what the British environmentalist Tom Burke has described as the easy politics of the environment of the last 25 years which has dominated much of environmental law, to the much more difficult issues of the next 25 years. We are entering a more fluid world of policies and politics. In this context sustainable development reflects a trajectory rather than a fixed state or goal. Reconciling that concept with the notion of environmental standards that inherently do represent an identifiable level of protection at a particular point of time is not easy.

How does one steer a route through these quagmires? It is, I think, a mistake to assume that a perfect methodology for standard setting can be devised. But some markers can be established. Scientific knowledge and understanding will still play a key element, but the idea, if ever if were true, that we can look for certainty from those quarters, or indeed have the time to do so, has to be resisted. The uncertainties and complexities involved in many contemporary environmental issues will lead to the development of new scientific procedures of arriving at scientific consensus, as witnessed in the workings methods developed by the scientific panel of the Inter-governmental Panel on Climate Change since 1988. On the other hand, rejection of the simplistic notion that environmental standards can be derived solely from 'sound science'

---

[17] See Part IV Environment Act 1995.

cannot be merely replaced by an equally simplistic invocation of the precautionary principle. Almost every activity has the capacity for harm, and the principle cannot be applied without some degree of risk analysis. Distinguishing more clearly the process of scientific assessment from risk analysis, as David Fisk has argued, is vital. Economic analysis has traditionally formed a key element in decision making, and while important the blind use of cost benefit analysis has to be treated with caution. Recent examples in the UK of its use in the environmental field illustrate clearly some of the underlying weaknesses of the conceptual approach, and the large degree of assumptions that must be made and which cannot derive from the discipline itself – before figures are arrived at.[18] But in future it will be all the more important for those responsible for standard setting to draw on other disciplines which can illuminate human behaviour in areas where economists should not tread. Socio-legal studies, and cultural anthropology have important roles to play, though not a traditional expertise which many Western governments have drawn upon.[19] To the extent that many of the future environmental and sustainable issues concern the behaviour of individuals these disciplines will be all the more important. We have to ensure that there is real feedback from the study of how laws are implemented back into the law-making processes. Too often governments devote time and effort to making new legislation with insufficient attention to the questions of implementation. As an MEP put it recently, 'We are good midwives but bad mothers'.

More significantly, it will be increasingly important to examine underlying principles behind the detail of environmental law, and be prepared to devise more rigorous mechanisms for their discussion and development. We have seen this recently in the field of biotechnology in the United Kingdom and the rest of Europe. There the complex regulatory machinery for controlled releases of Genetically Manipulated Organisms both on the market and for experimental purposes has consciously focused on the environmental risks.[20] Not surprisingly in a liberal economy the legal regulatory machinery is uncomfortable in engaging in a risk/need exercise. To that extent the procedures avoid

---

[18] In a recent major example of the use of cost – benefit analysis for environmental evaluation, the United Kingdom Environment Agency estimated the 'value' of the River Kennet to be £13.6 million, most of which was based on 'willing to pay' figures by consumers in the whole Thames Region. The Department of the Environment. Transport and Regions revised the figure down to £700,000 by reducing the number of consumers counted. See O Tickell 'Stream of Abust' *Guardian* 4 March 1998.

[19] Though in the United States the Environmental Protection Agency has recently drawn up a Co-operative Agreement with the Society for Applied Anthropologists - see http://www.telepath.com/sfaaleap/abouteap.html.

[20] See Part VI Environmental Protection Act 1990 (UK) and Directive 90/220/EEC *Deliberative Release into the Environment of GMO's*.

addressing ethical concerns that are apparent, and certainly alive with the general public. The simple answer is to say this is a political issue for decision by elected politicians. Yet our current institutional machinery – and certainly my own country's Parliamentary processes – are often ill-equipped to explore such issues in a convincing and rigorous manner. The phrase 'deliberative institutions' is currently in vogue amongst political scientists. Rather like 'sustainable development', the notion is readily dismissed as lacking clarity or straightforward solutions. Yet it represents a searching for new mechanisms to handle issues of genuine public concern which conventional methodologies have avoided.

In a short space of time I seem to have travelled from a bounded field of drinking water protection to the more uncertain world of political processes. For the environmental lawyer it would be more comfortable to remain in a familiar world of dealing solely with the implementation and enforcement of environmental standards. Yet if environmental law is to develop in a sophisticated way in tune with contemporary concerns it is important to appreciate some of the underlying tensions and complexities which is now apparent, even if our discipline cannot provide all the solutions.

CHAPTER 10

TECHNOLOGY AND ENVIRONMENTAL LAW ENFORCEMENT*

It would be entirely wrong to deny to the law of evidence the advantages to be gained from new techniques and new advances in science[1]

Introduction

One of Gerd Winter's strengths as an environmental lawyer has been his ability to consider the legal implications of developments of technology and science and from perspectives that often fall outside the immediate concerns of more conventional environmental law. He acknowledges the potential environmental benefits of man's continual inventiveness but has been prepared to explore difficult questions concerning the role of law in creating solutions that are both transparent and lead to a more environmentally sustainable society. In his seminal article, 'Perspectives for Environmental Law – Entering the Fourth Phase'[2] he questioned the capacity of interventionist approaches which have so characterised developments in environmental law over the past thirty years to handle the demands now being made on them. He argued that a preferable approach might be to reduce such burdens while at the same time injecting an environmental dimension and re-orientating substantive areas of law concerned with harnessing or emancipating the capacities of individuals and corporations, such as labour law, competition law, and company law : 'All of this must not be seen as a controlling law and administrative programme but rather as a programme which is inscribed into that body of law which at the outset releases the individual's economic energy'.[3] In a similar vein he has explored the fundamental concepts of patent law in the context of biotechnology,[4] noting that while legal debate has largely been concerned with developing regulatory techniques to handle environmental risks, the question of reforming intellectual property law had been largely untouched. Patent law in this context can been seen as a promotional body of law which should be reconsidered and refocussed rather than imposing every increasing burdens on an already over worked regulatory system: 'This is not a

* Macrory R (2003) Technology and Environmental Law Enforcement in Winter (ed) *Rechtund Um-Welt,* European Law Publishers, Amsterdam, pp 431-446

[1] Lord Justice Steyn, *R v Clarke* (1994) Criminal Division, Court of Appeal.
[2] *Journal of Environmental Law* (1989) Vol 1 No 1 pp. 38-47.
[3] ibid, p. 46.
[4] 'Patent Law Policy in Biotechnology' *Journal of Environmental Law* (1992) Vol 4 No 2 167-188.

mere doctrinal discourse, where new phenomena are subsumed under stretched old legal forms, nor is it a substantialist discourse where vitalists wage an idle war against materialist pervasiveness. Rather, it is a functionalist argument where patentability as opposed to other policy alternatives is assessed with regard to social, economic and ecological effects.'[5]

Remote Sensing in Court

Effective enforcement of environmental law is a challenge facing all governments, and the almost inevitable implementation gaps that pervade the use of traditional environmental regulatory techniques have been one of the motivations for Gerd Winter's search for new ways of thinking about the law and the environment. It is entirely in keeping with his intellectual curiosity that he has more recently been concerned with the potential use of satellite technology and remote sensing as a important technological tool in the application of environmental law. With ever increasing resolution and coverage, the technology can be presented as a cost-effective and reliable tool which will dramatically improve the ability of regulatory bodies in many areas of environmental law to detect and deter. Oil pollution from sea, illegal abstractions of water, damage to special protection sites for nature conservation, and even illegal disposal of waste can all in theory be determined by the use of remote sensing. Knowledge of the capacity of such satellites and the extent to which even the current generation can provide regular and detailed information is not yet generally pervasive among regulators, judges, environmental lawyers let alone the average citizen. More significantly, in the past few years there appears to have been a step change in the capacity of the technology. The Landsat systems which have been familiar to users of remote sensing for the past twenty years or so have a spatial resolution of between 30m and 50m, but in 2000 there were thirty one satellites in orbit with the capability of providing land cover data at spatial resolutions of 1–30 metres, while the Ikonos satellite, launched in 1999, has the capacity of 1 metre resolution, with high resolution and high frequency of revisits. Images from such resolution can distinguish, for example, individual vehicles. A new generation of satellites is planned for 2004 with 0.5 metre resolutions, and the future may well see the greater use of unmanned space vehicles which fly at 50,000 or so feet, lower than current satellites but considerably higher than an aeroplane. The potential for this technology in the assisting the implementation of environmental law is clearly enormous and of a quite different nature to what has been the experience to date, yet a more serious and intensive effort to harness this capacity in the interests

---

[5] ibid, p. 184.

of improved environmental protection raises potential conflicts with other well developed areas of law such as data protection, privacy, intellectual property ownership, and rules of evidence. Over 50 years ago the American lawyer, Thurman Arnold wrote that the law 'fulfils its functions best when it represents the maximum of competing symbols.' But unless the environmental lawyer is prepared to understand and engage with these 'competing' areas of law with their own important goals and precepts, progress with environmental law is likely to be stymied. The purpose of this contribution is therefore to consider a number of the legal issues likely to be raised in the context of the use of satellite technology for improved enforcement of environmental law.[6] The focus is on Europe, and many of the more detailed aspects of the law are provided are from the United Kingdom context, though they are likely to represent issues that will be common to most developed legal systems.

One could imagine a scenario of a regulator responsible for the enforcement of laws designed to prevent damage to special nature protection areas. Where such damage occurs the relevant legislation imposes criminal liability on the owner of the land unless, say, he can prove it was caused by a third party beyond his control. The constraints on public sector finances means that regular inspection by individual officers across last tracts of lands is not possible, and it is more cost effective to monitor remote sensing images of the land in question. The regulator decides to use one such satellite image to prove before a court that damage has taken place, and an offence committed. In all jurisdictions fairly complex rules of evidence have been developed to ensure that a defendant has a fair trial, and that evidence produced is as authentic as possible. In a common law jurisdiction such as the United Kingdom the rules and principles are especially coloured by the fact of the adversarial nature of the process and the strong lay element in criminal courts with juries determining facts in serious criminal cases, and a wide use of lay magistrates in less serious offences. In the scenario outlined above the likely immediate reaction of court faced with such an image as sole evidence will be to ask why the regulator did not investigate the situation at first hand. In this context a satellite image is likely to be of greatest value as providing a warning to a regulator of a potential problem, a valuable administrative tool particularly for regulators under financial pressure and tasked with monitoring expansive or remote tracts of land or the sea. In the United Kingdom, for example, set-aside schemes under the Common Agriculture Policy are regularly

[6] Much of the original analysis is based on a joint project involving both legal and technological research centres across Europe and conducted for the European Commission, APERTURE, ENV4-CT97-437 final report October 3 2000. Professor Winter led the German contribution.

monitored by remote sensing, and in at least one case have provided advance warning of fraud, later confirmed by visual inspection and leading to a successful prosecution of the farmer concerned[7]. Indeed, the use of remote sensing is positively encouraged under European Community rules concerning aid in the agricultural field, one of the few examples of Community legislation making such express reference to the technology for enforcement purposes.[8]

Nevertheless, we can also imagine situations where the relevant environmental law incorporates a temporal dimension, and where the capacity of remote sensing to build up data showing land changes over a period of years may provide the critical and only available evidence to contradict the defendant. An example might include laws requiring permits for new building but where the existence of the building for a number of years provides a good defence; or where new requirements for licences to abstract water do not apply to those who have abstracted water for a set number of years prior to the legislation coming into force.[9] In such cases the bank of images already obtained by remote sensing may prove critical to resolving conflicts of evidence over what took place in the past.

The use of photographs, tape-recordings, and other documentary evidence are now, of course, familiar to the criminal courts. As long ago as 1878, photography was held admissible as evidence in court proceedings : 'The photograph was admissible because it is only the visual representation of the image or impression made upon the minds of the witnesses by the sight of the person or the object it represents; and therefore, is, in reality, only another species of the evidence which persons give of identity, when they speak merely from memory'.[10] It is arguable that remote sensing from satellites is no different from the use of aerial photography, and should be treated as such. Nevertheless there are potentially significant distinctions. Rules of evidence concerning the

---

[7] R Macrory and R Purdy (2001) 'Use of Satellite Images as Evidence in Environmental Actions in Great Britain' *Droit et Ville* 51/2001, 71-88.

[8] Commission Regulation EEC 3887/92 laying down detailed rules for applying the integrated administration and control system for certain Community aid schemes. See Article 6, and the preamble which states, 'Whereas the conditions for the use of remote sensing for on-the-spot checks should be laid down and provision should be made for physical checks to be required in doubtful cases....'. The Regulation provides for financial contribution from the Community 'in order to encourage Member States in their efforts to develop remote sense.'

[9] The use of remote sensing images has already been the subject of extensive court proceedings concerned with the registration of existing water rights under the Spanish Water Act coming into force January 1 1986, and one of the few examples in Europe where the conflict between a satellite image and the evidence of an individual was directly in issue.

[10] Per Willes J, *R v Tolson* (1864) 4 F & F 103.

admissibility of documents in court proceedings in the United Kingdom were largely developed on the basis that there existed an 'original' (for analogue photographs, the negative) from which all copies derived. Common law jurisdictions, in particular, have long made an important distinction between 'real' evidence, that is, some material object such as a document or photograph from which the court may draw an inference, and what is termed 'hearsay' evidence, essentially evidence not of direct observation but what a witness heard others say. Clearly, the latter evidence may be given less weight because of the greater possibility of mistake or simply because there is another intervening level of human interpetation present. In jurisdictions based on an inquisitorial system and with a judge alone determining both fact and law, the distinction is less vital and simply goes to the weight of the evidence to be determined by the judges. Indeed, in civil cases in the United Kingdom where a judge determines both fact and law, hearsay evidence is admissible. In criminal cases, however, due to the tradition of lay citizens determining facts, there have long been rules forbidding its use in such cases: 'an assertion other than one made by the person while giving oral evidence in the proceedings is inadmissible as evidence of any fact asserted.'[11] Essentially the actual writer or originator of the statement must be present in court and available for cross-examination by the defence.[12]

Such rules may have been appropriate for a simpler era which was less rich in information technology, but clearly raise immense practical problems for the administration of justice where computer and similar data sources pervade almost every aspect of life. Legislation was therefore introduced in the United Kingdom[13] which permits the use of evidence produced by a computer but under the conditions that there was no reason to believe the information was inaccurate because of improper use of the computer and that at all times the computer was operating properly. Nevertheless, the conceptual difficulty of determining whether information derived from a computer or similar technological equipment is real rather than hearsay evidence are not always easy to determine, and require judgments to be made on the level of human intervention involved. In one case, for example,[14] the Criminal Court

---

[11] *R v Sharp* (1988) I All ER 65. See also Howarth (1997) 'Self-monitoring, self-policing, self-incrimina-tion and pollution law' 60 *Modern Law Review* 200.

[12] It is arguable that the prohibition of hearsay evidence in criminal cases is implied by Art 6(3) European Convention of Human Rights which provides that everyone charged with a criminal offence has the right 'to examine or have examined witnesses against him and to obtain attendance and examination of witnesses on his behalf under the same conditions as witnesses against him', though the European Court have not yet adopted such a strict interpretation., See C Osborne 'Hearsay and the Court of Human Rights' (1993) *Criminal Law Review* 255.

[13] See s 69 Police and Criminal Evidence Act 1984. See also s 23 and 24 Criminal Justice conditions, even though the writer may not be present.

[14] *John Eric Spilby* (1990) 91 Cr App R 186.

of Appeal upheld a trial judge's ruling that evidence from a computer automatically recording telephone calls in a hotel was real evidence[15] of those facts : 'This was not a print out which depended on its content for anything that had passed through the human mind...What was recorded was quite simply the acts which had taken place in regard to the telephone machinery and there was no intervening human mind.' But a year later, in a case concerning shop-lifting, the Appeal Court held that evidence[16] from a computer providing accumulated data from till rolls, and entered by individual till operators, was hearsay: 'In Spilby the computer was recording information automatically without the intervention of any human agency. It was that fact that as a consequence the documentary evidence did not infringe the hearsay rule. Here much of the information supplied by the till rolls was supplied by cashiers. So far as that information is concerned, it was clearly hearsay and would only be admissible if it could be brought into one of the exceptions...' The significance of the distinction can have immense implications as was seen in litigation concerning the use of computer records held by local authorities where local authorities sought liability orders for the failure to pay a new and politically controversial local tax. The ruling by the High Court[17] that such evidence was inadmissible as being hearsay threatened the whole viability of the enforcement system in this area, and led to the government introducing special legislative provisions to permit their use in such proceedings.

It is clear that digital images from remote sensing do raise particular evidential problems of categorisation and authenticity. There is no 'original' image, but essentially a visual representation of binary data in a computer memory, and a considerable amount of processing has taken place before that data is converted to a visual representation. Even at an initial stage, a degree of image pre-processing is likely to be conducted in order to reduce errors that were introduced during image acquisition with techniques such as geometric and radio-metric correction. Image processing itself involves a large degree of manipulation by the operator, for instance, in the assignation of colours designed to reveal particular features. Although it seems likely that the image itself would be considered 'real' rather than 'hearsay' evidence, expert evidence explaining the nature and implications of such resulting images are bound to be essential. All this is very different from the 'direct' photograph of the type more familiar to courts, and is clearly potentially vulnerable to legal challenge.

---

[15] The argument that computer evidence was real rather than hearsay was first suggested in Smith (1981) The Admissibility of Statements by Computer *Criminal Law Review* 387-391.

[16] *Hilda Shephard* (1991) 93 Cr. App R 140.

[17] *R v Coventry Justices ex parte Bullard and another, Times Law Report* 24 February 1992.

Nevertheless, the challenge of digital manipulation, lack of 'originals' and authenticity is no longer confined to satellite imagery but is increasingly experienced by courts handling evidence from video recordings, CCTV, and similar surveillance systems. But a 1998 Parliamentary inquiry into the use of digital images in court proceedings[18] could find no case where defence lawyers in a criminal case involving the use of video evidence had requested an audit trail – an omission which the committee attributed to a lack of technical knowledge amongst lawyers as to the nature of the technology and audits. In what continental lawyers might find a typically British pragmatic approach, the Committee nevertheless recommended against detailed legislation on the subject on the grounds that it would never keep up with technological development, and that it was best left to the courts to provide the necessary principles through case law. Already the Criminal Court of Appeal has provided ground-rules in the context of DNA evidence where it has held that a defendant must have access to all the individual stages involved in the production of such evidence, including the details of databases and specialist software upon which calculations have been based.[19]

The development of standardised procedures for audit trails in remote sensing is likely to be a crucial step in reassuring courts of the authenticity of the data presented, although as yet it is not a subject governed by legislation either in Britain or the at European level. At present, guidance has been issued by voluntary standards bodies such as the British Standards Institute concerning the best practice to be adopted in the case of computer generated evidence,[20] and though not legally binding, non-compliance with such a code could render the admissibility of such evidence vulnerable. Such a trail is likely to require the recoding of every step of enhancing and manipulating the date that the image goes through, ensuring that all processing and changes made to the document are recorded, and that the individuals who were responsible for this stages has the necessary authorisation. Although the concept of an 'original' image fits less easily into digital technology, bodies such as the British Standards Institute have recommended the hard copy original and original digital image be secured on a non-erasable image such as WORM (Write Once Read Many times), a practice now followed in financial and other business sectors. Even then such a procedure is not infallible, as in theory images could be altered and retransferred back to a second WORM, and any such alterations would be impossible

---

[18] House of Lords Select Committee on Science and Technology 'Digital Images as Evidence' 5th Report, HL Paper 64, 1998, HMSO, London.

[19] *R v Doheny, R v Adams* (1997) 1 Cr App Report 369 and 669.

[20] See, for example, British Standards Institution (1996) Code of Practice forn the Legal Admissibility of Information Stored on Electronic Document Management Systems DISC PD0008.

to detect. Watermark or digital signatures can also be incorporated with the computer data to preserve authenticity, although even these technologies are fallible.

Technological Equipment

Legal provisions concerned with the use of evidence produced by technological equipment have been introduced in some areas of pollution law, notably s 111 Environment Act 1995 which permits the use of information 'by means of any apparatus' used in connection with monitoring compliance with water discharge consents. A conviction based on evidence obtained by an automatic sampling device was first obtained by the then National Rivers Authority in 1993, by a device which was remotely operated to take effluent samples following a rise in pH levels.[21] The device, known as CYCLOPS, carried out continuous monitoring of the water quality and where consent levels were breached triggered a warning to a control centre, which permitted operators to instruct the machine to then take actual samples for potential use in a prosecution. The equipment containing the samples was opened in the presence of the defendant, and since the company in question decided to plead guilty, no legal points concerning the nature of the evidence came into play. Under s 111 of the 1995 Act where monitoring is carried out as part of a consent condition, the burden of showing that such apparatus is not recording accurately is placed on the defendant,[22] but in other cases it would be presumably be open to the defendant to question the accuracy of the device and the manner in which information is stored and processed. This does not appear to have occurred to date in criminal proceedings concerning water pollution offences, though it has be noted that there still remain legal doubts as to the precise nature of the evidence that is produced, and particularly whether it is to be categorised as real or hearsay, especially if computer equipment is involved.[23] The better view is probably that evidence from an automatic sampling device, where the only human intervention is to activate the device, would be classified as real evidence and admissible as such before the court and without the need to fall within any of the legislative exceptions.[24]

Probably the most developed use of digital imaging employed in the enforcement of criminal law is to be found in traffic speeding where

---

[21] Howarth and McGillivray (2001) *Water Pollution and Water Quality Law* Shaw and Sons, Kent, at 16.10.
[22] S 111 (3) Environment Act 1995.
[23] See Mumma (1993) 'Monitoring Data in Water Pollution Prosecutions' *Journal of Environmental Law* Vol 5 No 1 pp. 191-202 and Howarth and McGillivray, op. cit., 16.12.
[24] Mumma, op.cit. n 23

remotely operated speed cameras are now extensively used in the United Kingdom. The near impossibility of comprehensive enforcement by conventional means, which required corroborative evidence from a police officer, in some respects mirrors the problems facing environmental law, but in this context more elaborate and procedural changes have now been developed. According to s 20 Road Traffic Offences Act 1988[25], evidence of speeding offences may be given by the production of evidence produced by a device prescribed by the Secretary of State, accompanied by a police certificate as to the circumstances in which the record was produced. The statutory requirements relate to the type of equipment installed at the roadside, but an elaborate Code of Practice has been developed under the auspices of a government committee concerning operational requirements and the management and retention of data, especially important as digital imaging is replacing the use of conventional analogue photographic equipment originally used in the equipment. As the Code notes, 'The integrity and full acceptance of the evidence by the courts is of paramount importance. It is therefore essential this continues to be ensured by the use of data protection methods that will themselves be recognised as adequate by the courts.'[26]

As indicated above, current data from remote sensing is probably of most practical value as an administrative tool to provide advanced warnings to enforcement bodies of potential legal breaches which are then to be investigated and proved in court by more conventional evidential means. Yet the new generation of satellites with vastly increased spectral and spatial resolution which is on the horizon opens up new potentials for the direct use of imaging in court proceedings. Without more standardised procedures and the development of codes of practice across the industry to maintain authenticity – as have been developed in the case of CCTV – their direct use in court is likely to be vulnerable to challenge. The examples above illustrate that legal systems can adapt and develop evidential principles to accommodate the use of new forms of technology, and it may be in future that satellite images will be as familiar and unexceptional element of evidence as traditional photographs are today.

---

[25] The use of speed cameras was recommended by the Road Traffic Review Report (the North Report) 1988 HMSO, London who had become 'convinced that the legal issues could not sensibly be considered separately from practical considerations of enforcement and technology.'

[26] Para 4.3 Outline Requirements and Specification for Automatic Traffic Enforcement Systems, Home Office Police Policy Directorate, 1996, Home Office, London.

Privacy

This new generation of high resolution satellites may indeed offer dramatic scope for the potential improvement of the enforcement of environmental law, but it also raises important issues and potential conflicts with other areas of law, notably rights to privacy.

Such issues in relation to satellite imagery have barely been considered to date by the courts, even in the United States where privacy rights have been an inherent part of the constitutional law. As Slonecker has noted,[27] 'Until recently, the level of detail has been so gross as not be to be a concern, and the intrusion is one that society generally accepts as reasonable for some greater overall purpose, such as map making, effective land-use planning, or protecting human health and natural resources.' Yet the emerging technology raises real potential confrontations with the notion of individual privacy, and the extent to which those rights are protected in law. The analysis of Warren and Brandeis[28] in their seminar article of privacy written over 100 years ago and in the context of press intrusion may well resonate in this new context: 'The intensity and complexity of life, attendant upon advancing civilisation, have rendered necessary some retreat from the world, and man, under the refining influence of culture, has become more sensitive to publicity, so that solitude and privacy have become more essential to the individual.'

Within Europe, the European Convention on Human Rights provides in Article 8(1) the right of an individual 'to respect for his private and family life, his home, and his correspondence', and since the introduction of the Human Rights Act 1998, courts in Britain are increasingly being faced with challenges to the actions of public authorities based on a breach of these and other rights within the Convention. No case law exists to date concerning the application of Article 8 to possible intrusion by satellite imagery, and it seems unlikely in any event that images taken with today's generation of satellites would be considered a breach. But a world where resolution was such as to identify with certainty activities taking place on private property, vehicles, and perhaps even individuals clearly makes it a potentially live legal issue. Any analysis would have to consider first whether there was in fact a breach of Article 8(1), and second, if there were, whether it came within one of the public interest exceptions allowed for in the Convention. As for the first question, it is clear that from decisions that the European Court of Human Rights that

---

[27] Slonecker, Shaw, and Lillesand (1998) 'Emerging Legal and Ethical Issues in Advanced Remote Sensing Technology' *Photogrammetic Engineering and Remote Sensing* Vol 64 No 6 pp589-595.

[28] S Warren and L. Brandeis (1890) 'The Right to Privacy' *Harvard Law Review* 4, 103-220.

the case law on Article 8 reflect the need to allow for different degrees of privacy according to different circumstances. The more intimate the aspect of private life being infringed, the more serious must be the legitimate grounds for interference.[29] Certainly, the court has been reluctant to confine the notion of privacy solely to aspects of family life per se. As the Court noted in *Niemitz v Germany,*

> ..it would be too restrictive to limit the notion [of private life] to an 'inner circle' in which the individual may live his personal life as he chooses and to exclude therefrom from the outside world not encompassed within that circle. Respect for private life must also comprise to a certain degree the right to establish and develop relationships with other human beings.

Photography in a public place was been subject to decision of the European Court where in *Friedl v Austria*[30] the court held that this would not normally be a breach of Article 8:

> ..the reason why the taking of photographs and the retention of the photographs were not regarded as an interference could be said to be mainly that, when the photographs were taken, the applicant was in a public place where anyone is in principle free to take photographs and where the taking of photographs can, in most circumstances, be considered a trivial act which must be tolerated by others, although some persons may indeed consider it unpleasant that someone should take their photograph.

The reasoning was elaborated in *PG and JH v United Kingdom*[31], a case concerning listening devices used by the police and where the court made a specific reference to security monitoring in a public place:

> There are a number of elements relevant to the consideration of whether a person's private life is concerned in measures affected outside a person's home or private premises. Since there are occasions when people knowingly or intentionally involve themselves in activities which are or may be recorded or reported in public a person's reasonable expectations to privacy may be significant though not necessarily a conclusive factor. The person who walks down the street will inevitably be visible to any member of the public who is also present. Monitoring by technological means of the same public scene (e.g. a security guard viewing through closed circuit television) is a similar character. Private

---

[29] *Douglas v United Kingdom* (1981) 4 EHRR 149.
[30] *Friedl v Austria* (1994) A 305-B.
[31] 25 September 2001.

life considerations may arise however once any systematically permanent record comes into existence of such material from the public domain.

The Court of Human Rights will soon have to deal with a further elaboration of the use of CCTV images in the *Peck* case which was found admissible by the court last year[32]. In that case, security cameras in a shopping centre captured an individual attempting to commit suicide, with the result that rescue services were able to save him. The footage was subsequently sold to broadcasters by the local authority to boost the use of CCTV by showing that it could save lives, but without the individual's permission. The breach of Article 8 claimed refers not to the actual filming in the first place but to the subsequent passing on of the footage for broadcasting. As to the use of evidence by regulatory bodies in criminal proceedings, British courts have never gone as far as US courts in holding that illegally obtained evidence is inadmissible per se. Judges retained a discretion to exclude evidence, now codified under s 78 Police and Criminal Evidence Act 1984 which gives power to a judge to exclude 'unfair evidence' where the court considers that its admission 'would have such an adverse effect on the fairness of the proceedings that the court ought not to admit it.' The discretion has largely been used to exclude unreliable evidence rather than as a tool to persuade enforcement agencies to act within the law. In a recent case, for example, the court allowed the used of videotaped footage obtained by the police even though this was in breach of Codes of Practice and Article 8 of the European Convention[33], and the European Court of Human Rights has similarly refrained from holding that evidence obtained in breach of the Convention is thereby inadmissible in court proceedings.[34]

Even if surveillance by satellite were considered to intrude on rights of privacy according to Article 8(1), the Convention does not grant

---

[32] See Wadham (2000) 'Remedies for CCTV Surveillance' *New Law Journal* August 4 and August 11 2000 and Dodd (2002) 'Still life: For your eyes only' in 'Big Brother : The Secret State and the Assault on Privacy' Guardian Newspapers September 14 2002.

[33] *R v Loveridge and Lee* (2001) EWCA Crim 1034. As Lord Hope noted in *R v Sargent* (2001) UKHL 54, a case concerning the admissibility of evidence from unlawful telephone tapping : 'It is in the interests of everyone that serious crime should be effectively investigated and prosecuted. There must, of course, be fairness to all sides. But in the context of the criminal law the interests of the victim and the public interest must be taken into account as well as that of the accused. A rigid rule which excluded the use in all cases of all inadmissible intercepts at a person's interview would go further than was necessary to protect the accused. It could create an imbalance in his favour which would operate against the public interest, and that of the victim, when an alleged crime was being investigated. I do not think that a rule in such absolute terms can be justified.'

[34] *Schenk v Switzerland* (1988) 13 EHRR 242. In *Khan v UK* (2000) *Criminal Law Report* 68-1 (illegal surveillance of conversations), the European Court held that the discretionary powers under s 78 PACE were sufficient to ensure a fair trial.

unfettered rights. Article 8(2) provides a number of public interest justification including 'the prevention of disorder or crime', 'the protection of health or morals,' and 'the protection of the rights and freedoms or others.' No specific reference to the environment is made, and although the European Court has clearly held that the right to private life may include the right to a reasonable environmental quality for that life,[35] it is perhaps less obviously clear how it would handle claims that a breach of privacy was justifiable in order to protect the environmental quality of others. Nevertheless, especially where the enforcement of criminal law concerning environmental protection was involved, it seems likely that the public interest exceptions would apply, and the Court would be faced with applying a test of proportionality, essentially asking whether the degree of surveillance involved was justified by the nature of the public interest being protected. More troubling, perhaps, is the further requirement that any such interference with Article 8 rights must 'be in accordance with the law.' The lack of specific statutory provisions authorised the use of telephone tapping in the United Kingdom was found to be in breach of Article 8[36] – authorisation by the law implied explicit and transparent legal provisions rather than administrative procedures, and the decision required the introduction of new national legislation requiring warrants for carrying out telephone surveillance in respect of public telecommunications systems.[37] This approach to the need for specific statutory provisions concerning authorisations was confirmed by the European Court more recently in *Khan v United Kingdom*[38]

Against the background of human rights provisions, controversial recent legislation in the United Kingdom, the Regulation of Investigatory Powers Act 2000, has recently been passed in order to provide a more systematic means of regulating authorisations for the use of investigatory powers and with the establishment of Surveillance Commissioners to provide independent oversight.

Part II of the Act is concerned with surveillance, and distinguishes between 'directed surveillance' defined as being carried out for the purposes of specific investigation and operation and likely to result in the obtaining of private information, and 'intrusive surveillance' which refers to surveillance carried out in relation to anything taking place

[35] *Guerra v Italy* (1988) 26 EHRR 357.
[36] *Malone v United Kingdom* (1985) 7 EHRR 14.
[37] Interception of Communications Act 1985. This has now been replaced by more comprehensive provisions under Part I Regulation of Investigatory Powers Act 2000 which includes both public and private telecommunications systems, and was needed to comply with the judgment of the European Court of Human Rights in Halford v United Kingdom (1997) 24 EHRR 523.
[38] See n 34.

on residential premises. Both types of surveillance must be 'covert' to fall within the legislation, meaning that it is carried out in such a way 'to ensure that persons who are subject to the surveillance are unaware that it is or may be taking place.'[39] Although the Act does not require authorities to obtain authorisations for such operations, it is intended to ensure that if such authorisations are in fact obtained, the authority concerned will be guaranteed to have acted in compliance with the Human Rights Act. These aspects of the legislation have raised concern, and in any event it remains doubtful as to the extent to which the use of generalised remote sensing falls within the focused concepts of covert directed and intrusive surveillance defined in the legislation. Visible CCTV cameras, for example, would not appear to be covert within the meaning of the legislation, and in many cases are operated by private bodies for general preventative purposes – see, for example, the Home Office Code of Practice[40] which states, '…the provisions of the 2000 Act or of this code of practice do not normally cover the use of overt CCTV surveillance systems, since members of the public are aware that such systems are in use'. It is perhaps less obvious how members of the public would be aware of the existence of a surveillance satellite in the same way they are considered to be aware of (and implicitly consent to) the presence of CCTV cameras, but it is equally clear that the legislation was not drafted with the potential intrusiveness of satellite technology in mind.

Data Protection

Further legal issues of some complexity concerning privacy, data, and the use of remote sensing are to be met when considering the relevance of new data protection legislation. Under EC Directive 95/46/EC which came into force on March 1st 2000 and implemented in the United Kingdom by the Data Protection Act 1998, certain types of data processing systems must be registered, and with provisions concerning the fair obtaining of information, its retention, and the availability of copies to individual on personal data held by such systems. The Directive applies to 'personal data' meaning information relating to an identified or identifiable natural person and the 'processing of personal data' defined as any operation performed on personal data including collection, recording and storage[41], which has been processed by automatic means or within a filing system. Certainly in the United

---

[39] Regulation of Investigatory Powers Act 2000, s. 26(7).
[40] Home Offce (2002) Code of Practice on Covert Surveillance, which came into force August 1 2002. The Code acknowledges that where CCTV was being used by a public authority for specific investigatory purposes, authorizations under the Act might be necessary.
[41] Art. 2.

Kingdom, and under the domestic implementing legislation, it is accepted that CCTV systems falling within these basic concepts, and are liable to be registered with the Data Protection Registrar. It is less clear whether satellite imaging would fall within the controls, and much would depend on the interpretation of the concepts of personal data and their application to the type of images received. Again, on current resolutions, it may be dubious whether the provisions are applicable, but once such data is enriched or merged with information giving exact data on land use belong to an identified person the position might be different. Similarly, as resolutions become increasingly higher and are able to identify with precision individual parcels of land, it is arguable that the obligations are applicable.

The analogy between CCTV surveillance and the new generation of satellites, and the way in which law develops to balance the potential benefits to society from the new technology and the safeguards that individuals can legitimately expect needs is one that perhaps should not be taken too far. But there are some powerful similarities. In particular, public and private boundaries are no longer explicit, both in respect of the areas under surveillance and those responsible for operation.[42] Britain is considered to be the country with the most CCTV cameras in operations (perhaps some 300,000), and despite the developments of codes of practice, the legislative framework for their controlled use remains at an unsophisticated level, and a number of commentators expressing continuing concern with the adequacy of current arrangements.[43] Legislation such as the Regulation of Investigatory Powers Act 2000 is essentially aimed at action by public authorities rather than the private sector. Equally, the Human Rights Act 1998, implementing the European Convention, imposes duties on public authorities rather than the private sector. Here, though, the jurisprudence of the European Court of Human Rights has recognised that an artificial division between intrusions of privacy directly by public authorities and those made by private bodies would deprive the right of meaningful content, and has imposed positive obligations on the State to take action to protect those rights whatever the source of intrusion:

> The Court recalls that although the object of Article 8 is essentially that of protecting the individual against arbitrary interference by the public authorities, it does not merely compel the State to abstain from such interference: in addition to this primarily

---

[42] It is estimated, for example, that some 1000 satellites will be launched over the next decade, the vast majority being privately owned : Yaukey (2000) 'Satellites raise privacy questions' Gannet News Services, USA.

[43] See, for example, C Norris and G Armstrong (1999) *The Maximum Surveillance Society, the Rise of CCTV* Berg, Oxford, New York, D Lyon (2001) *Surveillance Society*, Polity Press, Cambridge.

negative obligation, there may be a positive obligation inherent in
an effective respect for private and family life. These obligations
may involve the adoption of measures designed to secure respect
for private life even in the sphere of the relations of individuals
between themselves.[44]

Governments, and indeed the courts, can clearly not wash their hands
of responsibility for ensuring legitimate protection of privacy even if the
private sector dominates the acquisition and exploitation of data from
remote sensing. Whatever the 'horizontal' duties of the State, in relation
to operations by the private sector, individuals may still, though, have
to rely on the protection of private civil law remedies. United Kingdom
law never developed an express tort of invasion of privacy, and others
forms of actions, such as trespass, libel, breach of confidence, have been
all been explored to protect personal privacy, particularly from the
press. More recently, though, the courts have been emboldened by these
provisions of the European Convention, and have apparently accepted
that the invasion of privacy should be recognised a distinct, though
qualified, right to be recognised by the courts.[45] And in doing so, the
courts have thrown doubt on a long standing decision that a landowner
had no rights of protection against aerial photographs being taken by
a private commercial operator on his property without consent on the
grounds that this did not amount to trespass.[46]

Gerd Winter himself has explored another legal aspect of the rich data
base that is obtained through satellite technology, which, as with CCTV,
is made more complex by the increasing privatisation of the industry.
In 'Access of the Public to Environmental Data from Satellite Remote
Sensing'[47], he explored the extent to which remote sensing information,
at least where it related to environmental matters, should be regarded 'as
part of the public sphere' rather than a commodity to be exploited and
sold, both as a matter of international, European and national law. In a
country such as the United Kingdom, the position is made more complex
because since the strong introduction of market force principles from
the 1980s even public sector bodies are expected to generate revenue
by the commercialisation of their data sets. In its most recent report,
the Royal Commission on Environmental Pollution[48] highlighted what

---

[44] *X v Netherlands* (1985) 8 EHRR 235, at 239-40. See also M Hunt (1998) 'The 'Horizontal
Effect' of the Human Rights Act' *Public Law* 423.
[45] See especially *Douglas v Hello* (2000) 9 BHRC 543 where the Court of Appeal refused
an injunction against a magazine publishing unauthorised wedding photographs,
but recognised that the claimants might still be able to secure damages for invasion of
privacy.
[46] *Bernstein v Skyviews and General Ltd* [1997] 2 All ER 902. see in particular, Sedley LJ in
Douglas v Hello, op.cit., at 119.
[47] (1994) 6 *Journal of Environmental Law* 43-54.
[48] RCEP (2002) 23rd Report *Environmental Planning* Cm 5459, HMSO London.

to them seemed a short-sighted situation where some public bodies were generating almost 60 per cent of their data sales through contracts with other public sector bodies, described as 'a merry-go-round of public finances with no net benefit and high transaction costs in which the full value of environmental information is not being realised.'[49] In this context, environmental law has provided a number of progressive pointers, notably within the European Community with the principles of public access to environmental information held by public bodies under the Directive of Access to Environmental Information[50] Similarly at international level, Principles X and XI of the 1986 UN Resolution 41/65 on Remote Sensing of the Earth from Outer Space contain explicit obligations on states to disclose information to other states which could advert environmentally harmful phenomenon or natural disasters. But as Gerd Winter notes, both the EC Directive and the UN Resolution were largely cast to reflect the obligations of the public sector and the State, and are less meaningful where the private sector and the market dominates the activity of data acquisition and processing. In this context, Gerd Winter concluded that 'remote sensing information should be seen not only as an economic good but also as an important element of public discourses.'[51] These sentiments resonate even more strongly as we enter an era of far higher resolution and more pervasive sensing technology. The environmental benefits to society are potentially immense, but unless we see concurrent developments in the legal frameworks for authenticity, privacy, and data access which anticipate both the nature of the technology and the structure of the industry, they are benefits that may not be fully realised or will be acquired at too high a price.

---

[49] Para 6.18 ibid.
[50] 90/313/EEC.
[51] G Winter (1994) op. cit. at 55.

CHAPTER 11

THE SCOPE OF ENVIRONMENTAL LAW*

1.   Introduction

Academic and practising lawyers in nearly all European countries now recognise that environmental law represents a distinctive and significant body of law and legal principle. Yet, when it comes to trying to define the boundaries of the subject, it is clear that there is little in the way of agreement. Certain commonly agreed elements exist such as the regulation of polluting activities by man and the protection of natural assets such as wildlife or landscapes, and these fields of law are what many environmental lawyers would describe as their core concerns. However, it is equally clear that there are many other areas of regulatory law such as health and safety at work, land-use planning, the protection of the manmade cultural heritage, and consumer protection law which have substantial environmental implications, even if environmental protection, as many would understand it, is not their sole focus. Looking further afield, the principles upon which apparently unconnected areas of law, such as competition or trade law, operate may be far from neutral in their potential impacts on the environment.

The need to integrate an environmental dimension into areas of policy hitherto largely unaffected by such concerns is one that is increasingly recognized by many countries, although the task is far from easy to achieve. In this chapter, I outline a number of legal considerations that appear to be involved in the challenge of integration. My underlying argument is that those who study and practise environmental law should be wary of limiting their attention to boundaries of law that are so narrowly confined that they fail to address what may prove ultimately to be far more significant issues of concern.

2.   Integrated Pollution Control

In the context of environmental law and policy there are different notions of what can be implied by integration. A significant element of environmental law is the regulation of industrial pollution, most

---

* R Macrory (1996) The Scope of Environmental Law in G Winter (ed) *European Environmental Law* Dartmouth, Aldershot, pp 3-14

commonly by means of various forms of consents or permits. The development of this type of pollution legislation has taken place at different times in different European countries, with examples in some countries to be found in the nineteenth century but with a rapid growth in scope and complexity in the last 30 years. The initial driving force behind such pollution controls was often a concern for the protection of human health and, at a later stage, the incorporation of wider environmental considerations. But common to many national legal systems is the extent to which such pollution laws regulate discharges into the environmental media of air, water and land on a quite distinct legislative basis, with different laws often being developed at different times. The UK, for example, had legislation regulating industrial discharges into the atmosphere dating back to the mid-nineteenth century, while a detailed regulatory system controlling discharges into waters did not appear until the early 1950s. No specialist controls over waste disposal on land emerged until the 1970s. These specialist controls are frequently enforced and applied by different agencies. The drawback of such a legal structure is that it may lead to inconsistent decision making and ignore or fail to consider the cross-media impact of control strategies, leading to results which are sub-optimal from an environmental perspective.

In 1975 the UK Royal Commission on Environmental Pollution identified these concerns, and coined the term, the *Best Practicable Environmental Option* (BPEO) as an appropriate criterion for the goal of all pollution control strategies.[1] It took some 15 years for the Commission's legal and institutional recommendations for the implementation of this approach to be fully taken on board by government. Part I of the Environmental Protection Act 1990 introduced the concept of *integrated pollution control* under which discharges of pollutants from specified industries into water, air and land are regulated by a single licence issued by a single authority.

Other countries, such as the Netherlands, have introduced 'one stop' licences for industrial discharges, and in 1993 the European Commission proposed European Community legislation which would introduce integrated pollution control throughout the Union.[2] The main aim of the proposal is to protect water, air and land against pollution from certain types of industries by introducing an integrated permitting regime and, as an underlying harmonising principle, requiring industry to employ

---

[1] Royal Commission on Environmental Pollution, *Air Pollution Control - An Integrated* ; *Approach*, 5th Report, London: HMSO, 1976. See also the Commission's follow-up j report, *Best Practicable Environmental Option*, 12th Report, London: HMSO, 1988.

[2] Proposal for a Council Directive on Integrated Pollution and Control, Com (93)230, 14 September 1992.

the 'best available techniques' of pollution prevention. At the time of writing the proposal has still not been agreed by Member States, and it is likely to be some years before the type of integration required by the proposed Directive is converted into a legal requirement throughout Member States.

But even where distinct legislation has existed for different pathways of industrial discharges, the obligation to conduct environmental assessment procedures for new projects, as required under the 1985 European Community Directive on the subject[3] has inevitably required a degree of integration. Where the Directive applies, the type of information generally required as part of the assessment process before consent is given for the project to proceed includes, *inter alia*, 'an estimate, by type and quantity, of expected residues and emissions (water, air and soil pollution, noise, vibration, light, heat, radiation, etc.) resulting from the operation of the proposed project'. The Directive does not oblige Member States to establish a single, unified consent procedure for projects subject to environmental assessment, but at the very least requires them to ensure improved coordination between decision-making agencies.

In countries such as the UK, where the assessment procedures were largely integrated into an existing land-use planning consent system rather than the specialist regulatory controls over pollution, the link between land-use planning and the pollution implications of land-based developments has been strengthened by the requirements.

Improved coordination between different pollution control agencies, the reorganisation of such bodies into unified agencies[4] and the establishment of 'one-stop' pollution consent procedures are developments that are now likely to take place in many jurisdictions, and represent one form, though a limited one, of integration.

3.   Codification

A further development of the concept of environmental integration may now be seen in a trend towards the codification of environmental legislation. At the very least, this may involve an updated restatement of existing laws into a single body of law and the removal of the

---

[3] Council Directive 85/337 of 27 June 1985 on the assessment of the effects of certain private and public projects on the environment, OJ L 175/40, 5 July 1985.

[4] See, for example, the creation of the French environmental agency, the Agence de l'Environnement et de la Maitrise de 1'Energie in 1990 and the establishment of the Irish Environmental Protection Agency in 1990.

more overt inconsistencies. For example, it was only recently that the European Community passed legislation which attempted to introduce a greater degree of harmonisation and standardisation concerning the requirements under various Community environmental Directives for Member States to provide regular national reports to the Commission containing the results of monitoring in the sector covered by the Directive in question.[5] Previously there were some glaring inconsistencies between different items of legislation even within the same general field; for example, Member States had an obligation to make regular reports concerning the state of bathing waters under the Bathing Water Directive, but no similar obligation in respect of drinking water under the Drinking Water Directive.

But, as Kiss and Shelton note: 'Codification involves more than the reproduction and restatement of applicable statutory texts; instead it constitutes a systematic consolidation and revision of the law, a major legislative effort.'[6] Examples of a moderate form of integration can been seen in the type of framework legislation adopted by Portugal in 1987, the Lei de Bases do Ambiente. Current work in Belgium, undertaken by the Interuniversity Commission for the Revision of Environmental Law in the Flemish Region, represents a more ambitious approach towards codification seeking to articulate underlying principles as well as consistent procedures.[7]

Yet, however laudable, even this approach towards codification generally restricts itself to the more familiar boundaries of pollution and nature protection legislation. This is not to underrate the intellectual challenges involved in such a task but, again, it by no means represents the full implication of environmental integration.

4.   Integration Into Other Policies Affecting The Environment

4.1   Article 130r Treaty of Rome

In 1985 the European Commission proposed to the heads of states and government that, as a basis of Community environmental policy, 'Protection of the environment is to be treated as an integral part of economic and social policies both overall (at macro economic level) and by individual sector (agricultural policy, industrial policy, energy policy, etc.); the point must be made that an active policy for the protection and

---

[5] Directive 91/692 OJL 377, p. 48 1991.
[6] A. Kiss, D. Shelton, *Manual of European Environmental Law*, Cambridge: Grotius Publications, 1993, p. 49.
[7] A Conference on the Codification of Environmental Law was held by the University of Ghent in early 1995.

improvement of the environment can help economic growth and job creation'.[8] This proposal eventually led to the insertion into the Treaty of Rome, following the Single European Act 1987, of the provision that 'Environmental protection requirements shall be a component of the Community's other policies'.[9] The requirement was altered and, I would argue, strengthened under the version of the Treaty as amended by the Maastricht Treaty, and coming into force on 1 January 1993, and now reads, 'Environmental protection requirements must be integrated into the definition and implementation of other Community policies'.[10] Similar integration requirements concerning culture have been introduced under Article 128 of the Treaty which requires that 'The Community shall take cultural aspects into account in its activities under other provisions of this Treaty', and concerning public health where, under Article 129, 'Health protection requirements shall form a constituent part of the Community's other policies'.

This environmental provision under Article 130r clearly represents a far more ambitious notion of integration than either the moves towards the coordination of pollution control or the codification of environmental laws described above. It is a challenging statement of principle and legal obligation which has yet to be replicated in the national legislation of many countries and has been described as perhaps the most important of all the environmental provisions contained in the European Treaty.[11] Yet, as Ludwig Kramer noted in his commentary on the 1987 version, '...the medium- to long-term consequences of this principle for the Community are a matter of speculation for the moment'.[12] Certainly, if one looks at the potential environmental impacts of important aspects of the Community's sectoral policies such as fisheries and transport, it is far from clear that any serious move towards environmental integration has yet been made. The longer-term environmental implications of those policies remain immense.

4.2   Principle of Law or Policy?

To a large extent such a statement of broad principle, even though expressed in legal language, is bound to be more an expression of policy aspiration than a specific legally binding requirement capable

---

[8] *Bulletin of the European Communities*, No. 3, 1985, p. 101.

[9] Second para., Art. 130r, European Treaty (pre-Maastricht).

[10] Third para., Art. 130r, Treaty Establishing the European Community as amended by the Treaty on European Union.

[11] N. Haigh, *EEC Environmental Policy and Britain*, (2nd edn), London: Longman, 1987, p.11.

[12] L. Kramer, *EEC Treaty and Environmental Protection*, London: Sweet and Maxwell, 1990, p. 65.

of enforcement by conventional legal routes.[13] Provided policy makers take at least some account of potential environmental consequences, courts are unlikely to wish to become overinvolved in determining the extent to which this should take place. Nevertheless, this does not mean that such a principle is devoid of legal consequence.

4.3   Legitimising Environmental Integration

An important area of potential legal dispute within the European Community concerns the identification of the correct Treaty legal provision on which to base subsidiary legislation. The choice of the legal basis is especially significant since it will determine the political procedures that must be followed for the adoption of the proposed measure, and different provisions in the Treaty provide quite distinct procedures giving differing voting requirements and differing degrees of influence to the Community institutions, notably the European Parliament.[14] Despite the political implications of the choice of legal basis, the European Court of Justice has consistently held that this choice must be based on objective factors amenable to judicial review rather than consideration of politics.[15] In *Greece v. EC Council*,[16] it was argued by the Member State that a Community regulation restricting imports of agricultural products from third countries following the Chernobyl nuclear accident should not have been adopted under Article 113 of the Treaty, dealing with common commercial policies, but should have more appropriately been based on either the express environmental provisions under the Treaty or under the parallel Euratom Treaty dealing with nuclear matters. The European Court upheld Article 113 as a correct legal basis, and rejected the idea that, because there was a clear environmental dimension to the measure, it should have been treated as part of the Community's express environmental programme of action. In so doing, the Court invoked the integration requirement in Article 130r: 'That provision which reflects the principle whereby all Community measures must satisfy the requirements of environmental protection, implies that a Community measure cannot be part of a Community action on environmental matters merely because it takes into account those requirements.'

---

[13] See L. Kramer, *EC Treaty and Environmental Law,* (2nd edn), London: Sweet and Maxwell, 1995, p. 59.

[14] See M. Hession, R. Macrory, 'Maastricht and the Environmental Policy of the Community: Legal Issues of a new Environmental policy', in D. O'Keefe (ed.), *Legal Issues of the Maastricht Treaty,* London: Chancery Publications, 1994. [15] *Commission v. Council,* (1987) ECR 1493.

[16] (1990) 1 ECR 1527.

4.4   Ensuring Environmental Integration

Such a legal analysis supports the legitimacy of environmental integration where it takes place. Policy makers who produce legislation in other sectors with strong environmental associations, such as transport or agriculture, will find their action less vulnerable to legal challenge on the grounds that such considerations were not legally relevant. But one task for environmental law in the future is to devise suitable provisions and techniques which will help to ensure that this process continues to take place to a far greater extent than at present, rather than to merely enable it to take place when policy makers so wish.

Implementing environmental integration principles

One approach is to supplement broad general statements of principles with far more express environmental requirements in subsidiary, 'non-environmental' legislation. For example, Article 7 of Regulation 2052/88, governing the distribution of structural funds within the Community, provides that

> measures financed by the Structural Funds or receiving assistance from the European Investment Bank or from another existing financial instrument shall be in keeping with the provisions of the Treaties, with the instruments adopted pursuant thereto and with Community policies, including those concerning the rules on competition, the award of public contracts and environmental protection.

This is clearly an important requirement which attempts to ensure greater consistency between policies on financial aid and the environment although, in reality, it has not proved easy to implement, not least because structural funds are given on the basis of regional programmes prepared by Member States whereas identifiable environmental impacts are often associated with specific projects which emerge from such programmes, probably at a later date.[17]

Nevertheless, the requirement provided the basis for a legal challenge by environmental groups before the European Court of Justice in 1994 - the first time that such a case had been brought. In Case T-461/93 *An Taisce* (the National Trust for Ireland) *and Worldwide Fund for Nature v. European Commission*,[18] two associations were concerned about the environmental implications of the proposed construction of an

---

[17] See Kramer (1995), *op.cit*, p. 29.
[18] Judgment of the Court of First Instance, 23 September 1994.

interpretative centre in a National Park which was to be financed under structural funds already approved by the European Commission under a Programme for Tourism submitted by the Irish government. The groups had alerted the Commission, and challenged what they alleged to be the Commission's decision not to withdraw the structural fund support on the grounds that the proposals were inconsistent with the requirements of the Structural Fund Regulation concerning compliance with Community environmental programmes. In the event, the Court decided that the Commission had not in fact taken any decision not to withdraw funds and that they were entitled to do so at any time, even after completion of the works. Since the case was rejected on its facts, the Court therefore did not have to determine whether the applicants had legal standing before the Court to bring such a case – clearly an extremely significant issue. However, despite the result of the case, it did underline the extent to which the integration requirements within the Structural Fund Regulation potentially have real legal purchase.

4.4.1 Enriching procedures

Another legal technique that may be employed to ensure improved integration is the use of procedural requirements in connection with policy and similar proposals in other sectors. The 1985 Community Directive on Environmental Assessment is expressly limited to proposals for projects such as industrial works and road schemes, but there has been considerable discussion concerning the possible extension of such assessment requirements to cover a much broader category of plans, policies and programmes. To date, any further development on such proposals appears to have been resisted within the European Commission, and would almost certainly be opposed by a number of Member States.

However, in dealing with policies at EU level, the parties to the Maastricht Treaty noted in one of its Declarations 'that the Commission undertakes in its proposals, and that the Member-State undertakes in implementing those proposals, to take full account of their environmental impact and the principle of sustainable growth'. In June 1993 the European Commission adopted internal administrative practices which were aimed at assisting the meeting of those goals; the measures included a commitment by the Commission to describe and justify the significant environmental impacts of proposed legislation, and the appointment of officials within each Directorate-General of the Commission with a specific responsibility to ensure that their Directorate takes on board the principle of environmental integration.

This sort of administrative management has been reflected at national level. In 1991 The UK Department of the Environment published a document intended to encourage other government departments to assess the environmental implications of their policies in a more systematic manner than had hitherto been the case,[19] and so-called 'Green Ministers' were nominated in each department. The document was followed up in 1994 with a series of case studies illustrating how such environmental appraisals were being carried out.[20] Yet the reality of the extent to which such a greening of government has genuinely taken place, against the background of such initiatives, has been consistently challenged.[21] To take one example, the 1994 report of the Royal Commission on Environmental Pollution on Transport and the Environment[22] provided a powerful critique of the extent to which UK transport trends were environmentally unsustainable in the longer run, and took to task the Department of Transport for failing 'to provide this country with an effective and environmentally sound transport policy'.[23]

4.4.2 Forming environmental integration principles

Another example of a legal technique designed to ensure greater environmental integration across departmental interests is the imposition of general duties concerning the environment. An early example to be found in British legislation is the provision in section 11 of the Countryside Act 1968 that 'In the exercise of their functions relating to land under any enactment every Minister, government department and public body shall have regard to the desirability of conserving the natural beauty and amenity of the countryside'. Although the parliamentary debates during the discussion of the provision displayed a surprising degree of passion and conflict,[24] the blandness and generality of the duty has meant that it is effectively unenforceable in law, and it is difficult to pinpoint any real effect that it has had on decision making over the years. Nevertheless, such broadly based duties, even if non-enforceable in a conventional sense, may still, as Ross Cranston has noted, give

---

[19] Department of the Environment, *Policy Appraisal and the Environment,* London: HMSO, 1991.

[20] Department of the Environment, *Environmental Appraisal in Government Departments* , London: HMSO, 1994.

[21] See, for example, J. Hill, M. Jordan, 'The Greening of Government: Lessons from the White Paper Process,' *ECOS,* 14, 1993.

[22] Royal Commission on Enviromnental Pollution, *Eighteenth Report: Transport and the Environment,* Cm. 2674, London: HMSO, 1994.

[23] ibid. para. 13.65.

[24] See R. Macrory, *Loaded Guns and Monkeys: Responsible Environmental Law,* London: Imperial College Centre for Environmental Technology, 1994. See also chap. 8 above.

'legitimacy to aspirations ... and can provide a backdrop against which specific decisions with legal consequence can be made'.[25]

In the mid-1980s there was an extended period of political controversy in Britain over the environmental implications of modern agricultural practices, criticism being focused on the relevant government department, the Ministry of Agricultural, Fisheries and Food, which was perceived to have sacrificed environmental concerns in favour of agricultural productivity. As one response, the government eventually introduced legislation which imposed a general duty on the minister to endeavour to achieve a reasonable balance between conservation, rural and agricultural interests.[26] Again, such a duty may be perceived as more of a gravitational rule rather than a enforceable legal obligation legitimising internal shifts of resources and priorities within a department. Certainly discussions with officials can frequently reveal the very real significance that such a duty can have on the internal administrative workings of such an organisation. But the difficulty with the implementation of such duties is not to devalue them by overuse, and in their drafting to achieve a sensible balance between being overgeneralised (and thereby ineffective or open to too many differing interpretations) and so specific that they lose the power to inject an environmental dimension across a broad area of activity.

5.   Integration into Policies with Remote Environmental Impact

In reality there is no single or optimum solution that will ensure greater environmental sensitivity across different industrial and economic sectors. A combination of broadly based legal principles, procedural requirements and the types of administrative restructuring described above must all contribute to reinforcing aspirational goals which are easy to state but infinitely less so to achieve.

But the challenge for environment law can go further. The types of measures so far taken to ensure integration tend to focus on the policies and decisions of non-environmental departments (whether at national or Community level) which demonstrably have significant physical impacts on the environment, energy, transport and agriculture being clear examples. Effective integration, however, goes deeper and implies that other areas of law must now be examined to determine the extent

---

[25] R. Cranston, *Law, Government and Public Policy*, Melbourne: Oxford University Press, 1987.
[26] Agriculture Act 1986, s. 13.

to which they are environmentally neutral or incur actual benefits or dis-benefits.

The potential conflict between free trade and environmental protection is one that is familiar at international level, and within the Community has had to be tackled by the European Court of Justice. In the landmark 1988 case of *Commission* v. *Denmark*[27] the European Court expressly permitted a Member State to introduce legislation concerning the recycling of drink cans even though it would have had some restrictive impact on the fundamental principle in the European Community Treaty concerning the freedom of movement of goods. A later case upheld the right of a regional authority to restrict the import of wastes from other regions and countries into its area on the grounds that such unrestricted free movement would have severe environmental consequence.[28]

Competition policy must similarly be examined. Article 85 of the European Community Treaty contains a general prohibition of price-fixing and similar agreements between competitive undertakings, but permits certain agreements which contribute 'to improving the production or distribution of goods or to promoting technical or economic progress, while allowing consumers a fair share of the resulting benefit'. The European Commission has now had to consider to what extent these latter conditions were fulfilled where environmental aims were involved, and in at least one case has confirmed this to be the case.[29] Ludwig Kramer[30] has also noted that the application of competition law principles to the types of voluntary environmental agreements and covenants between industry and government bodies, as favoured in some countries such as the Netherlands, is a new area of potential conflict that has yet to be fully explored.

In the search for integration, however, one can take a more profound approach which demands that the underlying rationale for principles that govern a much broader spectrum of law is examined to determine to what extent they are consistent with the contemporary challenge of the environment. Gerd Winter[31] has noted the extent to which modern environmental law takes an interventionist, regulatory form which has been imposed upon, and restrains, 'the inventiveness and energy of the individual'. The encouragement and release of such inventiveness had been one of the driving forces behind many developments of the law,

---

[27] Case 302/86 (1988), ECR 4607.

[28] Case C-2/90 *Commission v. Belgium* (1992), 1 ECR 4431.

[29] *XXIInd Report on Competition Policy 1992*, European Commission 1993.

[30] Kramer (1995), *op.cit*, p. 30.

[31] See G. Winter, Perspectives for Environmental Law - Entering the Fourth Phase, *Journal of Environmental law* 1 p 38, 1989.

particularly in the nineteenth century in countries such as Germany and the UK, and can be found in such diverse areas as patent legislation, corporation law and the promotion of freedom of trade. He argues that, set against the scale of environmental problems now facing society, the regulatory, interventionist approach cannot wholly succeed, and that it will be necessary to re-examine those underlying and pre-existing areas of law to ensure that they are more environmentally sensitive: 'The emancipatory law must therefore be inoculated with ecological considerations.'[32] This approach to integration has taken us a long way from the tentative moves towards seeking greater consistency between laws regulating discharges into water and air. Yet, ironically perhaps, the argument reflects, at a deeper level, the debate that has already taken place in the much narrower context of pollution control where the heavy reliance on 'end of pipe' solutions as a means of controlling discharges is seen ultimately to have only a limited role, and the fact that it is preferable to examine the total industry process to ensure improved waste minimisation and an eventual reduced burden on the environment. Environmental law, as it is conventionally written about and analysed, may represent a discrete and bounded field of law, but one role of the true environmental lawyer is to be prepared to re-examine all fields of law from an environmental perspective - ultimately, this is implication of the integration principle.

---

[32] ibid. p.45.

CHAPTER 12

CYCLE LORE*

The past few years has seen a remarkable revival in the use of the bicycle[1] in urban areas. Hoping no doubt to cut down on both transport costs and coronaries, many people now cycle to work, and there are even a fair number of bicycles to be seen chained to railings in the Temple. An All-party Parliamentary Cycle Group was established recently in the House of Commons, and staff solely concerned with cycles have been appointed at the Department of Transport. But as politicians and planners begin to examine seriously better ways of protecting and encouraging the cyclist, a number of intriguing problems and uncertainties have been revealed in the present law relating to cycles.

The legal difficulties surrounding the construction of cycle racks is just one example — though happily one that has now been resolved by the Transport Act 1978. Under the Road Traffic Regulation Act 1967, highway authorities possess general powers to provide on-street parking for all types of vehicles, including cycles. But the erection of a cycle-rack on the side of a carriageway or footway (ie the pavement) would create an obstruction of the highway, and a long line of cases has established that public authorities who wish to create such obstructions must have explicit statutory authority to do so. For instance, the statutory power to provide public lavatories in 'proper and convenient' places was held not to be sufficient to authorise their construction on any part of the highway: *Vernon v St James Westminster Vestry* (1860) 16 Ch 449. Public authorities have been given express powers in a number of statutes to erect street furniture such as traffic signs, lamp stands, bus-shelters and even, under the Public Health Act 1925, 'troughs for watering horses and cattle'. Somehow, they were never given similar powers to erect cycle-racks (though it is arguable that s 46 of the Road Traffic Regulation Act 1967 gives parish councils sufficiently explicit powers), and most highway authorities are therefore unwilling to construct cycle-racks on roads or pavements, even when this might be the most convenient position; one London borough council, however, eager to provide for cyclists, was known studiously to ignore the concern of their legal department, should a pedestrian be injured by such an illegal obstruction.

---

* R Macrory (1979) Cycle Lore, *New Law Journal*, June 21, 1979, 602-604
[1] This article is mainly concerned with bicycles, though the term 'cycle' would include tricycles and other pedal-powered vehicles.

The position over cycle-racks has now at long last been cleared up by the Transport Act 1978, s 12 of which provides, 'The powers of any authority under the Road Traffic Regulation Act 1967 to provide parking places shall extend to providing, in roads and elsewhere, stands and racks for bicycles'.

The cyclist who is on the search for newly erected cycle-racks may also experience some legal difficulties. Section 76 of the Highway Act 1835 makes riding a cycle on the footway a criminal offence, and despite the antiquity of the statute, it remains the main control over this activity.[2] Surprisingly, it may also be illegal to wheel or push a cycle along a pavement, since s 76 goes on to make it an offence to 'drive . . . any carriage' on the footway. A cycle is certainly 'a carriage' for the purposes of this section: *Taylor* v *Goodwin* (1879) 4 QBD 228, while the meaning of 'drive', a term which appears in a number of traffic offences, has been considered by the court in several cases, though all concerning motor vehicles. At one time these suggested that a person pushing a vehicle could be said to drive it, provided it was subject to his control and direction – a test that would include someone wheeling a cycle. But in *R v McDonagh* [1974] QB 448, an appeal from a conviction of driving while disqualified, the Divisional Court disapproved of an artificial use of the word. Where,

> ... the defendant was walking beside a vehicle which was being pushed or moving by gravity, we do not think that the mere fact that he had his hand on the steering wheel is enough to say he was driving in any ordinary sense of the word. (Lord Widgery CJ at p 452).

The Court went on to say that someone pushing a motorcycle, an example of a vehicle which 'must from [its] nature be manhandled from time to time', could not be said to 'drive' it in the context of licence and insurance offences. Despite this ruling, it could be argued that since the Highway Act 1835 creates an offence specifically designed to protect the rights of the pedestrian to free passage of the footway, the term, 'drive', in s 76 should be given a broader interpretation than in other traffic offences. At least one local authority is reported to be unhappy at exercising their new powers to erect cycle-racks on the pavement, because this would encourage cyclists to commit what, in its opinion, is the illegal act of pushing a cycle across the footway. And, while the writer has yet to hear of someone being successfully prosecuted for this, there was a cyclist in 1973 who was stopped by a policeman when pushing his bicycle along a pavement in Farnborough; he was later sent

---

[2] Written Answer, John Horam (Under-Secretary of State for Transport) House of Commons, 11/11/77.

a letter by the officer-in-charge, advising him that he had committed an offence under the Highway Act 1835, and trusting that, 'in future you will be more careful'.

The cyclist who wheels his machine across a zebra crossing appears to be at a legal disadvantage in comparison to pedestrians. The Pedestrian Crossing Regulations (SI 1971/1524) provide that, 'Every footpassenger on the carriageway within the limits of an uncontrolled pedestrian crossing shall have precedence within those limits over any vehicle and the driver shall accord such precedence to the footpassenger if the footpassenger is on the carriageway. . . .' Failure to give way to a footpassenger in these circumstances is an offence, but there is no statutory definition of the term, 'footpassenger', and it is unclear whether it would include someone pushing a cycle. The only reported case of relevance is *McKerril v Robertson* 1956 SLT 290, a Scottish case concerning similarly worded regulations. A driver was charged with failing to give way to a footpassenger on a zebra-crossing, namely a woman who had just pushed a child's go-chair onto the crossing. The court rejected the defence that she was not a foot passenger:

> In my view this is much too strict a construction of the regulations in question and would produce anomalous, if not ridiculous results. In my view it is essential to treat this lady and the go-chair which she was controlling as parts of one entity.

But it is possible to argue that a cycle, essentially treated in law as a vehicle to be ridden on the carriageway, is distinguishable from a go-chair or pram which cannot but be pushed by a pedestrian. *Wilkinson on Road Traffic Offences* (9th ed) supports this view at p 451, and in 1977 Staffordshire magistrates dismissed a charge, where a driver had failed to give way to a woman pushing a cycle across a zebra-crossing, on the grounds that she was not a 'footpassenger' for the purpose of the regulations.

Cyclists are often seen to dismount at traffic lights showing red, and push their machines across the junction. It is uncertain whether they thereby commit an offence, under s 22 of the Road Traffic Act 1972, of failing to comply with prescribed traffic regulation signs. And what of the cyclists who pushes his bicycle in the road – carefully avoiding the pavement and a possible charge under the Highway Act 1835 – the wrong way up a one-way street? A prosecution on these facts has been successful in a magistrates' court, reported in CXI JPJ 679

But it is probably the highway authorities, seeking to make positive plans for the cyclist, who suffer most from some of the present uncertainties in the law. The variety of schemes that can help cyclists has recently been outlined by the government,[3] but the legal method of implementing these schemes is by no means clear in all cases.

Section 66 of the Highways Act 1959 gives highway authorities specific power to construct 'cycle-tracks', but only 'in or by the side of' an existing highway. Some authorities are known to have been discouraged from building cycle-tracks which do not follow existing roads because of this apparent limitation in the Highways Act. However, it has been pointed out that authorities possess general powers to construct 'highways' under s 26 of the Act, and since a 'cycle-track' is defined in s 295 as a 'way *constituting* or comprised in a highway', the s 26 powers are available to build cycle-tracks that do not run beside a road.

There is not always the space or finance to build a new cycle-track, and, in some circumstances, it may make planning sense to move the cyclist off the carriageway and onto part of the footway beside the road. This might be appropriate where, say, there is a busy main road with a little-used, but wide pavement. But this cannot be achieved by simply painting a white line down the footway and revoking any existing bye-laws which may forbid cycling on the pavement. The 1835 statutory offence still remains, and anyone may bring a prosecution under the Act. Furthermore, it has been held that the fact that no pedestrian was present at the time of the alleged offence, and that the cyclist was exercising all due care is not a good defence: *McKee v McGrath* (1892) 30 LR Ir 41.

In these circumstances, it seems that the authority must 'remove' a proportion of the footway, using their powers under s 67(3) of the Highways Act, and then construct a cycle-track under s 66. But the powers under s 66 are limited to 'constructing', and there is no statutory definition of the term. It may be uneconomical to lay a new surface, but 'construct' seems to imply something more than simply painting white lines and erecting appropriate signs. As yet, the point does not appear to have been discussed in English courts, though a New Zealand case, *Kerridge Odeon Corpn Ltd v Auckland City* [1966] NZLR 266, concerned with building regulations, provides some guidance.

> Giving the phrase, 'construction of a building', its ordinary signification and natural meaning, I am of the opinion that it connotes something different from maintenance, repairs or alteration to an existing building or portion thereof' (per Greason J at p 269).

---

[3] Local Transport No'e 1/78 'Ways of Helping Cyclists in Built-up Areas' (Dept of Transport, Nov 1978).

The division of an existing pavement may not be possible if it is quite narrow. Where the pedestrian flow is extremely small, it may still sometimes be safer to allow cyclists to ride on it, but with an obligation to give way to pedestrians. Present traffic law does not appear to make provision for such a concept, and the closest analogy is that of bridleways, on which cyclists may ride but must give way to both persons on horse-back or foot (Countryside Act 1968, s 30(1). But the conversion of such footways into bridleways hardly seems an elegant solution.

A footpath (defined in the Highways Act 1959 as 'a highway over which the public have rights of way on fool only, not being a footway') also presents difficulties to the planner. In contrast to footways, cycling on footpaths is not a criminal offence, though it is probably actionable in nuisance and trespass, and may well be prohibited by local bye-laws. In some cases, it may be sensible to permit the use of cycles on footpaths, but there appears to be no general power in highway law to upgrade a footpath to a bridle-way or other form of highway on which cyclists have a right to ride. The solution suggested by the Department of Transport (Local Transport Note 1/78) is that the local authority should first obtain planning permission for development entailing a change of use of the footpath into a way usable by vehicles: 'The footpath could then be stopped up by an order under s 209 or s 210 of the Town and Country Planning Act 1971, and a new way provided along the same route but usable by a wider category of traffic'.

The law has to try to reflect the sometimes conflicting interests of users of the highway, whether they be on foot, cycle, or motor-vehicle. But the cycle possesses some unusual characteristics: it is extremely vulnerable to motor-traffic, is easily pushed or wheeled, but when ridden, potentially dangerous to pedestrians (though studies of foreign mixed cyclist – pedestrian facilities show surprisingly low accident rates). The special needs of the cyclist appear to have been somewhat neglected in traffic law, and for those highway authorities who now wish to initiate cycle schemes, especially in urban areas, some of the present legal difficulties may prove discouraging obstacles. Perhaps the time has come for a revival of the type of delightful but important case which was often brought by (and sometimes against) cyclists towards the turn of the century, at a time when the cycle had yet to feel the squeeze of the motor vehicle. Cases such as *Cannon v Earl of Abingdon* [1900] 2 QB 66, where an imaginative cyclists' club determined to test the applicability of an Act, authorising the Earl of Abingdon to collect tolls on a bridge over the Thames, to a number of different kinds of cycle. The Act provided a toll of 2d for 'carriages with less than four wheels', but no charge for the driver or any person riding in a carriage. The following cycles were solemnly ridden over the bridge: a bicycle carrying the rider alone; a bicycle with a valise fitted to its frame; a tricycle carrying the rider alone; a trademan's tricycle with a box fitted to its frame for carrying goods; and, finally, a bath-chair tricycle with a passenger (as well as the rider) seated in it. Unfortunately for the club's finances, in a special case stated for the opinion of the Court, all were held to be 'carriages with less than four wheels' within the meaning of the Act.

PART 4

THE COURTS AND THE ENVIRONMENT

Courts play a critical role in interpreting legislation and developing substantive principles of law, and in this country the last twenty years has seen an ever-growing influence of the higher courts in the environmental field. For many years I have reported on significant case law in the monthly environmental intelligence journal ENDS Report, and this chapter contains a selection of reports over the last decade as written at the time but with some additional footnote references. These of course are by means all of the important environmental decisions, but are intended to provide an impression of the range of issues the judiciary are faced with, and how they tackle them.

The period has seen an enormous growth in the scope and important of European Community environmental legislation, and as the final arbiter of the meaning of Community law, decisions of the European Court of Justice are critical. The European Court has generally been seen as environmentally progressive, though its reasoning can often be obscure and frustrating[1], as witnessed by the Court of Appeal's recent attempts in the OSS case to derive coherence from the ECJ's jurisprudence on when a recycled waste ceased to be waste in law. The influence of the European Treaty's environmental integration principle, discussed in more detail in the next chapter, can be seen in such cases as Concordia Bus *(competition law) and* British Aggregates *(environmental taxes and state aid). The distinctive enforcement mechanisms against Member States who fail to implement Community obligations are considered in Part 6, and the European Court of Justice remains the only supra-national court in the world which can directly impose financial penalties on states that fail to comply with its judgements.* Commission v Greece *was the first decision of the Court to use its new powers to impose such a penalty.*

One of the recent high points demonstrating the significance of Community environmental law in a national context was the 2000 House of Lords decision in Berkeley *dealing with the environmental assessment. There had been a failure to apply the requirements of the Directive, and the House of Lords, recognizing the public participation rights that were inherent in the European concept of environmental assessment, quashed the decision in question, refusing to follow the more traditional approach of British courts to exercise*

---

[1] For a recent review by the former British Advocate General see Francis Jacobs (2006) The Role of the European Court of Justice in the Protection of the Environment. *Journal of Environmental Law Journal of Environmental Law* Vol 18 pp 185-205

their discretion to uphold a decision on the grounds that the planning authority had all the necessary information and the result would not have been different had the proper procedures been followed. Yet the courts have been wary of allowing such an approach to give a green light to third parties looking for any procedural fault as an excuse to quash a controversial planning decision, as evidenced by Lord Justice Carnwath's comments in the 2003 Mansfield District Council decision.

Many of the decisions in this selection have come by way of judicial review. The 2004 Edwards *decision of the High Court demonstrates the liberal approach to standing that contemporary British courts now adopt in judicial review cases, though for the non-legally aided applicant, the potential costs involved in bringing a case remains a major deterrent. Yet equally – and in contrast to many courts, say, in the United States or in India, the British judiciary are clearly still cautious in trespassing too much on areas where they perceive specialist bodies are best equipped to make the complex technical and economic judgments so often inherent in modern environmental decision making – see, for example, the* Fisher *case (designation of nature conservation areas),* Marcic *(investment in new sewerage systems), and* OSS *classification of wastes. Similarly, where the words of the legislation appear clear* (National Grid Gas). *Applicants for judicial review who characterise the illegality as one of procedural impropriety rather than substantive mistake still remain on stronger ground – in this context the courts are not afraid of striking down decision making at the highest level of policy-making, as witnessed by the recent decision of the High Court in the* Greenpeace *case concerning energy policy and nuclear power. As discussed in Part 2, it remains to be seen whether we will see the development of a specialist environmental court or tribunal in this country, and what form it might take. In the meantime, it will remain the responsibility of the judiciary in the ordinary courts to grapple with the range, novelty, and complexity of legal questions that are consistently raised in cases concerning the environment.*

CHAPTER 13

EUROPEAN COURT OF JUSTICE

Nitrates Directive and polluter pays principle R *v Secretary of State for the Environment ex parte Standley and others* 1999

Free movement of goods and biodiversity *Re Criminal Proceedings against Bluhme* C- 1999

Designation under Habitats Directive *R v Secretary of State for Environment, Transport and Regions ex parte First Corporate Shipping* 2000

Fine against Member State for non-compliance with judgment *Commission v Greece* 2000

Greening public procurement *Concordia Bus Finland* 2002

Waste and by-products *Palin Granit Oy* 2002

Power of Member State to impose higher environmental standards than EC law *Denmark v Commission* 2003

Contaminated soil and waste law *Van de Walle* 2004

Agricultural slurry not a waste under EC law *Commission v Spain* 2005

Regional GMO ban illegal under EC law Land *Oberösterreich and Austria v Commission* 2005

Environmental assessment and UK planning procedures *Commission v United Kingdom; R on application of Barker v London Borough of Bromley* 2006

Environmental levy not a state aid *British Aggregates Association v Commission* 2006

EUROPEAN COURT OF JUSTICE

European Court Rules On Nitrate Directive

R v Secretary of State for the Environment and Ministry of Agriculture, Fisheries and Food ex parte Standley and Others (Case C-293/97 European Court of Justice [1999] ECR I-2603)

The European Court of Justice has provided its first authoritative interpretation of the 1991 EC Directive on nitrate pollution from agriculture, and has substantially upheld the UK Government's approach in implementing the Directive in the face of a challenge by a group of British farmers. *R v Secretary of State for the Environment and Ministry of Agriculture, Fisheries and Food ex parte Standley and Others* arose out of a challenge in the High Court by a group of farmers to the designation of nitrate vulnerable zones (NVZs) under British implementing regulations. In May 1997, faced with competing possible interpretations of the Directive, the High Court referred the questions of law to the European Court of Justice for an authoritative ruling – the first time it has made such a reference in an environmental case.

The Directive requires Member States to identify surface and groundwaters which contain or could contain more than 50mg/1 of nitrate. They must then designate as NVZs areas of land which drain into these waters and 'which contribute to pollution', and implement action programmes to curb nitrate leaching from farms within them. Regulations implementing the Directive were introduced in England and Wales in 1996, and an initial 68 NVZs were designated. The High Court challenge concerned the validity of the identification of three rivers and their tributaries, together with the designation of NVZs around them.

The government's approach to identification was essentially a three-stage process. First, bodies of water were identified which were either heavily polluted or showed the potential to be polluted with nitrate, whatever the source. Then areas of land draining into these waters were identified. Finally, an assessment was made as to whether agricultural sources were making a significant contribution to nitrate levels.

The first question referred to the ECJ was whether the initial identification method was legally correct. The farmers challenging the decision argued that the Directive's underlying purpose was to protect waters from agricultural pollution, so the initial identification had to concern waters in which the 50mg/l nitrate threshold was or could be exceeded by virtue of discharges from agricultural sources. Article 3 of the Directive refers to the identification of waters 'affected by pollution', and pollution is defined to mean the discharge of nitrogen compounds from agricultural sources. Member States, it was argued, therefore had to first establish the sources of nitrate giving rise to breaches of the 50mg/l threshold before making their initial identification.

The European Court disagreed. The identification of waters was to be carried out by applying criteria specified in Annex I of the Directive. In relation to surface freshwaters, this referred to the 50mg/l threshold if no action under the Directive was taken. According to the ECJ, 'it does not follow from the wording of the provision that Member States are required to determine precisely what proportion of the pollution in the waters is attributable to nitrates of agricultural origin or that the cause of such pollution must be exclusively agricultural.' The identification of waters was part of a process leading to the designation of NVZs and establishment of action programmes when the respective nitrate contributions from agricultural and other sources were to be taken into account.

The second issue referred to the ECJ raised more fundamental questions. The farmers essentially argued that if the Directive permitted the identification of waters where nitrate originated from sources other than farms, the fact that the main burden of the resulting action programmes would fall on agriculture rendered the Directive invalid. The farmers contended, first, that the Directive infringed the principle of proportionality, in that farmers alone would bear the responsibility of ensuring that the 50mg/l threshold was not breached even where drainage from farmland accounted for only a part of the nitrate levels. Second, the Directive was alleged to offend the 'polluter pays' principle contained in Article 130(2) of the EC Treaty, since farmers would bear the cost of reducing nitrate levels even where other sources were involved. Thirdly, the Directive was said to offend the principle that pollution should be rectified at source, as contained in Article 130(2). Where nitrate levels in water were increased by atmospheric deposition from sources such as industry or transport then those should be tackled first. Finally, the farmers argued that the Directive infringed their property rights, in that they were being faced with the entire financial responsibility of dealing with nitrate even where others might be the major cause of the problem.

It was never going to be easy to challenge the validity of the Directive on these grounds. The ECJ noted that action programmes established in NVZs had to take into account available scientific and technical data concerning sources of nitrate, and that any mandatory measures had to take account of the characteristics of each NVZ. Where these measures included limits on spreading of livestock manure which differed from those specified in the Directive, account had to be taken of objective criteria provided these did not prejudice the purposes of the Directive.

In the circumstances, the Court felt that the Directive contained provisions that were sufficiently flexible to allow the principle of proportionality to be respected. Similarly, it felt that the Directive did not imply that farmers had to take on burdens of eliminating nitrate pollution to which they had not contributed, and that the 'polluter pays' principle was not breached by the Directive itself. The same arguments applied to the principle of rectification of pollution at source. The Court recognised that restrictions on fertiliser and manure applications under the Directive could infringe a farmer's right to property. That right is recognised by general principles of Community law, but it was not an absolute right and could be restricted on public interest grounds, including, as here, the protection of public health. The validity of the Directive was therefore upheld.

The result was a victory for the government in its interpretation of the Directive – although it is currently facing a fresh challenge from the European Commission which may end in the designation of much larger areas of agricultural land as NVZs. However, when it comes to the implementation of action programmes, the ECJ's decision means that farmers and their advisers will be carefully scrutinising the measures required in each NVZ to ensure that they are not bearing a disproportionate cost in accordance with the principles outlined by the Court. Assigning nitrate levels in waters to their sources is no easy matter. It may not be part of the initial identification process - but clearly remains relevant to later stages.

Biodiversity, bees and free trade

Re Criminal Proceedings against Bluhme **(Case C-67/97 European Court of Justice [1998] ECR I-5121)**

The European Court of Justice has made it clear that the maintenance of local biodiversity can justify a Member State restricting imports and movements of animals which might interbreed with local species. The decision applies classically developed principles, but appears to be the first in which the Court has considered in detail the concept of biodiversity in the context of free trade. *Re Criminal Proceedings against Bluhme* arose out of a reference to the European Court by a Danish criminal court. In 1993, the Danish Ministry of Agriculture had issued a regulation banning the keeping of bees other than the Laeso brown bee on the small island of Laeso. The law also provided for the removal of swarms of other bees, together with compensation for any resulting losses. The underlying intention was to conserve local biodiversity by preventing interbreeding with other types of bees.

A local beekeeper was prosecuted for keeping bees other than the Laeso brown bee, but argued in his defence that the Danish law was in breach of Article 30 of the EC Treaty which prohibits national restrictions on the free movement of goods. Article 36, together with principles developed by the ECJ, permits Member States to invoke national restrictions on certain defined grounds, though before those principles can be applied it must be established that the issue is not in fact governed by existing Community legislation.

The Court initially considered whether a 1991 Directive laying down zootechnical and pedigree requirements for the marketing of pure-bred animals governed the situation. The Directive provides for the adoption of detailed rules for its application, but since no such rules had been made in respect of bees the Court held that the Directive was not applicable. The 1992 Directive on Habitats is concerned with the conservation of threatened biodiversity and the island of Laeso is designated under it, but the brown bee is not one of the species specified in the Directive.

The Court therefore had to consider whether the restrictions concerning Laeso bees amounted to a quantitative restriction or measure of equivalent effect prohibited under Article 30 of the Treaty. The Danish Government argued that Article 30 did not apply. The restrictions applied to only a very small part of the national territory, and the ban on imports of bees other than Laeso brown bees did not discriminate in respect of bees coming from other Member States.

Denmark also raised a more subtle point. In the 1970s and 1980s, the ECJ adopted an extensive interpretation of the meaning of a 'measure of equivalent effect' encompassing practically any sort of rule which could directly or indirectly affect trade. However, in an important decision in 1993 - the Keck case[1] – the Court, sensitive to the difficulties arising from challenges to national Sunday trading rules, drew back somewhat from its highly interventionist approach and redefined the boundaries by making a distinction between national rules concerning access to

---

[1] Joined cases C-267/91 and C-268/91 *Keck* [1993] ECR I-6097

markets, which remained subject to Article 30, and those governing arrangements for selling, which were no longer to be subject to Article 30. In the present case, Denmark argued that since the Laeso rules did not prohibit the import of bees into Denmark in general but merely limited their distribution in a small part of the country, this was equivalent to a 'selling arrangement' and therefore fell outside Article 30.

The Court rejected all these initial arguments. The national rules could not be described as concerning selling arrangements but were directly concerned with the intrinsic characteristics of the bees in question. The fact that the restriction affected only part of the national territory did not prevent it being a restriction of intra-Community trade. The key legal question was therefore whether the national measures could be justified under Community law. Article 36 permits national restrictions on certain grounds, including the 'protection of the health and life of animals'. The ECJ has itself established other grounds not expressly contained in the Treaty, including those of general environmental protection. The distinction between the two sets of grounds can be significant. Where an Article 36 ground is invoked, the national measures may discriminate between national and imported goods provided the discrimination is for good reason. But where one of the ECJ's general principles is invoked, no discrimination is generally permitted.

There was considerable argument before the Court whether the maintenance of biodiversity fell within the concept of the protection of the health and life of animals under Article 36. The Advocate General accepted that the threat of an animal population disappearing through slow interbreeding with other species was rather different from the protection of animals from hunting or disease, which has been held to fall within Article 36. In the former case, it was a 'slower, probably painless process' which would not 'necessarily endanger the life of any individual member of the population in question.' Nevertheless, he felt that Article 36 should apply, and the Court agreed: 'Measures to preserve an indigenous animal population with distinct characteristics contribute to the maintenance of biodiversity by ensuring the survival of the population concerned. By so doing, they are aimed at protecting the life of those animals and are capable of being justified under Article 36.'

However, simply coming within the terms of Article 36 is not sufficient to justify a national measure. Member States must also satisfy the Court that the measure was proportionate in the sense that it met a genuine need and was restricted to what was actually necessary to secure the public interest goals. Here, again, there was considerable argument, especially over whether the Laeso bee is a distinct subspecies, whether brown bees of the same subspecies exists elsewhere in the world, and whether the population was under immediate threat of extinction.

The Advocate General was prepared to give considerable latitude to the Member State in this context. He noted that the EC is party to the 1992 UN Convention on Biological Diversity which affirms that the conservation of biological diversity is a common concern of mankind, and is not confined in its application to species and subspecies but is more concerned with genetic resources generally. Even if the Laeso bee was not a distinct subspecies, he felt Denmark was entitled to seek to conserve what was a geographically and morphologically distinctive bee population. And even if there was no immediate threat – though Denmark contended that there was – the precautionary principle argued for anticipatory action.

The Court followed this line of argument. 'From the point of view of such conservation of biodiversity it is immaterial whether the object of protection is a separate subspecies, a distinct strain within any given species or merely a local colony, so long as the population in question have characteristics distinguishing them from others and are therefore judged worthy of protection either to shelter them from a risk of extinction that is more or less imminent, or, even in the absence of such risk, on account of scientific or other interest in preserving the pure population at the location concerned.' The ECJ concluded that the threat of the Laeso brown bees disappearing through interbreeding was genuine, and that the Danish national laws were an appropriate response and justified under Community law.

The Laeso decision is significant in the way that it explores the meaning of biodiversity and the latitude available to Member States to conserve what in their opinion are important local pockets of biodiversity. However, it is important to stress that the freedom of a Member State to invoke Article 36 applies only where no Community legislation on the subject exists. As such, the principles are unlikely to be applicable to, say, the current concerns in Britain over the potential local biodiversity impacts of genetically modified crops, to which specific EC legislation applies. Nonetheless, the sensitivities now raised concerning the vulnerability of local biodiversity, coupled with the potential impact of devolution in heightening local or regional concerns, are likely to increase the political and legal significance of the European Court's approach in the Laeso case.

UK shipping company loses case against habitat designation

R v Secretary of State for the Environment Transport and Regions ex parte First Corporate Shipping **(Case C-371/98 European Court of Justice, 11 November 2000 [2001] All E.R. (EC) 177)**

A rearguard action by a UK shipping company to block the designation of wildlife sites under the 1992 EC Directive on habitats has failed before the European Court of Justice. The Court ruled that economic and social interests, including those of industry, are not be taken into account when Member States tackle the task of designation. The decision is in line with Government policy. *R v Secretary of State* for *the Environment Transport and Regions ex parte First Corporate* was a referral to the European Court of Justice from the High Court. The case arose out of the Secretary of State's decision that he was minded to propose to the European Commission that the Severn estuary is eligible for designation as a Special Area of Conservation (SAC) under the Habitats Directive.

The Habitats Directive contains an annex specifying criteria for selecting sites, with preliminary lists to be sent to the Commission, followed by a complex procedure to establish, by agreement with Member States and the Commission, a network of sites of Community importance known as Natura 2000. Sites on the Commission's final list must be designated as SACs by Member States, though UK policy is to treat candidate sites submitted to the Commission as though they have been finally designated. Once a site is designated, Article 6 of the Directive kicks into play, requiring a Member State to avoid deterioration of habitats and disturbance of species. Plans or projects which might significantly affect SACs are subject to environmental assessment.

In 1991, the European Court of Justice held that the provisions in the 1979 Directive on bird conservation concerning Special Protection Areas (SPAs) did not permit any subsequent deterioration or incursion into such areas once they were designated unless human life was threatened.[2] Although most environmental groups welcomed that decision, there was real concern that such a strict ruling would make Member States less than enthusiastic in initial designation. In drafting the provisions of the Habitats Directive, Member States were clearly anxious to avoid such strictures. Article 6 therefore allows, under qualified conditions, that damaging plans or projects may be carried out for 'imperative reasons of overriding public interest,' including those of a social or economic nature. In such cases 'compensatory measures' must be taken by Member States to ensure coherence of the Natura 2000 network.

---

[2] *Commission v Germany* C-57/89 [1991] ECR I-883

In the Severn estuary case, the concern was with the criteria applied to initial designation. First Corporate Shipping is the port authority for Bristol, and had concerns that designation of the estuary could jeopardise future development of the port's facilities. It pointed to Article 2 of the Directive, which provides that 'Measures taken pursuant of this Directive shall take account of economic, social, and cultural requirements and regional and local characteristics.' The company argued that the identification and selection of candidate sites was a 'measure' within the terms of the Directive. In the European Court, it was supported by the Finnish government which argued that, provided the overall objectives of the Directive were not compromised, Member States should be entitled to take into economic, social and cultural requirements in preparing their lists. This might be the case where there was a large number of potential sites within a single territory, and where some pre-selection would not jeopardise the Directive.

Despite the general wording of Article 2, the European Court of Justice rejected the arguments. It noted that the Directive provides detailed and specific criteria for site selection, and that the criteria were defined exclusively in relation to the objective of conserving habitats or fauna and flora. The overall goal of the designation procedures was to establish a coherent European network of SACs. 'To produce a draft list of sites of Community importance, capable of leading to the creation of a coherent European ecological network of SACs, the Commission must have available an exhaustive list of the sites which, at national level, have an ecological interest which is relevant from the point of view of the Habitats Directive's objective of conservation of natural habitats and wild fauna and flora.'

The Court held that the Directive required that the conservation status of habitats and species must be assessed with regard to the entire European territory. It followed that when a Member State drew up its initial candidate list it would have no precise knowledge of the situation of habitats in other Member States. To allow Member States to fillet their candidate lists on non-scientific grounds would prevent the Commission having an exhaustive list of potential sites and thereby jeopardise the Directive's goals.

The decision is hardly surprising, especially in the light of the Court's ruling in the 1996 *Lappel Banks* case[3] which concerned SPAs under the Birds Directive. The Court held that initial designation of such areas could not involve economic and social considerations, and indicated that the same approach should apply to designation under the Habitats

---

[3] ECJ C-44/96, 11 July 1996

Directive though that matter was not directly in issue. Despite its predictability, the ruling is nevertheless valuable in ensuring that the process of initial selection and designation is not over-politicised. But it is equally clear that the resolution of potential conflicts is now likely to be down the line, and indeed the Directive is essentially structured on that basis. There is room for hard negotiation between Member States and the Commission concerning the initial list of European sites, and clearly there will be difficult decisions in the future concerning the extent to which designated sites may subsequently be damaged.

Greece gets first fine for breach of EC environmental laws

Commission v Greece (C-387/97, European Court of Justice [2000] ECR-I-5047)

The European Court of Justice has for the first time used its new powers to fine a Member State which fails to comply with its judgments. In *Commission v Greece* Greece has been ordered to pay 20,000 Euros per day until it complies with a 1992 ruling that it was in breach of two EC Directives on waste in respect of waste disposal in Crete. The significance of the decision is indicated by the fact that it was heard before a full panel of judges of the European Court, and the judgment very much supports the European Commission in its policy on estimation of penalties.

The provisions in what is now Article 228 of the EC Treaty were introduced in 1993 under the Maastricht Treaty, and strongly supported by the UK. They were designed to strengthen the ECJ's authority against a disturbing trend among some Member States which appeared to take little action in respect of adverse judgments. Under Article 228, if a Member State fails to comply with an ECJ judgment within a time limit laid down by the Commission, the Commission may bring the case before the Court, specifying a lump sum or penalty payment to be paid by the Member State. If the Court finds that the Member State has not complied with its judgment, 'it may impose a lump sum or penalty payment on it.' This appears to make it the only supra-national court in the world with powers to award direct financial penalties against a nation state.

The Treaty provides no further elaboration on how such penalties are to be calculated, and in 1996 the Commission issued a memorandum indicating the criteria it would apply. This was a followed by a Communication in 1997 which provided further details on methods of calculation.[4] Given

---

[4] See now SEC (2005) 1658 Commission Guidelines on Application of Art 228 of the EC Treaty 13 Dec 2005

the absence of more specific Treaty provisions, the Court accepted that it was within the Commission's powers to issue guidelines of this sort in order to ensure equal treatment between Member States, although it stressed that they could not bind it since Article 228 clearly gave the ultimate discretion on deciding a penalty to the Court. Nevertheless, according to the Court, the Commission's guidelines helped to ensure that it 'acts in a manner which is transparent, foreseeable and consistent with legal certainty and are designed to achieve proportionality in the amounts of the penalty payments to be proposed by it.'

The Commission's approach was to start with the basic aim of the provision which was the effective enforcement of EC law, and that there were three key criteria – the gravity of the infringement, its duration, and the deterrent effect of the penalty. The 1997 Communication suggested a starting figure of 500 ECU per day which was then multiplied by various coefficients which reflected different factors such as the seriousness and duration of the non-compliance, and the ability of the Member State to pay taking account of its gross domestic product and number of votes in the Council. The Court considered that this was a reasonable approach.

Commission v Greece concerned an uncontrolled municipal rubbish tip at the mouth of the river Kouroupitos in Crete. According to a 1996 study by the University of Greece, wastes were dumped into the top of a ravine some 200 metres from the sea without any other measures. The wastes had been burning uncontrollably for at least ten years. Well over ten years ago, Greece had told the Commission that the tipping would cease by the end of 1988 with the construction of new disposal sites, but essentially nothing had been done – in part, Greece argued, because of local opposition to new plans. Following an ECJ judgment against Greece in 1992, the Commission received no notification of any measures being taken to comply with the judgment, and began investigations.

Greece informed the Commission that preliminary approval for two new sites had been obtained, but the Commission considered that some four years after the judgment the measures were still at a preliminary stage and therefore initiated proceedings in respect of a penalty payment. Applying its guidelines, the Commission proposed a penalty of 24,600 Euros for each day's delay in complying with the judgment.

The ECJ considered the extent to which Greece had introduced measures to comply with the provisions of the 1975 Directive on waste and the 1978 Directive on toxic and dangerous waste which the Court found it to have breached in 1992. In 1992, the Court found that Greece had failed to draw up waste disposal plans in accordance with both Directives. The Commission argued that any such plans were still at a preliminary stage.

Despite the arguments of Greece that it had been taking a series of interventionist measures, the ECJ agreed that Greece had yet to fulfil its obligations concerning plans: 'Contrary to the claims of the Greek Government, legislation or specific measures amounting to only a series of ad hoc normative interventions that are incapable of constituting an organised and coordinated system for the disposal of waste and toxic and dangerous waste cannot be regarded as plans which Members States are required to adopt.'

The second breach concerned Greece's failure to comply with the general duty under Article 4 of the 1975 Directive to take measures to ensure that wastes are disposed of without endangering human health or harming the environment. The Court noted that while Article 4 did not specify the content of the measures to be taken, the obligation was binding on Member States as to the objectives to be achieved, although it gave a margin of discretion in assessing the need for measures. Nevertheless, according to previous case law, 'a significant deterioration in the environment over a protracted period when no action has been taken by the competent authorities is in principle an indication that the Member State concerned has exceeded the discretion conferred on it by that provision.' Although Greece argued that the volumes of waste being disposed off at the site have decreased significantly, it did not dispute that solid waste was still being tipped into the ravine, and the Court held that it has still not complied with the Article 4 duty.

The one crumb of comfort for Greece concerned its non-compliance with the 1978 Directive which imposed a similar general obligation with respect to toxic and dangerous wastes. In the 1992 case there was clear evidence that toxic wastes from military bases and other sources were being dumped at the site, but Greece produced evidence that this practice had ceased since 1996, and the Commission itself conceded that the volumes of toxic and dangerous wastes had been reduced. In the circumstances, the Court felt that the Commission had failed to produce the information necessary to prove the Greece was still in breach of this obligation.

In considering the proposed penalties, the ECJ concluded that the obligation to dispose of waste without endangering human health and the environment formed part of the very objectives of Community environmental policy as laid down in the Treaty, and that failure to comply with Article 4 must be regarded 'as particularly serious'. Since waste disposal plans were needed to achieve the Article 4 objective, failure to comply with the plan provisions must also be regarded as serious. The Court took account of the fact that the Commission had failed to prove the continuing breach of the obligation concerning toxic and dangerous wastes, and therefore reduced the penalty to 20,000 Euros per day – about £15,000 – starting from the date of the present judgment and continuing until compliance with the 1992 judgment is achieved.

The case will boost the Commission's confidence in its approach towards the calculation of penalty payments. This is clearly significant for the Environment Directorate, which has made most use of the provisions to date. According to a written answer in the European Parliament last year, it has formally requested payments in seven instances, including three cases against Germany. The proposed penalties appear to have had a strong influence in getting cases to be settled quickly, and now that it is clear from the ECJ that the Commission's basic approach towards calculation is legally correct, Member States will have to be sure of their facts to resist. Not all problems, though, have been resolved. The new provisions in the Treaty contain no specific clauses concerning the collection of payments should a Member State fail to pay a fine, nor does the Court have any sanction to award a final injunction against a Member State

Greening public procurement

Concordia Bus Finland Oy v. Helsingin kaupunki and HKL-Bussiliikeene **(Case C513/99 European Court of Justice [2002] ECR I-7213)**

In what has been described as a landmark decision, the European Court of Justice has ruled on the extent to which public procurement procedures under EU law can incorporate environmental criteria chosen by public bodies. The decision comes at a time when proposals for revising the existing legislation are in the pipeline, and will strengthen the arguments of environmental interests concerned that they will make the incorporation of environmental criteria more difficult.

Concordia Bus concerned a decision by public authorities in Helsinki to put out to tender the award of new contracts for running bus services in the city. Such procedures are subject to EU legislation concerning public procurement which is designed primarily to ensure economy and efficiency in the award of substantial public contracts, and based on principles of transparency and non-discrimination. The tendering requirements for the bus services included criteria relating to the overall price quoted for different routes, the quality of the bus fleet in relation to emissions of nitrogen oxides and noise, and the operators' quality and environmental systems. A weighting system was applied giving extra points for the environmental aspects of bids. The case concerned the award of one of the routes to HKL, a bus operator belonging to the city, which had not made the lowest bid in financial terms but had won extra points on the environmental aspects of its fleet. A rival bidder, Concordia, which had submitted the lowest price tender but had lost out on points for the environmental efficiency of its fleet, challenged the legality of the decision before a national court on the grounds that the points systems was unfair and discriminatory. Furthermore, it claimed that the criteria for NO_x emissions could only be achieved by buses powered by natural gas, and in practice only HKL had such a fleet and access to gas. The national court referred a number of questions of EU law to the European Court of justice for a definitive ruling.

The ECJ first considered the provisions of the key Directive 92/50 governing procurement in the field of public works contracts. Under Article 36 of that Directive, the criteria on which authorities are obliged to base the award of contracts are either the lowest price or, where the award is made to the economically most advantageous tender, various criteria relating such as quality, technical merit, aesthetic and functional characteristics, technical assistance and after sales service, and price. Drawing on case law, the ECJ noted that the criteria specified in Article 36 were not exhaustive. Furthermore, the express inclusion of aesthetic criteria as an example indicated that factors which were not purely economic could still influence the value of the tender from the point of view of the contracting authority.

As to environmental criteria, the Court noted that Article 6 of the EU Treaty provides that environmental protection requirements must be integrated into the implementation of EU policies and activities, and therefore concluded that Article 36 of the Directive 'does not exclude the possibility for the contracting authority of using criteria relating to the preservation of the environment when assessing the economically most advantageous tender.' However, it did not follow that public authorities had complete freedom to choose the environmental criteria they wished. Again, following case law and the context of the Directive, the Court noted that criteria must be aimed at identifying the economically most advantageous tender and must be linked to the subject matter of the contract. Such criteria must be expressly mentioned in the contract documents or tender notice, not allow the authority unrestricted freedom of choice as regards the award of the contract, and comply with fundamental principles of EU law, and in particular not offend the principle of non-discrimination.

Applying these principles to the Helsinki case, the Court concluded that criteria relating to NO_x emissions and noise were clearly linked to the subject matter of the contract. The points systems did not give unrestricted freedom of choice to the contracting authority, and the procedures concerning publication of the criteria had been satisfied.

In its 1998 Communication on public procurement, the European Commission argued that it was legitimate to take environmental considerations into account in order to choose the economically most advantageous tender, provided the awarding authority benefited directly from the ecological qualities of the product in question. In the present case, the city of Helsinki had argued that the procedures were consistent with this principle since the city authority was responsible for environmental protection and public health, and even modest improvements in health resulting from emission reductions would be of economic benefit In its judgment, however, the ECJ appears to have studiously avoided ruling on the Commission's interpretation that the authority must benefit directly from the environmental criteria. Instead, it now appears that provided the environmental criteria are linked to the subject matter in hand, and satisfy the other principles and procedural requirements, this is sufficient.

Concordia then argued that HKL already had a gas-powered bus fleet and was monopolising the only service station in Finland supplying natural gas. Against that background it argued that the environmental criteria discriminated in favour of one operator. The ECJ accepted that the criteria must not be discriminatory, but felt that that principle had not been breached here. It noted that the criteria were objective and applied without distinction, and that Concordia had in fact won the tender for one of the other routes even though that required gas-powered vehicles. The fact that one of the criteria could only be satisfied by a small number of undertakings did not in itself breach the principle of non-discrimination.

The decision comes at a politically sensitive time. In 2000, the Commission proposed a new Directive concerning public procurement which would restrict the inclusion of social and environmental criteria and insist, in line with the 1998 Communication, that any economic gains from environmental criteria directly benefit the awarding authority. Political agreement on the proposals were reached by the Internal Market Council last May, but the European Parliament is unhappy with the limitations. The ECJ has accepted that there must be a direct link between the environmental criteria and the subject matter of the proposed contract, but its more liberal approach on the question of who gains from their inclusion may persuade the Commission and Council to reconsider the proposals.

European Court rules again on the meaning of 'waste'

Palin Granit Oy v Vehmassalon Kansanterveystyon Kuntayhtifnan Hallitus (Case C-9/00, European Court of Justice [2002] 2 CMLR 560)

The European Court of Justice has given another significant judgment on the meaning of 'waste' under EU legislation, confirming its view that the needs of environmental protection require an expansive approach. The decision concerned left-over quarrying materials stored on site, but the principles have wider implications concerning the fine line between by-products and production residues. *Palin Granit* was a reference from the Finnish Supreme Administrative Court seeking guidance on the meaning of waste.

The case arose from a dispute between two Finnish administrative bodies as to which should grant a licence in respect of a quarry. An environmental licence had originally been granted in respect of a granite extraction works by the local municipal board. Some 65-80 per cent of the quarried stone could not be sold immediately because it was the wrong shape or size, and the application included provision for storage and management of the left-over stone on an adjacent site with the intention of using it for embankments, landscaping or possibly as gravel or infilling material.

However, another administrative body, the regional environment centre, claimed that the left-over stone was waste, and that only it had the authority under national law to grant a waste licence. The company argued that the left-over stone was identical in composition to the granite extracted and was stored for short periods for subsequent use without the need for any special recovery measures, and that there was no risk to human health or the environment. In those circumstances, the material should not be regarded as waste in law.

The governing EU legislation is the 1975 waste framework Directive as amended in 1991, and its complex structure has given rise to difficult issues of interpretation which have had to be considered by the European Court of Justice on a number of occasions. The Court has studiously avoided giving any definitive, all-embracing meaning of 'waste', though the body of case law has now clarified the principles to be applied in individual cases.

The starting point for the Court was the basic definition of waste as 'any substance or object in the categories set out in Annex I which the holder discards or intends or is required to discard.' Annex I of the 1975 Directive lists a large number of categories including 'residues from raw materials extraction and processing (e.g. mining residues).' But this is clearly an illustrative rather than a definitive list, since the last category includes 'any materials, substances or products which are not contained in the above categories.' The Directive also provides for the Commission to draw up a detailed list of waste categories in the European Waste Catalogue. But again this is essentially guidance, and the catalogue states that the inclusion of a material on the list does not mean it is necessarily waste in all circumstances.

The position is made more complex because the Directive also contains an annex listing various types of disposal and recovery operations which include deposit in or on land, permanent storage, and storage pending such operations, excluding temporary storage pending collection on the site where the waste is produced. Similar provisions concerning storage apply to recycling and similar operations listed in the annex. Establishments which carry out such disposal or recovery operations must be subject to a permit, though under Article 11 exemptions from the individual permit requirement may be granted where disposal is carried on at the place of production or for waste recovery operations, provided these are subject to general rules and that waste is recovered or disposed of without risks to humans or the environment. In previous case-law, Advocate General Jacobs had attempted to link these lists of disposal and recovery operations to the basic definition of waste in order to provide a degree of certainty – the so-called 'Tombesi by-pass' – but this approach has been rejected by the European Court as being unduly restrictive given the overall aims of the Directive. Material which is not subjected to one of these specified operations may therefore still be waste in law and, while no permit may be required in such cases, it is still subject to the general duty of Member States under Article 4 to ensure that waste is recovered or disposed off without risk to human health or the environment.

According to the Court, therefore, whether or not a substance is waste is primarily to be inferred from the holder's action, which depends on whether or not he intends to discard the substances in question. The term 'discard' is not defined in the legislation and, accordingly, it 'must be interpreted in the light of the aim of Directive 75/442 which according to its third recital is 'the protection of human health and the environment against harmful effects caused by the collection, transport, treatment, storage and tipping of waste.'

The company argued that storing the leftover stone was not a landfill of waste but a deposit of reusable materials. The fact that it was reusable, however, did not preclude it from being waste since the Court had held previously that materials capable of economic reutilisation could still be waste. Conversely, even if the storage did fall within one of the operations specified in the Directive, that was not conclusive since the Court accepted that the distinction between disposal or recovery operations from the treatment of other products was often a fine one. A key factor is to determine whether the substance was in essence a production residue, and this is largely affected by the primary purpose of the production: 'According to its ordinary meaning, waste is what falls away when one processes a material or an object and is not an end-product which the manufacturing process directly intends to produce.' Applying this test, the Court accepted that the left-over stone from the quarrying was not the primary product sought by the operator. The company, however, argued that in this case the left-over stone could be reused without any further processing, and that it should be regarded as a by-product rather than a production residue.

The Court appeared to have some sympathy with this analysis: 'There is no reason to hold that the provisions of Directive 75/442 which are intended to regulate the disposal or recovery of waste apply to goods, materials, or raw materials which have an economic value as products regardless of any form of processing and which, as such, are subject to the legislation applicable to those products.' But the Court then reiterated the need to avoid a restrictive definition of the term 'waste' as that might overlook its inherent risks and pollution. It concluded that the analysis concerning by-products as not being waste should be confined to those situations where their reuse was 'not a mere possibility but a certainty without any further processing prior to reuse and as an integral part of the production process.' The degree of likelihood of reuse was therefore another critical factor, and appears to be a newly developed principle of the Court. The Court noted that, 'if, in addition to the mere possibility of reusing the substance, there is also a financial advantage to the holder in so doing, the likelihood of reuse is high.'

Looking at the facts of the present case, the Court noted that that the only foreseeable uses of the left-over stone were not certain, and would in most cases potentially require long-term storage which constituted a burden to the holder and potentially the cause of environmental pollution. Such stone should be classified as waste in the view of the Court, though it noted that it might be subject to the national exemption requirements under Article 11 provided effective general rules were in place. The Court accepted that the left-over stone had exactly the same composition as the material being sold, but in the light of its analysis held this was not relevant to the question of its definition as waste, unless the material was actually being reused – in that case it might be treated as a by-product. Similarly, the location of its storage, whether on site, adjacent or at a distance, did not affect the definition of waste, though in some cases temporary on-site storage might exclude the need for a permit according to the Directive. Nor was the fact that the composition of the substance might be harmless to health or the environment decisive: 'Even assuming that the left-over stone does not, by virtue of its composition, pose any risk to human health or the environment, stockpiling such stone is necessarily a source of harm to, and pollution of, the environment since the full reuse of the stone is neither immediate nor even always foreseeable.'

It would be rash to hope that this will be the last word on the meaning of waste from the European Court of Justice. Clearly, its recent approach in this area has been to recognise the strongly subjective elements in the concept of waste, and, given the environmental goals of the legislation, the difficulties of providing definitive definitions in the absence of knowledge of the particular circumstances. Distinguishing between production by-products and production residues now seems to require greater knowledge of contractual arrangements in place and the certainties of the market for the items in question. All this will make life more challenging for waste regulators and businesses involved in potential waste production, and suggests the need for more sophisticated guidance, as well as greater flexibility in regulatory regimes which can reflect the differing environmental risks involved. The main government guidance on the meaning of 'waste' remains a 1994 circular, and at the very least this would now appear to require substantial revision to reflect recent case-law at both EU and national level.

Ruling from European Court on 'green guarantee'

Denmark v. Commission (C 3/00, European Court of Justice [2003] ECR I-2643)

The European Court of Justice has given its second important decision this year on provisions in the EU Treaty allowing Member States to maintain or introduce stricter environmental or health requirements than those contained in EU single market Directives. The provisions were substantially revised by the Amsterdam Treaty which came into force in 1999, and in a decision earlier this year the ECJ gave its first ruling[5] on them as they related to new national measures introduced after the adoption of a Directive.

---

[5] *Commission v Germany* C 512/99 [2003] ECR I-845

The latest case, *Denmark v. Commission* relates to the Treaty provisions permitting Member States to maintain stricter national measures that were already in force when a Directive is agreed. The case concerned standards for certain preservatives used in foodstuffs, though the principles will apply to equally to environmental measures. Under a 1989 framework Directive concerning additives in food, various daughter Directives established lists of foods and permitted uses of additives such as sweeteners, colouring and preservatives. A 1995 daughter Directive concerned preservatives, and was agreed under the Treaty's single market provisions by majority voting. Denmark voted against the Directive, arguing that it did not satisfactorily meet health requirements, especially as regards sulphites, nitrites and nitrates used as preservatives in certain foods.

Denmark implemented those parts of the Directive concerning additives other than sulphites, nitrites and nitrates, but in 1966 notified the European Commission that it was maintaining its own existing law concerning those additives by way of derogation. Following discussion with the Commission, further information was sent in 1998, and the Commission then sought opinions from other Member States, several of which expressed concern about Denmark's request. In making its notification, Denmark invoked the existing provisions of the Treaty permitting the maintenance of stricter national measures. But by the time it made its decision in October 1999, the new Amsterdam Treaty provisions were in force, and were the subject of the Court's ruling.

Article 95(4) of the Treaty provides that, in relation to single market measures, Member States may maintain an existing stricter national measure on grounds of major needs referred to Article 30, which includes the protection of public health, the environment or the working environment. However, the Commission has to be notified and be satisfied that the conditions are met, and that the measure is not a means of arbitrary discrimination, a disguised restriction on trade, or an obstacle to the functioning of the common market.

These grounds for maintaining a stricter national measure were a repeat of previous Treaty provisions, and it was in relation to new national measures that the Amsterdam Treaty broke fresh ground by introducing specific conditions, including the requirement for new scientific evidence after a Directive was agreed and a problem specific to the Member State seeking derogation. However, the Treaty also introduced new procedural requirements common to both existing and new measures, including a strict time limit for Commission decisions. In the case of the Danish notification, the Commission rejected the

Danish case in October 1999. It accepted that the Danish measures were aimed at protecting public heath, but decided that they were excessive in relation to the aim. It was the legal validity of this decision which Denmark challenged before the Court.

The first main ground of challenge related to the procedure adopted by the Commission. Denmark argued that it should have had a right to be heard before the Commission reached its decision. Article 95 makes no mention of such a right, but in other cases the ECJ has developed the principle of the right to a fair hearing, both for citizens and for Member States. Here, however, the ECJ noted that the procedure under Article 95 was not initiated by the Commission but the Member State, with the decision of the Commission 'being adopted merely in response to that initiative'. In its notification, the Member State has the opportunity to comment on the decisions it asks to be adopted, and the Court noted that the new Amsterdam Treaty provision which introduced faster decision-making would be jeopardised if the Commission was required to offer further hearings to the Member State. The Court concluded that the principle of the right to be heard was therefore not applicable to these procedures.

The second key ground of challenge concerned the conditions of Article 95(4) themselves. One of the Commission's grounds of rejection referred to Denmark's failure to demonstrate a particular health problem for the Danish population in relation to sulphites or the existence of a specific situation in Denmark relation to nitrites and nitrates. Denmark argued that Article 95(4) makes it clear that a reference to particular national problem was legally relevant only where new national measures were being proposed, not when a Member State proposed maintaining existing measures.

The ECJ agreed that there was a logic in the Treaty making the distinction between existing and new national measures. Where national provisions predate an EU measure, they are 'known to the Community legislature but the legislature cannot or does not seek to be guided by them for the purpose of harmonisation.' By contrast, new national measures were by definition unknown at the date of the EU measure, were more likely to jeopardise harmonisation, and stricter conditions were therefore justifiable. A problem specific to the Member State was therefore not a legally required condition for existing measures.

However, the Court went on to state that if there were such a problem, that would be highly relevant to the Commission's assessment, and in examining the Commission's decision letter it concluded that it had in fact treated the national situation as a relevant factor and not a pre-condition. Denmark's arguments on these grounds therefore failed. The Court added that the same approach would be applicable where there was new scientific evidence. However, in the case of an existing measure, a Member State was entitled to argue that its assessment of the risk to public heath was simply different from that made by the EU legislature when making a harmonisation measure: 'In the light of uncertainty inherent in assessing the public risks posed by, *inter alia*, the use of food additives, divergent assessments of those risks can legitimately be made without necessarily being made on new or different scientific evidence.'

The Commission's decision letter also referred to the possibility of the harmonisation measure being amended in future under the 1989 framework Directive. The Court agreed with Denmark that this was not a legally justifiable reason for rejecting the notification of a Member State, but concluded that the reference was in fact superfluous to the Commission's decision and had not affected its conclusions.

Denmark then raised various arguments claiming that the Commission's decision contained errors of law and fact in how it had assessed the risks posed by sulphites and had reached the conclusion that the Danish measures were disproportionate. One argument alleged that the levels of sulphites permitted in the Directive failed to take account of people with allergies to the additive. The ECJ, however, noted that the limit had been based on levels which would not constitute a danger to the health of the majority of consumers, while the issue of allergies was met by labelling requirements. It could find no sufficient errors in the Commission's assessment to warrant holding it invalid.

When it came to nitrates and nitrites, the ECJ noted that the scientific opinions which formed the basis of the Directive had concluded that the substances were potential carcinogens and that it was not possible to set a no-effect level. It was therefore necessary to set limits which were the minimum strictly necessary to meet the technological requirements of the additives as preservatives. In 1995, shortly after adoption of the Directive, the Scientific Committee on Food, the key EU advisory body in this area, had issued an opinion which criticised the levels fixed as being too high, and felt they could be reduced further without jeopardising the substances' technological function. The ECJ concluded that the Commission had failed to take sufficient account of this 1995 opinion, and indeed had not even mentioned in its decision that the levels fixed in the Directive had been called into question by the SCF. As such, its decision that the Danish national provisions were disproportionate were flawed, and this part of the decision was annulled.

Finally, Denmark claimed that the Commission's decision was flawed because it failed to address the question of whether the Danish measures were a means of arbitrary discrimination, a disguised restriction on trade, or an obstacle to the functioning of the common market. These are also conditions in Article 95 common to both existing and new national measures. The ECJ, however, held that once the Commission had decided to reject the national notification on the ground that the measures did not meet a major need to protect public heath, it was not obliged to address all or any other of the conditions in Article 95.

The Treaty provisions allowing Member States to maintain stricter existing legislation in spite of subsequent EU harmonisation measure have long proved controversial. Some commentators have argued, for example, that such a measure could never strictly meet the final condition in Article 95, since by definition it must be an obstacle to the functioning of the common market. As such, the wording must be assumed to imply an unreasonable or inappropriate obstacle. In the present case, the ECJ did not have to rule on this point, though the language of proportionality clearly permeates the judgement. The Amsterdam Treaty amendments introduced greater formality into the procedures, and Commission approval or disapproval is now in the form of reasoned decisions, opening them up to the greater scrutiny and more likelihood of legal challenge. The Danish case, however, suggests that the Court is likely to avoid an over-legalistic approach to the text of a Commission decision. Instead, it will look at the underlying reasoning and factors which determined the Commission's approach, and will overturn the decision only they are legally unsound.

Contaminated soil held to be waste by European Court

Van de Walle et al. (Case C-1/03 European Court of Justice [2004] ECR I-7613)

The European Court of Justice has continued its expansive interpretation of the meaning of 'waste' in EU waste legislation, ruling that an unintentional spillage from petrol storage tanks was waste. More significantly, it held that any soil contaminated by the spillage was also waste, even before it was excavated. In the UK the decision may have important implications for the difficult overlap between the contaminated land regime and waste clean-up powers.

Van de Walle et al. concerned a petrol station in Brussels leased by Texaco and operated by an independent manager under a service agreement. As a result of defects in the storage tanks, a quantity of hydrocarbons leaked into the soil. When the leak was later discovered, Texaco terminated the operating contract alleging negligence on the part of the manager and, without admitting any liability, carried out a partial decontamination of the site. The local authority was faced with the costs of full decontamination, and brought criminal proceedings against Texaco under local waste legislation which permitted it to recover costs.

The definition of 'waste' under the Belgian law reproduced the definition in the EU waste framework Directive 75/442, and the Belgian court referred the matter to the European Court of Justice seeking guidance as to whether an accidental spillage and any soil contaminated by the spill constituted waste in law. Under Article 1 of the Directive, 'waste' is defined as 'any substance or object in the categories set out in Annex I which the holder discards or intends or is required to discard.' The European Court noted that one of the categories in Annex I included materials that had been 'spilled, lost or having undergone other mishap.' However, in line with its case law, it held that this was not determinative in itself, and that the classification of waste 'is to be inferred primarily from the holder's action and the meaning of the term 'discard'.'

Again, following its case law, it held that given the environmental goals of the Directive, together with the principles of precaution and prevention, the term 'discard' should not be given a restrictive meaning. It followed that when a substance or object is a product which is not itself wanted or subsequent use and which the holder cannot economically use without prior processing, it must be considered a burden which the holder seeks to discard.

Applying this approach to the spillage in question, it was clear that the hydrocarbons were not a product which could be reused without processing. 'Those hydrocarbons are therefore substances which the holder did not intend to produce and which he "discards", albeit involuntarily, at the time of the production or distribution operations which relate to them.'

The next question was whether the contaminated soil was also waste within the meaning of the legislation. The European Commission argued that once soil contaminated with the spillage was excavated it would be waste, but argued that as a general rule unexcavated contaminated soil should not be considered a waste. The Advocate General, in his advisory opinion, also argued that the crucial test for the soil was whether the holder was required to discard it. He felt that the Directive itself contained no obligation to discard such soil itself, and that question would be determined by other relevant EU or national legislation.

The European Court was not prepared to apply these qualifications. It felt that the hydrocarbons could not be separated from the land which they had contaminated and could not be recovered or disposed of unless the land was also subject to the necessary decontamination: 'That is the only interpretation which ensures compliance with the aims of protecting the natural environment and prohibiting the abandonment of waste pursued by the Directive.' That fact that the soil had not been excavated had no bearing on its classification as waste.

Given the fact that the site in question was being operated by an independent manager, the court also considered the extent to which Texaco as the product supplier had responsibilities under the waste legislation. It noted that under the Directive the primary responsibility for disposal and recovery fell on the waste 'holder', defined in broad terms as the producer of the waste or the person in possession of it. However, according to Article 15 of the Directive and in line with the 'polluter pays' principle, the financial costs of disposal or recovery fell on the persons who cause the waste whether they are holders, former holders or the producers of the product from which the waste came.

In the circumstances of the case, the operating manager had the hydrocarbons in stock when they became waste and could therefore be considered to have produced them. He should therefore be considered to be the holder of the waste under the Directive. However, if the national court decided that the poor condition of the storage facilities and the subsequent leakage could be attributed to a disregard of contractual obligations by Texaco, then, the court held Texaco's activities could be considered to have produced the waste and it could accordingly be regarded as the holder.

The implications of the decision in the *Van de Walle* case will need to be carefully assessed. For the UK Government and the environment agencies, one immediate issue may be the need to reconsider the relationship between the clean-up powers under the contaminated land regime and the specialised waste legislation under the Environmental Protection Act 1995. Section 78YB(3) of the 1995 Act provides that remediation notices under the contaminated land regime may not be served in respect of contaminated land where it appears to the local authority that the powers of a waste regulation authority under section 59 of the Act, dealing with the removal of unlicensed disposal of waste, could be exercised. The potential burdens on the innocent occupier of land are, however, severely limited under section 59. If, according to the European Court, both unintentional spillages and any soil contaminated by the spillages are now to be considered as waste, local authorities may feel encouraged to pass the burden of exercising clean-up powers, and the potential difficulties of recovering costs, to bodies such as the Environment Agency.

European Court holds agricultural slurry is not waste

Commission v Spain **(C-416/02 European Court of Justice 8 September 2005)**

The European Court of Justice has held that agricultural slurry spread on fields as a fertiliser falls outside the legal definition of waste under Community law. The decision in *Commission v Spain* represents another exploration by the Court into the distinction between by-products of a process and a residue, and comes at a time when the Commission is developing a new discussion document on whether current legal definitions are appropriate.

The infringement proceedings brought by the Commission against Spain related to a number of environmental Directives, but the issue of particular general interest concerned the disposal of slurry from a pig farm in the Commune of Vera. The slurry was stored and spread regularly on fields up to 12 kilometres away. The Commission argued that as such it was waste and required express authorisation in accordance with the Waste Framework Directive. Spain argued that the slurry was a by-product of the pig farm being put to beneficial use and fell outside the legal definition of waste.

In accordance with previous case law on the subject, the Court noted that the critical question was whether the slurry could be said to have been 'discarded'. In the interests of the Directive's environmental goals the Court has adopted a generous approach to the meaning of that term. However, it acknowledged that, in line with its 2002 decision in *Palin Granit* (Case C-9/00) there were circumstances where a substance should be treated as a genuine by-product falling outside the Waste Framework Directive: 'There is, in such a case, no reason to hold that the provisions of that Directive, which are intended to regulate the disposal or recovery of waste, apply to goods, materials and raw materials which have an economic value as products regardless of any form of processing and which, as such are subject to the legislation applicable to those products, providing such re-use is not a mere possibility but a certainty, without any further processing prior to re-use and as part of a continuing process of production.'

The Commission accepted that slurry spread on the same agricultural holding on which it had arisen might be treated as a by-product, but argued that the analysis could not apply where, as in this case, the slurry was spread on fields belonging to third parties and many miles away. The Court, however, agreed with the UK that this was not a determinant factor and that slurry might still be treated as a by-product provided it was certain to be used to meet the needs of others.

As is so often the case with waste cases, conclusions were driven by an assessment of the facts. In his Opinion, the Advocate General noted that the slurry was being applied to land on a regular basis every two weeks, irrespective of growth phase or time of year. He considered it had not been established whether the fields were cultivated or whether the fertiliser spreading was necessary, and concluded that the re-use of the slurry fertiliser was not obvious and definitely not a certainty. In accordance with the previous principles of the Court, it had therefore been discarded and was waste.

The Court took a diametrically opposed view: 'It is clear from the contents of the case file that the slurry is used as an agricultural fertiliser and spread for that purpose on clearly identified land. It is stored in a pond awaiting spreading. The person running the farm in question is not therefore seeking to discard it, with the result that the slurry is not waste within the meaning of Directive 75/442.' The Court acknowledged that the spreading might have been contrary to requirements under the Nitrates Directive, but this did not affect the analysis as to whether it was waste for the purposes of the Waste Directive.

In relation to animal carcasses disposed on farms, the Court held that specific legislation under Directive 90/667 regulated their disposal and provided the equivalent degree of environmental protection as the Waste Directive. Since the waste Directive does not apply to wastes covered by the other Community legislation, it concluded that such carcasses were also not waste for the purposes of the Framework Directive.

DEFRA is now considering the implications of the judgment. In its consultation on draft waste management regulations, it has proposed a category of licence exemptions for slurry and other specified agricultural waste spread on land for beneficial use under certain conditions. In light of the ECJ judgment, DEFRA has acknowledged that such an exemption may now not be needed in most cases of slurry disposal since no waste is involved, though it is keeping open the possibility for residual cases which do not fall within the Court's criteria for by-products. The judgment in *Commission v Spain* appears to be applying existing principles of the Court to a particular set of facts. It might be argued that the Court's assessment of the facts, which were so contrasted to those of the Advocate General, are in fact a coded signal to member states and regulators to take a rather less expansive view of what is waste in order to encourage recycling and re-use. This may, however, have been reading too much into the decision.

European Court confirms Austrian GMO ban is illegal

Land Oberösterreich and Austria v Commission **(European Court of Justice 5 October 2005, joined cases T-3666/03 and T-235/04)**

The legal difficulties facing Member States that wish to introduce environmental measures stricter than those contained in European Community market-based legislation has been underlined by a decision of the European Court of Justice in a case concerning a proposed Austrian ban on genetically modified organisms. *Land Oberösterreich and Austria v Commission* raises important issues concerning the ability of national or regional governments to introduce GMO-free zones within their territory.

The release of GMOs within the European Community is now governed by Directive 2001/18/EC, which provides for a Community consent system based on a health and environmental risk assessment. Article 23 of the Directive gives a member state the power to restrict a GMO that has received a consent under the Directive in the light of new or additional information. However, such a restriction may only be provisional and must relate specifically to the GMO in question.

In 2003, the province of Upper Austria produced a draft law that would ban the cultivation of GM crops and breeding of transgenic animals in its territory for a three-year period. Since this was in effect a preventative measure and did not relate to any specific authorised GMO, Article 23 of the Directive could not be invoked. Instead, general provisions under the EC Treaty were relied on. If the Directive in question is based on the environmental provisions of the Treaty, Member States possess considerable discretion to maintain or introduce stricter environmental measures. But where – as in this case – the measure is based on the market provisions of the Treaty, the powers of a Member State are far more restricted, especially where it proposes a new measure as opposed to maintaining an existing one.

Article 95(5) provides that in the case of a new measure, this must be based on new scientific evidence relating to the protection of the environment or the working environment on grounds of a problem specific to the Member State. The proposed measure must be notified to the Commission, which must approve or reject it within six months. In the present case Austria duly notified the proposals to the Commission, which consulted the European Food Safety Authority about the value of the scientific information supplied by Austria. The Authority concluded that there was no new information justifying the ban and the Commission rejected the measure as not fulfilling Article 95. It was this decision that was challenged before the European Court of Justice

Before dealing with the substantive legal issue, the Court dealt with two significant legal points of procedure. The decision of the Commission had been addressed to the government of Austria, which had notified the proposed measures under Article 95. But the provincial governmental claimed that it should also have a direct standing before the Court since it had proposed the measures, and indeed under Austrian constitutional arrangements had the exclusive power to do so. The standing of parties other than member states before the European Court is limited under the Treaty to those who are 'directly and individually' concerned in the matter, and the Court has consistently adopted a strict interpretation of this provision. According to Court rulings, the decision in question must affect the party in a way that is distinct from others affected. However, in this case the Court accepted that because the provincial government itself had proposed the measure, and was prevented from exercising its powers by the Commission decision to reject, it was 'individually concerned' and had standing before the Court.

The provincial government argued that it should have had a right to be heard before the Commission reached its decision. Article 95 contains no such express right in a previous decision in 2003, *Commission v Denmark* (C-3/00, European Court of Justice, 30 March 2003) the Court had held that no such right should be implied. That decision was mainly on the grounds that Article 95 envisaged a speedy decision-making process, and it was initiated by a member state that therefore already had the opportunity to fully state its reasons. The applicants tried to distinguish that case on the grounds that it concerned an existing measure rather than a proposal, but the Court was not convinced: 'The authors of the Treaty intended the procedure should be speedily concluded in order to safeguard the applicant member state's interest in being certain of the applicable rules, and in the interest of the proper functioning of the internal market.'

As to the substance of the complaint, the Court noted that the Treaty was justified in placing much stricter rules where a Member State wished to introduce new measures, as opposed to maintaining existing provisions. The adoption of new national legislation is more likely to jeopardise harmonisation. It was for the member state concerned to prove that the conditions of Article 95(5) had been met. In this case, the Commission was not convinced that there was new scientific evidence or that it related to a problem specific to the member state. The province had noted that there were small farms and that organic production was important in the region. However, the Commission had argued that the small size of farms was not unique to Austria, and that no evidence had been provided to show that this region had unusual or unique ecosystems that required risk assessments separate from those conducted in other parts of Austria or in similar areas of Europe.

The Court felt that the applicants had failed to provide convincing evidence to cast doubts on the merits of this judgment by the Commission. The applicants argued that the proposed measures could be justified under the precautionary principle, but the Court gave short shrift to this. Since the basic conditions required by Article 95(5) had not been fulfilled, the Commission had had no option but to reject the application.

The so-called 'green-guarantee' clauses in Article 95 were introduced largely on the instigation of Scandinavian countries. But it is clear from the Court of Justice ruling that Member States wishing to introduce more stringent environmental measures following agreement of a market-based measure face a tough evidential hurdle, and the guarantee looks to be more of a chimera than a reality. In the 1980s there were large number of legal disputes about whether measures should be based on the market or environmental provisions of the Treaty, but these were largely brought because there were different procedural requirements in the legislative process. The procedures are now the same, thus removing that source of dispute. But member states concerned with maintaining greater local autonomy for stricter environmental measures may once again now pay greater attention to the legal basis of Community proposals.

European Court ruling prompts overhaul of environmental assessment rules

Commission v United Kingdom **(European Court of Justice 4 May 2006 C-508/03) and** *R on the application of Barker v London Borough of Bromley* **(Case C-290/03).**

Significant changes to UK legislation implementing the 1985 EU Directive on environmental assessment will be needed after a recent

European Court of Justice ruling. In *Commission v United Kingdom*, the court agreed with the European Commission that the UK regulations, which require assessments only at outline planning permission stage, failed to reflect the Directive's obligations.

Many projects potentially subject to environmental assessment fall within the UK planning control system, with the Town and Country Planning (Environmental Impact Assessment) (England and Wales) Regulations 1999 implementing amendments made in 1997 to the 1985 Directive. Most of the project types listed in the Directive are subject to discretionary assessment, meaning a full assessment is required only where the planning authority believes the project could have significant environmental effects. The problem raised here was the way the system fitted into the planning provisions concerning outline planning permission. British planning law has allowed land developers to first seek outline planning permission, which gives a project in-principle approval but reserves matters such a siting, design, external appearance and landscape for a later decision. This can be important for securing finance because a developer will be assured of project approval without needing to supply detail in the initial stages.

The Directive required any necessary assessment to be undertaken before 'development consent' is given. Under British law, outline planning permission has been treated as the consent. But at that stage, information relevant to the environmental assessment may have been left to reserved matters, which suggested that the Directive's requirements and the outline planning permission system were incompatible. British courts have tried to resolve the issue in several cases since 2000, suggesting that the two approaches could be made compatible but that much depended on the application type and nature of the reserved matters. The approach has been to require enough information to be provided at a outline stage to allow the main or likely significant environmental effects to be assessed recognizing that environmental assessment was required to deal only with significant effects, not all environmental effects. Both the British courts and the government circular on environmental assessment have accepted outline planning permission as the consent for the Directive's purposes, and that environmental assessment could not be carried out at the approval stage of reserved matters.

But the European Court of Justice rejected this approach. The Court noted that the Directive's definition of 'development consent' was the authority's decision entitling the developer to proceed with the project. The UK government argued that 'consent' under the planning system was granted when outline planning permission was given and not when subsequent reserved matters were approved. But the court observed that under British law a developer could not proceed with the development until reserved matters had been approved, and it followed that outline planning permission and the decision approving reserved matters must be considered to constitute, as a whole, a (multi-stage) 'development consent' within the meaning of Article 1(2) of Directive 85/337 as amended'.

It followed, according to the court that where national law 'provided for a consent procedure comprising of more than one stage, one involving a principal decision and the other involving an implementing decision which cannot extend beyond the parameters set by the principal decision, the effects which a project may have on the environment must be identified and assessed at the time of the procedure relating to the principal.' Where those effects cannot be identified until the time of the procedure relating to the implementing decision, then the assessment should be carried out during that procedure. Therefore the Court held that the rules providing that environmental assessment could not be carried out at reserved matter stage were incompatible with the Directive's obligations.

The decision in *Commission v United Kingdom* was based on infringement proceedings brought by the European Commission. But the Court also delivered on the same day a judgment on a reference from the House of Lords in a national case concerning the development of a major leisure complex in Crystal Palace – *R on the application of Barker v London Borough of Bromley (Case C-290/03)*. Although related to a specific planning project, the issue of law was the same as in the infringement proceedings, and the Court, cross-referencing to its infringement judgment, held that the inability of authorities to carry out an environmental assessment at reserved matters stage was incompatible with the Directive.

In doing so, it confirmed that the term 'development consent' in the Directive, though modelled on certain elements of national law, was a European Community concept that could not be dictated by the provisions of national law. The court ruled that in some circumstances an environmental assessment would need to be carried out when reserved matters are approved and that: 'This assessment must be of a comprehensive nature so as to relate to all aspects of the project which have not yet been assessed or which require a fresh assessment.'

The decision means the UK government will need to reconsider how environmental assessment requirements are integrated into current planning procedures – it will not necessarily be an easy task. A radical approach would be to concede that where a project is to be subject to environmental assessment, a full rather than an outline planning application must be made. But as the British courts have noted, this may place a straitjacket on the way commercial developments are conceived and evolve.

The European Court of Justice has acknowledged that further environmental assessment could be needed at the reserved approval stage where environmental effects could not be properly assessed at the initial stage. At reserved stage, a planning authority concerned about the detailed environmental implications of a development could, in theory, revoke the outline permission but only by giving compensation for the lost development rights.

The Directive carefully does not require consent to be refused where environmental effects are significant – simply that the decision-maker considers these effects. But the European Court might consider that the requirement under national law to pay compensation, should an authority refuse permission in a light of a subsequent environmental assessment, might constrain authorities in their handling of reserved matters of significance or where the situation had changed since outline permission was granted. The Court might decide this to be contrary to the Directive's underlying spirit. Once again the decision illustrates that when implementing a Directive into national law, it is often far more challenging to do so where there is an existing well-developed system which requires adaptation than where there is a blank slate.

European Court upholds legality of aggregates levy

British Aggregates Association v Commission (Court of First Instance, European Court of Justice, Case T-210/02, 13 September 2006)

The European Court has held that the European Commission acted correctly in deciding the UK aggregates levy was not state aid contrary to Community law. The decision by the Court should encourage the national development of selective environmental taxes, while recognising that these must still be consistent with the principles of Community law.

British Aggregates Association v Commission was the culmination of a long-running legal battle brought by a quarry owner who felt the tax, introduced by the UK government in 2002, was unduly selective in its application and gave an unfair competitive advantage to businesses falling outside it. The tax was designed to discourage the use of virgin aggregates in favour of recycled material, but contained significant exemptions, including a five-year derogation for Northern Ireland, exemptions for certain materials and exemptions for exports. Overall, the UK government projected it would reduce demand for virgin aggregates by 8-9 per cent a year.

Quarry owners had originally challenged the tax's legality before the British courts but in 2002 the Court of Appeal stayed proceedings pending the result of the present challenge. Following a complaint concerning the tax's legality, in April 2002 the European Commission decided it did not constitute state aid because its scope, including the exemptions, were justified by the logic and nature of the tax system proposed. It was this decision that the British Aggregates Association challenged before the European Court of Justice.

The first question for the Court was whether the Association had the standing to bring the challenge. The Court has long taken a restrictive view on standing, essentially holding that an individual must show they are directly and individually affected by the contested decision before they can mount a challenge. The Commission argued that its decision to approve the levy was one of general application and denied it had significantly affected the competitive position of any of the Association's members.

But the Court rejected the Commission's argument. It had previously held that an action by an association, acting in place of one or more of its member who would have the standing to challenge was admissible. It accepted the Association's evidence concerning a number of quarry owners whose businesses had been affected sufficiently by the tax to give them standing.

The Court considered the substantive issues raised and whether the Commission had made a manifest error in concluding the levy was not a state aid. A state aid for the purposes of Community law under article 87(1) of the EC Treaty was a measure that could confer a selective advantage to the exclusive benefit of certain undertakings or sectors. The basic test, according to the Court, was for the Commission to consider whether the differentiation between undertakings arose from the nature of the general system of the overall scheme. If differentiation was based on objectives other than those pursued by the overall scheme, the measure in principle would be considered selective and state aid.

The Court emphasised that, in the absence of Community measures, it was open to member states to introduce environmental levies designed to tax certain goods or services to internalise environmental costs and/ or render recycled products more competitive. 'In particular, Member

States are free, in balancing the various interests involved, to set their priorities as regards the protection of the environment, and, as a result, to determine which goods or services they are to decide to subject to an environmental levy.'

In a further endorsement of the general use of environmental taxes, the court noted that when it came to its own assessment of a national scheme, it was for the Commission to take into account the environmental integration principle expressed in Article 6 of the EC Treaty. This provided, according to the court, that environmental protection requirements 'are to be integrated into the definition and implementation of, *inter alia*, arrangements which ensure that competition is not distorted within the internal market'. The court noted that the aggregates levy was an environmental tax which was, in principle, a burden on the commercial exploitation of virgin aggregates. The association had argued that other parts of the quarrying and mining sector that fell outside the levy's scope had the same environmental impact, but the court held that the decision to impose a levy only on aggregates fell within a Member State's power to set its own priorities in economic, fiscal, and environmental fields.

The levy had also excluded materials such as shale, low quality slate and china clay that in some cases could, after extraction, be used as aggregates, but again, and perhaps somewhat surprisingly, the court held that this was open to the Member State. According to the UK government, such materials had until now rarely been used as aggregate because of high transport costs, but if the exemption encouraged their use, this would contribute to a rationalisation of the extraction and use of virgin materials.

The court held this was 'acceptable' in the light of the environmental objectives pursued. This might be the case with the use of old stocks of clay and similar materials which the UK government had noted often disfigured landscapes. But it is rather less easy to see how the logic applies to the extraction of virgin clay and other materials as an aggregate substitute. The applicants argued that some aggregates with a highly technical specification (such as red chippings used on footpaths and cycle paths) could not be replaced by alternative products, undermining the levy's substitution goal. But the court held that even in such cases, the levy was justified because one of the tax's objectives was to internalise the environmental costs of virgin aggregate production. A levy on products arising from the extraction of materials which cannot be replaced by alternative products was also justifiable according to the polluter pays principle.

A second major concern of the applicants, and one that they claimed showed inconsistency with the levy's environmental objectives, was that the levy did not apply to the export of virgin aggregates. The court noted the levy in effect was an indirect tax on consumption rather than a direct tax on producer incomes. The export exemption could not therefore be considered to confer a selective advantage on exporters as it was justified by the nature of the levy as an indirect tax which applied in principle in the member state in which consumption occurred to avoid double taxation of exported products. In such circumstances, 'it was open to the member state concerned to grant priority to considerations linked to the structure of the tax scheme concerned over the environmental objectives pursued'. The Court concluded that it could see no inconsistency in the levy's scope and structure, and held the applicant had failed to establish that the Commission had made manifest error in its assessment that the levy was not a state aid.

In reviewing a decision by the Commission in a case such as this, the Court is not attempting to second-guess the decision, but was essentially asking whether the Commission made a 'manifest error' in its appraisal, similar to the approach a British court would take in judicial review proceedings. Applicants therefore face a considerable hurdle, and it is perhaps not too surprising that the challenge was not successful. What is particularly significant is that the Court used the decision as an opportunity to state clearly the considerable legal discretion that member state possess in the design of environmental taxes, and that equally the Commission must take into account the environmental integration principle when assessing their legality against competition principles, such as those concerning state aid, embedded in the Treaty.

CHAPTER 14

HOUSE OF LORDS

Strict liability for water pollution offences *Environment Agency (formerly National Rivers Authority) v Empress Cars 1998*

Human rights and self-incrimination *R v Hertfordshire County Council ex parte Green Environmental Industries Ltd* 2000

Limits on Statutory Nuisance *Birmingham City Council v Oakley* 2000

Failure to comply with environmental assessment Directive Berkeley *v Secretary of State* 2000

Human rights and appeal to independent court or tribunal *R v Secretary of State ex parte Alconbury* 2001

Liability for sewerage flooding *Marcic v Thames Water* 2003

Liability for contaminated land and successor companies *R on application of National Grid Gas v Environment Agency* 2007

HOUSE OF LORDS

Strict Liability in water pollution offences

Environment Agency (formerly National Rivers Authority) v Empress Car Company (Abertillery) Ltd (House of Lords [1998] 1 All ER 481)

An important ruling concerning the meaning of the key water pollution offences under the Water Resources Act 1991 has been given by the House of Lords. The lead judgment of Lord Hoffmann in the *Empress Car* case provides a fresh analysis of what is meant by 'causing' water pollution, and implies that causation can apply even where the polluter takes no active steps. The decision will require industry and sewerage undertakers to pay extra attention to maintaining pollution control equipment and other preventative measures if they are to avoid criminal prosecution.

Under section 85(1) of the 1991 Act, a person commits an offence if he 'causes or knowingly permits any poisonous, noxious or polluting matter or any solid waste matter to enter any controlled waters.' Compliance with a discharge consent is a good defence. The wording repeats the formulation in previous legislation, and the lead 1972 decision of the House of Lords in *Alphacell Ltd v Woodward*[1] held that the drafting implied two distinct heads of liability – causing the entry of polluting matter, and knowingly permitting its entry.

The enforcing authority, now the Environment Agency, must choose the appropriate charge, but the critical legal distinction is that with the permitting offence some proof of knowledge on the defendant's part must be proved. In contrast, the offence of causing the entry is one of strict liability in that lack of awareness is no defence, though it may be reflected in any sentence imposed. As Lord Hoffmann put it in the *Empress Car* case: 'The notion of causing is present in both limbs: under the first limb what the defendant did must have caused the pollution, and under the second limb his omission must have caused it.'

The *Alphacell* decision insisted that the notion of causation in the offence must be given a common sense meaning. But since that case there have been a large number of High Court and Appeal Court decisions exploring what is meant by 'causing the entry' of polluting matter. Some of these appeared to suggest that there must be a 'positive' act on the part of the defendant, and that where the pollution was caused, say, by the failure of control equipment this could not be an offence under the first limb. Similarly, where the actions of a third party such as a trespasser had caused the direct entry of the polluting matter, the defendant could argue that the chain of causation had been broken.

These decisions now have to be re-evaluated in the light of the House of Lords judgment in the *Empress Car* case. The company maintained a diesel storage tank on its premises, which drained directly into a river. Although there was a bund around the tank, the company had overridden this by fixing an extension pipe to the tank outlet which connected to a drum outside the bund. The tank outlet was governed by a tap which had no lock. In 1995, someone opened the tap, allowing the full contents of the tank to run into the drum, which overflowed into the yard and drained into the river. The person who opened the tap was never identified. It could have been an employee or, since there had been local opposition to the company's business, an act of sabotage may have been involved.

---

[1] [1972] AC 824

Nevertheless, the company was charged with causing the entry of polluting matter into the river. It was convicted by local magistrates and lost an appeal to the Crown Court on the grounds that it had brought the diesel onto the site and had failed to take adequate preventative measures, such as fitting a lock on the tap and ensuring the integrity of the bund. On appeal, the Divisional Court held that, despite the intervening act of a stranger, the Crown Court was still entitled on the facts to find that Empress Car had caused the pollution. But it agreed that the case law was confusing, and certified that there was a point of law of general public importance for the House of Lords to consider.

The House of Lords agreed that the first limb of the section 85 offence required there to be some positive act on the part of the company – but the critical question was what counted as a positive act. Earlier case law, such as that of the Divisional Court in the 1992 case of *Wychavon District Council v National Rivers Authority*[2], held that the failure to maintain a sewerage system which resulted in sewage overflows into a river could not amount to a positive act. But in Lord Hoffmann's opinion, such decisions 'take far too restrictive a view of the requirement that the defendant must have done something. They seem to require that his positive act should not have been in some sense the immediate cause of the escape. But the Act contains no such requirement. It only requires a finding that something which the defendant did caused the pollution.'

Although the House of Lords reaffirmed that common sense notions of causality must apply, Lord Hoffmann emphasised that answers to questions of causation would differ according to the purpose for which the question was asked. Lord Hoffmann drew the analogy of the owner of a car who left his radio in overnight. A thief breaks the window to steal the radio and in law would be considered to have caused the damage to the car, and he could not argue that it was the owner's carelessness that had caused the damage. But if this had been the third such occurrence in a year, a common sense, non-legal approach might suggest that it was the owner's failure to take reasonable care of his possessions that had also caused the damage and the loss of his radio. Both approaches were correct in their own terms. In the case of a prosecution under section 85, it was therefore wrong to ask the question 'What caused the pollution?' and there might be a number of different answers to that question. Instead, one had solely to consider 'Did the defendant cause the pollution?'

When it came to questions of the acts of third parties or the influence of natural forces, there were situations where both as a matter of

---

[2] [1993] 1 WLR 125

common sense and the application of legal rules there were duties to take precautions to prevent losses being caused by external events. But before considering questions of causation, it was necessary first to consider the purpose and scope of the rule in question to determine whether it imposed a duty to require one to guard against the deliberate acts of third parties or the operation of natural forces. This question was not one of common sense but one of law, and in the present case one of statutory construction.

It was clear that Parliament had imposed a strict liability for the first limb of the offence 'in the interests of protecting controlled waters from pollution.' Lord Hoffmann agreed with statements in the *Alphacell* judgments that not every act of a third party could be said to interrupt the chain of causation, and to the extent that other cases such as *Impress (Worcester) v Rees*[3] in 1971 suggested that they did they were wrongly decided.

Although liability under the first limb of the section 85 offence was strict, 'it is not an absolute liability in the sense that all that has to be shown is that the polluting matter escaped from the defendant's land, irrespective of how this happened. It must still be possible to say that the defendant caused the pollution.' Some of the subsequent case law dealing with intervening actions of third parties had employed the test of foreseeability, asking whether the defendant could reasonably have foreseen what took place before he could be said to have caused the pollution. But Lord Hoffmann was unhappy with the use of such language: 'Foreseeability is not a criterion for deciding whether a person caused something or not. People often cause things which they could not have foreseen.'

In his view, the true common sense distinction was between acts and events which were generally a normal and familiar fact of life, and those which were abnormal or extraordinary. Acts and events which were familiar in that sense would often be foreseeable, but foreseeability was not strictly a necessary element. In this context, there was nothing extraordinary about leaky pipes, people putting substances unlawfully into the sewerage system, or ordinary vandalism. On the other hand, in the example given by Lord Hoffmann, a terrorist attack which damaged a defendant's works and gave rise to pollution 'would be something so unusual that one would not regard the defendant's conduct as having caused the escape at all.' The same distinction could be applied to natural events. In the *Alphacell* case, falling leaves and vegetation had

---

[3] [1971] 2 All ER 357

blocked the defendant's pumps, causing an overflow, but the House of Lords held that they had still caused the pollution in that there had been no abnormal weather conditions but precisely what one would have expected in the autumn. The situation would have been different if there had been some extraordinary natural event or 'Act of God'.

Lord Hoffmann ended his judgement by summarising the key principles to be applied in the case of a charge under section 85. These are now likely to be widely used by magistrates and other courts dealing with water pollution offences.

First, the prosecution must be asked to identify what it says the defendant did to cause the pollution. If he cannot be said to have done anything then the prosecution must fail, although the circumstances might still warrant a charge of knowingly permitting the pollution. But the prosecution need not prove that what the defendant did was the immediate cause of the pollution – maintaining tanks, lagoons or sewerage systems were all doing something, even if the immediate cause was something else. Courts must then consider whether what the prosecution alleged the defendant did could be said to have caused the pollution, and must not be diverted by questions such as: 'What was the cause of the pollution?' or 'Did something else cause the pollution?'

Where the actual escape was also caused by the act of a third party or a natural event, courts must consider whether this should be regarded as a normal fact of life or something extraordinary. 'If it was in the general run of things a matter of ordinary occurrence, it will not negative the causal effect of the defendant's acts even if it was not foreseeable that it would happen to that particular defendant or take that particular form. It if can be regarded as something extraordinary it will be open to justices to hold that the defendant did not cause the pollution.'

This distinction between ordinary and extraordinary was one of fact and degree which courts must apply with common sense and knowledge of what happens in the area. On the facts of the *Empress Car* case, the House of Lords felt that there was ample evidence to entitle the courts below to find that the company had caused the pollution.

The decision clearly throws light on what has proved a difficult area of law, and imposes greater duties on industries and sewerage undertakers to take appropriate preventative steps to guard against the actions of third parties, equipment failure, or natural events such as storm damage. Lord Hoffmann's analysis of what is implied by causation may be of relevance to other areas of environmental law, but the decision is strictly confined to section 85 water pollution offences. Many pollution offences are now contained in the Environmental Protection Act 1990, but these are often drafted in differing terms reflecting their distinct historical origins. The key offences concerning waste disposal, for example, use the term 'cause or knowingly permit' but the term 'knowingly' also qualifies the causation limb, making the distinction of less critical importance. However, there appears to be little rational justification for maintaining such a distinction between the water and waste regimes.The offences concerning integrated pollution control, in contrast, do not use the language of causation or permitting, but are directly related to operating without or in breach of an authorisation. The statutory nuisance provisions of Part III of the 1990 Act employ different terminology and place liability on the person 'responsible' for the nuisance or in some cases the owner or occupier of the land in question. The opportunity was taken in the Environment Act 1995 to introduce greater consistency across the enforcement provisions of the different regimes, but it may be that the time has come for a more detailed analysis of the rationale behind the conceptual distinctions that still exist.

Self-incrimination and human rights

R v Hertfordshire County Council ex parte Green Environmental Industries Ltd and Another (House of Lords [2000] 2 AC 412)

In an important judgment, the House of Lords has held that investigatory powers under the Environmental Protection Act 1990 do not offend against national or European principles against self-incrimination. The case concerned potential waste disposal offences, and the result will be welcomed by the Environment Agency. But it will also be of wider application to other environmental regulators who possess similar powers.

R v Hertfordshire County Council ex parte Green Environmental Industries Ltd and Another arose out of the discovery by Hertfordshire waste regulators of over 100 tonnes of clinical waste in trailers and a warehouse on a site being leased to Green Environmental. This was in 1995, shortly before enforcement responsibilities were transferred from local authorities to the Environment Agency. The site was not licensed under Part II of the Environmental Protection Act, and the local authority served a notice under section 71 requiring the company to supply certain information relating to the illegal storage – notably who had supplied the clinical waste, who kept the vehicles used to transport the waste, and the locations of any other sites used by Green. Most of the information sought clearly related to the 'duty of care' responsibilities under the Act.

Section 71 confers a general power to require anyone to supply such information as an authority reasonably considers it needs for the purpose of discharging its functions. Failure to comply without reasonable excuse is a criminal offence. The company's initial response was to seek confirmation that any answers it gave would not be used against it in a prosecution. It noted that using the statutory power under section 71 rather than an interview with a suspect under the Police and Criminal Evidence Act 1984, where the suspect would be cautioned that he need not answer, effectively deprived a company of the right to silence. The local authority refused to give such an undertaking, and brought a summons in the magistrates' court for failure to comply with section 71. The case was adjourned when the company sought to challenge the validity of the notice in the High Court, and then the Court of Appeal. Meanwhile, the company and its director were charged with waste management offences, and the director, John Moynihan, was eventually sentenced to 18 months in jail

The Court of Appeal upheld the validity of the notice but its analysis was largely concerned with national law. It noted that the rule against self-incrimination was a deep-rooted principle in English law, but that statutory interference with that right was as old as the right itself.

The House of Lords, in contrast, found itself more concerned with questions of EC law, in particular the European Convention of Human Rights. Lord Hoffmann, giving the main judgment, began by analysing the national legal position. The company had conceded – rightly in his view – that the possibility of self-incrimination was not a 'reasonable excuse' justifying refusal to provide information under section 71. It was all a question of construction of the relevant statute. In this case, the powers 'have been conferred not merely for the purpose of enabling the authorities to obtain evidence against offenders but for the broad public purpose of protecting the public health and the environment. Such information is often required urgently and the policy of the statute would be frustrated if the persons who knew most about the extent of the health or environmental hazard were entitled to refuse to provide any information on the ground that their answers might tend to incriminate them.'

Lord Hoffmann also noted that a request for information under section 71 did not form part of any criminal proceedings per se. There was no question of abuse of investigatory powers since no oral questioning was involved, and the recipient could answer after seeking advice. None of the questions in this case called for any admission of liability, and there was no certainty that the recipient would in fact be prosecuted. Moreover, where a prosecution did take place, the information provided in the answers could be excluded by the trial judge under section 78 of the Police and Criminal Evidence Act on the grounds that the confession would prejudice the defence,

The House of Lords was therefore satisfied that the notice requirements were valid under domestic law. The defendants, however, using one of the country's leading Community law barristers, argued that since Part II of the 1990 Act was giving effect to the Framework Directive on waste and other EC waste laws, it had to be interpreted according to principles of Community law. The Lords accepted that in this context it had to have regard to the European Convention of Human Rights, since the European Court of Justice had clearly developed doctrines of fundamental human rights as an inherent part of Community law. Article 6 of the Convention provided rights of a fair and public hearing, and a presumption of innocence.

The leading case in the European Court of Human Rights was the 1996 decision concerning the former Guinness director Ernest Saunders.[4] He had been subject to investigation by inspectors under the Companies Act, but successfully argued that the subsequent use of transcripts of these investigations in a criminal trial against him was in breach of the Convention. This was despite the fact that the Companies Act expressly provided that the answers given to investigators might be used in evidence against him. As a result of the decision, the Act was amended to exclude evidence of the answers given in prosecutions for certain offences. Lord Hoffmann, however, noted that the *Saunders* decision was concerned with the fairness of a trial itself rather than extrajudicial inquiries.

The European Court of Human Rights had expressly stated that the Article 6 guarantees should not hamper what were essentially investigative procedures, and Lord Hoffmann felt that the Saunders case provided no assistance to the defendants here. If any answers provided were to be used in a subsequent trial, then a judge had the discretion to exclude them, and would have to do so in the light of the *Saunders* decision. This in practice probably means that such evidence

---

[4] Saunders v United Kingdom (1997) 23 EHRR 313

will almost always be excluded. The defendants also referred to a number of other decisions of the European Court of Human Rights. One of these concerned the validity of the European Commission's extensive powers of investigation in connection with the enforcement of competition law. The European Court felt that the Commission was entitled to seek information of a factual nature even though this might subsequently be used in infringement proceedings. But it was not entitled to seek answers to questions which might directly require an admission of an infringement. Lord Hoffmann felt that in this case the enforcement authority had fallen on the right side of the line and that the information that it had sought was essentially factual and did not invite any admission of wrongdoing.

The decision in the *Green* case must be the first environmental case before the House of Lords where the question of human rights has been directly at issue. With the entry into force of the Human Rights Act 1998 later this year, many challenges involving its principles can be expected, particularly relating to enforcement and procedural aspects of environmental law. For the time being, the *Green* decision allows the Environment Agency to breathe a sign of relief, but the judgment does not give an unfettered green light to the use of section 71 notices. The House of Lords clearly recognises that the questions asked in such notices must be confined to factual questions only and not seek a direct admission of guilt. But there will not always be a clear dividing line. More significantly, Lord Cooke acknowledged that had the case been concerned with the admissibility in a trial of evidence obtained in consequence of the answers given to an information notice - the so-called 'derivative evidence' concept - the result would not have been so straightforward. In his view, a reference to the European Court of Justice might then well have been appropriate. The story of self-incrimination and fair trials is far from over yet.

House of Lords reins in statutory nuisances

Birmingham City Council v Oakley (House of Lords [2001] 1 A.C. 481)

In what appears to be its first decision on the statutory nuisance provisions contained in the Environmental Protection Act 1990, the House of Lords has, by a small majority, placed a restrictive interpretation on the scope of the controls. The case concerned washing facilities in a house, but the decision has wider implications for environmental law – not least in applying a brake on local authorities using the statutory nuisance procedure to impose responsibilities on those who design or let buildings with sub-standard noise insulation.

Birmingham City Council v Oakley concerned a house owned by the local authority. The ground floor included a bathroom with a wash-basin, a kitchen with a sink, and opposite the bathroom beyond the kitchen a lavatory with no basin and no room to insert one. The layout meant that anyone wishing to wash their hands after using the lavatory would have to cross the kitchen to the bathroom or use the kitchen sink. It was only in 1991 that Building Regulations made it compulsory for new houses to have a wash basin in lavatories, and the premises pre-dated those requirements. The tenant was concerned that the layout carried hygienic risks, and made a complaint to local magistrates alleging the existence of a statutory nuisance.

Part III of the 1990 Act provided a modern restatement of the law on statutory nuisances which is designed to provide an efficient legal procedure for remedying environmental and public health problems. Section 79 lists a number of forms of statutory nuisance which include under sub-section (a) 'any premises in such a state as to be prejudicial to health or a nuisance.' It was this provision that was at the heart of the case. Magistrates found that a statutory nuisance under section 79(a) existed, and ordered that the lavatory be moved to the bathroom with an extractor fan. The Divisional Court dismissed the appeal by the local authority, but permitted an appeal to the House of Lords on the grounds that a question of general public importance was involved.

The local authority was fully alive to the possible financial implications of the decision. There are apparently some 20,000 homes in its area where lavatories have no separate wash-basins, and many more elsewhere. In the House of Lords, though, Lord Slynn warned against being over-influenced by such figures. The case itself concerned the less common situation where access to washing facilities was through the kitchen or in the kitchen itself. It did not follow that in other cases the non-provision of a washing basin in the lavatory would give rise to the same health risks.

The question focused on whether the term 'state of the premises' could, encompass the layout and design of the building. At first glance, it seemed that it clearly could do so, but Lord Slynn, supported by two other Law Lords, felt that a narrower interpretation was possible. The layout of the building was not itself prejudicial to health - it was the use of the rooms, including a failure to wash hands or using the kitchen for washing that gave rise to possible health risks. He therefore concluded that it was necessary to examine the history of the legislation to determine which interpretation was most apposite.

Lord Slynn traced the history of the statutory nuisance provisions back to legislation in 1846 concerned with houses in a 'filthy and unwholesome condition'. Legislation in 1855 and 1875 used the contemporary phrase of premises 'being in a state' as to be a nuisance or injurious to health, as did the statutory nuisance provisions in the Public Health Act 1936 which were replaced by the 1990 Act. In analysing the case law, he concluded that the terminology was 'directed to the presence in the house of some feature which in itself is prejudicial to health in that it is the source of possible infection or disease or illness such as dampness, mould, dirt or evil-smelling accumulations or the presence of rats. The state of the house must be prejudicial to health.' It followed that if there was a defective drain or lavatory, that could clearly constitute a statutory nuisance if it was prejudicial to health. But that was not the position here. There was nothing in the premises themselves which was prejudicial to health, and it followed that 'it is not sufficient to render the house itself 'in such a state' as to be prejudicial to health that the lavatory and washbasin are in separate rooms or that to get from one to the other it is necessary to pass through the kitchen where food is prepared.'

Two of the other Law Lords agreed with Lord Slynn's analysis. But Lord Steyn and Lord Clyde took a more expansive view of the legislation. According to Lord Steyn, 'The Act of 1990 must be given a sensible interpretation in the modern world. The distinction between layout and the state of the premises is not be found in the statute.' Similarly, Lord Clyde concluded that a narrow construction excluding consideration of a layout which was injurious to health or the absence of a facility without which a risk to health would be likely to arise 'seems to me to run counter to the intent and purpose of the past and present legislation.'

The statutory nuisance provisions consistently use the phrase 'prejudicial to health or a nuisance', and case law has confined the 'nuisance' concept to types of nuisance which affected personal discomfort since it fell within the context of public health legislation. Although the same phrase is used in the modern legislation, most commentators have felt that since it now appears in an environmental protection Act, the same limitations to the concept of nuisance should no longer apply, and that it could encompass wider environmental damage. The *Oakley* decision did not deal with this specific point, though the majority approach suggests that the more generous view may not prevail. In any event, the decision will inhibit local authorities attempting to use the statutory nuisance provisions to cure defective designs leading to environmental problems.

A particular example is that of older houses and flats with poor noise insulation. In the *1989 Ince* decision,[5] Southwark Borough Council was successful in arguing before the High Court that poor sound insulation fell within the statutory nuisance provisions dealing with the state of premises. But though the case was not directly in issue, both Lord Hoffmann and Lord Millet in *Oakley* expressly doubted whether that decision could now stand in the light of the current ruling.

Under the legislation, notices are initially served on those responsible for the nuisance, though the concept of responsibility is not elaborated in the legislation. Another route for dealing with noise insulation problems, which was earlier successfully tested by Southwark in an unreported decision, is therefore to focus on the statutory nuisance provisions dealing expressly with noise, but to argue that landlords or designers rather than the occupiers are 'responsible' for the resulting nuisance. The *Oakley* decision also highlights the importance of ensuring that Building Regulations deal effectively with standards relating to noise insulation or issues such as energy conservation. The development of new Building Regulations has been an elaborate and slow process, and many have argued that in comparison with many other European countries, the UK's standards on energy conservation and similar matters are well below what is needed. Certainly in the *Oakley* case Lord Slynn was surprised that it was only in 1991 that regulations relating to washing facilities in lavatories were made. Last year, the government issued a consultation document on new Building Regulation standards for energy efficiency. Although Building Regulations generally deal only with new buildings, the decision in *Oakley* indicates the limitation of statutory nuisance provisions as an instrument for change, and the result may give a new sense of urgency to those in Government responsible for the development of new building standards. In that respect, the House of Lords decision may have done a service for environmental policy.

Breach of EIA Directive requires planning decision to be quashed

Berkeley v Secretary of State and Others **(House of Lords [2001] 2 AC 603)**

The House of Lords has held that a court has very limited discretion to uphold the validity of a planning decision where there has been a failure to apply the EC Directive on environmental impact assessment. The ruling sends a powerful signal concerning the importance of compliance with EC rules which may well have implications for other areas of Community environmental law.

---

[5] *London Borough of Southwark v. Ince* [1989] 21 HLR 504

Berkeley v Secretary of State and Others concerned the redevelopment of the Fulham Football Club ground. The club applied for planning permission in 1994 to build a new stadium and a block of flats, including a new walkway along the bank of the Thames. The planning authority, the London Borough of Hammersmith, consulted, among others, the London Ecology Unit, which opposed the development because it felt that the walkway would encroach on the river bank and damage the local ecology. A lengthy report on the application was prepared by the planning department summarising the views of those who had been consulted or made representations, and recommended that permission be granted. The Secretary of State, however, called in the application for his own decision in order to assess the implications of the proposed housing density on local car parking and the development's impact on the Thames. An eight-day public inquiry was held, with the inspector eventually recommending that permission be granted subject to conditions. In August 1996, the Secretary of State accepted the recommendation and granted planning permission. At no time, however, did it appear that either the planning authority or the Secretary of State had considered whether the project should be subject to environmental assessment.

Annex II of the 1985 EC Directive on environmental assessment, mirrored in Schedule 2 of the 1988 implementing regulations, contains a large number of project classes which must be subject to assessment where they are likely to have significant environmental impacts, and the Fulham FC development potentially fell within the category of 'urban development projects'. A local resident challenged the validity of the planning permission on the grounds that the Directive had not been followed. Under the 1988 regulations, the Secretary of State is barred from granting planning permission for a Schedule 2 application unless the information obtained during the assessment procedures has been taken into consideration. The regulations go on to provide that a grant of permission in breach of this requirement is taken to be ultra vires, allowing an aggrieved person to apply to the court to quash the decision.

In the High Court, Mr Justice Tucker had doubted whether the project fell within a category requiring assessment. But the Court of Appeal concluded that there had been a failure to comply with the Directive. However, the Court of Appeal noted that even where a planning permission is held to be illegal, the court has a residual discretion whether or not to actually quash the decision. The Court felt that given the extensive public inquiry and background documentation, all the information that would have been prepared under the assessment procedures was in fact considered by the Secretary of State, and therefore refused to quash the decision.

The House of Lords doubted whether this was the correct approach. Lord Bingham observed that if the Secretary of State had in fact considered that the project fell within a class subject to the EIA requirements, he could not have waived the procedures on the grounds that there had been substantive compliance with those requirements unless he had formally exempted the project under Article 2(3) of the Directive - a procedure that requires notification to the European Commission. 'It would, I think, be strange if the Secretary of State could lawfully achieve by inadvertence a result which he could not lawfully achieve if acting deliberately,' Lord Bingham observed.

Counsel for the Secretary of State conceded that the Court of Appeal had been wrong to imply that a court could exercise its discretion not to quash the permission on the grounds that compliance with the EIA requirements would have made no difference to the final result. This was a significant concession, and Lord Hoffmann elaborated why he felt it was correct in law. He noted that Article 10 of the EC Treaty imposes a general obligation on Member States to 'take all appropriate measures, whether general or particular, to ensure fulfilment of the obligations arising out of the Treaty.' The 1985 Directive grants a discretion to Member States concerning its application to Annex II projects, but clearly implies that they are 'under an obligation to consider whether or not an EIA is required. If it were not so, a Member State could in practice restrict the scope of the Directive to Annex I cases simply by failing to consider whether in any other case an EIA was required or not.'

Lord Hoffmann noted that the Directive 'requires not merely that the planning authority should have all the necessary information but that it should have been obtained by means of a particular procedure, namely that of an EIA'. The European Court of Justice had already held that the Directive gave directly effective rights to individuals, and Lord Hoffmann concluded that 'the directly enforceable right of the citizen which is accorded by the Directive is not merely a right to a fully informed decision on the substantive issue. It must have been adopted on an appropriate basis and that requires the inclusive and democratic procedure prescribed by the Directive in which the public, however misguided or wrongheaded its views may be, is given an opportunity to express its opinion on the environmental issues.' He concluded that a court was not therefore entitled retrospectively to waive the EIA requirements on the grounds that the decision-maker had all the relevant environmental information before him.

The approach of counsel for the Secretary of State was rather more subtle. He argued that on the facts of the case there had actually been substantive compliance with all the procedural requirements of the Directive even if the term environmental assessment had not been used. There is one decision of the European Court of Justice, in a 1995 case between the Commission and Germany[6] which supports this approach. The case involved a challenge by the Commission concerning an authorisation of a power plant at a time when Germany had failed to transpose the 1985 Directive into national law. The existing national procedures, however, already required an assessment, the developer to supply information, and the public to be consulted. The ECJ felt that the Commission had failed to produce sufficient details as to which provisions of the Directive had not been complied with, and dismissed its application.

In Lord Hoffmann's view, that decision established that an EIA by any other name 'will do as well', but he did not feel that the procedures followed in the Fulham FC case fell in the same league. He noted that there were in fact implementing national regulations in place which had not been followed, and felt that a court should be reluctant to validate an act in breach of the regulations on the grounds that different transposing regulations would have satisfied the Directive. Furthermore, he did not accept 'that this paper chase can be treated as the equivalent of an environmental statement ... the point about an environmental statement contemplated by the Directive is that it constitutes a single and accessible compilation, produced by the applicant at the very start of the application process, of the relevant environmental information and the summary in non-technical language.'

The House of Lords unanimously agreed that the planning decision should be quashed. Its reasoning marks a reversal of the traditional approach of British courts towards the exercise of their discretion to quash or not quash planning decisions. In cases of truly minor infringements, the House of Lords accepted that a court might uphold the decision. But it clearly expects a much tougher approach from the courts in future, and one more in line with the stance adopted by courts in countries such as the Netherlands. As Lord Bingham summarised the situation: 'In the Community context, unless the violation is so negligible as to be truly *de minimis* and the prescribed procedure has in all essentials been followed, the discretion (if any exists) is narrower still; the duty laid on Member States by Article 10 of the EC Treaty, the obligation of national courts to ensure that Community rights are fully

---

[6] Case C-431/93 [1995] ECR I-2189

and effectively enforced, the strict conditions attached by Article 2(3) of the Directive to the exercise of the power to exempt, and the absence of any power by the Secretary of State to waive compliance (otherwise than by way of exemption) with the requirements of the regulations in the case of urban development projects which in his opinion is likely to have significant effects on the environment by virtue of the factors mentioned, all point towards an order to quash as the proper response to a contravention such as admittedly occurred in this case.'

More than any other piece of EC environmental legislation, the EIA Directive is rooted in procedural requirements and rights of public consultation. These features clearly weighed strongly in the decision. Yet the signals given by the House of Lords in the *Berkeley* case may well stretch beyond town and country planning procedures, and colour the approach taken by courts when faced with judicial review challenges in other areas of environmental law such as IPPC and waste management licensing where breaches of Community law are alleged. A number of the environmental Directives have been held to give individuals legal rights to standards of environmental quality, and while public participation requirements are far less developed than in the EIA Directive, this may not remain the case for long. At a seminar in London in June organised by the UK Environmental Law Association, a senior Commission official revealed plans for a Directive to introduce public participation rights into a raft of existing environmental Directives as part of the Commission's preparations for ratifying the pan-European Aarhus Convention[7]. In the light of these developments, the Berkeley decision takes on an even wider significance for UK environmental law.

House of Lords rules on planning and human rights

R. (Alconbury) v. Secretary of State for the Environment, Transport (House of Lords (House of Lords [2001] 2 All ER 929)

In what same observers have described as the most important planning case for fifty years, the House of Lords has held that the current system under which the Secretary of State is able to decide important planning decisions is not inconsistent with principles of human rights introduced under the Human Rights Act 2000. The result of the *Alconbury* case is a setback for those arguing for an independent planning court or tribunal,

---

[7] see now Directive 2003/35/EC of the European Parliament and of the Council of 26 May 2003providing for public participation in respect of the drawing up of certain plans and programmes relating to the environment and amending with regard to public participation and access to justice Council Directives 85/337/EEC and 96/61/EC.

but still leaves open important issues concerning the impact of human rights principles on current procedures. The importance of the case was indicated by the unusual decision of five law lords to give separate opinions. In doing so they comprehensively overturned the decision of the High Court last December. The High Court had held that it was inconsistent with the 2000 Act for the Secretary of State to be both a policymaker and a decision-maker in planning and related matters. The position was not saved by the right of judicial review before the courts since their powers of intervention were limited, and did not involve a full appeal on merits.

The starting point for the case was Article 6 of the European Convention on Human Rights which states: 'In the determination of his civil rights and obligations or of any criminal charge against him, everyone is entitled to a fair and public hearing within a reasonable time by an independent and impartial tribunal.' It was accepted that the number of planning cases where the Secretary of State had called in an application for his own decision or recovered the power to do so from the Planning Inspectorate was tiny compared to the total number of planning applications - around 130 call-ins per year out of some 500,000 applications, and around 100 recovered cases out of 13,000 appeals. But the figures are somewhat misleading, since almost by definition these were likely to be the most important or controversial cases.

The House of Lords accepted, following decisions of the European Court on Human Rights, that disputes under planning rules and areas such as compulsory purchase did involve the determination of civil rights within the meaning of the Convention, even though, as Lord Hoffmann observed, this was not what was necessarily what the original drafters of the Convention had in mind. Although there was no suggestion of any bias against individuals, the Secretary of State did not argue that, in dealing with called-in or recovered matters, he was acting as an independent tribunal within the meaning of the Convention. As Lord Slynn observed, 'He accepts that the fact that he makes policy and applies that policy in particular cases is sufficient to prevent him from being an independent tribunal.'

The critical turning point in the analysis was the role of the courts in reviewing decisions of the Secretary of State, and the extent to which this provided sufficient consistency with the Article 6 principles. The House of Lords examined rather closely decisions of the European Court on Human Rights which accepted that many administrative decisions which affect civil rights are taken by ministers answerable to elected bodies. Assuming that this decision-making system did not involve an independent tribunal, compliance with the Convention required that these decisions be subject to control by an independent judicial body 'with full jurisdiction'. The meaning of 'full jurisdiction' was therefore critical. Despite some earlier, more extravagant judgments, developing case law of the European Court has indicated that in the context of administrative decisions, Article 6 does not provide a right to a full appeal on the merits of every administrative decision. As Lord Hoffmann put it, 'Subsequent European authority shows that `full jurisdiction' does not mean full decision-making powers. It means full jurisdiction to deal with the case as the nature of the decision requires.' The core conclusion of the House of Lords was that in the context of planning and similar disputes, it was not essential or even appropriate for a court to have the power to review questions of policy in a sense that it should substitute its own view of what the public interest required. What is required of the courts, according to Lord Slynn, 'is that there should be a sufficient review of the legality of the decision and of the procedures followed.' Their Lordships accepted that the British courts had in recent years extended the ambit of judicial review, and that a mistaken factual basis of a decision could be now a ground for judicial intervention. Lord Slynn went further and argued that the principle of proportionality, long recognised as important in European law, should now be expressly recognised as being applicable to questions of domestic law in place of the more traditional '*Wednesbury*' test of unreasonableness.

One of the cases before the Court involved a Government Department with a direct financial interest in the outcome of the planning application since it owned the land involved. Here, the House of Lords dealt rather more perfunctorily with the issue than some would have expected. They did so on the basis that the Secretary of State did not claim to be independent, and that a court could exercise powers of judicial review if irrelevant considerations, including financial ones, had been brought into play. In one sense this is a correct analysis, but it does not reflect the difficulties for those wishing to challenge such a decision in producing evidence of any such bias – which is certainly unlikely to be provided in express terms in a decision-letter or similar documentation. The House of Lords' decision will come as some relief to the government, but it by no means marks the end of the application of human rights principles to planning procedures. Indeed, by expressly recognising that the determination of planning issues does involve civil rights within the meaning of the Convention, their Lordships have kept open the exploration of other aspects of the Convention. The question of the rights of third parties – particularly those whose property is affected by planning decisions – still remains unresolved, and there will still be strong arguments that some form of third party right of appeal is required. The immediate pressure on the Government to introduce a new independent planning or environmental tribunal is relieved, though there may remain strong arguments for doing so, even in the absence of specific human rights principles. Finally, the decision indicates that in the exercise of judicial review functions, the courts need to scrutinise carefully the way decisions are reached and their factual basis, albeit without interfering with the policy functions of government. Proportionality as a principle of review will be more extensively applied than at present. In these respects it is likely that, far from diminishing the role of the courts, the decision may enhance their influence.

Key Ruling on Liability for Sewage Flooding

Marcic v. Thames Water Utilities Ltd (House of Lords [2004] 2 AC 42)

In a test case on the liability of sewerage undertakers for damage caused by flooding from overloaded sewers, the House of Lords has held that private remedies under nuisance law or breaches of the Human Rights Act have no part to play. In doing so, it overturned the decision of the Court of Appeal which held that both contemporary nuisance law and the Human Rights Act could provide a remedy for individuals affected. *Marcic v. Thames Water Utilities Ltd* (4 December 2003, UKHL 66) concerned the owner of a house in Stanmore who had suffered repeated and serious flooding from an overloaded public sewerage system since 1992, and had even resorted to constructing his own defence system at a cost of £15,000. The sewers affecting the claimant's property did not qualify for upgrading under the system devised by Thames Water for determining priorities, although by the time the case reached the House of Lords the necessary remedial works had eventually been completed.

The statutory provisions covering the provisions of sewers are contained in the Water Industry Act 1991. Under section 94, a sewerage undertaker has a general duty to provide a system of public sewers to ensure that its area is drained effectively. The Act empowers the Secretary of State and the water regulator Ofwat to serve an enforcement order on undertakers who are in breach of their statutory duties, and such an order can be enforced by an injunction if necessary. The legislation, however, expressly excludes an individual seeking damages for breach of a statutory duty. It is only where an enforcement order has been served that an individual may seek damages where breach of the order results in damage, although the undertaker may plead a due diligence defence in such cases. In the present case, no enforcement order had been served on Thames Water, and while the claimant had made complaints to both the company and the local authority he had not complained directly to Ofwat.

In its 2001 decision, the High Court did not feel that that statutory provisions excluded the application of common law remedies, but held that the existing principles of nuisance law only applied where an undertaker had carried out a positive act which resulted in damages, and were not applicable where, as here, there was failure to do something. Nevertheless, the court had held that the damage was sufficiently serious to amount to a breach of the Human Rights Act and its provisions concerning respect for privacy and the peaceful enjoyment of possessions. The Court of Appeal reviewed the old case law on nuisance, and held that a contemporary approach should permit a claim in case of failure to act. Much of its judgment was concerned with this aspect of the case, though it also upheld the claim based on the Human Rights Act.

In overturning the Court of Appeal's decision, the House of Lords gave far greater emphasis to the comprehensiveness of the statutory scheme under that Water Industry Act, which now governs both the provision of sewers and their financing through charges. It noted that, in the absence of an enforcement order, and individual could seek no statutory remedy against the undertaker, and that his only remedy was to seek judicial review proceedings against the Secretary of State or Ofwat to force them to make an order against the undertaker. As Lord Nicholls noted, in pursuing his claim under common law and the Human Rights Act, Mr Marcic was effectively seeking 'to sidestep the statutory enforcement code.'

Lord Nicholls considered the old common law cases concerning the liability of local authorities for sewerage overloads. The Court of Appeal had held that these could no longer stand in the light of more recent case law such as *Leakey v. National Trust* ([1980] I All ER 17), which had held that occupiers of land could be liable in nuisance for failing to take steps to prevent potential hazards in their property from causing damage to their neighbours. Lord Nicholls felt the Court of Appeal had been mistaken to apply principles concerning the duty of occupiers of land to their neighbours to the duties of statutory undertakers, which were now governed by the statutory scheme contained in the 1991 Act. Under the statutory provisions, Ofwat sets limits on the amount that undertakers can charge for their services, and in doing so has to balance the need to alleviate flooding with the costs of doing so, as well as other policy priorities such as those required under EU Directives. 'The existence of a parallel common law right, whereby individual householders who suffer sewer flooding may themselves bring court proceedings when no enforcement order has been made, would set at nought the statutory scheme. It would effectively supplant the regulatory role the Director [of Ofwat] was intended to discharge when questions of sewer flooding arise.'

In dealing with the claim under the Human Rights Act, their Lordships were clearly strongly influenced by the decision of the Grand Chamber of the European Court of Human Rights earlier this year in the *Hatton* case concerning night flights at Heathrow. There the Grand Chamber emphasised that the Convention rights did not grant absolute protection of privacy or property, and that in areas involving complex policy issues a large margin of discretion should be granted to governments in determining the appropriate balances that had to be made between private and public interests. As Lord Hoffmann noted: 'National institutions, and particularly the national legislature, are accorded a broad discretion in choosing the solution appropriate to their own society or creating the machinery for doing so.' Although the claimant had clearly suffered, there was nothing so suggest, according to their Lordships, that the statutory scheme as a whole did not comply with the Convention.

The decision reflects a general concern of the courts becoming involved in making decisions about the allocation of public resources for which they consider themselves ill-equipped, especially where, in the nature of litigation, they are normally faced with resolving a discrete dispute between an individual and a public authority rather than considering the wider policy context. Nevertheless, although Mr Marcic lost at the last round, the litigation has clearly had some positive impact. In March last year, Ofwat issued a consultation paper which acknowledged the seriousness of the problem of flooding from sewers, and made proposals for undertakers to deal more speedily with severe external flooding cases which should in future be included in their investment programmes.

Lord Nicholls also noted that existing regulations provided for modest compensation in respect of internal flooding for those who suffered while waiting remediation schemes. But the regulations made no provisions for compensation for the type of external flooding which had occurred in the present case, with some undertakers voluntarily providing compensation, but others not. Lord Nicholls felt this was unacceptable: 'The minority who suffer damage and disturbance as a consequence of the inadequacy of the sewerage system ought not to be required to bear and unreasonable burden.' Such compensation would eventually be funded through increased charges, but it was perfectly fair that the majority who benefited from an adequate system should compensate the minority who did not. He called on Ofwat and others to reconsider the provisions of compensation for external flooding.

Although the general scheme concerning the provision of sewers might be fair, Thames Water did not escape censure for its handling of Mr Marcic's repeated complaints. According to Lord Nicholls, 'It cannot be acceptable that in 2001, several years after Thames Water knew of Mr Marcic's serious problems, there was still no prospect of the necessary work being carried out for the foreseeable future. At times Thames Water handled Mr Marcic's complaints in a tardy and insensitive fashion.' As a result of the House of Lords decision, future complaints concerning the inadequacy of sewers must be directed to Ofwat, and it is equally clear that the robustness with which it deals with the problem will now be under increasing scrutiny.

Statutory successor not liable under contaminated land regime.

R on the application of National Grid Gas PLC (formerly Transco PLC) v Environment Agency **(House of Lords [2007] UKHL 30)**

The House of Lords has held that the contaminated land regime does not impose liability on statutory successors to companies whose gasworks caused contamination. In overruling last year's High Court decision, the Lords resisted allowing the 'polluter pays' principle to give an extended interpretation of the legislative language. The Lords ruling was a u-turn on last year's High Court decision and indicated that, where retrospective liability is imposed under a statutory regime, it is for Parliament rather than the courts to define who should be liable.

R on the application of National Grid Gas PLC (formerly Transco PLC) v Environment Agency concerned a site in Bawtry, Doncaster, which had been used as a coal gasworks by the Bawtry and District Gas Company and its successor bodies from about 1915. The site ceased operations shortly after nationalisation in 1948 and the land was sold to a private developer for housing by the East Midlands Gas Board in 1965. The gasworks had deposited coal tar residues under the land. Before the land was sold, it appears the residues had been drawn into underground containers – in line with contemporary practice – but these had probably been breached during development. In 2001 a pit filled with coal tar was found in the garden of one of the properties. The Environment Agency declared the whole area, including 11 residential properties, a special site under the contaminated land regime under Part IIA of the Environment Protection Act 1990. Remediation cost about £66,000 per property and the question in law was who should pay for it.

Liability under the regime is in essence imposed on the person or persons who 'caused or knowingly permitted' the presence of the contaminating substances. But if they cannot be found, liability for remediation rests on the current owner or occupier, subject to financial hardship provisions. The Environmental Agency had already indicated it would not impose any liability on the current householders in this case. The Agency determined that the developers and National Grid Gas, as the contemporary statutory successors to the original gas companies, were equally liable as the persons who caused the contamination. The developers were no longer in existence and the Agency carried out remediation works, seeking a 50 per cent contribution from National Grid Gas.

National Grid challenged the Agency's interpretation of the regime and Bawtry was seen as a test case for many other sites formerly occupied by previous statutory bodies. National Grid accepted that if it was the current owner of a contaminated site or had actually caused the contamination it might be liable under the regime, but in this case the land had been sold before the company had existed and before the gas industry was privatised.

The Agency's first argument rested on an extended interpretation of the meaning of the person who caused or knowingly permitted the contamination. National Grid was clearly a separate legal entity from its predecessor bodies, but the Agency argued that statutory succession provisions were intended to preserve legal continuity. The polluter pays principle underpinned the contaminated land regime, it said, and therefore it was permissible to give a more purposeful construction to the meaning of 'person' under Part IIA to avoid remediation costs falling on innocent owners or the public purse. This argument had been accepted in the High Court but was firmly rejected by the House of Lords. According to Lord Hoffmann: 'National Grid did not cause or knowingly permit any substances to be in, on or under the land. This was done by East Midlands Gas Board or its predecessors as gas undertakers many years before National Grid came into existence. There is nothing in the Act to say that an appropriate person shall be deemed to be some other person or which defines who that person shall be.' Lord Scott was even more dismissive of the High Court's approach: 'This is, in my opinion, a quite impossible construction to place on the uncomplicated and easily understandable statutory language.' The Agency has stressed that the contaminated land regime was based on the polluter pays principle and that innocent owners or occupiers of contaminated land should not to have to pay. Lord Scott noted: 'I have no doubt that was so and have no quarrel with that principle. But Transco was not a polluter and is no less innocent of having "caused or knowingly permitted" the pollution than the innocent owner or occupiers of the 11 residencies.'

The Agency's second main line of argument related to the various Acts of Parliament that had created successor gas companies, and the provisions concerning the transfer of assets and liabilities. Both the Gas Acts 1948 (nationalisation) and the Gas Act 1986 (privatisation) transferred liabilities that existed 'immediately before' the transfer took place. The Agency argued that the contaminated land regime has imposed retrospective liability in the sense that bodies that have caused contamination could now be liable for actions that were legal at the time. Given that approach, it was acceptable to interpret the previous statutory provisions concerning the transfer of liabilities to now include liabilities under the Part IIA of the Environment Act 1995.

Their Lordships dismissed this interpretation. Lord Hoffmann noted it was true that the contaminated land regime was retrospective by creating a potential present liability for acts done in the past. 'But it is not the same as creating a deemed past liability for those acts. There is nothing in the Act to create retrospectively in this sense,' he said.

In this context, Lord Scott was particularly concerned that on privatisation in 1986, the public were invited to invest on the basis of liabilities in the new company as being limited to those existing immediately before the Act. 'I find it extraordinary and unacceptable that a public authority, a part of government, should seek to impose a liability on a private company, and thereby reduce the value of the investment held by its shareholders, that falsifies the basis on which the original investors, the subscribers, were invited by government to subscribe for shares,' he said.

Lord Neuberger, though, gave a more nuanced view on the issue of shareholder expectations. People who had bought shares before 1995 in a company that had caused contamination might be equally aggrieved that the application of the polluter pays principle had now unpredictably falsified the basis on which the original investors, the subscribers, were invited by government to subscribe for shares. But he accepted that this might be a consequence of imposing retrospective liability and that in such circumstances public and private interest in decontaminating land outweighed shareholder interests. The increasing awareness of the seriousness and extent to which land has been contaminated must inevitably have both unexpected physical and economic consequences. 'Where a polluter has ceased to exist and the whole of its business, or at least the whole of its relevant business, has been acquired by another company, it might well appear to many people to be similarly justifiable, at least in some circumstances, if liability for decontamination was extended to apply to that other company.' But in Lord Neuberger's view, the circumstances where it would be right to extend the polluter pays concept in such a way is a matter of policy for the legislature, not for the courts. 'The role of the courts is to interpret the relevant statutory provisions which the legislature has enacted, in order to determine whether they have that effect,' he said. He agreed it was not possible to interpret the relevant statutory provisions in the way contended for by the Agency.

The decision in *National Grid* does not necessarily imply that all statutory successor bodies, whether in the public or private sector, are relieved from liability under the contaminated land regime. Much will depend on the words actually used in specific transfer schemes. For instance, the legislation which privatised the water industry – the Water Act 1989 – provided that a transfer scheme made by the Secretary of State could provide that a successor body is to be treated as the same person in law as the water authority from which it is transferred. If a transfer scheme contained such a provision, it is likely that the successor body would be liable as an appropriate person where the previous water authority had caused the contamination. Similarly, some liability transfer provisions expressly include liabilities arising under future legislation, and such provisions could also impose liability under the contaminated land regime. Government no doubt will now have to evaluate carefully the implications of the decision against the different regimes governing statutory bodies. It must decide whether in reality it is confined to a narrow set of circumstances or whether it implied such a significant problem for the contaminated land regime as to require new amending legislation. As their Lordships noted, Parliament can impose what liabilities it sees fit on whom it chooses. But Lord Scott warned that 'very careful statutory language would be needed to impose on a company innocent of any polluting activity a liability to pay for works to remedy pollution caused by others to land it had never owned or had any interest in'.

CHAPTER 15

COURT OF APPEAL

Liability for nuclear contamination *Blue Circle Industries v Ministry of Defence* 1998

Landowner's liability in public nuisance *Railtrack plc v London Borough of Wandsworth* 2001

Environment assessment and review by courts *R on application of Jones v Mansfield District Council* 2003

Designation of nature conservation sites and human rights *R on application of Fisher v English Nature* 2004

Waste derived fuels are not waste *R ex parte OSS v Environment Agency* 2007

COURT OF APPEAL

Liability for Nuclear Contamination

Blue Circle Industries v Ministry of Defence (Court of Appeal (Civil Division) [1998] 3 All ER 385)

The Court of Appeal has upheld the 1998 decision of the High Court to hold the Ministry of Defence liable for over £6 million in respect of a radioactive contamination incident at the Atomic Weapons Establishment at Aldermaston in 1989. The judgment is one of a handful interpreting civil liability provisions in the Nuclear Installations Act 1965 and will be relevant to the operators of any nuclear establishment.

Blue Circle Industries v Ministry of Defence arose from a storm which caused ponds at Aldermaston to overflow via a stream into a marshland and lake on an estate owned by Blue Circle. The marshland was contaminated with radioactive material, including plutonium, which it was not practically possible to separate from the soil. Although the marshland was not a principal feature of the 137-acre estate, expert valuers agreed that the economic value of the entire estate had been affected. Furthermore, it was agreed that the estate was unsaleable until the contaminated soil had been removed. Blue Circle sought damages for the loss it had suffered as a result.

Generally in cases concerning civil liability negligence on the part of the defendants has to be proved. But the Nuclear Installations Act provides a special regime for radioactive contamination from nuclear installations. Essentially, it imposes absolute liability on the operator without the need to prove negligence, together with greatly extended time limits for bringing claims. As a sort of *quid pro quo* for this extra exposure to liability, the Act also introduced ceilings on liability in respect of any incident, in line with international conventions. Furthermore, as the High Court held in the *Merlin* case in 1990[1] – its first decision on these provisions – liability is limited to compensation for personal injury and damage to property. Pure economic damage without any physical injury is not covered.

In the *Blue Circle* case, the High Court had concluded that the incident had resulted in radioactivity levels well above normal background levels and in excess of statutory limits, though below levels which would have posed a risk to health. In the Court of Appeal, the Ministry of Defence (MoD) argued that section 7 of the 1965 Act imposed liability for damage to property which 'arose out of or resulted from radioactive properties.' While there had clearly been contamination, the MoD contended that it could not be said that the soil had been 'damaged' by the radioactive material. It was physically the same as before although mixed with a small amount of plutonium. Nor was there any potential or actual risk to humans or the environment. Although the soil had to be removed, this was not because it had been damaged, but in order to comply with statutory limits.

The Appeal Court, in line with the High Court, rejected the argument. Although section 1 of the 1965 Act related to physical damage it was not limited to particular types of damage. According to the Court, 'damage within the Act would occur provided there was some alteration in the physical characteristics of the property, in the present case, the marshland, caused by radioactive properties which rendered it less useful or less valuable.' It was clear from the valuation evidence that the marshland was less valuable than it had been, and that the contamination was such that the soil had to be removed in order to comply with the regulations.

---

[1] *Merlin v British Nuclear Fuels Ltd* [1990] 3 All ER 711

English courts have generally been reluctant to impose liability in cases involving pure economic loss without any physical damage, mainly on policy grounds to restrict exposure to liability. But the Court was satisfied that this was not the case here: 'The consequence was economic in the sense that the property was worth less and required the owner to expend money to remove the topsoil but the damage was physical.'

The MoD's second main argument concerned the extent of its liability. It maintained that any liability should be restricted to compensation for the property damage due to the radioactive contamination. In this case, this meant the damage to the marshland as being the only property directly affected, and should not extend to the consequential losses arising from the drop in value of the estate as a whole.

Again the Court of Appeal disagreed. The 1965 Act did not contain any limitation on applying the normal principles concerning remoteness of damage in civil liability. Once an operator was in breach of the duty not to damage property imposed by the Act, liability should extend to all losses caused by the damage which were reasonably foreseeable and not too remote. There was no reason to restrict such losses to damage to the marshland itself.

In this case, although not a principal feature of the estate, the marshland was situated close to the centre of the property, and it 'must have been reasonably foreseeable that damage to the marshland would affect both the use and the value of more than the marshland.' The High Court's decision to award damages, including interest, of just over £6 million was therefore upheld. The decision underlines the potential exposure to strict liability for operators of nuclear installations, and neither the High Court nor the Court of Appeal were persuaded to adopt a restrictive interpretation of the statutory provisions. But the way in which the Court interpreted the meaning of physical damage, and the application of principles concerning liability for consequential economic damage, may now be significant in a wider context.

Landowner's liability in public nuisance

Railtrack plc v London Borough of Wandsworth **(Court of Appeal (Civil Division) [2001] EWCA Civ 1236)**

The Appeal Court has held that Railtrack was liable in public nuisance for the environmental problems caused by pigeons roosting on a railway bridge across a busy urban street. The decision contains an important review of the principles of legal liability where nuisances are permitted to occur though not directly caused by a party, and as such has wider implications for environmental responsibilities of landowners.

Railtrack plc v London Borough of Wandsworth concerned a railway bridge owned by Railtrack crossing Balham High Street in South London. Complaints about the prevalence of droppings from pigeons roosting on the bridge began about twenty years ago. The most likely explanation was the increased number of pigeons due to an expansion of food outlets in the vicinity, although the court accepted it may have equally been due to heightened public sensitivity. As a result, and with the agreement of Railtrack's predecessor, British Rail, the local authority installed netting on the bridge in 1990 to prevent pigeons roosting there. Five years later, however, this was removed because pigeons were being trapped in the netting and dying. The local authority then arranged for daily cleaning of the streets at a cost of £12,000 per year, while Railtrack offered the opportunity to the authority to fix improved, permanent netting on the bridge – provided the authority paid the cost, estimated around £9,000. The authority felt that it should not have to bear this cost and brought proceedings against Railtrack, mainly based in public nuisance.

A public nuisance is generally defined as a nuisance that affects a large number of people or interferes with public rights such as the use of a highway, and as such is a crime. Civil proceedings for damages and an injunction may also be brought in public nuisance, but a private individual who sues in public nuisance must show that he has suffered damage which is distinct from other members of the public who have suffered. Local authorities, however, have specific statutory powers, under both the Local Government Act 1972 and the Highways Act 1980, to bring such proceedings to protect the interests of the public in the area without the need to show such special damage. There was no disagreement with the findings of the trial judge that the extent of the pigeon infestation and the amount of droppings were sufficient to be a public nuisance in law. He also found that Railtrack could not be said to have made an unreasonable use of its land, nor had the nuisance been due to any act or default by the company. Nevertheless, the judge held Railtrack liable on the grounds that it had been aware of the situation arising on its land but failed to take steps within its powers to remedy the situation. Railtrack appealed on the grounds that the judge had failed to apply proper legal tests of liability.

Nuisance liability generally occurs where a defendant has actively caused the problem at hand, but the courts have developed principles where a defendant did not actually create the nuisance but can be said to have allowed nuisance to continue on his property. At one stage, the courts were reluctant to impose any liability where the nuisance could be said to be due purely to natural causes, such as the spreading of weeds or landslips. But in a leading case in 1980 involving the National Trust[2] the Court of Appeal established that such liability could arise. However, it also accepted that the principles should be somewhat modified from situations in which a defendant had actively caused the problem, and held that a landowner was under a duty to do what was reasonable in all the circumstances to prevent a known risk of damage or injury to neighbouring property. The relative financial strength of the parties involved was also a factor to be taken into account. An impoverished landowner, for example, might discharge his legal liability by advising his wealthier neighbour to enter his land to carry out remedial steps.

Railtrack argued that the case law concerning liability for nuisance caused by natural events showed that there was a strong element of negligence that had to be proved, and that the trial judge had not sufficiently taken this into account. The Court of Appeal, however, emphasised that the cases on which Railtrack relied involved private nuisance disputes between private parties. The Court noted a Victorian case in public nuisance, *Attorney General v Tod Heatley*,[3] where the owner of a vacant piece of land was held liable for a public nuisance caused by people throwing rubbish on his land even though he had put up a hoarding to prevent it. The Court held that the principles in that case should apply, whatever the position in private nuisance. According to Lord Justice Kennedy, where there was a public nuisance on the defendant's land, it did not matter whether it was created by him, a third party, or by natural causes: 'If the defendant was aware of it, has a reasonable opportunity to abate it, has the means to abate it, and has chosen not to do so, then he is liable, and there is no reason to approach the matter as though it were a claim in negligence or private nuisance.'

Railtrack then tried to argue that the court should distinguish liability where physical damage was caused by the nuisance from those situations, as here, where there was essentially an interference with the enjoyment of property or the use of the highway. The Court of Appeal accepted that it was generally easier to prove a nuisance where physical damage was involved, but that the distinction between physical and non-physical damage did not affect the principles of liability.

Finally, Railtrack argued that the local authority should have dealt with the problem by using its statutory powers of cleaning streets, and its

---

[2] *Leakey v National Trust* [1980] 1 All ER 17
[3] [1897] 1 Ch 560

general powers under the Public Health Act in 1961 to deal with nuisance problems caused by pigeons in built-up areas. But the court held that the case was not concerned with the general problem of pigeons, but with a particular nuisance which Railtrck had a clear legal duty to address. In such circumstances, there was no reason why the costs of dealing with the problem should fall on local residents.

The *Railtrack* case is an important reassertion of liability principles where a public nuisance is involved. The Court of Appeal appears to have accepted that the financial implications for a landowner may be relevant in determining liability where natural occurrences are involved, though in this case it felt that they were not excessive for Railtrack even though the principles will clearly apply to other bridges owned by the company. It is perhaps unfortunate that the court was not more explicit in justifying the application of tougher principles in public nuisance as opposed to private nuisance rather than simply relying upon earlier case-law. But it is now clear that landowners will need to consider carefully their liabilities where problems occur on their land that are sufficiently extensive to be considered a public nuisance, and it will generally be insufficient simply to invite a local or public authority to deal with the problem at its expense.

Environment assessment and 'discretionary' projects

R on the application of Jones v Mansfield District Council (Court of Appeal (Civil Division) [2003] EWCA Civ 1408)

The Court of Appeal has recently reviewed the principles to be applied where a planning authority decides that a proposed project does not require environmental assessment. Resisting arguments that case law of the European Court of Justice called for a more intensive review of the issue by the courts, it ruled that the decision was essentially a matter of judgement by the planning authority, subject only to review by the courts on standard grounds that no reasonable authority could have come to such a decision.

R on the application of Jones v Mansfield District Council concerned an application for outline planning permission for the development of 28 hectare plot of farmland as an industrial site. It was accepted that the proposed development fell within one of the 'discretionary' project classes in the EC Directive on environmental assessment and national implementing regulations. Projects falling within any of these classes must be subject to assessment where they are 'likely to have significant effects on the environment'. The national regulations which implemented the Directive in relation to projects requiring planning permission essentially oblige the planning authority in the first instance to determine the question of likely significant effects, although there is no provision in the regulation precisely to that effect. The Secretary of State is given the power to give a definitive direction that in his opinion the proposal is likely or not likely to have significant effects, and before submitting a planning application the developer may also seek a prior opinion from the local authority as to whether the proposal will require an environmental assessment. Neither of these provisions was invoked in the present case.

The local authority considered the question of likely significant effects. There were no designated conservation sites in the area, but there was evidence that the proposal might have an impact on bats and on the habitat of birds in the area, in particular the golden plover. On this latter issue, English Nature was consulted, and said it was 'far from clear' that the proposal would have a measurable impact on the current bird population within the wider area available to the species in the county. The local authority concluded that no significant environmental impact was likely and that no environmental assessment was therefore required. It subsequently granted outline planning permission. That decision was challenged in the courts by a local resident on the grounds that the application should have been subject to environmental assessment. Earlier this year, the High Court held that the local authority's decision was reasonable and dismissed the application for judicial review, and the applicant was granted leave to appeal to the Court of Appeal.

During the course of arguments before the Court of Appeal, it was suggested by one of the judges that the question of whether a project was likely to have significant environmental effects might be a question of primary fact for determination by the court, rather than leaving it to the discretion of the planning authority, subject only to traditional grounds of legal review based on so called '*Wednesbury* principles' of unreasonableness. Not surprisingly, the applicant seized on the suggestion, and the Court of Appeal admitted that it was unfortunate that the issues were not subject to detailed argument before the court.

In the *Berkeley* case[4] in 2001, the House of Lords had indicated that in relation to the power of the Secretary of State to issue directions concerning likely significant environmental effects, this was subject to judicial review where no reasonable Secretary of State could have come to such of conclusion. The role of the courts in relation to a local

---

[4] *Berkeley v Secretary of State and Others* [2001] 2 AC 603)

authority making that decision was not dealt with directly in *Berkeley*, but the Court of Appeal felt that it would be very surprising if a court's reviewing function was different where the decision of the local authority rather than the Secretary of State was an issue. According to Lord Justice Dyson, who gave the lead judgment, 'Whether a proposed development is likely to have significant effects on the environment involves an exercise of judgment or opinion. It is not a question of hard fact to which there can only be one possible correct answer in any given case.' He concluded that the role of the court in reviewing such a decision should be limited to *Wednesbury* review grounds.

As to the correct approach to be taken by the local authority in making its judgment, that applicant argued that where there were any uncertainties about the environmental effects of a development, it cannot be said that that it would be unlikely to have significant environmental effects and therefore should be subject to environmental assessment. The approach underlined what is in some respects an inherent contradiction at the heart of the Directive in relation to discretionary projects. Without undertaking an environmental assessment, how can an authority judge whether likely significant effects are involved?

The court considered a number of judgments of the European Court of Justice relating to the Directive and discretionary projects. However, as it noted correctly, these cases dealt essentially with whether the Directive gave sufficient discretion to a Member State to exclude in advance whole classes of projects or a specific project from assessment as not likely to have significant effects. Though it rejected such 'blanket' approaches, the ECJ did not deal directly with the principles governing the exercise of the discretion, other than that it should be exercised. The Court of Appeal concluded that whether or not a project was likely to have significant effects was a question of degree calling for exercise of judgment. It adopted the approach of the High Court which rejected any overriding principle that unless an authority was confident of there being no likely significant effects it must require an environmental assessment, and that any uncertainty must be resolved in favour of an assessment. It was only 'significant' effects that came into play, and any minor environmental effects would be potential material considerations in considering the planning application.

The principles, according to Mr Justice Richards in the High Court and endorsed by the Court of Appeal, were that the planning authority 'must make an informed judgment on the basis of the information available to it and having regard to any gaps in that information and to any uncertainties that may exist, as to the likelihood of significant effects. The gaps and uncertainties may or may not make it impossible reasonably to conclude that there is no likelihood of significant environmental effects. Everything depends on the circumstances of the individual case.' Reviewing the actual facts of the case, the Court of Appeal agreed with the High Court that the planning authority had come to a reasonable conclusion on the basis of the evidence before it. Earlier this year, the Court of Appeal held in the *Gillespie* case[5] that authorities should not over-rely on the effect of mitigating measures imposed as part of the planning permission to assume that no significant effects were likely. In the present case, the developer had formally undertaken to carry out further ecological surveys, and various conditions concerning nature conservation were imposed. But the Court of Appeal rejected the applicant's argument that the planning authority had relied upon the undertaking and conditions in its determination about significant effects. The comments of English Nature were important, and according to the court it was reasonable for the planning authority to decide that the development was unlikely to have significant effects in relation to birds and bats.

The decision emphasises the large degree of discretion which planning authorities enjoy in relation to discretionary projects. Once a proposed project falls within one of the discretionary classes and this question probably is one of the law and fact reviewable by the courts – the authority must address the question of likely significant effects. But the judgement is essentially one for it to make, not the courts. The Court of Appeal rejected an overly legalistic approach towards interpreting the requirements, and was wary of it being used as technical grounds by third parties seeking to prevent the development. Lord Justice Carnwath in particular was concerned at the protracted procedures involved in the case, and noted: 'It needs to be borne in mind that the EIA process is intended to be an aid to efficient and inclusive decision-making in special cases, not an obstacle race.' No doubt this will not be the last judicial review concerning the environmental assessment requirements, but the courts are hinting strongly that they do not wish to usurp roles best suited to others bodies in the planning process.

Nature conservation and human rights

R on the application of Fisher v English Nature **(Court of Appeal (Civil Division) [2004] EWCA Civ 663)**

The legal validity of English Nature's procedures for designating Sites of Special Scientific Interest has been upheld by the Court of Appeal.

---

[5] *R (Gillespie) v First Secretary of State* [2003] EWCA Civ 400

The decision contains important principles concerning the significance of government policy and confirms that at the end of the day English Nature must exercise its independent judgment according to the criteria laid down in the legislation.

R on the application of Fisher v English Nature arose out of English Nature's decision to designate some 30,000 acres of arable land on the Norfolk/Suffolk border as an SSSI. The site is home to a substantial proportion of the UK's population of stone curlews, a migratory species present between March and October, and protected species under the EU birds Directive. Patrick Fisher, a farmer with land in the SSSI, challenged the designation. It was clear that the site would qualify as a Special Protection Area under the Birds Directive since it supported more than 1 per cent of the country's population of the species in question, and that designation was not questioned.

The applicant had voluntarily been involved in the protection of the stone curlew population, but questioned whether once an area was designated as an SPA it was always appropriate to designate it as an SSSI under national law. This was especially the case as, following amendments to the legislation brought about by the Countryside and Rights of Way Act 2000, SSSI status brought with it a much tougher system of regulatory controls. Between 1994 and 2000, it had indeed been the policy of English Nature not to designate large areas as SSSIs where migratory species, of necessity present only part of the time, were involved. In a letter to the then Department of Environment, Transport and the Regions, English Nature argued that such areas should still be designated as SPAs, but 'the conservation interest and pattern of ownership means that adequate protection and management action can be taken without SSSI designation.' This was essentially the position that the applicant adopted. However, the Department's policy was that any SPA designation must be underpinned by SSSI designation – otherwise a site deemed of international importance would not be considered of national importance. In February 2000, the general committee of English Nature's council approved the designation of three SPAs as SSSIs, marking a departure from its previous policy. A key argument of the applicant was that the change of policy was irrational, and that English Nature had been unduly influenced by the government's preferred policy on the issue.

The Court of Appeal examined the procedures leading up to designation in considerable detail. It was clear from the paperwork that English Nature recognised that voluntary measures for protecting stone curlews on arable land had achieved much, and that formal designation as an SSSI was novel in this context and might jeopardise existing relationships with landowners. Although it was not legally required to do so, English Nature had engaged in considerable consultation prior to notification, recognising the contentious nature of the proposal. The decision to confirm was taken by the council of English Nature itself, and in accordance with its practice it allowed objectors an opportunity to make oral representations. These procedures had been significant in safeguarding English Nature from a human rights challenge based on a lack of an independent court or tribunal.

The court reviewed a transcript of the discussion by council members with a view to determining what factors had influenced their decision. It felt it to be clear that the council did not consider that SSSI designation automatically followed from SPA designation, but that it had considered whether the site in question was of national importance under the terms of the national legislation, section 28 of the Wildlife and Countryside Act of 1981. SPA status was a relevant factor to this question, but not compelling. The applicant's main concern was that it was a flawed analysis to assume that SSSI designation must automatically apply to land with an SPA status. Although the national legislation used the term 'special scientific interest' it was important, he argued, to interpret the term in the context of both the purposes of the legislation in question and the statutory consequences which followed SSSI designation. On that analysis, the fact that it was important under EU or international law did not necessarily mean that it was important under national legislation.

The Court of Appeal was not convinced by these arguments. It was clear that the court was influenced by the fact that this was a decision by a specialist body, which should only be challenged before the courts on limited grounds of judicial review. Second, the court could not see how English Nature could reasonably have not made a designation of national importance when the site was considered to be of European significance, and rejected the applicant's arguments considering the 'purposeful' construction of the 1981 Act. According to Lord Justice Wall, 'English Nature reasonably formed the opinion that the area of land was of special interest by reason of its internationally important population of stone curlew. This led to the duty to notify under section 28(1) of the 1981 Act. There is nothing in the process of consultation, or in English Nature's considerations of the objections, to which objection can be taken.'

There was another, rather subtle argument concerning the Human Rights Act which the court was also asked to consider. According to the High Court, once English Nature had decided to notify the potential designation, it had a duty to confirm if it maintained that opinion as to its special status after hearing the objections. The question raised before the court was whether English Nature should also have considered the potential impact of designation on the applicant's rights under Article 1 of the First Protocol of the Human Rights Convention concerning the protection of private property rights. Essentially the applicant argued that SSSI designation was a disproportionate response to the need to protect SPA status which could achieved by other, less intrusive means.

Lord Justice Wall argued that the decision to confirm SSII status was clearly not simply a rubber stamp process following notification: 'I would prefer to construe section 28(5) of the 1981 Act as giving rise to the exercise of a power not to confirm, which is to be exercised in accordance with the conclusion reached as a result of the outcome of a genuine, open-minded consultation/investigation process.' As to the human rights points, he did not find any evidence as presented in objections by the applicant as compelling, and indeed English Nature has clearly made efforts to ensure that there is no undue restraint on farming operations. The specific question as to whether English Nature was under a duty to consider the human rights issues in its confirmation decision was not directly addressed by the court, which preferred to state simply that on the facts there was no disproportionate intrusion on the applicant's rights.

The *Fisher* case is one of a series of recent legal challenges against English Nature on designation procedures brought by landowners. This development has probably been an inevitable consequence of the recent shift from the largely voluntary system at the heart of the 1981 legislation to a tougher regulatory regime, largely brought about by the need to implement EU conservation legislation. The current procedures have survived legal challenges, although last July in the *Bown* case[6] the Court of Appeal was highly critical of complexities and lack of transparency in the UK procedures for designating SPAs. The present case underlines the extent to which the Government has largely used existing nature conservation legislation, strengthened in parts, to implement EU requirements. Although the *Fisher* case did not question the legality of this approach, it may still give policy-makers some pause for thought as to whether certain types of conservation designation under EU law might be more effective with a more dedicated regulatory

---

[6] *Bown v Secretary of State for Transport* [2003] EWCA Civ 1170

regime than that provided by SSSIs which was originally developed in a vary different context.

Waste-derived fuels are not waste

R ex parte OSS Group Ltd v Environment Agency and Department of Environment Food and Rural Affairs **(Court of Appeal (Civil Division) [2007] EWCA Civ 611)**

The Court of Appeal recently wrestled with the question of whether waste-derived fuels can cease to be waste in law before being burnt. The court rejected the Environment Agency's strict interpretation of the law with a decision likely to encourage greater use of fuels derived from waste or recycled products. Some observers hoped that the decisions in the *OSS* case would provide legal certainty regarding when a waste product ceased to be waste. The lead judgment was given by Lord Justice Carnwath, who is well-versed in environmental law and provided an extensive review of the European and national case law on the subject. But even he felt the European law as interpreted by the European Court of Justice made it impossible to provide a definitive ruling, and he urged the Agency and the Environment Department (DEFRA) to co-operate to produce practical guidance on the issue.

The OSS Group was in the business of reprocessing waste oils into fuel products. Its most recent product was known as 'clean fuel oil' which the company argued was materially indistinguishable from a natural fuel – a point which remains in dispute between OSS and the Agency. However, the key question was whether the product remained a waste in law. If it was waste, then any combustion processes would be treated was waste incineration and be subject to the Waste Incineration Directive's strict requirements. This would be likely to jeopardise any economic advantages of the recycled fuel over non-recycled 'natural' alternatives.

Waste legislation both at a national and European level has tended to focus on whether a material is waste in the first place, rather than on the issue – which is at the heart of this case – of when what is admittedly a waste can cease to be waste. The European Court of Justice has considered the issue on several occasions, but as Lord Justice Carnwath noted with a degree of frustration, its judgments often lacked clarity.

The starting point for any analysis is the definition of 'waste' in the Waste Framework Directive which applies to substances or materials 'which the holder discards or intends to discard'. Annex IIA and IIB of the Directive list operations which amount to 'disposal' and 'recovery of waste' including as recovery its use principally as a fuel and solvent reclamation. But the European Court of Justice has consistently held that 'discard' has an extensive meaning and can encompass the operations listed in Annex IIA and IIB. But it does not follow that if a substance is subject to one of those operations it is automatically a waste – one has always to ask whether it was 'discarded'.

Lord Justice Carnwath derived several core principles from the case law. The concept of waste should not be interpreted restrictively and 'discard' was to be considered in the context of the Directive's overall aims to protect human health and the environment, and the general principles of the European environmental policy, including the prevention and precautionary principle. In deciding whether burning a substance amounts to discarding it, the European Court has held that it was not relevant that it could be recovered as fuel in an environmentally responsible manner and without substantial treatment. The Agency, relying on its interpretation of the case law of the European Court of Justice, had adopted a tough but clear test: materials contained in lubricating oils that have been discarded and have become waste only cease to be waste when they are finally burnt. The standard of the prior processing was not relevant. The only exception would be waste fuel oil that was recovered for use as fuel oil which was chemically and physically identical to the original product and required no further processing. But here one was dealing with waste lubricating oil turned to a different use, and the limited exception could not apply. DEFRA had a more generous formulation. It accepted that material derived from waste lubricating oil to be used as fuel was not being discarded as waste provided it had 'the same characteristics' as the virgin fuel which it replaced. It was not a question of 'never' but 'if', and this would be a question of fact. For its part, OSS in the Court of Appeal reduced the test to two simple questions: was the material sufficiently analogous to the virgin product or material which it replaced; and was the material analogous in term of environmental risks in use? In its view the product in question met these tests.

Much turned on the key 2002 decision of the European Court of Justice in ARCO[7] which was concerned with waste materials transformed for use a fuel. A key question was whether a waste product which had already been subject to recycling operations listed in Annex II to turn into a fuel remained a waste until burnt. The court did not consider the application of the specified operations definitive: 'Whether it is waste

---

[7] Joined Cases C- 418/97 and C-419/97 (*ARCO Chemie Nederland Ltd* etc) 15 June 2002.

must be determined in the light of all the circumstances, by comparison with the definition set out in Article 1(a) of the Directive, that is to say the discarding of the substance in question or the intention or requirement to discard it, regard being had to the aim of the directive and the need to ensure that its effectiveness is not undermined.'

Lord Justice Carnwath found the passage unfathomable. The European Court has accepted that the fact that a waste substance had undergone a recovery operation was a factor in determining whether it was still waste. As such it had impliedly accepted that a substance which was waste could cease to be a waste even if it was destined for use as a fuel. But then the European Court had simply said the decision must be taken in light of 'all the circumstances' but without specifying the other factors to be considered, other than saying this must be done against the discarding definition in Article 1A. Lord Justice Carnwath felt this was meaningless as a response. The product's user wanted to reuse it not discard it and 'no amount of reference to 'all the circumstances'' would change that fact. No doubt the material was discarded by the original user: but the issue was not whether it was then waste, but whether it had since ceased to be waste.

The European Court in ARCO also noted that even where a waste had been completely recovered resulting in the substance having the same properties as a raw material, it could still be regarded as waste if the holder discards it or intends to discard it. Lord Justice Carnwath found the reasoning 'extremely obscure'. There were clearly objective factors relating to the product's characteristics and environmental impacts, but he could not see why the subjective intentions of the holder should acquire such significance when dealing with the question of whether waste ceased to be waste. Lord Justice Carnwath concluded that 'a search for logical coherence in the Luxembourg case law is probably doomed to failure'. A fundamental problem, he felt, was the European Court's continued adherence to the discarding definitions which had little relevance to the issue where the holder intends to use the material rather than discard it on any ordinary sense. What should be key was whether the material should continue to be treated as waste until acceptable recovery or disposal had taken place, because of the Directive's environmental policy aims. But as he noted, the European Court had consistently declined invitations to provide workable criteria to decide that question.

It followed that it was up to national courts to apply value judgments in the light of the indicators derived from the Directive's policy goals. Lord Justice Carnwath noted with approval a 2003 decision of the Dutch Council of State which held that waste-derived fuel pellets produced with the sole aim of being used as fuel, in the same way as regular fuel, and containing no contaminants should be considered equivalent to regular fuel and no longer a waste. Lord Justice Carnwath felt that such a decision showed a common sense approach, consistent with the aims of the Directive and the case law, and with the aim of encouraging waste recovery and reuse. 'It should be enough that the holder has converted the waste material into a distinct, marketable product, which can be used in exactly the same way as an ordinary fuel, and with no worse environmental effects. It cannot be said that such a material is being 'discarded' in any ordinary sense of the term and there is nothing in the objectives of the Directive which requires any fictitious assumption of that effect.'

Turning to the various tests proposed, the court concluded that the Agency's test was too narrow and not consistent with the case law, and overturned the decision of the High Court which had followed the Agency's approach. Similarly, although DEFRA's arguments were found generally more persuasive than the Agency's, the Court felt DEFRA's 'hardly distinguishable' test was equally too narrow Equivalence in both environmental implications and usage appears to be the preferred approach, though the Court felt that given that the European Court had declined to provide a definitive test, it was not the domestic court's function to fill the gap. It may be that the European Commission's current work on revising the waste framework Directive will provide greater clarity. In the meantime, Lord Justice Carnwath urged the Agency and DEFRA to pool their expertise to give practical guidance to those concerned with waste treatment and handling. In this context, he noted that the difficulties in interpreting the European Court of Justice case law were compounded by DEFRA and the Agency not being able to agree a common approach. He acknowledged the Agency's concerns of applying a more generous test and finding suitable comparators, but felt that the difficulty was not as great as the Agency suggested. It would be rash to assume that the OSS decision will be the last legal ruling on when a waste product ceases to be waste. Nevertheless, the Court of Appeal has indicated that the issue should be determined by the application of technical criteria and expertise rather than rigid application of legal principles. Lawyers may feel frustrated, but many will see this as a welcome signal.

CHAPTER 16

HIGH COURT

Habitats Directive and off-shore waters *R v Secretary of State ex parte Greenpeace* High Court 1999

Packaging Directive and garden centres *Davies v Hillier Nurseries Ltd* 2001

Noise nuisance and defence of public interest *Dennis v Ministry of Defence* 2003

Liability for water pollution offences *Express Ltd v Environment Agency* 2004

Third party standing and judicial review *R (on application of Edwards) v Environment Agency and others* 2004

Integrated Pollution Prevention Control and Best Available Techniques *R on application of Rockware Glass v Chester City Council* 2005

Consultation on energy policy flawed *R on application of Greenpeace v Secretary of State for Trade and Industry* 2007

HIGH COURT

Habitats Directive and Off-Shore Waters

R v Secretary of State ex parte Greenpeace (Queens Bench Division [2000] 2 CMLR 94)

The High Court has held that the government was wrong in its view that the 1992 EC Directive on Habitats does not extend beyond the UK's 12-mile territorial limit. In an important case, the court concluded that the Directive applies to the Continental Shelf and the 200-mile fishing limit. The decision will require new implementing regulations[1], and may impose significant constraints on continued deep sea exploration and eventual exploitation of oil and gas, especially in the North East

---

[1] See now Offshore Marine Conservation (Natural Habitats, &c.) Regulations 2007 SI 2007/1842

Atlantic. *R v Secretary of State ex parte Greenpeace* was an action for judicial review brought by Greenpeace challenging the 19th licensing rounds for offshore exploration and drilling initiated by the Secretary of State in 1997. In October 1997, the High Court[2] had ruled against Greenpeace in a challenge based on an earlier round of licences, based on similar legal arguments concerning the Habitats Directive. That case, however, had concentrated on procedural rather than substantive questions, and the court had held that Greenpeace had been too late in its challenge.

In the present case, both the Secretary of State and the main oil companies concerned again argued that Greenpeace was out of time. But, in contrast to the first case, the court had earlier ruled that the hearing should consider fully both the questions of delay and the detailed issues of law at the same time. The essence of Greenpeace's challenge was straightforward. When the UK implemented the Habitats Directive under the Conservation (Natural Habitats etc) Regulations 1994, the regulations expressly did not extend beyond the 12-mile limit of UK territorial waters. Greenpeace argued that this was a mistaken interpretation, and that the Directive extended to areas of the sea and seabed within the UK's jurisdiction, including the Continental Shelf. Environmental obligations in the Directive were relevant to the award of the deep sea licences – specifically the protection of cetaceans and reefs – and had clearly not been considered by the Secretary of State when it came to the licence awards. There was no question that Greenpeace had standing to bring the case. But the oil companies kept open the question as to whether the Directive had 'direct effect', with the implication that its provisions could not be argued before a national court, and that any legal action could be brought only by the European Commission. The Secretary of State disassociated himself from that argument, and the court had little doubt that it had direct effect.

Mr Justice Kay began by considering the UN Convention of the Law of the Sea, to which the EC and all Member States are parties. The Convention contains a number of concepts concerning the jurisdiction of countries over neighbouring marine waters. First, the territorial sea extending 12 miles from the coast over which a country has sovereignty. Then, the Continental Shelf over which a country has rights of seabed exploration and exploitation. And finally an Exclusive Economic Zone extending 200 miles beyond the coast, in which a country has rights of exploration, exploitation and management of both the seabed and waters above it. National legislation in 1964 related to the UK's rights over its Continental Shelf, and although no Exclusive Economic Zone

---

[2] *R v Secretary of State for Trade and Industry ex parte Greenpeace* [1998] COD 59

has been formally declared, the UK has also designated a 200-mile exclusive fishery zone.

The EC Treaty itself does not explicitly deal with the territorial application of Treaty rules, and simply states under Article 299 that it shall apply to 'the United Kingdom of Great Britain and Northern Ireland.' Most commentators have agreed that Article 299 implies that the Treaty extends to areas within the jurisdiction of Member States under international law principles, and this has indeed been the practice in many areas of Community law. The UK, for example, recently conceded the point in relation to the Directive on environmental impact assessment, when amending regulations applying the Directive to offshore installations were introduced earlier this year.

The Government rightly did not therefore argue the general principle of the potential scope of Community law, but claimed that by its very nature the Habitats Directive was restricted to the land and territorial waters of Member States. Article 2.1 of the Directive states that its aim is the conservation of habitats and wild fauna and flora 'in the European territory of the Member States to which the Treaty applies' without defining jurisdictional scope any further. Both sides pointed to the Directive's drafting history. The government noted that an earlier draft applied to the European territory of Member States 'including maritime areas under the sovereignty or jurisdiction of the Members,' but that this phrase did not appear in the final version. The Government argued that this demonstrated a deliberate intention to restrict the Directive's geographical scope. Greenpeace countered with an affidavit from Stanley Johnson, a former senior Commission official with a key responsibility for negotiating the Directive and last seen dressed as a turtle at the Seattle WTO demonstrations. He thought that the change was merely to bring the Habitats Directive into line with the older Directive on bird conservation, and did not affect its geographical scope.

In the event, Mr Justice Kay found little assistance from the drafting history. But looking at the particular aims of the Directive and in particular the inclusion of cetaceans and reefs – in this case *lophelia pertusa*, sometimes known as 'cold coral' reef – as among the species to be protected, he concluded that Greenpeace's argument on scope was correct: 'It seems to me that a Directive which includes in its aims the protection of, inter alia, *lophelia pertusa* and cetaceans will only achieve those aims, on a purposive construction, if it extends beyond territorial waters. Although much of the concern of the Directive and some of the language can properly be described as 'land-based' it also deals specifically with some habitats and species which are sea-based and to a large extent flourish beyond territorial waters.'

The argument then moved to the question whether in fact these species were present in the areas subject to the 19th licensing rounds and were likely to be affected by licensed activities. Clearly if they were not, the Secretary of State's actual decision could not be challenged. The Directive does not refer specifically to *lophelia pertusa* but 'reefs' are included in its list of natural habitat types. There is no definition of the term 'reef', and while the Secretary of State accepted that *lophelia pertusa* is a reef-forming coral, the oil companies had one expert witness who argued that it is not. The court preferred the expert evidence produced by Greenpeace and concluded that it was a reef within the meaning of the Directive, and that 'oil exploration activities will be at least likely to have an adverse effect on *lophelia pertusa* in relation to the area included in or affected by the Nineteenth Round.' In relation to cetaceans, Mr Justice Kay also concluded that the Atlantic Frontier contains a high variety of cetaceans, and that that there had been no substantial challenge to Greenpeace's expert evidence that oil exploration, including seismic activity, is harmful to cetaceans and has serious implications for conservation.

Greenpeace did not, however, succeed on all the legal arguments. In relation to cetaceans, Article 12 of the Directive requires Member States to establish 'a system of strict protection' of animal species listed in the Directive. It also prohibits, among four listed activities, 'all forms of deliberate capture or killing of specimens of the species in the wild,' deliberate disturbance of the species especially during breeding seasons, and deterioration or destruction of breeding sites. The 1994 regulations reflected these categories, making them an offence, but provided a general defence where it is shown that a damaging act was an 'incidental result of a lawful operation and could not reasonably have been avoided.' Greenpeace argued that the four categories of prohibited activities were merely illustrative of the overarching requirement to establish a strict system of protection. But the Court agreed with the Government and the oil companies that they are an exhaustive list of the means of protection.

The Court then considered the meaning of the word 'deliberate' which qualified the prohibition an capture, killing and disturbance of species. The word is not defined in the Directive, and, as the Court noted, it is not a concept normally used in British criminal law. Greenpeace argued that where an oil company conducted operations which it knew were likely or possible to result in killing or disturbance, that was a deliberate act which fell within the Directive's prohibition. Again the Court agreed with the Government and the oil companies: 'I do not consider that it could properly be said that the oil companies engage in the deliberate disturbance of cetaceans.' But the fourth category of prohibited acts, under Article 12(1)(d) – the deterioration or destruction of breeding sites - is not qualified by the word 'deliberate'. The question then was whether this was an absolute prohibition, which was therefore incompatible with the general defence under the 1994 regulations which related to incidental actions. The court noted that Article 12.4 specifically obliges Member States to establish a system to monitor the incidental killing or capturing of protected species, but that they have some degree of discretion in transposing this requirement. Mr Justice Kay agreed with the oil companies that while the Directive requires a prohibition, it did not follow that it obliged Member States to create criminal offences. 'This Member State has chosen to express the prohibition in the form of a criminal offence. In the circumstances, it is entirely natural, reasonable, and within the degree of discretion, that the criminal offences are defined (whether by reference to a defence or otherwise) in a manner which is clear and consistent with the style and ethos of our criminal law.' He therefore concluded that the general defence was compatible with Article 12, even in relation to the fourth category. Otherwise, 'the range of criminality which might arise in the course of carrying out activities which are in other respects lawful would be intolerable, especially if Article 12.1(d) were allowed to create a crime of virtually strict liability.'

The other main issue which the court was required to consider was the question of delay. The general rule under national law is that applications for judicial review must be made within three months 'from the date when grounds for the application first arose.' A court may extend this period for 'good reason'. But it may also decide that an application even within the three-month period involves undue delay. In the first Greenpeace challenge, Mr Justice Laws decided on grounds of delay that leave should not be granted. He agreed that the clock did not start running as soon as the implementing regulations were made in 1994, but felt that the 1997 date of the announcement by the Secretary of State of the blocks that were to be offered in the 17th licensing round was the executive act that was susceptible to judicial review. Greenpeace had waited until the actual award of licences, and he felt this to be too late. Moreover, because Greenpeace was a public interest plaintiff, he suggested that delay would be tolerated much less readily.

In the present case, the challenge was mounted at an earlier stage, and at a time when the Secretary of State had not yet indicated precisely the areas for which he would be inviting licence applications. The government suggested that Greenpeace was using the 19th round simply as a second run at a case previously lost. But Mr Justice Kay did not feel this was a bar to Greenpeace making another application in relation to a later round. 'The notion of a 'second bite at the cherry' or other language more redolent of abuse of process is not appropriate in relation to the present application,' he concluded.

The judge accepted that where third party interests are involved the requirement to act promptly was all the more important. But he was distinctly unhappy with Mr Justice Laws' suggestion that the principle of promptness must be applied 'with special force' where a public interest litigant was involved. He felt it was necessary to avoid creating too high or too early an hurdle for litigants, including public interest plaintiffs: 'The precipitation of premature applications on incomplete evidence is hardly desirable.'

But in the present case, Mr Justice Kay felt that given the basis of the arguments a challenge should have been in respect of the government's initial announcement of the forward programme for plans for the 19th round in July 1997. However, at this time the decision of Mr Justice Laws in the first *Greenpeace* case had not yet been given, and he accepted that the group could reasonably have waited until the judgment, some two and a half months later. Greenpeace did not commence proceedings until April 1999, and even though this was before any specific decisions concerning the licence awards were made, the Court agreed with the Government that 'this is one of those cases in which it is appropriate to move ahead of an anticipated decision.'

The national rules, though, still permit a court to allow a late challenge. Mr Justice Kay could not find a 'reasonable excuse' on the part of Greenpeace for the delay. However, the judge also needed to have regard to the interests of third parties and detriment to good administration. He could see that these were powerful in respect to the original Greenpeace challenge where the licences had already been awarded. But here the challenge was at an earlier stage anyway, and both the government and the oil companies were fully aware of the potential for challenge. Greenpeace had made a formal complaint to the European Commission in 1998, and the Commission had still to make a decision concerning possible infringement proceedings. It followed that 'any increased activity or expenditure since then has been undertaken with knowledge of the risk.' The court concluded that that there was sufficient public interest in extending the time for the application. 'The finding that, in these circumstances, the 1994 Regulations were and are not a complete and lawful implementation of the Habitats Directive is a matter of substantial public importance, as is the fact that the approach of the Secretary of State to the Habitats Directive, i.e. his failure to consider it in the licensing process, is legally erroneous.'

The decision in the second *Greenpeace* case will no doubt be welcomed by the European Commission, which had indicated that it agreed with the group's interpretation of the geographical scope of the Habitats Directive. It is too early to predict what effect the result will have on future exploration in the North East Atlantic. The oil companies will be relieved by the interpretation of the Directive which permits defences concerning non-deliberate killing or disturbance of cetaceans. As the Court noted, some environmental controls are already in place in respect of exploration and drilling, though none as specific as those under the Habitats Directive. Certainly there is bound to be delay in the process for the next licensing round, since the Secretary of State will now have to consider whether Special Areas of Conservation (SACs) should be designated under the Habitats Directive in respect of *dophelia pertusa* – in the face of limited scientific understanding of the habitat's extent and significance. Under the Directive, even SAC designation does not provide absolute protection against interference. But it does result in considerable restrictions. Environmental assessments must be carried out in respect of plans or projects which might significantly affect SACs, and generally Member States may not approve plans which will adversely affect their integrity. However, in the absence of alternative solutions, Member States may permit interference for 'imperative reasons of overriding public interest' – which expressly include social or economic interests – but in such cases appropriate compensatory measures must be provided to preserve the coherence of Community habitats. 'Priority' habitat types, however, generally may only be interfered with for environmental, human health or public safety reasons. Other reasons of overriding public importance may only be invoked 'further to an opinion from the Commission.' At present, reefs are not listed in the Directive as a priority habitat type, though there may be pressure for amendment. The language of the Directive continues to contain areas of doubt – for example, does an 'alternative solution' encompass a non-fossil fuel policy, and what is the precise meaning of compensatory measures? As a result, the next stage in the licensing process will be scrutinised closely by both conservationists and lawyers.

Packaging Directive and garden centres

Davies v Hillier Nurseries Ltd (Divisional Court [2001] EWHC Admin 587)

In the first High Court decision concerning the interpretation of the 1994 EC Directive on packaging and the UK's implementing regulations, the court has given a broad meaning to what is meant in law by packaging, and has held that it can encompass plastic pots used during the sale of plants and shrubs. If the court had upheld the original approach of the magistrate, it could have given a green light for many manufacturers to have products excluded from the scope of the regulations. *Davies v Hillier Nurseries* was a dispute between the Environment Agency and a Hampshire nursery with eight garden centre outlets, and backed by the Horticultural Trades Association, as to whether the company should be registered as a producer under the 1997 packaging regulations. The Agency had prosecuted Hillier but the stipendiary magistrate had agreed with the company's arguments that its plastic pots did not fall within the scope of the regulations. The Agency appealed on the grounds that the magistrate had applied the wrong legal test.

The packaging regulations contain a definition of 'packaging' which is transposed directly from the EC Directive. The Hillier case was concerned with primary packaging, defined as 'packaging conceived so as to constitute a sales unit to the final user or consumer at the point of purchase.' In most cases it would be perfectly obvious to a consumer buying a product as to what constitutes its packaging. But when it came to plastic pots used by nurseries the position was less clear because of their dual function. Although the plants and shrubs were sold in plastic pots and it was accepted that in most cases the consumer would remove the plant from the pot for replanting, Hillier argued that the container's main purpose was to act as a growing environment for the plants.

Evidence was presented about the views of other Member States as to whether plant pots are packaging within the meaning of the Directive. France has decided they are not, but nine Member States have decided they are. The evidence showed that plants were grown from cuttings, and once rooted were transferred to a plastic pot for growing for a month or two until ready for sale and planting out. According to the Court, 'the purpose of putting them in the pot is to nurture them to a size at which they can be sold to the public and in good condition.' The magistrate had therefore concluded, as did the High Court, that the pot's primary purpose was for the growing of the plant, that the pots were integral to the manufacturing process, and therefore not conceived as packaging within the Directive.

The Agency was particularly concerned to challenge this 'integral' test since if it stood it could have opened the door to many other companies claiming that their products fell outside the scope of the regulations. Wine bottles, where the wine was fermented in the bottle itself, would be a prime example. The Agency's first argument was that once the pots in question fell within the broad scope of the meaning of packaging as material used for the containment of products, the only question was whether such material was still being used at the point of sale. The High Court, however agreed with Hillier's counter-argument that this is not what the definition said, and that the question for the court was whether the pot was 'conceived so as to constitute a sales unit'. This implied looking back at the purpose for which the item in question was formulated, and Mr Justice Newman held that the use at the time of sale was not the determining issue, though it might be relevant to the overall question.

The Agency's second approach was to accept that 'conceived' must be given a meaning beyond the factual circumstances of the sale, but that the relevant point of conception was when the pot was on sale. Again, the Court rejected this line of argument. It was obvious that when a plant or shrub was offered for sale it was still in the pot for growing or nurturing, and all that could be said was that at the time of sale its primary purpose had changed from nurturing to selling. The primary purpose test had in fact been the test applied by the magistrate in interpreting the term 'conceived', but had been applied only to the time at which the plants had been placed in pots, thereby leading to a different conclusion.

It was the Agency's third argument, developed during the course of the hearing, that the High Court accepted as the right approach. According to this approach, it was correct to focus attention on the time at which the plants were placed in the pots, but it was not necessary to concentrate solely on the primary purpose at the time. If it was also planted with the purpose of selling the plant in the pot, this was sufficient to bring it within the meaning of being 'conceived so as to constitute a sales unit.' According to Mr Justice Newman, the word 'conceived' 'requires the court to consider all the circumstances present at the time the plant was put in the pot, and to determine, according to the circumstances, whether its use at the time included use of the pot in the process of sale, so as to form part of the sales unit of the plant.' The case was therefore remitted back to the magistrate with a direction to convict. In a statement following the case, the Agency accepted that Hillier had acted in good faith on advice from its trade association, and that the purpose of the case was to test the law. In that context, it is unlikely that a court would impose more than a nominal fine.

The case received considerable publicity in the popular press, and attracted critical comment from Eurosceptic MPs on the apparent absurdities of over-bureaucratic laws and an over-zealous regulator. Yet the Environment Agency has faced consistent criticism from industry for failing to enforce the regulations properly, allowing too many free-riders, and thus increasing the potential burden on those producers who had registered. The Agency had already allowed a six-month leeway beyond the legal deadline for registering, but this amnesty was withdrawn at the end of 1998, and since then the Agency has taken an increasing number of prosecutions for non-registration. The Agency can perhaps be criticised for failing to ensure that the prosecution was to be seen in that light, and against a concern at the large amount of plastic now passing through garden centres. Hillier's declared tonnage in 1998 was an annual 30 tonnes of plastic pots which, together with other forms of packaging arising from its garden centres, brought it well over the current 50 tonnes per annum threshold. One of the largest wholesalers in England is known to sell around 30 million plastic pots per year.

Noise Nuisance and Public Interest

Dennis v Ministry of Defence (Queen's Bench Division, High Court [2003] 2 EGLR 121)

The High Court has broken new ground in developing the principles of common law nuisance in a case brought against the Ministry of Defence in respect of noise from military aircraft. The judgment demonstrates the influence of the Human Rights Act in how the courts now approach such cases, and the outcome could have significant implications for governmental and other public works giving rise to potential nuisance claims.

Dennis v Ministry of Defence had all the hallmarks of a classic nuisance case. Mr and Mrs Dennis lived at Wilmont Hall, a large estate near Peterborough, and close to the RAF station of Wittering. This had been developed since the First World War and was now the main base for a squadron of Harrier vertical take-off jets. It was the training and circuit flying of these jets which gave rise to the claim, and Mr Justice Buckley noted that no-one has suggested there was a noisier aircraft, particularly when it came to vertical landings. The Court accepted that it was not practicable for the MoD to alter the layout of the circuits, and although at one stage it had considered moving to another base this was felt to be too costly. The MoD had clearly acknowledged the intrusion which the operations caused local residents and had provided a voluntary scheme of grants of double glazing and made offers to buy out properties especially affected. Wilmot Hall, however, was a listed building and double glazing was therefore not practicable, and in any event would not have affected the noise experienced outside the building. Experts for both sides agreed that noise levels from the jets caused disturbance and interference with the normal domestic and business activities at Wilmot Hall, though they disagreed as to their seriousness. Experts for the claimants considered that the market value of the property was reduced substantially, and that the aircraft noise effectively destroyed any opportunities to exploit the Hall for corporate entertainment and similar business activities. Lay witnesses gave evidence, and Mr Justice Buckley considered their testimony convincing. He concluded: 'It seems plain to me that the noise is, on the face of it, a nuisance.'

The courts' traditional approach in this type of nuisance claim, which involves interference with the enjoyment of property rather than actual physical damage, has been to look for a balancing of interests. Nobody is entitled to absolute peace and quiet, but must accept a degree of give and take in the light of reasonable usages of land. The character of the neighbourhood is also a relevant factor in determining what sorts of interference are to be considered reasonable in this context. The Court rejected the MoD's arguments that training pilots could be considered an ordinary use of the land: 'I regard such activities which generate extreme noise and other pollution as extraordinary uses of land, even in this day and age.' Nor did Mr Justice Buckley accept the arguments that the operations had changed the character of the neighbourhood for nuisance purposes, but felt that it remained essentially rural. It was true that the base had been in operation for many years, but it was the development of the jet engine and vertical take-off aircraft that had escalated the problem. He also noted that many types of industrial development had taken place within the context of planning controls or specific Acts of Parliament such as those relating to railways or roads, and that these usually provided various mechanisms for accommodating private interests affected by such developments. These factors were absent here since the MoD required no authorising statute nor planning permission for its operations.

Having rejected the more familiar lines of defence available in nuisance actions, the key legal issue was whether the MoD could justify its operations on the grounds that they were in the public interest, namely that they were concerned with the defence of the realm. Older UK case law has long rejected a public interest defence *per se*, but it had never been as starkly raised as in this case. According to Mr Justice Buckley: 'It seems to me the nettle must be grasped. Either these Harriers constitute a nuisance, or public interest, as represented by the MoD maintaining a state-of-the-art strike force and training pilots, provides immunity.' The Court accepted that if public interest did provide a good defence, it would not provide unlimited immunity. In line with principles developed where an Act of Parliament specifically authorises works or activities that cause a nuisance, the defendants would have to do everything they reasonably could to avoid or minimise damage. But in this case this would not help the claimants, since the Court accepted that the MoD had made reasonable efforts to keep local annoyance to a minimum within the constraints under which it was operating.

Mr Justice Buckley, however, felt uncomfortable with the idea of a public interest defence, and it was here that the impact of the Human Rights Act made itself felt. 'The problem with putting the public interest into the scales when deciding whether a nuisance exists is simply that if the answer is no, not because the claimant is being over sensitive but because his private rights must be subjugated to the public interest, it might well be unjust that he should suffer the damage for the benefit of all. If it were to be held that there is no nuisance, there can be no remedy at common law. As this case illustrates, the greater the public interest, the greater may be the interference.'

The claimants had also raised separate claims under the Human Rights Act, alleging breaches of Article 8 (interference with respect for private and family life and home) and Article I of the First Protocol (interference with the peaceful enjoyment of possessions) of the European Convention on Human Rights. There are defences available to the state where, *inter alia*, interference is necessary in the interest of national security. But the Court accepted that rulings of the European Court of Human Rights implied that principles of proportionality applied, and that a fair balance between competing interests had to be struck. In the *Marcic* case last year concerning nuisance from sewerage overflows, the Court of Appeal had accepted that breaches of the Convention were involved, and that this might require the payment of compensation to the individual concerned as a way of resolving the competing public and private interests.[3]

Mr Justice Buckley felt that it would be a second best solution to deny the claim in nuisance, but allow one under human rights: 'It would be one that reflected adversely on the flexibility of the common law.' He felt that the principles now being developed were that the public interest should be considered and that selected individuals should not bear the cost of the public benefit: 'I am in favour of giving effect to those principles. I believe it is necessary to do so if the common law in this area is to be consistent with the developing jurisprudence on human rights.'

The solution was to allow the MoD operations to continue, but to require compensation be paid to the claimants, for both past and future damage, including the diminution in value of their property. The evidence of

---

[3] But subsequently overruled by the House of Lords: *Marcic v. Thames Water Utilities Ltd* [2004] 2 AC 42 see p.495.

the MoD indicated that the Harriers would be phased out by 2012, and the Court approached the estimation of damages on the basis that the nuisance had existed since 1984 and would continue until that end date. After considering all the evidence concerning blight, loss of potential commercial use and loss of amenity, Mr Justice Buckley held that the overall damages to the awarded should be £950,000. He went on to hold that this was just satisfaction of the alternative claims under the Human Rights Act. Furthermore, if he was wrong about the common law nuisance claim, he would have held that the claims under the Act would succeed in their own right and awarded the same amount.

His approach appears to run directly counter to that traditionally taken by the British courts when considering the award of injunctions to prevent a continuing nuisance.

The award of injunctions is at the discretion of a court, but in nuisance claims injunctions have generally been granted as a right to a successful claimant. Any public interest in the activity concerned has not been considered relevant. As observed in one notable Victorian case on sewage pollution: 'So far as this court is concerned it is matter of almost absolute indifference whether the decision will affect a population of 250,000 or single individual.' It is what is in effect an entitlement of right to an injunction which gives common law nuisance its particular strength as a legal remedy in tackling pollution and environmental problems. Since the 1850s, the courts have had a general power to award damages in lieu of a injunction, but in *Shelfer v City of London Electric Lighting Corp*[4] general principles were laid down stating that such damages should be awarded only where the interference was small and where they were capable of being estimated in monetary terms, and where it would be oppressive to grant the injunction.

This restrictive approach appears to be based on an aversion to the idea of rich defendants being able to buy the right to continue a wrongful nuisance, even though many pollution economists would argue that this could be an economically correct solution. In the mid-1970s, the innovative judge Lord Denning tried to suggest a more flexible approach where public interests were involved. But in a 1981 case involving speedboat racing in the Lake District,[5] the Court of Appeal resolutely struck down a High Court award of £15,000 in lieu of an injunction on the grounds that it breached the long standing *Shelfer* principles which confined such awards to small claims. The *Dennis* case clearly

---

[4] [1895] 1 Ch 287
[5] *Kennaway v Thompson* [1981] I QB 88

suggests that the time has come for a far more flexible approach towards awarding compensation for continuing nuisances. In many ways, it may bring the British courts closer to their US counterparts, where judges in nuisance cases have generally examined closely the social utility of the defendant's activities in deciding whether to grant an injunction. The facts in *Dennis* were extreme, and the defendants a direct arm of the state. But lawyers will now be looking to see whether the approach will filter down to less dramatic cases, and where a defendant is a private body but one which argues that its activities are in the public interest by, say, creating local employment or creating export markets.

Mr Justice Buckley had one final warning shot for the MoD. He noted that the evidence suggested that the eventual replacement aircraft for the Harriers in 2012, the carrier-borne aircraft FCBA, would be even noisier. The present claim related to the Harriers, and should the FCBA be introduced they could give a new case of action. Without prejudging any such case, he warned that a court might conclude that the use of such aircraft would be simply intolerable for local residents: 'To put it bluntly, the MoD would be well advised to train their pilots for FCBA in the wide-open spaces the USA can provide or reconsider the location of training fields here.'

Liability for Water Pollution Offences

Express Ltd v Environment Agency (Divisional Court, High Court [2004] EWHC 1710)

The High Court has ruled that businesses must carry out adequate risk assessment if they are to escape prosecution of water pollution caused by third parties on their premises. The court also held that substances entering water can still be polluting within the legislation even if no actual harm occurs.

Express Ltd v Environment Agency concerned a pollution incident at a depot belonging to Express Dairies in Redditch in January 2002. The customer, Pardy's Dairies, was transferring cream contained in a 'grundy', described by the court as a 'somewhat unwieldy drum on wheels', by means of a forklift truck into the back of a van. The grundy collided with a milk crate and toppled over, spilling about 10 litres of cream. The area was served by surface water drains leading to a brook. Immediate efforts were made to contain the spillage by covering the drains and using sand to mop up the cream, and the company reported the incident. But some of the cream ran into a road and eventually entered the brook, causing discolouration for 150-200 metres. As a result

Pardy's was charged with an offence under section 85(1) of the Water Resources Act 1991 of causing poisonous, noxious or polluting matter to enter waters, and pleaded guilty.

It was, though, the liability of Express Ltd which was at issue in the case. The company was charged under section 217(3) of the 1991 Act, which provides that where the commission of a water pollution offences is 'due to the act of default of some other person', that person may also be charged with an offence. Express accepted that the core pollution offence with which Pardy's was charged was one of the strict liability, meaning that no evidence of intent or negligence was necessary. But it argued that in relation to an offence under section 217(3) the words 'act or default' did not imply strict liability, and that it was not sufficient simply to show that Express gave the company an opportunity to cause pollution. Counsel for Express acknowledged that a full risk assessment of the cream transfer operation had not been carried out but argued that there was no statutory duty to do so, nor was Express under any duty to prescribe how Pardy's should carry out its work. Surprisingly, this appears to be the first time that a higher court has considered the meaning of section 217(3) or its predecessor in section 121(1) of the Water Act 1989, and the Divisional Court looked to analogous case-law for guidance on the meaning of 'act or default'.

A key recent authority was the 1999 decision of the House of Lords in the *Empress Car* case[6]. That case concerned liability under section 85(1) where a third party had opened a tap on the company's premises causing a diesel spillage into a river. The House of Lords held that causation under the offence did not mean a prosecutor had to show that the defendant did something which was the immediate cause of the pollution, nor was there always necessarily one cause of a pollution incident. If the act or event was something that could be described as a normal fact of life – and this might include vandalism by third parties – then a company which maintained tanks full of noxious liquids could be said to have caused the pollution as well as the third party.

In the present case, the High Court held that to establish liability the prosecution had to show that Pardy's contravention of section 85 was due to the act or default of Express Diaries. Lord Justice Kennedy disagreed with the argument of Express that it had no obligation to take action. The source of the obligation was statutory and not be found from principles relating to civil obligations between parties. 'If a landowner, such as Express, is going to permit and operation on his land which

---

[6] [1998] 1 All ER 481, see ch 14 above.

gives rise to a risk of pollution then, as it seems to me, in order not to fall foul of section 85(1) he must carry out a risk assessment and respond to what the assessment reveals. Otherwise if pollution does occur it may be impossible for him to say that the offence committed by those using his land is not due to one or more of his acts of defaults.'

The second main line of argument by Express was that since the magistrates had found as a matter of fact that there was no actual harm caused by the cream entering the brook it could not be said that the substance was polluting within the meaning of the legislation. It was accepted that there had been discolouration, and that analysis of samples revealed increased biochemical oxygen demand, suspended solids and ammoniacal nitrogen, but there had been no fish kill nor any evidence that the cream was toxic. Express argued that there was no statutory definition of 'polluting matter' in the 1991 Act, and pointed to dictionary definitions of 'pollute'. However, its argument was not helped by a 1995 decision of the Court of Appeal in the *Dovermoss* case[7] where it was held that the term 'polluting' was clearly distinguished from 'poisonous' or 'noxious' in the definition of the offence, and did not imply that a harmful effect had to be shown.

The court was prepared to adopt dictionary definitions of pollute such as 'to make physically impure...to dirty, stain, taint.' Even the term 'noxious', according to the court, did not imply actual harm – the likelihood or potential of causing harm were sufficient for a substance to be noxious. The court could see no good reason for not following the approach in *Dovermoss*. According to Lord Justice Kennedy, 'section 85(1) is worded in such a way as to make clear that pollution matter need not be either poisonous or noxious. It is sufficient if it, for example, stains or taints as the cream did.'

The *Express* case is consistent with recent authorities on water pollution offences, which emphasise the very strict nature of the offences, and the extent to which extenuating circumstances are relevant to the mitigation of sentencing rather than as a defence to conviction.

Standing issues in judicial review

R (on the application of Edwards) v Environment Agency and another **(Queens' Bench Division (Administrative Court) [2004] EWHC 736)**

The High Court has given a liberal interpretation of standing rules where an individual seeks to challenge the legality of an environmental

---

[7] [1995] Env LR 258

permit. A local resident who was apparently homeless at the time of the application and played no significant part in statutory consultation processes was nevertheless held to have sufficient standing to apply for judicial review, and the fact that he was probably chosen as a test applicant who would qualify for legal aid did not amount to an abuse of legal process.

R (on the application of Edwards) v Environment Agency and another concerned Rugby Cement's works in Rugby. Last year, following an extended consultation exercise against a background of considerable local opposition, the Environment Agency granted the company a pollution prevention and control (PPC) permit authorising it to burn waste tyres on a trial basis. The judicial review application raised two key issues concerning the legality of the permit: whether a PPC permit was a 'development consent' within the meaning of the 1985 EC Directive on environmental assessment, implying that the permitting procedure should have been subject to the assessment requirements, and whether the Agency had failed to ensure that the company used the 'best available techniques' (BAT). The present decision, though, was not concerned directly with these issues, but with the initial question of whether the applicant had sufficient standing to bring the case in the first place. The court also had to consider whether, even if he had standing, it was an abuse of process to bring the claim given the circumstances of the case.

The Environment Agency noted that the claim for judicial review had not been brought directly by known opponents of the permitting decision such as the local council or the campaign group, 'Rugby in Plume'. The applicant had made no representations to the Agency during the consultation process, and did not seem to have attended any of the public meetings. The claim form stated that Mr Edwards was a resident of Rugby but no address was given, and according to a local councillor he was currently homeless, though in the past he had lived at a number of addresses in Rugby. However, it did not follow that he was not concerned about the environmental effects of the permit decision. According to the councillor, he had expressed concern to her about the cement works, and in his witness statement said that he had attended meetings, even if he was not an active member of the local campaign.

According to the court, the leading light of 'Rugby in Plume' was Mrs Lillian Pallikaropoulos, who had instructed solicitors now acting for Mr Edwards, had committed substantial funds of her own to the campaign, and was committed to challenging the legality of the Agency's decision. Following advice from leading counsel, Rugby Borough Council had decided not to seek judicial review itself. Mrs Pallikaropoulos was then reported as stating that since she owned her house she would not qualify for legal aid, and the campaign needed someone who could take the case forward on public funds.

Mr Justice Keith acknowledged that Mr Edwards did not say that he had responded to this request for assistance, but nevertheless concluded: 'It is difficult to resist the inference that Mr Edwards has been put up as a claimant in order to secure public funding of the claim by the Legal Services Commission when those who are moving force behind the claim believe that public funding for the claim would not otherwise have be available.'

It was against this background that the court considered whether Mr Edwards should be entitled to proceed with the claim. The test for standing in judicial review is that the claimant has 'sufficient interest' in the matter at hand. A generation ago, courts would tend to interpret this phrase to mean that the individual needed to own property that was affected, but they have since adopted an increasingly liberal approach. In the present case, however, the Agency argued that a central plank of the legal challenge was the failure to apply the environmental assessment requirements to the PPC permitting procedure. This in turn affected the nature of the public consultation process and the way that information was available to the public. Mr Edwards appeared to have played no part in the consultation process and therefore, according to the Agency, could not be said to have sufficient interest in the matter.

Mr Justice Keith was quick to dismiss this line of argument. It failed to deal with the second main line of challenge concerning BAT. Furthermore, it did not acknowledge that Mr Edwards was entitled to leave it to others such as the local authority or Rugby in Plume to act on his behalf: 'You do not have to be active in a campaign yourself to have an interest in the outcome...You should not be disbarred from subsequently challenging the decision on the grounds of inadequate consultation simply because you choose not to participate in the consultation exercise, provided you are affected by this outcome.' The court was satisfied that Mr Edwards, even if temporarily homeless, was an inhabitant of Rugby and therefore would be affected by any adverse environmental impact which might result from the permitted operations. Accordingly, he had sufficient interest for the purpose of standing.

The court still had to deal with the question of whether bringing the claim in the name of an individual chosen solely for the purpose of qualifying for legal aid was an abuse of process. The Agency referred the court to two recent cases concerning parents challenging decisions of local education authorities, where the actual proceedings had been brought in the name of their children. In one case, it was clear that the child had been chosen to qualify for legal aid and protect the parents against adverse costs orders. The claim had been dismissed as an abuse of the court process. In the second case, the Court of Appeal had allowed the claim to proceed, but accepted that if there were clear evidence that proceedings had been brought in the name of the child in order to obtain public funding, this might amount to an abuse.

However, Mr Justice Keith doubted whether these cases were on all fours with the present application. There, it was in reality the parents' claim rather than the children's interest that was directly at stake. In the present case, in contrast, Mr Edwards himself was affected by the permit decision and there was nothing in addition which prevented him from having a sufficient interest. Moreover, he felt that if there were an abuse it was one that really was a matter for the Legal Services Commission. It was clear that the Commission was fully aware of Mr Edwards' circumstances, since Rugby Cement had written to it to question whether the proceedings were really for his benefit rather than that of other individuals. Mr Justice Keith noted that if the Commission had really felt that the claim was for the benefit of others who could reasonably be expected to contribute to the costs of litigation, they could have been required to contribute as a condition of the grant of funding. In the event, it was clear that the Commission had granted the certificate in the knowledge of all the surrounding circumstances, and must have addressed the question of whether the grant would or would not be an abuse. The court therefore concluded that no abuse of process was involved. The legal issues at the heart of the dispute over the Agency's grant of the permit will now be aired at a full hearing. Although questions of standing and abuse often turn on their own facts, the present decision is a significant development of principles. Certainly, it indicates that in future it will be difficult to refuse standing to local inhabitants where environmental decisions are involved.

IPPC and Best Available Techniques Scrutinised in Rockware Glass Case

R on the application of Rockware Glass Ltd v Chester City Council **(Administrative Court, High Court of Justice [2005] EWHC 2250)**

The High Court has emphasised that regulators determining best available techniques under and IPPC permit application must not be constrained by the production process proposed by the applicant. *R on the application of Rockware Glass Ltd v Chester City Council* is a significant decision that underlines the scope and complexity of judgments to be made under the IPPC regime and its linkages with the planning system. The case arose from proposals by Quinn Glass for a major container glass factory in Elton, Cheshire. The proposals required both planning permission and an IPPC authorisation under the Pollution Prevention and Control (England and Wales) Regulations 2000, both of which would initially be handled by the local authority. It is normal practice for a planning application to be obtained first, but as His Honour Judge Gilbart (sitting as a High Court judge) noted, there was nothing in law to prevent the IPPC application being considered and granted in advance of a planning application. Only waste legislation expressly requires relevant planning permissions to be in place before waste management licences can be issued.

In this case, the planning permission for the plant granted in 2004 had been challenged successfully by Rockware Glass on the grounds that it should have been subject to environmental assessment requirements. A revised planning application was submitted to Chester City Council with the IPPC application being made shortly afterwards. The Council granted the IPPC application the day before it was due to consider the planning application. However, the planning application was in fact called in by the Secretary of State – apparently without the knowledge of the officer granting the application. In the meantime, Quinn Glass had proceeded with the development and made contractual commitments. His Honour Judge Gilbart observed that while this was a considerable gamble and against the spirit of the environmental assessment regime, development without planning permission was not a criminal offence in itself until an enforcement notice had been issued. He emphasised that the unusual planning background should not influence the judgment as to the legality of the IPPC permit granted.

In terms of potential pollutants, the main concern was the release of oxides of nitrogen (NO_x) from the furnaces used in the plant. The court noted from the Government's Air Quality Strategy, published in 2000, that whereas NO_x was a pollutant with local health impacts and subject to air quality standards, it also contributed to the formation of ozone in the lower atmosphere. The strategy emphasised the transboundary nature of ozone which could arise from NO_x emissions many hundreds or thousands of kilometres away. In this case, many of the local authority's considerations appear to have been driven by local air quality concerns, but as the Court noted, '...the effects of NO_x as a pollutant are not assessed adequately by local measurements nor by measurements of NO_x.' The Court went on to observe that the amount of NO_x produced by a furnace was critically affected by the design of the plant, and in this case there was a key choice of processes: a cross-fire regenerative plant fed by air and an oxyfuel plant using oxygen rather than air, and as such producing much less NO$_x$. The furnaces proposed by Quinn were the former type.

A key issue at the heart of the case was whether the local authority should consider what was best available techniques (BAT) in relation to the plant proposed by Quinn, or whether it was obliged to consider other types of plant, and especially oxyfuel plants, as a comparison. His Honour Judge Gilbart conducted a lengthy analysis of the 1996 EC Directive on integrated pollution prevention and control (IPPC), the national implementing regulations and guidance documentation, including the relevant BREF note published in 2000, and the Secretary of State's guidance on general principles and the sector guidance note on glass manufacturing, which were both issued in 2003. As a matter of general principle, he noted that regulators must have regard to the statutory guidance where required to do so, and must give clear and cogent reasons for departing from it: 'This is particularly important in the context of technical guidance relating to national industry, where the bodies being regulated can reasonably expect decisions to be guided by consistent and scientifically informed national policy.'

The Court accepted that in determining BAT, a regulator was entitled to take into account and have regard to the individual characteristics of the proposed installation, but rejected Quinn Glass's argument that it could not question basic design choice. In his view it was clear from the basic principles of the legislation and made explicit in the relevant guidance, that the regulator must have regard to other configurations or design which would result in lower emission levels: '…if a BAT analysis is carried out, then the choice of process has to be examined, as does the design of the furnace. It would be quite illogical and inconsistent with the fundamental objectives of the statutory code if the aspects of design which could be examined were to exclude the size of the furnace or (as in this case) the choice of a two-furnace as opposed to three-furnace design to reach the proposed production capacity.'

His Honour Judge Gilbart went on to consider the relationship between BAT and any environmental quality standards as prescribed in Community legislation. He noted that under the Directive and implementing regulations, techniques beyond BAT had to be applied if BAT would cause an environmental quality standard to be exceeded, and that a permit could be refused if the standard were to be breached. But it did not follow, as Quinn appeared to argue, that there was no requirement to reduce levels below the standard. The basic objective in the Directive referred to a 'high level of protection of the environment as a whole' which implied that the goal was 'to prevent to reduce to the irreducible minimum the emission of pollutants at source.' Given that NO_x has effects beyond local impacts, it followed that downward pressure on NO_x generation was important in its own right, irrespective of local readings of environmental quality standards.

The Court then examined the evidence concerning the factors that had influenced the regulator's decision to grant the authorisation. The judge was clearly unimpressed with the lack of written detail and records of critical meetings: 'Both the claimants and the Court has had some real difficulty establishing what Chester took into account and why it took the decision it did.' Eventually, he concluded the reasoning was fatally flawed. In particular, Chester had failed to consider adequately whether alternative configurations and design would have produced lower emissions, including the use of the alternative oxyfuel process. It also failed to take into account that NO_x was a global as well as local pollutant.

The case also raised issues of principle about the extent of local authority powers. The final decision to grant the permit had been taken by the Council's chief executive under delegated powers, but the Court concluded that the scheme of delegation essentially only related to routine, technical matters where there was little room for discretion. This was not the case here and the officer had acted outside the scope of the delegated authority.

The judicial review had been brought by a rival glass manufacturer and its standing to do so was challenged. The Court agreed that the mere fact that a claimant is a competitor company does not provide the necessary standing to challenge a decision within the IPPC system. But here in a regulated field where substantial investment decisions are to be made on capital works, it was proper to ensure that one's competitors were subject to the same consistency of approach by regulators. A minor defect in the process might not be enough to give sufficient interest to others, but 'the deficiencies in Chester's approach are so serious, and have such serious implications for the regulation of the whole sector, that I am satisfied that a sufficient interest exists to grant relief.'

The *Rockwell* decision clearly raises important questions of principle and process concerning the handling the IPPC applications, and the range of the factors that need to be considered by regulators. It will raise concerns as to whether local authorities are best suited to handling such applications at all, and whether it would be preferable for the Environment Agency to deal with all IPPC permits. And the factual background suggests the relationship between planning and IPPC applications needs to be handled more rigorously, as suggested by the Royal Commission on Environmental Pollution in its 2002 report on environmental planning.[28]

Court finds procedures on nuclear energy policy legally flawed

R on the application of Greenpeace v Secretary of State for Trade and Industry **(Administrative Court, High Court, [2007] EWHC 31)**

The High Court has held that the government's policy decision last year to support the building of new nuclear power stations was procedurally flawed on the grounds of inadequate public consultation on key aspects of the conclusions. The government will now have to rethink its consultation procedures on nuclear policy.

Following a review by the Prime Minister's Performance and Innovation Unit on future energy strategies, the government published a consultation document on energy policy in 2002, seeking views on a wide range of options including continued use of nuclear power. The court agreed that this exercise was thorough and well-informed. An Energy White Paper was published in 2003 which concluded that current economics made new nuclear build an unattractive option, and that the government did not propose to support this option for the present. It did not rule out the possibility of new nuclear build being needed in the future to meet carbon reduction targets, but that 'before any decision to proceed with the building of new nuclear power stations, there would need to be the fullest public consultation and the publication of a White Paper setting out the government's proposals.'

It was this statement and what it implied that formed the crux of the legal challenge in *R on the application of Greenpeace v Secretary of State for Trade and Industry*. At the end of 2005, the government announced there would be a review of the energy White Paper with a team of civil servants reporting to the Prime Minister and the Secretary of State for Trade and Industry . Answering questions from a parliamentary select committee, the Secretary of State indicated the process was a review of progress since 2003 rather than one leading to a new White Paper, but that one of the key questions was whether to keep the nuclear option open or close it. If the decision were taken to keep the nuclear option, he said there would need to be a new White Paper.

[28] Royal Commission on Environmental Pollution 23rd Report *Environmental Planning* Cm 5459 2002 HMSO, London

A consultation paper was issued in January 2006. In dealing with nuclear policy it indicated that, while the 2003 White Paper concluded new nuclear build was uneconomic, the issue should be revisited in light of rising fossil fuel prices. The recommendations of the Committee on Radioactive Waste Management, due to report on long-term management options in July 2006, should also be taken into account. A four-month public consultation period followed, and the review report was published by the government in July. This concluded that new nuclear power stations 'would make a significant contribution to meeting our energy policy goals'. It proposed that a new White Paper be published later in the year setting out a proposed framework for the consideration of issues relevant to new nuclear build and the context in which public inquiries as part of the planning process should be held. As the review indicated, this was intended to include a nuclear 'statement of need' which would provide a context for future planning inquiries into individual proposals.

Greenpeace challenged the review report decision concerning support for new nuclear build by way of judicial review. The core argument was that the 2006 review process was inconsistent with the government's commitment in the 2003 White Paper to hold the fullest possible public consultation process before supporting new nuclear build. The 2006 process was ambiguous as to its intentions. It could be seen in the nature of an issues paper seeking views as to which issues should be examined by the government before deciding whether the support new nuclear build. In this case the review report cut corners by reaching conclusions on the policy. On the other hand, if the 2006 process was intended to review the substantive issues the process was flawed in that consultees were not told in clear terms what they were being asked to respond to and the information provided by the government was inadequate. The government argued it was clear that the 2006 review was examining the substantive issue as to whether the nuclear option should now be endorsed as part of an energy mix. While it did not claim the issue should not be subject to legal review, it argued a court should be slow to intervene regarding such a high-level strategic document.

Mr Justice Sullivan began by considering the question of justicability. He noted the government had promised at the highest level in a White Paper to carry out the fullest public consultation should the nuclear option be reopened: 'It would be curious, to say the least, if the law was not able to require the government to honour such promise, absent any good reason to resile from it.' He pointed out that in the environmental field, consultation was no longer a privilege to be granted at will by the executive. Article 7 of the Aarhus Convention, to which the UK was a party, required parties to endeavour to provide opportunities for public participation in the preparation of policies relating to the environment. In this context, it was 'difficult to see how a promise of anything less than the 'fullest public consultation' would have been consistent with the government's obligations under the Aarhus Convention'. In his view, the government's decision following the 2006 review was the critical stage in the formulation of government policy in respect of new nuclear build, and represented the key principle from which any more detailed policy framework would follow.

Mr Justice Sullivan accepted it would be almost impossible to challenge the substantive conclusions of such a high-level strategy on the grounds they were irrational, and that in the absence of statutory or well-established procedural rules, it would not be easy for claimants to attack procedural impropriety. But this did not mean courts should not review decisions simply because they were matters of high policy. Looking at previous case law concerning consultation, it was clear the overriding requirement was that any consultation must be fair. Nevertheless, what was fair had to be judged by circumstances of the case, and he accepted there was generally a large degree of discretion as to how to carry out of consultation exercise, particularly one which was with the public at large. In such a case, in reality, he felt, a court would strike down a decision not merely because something went wrong but only when that something went 'clearly and radically' wrong with the process. Using these broad principles at a test, Mr Justice Sullivan examined the documents and consultation procedures that followed the publication of the January 2006.

He concluded that whatever the intentions might have been, the 2006 consultation gave every appearance of being an issues paper and no more, and this is what any reasonable consultee would have thought. Greenpeace and other core environmental groups suspected the government might have been conducting a substantive review and sought clarification as to the status of the exercise. Mr Justice Sullivan criticised the lack of clarity given by the government, noting tartly in respect to one DTI response to Greenpeace: 'As an exercise in avoiding giving the claimant the clarification it had sought, the reply could not be improved upon.' But even if those most closely engaged were deeply sceptical about the nature of the consultation process, a key issue was how ordinary members of the public would have viewed what was taking place.

Mr Justice Sullivan then reinforced his decision by considering whether he was wrong to regard the consultation paper as one dealing with the identification of issues only, but in fact it was a paper that a reasonable consultee would regarded as inviting comments on the question of substantive principle. If this was the case, he considered the information in the paper was simply inadequate in this context. If this was to be regarded as the final consultation paper on the substantive issue, the thumbnail sketches of the issues contained in the paper, especially on costs and waste, 'are so devoid of content that they could not realistically be said to have told consultees what the proposal was, much less to have told them enough to enable them to make an intelligible response.' He noted in particular that on the issue of economics the public had been presented with little more than an 'empty husk' and that the kernel of the economic issues had been contained in numerous reports that emerged only after the consultation paper expired.

As a matter of law, fairness did not always require the disclosure of and further consultation on all new information that emerged after consultation, but in this case where the contrast between what was contained in the consultation paper and the subsequent material relied upon was so striking, the process was 'manifestly unfair.' Mr Justice Sullivan concluded that the consultation exercise was seriously flawed. If the 2006 paper was merely an issues paper to be followed by a full consultation it was perfectly adequate, but as a consultation on an issue of such importance and complexity it was manifestly inadequate. It followed that the decision in the energy review in July 2006 that new nuclear build had a role to play was unlawful.

The Greenpeace decision is a powerful reminder that the courts are not afraid to engage in review of even the highest policy decisions of government, but that, as so often in judicial review, they are better equipped in dealing with issues of procedural fairness rather than substantive review. It is particularly striking that the court implied that even if the government had not committed itself in the 2003 White Paper to the widest possible consultation should the nuclear option be reopened, it might have had to do so in any event because of its obligations under the Aarhus Convention. It maybe that until ministerial diaries are published we will never be quite sure whether ministers and civil servants were clear in their minds as to the purpose of the 2006 consultation review, whether the ground rules changed during the process, or whether there was deliberate obscuration from the start. The decision will now require the government to reconsider the consultation process. What is clear from the judgment is that it would be rash to take procedural short cuts on such an important and complex issue.

EUROPE AND THE ENVIRONMENT

PART 5

EUROPE AND THE ENVIRONMENT

The European Community is a dynamic source of environmental legislation and legal principles, and for many Member States Community law is now dominant source of new environmental law. More recent substantive legislative initiatives such as those on carbon emissions trading, chemicals legislation, and producer responsibility for waste provide offer models of new legal approaches that are increasingly being considered by jurisdictions outside Europe. But above all the European Community presents a unique form of supra-national legal arrangement that provides both challenges and opportunities for the development of environmental law.

__The Amsterdam Treaty: An Environmental Perspective__ (1999) considers some of the main environmental implications of the Amsterdam Treaty. Compared to previous treaty amendments, the environmental changes were modest, but nevertheless significant in the signals they provided. Sustainable development entered the language of the Treaty with the achievement of a 'balanced and sustainable development' being defined as one of the core tasks of the Union. The duty to integrate environmental policies into other areas of Community policy was repositioned from semi-obscurity in the environmental provisions to the Treaty to Article 6 containing the core principles of the Treaty. In strict legal terms, the positioning of the duty may make no difference to its legal interpretation but undoubtedly gives heightened political significance.

The integration duty has been described as perhaps the most important environmental provision in the Treaty, and the EU Treaty is the only constitutional or quasi-constitutional document in the world that has given expression to the concept. __The Legal Duty of Environmental Integration: Commitment and Obligation or Enforceable Obligation?__ (1998) is an analysis of the duty very much from a legal perspective, and written with my then academic colleague, Martin Hession, now a distinguished government expert on international climate change. This was written shortly before the Amsterdam changes, when the duty was contained in the environmental provisions of the Treaty. We recognised that environmental integration can imply a raft of new administrative processes, but our focus was that of the lawyer – how would a court interpret such a duty and who could enforce it? The European Court of Justice had already indicated that the duty could empower the Community institutions to introduce environmental dimensions into other policy areas, but more challenging was the question whether the duty might be used to constrain environmentally damaging policies.

Since the Article was written, the integration duty has proved of significance in a number of cases, and while the Court has not yet taken the tough line on process we suggested, there are indications that it does take it seriously - in the Preussen Elektra case, for example, Advocate General Jacobs noted that the duty was not simply programmatic but of a binding nature.[1] The narrative of the integration duty is set to continue. The duty had already appeared in slightly different form in the 2000 EU Charter of Human Rights, Article 37 of which declares that "A high level of environmental protection and the improvement of the quality of the environment must be integrated into the policies of the Union and assured in accordance with the principle of sustainable development." Environmental integration might be considered a rather bizarre form of human right, but under the 2007 EU Reform Treaty where the Treaty integration duty is now repositioned in Article 7, the new Article 6 recognizes the Charter of Human Rights and declares them to have the same values as the Treaties. What this will imply in legal terms for the integration duty remains to be seen, but the arguments concerning enforceability and legal interpretation identified in **The Legal Duty of Integration** *are likely to be worth revisiting in the context of environmental integration being characterized as an individual human right.[2]*

Environmental Citizenship and the Law – Repairing the European Road
(1996) considers the notion of citizenship of the European Union, introduced in 1993, and what it might imply from an environmental perspective. It is clear from the case law of the European Court of Justice that some Community environmental legislation could be interpreted as giving rights to individuals, whether of a procedural nature such as environmental assessment or to substantive environmental quality standards. But it seemed to me to go much deeper than that. From a legal perspective, citizenship also raised important questions such as those concerning access to the courts, an area where the European Court of Justice continues to demonstrate a restrictive approach to direct access by individuals or non-governmental organizations that wished to challenge the legality of action by Community institutions.

The European Community had its origins as a purely functionalist economic institution, with a free market and all it implied designed to bring about closer political cooperation and union between Member States. It is clear that this is no longer the case – successive amendments to the Treaty have indicated a much broader set of tasks and goals including that of sustainable development

---

[1] "As its wording shows, Article 6 is not merely programmatic; it imposes legal obligations." Advocate General Jacobs. Opinion in *Preussen Elektra AG v. Schleswag AG [2001] ECR I-2099* Case C-379/98
[2] But less relevant for a country such as the United Kingdom proposing to opt out of the legal binding nature of the Charter.

and a high level of environmental protection. As the then Advocate General, Francis Jacobs succinctly observed in the mid 1990s, the 'mercantilist approach is simply no longer tenable.'[3] But **Environmental Citizenship and the Law** *notes how from a legal perspective the environment still was treated differently from economic rights. The core economic rights in the Treaty such as the free movement of goods have been interpreted by the European Court of Justice as individual legal rights that may be invoked to challenge the legality of national legislation that inhibits them. In contrast, the environmental principles in the Treaty grant no equivalent general individual rights, and any such rights may only be determined from individual pieces of Community environmental legislation. In essence, the Community has granted its citizens individual economic rights but in the absence of Community legislation no equivalent environmental rights.*

Balancing Trade Freedom with the Requirements of Sustainable Development *(1996) is a more detailed analysis of the balance between trade and sustainability within the European Community, and how legal principles and the courts handle the inevitable conflicts that may occur. The tension continues to this day, and the European approaches are echoed in the decisions of the World Trade Organization at international level.*

Both **Environmental Citizenship** *and* **Balancing Trade Freedom** *argue that if we are to truly ensure a greater legal balance between trade and the environment, we should consider redefining in the Treaty more explicitly the purposes of free movement of goods as being the 'rational and prudent use of natural resources', reflecting one of the environmental principles of the Treaty. This would transform the basic legal structure and hierarchy of principles, though as with any significant constitutional change, one that consciously leaves open the precise direction that would be taken in the future in its interpretation. In 2003 the Avosetta Group of European environmental lawyers proposed as an input to the then European Convention an alternative but equally radical legal formulation which was also aimed to redress these fundamental legal imbalances between trade and the environment.[4] This would insert a new general provision in the Treaty that, "Subject to imperative reasons of overriding public interest, significantly impairing the environment or human health shall be prohibited.' Such a provision would – as are the current free trade provisions – be invocable by individuals and be directly applicable to the activities of all Member State's governments and legislatures, as well as Community institutions. It is perhaps hardly surprising that these sorts of profound structural change are not reflected in the current EU Reform Treaty, yet they raise challenging questions of core principle that still need to be faced.*

---

[3] Jacobs (1994) *Human Rights and the European Union* Durham: European Law Institute
[4] *Resolution of the Avocetta Conference* 11/12 October 2002 in Jans (ed) (2003) The European Convention and the Future of European Environmental Law Europa Law Publishing, Groningen.

Another core principle of the EU Treaty is the principle of subsidiarity which is still given high prominence. First written into the Treaty under the Maastricht amendments, the principle was famously described by a former President of European of the Court of Justice as 'legal gobbledygook' and capable of at least thirty different meanings. **Subsidiarity and European Community Environmental Law** *(1999) does not attempt to unravel all those interpretations, but explores the principle in relation to European Community environmental law. The environmental policies of the Community represent a concurrent area of competences between the Community and Member States to which the subsidiarity principle will apply. When the principle was originally introduced some Member States hoped that it would roll back the frontiers of Community legislative intervention and even lead to the repeal of a substantial number of existing Directives. This has not happened in any dramatic fashion, and the European Court of Justice has recognized that the test requires a considerable degree of political judgment to which the Community institutions are entitled a large margin of discretion. Yet the principle has influenced in more subtle ways the substantive content of more recent Community environmental legislation that is rather less dirigistic in tone than earlier examples, and contain more flexibility for Member States in their interpretation and implementation. This may more truly reflect the complexity of designing contemporary environmental solutions across some 26 countries, but raises challenges for effective supervision and enforcement at Community level, which is discussed further in Part VI.*

The shift in substantive content of Community environmental legislation also provides the stimulus for the analysis in **Participatory Rights, Transboundary Environmental Governance and EC Law** *(2002). Written with Sharon Turner of Queens University, Belfast, it argues that as the imperative to achieve democratic accountability in environmental governance has moved to the heart of Community policy making on the environment, Community legislation has increasingly granted individuals rights to participate in environmental decision making. In the European context, a distinctive feature of such participatory rights has been the extent to which Member States have been required to take into account transboundary environmental impacts of decisions, and in doing so to consult not just the governments of potentially affected states (a feature of international environmental law) but also citizens and non-governmental organizations within those countries. So pronounced is the pattern is that it is arguable that transboundary participatory rights are fast emerging as a minimum procedural requirement of good environmental governance.*

It is now over thirty years since European Community environmental legislation was first developed. Ten years after the initiation of the first Community action programme on the environment, I organised a conference at Imperial College to reflect on progress to date from both a policy and legal perspective. **Underlying Themes in the Policy Process** *(1983) is an analysis of some of the core themes* *that emerged from the conference, and written with a colleague, the late John Peachey, a resource analyst who had previously worked in government. At the time, the United Kingdom was strongly resisting the proposed Directive on environmental assessment (this was when unanimous voting at Council level was required to agree legislation), and we were intrigued with the vigour with which the UK government was protecting the more informal approach to assessment then practised in the United Kingdom to the apparently more formalized requirements being proposed by the European Commission. The Directive, which was agreed two years later, was the first environmental directive almost wholly concerned with prescribing a procedure for decision making rather than substantive outcomes, a feature than has since become more significant in subsequent directives, and this aspect of the proposal appeared to exacerbate potential national and community conflicts. Many of the issues identified in **Underlying Themes** continue to resonate in contemporary negotiation of Community environmental law and policy making.*

CHAPTER 17

THE AMSTERDAM TREATY:
AN ENVIRONMENTAL PERSPECTIVE*

Introduction

From an environmental perspective, the Amsterdam Treaty amendments reflect a consolidation of existing themes rather than wholesale innovation. During the build-up to the Treaty negotiations the then Commissioner for the Environment, Ritt Bjerregaard, identified three key goals for effective environmental revisions in the new Treaty: (a) simplification of decision-making procedures and increased use of qualified majority voting; (b) sections of the Treaty dealing with sectoral areas such as agriculture, transport and regional policy to be amended to make express reference to environmental protection; and (c) a right to a clean and healthy environment to be included in the Treaty.[1] In the event only the first of these goals was realised, and even here the amendments did not go as far as the Commission had originally hoped. No-one could yet conclude that the Treaty has been 'greened', but the changes to the Treaty that did take place are not insignificant, and will impact on the future direction of Community environmental law and policy.

The Task Of Sustainable Development

The pervasive concept of sustainable development was already fully alive during the Maastricht negotiations, and attempts were made formally to introduce it as one of the goals of the Community. In the event, Maastricht resulted in a rather unholy compromise between economic and political interests, and in the English-language version introduced as a task of the Community the promotion of 'sustainable and non-inflationary growth respecting the environment'.[2]

---

* R Macrory (1999) The Amsterdam Treaty: An Environmental Perspective in O'Keeffe and P Twomey (eds) *Legal Issues of the Amsterdam Treaty* Hart Publishing, pp 171-183

[1] Speech of Commissioner Bjerregaard, SPEECH/97/19 quoted in Calster and Deketelaere, Amsterdam, the Intergovernmental Conference and Greening the EU Treaty' [1998] *E Env. LRev.* 12-25.

[2] See Hession and Macrory. 'Maastricht and the Environmental Policy of the Community' in O'Keeffe and Twomey (eds.), *Legal Issues of the Maastricht Treaty* (Chancery, 1994), 151. Nigel Haigh has enumerated the different language versions of this provision in the Treaty, and notes in particular that the German version refers to continuous or lasting *(beständiges)* non-inflationary growth rather than sustainable as such: Haigh, 'Introducing the Concept of Sustainable Development into the Treaties of the European Union' in

Continued

The Amsterdam Treaty has now firmly inserted sustainable development as an explicit Treaty concept, with Article 2 of the TEU introducing as one of the objectives of the Union the achievement of 'balanced and sustainable development'. In theory this should mean that the language of sustainable development should in future enter the development of policies under all three pillars of the Union, including justice and home affairs and common security and foreign policy. When it comes to the Treaty on the European Community, the position is a little less clear-cut. The Article 2 task of sustainable and non-inflationary growth is retained, but no longer expressly linked to or qualified by the words 'respecting the environment'; the separate task of promoting the development of economic activities must now be 'sustainable' as well as harmonious and balanced,[3] and a new task of promoting a 'high level of environmental protection and improvement of the quality of the environment' is inserted. Sustainable development is expressly introduced as a goal for the integration principle contained in Article 3 which is discussed below. In terms of drafting, therefore, the Amsterdam amendments to the tasks of the European Community Treaty remain somewhat confused. There is no hierarchy of tasks, and no expanded definition of the meaning of sustainable development. From a legal perspective, the concept is, according to Krämer, 'more than vague',[4] and by themselves the new words are likely to have more political than legal importance. The means to achieve the range of Community tasks remain defined and constrained in Article 2 – 'by establishing a common market and an economic and monetary union and by implementing common policies or activities referred to in Articles 3 and 4'. To those who view sustainable development as requiring a fundamental restructuring of economic and political hierarchies, the changes are largely symbolic rather than structural,[5] and in the absence of explicit Community policies, the underlying legal structure of the Treaty and the judicial interpretation given to it continue to favour economic over environmental interests rather than ensure a deeper realignment.[6] The elaboration and

---

...O'Riordan and Voisey, (eds.), *The Transition to Sustainability: The Politics of Agenda 21 in Europe* (Earthscan, 1998), 64.

[3] The German version still uses the word *'beständiges'* (continuous) rather than ,sustainable': Bar and Kraemer, ,European Environmental Policy After Amsterdam' (1998) 10 *JEL* 315 at 316.

[4] Krämer, *EC Treaty and Environmental Law* (3rd edn., London, Sweet and Maxwell, 1988) at 56.

[5] Hession, 'The Legal Dynamics of European Integration and Sustainable Development' in O'Riordan and Voisey, *supra* n.2 at 76-99. As Hession notes at 85, 'European sustainable development is part of the Community's existing model rather than fully transformative of it'.

[6] The clearest example is that Art. 28, prohibiting quantitative restrictions on imports and measures of equivalent effect, continues to have direct effect, permitting individuals or economic interests to challenge national legislation inconsistent with the principle; there

Continued

development of sustainable development concepts will therefore be found in the future content of Community policies rather than legal rules and judicial principles. Member States were unwilling to accede to detailed amendment of individual sections of the TEC dealing with sectoral areas such as transport and agriculture to incorporate explicit environmental and sustainability objectives which the Commission and other interests had proposed.[7] Instead, an alternative approach was adopted with the strengthening and repositioning of the general principle of environmental integration, and the new express reference that it should be pursued 'with a view to promoting sustainable development'. In this way, the Amsterdam Treaty identifies one method for securing sustainable development, and in a form that has some legal meaning.

The Principle Of Environmental Integration

From a policy and administrative perspective, the significance of ensuring that sectoral areas not traditionally considered as environmental are nevertheless imbued with environmental considerations has for many years, both nationally and internationally, been considered a key challenge for contemporary government. The TEC is legally significant in being perhaps the only constitutional document where the concept has been given explicit expression in law. First inserted into the Treaty under the Single European Act, it was strengthened under Maastricht by the requirement in Article 130Rr that '[e]nvironmental protection requirements must be integrated into the definition and implementation of other Community policies'. Amsterdam now places the duty at the head of the Treaty in Article 6, and is more explicit about its remit of application, expressly applying it to all 'activities and policies' listed in Article 3. This removes the grounds for a restrictive interpretation of the duty under Article 130r which would have confined its application to express 'policies' of the Community listed in Article 3, such as transport and agriculture, but excluding areas such as competition and free movement of goods which are not stated to be policies as such.[8]

Repositioning the duty in itself does not appear to change its legal significance, but will undoubtedly increase the political and administrative attention given to it. Hallo, for example, notes that the

---

...is no equivalent Treaty right to challenge national legislation contrary to environmental interests. See Macrory, 'Environmental Citizenship and the Law' (1996) 8 *JEL* 219, especially 230-3. See also chap.19 below.

[7] Some Member States, including Austria and Denmark, did favour amendments to Treaty Arts, dealing with sectoral areas: see Calster and Deketelaere, *supra* n.1, at 17.

[8] Probably in any event an over-legalistic approach which would not have been supported by the European Court of Justice: Hession and Macrory in O'Riordan and Voisey (eds.), *supra n.2*, at 105. See chap. 18 below.

relocation of the subsidiarity principle under the Maastricht Treaty from one tucked away in the environmental Articles to a general principle at the head of the Treaty greatly increased the policy attention given to it, particularly in the environmental field.[9] The same administrative impact may well follow from the new location of the integration duty. The Commission itself has already developed important administrative and procedural initiatives in a bid to secure improved integration justified in part by reference to the legal requirements contained in the Treaty,[10] and in recent years more Council of Ministers meetings have been held which jointly cover areas such as Transport and the Environment and Energy and the Environment.

Nevertheless, Directorate General XI's relationship with other Directorates General has to date largely relied 'upon persuasion rather than power'.[11] The significance of the duty has been acknowledged by legal experts, with Jans, for example, describing it as 'perhaps the most important of all the principles mentioned, in Article 130r'.[12] The duty as reformulated at Amsterdam carries a heavy political burden since its agreement by Member State governments effectively bought off demands both for a line-by-line Treaty amendments in sectoral areas *and* the introduction of a general citizen's right to a healthy environment.[13] Yet the legal, as opposed to the policy, importance of the duty, both for Community institutions and external interests, remains to be fully tested.

The new positioning of the duty may be distinct, but legal duties of integration are now to be found in other areas apart from the environment, notably public health which now mirrors almost word for word the environmental principle (Article 152),[14] employment (Article 127),[15] consumer protection (Article 153)[16] and in a rather different formulation which has not changed since Maastricht in the area of Culture (Article

---

[9] Hallo, 'Sustainable Development and the Integration of the Environment into Other Policies' unpublished Conference Paper (1997) *IGC and the Environment*, 27 Jan. 1997.

[10] See, in particular, CEC Internal Communication *Integration by the Commission of the Environment into Other Policies* (1993) SEC(93)785/5, 28 May 1993.

[11] Wilkinson, 'Steps Towards Integrating the Environment into Other EU Policy Sectors' in O'Riordan and Voisey, *supra* n.2, 113.

[12] Jans, *European Environmental Law* (Kluwer, 1995), 25.

[13] See proposals of the European Council, Bull. EU 6-1996, para. 1-84.

[14] 'A high level of human health protection shall be ensured in the definition and implementation of all Community policies and activities' (Art. 152(1). Under the Maastricht version, the form of wording was weaker: '[h]ealth protection requirements shall form a constituent part of the Community's other policies' (Art. 129(1)).

[15] 'The objective of a high level of employment shall be taken into consideration in the formulation and implementation of Community policies and activities.'

[16] 'Consumer protection requirements shall be taken into account in defining and implementing other Community policies and actions.'

151)[17] and industry (Article 157)[18]. Under Protocol 33 due regard must be paid to the requirements of animal welfare in formulating and implementing Community policies in the field of agriculture, transport, the internal market and research. The strongly worded environmental integration duty as it appeared in Maastricht was unique amongst other policies, and some writers argued, not altogether convincingly, that as a result the environment was to be given priority over all areas of Community law and policy.[19] Imitation may be a form of flattery, but the proliferation of integration duties must weaken the concept, and, aside from its positioning, it is no longer possible to argue so convincingly that the environment is given a unique and distinctive legal status in the scheme of the Treaty.

In the case law to date which makes references to the environmental integration duty, the European Court of Justice has treated it essentially as an enabling provision, justifying measures taken by the Community under non-environmental Articles of the Treaty even though they have an environmental dimension.[20] The more significant question is the extent to which the duty could be invoked to constrain Community measures which are claimed to fail to respect the environmental requirements. There are difficult issues of pure legal interpretation. For a start, what is meant by 'environmental protection requirements'? A narrow approach would imply solely those environment requirements already contained in existing Community legislation, the approach that was adopted by the Commission in its application of the principle in the context of the award of structural funds.[21] Although this has the merit of some defined certainty in the criteria to be applied, it results in a duty largely devoid of any legal significance beyond the existing obligation of Member States to ensure compliance with Community obligations.[22] A more radical interpretation would look towards some objective standard of environmental protection against which to judge measures even where none has been defined in Community secondary legislation,

[17] 'The Community shall take cultural aspects into account in its action under other provisions of the Treaty, *in particular in order to respect and to promote the diversity of its cultures.'* The italicised words are inserted by the Amsterdam Treaty.

[18] 'The Community shall contribute to the achievements of the objectives set out in paragraph 1 through policies and activities it pursues under other provisions of the Treaty.'

[19] See, e.g., Scheuing, 'Umweltschutz auf der Grundlage der Einheitlichen Akte' (1989) 2 *Europarecht* 152, quoted in Bar and Kraemer, *supra* n.3, at 318.

[20] See, e.g., C-62/88, *European Parliament v. EC Council (Chernobyl I)*, [1990] ECR 1-1527; Case C-300/89, *Commission v. Council (Titanium Dioxide)*, [1991] ECR 1-2867.

[21] See, e.g., Art. 7 of Reg. 2081/93 on Structural Funds, which requires that measures financed by the funds 'shall be in conformity with the provisions of the Treaties, with the instruments adopted pursuant thereto and with Community policies, including those concerning environmental protection'.

[22] Art. 10 (*ex* Art. 5).

and taking as its starting point the express objective of the Treaty inserted at Amsterdam, 'a high level of protection and improvement of the quality of the environment'.[23] Yet this would involve the Court of Justice directly in making the complex economic and ethical questions inevitably involved in the establishment of environmental standards,[24] and inherent in the political processes involved in the making of Community legislation. It is, of course, arguable that the Court is already prepared to make these types of decisions in economic areas of Community law,[25] and that, at least in cases of severe environmental impact, they should be prepared to intervene.[26] But if the duty is to have a legal meaning, it is more indicative of a procedural duty rather than one that guarantees a substantive result. The Declarations to the Protocol to the Amsterdam Treaty already anticipate such a procedural significance, with Declaration 12 providing that '[t]he Conference notes that the Commission undertakes to prepare environment impact assessment studies when making proposals which may have significant environment implications', a strengthening of the wording found in the Maastricht Treaty. The legal status of a Declaration may be dubious, but when taken in conjunction with the express integration duty a failure to undertake such a assessment might well be an appropriate subject for legal action. More difficult (and perhaps more likely) would be the position were such a study to suggest significant environmental impacts but the Community were to continue to promote the measure in question for other legitimate goals. Would the Court feel that the environmental implications had at least been considered and that it was a matter and discretion for the legislative Community institutions rather than the Court to resolve the conflicting interests involved? At the very least, it might consider that in such cases the duty to gives reasons for Community regulations, directives and decisions contained in Article 254 must fully address the issue,[27] and not simply provide a descriptive statement of procedures followed.[28]

---

[23] Art. 2.

[24] See Royal Commission on Environmental Pollution, *Setting Environmental Standards,* 21st Report (London, HMSO, 1988). The same concern can be applied to the concept of general rights to a clean environment which must be interpreted into concrete standards of some sort.

[25] See Macrory and Hession, 'Balancing Trade Freedom with the Requirements of Sustainable Development' in Emilou and O'Keeffe, *The European Union and World Trade Law* (Wiley, 1996). See also chap. 20 below.

[26] In a similar way the European Court of Human Rights has tentatively interpreted Art. 8 of the European Convention (respect for privacy and family) to be breached in cases of 'severe environmental pollution': sec Case 116/1996, *Guerra and Others* v. *Italy,* 19 Feb. 1998.

[27] See Hession and Macrory, ,The Legal Duty of Environmental Integration' in O'Riordan and Voisey (eds.), *supra* n.2, at 111-12. See also chap. 18. below. We go on to argue that the principles of environmental action contained within the Treaty (prudent use of natural resources, precautionary principle, polluters pay, etc.) could be used as a set of rational

Continued

The issue of the substance of the integration duty and the question to whom it is owed are difficult to separate. Clearly, Member States and Community institutions have rights to challenge the legality of Community measures directly before the European Court,[29] although in areas such as structural funds, Member States have been reluctant to initiate such action. The increased use of qualified majority voting might be expected to increase the likelihood of minority Member States challenging the legality of measures considered to be lacking in environmental sensitivity, but to some extent the availability of rights for Member States to adopt stricter environmental standards than those contained in Community measures (see below) may act as a counterbalance. The political reality is that any legal challenge is most likely to be initiated by external environmental interests. During the Amsterdam negotiations Member States resisted proposals to broaden the ambit of *locus standi* for direct action before the European Court, and the case law to date suggests that where general environmental interests are concerned, it will be extraordinarily difficult for a non-privileged applicant to satisfy the 'direct and individual concern' test now repeated in Article 230.[30] A more profitable course for such interests in many cases would be to seek to challenge the legality of the Community measure before a national court, and secure a reference to the European Court.[31] Yet there will remain situations where a national challenge is not possible, either because the measure in question does not directly involve a decision that is justiciable at national level (the award of structural funds by the Commission to a Member State being

... and demanding criteria for substantive legal review of Community action in this context.

[28] However, in relation to the subsidiarity principle, the ECJ did not feel that the issue need be expressly addressed on proposed measures in order to satisfy the duty to give reasons, since it had been implicitly considered by the Council and Parliament: *Germany v. European Parliament and EU Council* [1997] 3 CMLR 1379 at 1413. Contrast the Opinion of Léger AG who considered, at 1397, that, given the importance of the principle of subsidiarity in allocating powers between Member States, 'it does not seem excessive to expect (Community] institutions in the future systematically to state reasons for their decisions in view of the principle of subsidiarity'. The question is whether the integration principle could assume such significance.

[29] Art. 230. With respect to the European Parliament, the Court of Auditors and the European Central Bank such action may be taken only to protect their prerogatives.

[30] Case T-585/93, *Stichting Greenpeace Council and others* v. *Commission* [1995] ECR 11-2205, upheld on appeal in Case C-321/95P [1998J 3 CMLR 1; *Danielsson* v. *Commission* [1995] ECR 11-3051.

[31] Art. 234 clearly gives the Court the jurisdiction to make rulings on the validity of acts of the Community institutions. Sec also Case 314/85, *Firma Foto-Frost* v. *Hauptzollamt Lübeck-Ost* [1987] ECR 4199, where the ECJ held that national courts could not declare acts of the Community institutions invalid but should refer the matter to the ECJ. The doctrine denying the power of national courts to hold Community measures illegal, is by no means accepted by the higher national courts in many Member States: for a recent review, see Sweet, ,Constitutional Dialogues in the European Community' in Slaughter, Sweet and Weiler (eds.), *The European Courts and National Courts* (Oxford, Hart Publishing, 1998), 305.

a good example) or where national rules on *locus standi* or costs inhibit such a challenge. In this respect, Amsterdam fails to address the issue of devising more effective means to secure review of the legality of measures taken by Community institutions, and there seems little likelihood that the Court of Justice will, without clearer signals in the Treaty, develop such principles itself.[32]

Legislative Procedures

The development of the integration principles underlines the extent to which it is difficult to characterise the environment as a confined area of policy, yet the need to choose a legal basis for a particular measure requires a discrete choice to be made. Maastricht introduced qualified majority voting for many areas of environmental policy under the then Article 130s, yet inter-institutional legal disputes over the correct choice of legal base continued,[33] particularly between Article 100A and Article 130s. The very different legislative processes involved, with co-decision attached to the former and co-operation to the latter, formed the motive for legal action and justified the Court in denying the possibility of a joint legal base.[34] Despite the underlying political background to the cases, the Court insisted that the choice of measure was to be based on objective criteria, but difficulties of identifying a 'centre of gravity' for an environmental measure which in reality *does* have a number of joint objectives is fully apparent in the reasoning of the Court, and the resulting decisions have not lacked for critics.[35]

The Amsterdam Treaty should now remove this particular source of legal dispute since Article 175 now introduces the codecision procedure under Article 251 for the majority of environmental measures, bringing it in line with Article 95 approximation measures. The codecision procedure has also been introduced for transport measures made under Article 71. Amsterdam has somewhat simplified the codecision procedure, but its application to pure environmental measures clearly increases the political significance of the European Parliament in the future direction and content of environmental policy. Furthermore, both

[32] I see real difficulties in giving unlimited access to the ECJ by third parties under Art. 230, as argued by some environmental organisations, especially with procedures that incorporate no filter or leave element. An alternative mechanism might be to create a new body, equivalent to the European Ombudsman, with power to investigate and bring cases concerned alleged illegality where privileged parties are unwilling to do so.

[33] Case C-300/89, *Commission v. Council* [1991] ECR 1-2867; Case C-70/99, *European Parliament v. Council* [1991] ECR 1-4529; Case C-155/91, *Commission v. Council* [1993] ECR 1-939; Case C-233/94, *Germany v. Parliament and Council* [1997] ECR 1-2405.

[34] The Court has not, however, always been consistent on this point and, as Jans notes, *supra* n.12 at 59, has held that a joint legal base involving different procedures is possible, with the result that the 'modalities of the two procedures are combined'.

[35] See Kramer, *supra* n.4, at 86-91; Jans, *supra* n.12, at 50-66.

Articles 175 and 251 now require the Council of Minister to consult with the Committee of the Regions on proposed measures. Nevertheless, despite the alignment of the legislative procedures, it would be unwise to assume that disputes over the choice of legal base will not continue or that joint legal bases can be adopted. As discussed below, the legal powers of Member States to apply higher national environmental standards than those contained in the Community measure continue to differ according to the choice of legal base. Furthermore, the co-decision procedure has not been introduced into other Articles of the Treaty which in the past have provide a basis for environmental measures, notably Article 37 (agriculture) and Article 166 (specific research and technological development programmes).[36]

Not all environmental measures under Article 174 require co-decision procedures. Amsterdam retained the list of environmental areas still requiring unanimous voting by the Council of Ministers included under Maastricht, and failed to attempt any clarification of the ambiguities in the terms employed.[37] The increasing potential importance of fiscal measures as a mechanism of environmental policy was recognised in proposals during the Amsterdam negotiations to include a protocol declaring that certain environmental taxes were not to be regarded as fiscal provisions, but this failed to secure the approval of all Member States.[38]

Higher National Environmental Standards

Article 174 (environment) has retained the form of wording introduced under the Single European Act, which permits Member States to maintain or introduce 'more stringent protective measures' provided these are notified to the Commission and compatible with the Treaty. Before the introduction of the principle in the Treaty itself a number of environmental Directives and regulations contained clauses to similar effect, although it remains to be decided whether Article 174 still applies where a Community environmental measures specifically excludes the possibility of higher national standards.

---

[36] Art. 157 (industry) is another area where co-decision procedures do not apply, although it appears that this has not been used as a legal base for environmental measures even with a strong industrial content: see Kramer, *supra* n.4, at 44-7.

[37] For a discussion of the various headings and a rationale for the retention of unanimous voting, see Kramer, *supra* n.4, at 94-100. The recent announcements from the German Government on the future institutional changes to the Union call for a wholesale reduction in unanimous voting, including fiscal matters: 'Germany wants full political union in EU', *The Guardian*, 13 Jan. 1999.

[38] Calster and Deketelaere, *supra* n.1 at 19. Art. 175(2) reserves for unanimous voting 'provisions primarily of a fiscal nature', clearly allowing for fiscal measures which are a subsidiary element of a substantive environmental measure to be decided by qualified majority.

The most substantive amendments concerning higher national standards are contained in Article 95. These build upon, and in some respects clarify, the provisions contained in the former Article 100A, and introduced under the Single European Act. But significant legal ambiguities remain, and while on the surface the amendments appear to increase the powers of Member States the conditions attached to their application are likely to have the reverse effect. There is an inherent contradiction in the concept of single market harmonising legislation and the retention of powers to apply higher national environmental standards,[39] and the provisions reflect the continuing conceptual ambiguities involved.

The provisions in Article 95 now apply to both approximation measures adopted by the Council[40] and those adopted by the Commission. This is potentially an important extension, since many Directives and regulations permit the adaptation of technical aspects of the measures by the Commission using the various comitology procedures, and it is precisely in the detail of technical standards that Member States may wish to see a more stringent national approach. The provisions are no longer restricted to where measures were adopted by qualified majority, removing former legal arguments whether only Member States voting against or abstaining could invoke the rights. The former Article 100A permitted Member States to 'apply' more stringent standards, but the new wording makes it expressly clear that Member States may both maintain *and* introduce more stringent standards, thus rendering largely obsolete the considerable arguments in the legal literature about whether 'apply' could encompass the introduction of new standards. But the distinction remains importance since the conditions applicable to the derogation rights differ considerably between existing and new national standards.

The justification for the maintenance of existing standards has not changed under Amsterdam, and Member States may do so on grounds of major needs referred to Article 30, or relating to the protection of the environment or the working environment. In contrast, grounds of major need are excluded in the case of the introduction of new standards which

[39] See, e.g., Pescatore, 'Die "Einheitliche Europäishche Akte" — Eine ernste Gefähr für den Europäischen Markt' [1986] *EuR* 153. On the other hand, a number of directives made under Art.100A specifically contained 'safeguard' clauses allowing Member States to apply higher standards. Such clauses were expressly permitted under Art. 100A(5) and continued under Art. 95(10), and the ECJ has held that the goals of minimum harmonisation (as opposed to complete harmonisation) and Art. 100A are not incompatible: Cases C-11/92, *Gallaher* [1993] ECR 1-3545 and C-222/91, *Phillip Morris* [1993] ECR 1-3469, quoted in Jans, *supra* n.12 at 102.
[40] As Kramer notes, *supra* n. 4 at 131, this must be interpreted to include measures adopted jointly by the Council and Parliament where the codecision procedures under Art. 251 are fully brought into play.

may relate only to the protection of the environment and the working environment.[41] Furthermore, there must be 'new scientific evidence' and the problem must be 'specific to that Member State arising after the adoption of the harmonisation measure'. Both conditions are fraught with ambiguity, but clearly present real difficulties for a Member State. Scientific evidence does not necessarily mean the same as scientific proof,[42] and it is increasingly recognised that conventional notions of scientific causation are often inappropriate or unattainable, given the complexities of contemporary environmental science.[43] Nevertheless a Member State would have to provide some degree of detailed scientific justification. Evidence of a problem that is both new and specific to the Member State makes the application of the principle even more of a challenge, and it is difficult to see how it would apply to standards concerning the effect of pollutants on, say, human health. It is true that in its case law concerning the justification of measures under Article 30 for public health grounds in areas such as food additives, the European Court of Justice has often had to deal with question of different perceptions by Member States of risks posed, and subject to the principle of proportionality, has generally accepted that it was for the Member State to determine what degree of protection is appropriate for its citizens.[44] But satisfaction of the Article 30 necessity test by a Member State is all the more difficult where there is a degree of international scientific consensus on the issue in question,[45] and by definition these principle apply in the absence of a harmonisation measure. It is likely therefore that the application of Article 95 would require more convincing evidence of the specificity of the issue that has been apparent in existing case law.[46] Furthermore,

---

[41] It could been argued that since one of the grounds of major need in Art. 30 is the protection of public health, its exclusion here means that the protection of the environment-must be interpreted restrictively to include only measures concerning the protection of the natural environment, such as habitats and flora and fauna. My own view is that this is unduly legalistic and an artificial division – many Community environmental measures are designed to protect public heath by the improvement of environmental standards.

[42] Bar and Kraemer, *supra* n.3 at 321-2, note that the German language version uses the term *'wisssenschaftliche Erkenntnisse'* (scientific knowledge) rather than *'Bewies'* (proof), although the French version uses the phrase, *'preuves scientifiques'*, which seems rather stricter.

[43] See Fisk, 'Environmental Science and Environmental Law' (1998) 10 *JEL* 3-8. The difficulties involved have provided one the main justification for the introduction of the precautionary principle in environmental policy-making, and expressly provided as a basis for Community environmental policy under Art. 174(2).

[44] E.g., Case C-272/80, *Frans-Nederlandse Maatschappij voor Biologische Produkten BV* [1982] 2 CMLR 497; Case C-174/82, *Officier van Justitite v. Sandoz* BV [1983] ECR 2445.

[45] See Case C-178/84, *Commission v. Germany* [1987] ECR 1227; Case C-293/94, *Brandsma* [1996] 3 CMLR 904.

[46] The difficulty of applying these provisions particularly to public health issues is confirmed by the new para. (8) of Art. 95 which requires the Commission to consider the need to amend harmonisation measures in the light of public health problems notified by Member States – i.e. in the case of public health issues the Commission can be required

Continued

in considering the issue, the Court of Justice would be alive to the fact that in its proposal for a harmonisation measure the Commission must have taken as a base a high level of protection, 'taking into account any new development based on scientific facts' (Article 95(3)), a new clause inserted by Amsterdam, and that the European Parliament and the Council must also seek to achieve the objective of a high level of protection in the exercise of their powers, again a new provision.[47] The starting point, therefore, against which to judge a Member State's application to introduce higher standards must be that the harmonisation measure in question is already based on the recent scientific evidence and is intended to ensure a high level of protection.[48]

The new provisions in Article 95 set out a far more explicit procedural route for handling applications by Member States in relation to both existing and new national measures, reflecting the decision of the European Court of Justice in its only decision to date on the issue.[49] As before, Member States must notify the Commission, but for both existing and new measures the Member State must provide the grounds for doing so. The Commission itself is given the specific power to approve or reject the provisions, but a time-limit of six months is imposed,[50] with the important proviso that in the absence of a decision the measure is deemed approved. Until a decision is made or deemed approval given, it must be assumed that the national provisions cannot be applied, in line with the decision of the European Court in the *PCP* case.[51] The deemed approval proviso is clearly intended to ensure that decisions do not remain in limbo.[52] As before the Commission must ensure that the

---

...to consider the need for higher standards without the need for Member States to satisfy the specificity test.

[47] It has been correctly observed that the phrase 'seek to achieve' is a legal duty that is unlikely to be enforceable by the judiciary: see Calster and Deketelare, *supra* n.1 at 15; Bar and Kraemer, *supra* n.3 at 324. But this does not diminish the view likely to be taken of the context in which a harmonisation measure is taken.

[48] This analysis is based on what some might argue is a narrowly based view of science, essentially equating it with the physical sciences. A more radical interpretation would widen the ambit to encompass social sciences. Could, for example, Art. 95 be invoked by a Member State which relied solely upon social science surveys pointing to unease amongst its citizens with the ethical implications of genetically manipulated organisms? Given an approach which is likely to judge these derogations from the principle of harmonisation restrictively in any event, it seems unlikely that the judiciary will feel comfortable in moving beyond more conventional views on the meaning of scientific evidence in this context.

[49] Case C-41/93, *France v. Commission (Re Pentachloropenol)* [1995] 3 CMLR 733.

[50] In the absence of human health danger and when justified by complexity, the period can be lengthened to 12 months: Art. 95(6).

[51] *Supra* n.49 at para. 30.

[52] Kramer, *supra* n.4 at 130, notes that by 1997 the Commission still had not reached decisions concerning notifications from The Netherlands in two cases *(PCP* and *Cadmium)* sent in 1992. Commission pressure persuaded The Netherlands to withdraw the application concerning cadmium in 1998.

measure is not a disguised restriction on trade or a means of arbitrary discrimination, but a new ground of rejection has been inserted – that the measure 'constitutes an obstacle to the functioning of the internal market' (Article 95(6)). The meaning of this phrase is ambiguous, since by definition any higher national standard must constitute at least some obstacle to the functioning of the market. Given that the provisions represent a derogation from the market principles, it seems clear that the principle of proportionality applies in any event, i.e. the national measures must be the least restrictive possible,[53] suggesting that the phrase is not simply to be equated with the conventional application of the proportionality test. It would follow that the Commission would be justified in rejecting an national measure which had a significant impact on the market, without the need to weigh up the environmental benefits.[54] Only three national measures were confirmed by the European Commission under the old Article 100A between 1987 and 1997, and the new Amsterdam provisions are unlikely to result in a dramatic increase in numbers. It is clear, however, that the need to preserve the integrity of market harmonisation measures is strengthened by the new feedback provision in Article 95(7) which requires the Commission to 'immediately examine', upon authorisation of an existing or new national measure, the need to amend the Community measure in question. Similarly, the new provision in Article 95(8) requires Member States to notify the Commission of problems concerning public health in a field covered by a harmonisation measure with the Commission, and again the Commission is required immediately to examine the issue with a view to proposing amendments to the Community measure. These two provisions are intended to assist in ensuring that harmonisation measures are ratcheted up to meet contemporary demands and in response to developments within Member States, forestalling the proliferation of more stringent national measures. In this context, while the new Article 95 provisions may raise the legal obstacles to maintaining or introducing more stringent national measures, their overall effect may be increase the political power of individual Member States to press for higher standards to be inserted into harmonisation measures.

Conclusions

Treaty amendments inevitably reflect the political and social contexts in which they were negotiated, and Amsterdam is no exception.

[53] Argued by Teasuro AG in the *PCP* case, *supra* n.49 at para. 5, though not expressly confirmed by the ECJ.

[54] Kramer, *supra* n.4, at 134 and Bar and Kraemer, *supra* n.3, at 326 appear to equate this provision with the proportionality principle, but for a contrasting view see Jans, 'Environmental Protection and the Amsterdam Treaty' (1997), unpublished paper at the Conference marking the 3.0th Anniversary of the Groningen Chair of European Law, University of Groningen.

Environmental policies, at both national and supra-national level, have entered a strangely contradictory period where there is greater awareness of the international dimension to many environmental challenges, but less confidence in conventional regulatory methods and prescriptive 'top-down' governmental intervention as a means of meeting those challenges. Community environmental policy is coming to terms with these new dimensions. We have yet to see the wholesale demise of Community-wide environmental standards which so characterised Community policy instruments in the 1980s, but already the application of the subsidiarity principle, strengthened by the Protocol agreed at Amsterdam,[55] has influenced the content of recent environmental measures, giving greater discretion to Member States in their interpretation and application. The increased consultative powers of the Committee of the Regions, and the possible application of the new provisions concerning closer co-operation between individual Member States[56] on environmental matters suggests an unsettling period of asymmetry in the substance of environmental policy, and one which has not been counterbalanced by the inclusion of any general Community legal rights to environmental quality. In the context of the constitutional architecture of the Union, Weiler has described the Amsterdam Treaty as 'generally more anæmic' than its predecessors,[57] and the environmental revisions are modest in terms of fundamental legal restructuring. The implications of accession and enlargement remain to be tackled, and devising more effective legal means to ensure effective review of the legality of Community activities was a missed opportunity – although the new general principles concerning access to documents held by Community institutions may prove a significant check in the environmental field.[58] Monetary union is likely to prove to be the stalking horse for a deeper discourse over the political and constitutional direction of the European Union. In that context, the Amsterdam strengthening of the key principles concerning sustainable development and environmental integration, despite their insusceptibility to formal legal analysis, can be seen as providing the underpinning legitimisation that ensures these concepts are at least firmly embedded in future debate.

---

[55] Prot. 30 on the Application of the Principles of Subsidiarity and Proportionality.

[56] Arts. 43-44 TEU and Art. 11 TEC.

[57] Weiler, 'The European Courts of Justice: Beyond Doctrine or the Legitimacy Crisis of European Constitutionalism' in Slaughter, Sweet and Weiler, *supra* n.31, at 366.

[58] Art. 255. General principles and limits on public access are to be determined by the Council under the co-decision procedure within 2 years of the entry into force of

CHAPTER 18

THE LEGAL DUTY OF ENVIRONMENTAL INTEGRATION: COMMITMENT AND OBLIGATION OR ENFORCEABLE RIGHT?*

Environmental protection requirements must be integrated into the definition and implementation of other community policies.
article 130r(2), European Community Treaty

Why A Legal Analysis?

In its 1992 report to UNCED, the European Commission described environmental integration as 'the lynch-pin in the process of establishing sustainable social and economic development patterns'. All Member States may now politically subscribe to the goals of sustainable development, but no national constitution or legal system contains an explicit legal requirement concerning the integration of an environmental dimension into other policy sectors. Only within the European Community Treaty, under article 130r, has the idea been given such an overt and broadly drawn expression in law. The presidency conclusions from the 1997 Amsterdam Treaty reaffirm the integration duty and expressly relate it to the promotion of sustainable development:[1]

> Environmental protection requirements must be integrated into the definition and implementation of community policies and activities referred to in Article 3, in particular with a view to promoting sustainable development.

Other chapters in this collection consider the policy and political implications of environmental integration, together with the tensions and difficulties apparent at European Community and national level as efforts are made to respect the requirement. The approach here is somewhat different. Given the distinctive legal dimension to the integration duty in the treaty, we feel it is important to consider the

---

* M Hession, and R Macrory (1998) The Legal Duty of Environmental Integration: Commitment and Obligation or Enforceable Right? In T O'Riordan, and H Voisey, (eds) *The European Union and Sustainable Development* Frank Cass, London, pp 100 - 112
[1] Referred to in the rest of this chapter as the Amsterdam Treaty amendments. At the time of writing (August 1997) the Conclusions of the Presidency had still not been formally agreed upon and signed by the parties. Formal amendment of the treaty (which requires referenda in some countries) is probably still several years away. Under the Amsterdam amendments, the integration duty would be repositioned as a new article 3d at the head of the treaty.

nature of a duty from a legal perspective, bringing to bear principles and conceptual approaches developed in the context of the discipline of law. In particular, we need to ask: to what extent does the provision, as a matter of law, require, provide, and constrain the operational criteria for its implementation?

It is tempting to dismiss a duty which is expressed, in such broad and apparently political terms, as merely 'symbolic reassurance' (Edelman, 1963) or one that implies no more than a reflection of existing policy developments. It is true that the community commitment to a policy of environment integration predates its express inclusion in the treaty in 1987 by some five years.[2] As Haigh describes in Chapter 3, the duty first entered the legal language of the treaty under the Single European Act 1987 and the wording was strengthened under the Maastricht Treaty in 1992.[3]

These developments, however, do not answer the question of the legal significance attached to the duty. Despite the Single European Act requirement, the European Commission made little progress in strengthening its own policy-making procedures to reflect the obligation. It did publish integrative policy documents in a number of sectoral areas (see Wilkinson, 1992). But it is only fairly recently, as considered by Wilkinson in the next chapter, that more substantial internal administrative changes have been made by the commission in order to pursue the goal of integration. A number of these reflect similar administrative initiatives already introduced by member state governments at national level. It is fairly fruitless to speculate whether these developments were brought about by the existence of the duty in the treaty, or whether these provisions simply reflected pressures for policy changes that were occurring in any event. Certainly, the developments that have taken place at community level cannot be said to have been the result of any dramatic, interventionist decision by the Court of Justice. This has happened in some other policy areas, such as the common transport policy.[4] The fact that the legal duty existed for almost ten years without any significant internal administrative change at community level indicates that the motor for change was not sparked by a legal dynamic.

---

[2] Council resolution endorsing the Third Action on the Environment (1982-86) established the integration of an environmental dimension into other Community policies as a priority, and in 1985 the European Council 'affirmed its determination' to give Community environmental protection policy 'the dimension of an essential component of the economic, industrial, agricultural and social policies implemented by the community and by its member states'.

[3] A number of expert commentators soon noted the potential significance of the provision. Ludwig Krämer (1990) that it 'must be considered the most important provision in the entire section on the environment': Nigel Haigh (1987) also commented that it is 'potentially the most important new provision'.

[4] See, in particular, C 13/83 *European Parliament v EC Council* [1985] ECR 1513.

It does not follow, however, that the duty is devoid of legal significance. It has already been referred to by the Court of Justice in a number of cases concerning the appropriate legal basis for community environmental legislation.[5] The thrust of the case law to date has been to interpret the duty in the light of measures based on the Treaty's non-environmental provisions even where their substantive content has an environmental dimension.[6] In that sense, the integration duty can be said to have an enabling or legitimising effect on Community action already being proposed. But from a legal perspective, perhaps the more critical question for the future is whether the requirement goes further: does it imply a duty which *constrains* Community activities, and which fails to reflect the integration concept or *requires* positive steps to be taken? In other words, the duty to integrate must fall somewhere in the continuum of an expression of general interest in environmental protection and a general duty to protect the environment.

The bald conclusion of the European Court in the Chernobyl I case, namely that the integration provision under article 130r in its pre-Maastricht version implies that 'all Community measures must satisfy the requirements of environmental protection', hints at something more than a mere enabling provision.[7] But closer analysis is required to test the validity and practicality of that assertion. Ordinarily, the expression of a legal duty implies a concomitant right, as a consequence of the general need that duties should be enforceable. Therefore, in seeking to define its place on the continuum, it is important to consider how and by whom the duty/right is enforceable. In the absence of any enforcing power a duty risks becoming 'a statement of public policy that is contradicted by practice' and 'is nothing but an empty shell ... It may even be pernicious to the reputation of the constitution as a whole and detract from the credibility of the constitutional system derived from it.'[8]

In pursuing the analysis further we can identify five interrelated but essentially distinct lines of inquiry. These are purposely framed in terms of a legal perspective on the issue.

---

[5] For example, case C-62/88 *Greece v EC Council* [1990] 1 ECR 1527.

[6] The rule of law underlies the operation of the Community in that any legal measures taken by the Community (such as legislation) must expressly be founded on a specific provisions of the treaty (such as those concerning agriculture, transport, the environment, etc). Ultimately the European Court has the power to determine whether a particular measures falls within the remit of the provision claimed. Since different procedural consequences can flow from the choice of Treaty provision, there have been frequent legal disputes between the European Council, the European Commission, the European Parliament and Member States over the correct legal base.

[7] For example, case *Greece v EC Council* [1990], ECR 1527.

[8] This was said of the constitution of the German Democratic Republic, which included a mandate to the legislature and a fundamental duty to protect nature (Brandi and Bungert, 1992).

1   Is the integration duty legally binding or merely exhortatory in character?

2   What does the duty apply to?

3   By whom is the duty owed?

4   What is the substance of the duty: what must be integrated, and when is the duty satisfied? Is it a substantive or procedural requirement?

5   To whom is it owed, and if it is legally binding, by whom is it enforceable?

The Integration Duty in Context

Before considering these questions in more detail, it is important to place the duty in the context of the environmental provisions of the treaty. Although these represent something of a mishmash from a legal perspective, one can provide an analytical overview of the structure.

• Ostensibly the treaty does not guarantee environmental quality or sustainable development nor does it place a duty on the Community to achieve these goals. To paraphrase article 2, the Community has as one of its fundamental tasks to promote sustainable growth while respecting the environment, which it will achieve by various measures (establishing a common market and an economic and monetary union and by implementing common policies or activities, including the environmental policy). The Amsterdam amendments would expressly add as one of the tasks 'a high level of protection and improvement of the quality of the environment'.

• The Community does, however, have a recognised *interest* in environmental protection, and has legal authority to adopt measures with reference to a range of policies including those contained in article 130r of the treaty relating to community policy on the environment.

• The three key objectives are: preserving, protecting and improving the quality of the environment; protecting human health; and the prudent and rational utilisation of natural resources.[9] These

---

[9] There is an important fourth objective of promoting measures at international level to deal with regional or worldwide environmental problems, but this relates more to geographical competence than to substantive content.

indicate that environmental protection is defined according to a variety of philosophical approaches – ecocentric, anthropocentric and what might be described as economic rationality (the rational use of resources).

- The Community authority for action is confined to the range of Community policies listed in article 3 and their relevant legal base. For those policies which are not exclusively the preserve of the community but exist concurrently with those of Member States (of which the dedicated environmental policy is one), Community authority is further constrained by the principle of subsidiarity.

- Nevertheless, where the Community does take action, there is an identified standard of protection to be achieved, albeit expressed in qualitative terms. In its proposals concerning the internal market and environmental protection, it *must take as a base* a 'high level' of protection (article 100a), or alternatively in proposals under the environment policy it must aim at a 'high level' of protection, taking into account the diversity of situations in various regions of the Community.

- According to article 130r, there are express principles upon which environmental policies must be based, notably: the precautionary principle; the principle that preventative action should be taken; the need to rectify damage at source; and the principle that the polluter should pay. Again under article 130r, additional factors must be taken into account when preparing environmental policy. These are: available scientific data; environmental conditions in the various regions of the community; the potential costs and benefits of action or lack of action; and the socio-economic development of the community and its regions.

- Finally, there is the integration duty, currently contained in article 130r and analysed in more detail in the chapter that follows. The positioning of the duty is potentially significant, as are the Amsterdam amendments which place it higher up in the Treaty, in a new article 3. Currently, it falls within the definition of the Community's competence on environmental matters, and after the stated objectives for environmental policy and the principles of environmental action. Its position suggests a requirement that is exercisable only in the context of community policy formulation and implementation rather than any absolute duty in respect of existing and presumably superior legal principles. Repositioning the provision is intended to give the principle far greater policy significance. As Hallo (1997) has noted, there may be an analogy with the repositioning and reformulation of the subsidiarity duty as a general principle following Maastricht, which brought in its wake considerable political attention designed to flesh out the implications of the requirement.[10]

Is the Integration Duty Legally Binding or Exhortary?

> From a practical point of view, only a self executing [judicially enforceable without the enactment of implementing legislation] constitutional provision seems to be worthy of adoption, since it alone has true constitutional value. Any other type of clause could be easily ignored: it would lack the weight and timeless authority of a constitutional provision. *[Brandi and Bungarth, 1992]*

Most systems of public law, and especially those that require the interpretation of written constitutional provisions, recognise two categories of legal statement:

- *directory duties* which are essentially exhortatory or policy statements not intended in themselves to be legally enforced, though they may colour the interpretation of other duties; and

- *mandatory requirements* which are self-executory in the sense that they impose duties which are enforceable in themselves, without requiring the implementation of further legislation.

The fact that a directory duty may not be legally enforceable does not necessarily render it mere rhetoric. It may influence the legal interpretation of other provisions, as has already happened with the integration duty.[11] Moreover, the existence of such a duty may elevate the status and influence of those parts of government already convinced of the need for such goals, and in turn affect the approach of others. As Cotterrell (1984) put it, 'the behaviour of officials and individuals may change even though the legislation does not create enforceable rights and duties ... non-justifiable legislation performs important functions'.

There are a number of arguments for considering the duty to be directory in character only. The duty is expressed in positive terms

---

[10] Hallo draws an analogy with the subsidiarity principle which 'underwent a similar migration in the Treaty of Maastricht, moving from the environment article to a new separate article at the beginning of the Treaty'. He notes how following that move, serious political attention was given to refining and developing the principle into workable criteria.

[11] See case C-13/83 *European Parliament v EC Council* [1985] ECR 1513.

('environmental protection requirements must be...'), and therefore, from a legal perspective is generally less susceptible to enforcement than is a negative requirement ('the Community may not promote policies damaging the environment...'). It relates to the exercise of judgment in policy development and implementation in which a court would ordinarily allow a greater margin of discretion to the decision-maker. The provision can be said to be ambiguous in that it fails to identify specific environmental protection requirements, an issue considered further below. This is a common response to environmental duties, but not necessarily fatal. Given the unconditional character of the duty, a proactive Court of Justice might insist that it has the authority to seek out the environmental protection requirements of the duty. But some commentators have detected a palpably less activist and more consolidatory phase in the court's current approach – and in any event the court has generally been less inclined to hold the Community's actions as contrary to Community law when compared to its tougher approach to the enforcement of community law against member states. Finally, as a general comment where duties exist with respect to the environment in national constitutions, experience has revealed considerable reluctance on the part of the courts to implement such environmental duties, in whatever language they are expressed (see Brandt and Bungert, 1997).

These are powerful arguments. But despite the ambiguity of the language, the literal meaning and legislative history of the integration provision tend to suggest that it is more in the nature of mandatory requirement. As Haigh notes[12] at Maastricht the member states consciously took the opportunity to reinforce the mandatory tone of the provision by strengthening the language of the obligation. Furthermore, in the context of community law, it would be unusual for the court not to ascribe some effect to such a statement pursuant to the principle of *effet utile* - the idea that treaty provisions must have some useful purpose.

To What Does the Duty Apply?

The duty applies integration to 'other community policies' without defining the meaning of that term. Article 2 of the treaty sets out a range of European Community activities, but only a limited number of these are referred to explicitly as policies:

- a common commercial policy (external trade to developing countries);

---

[12] T O'Riordan, and H Voisey, (eds) *The European Union and Sustainable Development* Frank Cass, London

- a common policy in the sphere of agriculture and fisheries;

- a policy in the social sphere comprising a European social fund –
  a common policy in the sphere of transport;

- a policy in the field of the environment; and

- a policy in the sphere of development cooperation.

A restrictive legal interpretation would suggest that the integration duty is confined to these areas only and does not cover other areas of community activity, such as competition law or free movement of goods, which are not explicitly on that list. The drafters of the integration duty could have used, if they wished, broader language. Our own view is that this is too limiting an approach. If the issue were to come before the European Court of Justice it would adopt a more generous interpretation, and not feel confined by the explicit list of policies in article 3. For a start, the treaty itself is not consistent in the use of the term 'policies'.[13] The court would be justified in considering the duty's underlying rationale and subject those policy-making activities of the Community, whether or not they are formally described as policies, to the integration duty.[14] In any event, the Amsterdam amendments will remove the doubt. The new version of the integration duty applies to 'policies and activities' (our emphasis) referred to in article 3. This extends the scope well beyond narrowly defined policies to encompass, amongst others, free movement of goods, competition, consumer protection, and measures of energy.

So much for the substantive areas encompassed by the duty. But we also need to ask what exactly is meant by policies (and 'activities' if the Dublin proposals are agreed). Does it encompass only binding legal acts such as directives, regulations and decisions? Or would it include formal, but non-binding, acts such as decisions, or go further to include informal documents and statements which do not necessarily have a legal status under Community law? Again, our view is that the court would be tempted to adopt a generous view, looking not so much at the legal form or status of the measure in question, but considering its significance in practice – is it, for example, a formulation of principles

---

[13] Part 3 of the Treaty, for example, is entitled *Community Policies* and includes competition policy, economic policies, and free movement of goods, and includes sections entitled 'economic policy' and 'monetary policy'.

[14] This approach is reinforced by the historical background to the proposal and the declaration at the Maastricht Conference that the commission undertakes to take full account of the environmental impact and the principle of sustainable growth in implementing its proposals — no qualification confining the scope of those proposals is provided in the declaration.

intended to guide or influence action within a field of community activity? Again the Amsterdam amendments would strengthen that view.

By Whom is the Duty Owed?

No particular institution or body is identified by article 130r(2), but it is clear that it applies to those bodies with primary responsibility for defining and implementating the community's other policies. These include all relevant Community institutions and Member States in so far as they are charged with implementing Community policies. The Declaration to the Maastricht Treaty refers to the Commission's undertakings in respect of environmental integration, and most attention to date has been focused on the Commission's internal administrative initiatives. But the above interpretation suggests a broader range of subjects than envisaged in current proposals, and would encompass at the very least all those community bodies involved in defining or implementing community policy, including the Council of Ministers, the European Investment Bank and the European Parliament.[15]

As to Member States, they are clearly bound by the duty when acting within the Council of Ministers.[16] The duty, however, refers to 'implementation' as well as to 'design', and since implementation is often the responsibility of Member States, it is arguable that the integration duty must apply here as well. This interpretation has considerable implications for Member States. Much would depend on the level of discretion granted at national level, and the extent to which a failure at national level to integrate an environmental dimension could frustrate the effect of article 130r. To take one example, a national body such as a transport department might be given the responsibility to define routes for Trans-European networks under article 129b of the treaty and would, we suggest, be legally vulnerable if no regard were paid to the duty at the time it exercised its responsibilities. Or a national body might be given responsibilities concerned with implementing community policy, such as the distribution of community funds. Again, we would argue that it would be bound by the integration duty. This would be especially

---

[15] Both the Council of Ministers and the committees of the European Parliament have been organised along traditional functional lines (transport, agriculture, environment, etc) which does not necessarily assist the integration process. The Council has occasionally held joint meetings (energy and environment) but the European Parliament has yet to establish any 'cross-cutting' committee structure.

[16] UK case law has held that the precautionary principle as expressed in article 130r binds member states only when developing a community policy and does not apply to other fields unencompassed by Community legislation: *R v Secretary of State for Trade and Industry ex parte Duddridge* (Court of Appeal 6 October 1995; see case note by Hughes (1995) *Journal of Environmental Law, 1* (2) 224,226).

relevant where the body has a margin of discretion and choice – in other words, where regard to the duty could have a real influence on the outcome of its decision.

The Substance of the Duty: Regarding Environmental Protection Requirements

The core of the duty refers to the integration of 'environmental protection requirements' and both phrases require interpretation in order to understand the substance of the requirement. But in the legal analysis of similar duties on governmental bodies, it has usually been difficult to disentangle the nature of the duty from the question: to whom the duty is owed. Each inquiry influences the other. The issue of enforceability is considered in more detail in the next section, but at this stage we can usefully identity three broad possible classifications of the duty.

1) *Internal integration:* this implies that the duty is one owed by Community policy-makers only to other Community policy-makers. The duty could take the form of one that is owed and legally enforceable by each institution, or one that is owed by Community institutions to the others but is implemented only by internal administrative methods. The current administrative initiatives considered by Wilkinson in the following chapter can be considered as an example of the latter.

2) *Weak constitutional integration:* here the duty is treated as one that is owed by Community institutions to Member States as well as to other Community bodies. This would permit Member States to challenge, in law, policies and decisions on the grounds that they were in breach of the integration duty.

3) *Strong constitutional integration:* this classification of the duty treats it as one that is owed by the Community to individual citizens, in effect creating an external individual right. Recent case law of the European Court has already treated the code of conduct on public access to information, developed by the European Council and European Commission and the decisions of those bodies to adopt it, as creating such external rights.[17] Nevertheless, as we discuss below, we see considerable difficulty in treating the integration duty as creating similar rights.

---

[17] See case T–I94/94 *Carvel and Guardian Newspapers v Council* [1995] ECR II-2765 and case T–I05/95 *WWF UK v Commission* 5 March 1977. Here the Court concluded that although the Commission's decision to adopt the code of practice was 'in effect, a series of obligations which the Commission has voluntarily assumed for itself as a measure of internal organisation, it is nevertheless capable of conferring on third parties legal rights which the Commission is obliged to respect'.

When considering the meaning of 'environmental protection requirements', there are several possible interpretations. The first, which we call conservative, is the simplest and most narrow. The word requirement implies a legal obligation and thus encompasses only those obligations concerning the environment contained in Community environmental legislation. This has the advantage of providing a clear benchmark and avoids the difficulties elaborated below when determining other, more elusive reference points. This is the approach that appears to have been adopted by the commission in relation to structural funds, as indicated in the analysis by Clare Coffey.[18]

Whatever its superficial attraction, this narrow approach hardly makes long-term sense. All it contributes to the existing legislative framework is an added mechanism for ensuring compliance with existing community environmental law – that is, a requirement to prevent other community policies from undermining compliance by Member States with their obligations under community law. General principles of Community law already exist to prevent this from happening. The general duty under article 5 of the treaty requiring Member States to take all appropriate measures to fulfil Community obligations imposes a reciprocal duty on the Commission to assist Member States, and by implication to refrain from action which inhibits implementation. Furthermore, the conservative approach fails to reflect the aspirations of the integration requirement.

The second approach to interpreting environmental protection requirements looks to objective standards of protection. According to this argument, in order to judge whether or not the integration duty has been followed, it is both legitimate and necessary to determine some standard of environmental protection which is neither contained in the treaty nor, necessarily, in community secondary legislation. To an extent, the idea that there are objective environmental protection requirements derives from the environmental rights ethos – wherever those rights are placed, it is possible to objectively determine what is necessary to protect the environment.

There are considerable difficulties in endorsing this interpretation. By cutting adrift the definition of environmental protection requirements,

---

[18] T O'Riordan, and H Voisey, (eds) *The European Union and Sustainable Development* Frank Cass, London. Whether the conservative interpretation was correct was at the heart of the *Mullaghmore* case, case T–461/93 *An Taisce and WWF (UK) v Commission* [1994] ECR II-733. The applicants challenged the commission's narrow interpretation of the structural funds regulation that measures financed by such funds must be in keeping with 'Community policy on environmental protection'. Unfortunately, the substance of the argument was not considered since the case was ruled inadmissible on procedural grounds, a decision confirmed on appeal, case C-325/94 [1996] ECR 1-3727.

a court would potentially be involved in substantive moral and ethical choices with respect to the factors that ought to be integrated and the standard of protection to be adopted. The reference to a 'high level' of environmental protection in article 130r of the treaty might act as a useful pointer for a court, but remains an aim rather than an obligatory requirement. In general terms, the essential difficulty with enforcing an objective standard of environmental protection is that the standard is not one amenable to judicial application or confidence.[19] The essence of judicial reluctance to become involved in such issues lies in the difficulty of describing an effective dividing line between the application of a rule based on solid criteria and the substitution of judicial judgment for what should be a matter of political discretion. In contrast, reviewing a decision for its procedural regularity is more easily performed. Here, what is examined is the reasoning process of the decision-maker; the substantive result of the decision is not directly tested for its compatibility with some putative environmental protection requirement. Even this approach does not always let a court completely off the hook. Assessing procedural regularities requires some consideration of the facts leading to the decision, their relevance or irrelevance, and some minimum basis to justify the decision.

The limitations of the conservative interpretation and the conceptual challenges of the objective standards suggest that a third approach is required. The Treaty itself contains certain obligatory policy requirements concerning the environment, which can be summarised as follows:

• a contribution towards the objectives of preserving, protecting and improving the quality of the environment, protecting human health, and the prudent and rational utilisation of natural resources;

• a high level of protection;

• adherence to the four principles of precaution, prevention, rectification at source, and polluter pays; and

• the need to take into account certain additional factors including the diversity of situations within various regions of the community,

---

[19] In a slightly different context, in the *Danish Bottles* case, *Commission v Denmark* [1989] 1 CMLR 619, the European Court was called upon to define an objective standard of environmental protection which was reasonable for a Member State to pursue, where this would inhibit the free movement of goods. The Court studiously avoided providing an answer, and refused to interfere with the judgment of the Member State on the issue. Posing the question of what is a reasonable degree of environmental protection, Kramer (1993) succinctly replies, 'the answer is relatively simple: we do not know'.

available scientific and technical data, and the potential costs and benefits of action or inaction.

These principles indicate the basis and direction of policy rather than specify a substantive result. The language used and the gradation of terminology (a 'basis in' to 'taking into account') suggest that they are guidelines – directional rather than prescriptive – and indicate a real difficulty in challenging measures claimed to be in breach of such principles, other than in the most clear-cut case of consciously avoiding their consideration. Nevertheless, if the integration duty is to be given any legal significance, we suggest that it represents a basis for interpretation which is consistent with the Treaty rather than relying on the contents of existing secondary legislation.

The Substance of the Duty: Integration

Article 173 of the Treaty, which provides the means to review the legality of community acts, makes a classic distinction between infringement of a rule of law and infringement of an essential procedural requirement. Generally speaking, the former guarantees a particular substantive result, while a procedural right guarantees some form of participation in the process of determining a result. The distinction is important, though in practice it can become blurred.[20] As we have indicated, courts are more inclined to recognise a procedural right with respect to the environment rather than a substantive right.[21]

The duty to integrate environmental requirements is suggestive of procedural rather than substantive protection. The dictionary definition supports the idea of a duty with respect to formulating policy rather than identifying a *ne plus ultra* of policy results. At the very least, the duty requires that regard must be given to environmental requirements when developing other community policies. As Kramer (1990, para 4.45) points out, in the context of the 1987 version of the duty, all Community measures 'must have one eye on the existing community legislation and the other on the environment, which is now a factor in all action [taken] by the community'.

A familiar requirement often imposed on administrative bodies is to 'take into consideration' certain factors, implying that once taken on

---

[20] For example, the right to procedural protection can include cases where the only evidence of a breach of procedures is the evidence of an inadequate substantive result which would not have occurred if adequate procedural protection had been given.

[21] In the general scheme of rights, individual substantive rights which are guaranteed exclusively to them, whereas collective rights, such as those relating to the environment, do not. The only sense in which a collective right may be ensured is by way of a guarantee in individual participation.

board they may be rejected if they conflict with other goals. But the terminology of the integration duty implies more than this; conflict with other areas does not entitle environmental requirements to be dismissed. Courts frequently have to make sense of competing goals which appear oh the face of law. The European Court is no stranger to this challenge and could adopt a number of tried and tested approaches. The first would be to apply principles of proportionality already seen in the context of conflicts between free movement of goods and environmental protection. According to this model, transport or competition policy, for example, would have to be the most environmentally compatible with the goals of these policies. This approach is not entirely satisfactory since it gives a predominance to those other policy objectives, whereas the integration duty is designed to redefine and redirect those policies.

Another approach that the Court could adopt would be to accept that determining the balance of competing objectives should remain at the discretion of Community institutions rather than within the Court's domain. This essentially is the stance adopted by the court in the agricultural field where the Treaty objectives are themselves potentially in conflict, and where the Court has been reluctant to interfere with the Commission or Council's determination of the purpose or scope of particular measures – even accepting that at any particular time one objective may legitimately take precedence over another.[22] The third approach is to develop a restrictive attitude towards parties entitled to bring legal challenges before the courts, thus relieving the Court of the difficult choices involved. This demonstrates the clear connection between the nature of the substantive duty and the question of locus standi, considered in the next section.

To Whom is the Integration Duty Owed?

This is perhaps the most difficult of all the questions raised and the most important. It determines the true nature of the duty, and whether it gives rise to a responsibility in the sense that somebody has the right to enforce it. As we indicated in the section on environmental protection requirements, three categories of potential beneficiaries can be identified: Community institutions; Member States; and, individual citizens.

With respect to the Community institutions, under article 173 of the Treaty, they have general rights to challenge the legality of Community acts and could conceivably enforce the integration duty against each other in this way. It must be observed that as the institutions share the responsibility of adopting Community acts in most cases, breach

---

[22] See, for example, case 5/73 *Balkan-Import-Export GmbH v Hauptzollamt Berlin-Packhof* [1973] ECR 1091.

of the duty to integrate during this process might arise in the context of disputes over the legal basis of measures. Here, both the European Parliament and the European Investment Bank may act only in respect of their own prerogatives (to protect their own particular rights), and it seems unlikely that either could hold rights with respect to the integration duty *per se*.

Similarly, Member States are able to challenge the validity of Community acts. Against a background of increased majority voting at Council level, it is possible to predict that a minority country, concerned with the lack of environmental sensitivity in a proposed Community measure, might take advantage of the remedy. But in areas such as structural funds, there has been a marked reluctance by Member States to initiate any legal challenges – perhaps for the simple but cynical reason that all member states expect to gain from structural funds at some point and have been unwilling to rock the plentiful boat (Kramer, 1996, p9).

To the extent that the integration duty also applies to Member States when defining or implementing Community policy, the European Commission would have a primary duty to initiate enforcement procedures under Article 169 of the treaty. The decision whether or not to initiate such action is essentially a matter of discretion for the commission and is not reviewable by the Court.[23]

Individuals bringing action before the national courts may also claim the benefit of treaty provisions, which are considered sufficiently precise and certain to have 'direct effect'.[24] In one sense, the integration duty is relatively precise and unconditional, but it is most unlikely that it would have such direct effects. There are sufficient ambiguities in the terminology (both of court overload and the substantive judgments demanded of the courts) to allow direct challenges of all Community policies by almost anyone; these weigh heavily against such an interpretation.

The treaty also permits individuals to challenge the legality of Community action directly before the European Court of Justice, although there are two critical limitations to the remedy. Firstly, the treaty rules, under article 173, only permit challenge to regulations or legal decisions. They do not allow individuals to challenge directives, resolutions and other non-binding actions of the community. Secondly,

---

[23] Member States may also initiate enforcement actions under article 169 against other Member States but are highly reluctant to do so, again for the fairly cynical reason of mutual reassurance.

[24] See case 26/62 *Van Gend en Loos* [1963] ECR 1, where the Court commenced its extensive jurisprudence on this doctrine.

the applicant must show 'direct and individual concern' and the Court of Justice has consistently given a restrictive interpretation of this phrase. Essentially, individuals making the challenge must demonstrate that they are affected in some way which differentiates them from all others affected,[25] and recent decisions of the Court of Justice which deny standing to environmental groups and individuals demonstrate that the test is almost impossible to satisfy where an issue of general environmental concern is raised.[26] During the build-up to the Intergovernmental Conference, environmental interests made proposals to liberalise the standing rule, and in effect to introduce an *actio popularis* (Climate Action Network *et al*, 1995), but the current overload in the European Court and concerns about opening the floodgates makes any radical change unlikely. Nevertheless, for a system that is so fundamentally based on the rule of law, the present procedures represent a worrying lacuna (Kramer, 1996; Macrory, 1996).

Procedure and Substance Revisited

It is clear that to the extent that the integration duty amounts to a procedural requirement for adopting and implementating Community legislation, the Community institutions are at least bound by the obligation, and there is liberal standing for them and Member States to challenge the legality of decisions made in breach of them. Article 190 requires that Community regulations, directives and decisions must state the reasons upon which they are based – an important requirement to promote transparency in decision making. It is a broad principle which is deeper in scope than are most equivalent rules under national legal systems.[27] The substantive content of the duty to give reasons has varied according to the nature of the act in question, and although a margin of discretion is afforded to the institutions with respect to the detail of reasoning required, the obligation can act as a significant lever to reinforce the application of the integration duty.[28] Interpreting the duty as a procedural requirement would imply a guarantee of certain procedural minima before a policy is agreed upon and implemented.

[25] Case 25/62 *Plaumann v Commission* [1963] ECR 95 established the key test and has been consistently applied in subsequent cases.
[26] *Stichting Greenpeace Council and others v Commission*, case T-585/93 12 February 1994; 1996 *Journal of Environmental Law* vol 8, no 1; *Danielsson and others v Commission*, case T-219/95R 22 December 1995.
[27] In *WWF UK v Commission*, case T-l05/95 Court of First Instance 5 March 1997, the court argued that article 190 served two purposes - first, to permit interested parties to know the justification of a measure in order to enable them to protect their rights; and second, to enable the Community courts to exercise their power to review the legality of decisions.
[28] Case 5/67 *Baus* [1968] ECR 83. See also case C-350/88 *Delacre v Commission* [1990] ECR 1-395.

We have already identified the difficulty of viewing the duty as substantive and relating to specific results. The problem of determining by legal process (as opposed to political means) an objective environmental standard is one that bedevils the whole field of substantive environmental rights. We suggested, however, that the principles of environmental action contained in the Treaty might serve as a basis for more substantive review. And, indeed, in case law concerning the conflicts between free movement of goods and environmental protection, recent legal developments have hinted that the integration principles have given a higher status to those principles of environmental action than previously.[29]

If, as we have suggested, the integration duty forms an essential procedural requirement, one can argue that a precondition of the legality of Community measures should be a demonstrable compliance with an environmental appraisal based on the principles of environmental action contained in the Treaty.[30] Difficult though this sounds, it merely supports the simple notion that policy development leading to European Community acts must display a minimum standard of reasoning. The environmental integration requirement is now an essential element of that reasoning process. Failure to reflect the broad criteria of the Treaty's environmental principles should open the institution in question to at least a minimum review of the stated reasons. Where no reference is made to the basic environmental criteria, or the reasoning is unsupported by substantial evidence, the decision in question must be open to challenge. Applying legal analysis to the integration duty suggests that, despite the conceptual difficulties involved, it can be considered as something more than a political aspiration. But it will require a degree of bold foresight on the part of lawyers and judges to bring about that change.

---

[29] In the Wallonia waste case, *EC Commission v Belgium* [1992] 1 ECR 4431, the Court was prepared to invoke the principle of Community environmental action that damage should be rectified at source to justify a local ban on the import of wastes. Although the reasoning in the decision has been much criticised, the Court in essence recognised that Member States could claim the benefit of the principles of Community environmental policy in the face of preemptive Community rules concerning free movement.

[30] Under the Declaration to the Final Act of the 1997 Amsterdam Conference, the conference noted that 'the Commission undertakes to prepare environmental impact assessment studies when making proposals which may have significant environmental implications'.

CHAPTER 19

ENVIRONMENTAL CITIZENSHIP AND THE LAW: REPAIRING THE EUROPEAN ROAD*

The English are incurious as to theory, take fundamental principles for granted and are more interested in the state of the roads than their place on the map.

R. H. Tawney

The European Council invites the Conference which should finalise its work in about one year, to adopt a general and consistent vision throughout its work: its aim is to meet the needs and expectations of our citizens while advancing the process of Europe's construction and preparing the Union for its future enlargement.

Presidency Conclusions, Turin European Council, 29 March 1996

Introduction

On I January 1993, as a result of the Maastricht amendments to the European Treaties, all nationals of Member States acquired under the Treaty something called citizenship of the European Union.[1] This new citizenship may not be uppermost in the civic consciousness of many, and my starting point will be to consider to what extent it can be said to incorporate an environmental dimension. The second half of the title is derived from R. H. Tawney's well-known observation about the English, and to pursue his analogy, there already exist a number of pretty substantial potholes. As someone who in his approach to environmental law has attempted to combine both an academic and a practitioner's perspective I will be suggesting some practical repair jobs.

* R Macrory (1996) Environmental Citizenship and the Law – Repairing the European Road. *Journal of Environmental Law* 8 no 2, pp 219 - 235
This article is a revised text of the inaugural Nathan Environment Lecture, sponsored by Denton Hall, Solicitors, and delivered by the author at the Royal Society of Arts on 25 April 1996.
[1] Treaty Establishing the European Community, Article 8: '(I) Citizenship of the Union is hereby established. Every person holding the nationality of a Member State shall be a citizen of the Union. (2) Citizens of the Union shall enjoy the rights conferred by this Treaty and shall be subject to the duties imposed thereby.' The Maastricht Treaty established both a European Union and a European Community. The Union is essentially a forum for political co-operation, and only the Community possesses legal entity, and it is within the Community structure that legislation is made. My paper will, therefore, for the most part refer to the European Community.

But I will also argue that there are some deeper issues concerning the way that the Treaty is currently structured and has been characterized in law. However effective the repairs, these also need to be addressed if the route on which we are embarked is to lead to a more environmental sound destination.

Citizenship is of course both a political and legal concept. Yet I will make no excuse for concentrating on legal conception and principle. The law and legal analysis permeates the structure and operation of the European Community. Some years ago, also at the Royal Society of Arts, Lord Dahrendolf observed that, 'In fact almost everything is wrong about the European Community except that it exists as a community of law which united developed democracies in Europe'.[2] Certainly for my part, I subscribe to the immense significance of the unifying and legitimising concept of the rule of law. In taking this argument further, I am not going to describe or analyse in detail the substantive content of European environmental policy since my concern will be more with institutional and legal structure. But as a matter of general background, and whatever the precise content of future environmental policies, I start from the assumption that the European Community and Union will remain a reality. The role of law in that structure will retain its pervasive significance, and the task of reconciling environmental and economic interests, encapsulated in the notion of sustainable development, will continue to provide a major political and intellectual challenge. At the same time, we have nine applicant countries from Central and Eastern Europe together with Malta and Cyprus. We may be many years away from accession but with negotiations due to formally commence after the end of the Intergovernmental Conference, the institutional implications of this prospective enlargement must be addressed.

The concept of citizenship is clearly stated in the Treaty to involve both rights and obligations. The Treaty itself goes on to express a number of individual rights, including the right to move and reside freely,[3] and the right to vote or stand as a candidate in municipal countries in the country in which he or she is residing.[4] Important procedural rights are provided in the rights to petition the European Parliament and to apply to the newly established Ombudsman.[5] The Treaty in its present form does not, however, provide any legally expressed rights to a healthy environment or indeed quality of life.

The Declaration of the first major international conference on the environment, the UN Conference on the Human Environment held in

---

[2] Lord Dahrendorf, 'Education for a European Britain', Royal Society of Arts, 9 June 1991.
[3] Article 8a.
[4] Article 8b.
[5] Article 8d.

Stockholm in 1972, clearly emphasised a link between human rights and the environment: Principle I declares that, 'Man has a fundamental right to freedom, equality and adequate conditions of life, in an environment of quality that permits a life of dignity and well-being, and he bears a solemn responsibility to protect and improve the environment for present and future generations'. Similarly, the Declaration following the UN Conference on Environment and Development held in Rio de Janeiro in 1992, though giving greater emphasis to the concept sustainable development, made a reference to rights and the environment.[6] Neither Declaration is a legally binding instrument as such, and neither attempt to establish specific environmental rights. Now, however, in the present preparations for the IGC Conference, both the European Commission and a number of Nordic countries are beginning to promote the idea that the Treaty should contain an express inclusion of a right to a healthy environment or some similarly worded phraseology.[7]

Many would argue that there are conceptual impossibilities to formulating an individual right to the environment in general terms which has any legally meaningful sense. The experience of those European countries and of certain States in America, whose constitutions do contain some expression of environmental rights, tends to confirm this.[8] They may end up influencing the interpretation and operation of other legal principles and rules, but are near impossible to invoke in themselves.[9] It is an issue to which I will return to later.

Environmental Rights in Community Law

Yet when it comes to specific items of Community environmental legislation concerning environmental quality, the European Court of

---

[6] Principle 1 states that, 'Human beings are at the centre of concerns for sustainable development. They are entitled to a healthy and productive life in harmony with nature'.

[7] The 1994 Report of the European Parliament's Committee on Institutional Affairs proposed a model constitution for the European Union which included a Title on Human Rights Guaranteed by the Union. These rights included, *inter alia*, 'Everyone shall have the right to the protection and preservation of his natural environment'. Doc EN/RR/244/244403 27 January 1994.

[8] Article 66 of the Portuguese Constitution contains the most explicit expression of environmental right in European Constitutions by providing that everyone shall have 'the right to a healthy and ecologically balanced environment and a duty to defend it'. Nevertheless, only where the state has determined what makes up such an environment are these rights enforceable. For a valuable comparative study which demonstrates the problem of constructing enforceable environmental rights: see, E. Brandi and H. Bungert, 'Constitutional Entrenchment of Environmental Protection: A Comparative Analysis of Experiences Abroad', 1992 *Harvard Environmental Law Review* Vol 16 No 1.

[9] Nevertheless, the UN Sub-Commission on Prevention of Discrimination and Protection of Minorities recently produced an elaborate Draft Declaration of Principles on Human Rights and the Environment: see *Environmental Law Network International Newsletter* 2/1994 at 120, and *RECIEL* 1994 Vol 3 No 5 261. See also, Aguilar and Popovic 'Law-Making in the United Nations: The UN Study on Human Rights and the Environment',1994 *RECIEL* Vol 3 No 5 197-205.

Justice has been prepared to characterise certain provisions as giving individual environmental rights. Thus in 1991, in a case brought by the Commission against Germany, the Court held that the 1980 Directive prescribing air quality standards for sulphur dioxide and smoke in effect gave individuals the right to air meeting those standards.[10] One characteristic mark of the Directive as a legal instrument is that while Member States are obliged to achieve its goals, it gives Member States a degree of discretion as to how to implement it within their national systems of law and administration.[11] But by characterising the SO_2 Directive as creating individual rights, the Court felt justified in insisting that the Member State no longer had complete discretion as to the means of transposing the obligations within its own legal and administrative system. Instead it held that individuals 'must be in a position to rely upon mandatory rules in order to be able to assert their rights'.

This firm nexus between the concept of a right and its expression in legally binding national law can be traced back to the mid 1980s in case law concerning rights of free movement of professionals within the Community. Here the Court held that the legal position for individuals must be 'sufficiently clear and precise and the persons concerned are made fully aware of their rights and where appropriate afforded an opportunity of relying upon them before the national courts'.[12]

Yet it is significant that the SO_2 Directive was to a large degree concerned with the protection of human health.[13] Other environmental Directives have granted what might be termed procedural rights, such as those concerning Access to Information[14] or rights to be consulted during Environmental Assessment procedures.[15] Again, the same justification for insisting that such rights appear in formal national law must apply. But many Directives are concerned purely with the protection of the environment per se rather than the direct protection of individuals. Here,

---

[10] *EC Commission v Germany* [1991] 1 ECR 2567.

[11] Article 189 EC Treaty. 'A directive shall be binding as to the result to be achieved, upon each Member State to which it is addressed but shall leave to the national authorities the choice of form and methods.'

[12] *European Commission v Germany* [1986] 3 GMLR 579. There is another line of authority within the European Court of Justice where the Court has required the formal transposition of Directives into national law but concerned with Directives based on Article 100 or 100A (harmonisation in relation to functioning of the common market). Here the justification for formal transposition is distinct and based on the concept of harmonisation rather than individual rights. See R. B. Macrory, 'EC Directives and UK Control Policy and Practice*, *55th Conference Proceedings National Society of Clean Air*, 1988.

[13] Article 2 of the Directive provides that the specified limit values must not be exceeded 'in order to protect human health in particular'.

[14] Directive 90/313 on Freedom of Access to Information on the Environment OJ 1990 L 158/56.

[15] Directive 85/337 on the Assessment of the Effects of Certain Public and Private Projects on the Environment OJ 1985 L 175/40.

the position in Community law remains less clear, and exposes one of the constant dilemmas of the use of the language of rights in relation to the environment – to what extent can they only be conceived of only in anthropogenic terms and thus largely confined to human health and welfare contexts, or can they extend to all areas of the environment whether or not individuals are affected – in which case who should entitled to ensure their protection?

Yet, the case law of the European Court remains rather ambiguous. Another case brought by the Commission against Germany in 1991 concerned the Groundwater Directive.[16] This Directive is clearly aimed at the protection of the environment rather than human health as such, yet the Court stated that the Directive, in order to guarantee effective protection of groundwater, laid down precise and detailed rules which are intended to create rights and obligations for individuals. Having so characterised the Directive, it justified the Court in again insisting that it had to be incorporated into national law with the precision and clarity necessary to fully satisfy the requirements of legal certainty. Unfortunately the Court did not spell out precisely the rights and obligations it found in the Directive, but it appeared to have been referring to the various prohibitions and requirements for authorisations under the Directive. Industry and other consumers of the environment who may have obligations imposed upon them under Community law are entitled to know precisely what these entail.[17] But we are still left with some degree of uncertainty over the question of rights where provisions are solely aimed at environmental protection.[18]

Despite the ambiguities, these principles concerning the transposition of Community obligations into formal national law have had immense significance not least for the structure of UK environmental law. They are entirely the creation of the Court and if anything goes against the apparent wording of the Treaty. And they form what could be described as a family of doctrines developed by the court designed to ensure that Community law has genuine bite within national systems. They include

[16] *EC Commission v Germany* [1991] 1 ECR 825.

[17] A similar argument is found in Case C-13/90 *Commission v France* [1991] ECR 1-4327 which again concerned the air quality Directives. In insisting upon formal transposition into national law, the Court in part justified their argument by suggesting that these Directives imposed obligations on potential polluters.

[18] It has been suggested that the Court will in practice be liberal in interpreting that Environment Directives create or imply rights, as the case law quoted above suggest: I. Pernice, 'Kriterien der normativen Umsetzung von Umweltrichtlinien der EG Lichte der Rechtsprechung des EuGH', 1994 *Europareckt* 325. For a lengthier discussion on various forms of transposition see, J. Jans, 1995 *European Environmental Law* at 119 seq (Kluwer: London).

the direct effect doctrine,[19] the doctrine of sympathetic interpretation,[20] and the more recent emergence of principles concerning the right to damages where a Member State has failed in its Community obligations,[21] Each of these doctrines raise difficult issues, but at their root, they can be seen as attempts by the Court to ensure that Community law is fully applied. And they are in effect an implied criticism of the institutional mechanisms already built into the Treaty and specifically designed to ensure compliance with Community obligations. If they were working fully and effectively, the Court would not have had to develop these doctrines in the way they have.

Improving Community Enforcement Mechanisms

Persuading countries to comply with supra-national obligations is not, of course, a problem confined to Community law. The last twenty-five years has seen a rapid expansion and growth of international environmental treaties between sovereign states, but ensuring implementation of international treaties has long been the familiar Achilles heel of public international law. Earlier environmental treaties made little or no reference to the question of implementation but left it entirely to the goodwill of the parties concerned.[22] Modern practice is commendably different. In many of the more recent environmental treaties, far more attention has been paid to the issue of implementation and enforcement,

---

[19] Under this doctrine, even where a Member State has not implemented a Directive properly into national law, certain provisions of Directives provided they are precise and certain may be invoked before national courts but only against government or other 'emanations of the State' and not other individuals; see, Gase-91/92 *Don v Recreb Srl* [1994] ECR 1-3325 which confirmed that the doctrine could not be invoked against private parties. See generally, S. Prechal, *Directives in European Community Law*, 1995 (Oxford University Press: Oxford). In the environmental field, see especially, L. Kramer, The Implementation of Community Environmental Directives: Some Implications of the Direct Effect Doctrine', 1991 *Journal of Environmental Law* Vol 3 No 1 39. In practice, both in the United Kingdom and before the European Court of Justice (but not in countries such as the Netherlands), it has proved difficult to date to convince the courts that environmental directives have direct effect: see, J. Holder, 'A Dead-End for Direct Effect?', 1996 *Journal of Environmental Law* Vol 8 No 2.

[20] Case C-106/89 *Marleasing SA v La Commercial International de Alimantiacion SA* [1990] ECR 1-4135 where the European Court of Justice held that national law whether or not introduced to implement Community obligations must be interpreted in such a way as to ensure conformity with Community Directives 'in so far as possible'. The limits of the doctrine are still being worked out.

[21] Cases C-6/90 and C-9/90 *Frankovitch v Italian State* [1991] 1-ECR 5357. For the most recent judgment concerning the principles see, Cases C-46/93 and C 48/93 *Brasserie du Pêcheur SA v Germany; R v Secretary of State for Transport ex parte Factortame and others* ('Factortame IIP), [1996] 75 CMLR 889.

[22] See generally, P. Birnie and A. Boyle, *International Law and the Environment* 1993 (Oxford University Press: Oxford), esp 160 seq; P. Sand, *The Effectiveness of International Environmental Agreements* 1992 (Grotius: Cambridge); D. Freestone, The Road from Rio: International Law after the Earth Summit', 1994 *Journal of Environmental Law* Vol 6 No 2 193.

and treaties such as the Ozone Convention and the Climate Change Convention provide for the establishment of implementation committees composed on signatory states with the express task of reviewing the effectiveness of implementation.[23] Ultimately, however, the pressure that can be brought to bear on recalcitrant states is largely one of peer or political pressure, though the Montreal Protocol has taken steps somewhat further by providing an elaborate procedure for allegations of non-compliance and an express list of measures that might be brought on respect of non-compliance, including both inducements in the form of financial and technical assistance, and sanctions in the form of the suspension of rights and privileges under the Protocol.[24]

Yet in its formal institutional mechanisms for ensuring the Member States implement their obligations under Community law, the European Community has clearly established a far deeper and potentially more effective structure than anything yet devised under other international arrangements. And I would argue that one mark of citizenship within the Community and Union should be an effective legal structure which can guarantee that both national governments and Community institutions will bona fide implement those Community obligations to which they are a party. The Treaty imposes an obligation on the European Commission to ensure that Member States fulfil their duties under Community law,[25] and quasi-legal procedures are provided allowing eventually the Commission to take Member States before the European Court for failure to implement.[26] And since Maastricht, the Court now has power to fine Member States that do not comply with its judgments – amendments to the Treaty that were promoted by the UK government, and giving the Court a direct sanction power that is unique among international courts.[27]

Much could be done to improve the effectiveness of current procedures, especially in the light of prospective enlargement of the Community. This is not to belittle efforts that have been made in recent years: greater consistency in the reporting requirements by Member States concerning

---

[23] Annex IV, Montreal Prototcol on Substances that Deplete the Ozone Layer, 1987; Article 10, Framework Convention on Climate Change, 1992.

[24] Annex V, Montreal Protocol. Freestone, op cit, describes the enforcement regime as 'one of the strictest devised for a global treaty of this kind'.

[25] One of the four defined functions of the Commission under the Treaty is to 'ensure that the provisions of this Treaty and the measures taken by the institutions pursuant thereto are applied'. The existing case law on standing, however, means that it is not a duty which could be enforced in law by third parties.

[26] In the environmental field see, R. Macrory, 'The Enforcement of Community Environmental Laws: Some Critical Issues', 1992 *Common Market Law Review* 347. Se chap. 26 below

[27] Article 171. The Court has yet to fine a Member State under these procedures.

various aspects of environmental quality;[28] improved mechanisms for contact between those working within national regulatory bodies though at present this is largely confined to pollution control bodies,[29] and does not involve, for example, those in nature conservation; the acknowledgement by the Council of Ministers of the importance of implementation; and the establishment of the new Environment Agency[30] which may bring a more rigorous approach towards the comparative analysis of the state of environmental quality within different Member States.

It could be argued that many of these developments were in a sense making up for lost time. One of my main concerns is to improve the procedures for ensuring the national transposition of Community obligations. If Community obligations were faithfully reflected in national law, both in substance and within the time-limits specified, we would be a long way down the path of more effective implementation. Not the whole way by any means, since much would then depend on the effectiveness of national procedures, including such questions as ease of access to the courts or other administrative bodies, but at least there would be a common starting position. The current practice is that the Community obligation under Directives requires the Member State to send texts of their national measures to the Commission within the time-limit specified in each Directive, normally two years, of its being agreed.[31] In practice, this often happens at the last moment, and generally no guidance is given by the Member State to the Commission to relate the national measures to the provisions of the Directive. Indeed, some Member States seem to take an almost perverse pleasure in leaving it to Commission officials to puzzle out the intricacies of what are often complex national laws themselves and relate them to the Directive in question.

For a start, then, I would like to see a requirement for Member States to provide the Commission with a systematic explanation of the relationship between the national measures and the provisions of the Directive – an article by article guide if you like. And, as a

---

[28] Council Directive 91/692/EEC, Standardising and Rationalising Reports on the Implemention of certain Directives relating to the Environment.

[29] Originally known as the 'Chester Network' after the place of its first meeting and established in 1992, now called IMPEL.

[30] Established under EC Regulation 1210/90. Despite pressure from the European Parliament, the powers and duties of the Agency were at the time deliberately restricted to avoid it becoming directly involved in issues of implementation and enforcement, but its terms of reference are to be reviewed.

[31] Sometimes three years as in the Environmental Assessment Directive.

acknowledgement of citizen interest in this issues, these should be documents that are publicly available.[32]

Secondly, it needs to be recognised that the reluctance to lose face is a general feature of institutional behaviour. Once national laws have been made, whether in primary legislation or regulations, Member States are likely to resist change or at least will give an exaggerated defence of them against differing interpretations. So I would like to see a general requirement that *draft* legislation proposed to implement a Directive is sent to the Commission at least six months before the date for compliance. This may require longer time-limits for compliance – perhaps a general move from two years to three – but is, I believe a price worth paying if the result is a greater opportunity to ensure a truer reflection in national law of Community obligations. The 1994 Packaging Directive does provide something of a model in this respect in that it contains a provisions concerning the requirement of Member States to notify draft measures, though no time limits are provided.[33] Of course, the Commission cannot give a final legal interpretation of Community law which remains the responsibility of the European Court of Justice, and there will remain instances where both Member States and the Commission refuse to compromise on their respective interpretations— but at least there will be greater advance notice of trouble ahead. In practice discussions are sometimes held between Member States and the Commission over draft legislation[34] but it appears to be done in an ad hoc manner. I accept that these discussions will not always be plain sailing or conducted in the spirit of perfect rationality, but my complaint is that there is little consistency in the current approach nor is there apparent acknowledgment by Member States that it is important.

The drafting of Community legislation still often leads to ambiguities and inconsistencies, though the blame cannot always be laid at the Commission; late night negotiations at the Council of Ministers can lead to oddly drafted provisions. But certainly there seems to me to be the need for greater attention to drafting, including the use of interpretation sections, together with the greater use of advisory material, akin to Circulars, issued by the Commission and explaining their understanding of the new Community legislation and containing, for instance, worked examples of its application. And there are times when the Commission

---

[32] It may be that under the Access to Environment Information Directive there would be a legal right to obtain such documentation.

[33] European Parliament and Council Directive 94/62/EG on Packaging and Packaging Waste, Article 16. Reproduced *in JEL* Vol 7 No 2.

[34] Considerable discussions were held between the UK government and the European Commission over the enforcement provisions in the Water Bill 1989 leading to amendments to the text of the Bill.

could play a more proactive role in assisting national institutions. Art 5 of the Treaty imposes a general duty on Member States to facilitate the achievement of the Community's tasks. Although the provision refers only to Member States, the duty has been interpreted by the European Court to impose a reciprocal duty upon the Commission to cooperate with national authorities.[35] In the field of competition policy and state aid, the Commission in 1993 and 1995 respectively, issued Notices of Cooperation providing guidance on when it would provide assistance to national courts in the provision of relevant information, including information on points of law.[36] I recognise that developing a more proactive approach is not without difficulties. One reason for the Commission's reluctance to over-commit itself in advance of its view of the law is a fear that this will inhibit it from bringing enforcement procedures against a Member State should its opinion later change, akin to a principle of estoppel. My own view is that it should not.[37] But if a Member State were sued for damages under the *Frankovitch* principles in respect of non-implementation under the principles now being developed by the ECJ, reliance on prior legal interpretation and advice given by the Commission could well provide a justifiable defence. This is acknowledged by the European Court in the latest decision on this issue, *Factortame III*.[38]

In accordance with one of the Declarations attached to the Maastricht Treaty, one of the tasks during the forthcoming intergovernmental conference will be to reconsider the whole question of the hierarchy of Community legislation.[39] As happened before Maastricht, no doubt it may again be argued that Community Directives, one of the major forms of Community legislation which have existed since the foundation of the Community and are really quite distinct to the Community, are now an

---

[35] Case G-2/88 *Zwartweld* [1990] ECR 1-3365-

[36] Notice of Cooperation between National Courts and the Commission in Applying Articles 85 and 86 of the Treaty, OJ 1993 C39/6; Notice of Cooperation between National Courts and the Commission in the State Aid Field, OJ 1995 C312/8.

[37] Once enforcement proceedings are commenced, however, the Commission may find itself inhibited from redefining issues or raising new points as stated in the Reasoned Opinion.

[38] Joined Cases C-46 and C-48/93 *Brasserie du Pecheur SA v Germany R v Secretary of State for Transport ex parte Factortame* [1996] 75 CMLR 889. According to the Court of Justice, one of the factors to be taken in account when determining whether a Member State should be liable was 'the fact that the position taken by a Community institution may have contributed towards the omission', (para 56).

[39] 'The Conference agrees that the Intergovernmental Conference to be convened in 1996 will examine to what extent it might be possible to review the classification of Community Acts with a view to establishing an appropriate hierarchy between the differing categories of Act.' This Declaration followed unsuccessful proposals made at the time, notably by the European Parliament to reclassify Community acts, which included the abolition of Directives and the creation of a new form of general legal instrument, a 'Loi': see, Resolution of the European Parliament on the Nature of Community Acts, OJ 1991C/129/136.

outmoded legal instrument. By leaving so much room for manoeuvre for Member States, their form has given rise to the sorts of implementation problem I have already outlined. We do of course have another key form of Community instrument, the Regulation, which generally requires no national implementation measures but has immediate effect within national legal systems. Directives have dominated the environmental field, but there are examples of Regulations being used. But it surprised both Lord Nathan and his colleagues when he chaired a House of Lords subcommittee investigating the implementation of Community environmental law[40] to hear how little in the way of principle has been developed by either the Council of Ministers, or the European Commission, in determining in what circumstances one or other of the instruments is most appropriate. Nor is it an issue that the European Court of Justice has yet been called upon to consider. In 1992 the Sutherland Report called for the transformation of all Directives into Regulations after a period for harmonisation, but my own view is that Directives should continue to play a significant role.[41] They acknowledge and attempt to accommodate the diverse legal and administrative cultures which exist within Member States, and may be all the more appropriate should further expansion of the Community take place. But as I have indicated they place considerable demands on the institutional machinery if effective and consistent implementation is to be achieved.

Applying the Rule of Law to the Commission

The Community system is as the Court of Justice has consistently argued based upon the rule of law. The procedures I have just mentioned concern Member States' obligations. Yet there remain serious problems when it comes to ensure that the Commission itself complies with the rule of law. A central problem is the question of standing before the courts. All jurisdictions develop rules concerning who may or may not bring cases before the courts, especially where issues of public law are concerned. Standing, especially in the field of the environment where private interests in the conventional sense may not be at risk, has long proved a problem. For the most part in the field of public law the UK courts have shown an increasingly liberal approach in their interpretation of the basic test that the person or organisation bringing the case must have 'sufficient interest' in the matter concerned[42] and I do not believe it now presents a major inhibition.

---

[40] House of Lords, 9th Report Session, *The Implementation and Enforcement of Environmental Legislation* 1991-92 (HMSO: London).

[41] See also, G. Winter (ed), The Directive: Problems of Construction and Directions for Reform' in *Sources and Categories of European Union Law* 1996 (Nomos Verlagsgesellschaft: Baden-Baden).

[42] For a recent and firmly argued liberal approach see the judgment of Otton J in *R v Her*
Continued

The Treaty provides for challenges of the legality of acts by the Commission directly before the European Court. Member States and the Council of Ministers basically have unrestricted access, and the European Parliament may bring action to protect their own prerogatives. Individual applicants may take action in respect of decisions actually addressed to them personally, but this will be unusual in the environmental field. In those cases where the decision is directed to another person (say the grant of financial assistance to a member state) a third parties may still bring action but must, according to Article 173 of the Treaty, show that the decision or regulation[43] is 'of direct and individual concern' to them. Early case-law of the European Court, going back over thirty years, has held that this phrase, 'direct and individual concern', implies that the individual is affected by reason of certain attributes which are peculiar to them or by reason of circumstances in which they are differentiated from all other persons, and the European Court has consistently adopted that interpretation in subsequent case law.[44] The result of this restrictive approach was confirmed last year in the environmental field where environmental groups and local residents attempted to challenge the legality of the Commission grant of structural funds in respect of the construction of power stations in the Canary Islands.[45] The complaint was essentially that the award of the aid had not been in compliance with environmental requirements contained in the relevant structural fund regulations especially those concerning environmental assessment. But whatever the merits of the case, the Court never considered these issues, ruling that the applicants had no standing. It could find no evidence that the applicants, or the members of the association, were affected in some way different from other residents in the area.[46] A similar approach was adopted in the case concerning the challenge to the legality of the Commission not intervening in the French nuclear testing in the Pacific.[47]

...*Majesty's Inspectorate of Pollution and the Minister of Agriculture Fisheries and Food ex parte Greenpeace Ltd* 1994 *Journal of Environmental Law* Vol 6 No 2, and case analysis by Purdue, ibid.

[43] The Court has also recently confirmed that there is no provision in the Treaty for third parties to challenge the legality of Directives, as opposed to Regulations or Decisions: *Asocarne v Council* Case T-99/94, quoted in M. Beloff, supra.

[44] Case 25/62 *Plaumann v Commission* [1963] ECR 95. It would seem that the Court would prefer such issues to be brought to its attention by a reference from the national courts under Article 177, but this will not necessarily deal with the legal control of the Commission's activities.

[45] *Stichting Greenpeace Council and others v EC Commission*, Case T-585/93 12.2.94, 1996 *Journal of Environmental Law* Vol 8 No 1.

[46] For a similar result see, Case T-117/94 *Associazione agricoltori della provinca di Rivigo et all v EC Commission*, concerning a challenge to a decision of the Commission to grant financial assistance for conservation measures under the LIFE fund.

[47] Case T-219/95R *Danielsson and others v Commission of the European Communities*, 22 December 1995.

Of course, it could be argued that another Member State could have made the challenge and would not have be inhibited by the standing rules. But the political reality is that this is most unlikely, especially in the case of structural funds, if only because most Member States benefit from such funds to a degree.[48] The result seems to be a lacuna in ensuring compliance with law. And I am reminded of the position some years ago when there was no express legal base for Community environment legislation under the Treaty. Other legal bases under the Treaty were sought to justify the legislation, and in certain cases, they were extremely dubious had they been subject to proper legal scrutiny. But, as I remember the late Lord Diplock eloquently espoused at a conference at Imperial College, the problem then was that all Member States had agreed to the legislation in question, with the result that effectively there was no one with standing who could or would challenge the legality of the laws in question.[49] Political expedience and priorities in effect subsumed the rule of law.

It should also be said that the Court of Justice itself has not been consistent in its approach towards standing, at least, in the non-environmental field. A slightly less restrictive approach is apparent in the fields of competition law and anti-dumping. And a rather more liberal approach appears to have been adopted in a recent decision in 1994 falling within the sphere of the Common Agricultural Policy.[50] In that case, a sparkling wine producer in Spain challenged a regulation stipulating that a particular term concerning sparking wine could only be used in respect of wines from France or Luxembourg. Although there were other sparkling wine producers in Spain in the same position, the European Court was prepared to accept that the Regulation in question was of individual and direct concern to the complainant producers, and that they had standing.[51] They had a protected economic interest at stake, a registered trade-mark, and were by far the largest producer of the wine in question, and these factors were sufficient to give them a position distinguished from other producers.

The economic factors clearly in play may permit the Court to develop a rather more liberal test of standing in these sorts of cases as opposed

---

[48] See, L. Kramer, 'Public Interest litigation in Environmental Matters before the European Courts' 1996 *Journal of Environmental Law* Vol 8 No 1.

[49] R. Macrory (ed), (1982) *Britain, Europe and the Environment* (Imperial College Centre for Environmental Technology: London).

[50] Case G-309/89 *Cordorniu v EC Council* [1995] CMLR 561.

[51] In other cases, the Court appears to have adopted the view that if the challenged act was truly a Regulation which by its nature had general application, third parties would not the right to challenge it: see, T-472/93 *Campo Ebro v EU Council* [1996] CMLR 1038. In *Cordorniu* the Court appeared to have accepted that an act could both be a true Regulation and of individual and direct concern at the same time.

to those concerned with the environment, and maybe we will just have to wait for developing jurisprudence. But the present position is hardly satisfactory, and does not meet my test of citizenship. One political response, at least over the question of structural funds, has been the recent flexing of muscle by the European Parliament using its budgetary powers to impose a greater commitment on the Commission to ensure that the environmental implications of the use of structural funds are more effectively considered. This in fact may have the effect desired in that field,[52] but in many ways represents a failure of the legal system to come to grips with the issue.

Although the Court does not say so explicitly, its restrictive approach towards the definition of standing must to a large degree be due to the familiar floodgates arguments. Time delays before the Court at present are sufficient to raise alarms at the prospect of a whole new tranche of litigation. There will be arguments for amending the provisions of the Treaty to provide for a total liberalisation to allow any individual or organisation to have standing,[53] but I am not convinced that this would be practicable or necessarily the correct response. One approach might be to relax the standing rules, and develop a more vigorous filtering process for applications, akin to the procedure for leave of application to judicial review in this country – this would help to ensure that cases with little merit would not reach the court. Or perhaps, rather than broadening the standing tests, we need a new independent body with power to bring such cases in the public interest against the Commission and other Community institutions. The Maastricht Treaty did establish a new Community post, the Ombudsman, with the duties to investigate complaints concerning maladministration within Community institutions.[54] The Ombudsman, however, is very much the creature of the European Parliament reporting to the European Parliament. As yet the jury is still out on the effectiveness of this new position, and it is very unlikely that the Ombudsman would have independent standing before the Court.[55] Nor am I satisfied that a body concerned with maladministration can be an effective substitute for one responsible for ensuring legality.

---

[52] See in particular, European Parliament Committee on Budgets, Report on the 1996 Draft Budget as modified by the Council A4-0305/95 11.12.95, and Final Adoption of the General Budget of the European Union for the financial year 1996 OJ L 22 29.1.96. I am grateful to David Wilkinson of the Institute for European Environmental Policy for information on these political developments.

[53] See e.g., 'Greening the Treaty II: Sustainable Development in a Democratic Union', Climate Action Network et al, 1995.

[54] EC Treaty Article 138e.

[55] Other than to protect the interests of the position.

Environmental and Economic Rights: The Uneven Hierarchy

It is perhaps no coincidence that the Court's rather more liberal approach towards standing has appeared in more purely economic areas of the Community interest rather than the environment. And similarly, it is telling that in relation to enforcement some of the Commission's more recent procedural initiatives concerning enforcement appeared in economic fields. In my final theme, then, I want to consider some deeper structural features of the Community as a legal system in its treatment of economic and environmental interests. Whatever precisely the meaning of sustainable development, it clearly implies a far deeper integration of economic, social and environmental concerns that has hitherto been the case. Sustainable development, albeit in rather garbled form, was inserted at Maastricht as one of the tasks of the Community.[56] The Treaty also contains an obligation to integrate environmental protection requirements into other areas of Community policy,[57] again one of the necessary implications of sustainable development.

The Community may have had its origins as a functionalist economic institution, but clearly has developed beyond those boundaries. The acknowledgment by the Court of Justice of the significance of human rights as an element of the Community legal order which is now reflected in the Maastricht Treaty,[58] and even the change of name of the European Economic Community to the European Community and Union under the Maastricht Treaty underlines those developments. As Advocate General, Francis Jacobs put it in a recent lecture,[59] 'This has among other things put an end to the idea that the Community is a purely economic entity and that it is only as a factor of production that an individual has to be considered under Community. That mercantalist approach is simply no longer tenable'.

---

[56] Among the general tasks of the Community defined in Article 2 of the Treaty as amended are the promotion of 'sustainable and non-inflationary growth respecting the environment*. See generally, R. Macrory and M. Hession 'Maastricht and the Environmental Policy of the Community: Legal Issues of a New Environment Policy' in *Legal Issues of the Masstricht Treaty,* O'Keefe and Twomey (eds), 1993 (Chancery Publications: London).

[57] Article 13 or EC Treaty. 'Environmental protection requirements must be integrated into the definition and implementation of other Community policies.' Although the sentiment is clear, the precise legal meaning of this requirement, let alone its institutional implementation, remain unclear.

[58] Article F_2. 'The Union shall respect fundamental rights as guaranteed by the European Convention for the Protection of Human Rights and Fundamental Freedoms signed in Rome on 4 November 1950 and as they result from the constitutional traditions common to the Member States as general principles of Community law.' But under Article L this provision is excluded from the jurisdiction of the European Court of Justice.

[59] F.Jacobs, 'Human Rights in the European Union', 1994, Durham: European Law Institute.

But when one looks closer at the current legal structures there is still a long way to go. All systems of law and legal principle are ultimately based on a hierarchical structure – some principles overriding or qualifying others, some mandatory, others merely giving power, some enforceable before the courts, others existing merely as what might be described as gravitational rules. The European Treaty contains no explicit hierarchy as such – indeed the fundamental principle that in case of conflict with national law Community law is supreme is not expressed as such in the Treaty but is entirely a creation of the judiciary. Nor within its own confines does the Treaty explicitly create a structured hierarchy. Yet when one examines its format and the way that it has been interpreted and approached by legal practitioners and the Court of Justice, one can construct a set of interlocking principles and rules, some of which clearly take precedence over others. Understanding the nature and rationale for this approach is of key importance if we are to ever to see a more balanced integration of economic and environmental interests.[60]

At the pinnacle of this pyramid are statements of what can be described as preemptive norms given the highest value by the Court. These are binding, have direct effect, and are invocable against Member States, Community institutions, and in many instances by and in some cases against individuals before their national courts. The most obvious are the provisions in Article 30 guaranteeing free movement of goods, and those principles in Articles 85 and 86 relating to competition. We can identify further categories of principles, including a duty on the Community to act in favour of particular goals which may include the environmental integration requirement,[61] down to what may described as statements of interests which provide a legal justification for action by the Community or Member States but do not require any such action to be taken.

If we just contrast two sets of important provisions the dilemma is clear. The Treaty now contains a set of environmental principles, but these do not have any pre-emptive effect; rather, they guide and influence Community action where it is taken. Similarly, the environmental integration requirement is a principle that binds the Community where it takes action, but as the cases on standing illustrate is unlikely to be enforceable other than by another Member State or perhaps the European Parliament. In contrast, Article 30 concerning the free movement of goods has been held to have direct effect, and in essence can be described as a constitutional right. Indeed the freedom of trade has

---

[60] See generally, R. Macrory and M. Hession 'Balancing Trade Freedom with the Requirements of Sustainable Development' in *The European Union and World Trade Law*, Emilou and O'Keefe (eds) 1996 (Wiley: Chichester).
[61] Article 130r.

been described by the European Court as a fundamental right of those living within the Community.[62] It can be invoked by individuals and companies before the national courts. It exists quite independently from any measures or policies initiated by the Community or Member States. Any national legislation and any other equivalent measures taken by national governments, whether concerned with Community policy or not, which conflict with the principle can be challenged as illegal.[63] Even Community legislation is in theory subject to the principle.[64] It is true that under both express provisions of the Treaty[65] and principles developed by the European Court[66] Member States in certain circumstances and for certain reasons are permitted to retain measures which conflict with the general principle in Article 30, and environmental protection is one such ground.[67] But the burden is very much on the Member State to justify an incursion into the general principle, and does not detract from its general pre-emptive quality.

The whole issue of trade and environment is, of course, high on the international agenda, in the context of General Agreement on Trade and Tariffs and the World Trade Organization and the forthcoming Singapore meeting. Much of the language in the Treaty concerning free movement and the exemptions that are permissible is very similar to GATT. Yet in terms of their internal legal significance, and one might describe as the constitutionalisation of economic rights, it is clear that the Treaty has gone further than anything yet attempted internationally.

The rationale for the priority given to these principles and others such as competition law principles is not hard to find. In part it lies in the historical origins of the Community, where following the failure of the proposed European Political Community in 1954, the central thrust was given to the establishment of economic integration, based on a liberal economic order, as a prelude to further political integration.[68] But there

---

[62] *ADBHU* [1985] ECR 531. The principle of free movement of goods and freedom of competition together with freedom of trade as a fundamental right are general principles of law which the Court ensures observances.'

[63] Since 1969 the Court of Justice has recognised that Community Institutions must comply with basic human rights, and that these doctrines may also apply to Member States when applying Community law. But under Community law they do not apply to national legislation per se, and in this respect can be contrasted with the economic rights granted under the Treaty; see Jacobs, op cit.

[64] Confirmed in ADBHU supra, though in practice the Court is more likely to find other Community policy objectives justify action despite its conflict with Article 30.

[65] Article 36.

[66] The sole called 'rule of reason'.

[67] In Gase 302/86 *Commission v Denmark* [1988] ECR 4607 (*Danish Bottles*), the European Court explicitly recognized that environmental protection, though not mentioned as such in Article 36, was such a ground.

[68] See the Spaak Report, Brussels 1956.

are further reasons why from a legal perspective economic rights are likely to be conceptualised and invocable as legally protected interests more readily than environmental concerns. Lawyers traditionally characterise trade freedom as a classical individual right, which should be equivalent to familiar rights of property, and capable of legal protection as such. In contrast, environmental concerns are viewed in law not so much as an aspect of individual freedom or entitlement but rather as an interest which restricts the freedom of what people may or may not do. As such it is an area appropriate for intervention by government but cannot readily be conceived of as a right directly enforceable before the courts in the same way as the freedom to trade.

There are further important underlying differences in the way that trade and environment interests are conceived which inevitably compound the difficulties of giving them equal or equivalent legal status. The economic market in which the freedom to trade or to enjoy other economic rights is a purely human construction, and demands a certain unity of conditions for its effective operation; this reinforces the attraction of a legally and universally applicable right. In contrast, the environment is not of course an artificial concept, but a physical and heterogeneous reality. Effective and efficient environmental management frequently has to be sensitive to very differing natural conditions in the receiving environment, demanding different responses and hardly consistent with the legal concept of universally invocable rights. Furthermore, the apparent absence of any truly objective standard of environmental protection means that it is all the more difficult to construct an enforceable right. It may be within the capacity of the judiciary to judge what is or is not trade restrictive since this can be legally viewed as an objective test, but the courts should not be burdened with the more political task of determining what level of environmental protection is appropriate,[69] especially when in many areas the nature of environmental science cannot provide hard and fast answers. The dilemma for the courts can already be seen in case law of the European Court of Justice concerning the legality of measures taken by Member States which infringe the right of free movement of goods. As I have already mentioned, Member States may invoke environmental reasons for so doing but do they have right to determine the level of environmental protection desired, or should the Court's apply some objective test? In the *Danish Bottles* case[70] Advocate General Slynn, as he then was, did indeed call for an objective test – 'The level of protection sought must be a reasonable one' – but

---

[69] The contrast between the objective examination of trade restrictive measures and the more political evaluation of environmental appears plausible. But it has to be said that when one examines the cases concerning alleged trade restrictive measures, it is clear the court is often equally faced with many ambiguities, and is often engaged in complex social and political choices.

[70] n 67 above.

despite requests from the Court, the European Commission refused to provide guidance on what than reasonable level might be in that case, and the Court decided that it would not interfere or question the Danish government's determination of the standard of environmental protection they desired to be achieved by the proposed measures.[71] *Danish Bottles* concerned economic rights of free movement of goods being pitched against government action on the environment, and since such an action implies that a choice as to an appropriate level of environment protection has already been made by a government, it is hardly surprising that the Court felt it did not need to reconsider the question. But if an environmental right was to be invocable to the same extent as an economic right, we would be faced with situations where, unlike *Danish Bottles*, there was no necessary explicit decision taken by a government on the environmental issue at hand. Courts would be constantly faced with determining the standards themselves. The reluctance to develop environmental rights is understandable.

My argument then is that despite the views of Advocate General Jacobs, the Treaty and its legal interpretation has granted us as citizens general individual economic rights but, in the absence of Community legislation no equivalent environmental rights. Giving greater predominance to the notion of sustainable development within the overall aims of the Treaty, or increasing qualified majority voting for Community environmental measures may be the preoccupation of many environmental interests at present during the Inter-Governmental Conference. But these changes will not in themselves alter that fundamental legal construction and bias contained in the current structure.

A New Goal for the Market?

There are no easy solutions, but it is an intellectual challenge that needs to be faced if we are serious about the greater integration of economic and environmental interests implied by sustainable development. One way forward might be to include within the Treaty an individual right to environmental quality, as already been proposed by some quarters.[72] But as I have indicated, there are very real difficulties whether such a right could be expressed in genuinely enforceable or legally meaningful terms, certainly where it concerned environmental quality. This is not to argue that the incorporation of such an statement of rights would be without any legal or political effect, and certainly the more that

---

[71] Alternative approach might be that the role of the Court should be determine whether an activity harmed the environment but to leave it to the national authority to dermine what level of harm should be permitted, subject to proportionality.

[72] See supra 7. Some Nordic countries are thought to support the inclusion of such a right during the current Inter-Governmental Conferencve.

such rights are concerned with procedural requirements (such as the right to information) rather than rights to a particular quality of the environment, the more are they likely to be genuinely enforceable before the Courts. Even statements expressed in general terms may guide the legal interpretation of other rules and principles in a more environmentally sensitive manner. But it needs to be appreciated why such rights are unlikely ever to achieve equal legal status with economic rights. Certainly, the juxtaposition of such an environmental right within the Treaty alongside the existing norms and principles of necessity would create difficult and continuing tensions.

Another response – and in essence what has been taking place for the last twenty years – is to simply carry on with the development of explicit Community environmental legislation as a sort of counterbalance where existing fundamental principles are considered to run counter to environmental interests. This is likely to happen in certain fields, but, although it is too early to determine a definite trend, the pace of Community environmental legislation appears to have slowed in recent years, reflecting in part a greater sensitivity to the subsidiarity principle that now appears in the Treaty. In 1993 and 1994, for example, nearly 50 items of environmental legislation were adopted, dropping to 19 in 1995.[73] Even if qualified majority voting in the Council of Ministers were extended to all environmental matters, the accession of new member states could be expected to make the agreement of new environmental legislation more rather than less difficult.

In any event, such an approach is perhaps over dirigist. Another method, which is more fundamental and long lasting, is to reconsider the purposes of the market whose goals are not defined with precision in the Treaty. Under this model, which I and a colleague have recently suggested,[74] one would take as a starting point the concept of the 'rational and prudent use of natural resources', which is now one of the express principles of Community environmental policy, and could be said to be one of the underpinning goals of sustainable development. It is also a goal with which one would hope an economist would have little to disagree with as a general preferred outcome of market principles. If this were expressed explicitly in the Treaty as one of the goals of the market, the basic legal structure and hierarchy of principles would be transformed. Legislation and policies both at national and Community level which conflicted with these goals would in accordance with the existing principles be susceptible to legal review. Policy-makers at both national and Community level would develop an increased sensitivity in the design and development of measures which might conflict with

[73] N. Haigh, *Manual of Environmental Policy: the EC and Britain,* (Longmans: London).
[74] Supra 60.

those principles, as they do at present in respect of free movement of goods.[75] Activities of the State which caused or permitted environmental damage would prima facie be contrary to the Treaty as are activities that distort free trade.[76] A true legal integration between market and environmental concerns would lie at the heart of the legal structure, and in essence one would be bringing to bear the full weight of the power of market law and principles developed within the Community behind at least some of the goals of sustainable development.

It takes some imagination to consider the likely outcome of such a change. Indeed far from being a top-down prescriptive solution, it deliberately leaves open the detailed future development of policy and law but against a new, and more balanced legal framework which might be more appropriate for the next century. But in suggesting such a proposal, it will be argued that far from carrying out repairs, I am now pulling up the whole road. My response would be – perhaps echoing the 18th Report of the Royal Commission on Environmental Pollution[77] – that over-obsession with one form of propulsion may end up eventually restricting rather than increasing freedom of choice. Or, in the words of Father Brown 'It isn't that they can't see the solution. It is that they can't see the problem?[78]

---

[75] N. Neuwahl, ,Individuals and Gatt: Direct Effect and Indirect Effects of the General Agreement on Tariffs and Trade in The European Union and World Trade Law', 1996, op.cit.

[76] No doubt the courts would have to develop thresholds since so many activities are environmentally damaging but the same developments and drawing back can be seen in the case law on restrictions of trade and measures of equivalent effect. But the purpose of the proposal is to permit the development of principle rather than lay down over-prescriptive rules in advance.

[77] *Transport and the Environment*, 1994 (HMSO: London).

[78] G. K. Chesterton, *The Scandal of Father Brown*, 'Point of the Pin', 1935.

CHAPTER 20

BALANCING TRADE FREEDOM WITH THE REQUIREMENTS OF SUSTAINABLE DEVELOPMENT*

Introduction[1]

The integration of social, environmental, and economic concerns lies at the heart of the commitment to sustainable development to which the European Community, the Member States and many members of GATT are at least formally dedicated.[2] In purely legal terms the principle of sustainable development, while much talked about, defies precise definition and risks dismissal as a political aspiration rather than a legal concept. Nevertheless, inspirational provisions lie at the heart of many constitutional legal systems, motivating the interpretation of substantive and procedural rules and establishing general principles of law which have a substantial influence in practice. Integration forms the formal kingpin of the Community's sustainability strategy – the legal integration

* M Hession and R Macrory (1996) Balancing Trade Freedom with the Requirements of Sustainable Development. In: N Emilou, and D O'Keeffe (eds.) *The European Union and World Trade Law: After the GATT Uruguay Round*. John Wiley & Sons, London. pp 181-216
[1] Martin Hession is a lawyer and senior research scientist at the Environmental Change Unit at Oxford University; Richard Macrory is IBM Director of the ECU and Professor of Environmental Law.
This article is derived from work undertaken for a research project funded by the European Commission (DG XII) entitled 'Institutional Adjustment to Sustainable Development'' coordinated by CSERGE at the University of East Anglia.
[2] While the fundamental task of the Community has always centred on free trade it has also always incorporated other social and political objectives. The question whether free trade is an objective in itself or the means of attaining a broader range of objectives is answered in Article 2. which makes clear that the market is a means to an end rather than an end in itself. Article 2 was amended to reflect the Community's interest in environment protection; 'Article 2 The Community shall have as its task by establishing a common market and an economic and monetary union and by implementing the common policies or activities, to promote throughout the Community a harmonious and balanced development of economic activities, sustainable and non-inflationary growth respecting the environment, a high degree of economic convergence of economic performance, a high level of employment and of social protection, the raising of the standard of living and quality of life, and economic an social cohesion and solidarity among the member states'. The recently adopted WTO contains similar language: Preamble to the WTO 'Recognising that their relations in the field of trade and economic endeavour should be conducted with a view to the raising of standards of living, ensuring full employment, and a large and steadily growing volume of real income and effective demand, and expanding the production and trade in goods and services, while allowing for the optimal use of the worlds' resource in accordance with the objective of sustainable development, seeking both to protect and preserve the environment and enhance the means of doing so.'

of the principles of free trade with those of environmental protection perhaps its most difficult task.[3] In the process of fulfilling the obligation to integrate it will be demonstrated whether the interests of trade and the environment are ultimately reconcilable and by what institutional framework this may be achieved – if at all. The balance achieved at a community level displays some of the difficulties of integration adopted and implemented at a supranational level. Though reinforced by recent amendments to the Treaty, the process towards sustainability might be described as in its early stages, and there is already ample evidence in the eyes of some that the process cannot be completed while leaving protection afforded to both interests undiminished.

Historically, the Legal Order of the European Community has provided a framework within which provisions relating to the free market have been developed and applied in a manner unique between states.[4] Though in many instances the legal language is the same, the essential provisions of the Treaty relating to goods, services and capital go far beyond anything suggested by the Uruguay round of GATT. In particular the existence of an independent enforcement agency and the principles of superiority and direct effect of Community law provide for a particular style and level of enforcement within the EC to which GATT may only distantly aspire. The recognition that individual provisions of the Treaty relating to free trade can have the effect of invalidating national law and that these provisions can be invoked even by individuals has had a profound effect on Member States, ability to regulate the national public interest in matters affecting trade.

Article 30 in particular has been broadly interpreted to invalidate measures which potentially indirectly hinder interstate trade – a test very little legislation appears to pass. Adopted by the Court in the interests of establishing an integrated market, this broad interpretation of Article 30 of the EC Treaty[5] has, in the absence of a formal division of powers between the Member States and the Community or an express bill of rights respecting individuals[6], lead to a commensurate

---

[3] Art. 130r(2) reinforced at Maastricht requires that environmental protection requirements be integrated in the definition and implementation of other policy. Integration has been adopt as a formal policy objective in the 5th Action Programme 'Towards Sustainabihty' 1993.

[4] See Petersmann 'The EC And GATT on the Economic Functions of GATT Rules' 1984 *Legal Issues of European Integration* 37 who characterises the Community and GATT as incorporating the liberal market idea in legal constitutional form (see also Petersmann n 25 below). But see Staker 'Free Movement of Goods in the EEC and Australia: A Comparative Study' 1990 YBEL 10 on Art. 92 of the Australian Constitution for a description of a similar federal provision guaranteeing free trade.

[5] Prohibiting quantitative restrictions and measures having equivalent effect which have been interpreted in the light of the objective of attaining a single market see note infra.

[6] 291/69 *Stander v Ulm* 1969 ECR 419, 11/70 *International Handelsgesellschaft* 1970 ECR 1125, 4/73 *Nold II* 1974 ECR 491. 44/79 *Liselotte Hauer v Rheinlandpfalz* 1979 ECR 3752-3765.

expansion in recognised socially motivated justifications from the general prohibition. These justifications in the form of general principles and interests commonly recognised in the European legal system are interpreted by the European Court of Justice which therefore has a broad power to review national legislation adopted under them. In a similar manner, where the Community has regulated, the Court has allowed an extensive interpretation of the Treaty and Community tasks to justify Community legislation in respect of these concerns. In both cases the principles of legality and certainty have been undermined.

Essential competences relating to the harmonisation of domestic standards and the Common Commercial Policy, both ostensibly directed at the establishment of a single market within the Community, have always necessarily encompassed other considerations for which trade is commonly regulated. But, ever broader interpretation of the legal bases for market action is, ultimately, an unsatisfactory legal foundation for Community measures which have had only a tenuous connection to the objectives. Even so, the express recognition provided by recent Treaty amendments of separate bases defined according to independent objectives demonstrates the limitations of a system of separate legal bases operated according to a teleological approach, where legitimate objectives and measures adopted to satisfy them increasingly overlap. Resulting tensions within the definition of each basis are reinforced both by the division between broadly unitary trade policy and concurrent policies representing other aspects of the public interest and the proliferation of legislative procedures required for their adoption.

At an international level the increased interrelationship between trade and other issues has caused the Court of Justice to hesitate between an inclusive interpretation of Article 113 and the recognition of competence in the Member States.[7] Similarly within the Community while the concept of the market effect was used to justify particular environmental measures under Articles 100 and 235 in the absence of an alternative specific competence, the adoption of a separate legal basis (Article 130r-t), for the environment has outlined a conflict between the interests of competitive equality and market unity and the legally reinforced recognition of a decentralised pursuit of environmental protection.

---

[7] Most recently the balance has come down in favour of a less monolithic Common Commercial policy than some have argued for, Opinion 1/94 *Re the Uruguay Round Treaties Commission* v *Council* 1995 Common Market Law Reports 205. For critique see Bourgeois 'The EC in the WTO and Advisory Opinion 1/94: An Echternach Procession' (1995) 32 No 3 CMLRev 736-787.

Developing a Community Framework

To date an holistic approach to the Treaty and judicial testing of legislative discretion according to developed principles of non-discrimination, necessity and proportionality[8] as well as the objective factors for review of legal bases have formed the geography of the Trade and Environment Division in Community law. The place and influence of the newer principles of integration and subsidiarity in the review of action pursued in the general interest remain to be determined according to a defined framework of Community constitutional law itself as yet in its early stages.[9]

The following is suggested as a possible framework within which the principles of free trade and environment might be reconciled or integrated at Community level. While nowhere defined in the Treaty, a broad outline can be gauged in the application of particular community rules.

Statements of Pre-Emptive Norms

These are Treaty provisions and General Principles of Law given highest value by the Court, of a binding character invocable against and by the Community institutions, or the Member States, but also in some circumstances are also invocable by and against individuals (in that sense giving rise to what might be termed personal constitutional rights). Article 30 of the Treaty guaranteeing free trade, and fundamental rights recognised as general principles of law fall into this category.[10]

A Duty to Act or to Respect Particular Interests

An obligation on the part of the Community to act in favour of a particular interest. Such a statement is suggestive of a pre-emptive norm, but may perhaps be distinguishable in that it is invocable only by the Community institutions and the Member States between each other.

---

[8] 138/79 *Isoglucose* 1980 ECR 333, 113/76 *Skimmed Milk, Benuhle* 1977 ECR 1211 and *Buitoni* 1979 ECR 677-686 for examples in practice. Generally De Burea 'The principle of proportionality and its application in EC Law 1993 YEL 105'.

[9] For the constitutional character of the Community Parti Ecologiste *'Les Verts* v *European Parliament'* 1986 ECR 1339. and see generally Lenearts 'Fundamental Rights to be Included in a Community Catalogue' 1991 *European Law Review* 367.

[10] Confirmed in *ADBHU* 1985 ECR 531 at 549 See also Quinn and MacGowan 'Could Article 30 impose obligations on individuals' 12 ELR 163. It should be remembered that whereas the right to trade across frontiers recognised in *ABHU* applies to Community and national legislation alike, the court recognises the application of other 'human' rights to Community provisions only (see John Temple Lang 'The Sphere in which Member States are obliged to comply with General principles of Law and Community Fundamental Rights Principles' 1991/1 Legal Issues of European Integration 23.)

Such obligations may be found in many of the early Treaty articles establishing the common external tariff and the common market and have formed the basis for the courts' jurisprudence on exclusivity.[11] A duty on the Community to respect a particular interest forms a limitation on the exercise of power in judicial review but may not amount to the grant of a right. The integration requirement may fall into this category.[12] And perhaps even the duty to fulfil elements of the general action plan in Article 130s(3) falls into this category.[13]

General Principles of Law

General duties operate in the sphere of Community discretion. These principles are binding but operate in respect of the application of other interests and norms: their effect is therefore dependent on the operation of a norm or interest: Article 5 Duty of Solidarity[14], Article 7 Nondiscrimination or Equality are examples.[15] Necessity, Proportionality and Subsidiarity (Article 3b) and perhaps at least some of the Principles of Environmental Action detailed in Article 130r(2), in particular proximity (see below) are similar principles though perhaps lower-order principles regulating the application of pre-emptive norms, duties and basic principles on recognised interests.[16]

Statement of Community Interest

The Community's interest in a particular objective authorising the adoption of particular measures pursuant to the appropriate legal basis and forming the legal boundaries of a Community power: (Article 130r (Environment). Article 43 (Agriculture)). These interests justify an intrusion upon pre-emptive norms subject to the basic principles of nondiscrimination, necessity and proportionality.[17]

---

[11] In particular duties to adopt particular measures by particular dates appear to have this effect see particularly *Commission* v *United Kingdom* 1980 ECR 1045.

[12] It appears that whether by sympathetic interpretation or by formal recognition of the duty to integrate contained in Article 130r(2) the proximity principle has been allowed to modify the application of a Community law rule (derogations to Article 30) in the *Wallonia Waste* Case 2/90 *Commission* v *Belgium* [1993] CMLR 365 (see below).

[13] Hession and Macrory 'Legal Issues of a New Environment Policy' Chap 10 O'Keeffe and Twomey (eds) in *Legal Issues of the Maastricht Treaty* (Wiley 1994) 163-164.

[14] Giving rise to ERTA implied powers and pre-emption which derives ultimately from Art. 5 but gives rise to other duties *Fisheries Commission* v *UK* 1980 ECR 1045 and *Opinion ILO Convention No 170* [1993] Common Market Law Reports 800 and Opinion 1/94 Uruguay Round Agreements 1995 CMLR 205.

[15] See discussion on non-discrimination below and for relevance of environmental principles on *Wallonia Waste* case (n 12 *supra)* also below.

[16] *Wallonia* supra n 12.

[17] The existence of such an interest is a matter of interpretation and not limited to express policy statements, as the *ADBHU* case *(supra* n 10) concerning the environment demonstrated prior to the adoption of an express legal basis.

Statement of Member States' Interest

The Treaty also recognises Member States' interests which also justify limited exceptions to the pre-emptive norms of Community law subject to the principles of necessity, proportionality and equality: (Article 36, and the Mandatory requirements Cassis di Dijon).[18]

Statements of Interpretative Value

Principles which are suggestive but have no autonomous effect (but nonetheless are likely to have some interpretative value in a legal framework): Subsidiarity may fall into this category.

Pre-Emptive Trade Norms and the Environmental Interest

A fundamental assumption is made as to the effects of trade and environment provisions, the reasons for which are rooted in politics and the nature of the interests themselves. Whereas Article 30 of the Treaty presents a pre-emptive and directly effective provision establishing an area of individual protection equivalent to that of an individual right, environmental protection provisions are defined as legislative interests in language which denies the possibility of such effects.[19] The traditional justification for this lies with the difficulty in determining the limits and standard of protection required by the latter. And yet the limits of what represents the common market are no more certain than those of environment. Both definitions incorporate questions of scale and degree linked to social and political choices. Indeed the Community definition of the market (single, common and internal) is uncertain and finds an unsteady application in the substantive rules governing its establishment.[20] Nonetheless the current broad hierarchy of principles

[18] While the Member States may be said to retain all powers not ceded to the Community the interpretation of the extent of Community power is difficult. Art. 36 is one of the few places in the Treaty where state interests are indirectly recognised and listed. Until the formal identification of concurrent policies permanently preserving state rights to legislate under the subsidiarity principle (Art. 3b) and more stringent measures powers provisions (Art. 130t) these 'police powers' remained subject to the possibility of permanent and absolute harmonisation in so far as this was possible through Art. 100.

[19] The Constitutions of Portugal and Greece recognise a right which while not self-executory for these reasons has a certain legal/discretionary value in review. The Court's recognition of a constitutional right to be found in national constitutions would be one alternative approach to founding an environmental norm at Community level.

[20] The single market is implemented or enforced through several substantive rules. Arts 85 and 86 on Competition (Fair and Perfect Competition between undertakings); Art. 12 (prohibiting the introduction of new duties on imports and charges of equivalent effect while further articles provide for the abolition of existing standards now achieved (Art. 16); the central Art. 30 prohibiting quantitative restrictions on imports and measures having equivalent effect interpreted to establish the principle of mutual recognition of product-

continued

reflect a legal presumption in favour of trade freedom and economic growth over scientific uncertainty as to the environmental consequences of these choices. This presumption lies at the heart of a liberal economic and social order based on competition and risk.

One element of the distinction is traditional in that trade freedom reflects a classical individual right, falling within traditional notions of property, capable of objective legal protection to the holder of such rights.[21] As a result, Free Movement of Goods in particular[22] has been interpreted to include a sufficiently substantive set of criteria to provide an adequate standard for the judicial review of Community and Member State legislation.[23] This character – one of individual right – derives from the special nature of the Community Treaty which acts increasingly as a constitutional charter. Member States are policed not only by themselves but by the Commission under Article 169 and by individuals in accordance with the doctrine of direct effect.[24] The Community itself is policed under the provisions of Article 173 by the Member States and its own institutions and individuals insofar as a Community decision is of 'direct and individual concern'.[25]

...related standards throughout the Community. This mutual recognition principle is applied to a lesser but increasing extent in other areas notably Arts 52-62: Services prohibition on the introduction of new Arts 71 and 73b Capital (weaker provisions). Art. 48: Free Movement of Workers (standstill plus): Arts 52-53: (standstill plus) Right of Establishment, (standstill plus) and Art. 72 on Transport.

[21] Rene Barents 'The Community and the Unity of the Common Market: Some Reflections on the Economic Constitution of the Community' 33 (Dunker and Hamblot. 1990) *German Year book of International Law* 9-36.

[22] Art. 8a provides that the internal market is based on four freedoms: Free movement of Goods. Workers, Services and Capital which are elaborated in individual provisions of several articles of the Treaty: Arts 12, 30, 59 etc.

[23] Nonetheless the concept of a 'common market' is nowhere defined though it is mentioned in several provisions: Arts 9-102 assist in its definition through detailing aspects of public and private activity which is incompatible with the establishment and functioning of the market though these provisions. The Court has attempted to define the essential character of the market in several cases; 270/80 *Polydor* v *Harlequin* 1982 ECR 329 'The Treaty seeks to create a single market reproducing as closely as possible the conditions of a domestic market' and 15/81 *Schul* 1982 ECR 1409 'the elimination of all obstacles to intra-Community trade in order to merge the national markets to those of a genuine internal market'. These cases themselves contain some margin for interpretation - see *supra* n 21 at p 10.

[24] Arts 12 (Customs Duties and Charges having equivalent effect) 26/62 *Van Gend en Loos* 1963 ECR 1 and Art. 30 (Quantitative Restrictions and measures having equivalent effect) are directly effective: 13/68 [1968] *Salgoil* ECR 453. 74/76 *Ianelli* 1977 ECR 557 and *Pigs Marketing Board* v *Redmond* 1978 ECR 2347.

[25] As to the desirability of a trade norm and individual access to it see Petersmann 'Limited Government and Unlimited Trade Powers. Why Effective Judicial Review of Foreign Trade Restrictions Depends on Individual Rights' in Hilf and Petersmann *National Constitutions and International Economic Law* (Kluwer 1993).

In contrast, environmental protection rather than embodying a freedom more commonly implies a restriction on individual activity mediated through the legislative activities of a state which is either duty bound to protect the environment or is recognised to have a discretionary interest in doing so.[26] As such a right to the environment is not easily associated with an individual for enforcement save in so far as some element of the environment amounts to an asset falling within traditional notions of private property or another more traditional right and is protected in this way.

One suggested method of achieving an individualisation of rights and responsibility over the environment is the internalisation or monetisation of environmental costs.[27] Even if distribution of rights according to a market were desirable and could negate all the disadvantages of a more inflexible approach through central regulation it must be doubted whether all environmental problems can be given a value. Reference to such an approach demonstrates nonetheless that the extent to which a market incorporates environmental assets and liabilities may vary in different Member States and this is one way the application of trade rules to environmental problems is delimited.[28]

The central objection to the recognition of an environmental right remains the absence of an objective standard of protection and the judgment than any standard must be set through the legislative rather than the judicial method. The Treaty of Rome has endorsed though not defined a high level of protection but 'normativity' of this statement is doubted or at least limited.[29] The objection is not consistently applied however as while it is used to deny the possibility of a norm against which legislation may be measured in terms of its environmental component, judicial testing of measures against an objectively determinable standard of protection has been suggested where it has been alleged it is trade

---

[26] The extension of the state's interest in the environment to include precautionary as well as preventive or protective measures implies an extension of public power without an appropriate mechanism for rational review of such policies against objectively determinable facts or reasons (see discussion on precaution and proportionality below). See McGarity *Reinventing Rationality The Role of Regulatory Analysis in the Federal Bureaucracy* (Cambridge University Press 1991) for a US discussion of the problem, (particularly Chap 9). This difficulty has led to warnings of a danger of an authoritarian ecological state see Michael Kloepfer 'An Authoritarian Ecological State?' 1994 EELR112.

[27] Nonetheless in conditions of uncertainty environmental risks themselves unquantifiable are still less capable of market valuation. The process of cost benefit analysis of environmental messages displays some of the problems of such an apples and oranges approach (McGarrity).

[28] Vide discussion whether waste is a good in *Wallonia*. The issues of patenting living organisms in the area of biotechnology and discussions on civil liability for environmental harm also come to mind.

[29] Lenaerts 'Fundamental Rights to be Included in a Community Catalogue' 1991 European Law Review 367.

restrictive. Inherent scientific uncertainty as to the effects of particular actions operating through a complex system of possible processes, interactions and cumulative effects makes an excessive reliance on science to determine an objective assessment of risk or harm of human activity.[30] This is not to deny that the conditions for a trade restriction nor indeed a test insuring protection is not judicially determinable even in conditions of uncertainty, but merely to state that science on its own cannot be relied upon to establish an objective standard against which particular measures may be judged in all cases.

In addition the philosophy of both interests is different. Whereas the single market is a human construction and of its nature requires a certain unity of conditions, the environment is not, and must be regulated according to a hierarchy of provision with regard to the global, regional and local levels according to different conditions and circumstances.[31] In contrast Non-discrimination and universally applicable uniform standards are the foundation of Community trade policy, while Subsidiarity[32] and Minimum Standards[33] provision reinforce the non-unitary nature of the environment policy.

Different physical and social conditions logically suggest local regulation. Hence restrictions on trade in environmentally hazardous material are justifiable to protect the local environment (though perhaps invidious to the market). Regulation in the interest of the environment, at a Community level must be justified as being more effective than that at local level suggesting some trans-boundary element. This is supported by criterion of effectiveness - the use of national trade instruments to protect the local environment from external sources of pollution is indirect enforcement of local standards at the best of times. It is also apparently unjustified on environmental grounds given that the definition of environmental interest seems to be restricted to state

---

[30] John Stonehouse 'Science Risk Analysis and Environmental Decisions' **UNEP** Trade and the Environment Series No 5. ISSN 1020-1610.

[31] A rather crude attempt to define what is appropriate can be made with reference to physical or trans-boundary nature of particular environmental problems:
Global Environmental Problems: Climate, Stratospheric Ozone, Highly Migratory Species, the High Seas.
Regional Environmental Problems: More limited trans-boundary problems. Sulphur Dioxide, NO_x. migratory species. Rivers, Regional Seas.
Local Environmental Problems: Suspended Particulates, Waste Disposal, other localised pollution.

[32] Community action is permissible only if *and* only in so far as the objectives of the proposed action cannot be sufficiently achieved by the Member States and can therefore by reason of the scale and effects of the proposed action be better achieved by the Community (Art. 3b).

[33] Art. 130t authorising the introduction of more stringent protective measures *compatible with the treaty* and Art. 100a(4) authorising the *maintenance of* more stringent environmental protective measure in limited circumstances.

boundaries.[34] Regulation to achieve conditions of competitive equality or the application of Article 30 to achieve this have no such limitation however and the consequent harmonisation need not reflect local conditions allowing an equalisation of standards.[35]

Article 30 and the Extent of the Free Market in Goods[36]

The Common Market created by the European Community is far more ambitious than anything attempted in the GATT Agreements. The substantive elements of the market defined by the Treaty are a free trade area established in accordance with Articles 12-17 which provide that all customs duties and charges of equivalent effect be progressively abolished between the Member States and a customs union established under Articles 18-28a providing for a common tariff to apply with respect to third states. Much of the effective bite of the internal market in goods has been established by Article 30 which provides that quantitative restrictions and measures having equivalent effect are prohibited.[37] The Treaty as amended provides that the Community may adopt measures to harmonise provisions which directly affect the establishment or functioning of the Common Market,[38] or measures which have as their object or effect the establishment of the internal market[39] – the latter defined as an area without internal frontiers in which free movement of goods, persons, services and capital is ensured.[40] Both the concept of Common Market and Internal Market are difficult to define further. Even so, on the basis of these provisions and particularly Article

---

[34] The argument whether an interest in environmental protection justifies unilateral regulation of trade in respect of the external environment (process standards) for Member States or the Community remains untested. *Dassonville* Case 1974 ECR 837 at 840 suggests that Art. 36 justifies measures for the protection a state's own interests and not for the protection of interests of other states. The *Scottish Grouse* Case (169/89 *Goumeterrie van den burg* 1990 ECR. 2143) suggests a similar analysis. See also Krämer 'Environmental Protection and Article 30 of EEC Treaty' 30 *Common Market Law Review* 1990 111-143 at 119-120 for a contrary view.

[35] For discussion of unilateral trade restrictions at an international level see Schoenbaum 'Trade Sanctions Domestic, Enforcement of Agreement, Anti-Competitive Factors'. AJIL Vol. 86 1992 701. Principle 12 of Rio Declaration, differentiates between direct and indirect regulation.

[36] A subject on which much has been written: see *supra* n 21: Wils 'The Search for a Rule in Article 30. Much Ado about Nothing' Vol. 18 No. 6 ELR 475; J Steiner 'Drawing the Line: Uses and Abuses of Article 30 EEC' 1992 (29) *Common Market Law Review* p 754; Mortelmans 'Article 30 of EEC Treaty and Legislation Relating to Market Circumstances: Time to Consider a New Definition' 28 *Common Market Law Review*: White 'In Search of the Limits of Article 30 of the EEC Treaty' 26 *Common Market Law Review* 235-280.

[37] One of the shorter treaty articles: Art. 30: Quantitative Restrictions on Imports and on all measures having equivalent effect shall without prejudice to the following provisions be prohibited between the Member States.

[38] The formula of Art. 100.

[39] The formula of Art. 100a.

[40] Art. 7a.

30 the Court has confirmed that 'the principle of Free Movement of Goods and Freedom of Competition, together with freedom of trade as a fundamental right are general principles of law of which the Court ensures observance' [*ADBHU supra* n 10]. These fundamental principles define a pre-emptive norm of free trade applicable to the Community[41] and the Member States alike, and are invocable as individual rights in the national legal systems, rendering contrary measures inapplicable.[42]

Defining the extent of this putative human right has proved fraught and while it is clear that the prohibition incorporates elements of nondiscrimination and distortion of intra-community trade the latter element in particular has caused some difficulty in application leaving the law in a state of confusion.[43]

Non-Discrimination or Equality[44]

The presence or absence of discrimination cannot be established in the absence of other substantive criteria applicable in one situation and not in another in which it is claimed there is discrimination. Here we are concerned with a general freedom to trade across frontiers attaching to goods. Equality of treatment, according to an Aristotelian conception requires consistency in some circumstances and differentiation in others.[45] Discrimination therefore consists in treating either similar situations differently or different situations identically.[46] The basic requirement in Community law is that there be no discrimination on

[41] 80 & 81/77 *Société les Reunis Sarl et al v Receveur des Douanes* 1978 ECR 927 at 946-947 (provision authorising charge having equivalent effect to custom duty in Art. 31 (2) of Reg. 816/70)and 61/86 *United Kingdom v Commission* 1988 ECR i 37/83 *Rewe Zentral* 1984 ECR 1229 and 15/83 *Denkavit* 1984 ECR 2171 (disparities ruled justifiable or inevitable)

[42] *Salgoil* 13/68 ELR. 453, *Ianelli v Mer* 74/76 1977 ECR 557, *Pig Marketing Board v Redmond* 1978 ECR 2347 (direct effect of Art. 30).

[43] To quote Advocate General Jacobs 'The European Court of Justice: Some Thoughts on its Past and its Future' in *The European Advocate* Winter 1994-95 (Bar European Group UK) ISSN 1351-4172.

[44] Art. 6 'Within the scope of application of this Treaty . . . any discrimination on grounds of nationality shall be prohibited' – Non-discrimination is a general principle not limited to free movement of goods but can mean different things in different places (see standstill prohibition on discriminatory treatment under the transport title Case 195/90 *Commission v Germany* and the case confirms that pre-existing inequality forms no justification for the adoption of more discriminatory measures with respect to charges for heavy goods vehicles).

[45] Nicomedean Ethics: Aristotle.

[46] (Art. 36, 13/63 ECR *Italy v Commission* 1963 ECR 165 'The different treatment of non-comparable situations does not lead automatically to the conclusion that there is discrimination. An appearance of discrimination in form may therefore in fact correspond to an absence of discrimination in substance. Discrimination in substance would consist in treating either similar situations differently or different situations identically'.

grounds of origin.[47] This requirement is essentially a negative and rather limited requirement which states grounds which are insufficient to justify different treatment but fails to address justifiable grounds upon which products may be differentiated.

The distinction between similar and dissimilar situations can be presented in two ways.

The first involves searching for a physical difference inherent in the object of the freedom (in the case of goods a like products approach). The second alternative involves searching for an objective justification for the distinction made between products (which may be broader than differences in the physical nature of the goods themselves).[48] It is suggested that elements of the general interests recognised by Community law are grounds which justify distinction and render it non-discriminatory.[49] The second alternative allows a greater range of distinguishing features than the former including distinctions justified according to environmental effects of production as well as those inherent in the goods themselves or indeed the objective general principles of environmental policy.[50]

In addition the Court recognises that there may be natural advantages and disadvantages which do not amount to discrimination and are allowed to lie where they fall. These might be said to form the basis of the comparative advantage the internal market is intended to exploit.[51]

---

[47] Art. 6 above and the final sentence of Art. 36 'such prohibitions shall not constitute a means of arbitrary discrimination . . .'.

[48] In this sense discrimination is not 'arbitrary discrimination' (final sentence para 36) and see 13/63 *Italy v EEC Commission* ECR 165.

[49] See *Servinde* 1984 ECR 4209 para 28: difference in treatment is objectively justified *inter alia* in the light of particular provisions of Community law. The question whether the process by which a good is produced is a valid ground for distinction is obviously related to the question whether the decision to restrict access of goods on this ground is justifiable on criteria of effectiveness (it is necessarily indirect regulation after the event). If discrimination on the only criterion upon which a measure might be found trade restrictive the question whether Art. 36 applies with respect to the external environment becomes irrelevant. As this is patently not the case the legitimacy of a process standard must be related to on this question. See n 34 *supra*.

[50] Such as precaution, prevention at source and polluter pays. See *Wallonia Waste* Case *infra*. The discrimination must necessarily be proportionate to the legitimate differences recognised by the Treaty – which in the case of environment can be difficult to assess and enforce. The principle that damage ought as a priority be prevented at source for instance might work both ways, to encourage process standards dealing with pollution arising at source, or to preclude them, if use of such indirect sanctions rather than direct regulation of the source were considered to breach the principle.

[51] The burdens of natural differences such as physical location and transport costs are allowed to rest where they lie (Case 52/79 *Procureur du roi v Marc JVC Debarre & Others* 1980 ECR 833) and Case 63-69/72 *Wilhelm Werhahn Hansmulne & Oth v Council* 1973 ECR 1229).

Continued

Distortion or Restriction of Intra-Community Trade

National treatment of imported goods-regulated by a provision on nondiscrimination may still have the effect of partitioning the Single Market as goods marketable in one state may not be marketable in another state because of different applicable standards. It is clear that what is prohibited by Article 30 goes beyond simply discriminatory measures as the limited exceptions to the rule provided for are still stated to be the subject of a requirement of non-discrimination. It is equally clear that Article 30 could not have been envisaged to invalidate all measures adversely affecting the operation of the market as the Treaty affords a legal basis for the harmonisation of national measures which do so.

The central problem is determining what is restrictive of *intra-Community trade* without some even indirect discriminatory element. Indistinctly applicable measures may have discriminatory effects when applied to products from different countries.[52] Here the question becomes one of assessing the probity of the distinction adopted: essentially whether the justification provided is objectively justified when compared with its discriminatory effects.[53]

The Court in the *Dassonville* case has drawn a very wide circle about Article 30 ruling that 'all trading rules which are capable of hindering directly or indirectly, actually or potentially, intra-Community trade must be considered measures having an effect equivalent to quantitative restrictions'. Such measures may even include measures which show no discrimination on their face and even measures which do not have a heavier impact on foreign goods per se.[54] In essence indistinctly applicable measures which have a general restrictive effect on trade are technically within the ambit of Article 30. For a time it appeared that there were few areas of market regulation where Article 30 would not apply.[55]

…Art. 130r(3) itself seems to confirm this as a general principle in environmental legislation requiring that differences in physical factors be taken into account in Community legislation.

[52] Amount to 'disguised restrictions on trade' (final sentence of Art. 36).

[53] In this way the question whether indistinctly applicable measures are trade retraction and whether they may be justified are intimately interlinked, though the Treaty itself requires these questions are treated separately (Arts 30 and 36).

[54] Interestingly a recurring argument is that not all measures impinging on trade may be considered restrictive – the Advocate General even suggested that veterinary inspection in the general Community interest assisted rather than interfered with trade 46/76 *Bauhuis* 1977 ECR 5 Opinion of Advocate General para 7.

[55] This is particularly important in environmental terms as regulation of use and disposal of goods even if indistincüy applicable and factually non-discriminatorv are still plainly capable of causing an indirect trade restriction – as *Danish Bottles* demonstrates.

It has been suggested that there has been an attempt by the Court to make the trade rules applicable to states coextensive with those applicable to undertakings under the competition policy.[56] The result has been that the broad *Dassonville* definition 'of measures having equivalent effect' means that Article 30 operates as a quasi-presumption against rules regulating trade rather than a substantive rule invalidating measures restrictive of intra-Community trade.[57] In the absence of a clear standard of competition and trade freedom applicable to trade in a single market[58] the formula is ultimately unsatisfactory.

This test is therefore very broad indeed as the *Cassis de Dijon* Case confirmed. Here the Court found that any product legally marketable in the country of origin (and by analogy in free circulation within the Community) must be admitted to the national market in the absence of justification provided for by the Treaty. The presumption becomes one that products legally on the market in one Member State must be admitted without restriction to the domestic market.[59]

Under this test it is difficult to overcome the presumption that any legislation with only a potential and indirect effect on trade is not prohibited. Measures found to fall within the prohibition have included such diverse regulation as limits on production[60], checks and inspections on goods[61], packaging requirements[62], national goods buy-only policies[63] or even restriction on video rentals.[64]

In recent years the full consequences of *Dassonville* and *Cassis de Dijon* has led the Court into difficulties and the Court has found certain restrictions (on working hours or sales outlets for spirits and limitations on Sunday trading[65] etc) to fall outside the scope of Article 30. The ground upon which certain indistinctly applicable measures have been found to fall outside the prohibition remain confused despite an attempt to clarify the Court's policy in the recent *Keck and Mithouard*

---

[56] See this consequence made explicit *Cassis de Dijon Rewe-Zentrale AG v Bundesmonopobverwaltung fur Branntwein* 1979 ECR 649.

[57] Kapteyn and van Themaat *Introduction to the Law of the European Community,* 2nd ed (Kluwer, 1992) p 380-381.

[58] See three connotations in Kapten and van Themaate p356.

[59] *Cassis di Dijon: Rewe-Zentrale AG v Bundesmonopoloverwaltung fur Branntwein* 1979 ECR 649.

[60] Quotas on milling wheat 190/73 *Van Haaster* [1974] ECR 1123

[61] 251/78 *Denkavit* [1979] ECR 3369.

[62] *Prantl* [1984] ECR 1299 *Ran v Smedt* 1982 ECR 3901.

[63] 249/81 *Commission v Ireland* [1982] ECR 4005.

[64] Ban on release within one year to protect cinema viewing *Cinetheque v FNCF* 1985 ECR 2605.

[65] 155/80 *Oebel* 1981 ECR 3147 and 75/81 *Blesgen* 1982 ECR 11211, 69/93 and C-258/93. *Punto Cas Spa.* ECR. 1994.C-23/89 *Quietlynn v Southend Borough Council* [1990] ECR 3059.

case.[66] Here the Court expressly recognised that its policy of regulating all potentially restrictive legislation through granting exceptions has its limits and that there are indeed areas of legislative policy the effect of which on intra-Community trade is not sufficient to bring them within the ambit of Article 30.[67]

The Recognition of General Interests of the Community and the Member States

A narrow interpretation of Article 30 which is applicable to the Community and the Member States alike would create a Single Market based on competition of regulatory orders in which Member States wishing to preserve higher standards would be in the position of having to pay for them through a commensurate loss in comparative advantage.[68] Alternatively a broad interpretation brings into question the need for a legislative basis for harmonisation of standards where Article 30 appears to achieve a dismantling of trade barriers in the absence of formal harmonisation. The former has the disadvantage of leading to a downward pressure on standards in a race to match the lowest common denominator as to cost, and the latter to a great deal of legal uncertainty.

The broad interpretation favoured in the *Cassis* formula has enabled the review of national regulation of markets and ultimately derives from the Courts dissatisfaction with the pace of harmonisation through legislation. Judicial harmonisation of national standards is effected through the application of Community principles through an extended list of justifications-mandatory requirements. *Keck and Mithouard* notwithstanding, the basic formula of broad prohibition and regulated exception continues. The process initiated by *Dassonville* by which a greater number of trading rules have been caught by an extensive definition of the pre-emptive norm but have been saved by an ever-growing legion of mandatory requirements may be criticised if only because legal certainty has been compromised.

[66] C-267 And C-268/91 *Keck and Mithouard* [1993] ECR 1-6097, para 16 and 17 in particular. Comment Roth 31 (1995) *Common Market Law Review* 845.

[67] See also Chalmers 'Repackaging the Internal Market – Ramifications of the *Keck* Judgment' 19 (1994) European Law Review 385. This is again important in environmetal terms as common use restrictions based on planning or licensing of activities are just the sort of measures the *Keck* Case appears to exempt from the full rigours of the *Dassonville* formula. Measures restricting traffic or the local use of non-biodegradable materials appear to have escaped application of the principle in two cases: *R v London Boroughs Transport Committee ex. P. Freight Association Ltd* 63 CMLR p 5 and *Enichem Base spa and others v Comune di Cinisello Balsamo* 989 ECR 2491.

[68] Norbert Reich 'Competition between Legal Orders: a New Paradigm for Community Law' 29 (1992) *Common Market Law Review* 861-896.

The Community Interests: Objectives in the General Interest

In the *ADBHU* Case[69] the Court confirmed that Article 30 is generally binding on the Community as well as the Member States, but recognised that the Community may adopt measures in pursuit of objects in the general interest which include environment protection: 'the principle of freedom of trade is subject to certain limits justified by the objectives of general interest pursued by the Community provided the rights in question are not substantially impaired'. Here certain provisions of a Community Directive derogating from absolute free movement with respect to waste oil were confirmed by the Court.[70] Judicial review of Community legislation is difficult to effect and the Community has a broad discretion to regulate trade in accordance with the provisions of the legal powers it is granted in pursuit of Community objectives.[71] Nonetheless restrictions on trade adopted by the Community are clearly subject to the requirement that they be non-discriminatory and that they are necessary and proportionate to the end in view, as well as a general obligation not to infringe individual human rights.[72] The discretion afforded to the Community is clearly broad: the Court in *ADBHU* stated that Community measures were reviewable only if they were manifestly inappropriate having regard to the objective being pursued.[73]

The Member States' Interests: Article 36 and Mandatory Equirements

Similarly Member State restrictions can be justified according to a list of interests exhaustively listed in Article 36.[74] The extension of Article 30 implied in *Dassonville* lead the Court to establish a further non-exhaustive list of mandatory requirements which might also justify unilateral action.[75] The *Danish Bottles Case*[76] has confirmed that the protection of the environment is a mandatory requirement. It is clear that measures taken in pursuit of Article 36 or the mandatory requirements

---

[69] *ADBHU* 1985 ECR 531 at 549.

[70] 75/439 Directive on Waste Oils see p 549 of the *ADBHU* judgment

[71] *Supra* n 21.

[72] This is confirmed by Art. 3b of the Treat. 'Any action by the Community shall not go beyond what is necessary to achieve the objectives of this Treaty'.

[73] 331/88 *The Queen* v *Ministry of Agriculture ex. P. FEDESA & Others* 1990 ECR 4032.

[74] Art. 36 'The provisions of Arts 30-34 shall not preclude prohibitions or restrictions on imports, exports or goods in transit justified on grounds of public morality, public policy or public security, the protection of health and the life of humans, animals or plants; the protection of national treasures possessing artistic, historic or archaeological value; or the protection of industrial or commercial property. *Such prohibitions shall not however constitute a means of arbitrary discrimination or a disguised restriction on trade between Member States.*'

[75] In *Cassis di Dijon supra* n 59. But the interests listed are justifications not reserved powers and are therefore amenable to review by the Court 35/76 *Simmenthal* 1976 ECR 1871.

[76] 302/86 *Commission v Denmark* 1986 ECR 4607.

may not be discriminatory.[77] Nonetheless in certain circumstances different treatment of imported products may be justified according to objective criteria provided equivalent measures are taken with respect to domestically produced products.[78]

In contrast with the position internally, in the external sphere the right of Member States to take independent protective action is uncertain. The Treaty appears to provide that the Member States are at once required not to agree external trade measures outside the Community framework, but may introduce independent trade restrictions in respect of internal trade. In practice power is delegated to the states acting as trustees of the Community interest; Regulation 288/82[79] provides that Member States may introduce restrictions on grounds similar to those listed in Article 36 but nonetheless there is some uncertainty as to whether this includes environment protection.[80]

Community harmonisation retains as a purpose the harmonisation of national standards justified by Article 36 and mandatory requirements at a Community level, and once this legislation has been adopted it appears to restrict or extinguish recourse to Article 36 in so far as it is exhaustive.[81] The adoption of general provisions authorising the retention or adoption of more stringent measures apparently precludes this restriction in certain circumstances but the Community cannot add

---

[77] Second sentence of Art. 36 and for example *Gilli and Andres* 1980 ECR 2071 confirms the same limitation on action taken in pursuance of a mandatory requirement; 'it is only where rules which apply without discrimination to both domestic and imported products may be justified as necessary in order to satisfy imperative requirements that they may constitute an exception to the requirements arising under Article 30'

[78] 4/75 *Rewe Zentralfinanz-LandwirtschaflsKammer* 1975 ECR 843 'different treatment of imported and domestic products based on the need to prevent the spread of harmful organisms could not be regarded as arbitrary discrimination if effective measures are taken in order to prevent the distribution of contaminated domestic products and if there is reason to believe in particular on the basis of previous experience that there is a risk of the harmful organism spreading if no inspection is held on importation'.

[79] See the replacement of national with Community quotas see Kapteyn and van Themaat at p803 *supra* n 57. Regulations 288/82. 1765/82 and 2603/69 include national safeguard clauses similar to Art. 36.

[80] Demeret, 'Environmental Policy and Commercial Policy: The Emergence of Trade Related Environmental Measures (TREMS) in the External Relations of the European Community' in Maresceu (ed) *The European Community's Commercial Policy After 1992: The Legal Dimension* (Martinus Nijhoff, 1993) 315-319 at p346-347.

[81] 29/87 *Denkavit v Danish Minister for Agriculture* [1988] ECR 2965. 169/89 *Gourmeterne van den Burg* BV1990 ECR 2143 para 8, 2/90 *Wallonia* [1993] CMLR 365 itself, (vide the rather restrictive interpretation of Art. 14 of Dir in *Scottish Grouse* Case 169/89), as the ability to adopt more stringent standards is confirmed in the Treaty text which is superior to secondary legislation adopted under it (Art. 130t). More stringent standards are still required to be consistent with the treaty (Art. 130tand 100a(4)).

to the discretion afforded to the Member States under Article 36 or the Mandatory Requirements.[82]

Discrimination and the Principles of Environmental Action

It has been assumed that the principles of environmental action detailed in Article 130r(2) had a limited, if any, legal effect. The *Wallonia* case[83] provides an interesting precedent for the use of one of these principles to modify the operation of the general non-discrimination requirement relating to measures restrictive of trade.[84] Though no express reference is made to the integration requirement the case appears to mark the first positive integration of environmental protection requirements into the definition and implementation of the Community's other policies.

In the *Wallonia* Case a blanket ban on import of non-hazardous waste into the province of Wallonia was upheld by the Court. Much of the judgment was concerned with whether waste amounted to a 'good' subject to the provisions of Article 30. The Court determined that it was and gave little consideration to necessity and proportionally, merely noting that the influx of waste into Wallonia was a serious problem. Most controversially the non-discrimination requirement was held inapplicable on the grounds that waste originating outside Wallonia was legally distinguishable from waste originating within Wallonia by reference to the proximity principle recognised in Article 130r(2) of the Treaty.

The Court failed to deal with Advocate-General Jacob's observation that proximity had not been expressly incorporated in the Wallonian legislation giving grounds to his opinion that the regional ban was not sufficient to claim the benefit of the principle.[85] The argument appears to be that either proximity was not the interest actually pursued by the legislation or, alternatively, that the regional ban was not proximate enough to satisfy such a justification. It appears to be conceded that if proximity is relevant to justification for a restriction of trade it would be difficult to rule a measure unjustified simply because it is not sufficiently restrictive of trade.[86] A rule as to the appropriate geographic scope of a

---

[82] *De Peijper* 1976 ECR 613-640 para 31 see *infra* [Oliver].

[83] *(Walionia Waste) Commission* v *Belgium* 1993 Common Market Law Reports 365.

[84] For a comparable case in the United States where a waste import ban was ruled discriminatory see *Philadelphia* v *New Jersey* 437 US 617 1978.

[85] Citing perhaps the requirement that there should be equivalent treatment of domestic products having the same harmful effects *Rewe ZentralFinanz* v *Landwirtchaftkammer* 1975 843-863. The important point was proximity allowed discrimination on grounds of origin and not the environmentally deleterious character of the waste per se.

[86] It might be argued that a ban at city level would affect intra-Community trade less

Continued

waste transport ban might ultimately encourage greater environmental protection but imply a harmonisation of the size and authority of local and regional authorities dealing with waste and invalidate many imperfect measures along the way.

In the same judgment the Court ruled that national legislation might not be applied against provisions of a directive which provided an exhaustive regime for inter-state trade in hazardous waste. A breach *by the Community* of the proximity principle in this case was neither argued nor considered. As a result, and a matter of some criticism, the more hazardous waste remained subject to a more liberal trade regime.

Necessity and Proportionality: Relating the Restriction to the Interest

Two principles directed towards the relationship between the objective authorising a restriction and the means adopted to do so and a test comparing objectives are often rolled into one.[87] In fact proportionality encompasses at least three separate tests factors.[88]

- *Effectiveness:* that the measure is sufficient to achieve the stated objective (and in that sense is necessary to achieve it).[89]

- *Minimum Restrictiveness:* requires that the least restrictive effective option is adopted to achieve the stated objective.

- *Proportionality in the strict sense:* which balances not the means to the ends but two ends, where the means adopted to enforce one objective are considered against the seriousness of the infringement of an alternative objective of equal or other value.

It is apparent that measures must show a reasoned relationship to the interest pursued. Establishing this is a matter of some complexity. Both

---

...directly than one effected at state or regional borders and it is not clear whether a ban at national level say in Luxembourg could be supported by the principle expounded in the judgment.

[87] 122/78 *Buitoni* (1979) ECR 677 defines a proportionate measure as 'what is appropriate and necessary to attain the objective sought'.

[88] Schwarz, *European Administrative Law* (Sweet and Maxwell 1992).

[89] *Cassis de Dijon op cit* 'Obstacles to movement within the Community must be accepted insofar as those provisions may be recognised as necessary in order to satisfy mandatory requirements'.

an objective test, based on the actual effects of a supposed restriction, and a subjective test, which looks only to the interest pursued by the legislator, have their attractions.[90] However, the Court is extremely restricted in its capacity to examine factual evidence and relies for the most part on the formal reasoning for a particular measure supplied by the Community or the Member State.[91] The objective test is theoretically the more verifiable but requires the greatest factual input. The subjective test requires that the Court look into the 'mind' of the legislature but even where there is a duty to give reasons for a measure these may be disguised. The real motivation behind the subjective approach is the detection of some failure underlying the reasoning supplied. It is suggested that the terms arbitrary and disguised restriction ought to be interpreted in this light.

The difficulties encountered in establishing an objective standard of environmental protection recur in this context, as assessing the formal necessity of a particular action to achieve the interest requires some appraisal of the standard implied by the interest itself. As already commented upon an objective standard is difficult to come by. It is submitted that whether a particular standard is justified or not in the interests of environmental protection ultimately must be within the discretion of the legislator to determine. If it is inappropriate to substitute the judgment of the Court for that of the political authorities in one context it must be so in another.[92] If not, environmental protection is as capable of becoming a pre-emptive and directly effective norm as any other.

Nevertheless statements in *ADBHU* that the Community 'cannot go beyond the inevitable restrictions which are justified by the pursuit of an objective standard of protection'[93] seem to suggest that an objective standard is available. In more recent cases the Court has managed to avoid the problem directly and has given contradictory signals. The judgment in *Danish Bottles* seems to suggest that there is a reasonable standard of protection to which the Member States will be held. In the *Wallonia* case[94] the objective justification of a trade ban and its relative justification when compared with possible less restrictive measures was accepted by the Court without discussion.[95]

---

[90] *Commission v UK Poultry* 40/82 1982 E.C.R 2793 the real purpose was not to protect health but domestic production.

[91] Art. 190 requires that Community measures be reasoned.

[92] Kramer 'Environmental Protection and Article 30', 30 CMLR 111 1993 at 123 is of the opinion that Member States are free to choose the level of protection.

[93] Para 15 of judgment.

[94] *Re Imports of Waste EC Commission v Belgium* 1993 CMLR 365 Vol. 66(8) see Hancier & Sevenster (1993) 30 CMLRev 351.

[95] Such as a licensing system as applied in the case of hazardous waste.

Generally speaking, Community law recognises some discretion whereby Member States may choose to apply standards in pursuit of recognised interests. However as 'such standards cannot be determined unilaterally by the Member States'[96], this discretion is reviewable according to Community law. The level of discretion appears to vary according to the interest pursued.[97]

For example with regard to human health (an objective of environmental protection) Member States have a wide margin of discretion. In particular the health and the life of humans rank first among their property or interests protected by Article 36 and it is for the Member States within the limits imposed by the Treaty – to decide on the degree of protection they intend to pursue and in particular how strict the checks to be carried out are'[98] but even here the Court has suggested the discretion is limited according to objective factors by the requirement that measures may be adopted only in so far as necessary for the effective protection of health and life of humans'[99]

If the guarantee of free movement afforded by the Treaty is viewed as a presumption rather than an absolute standard of protection the problem can be approached as one relating to the onus and standard of proof necessary to rebut this presumption. It is clear in this sense that while the Community must raise evidence establishing the presumption, the onus of justifying trade restrictive measures lies with the Member States.[100]

It is clear that scientific evidence alone may not be sufficient to dis -charge the standard required. While a measure may be shown to be discriminatory if scientific evidence clearly establishes that there is no difference between products justifying discrimination on health grounds[101] establishing the positive and objective necessity of particular restrictions through scientific evidence can be extremely difficult in many cases.[102] Innumerable factors militate against complete reliance on scientific evidence for environmental protection. The development of

[96] 41/74 *Van Duyn* v *Home Office* [1974] ECR. 1337.
[97] *De Búrca supra, Sedemund* and 121/85 *Conegate* 1986 ECR 1007 and 34/79 *Henn and Darby* 1979 ECR 3795.
[98] Case 174/82 *Sandoz BV* 1983 ECR 2445 at para 19
[99] Sedemund p 31-32 and 104/75 *De Peijper* 1976 ECR 613: liberal interpretation of risk which was ruled genuine if claimed one life over 20 years
[100] The onus on the Member State to prove justification of necessity 227/8? *Van Bennekom* 1983 ECR 3883 para 40 It is for the national authorities to demonstrate in each case that the marketing of the product in question creates a serious risk to health'
[101] 124/81 *Commission* v *UK* 1983 ECR 205 Retreatment of UHT milk was not justified as the technical data showed retreatment made no difference to the milk.
[102] Sedemund 'Statement on the Concept of Free Movement of Goods and the respect for National Action under Article 36 of *the* EEC Treaty' in Schwarze *Discretionary Powers of the Member States in the Field of Economic Policies* (Baden-Baden 1988)

new processes and substances far outpaces adequate testing, even where testing the results cannot be reliably extrapolated to conditions in the field etc. The precautionary principle designed to meet these limitations seems to demand at least a certain discretion for Member States where a scientific assessment of effects and risks result in uncertainty. In consequence the application of precaution to the necessity test would provide that uncertainty is in itself a justification for action in restraint of trade.

Several cases in the area of product standards appear to confirm this approach – a recognition of uncertainty as a factor in establishing the Member State discretion to apply trade restrictive measures Indeed the application of proportionality to test measures adopted on this justication risks becoming meaningless.[103] Nevertheless other cases imply that states must at least take steps to establish the uncertainty upon which they rely before a precautionary approach may be relied upon.[104] The adoption of a duty on individuals to establish that there are no harmful effects prior to release of a new substance into the environment is therefore precluded.[105]

The concept of technical need for a particular additive in a foodstuff may reduce still further the importing state s discretion.[106] In *German Beer* Advocate General Slynn adopted a broad interpretation of this concept.[107] The test in *German Beer* points to a case-by-case assessment of particular substances to establish the legality of a ban or restriction in use. Sedemund points out that contrary to a common understanding of precaution the solution adopted in a case-by-case assessment of risk

[103] See generally Sedemund but particularly Case 53/80 *Kaasfabriek Eyssen* 1981 ECR 409 paras 13 and 14 and *Heijn* 1984 ECR 3280. 97/83 *Melkunte* 1984 ECR 2367 at 2385
[104] 178/84 *Van Bennekom* 1988 para 35 CMLR 1 *Muller* 1980 ECR 1511 *German Beer* 1987 ECR 1227 'it is for the national authorities to demonstrate in each case that the marketing of the product in question creates a serious risk to public health'.
[105] Case 174/82 *Sandoz BV1983* ECR 2445 'in so far as there are uncertainties at the present state of scientific research it is for the Member States in the absence of harmonisation to decide what degree of protection of the health and life of humans they intend to assure having regard however to the requirements of the free movement of goods within the Community and their limits under the EEC Treaty: here a requirement that manufacturers supply proof that a partial lar additive was safe was found unlawful (para 24) but in Case 251/78 *Denkavit Futtermittell* 1979 ECR 3369 the Court failed to decide whether a blanket assumption that additives were harmful unless the contrary was proved amounted to a unjustified restriction on trade.
[106] *Sandoz supra* at para 19.
[107] *Commission* v *Germany* (Beer) 1987 ECR 1227 The case involved additives in beer, where the chemical was authorised in another state for use in imported products, the importing state must authorise the chemical in question: (1) provided international scientific data shows it to be harmless to individuals with dietary habits of its population, or otherwise, if it meets a genuine technical need and there is a procedure for authorisation, the state has taken steps to establish whether it is harmful and action is available for refusal of audionsation. Technical need is to be determined with reference to the imported.

still ignores the possible cumulative effects of chemicals and disallows a policy based on reducing an overall risk to the public by a limitation on the amount of chemicals in the food supply.[108]

Given the reality of these factors a full integration of the precautionary principle suggests less reliance on a scientific assessment of risk to justify restrictive measures in the absence of evidence establishing that no harm may result not only from the substance in question but a clearer recognition that the presence or absence of a scientific assessments of risk cannot on its own be relied upon to establish the legality or otherwise of Member State action.[109] The development of a comprehensive framework through which the law may deal with scientific uncertainty and avoid an over-reliance on mechanistic quantitative assessments of risks remains a matter of some controversy world-wide.

Acting in the Community Interest and Finding an Appropriate Legal Basis[110]

In contrast with the GATT system the pre-emptive provisions of the Treaty concerning the customs union and the internal market are supplemented by provisions creating an interest in measures which supplement and support the basic scheme. The Community is expressly provided with the power to adopt measures for the establishment and functioning of the Market and the regulation of international trade. The interaction between trade provisions and environmental principles is therefore not limited merely to that of pre-emptive norms and public interest (at whatever level) described above.

The definition of the Community task detailed in Article 2 of the Treaty is supplemented by particular provisions which confirm the Community's powers to adopt measures which will ultimately contribute to its

---

[108] At p 30

[109] In the context of Art. 100a(4) and the Courts approval of national standards under that provision. The recent *Pentachlorophenol* Case 41/93 *French Republic v Commission of the European Communities*. 1994 ECR 1829 appears to confirm the requirement that measures must be legally if not scientifically justified or reasoned. As the reasons given by *the* Commission for confirmation in this case were ruled insufficient the judgment does not in itself rule out a precautionary-approach

[110] Bradley 'The European Court and the Legal Basis of Community Legislation' Vol. 13 (1988) *Common Market Law Review* p379. Barents 'The Internal Market and some Observations on the Legal Basis of Community Legislation' (1993) 30 *Common Market Law Review* 85; Geradin 'Trade and Environment: The Community Framework and National Environmental Standards' 1993 YEL 151; Lenearts 'Some Reflections on the Seperation of Powers in the European Community' 28 *Common Market Law Review* 1991; Emiliou 'Opening Pandora's Box: The Legal Basis of Community Measures before the Court of Justice' (1994) 19 ELR 488.

attainment.[111] The interpretative value of Article 2 may modify or reinforce these provisions in the ultimate attempt to ensure a holistic interpretation of the whole Treaty, but the difficulty in reconciling individual policies suggests that the final balance of measures adopted in fulfilment of Article 2 remain political choices open to the Community institutions to investigate.[112] Nonetheless the Court maintains a policing role even in the balance of legislative choice through its insistence that an express choice of legal basis is necessary and that this choice must be exercised according to objective factors amenable to judicial review.

The diversification of legal bases for Community action with the adoption of the Single European Act and reinforced at Maastricht has presented the Court with a clear choice between legislative models and little guidance on the factors relevant to their respective application (see table on page 645). Initially at least the Court has hesitated in response to the increased complexity of the system and encountered considerable difficulty in the identification and application of objective factors for the review of the selection of particular bases. Caselaw suggests that the addition of new legal bases to the Treaty have initiated a process of adaptation by the Court.

As already mentioned, in addition to the interposition of additional legal bases, the Community's task has recently been recast by Maastricht to reflect a more equal balancing of economic and environmental considerations.[113] The approach taken is closely mirrored in the preamble to the agreement establishing the World Trade Organization.[114] The Treaty is therefore ambiguous as to the model whereby a sustainable balance of interests may be achieved. It recognises both a system of separate bases dedicated to ostensibly distinct interests and the necessity of integration through the obligation to integrate environmental protection requirements into all policies. The following sections are intended to show both the inherent complexity of operating a series of distinct bases and the particular difficulties arising from the interposition of an obligation to integrate on an already difficult system.

---

[111] In addition (III) Art. 43 (Agriculture), and (IV) 76 (Transport) may be mentioned as regulatory bases designed to promote integration in particular sectors (V) Art. 130s in common with (VI) Art. 118 and others are bases which are dedicated towards social, political or perhaps ethical interests and do not directly promote integration.

[112] See Art. 3 listing the Community policies 'for the purposes set out in Article 2 the Community's activities shall include . . .'.

[113] Art. 2 *supra*.

[114] Preamble to WTO Agreement see *supra*.

Procedural and Substantive Consequences of the Choice of Legal Basis

The question of choice of legal basis for Community measures is fundamental for two basic reasons concerned with preserving the legitimacy and coherence of Community action, each elements of the rule of law.

Firstly, the requirement of legitimacy and rationality, derived from Article 3b[115] and Article 190[116] of the Treaty, relies on establishing the appropriate Treaty basis which both delimits Community competence (at least theoretically) and determines the division of powers through the procedures according to which measures designed for particular ends may be adopted – unanimously or by qualified majority vote, with parliamentary consultation, co-operation[117] or co-decision.[118] The exercise of a choice between bases is therefore politically charged and constitutionally important, and the courts review the principle method of policing the Communities division of powers.

Secondly, the choice of legal basis has substantive consequences with relation to the nature of the legal order thereby created and affects the coherence of Community law. There are several modes of policy: according to one framework there are those which are exclusive and unitary *per se*, such force being derived from the Treaty itself[119], and those which are concurrent allowing Member State action, in accordance with the doctrine of pre-emption, only in so far as Community measures have not yet been adopted.[120] Recent amendments to the Treaty system have added another suggesting that the old assumption that many areas of concurrent policy would ultimately become exclusive by reason of legislative preemption has been abandoned.

Firstly, several of the newer areas of policy expressly preserve the ability of Member States to adopt more stringent measures, a factor which the Court has ruled has a fundamental effect on the pre-emptive effect of measures adopted by the Community within the context of these policies.[121] Secondly, Article 3b provides that in non-exclusive areas the principle of subsidiarity applies, which would tend to entrench

---

[115] 'The Community shall act within the limits of the powers conferred upon it by this treaty and of the objectives assigned to it therein'.

[116] '[Measures] adopted . . . shall state the reasons on which they are based . . .'.

[117] A procedure detailed in Art. 189c.

[118] Detailed in Art. 189b

[119] *e.g.* the common commercial policy or aspects of manne fisheries conservation.

[120] Such as the Environment Policy.

[121] Opinion 2/91 ILO No 170[1993] Common Market Law Reports 800.

the concurrent nature of policies deemed not exclusive (though what exclusive means in this sense has yet to be interpreted).

Balancing Pre-Emptive Norms Interests and the Trade Environment Relationship

In the ebb and flow of interpretative relationships between various elements of the Treaty system three principle tensions may be described.

Pre-emptive norm and interest

Firstly, a tension between 'negative harmonisation', through the disapplication of national rules, and positive harmonisation, through the adoption of Community measures, rests in the relative interpretation of Article 30, and the pre-emptive norm of free trade it contains, and, the Community power to establish the market through legislation detailed in Article 100 and 100a.[122] There is a direct relationship between the extent to which national measures are rendered inapplicable by Article 30 and saved by Article 36 or mandatory requirements and the extent to which measures may be adopted which have as their object the establishment of the internal market. Article 100-100c must be necessary only to the extent that the measures it is proposed to harmonise are not already invalidated automatically. Thus the legislative space for the Community and the Member States in environmental matters is as has been described in the first section limited by the extent of Article 30 and recognised interests justifying departure from this rule.[123]

Exclusive and concurrent policies

Secondly, there is a tension between two models of harmonisation within the Community system. The first is a system of progressive adaptation of national rules to conditions of absolute uniformity necessary to ensure non-discrimination and competitive equality between states in a single market upon which the trade policy is based. The second is a system of minimum standards with a concurrent freedom on the part of Member States to adopt more stringent standards with regard to a particular interest where diverse situations are recognised to require a diversity of solutions.

---

[122] Vide the extension implied by *Cassis de Dijon supra*.

[123] Remembering always that Art. 30 is pre-eminent but still only one of the Market rules which might invalidate state or individual action with an environmental motivation. See particularly Reto Jacobs 'EC Competition Policy and the Protection of the Environment' 1993 Legal Issues of European Integration 1993 37.

Regulatory and Deregulatory Interests

The third tension lies in implicit regulatory and deregulatory elements of the Treaty system: Harmonisation of Law on whatever basis necessarily includes both deregulatory and regulatory elements. Nonetheless the Court has attempted to draw a distinction between harmonisation pursuing the establishment and functioning of the market which is deregulatory, and harmonisation directed at environmental protection which is necessarily regulatory or restrictive of trade.[124] Whether this can be properly justified given that the trade basis (100a) expressly recognised that harmonisation may have regulatory effects, and more generally it is submitted that even liberalising measures leave intact a degree of market restriction justified in terms of some public interest.

These modes of legal order attributed to the interests represented in the several Community policies reflect not only the division of powers between the Community institutions and between the Community and the Member States, but also fundamental conceptions as to the nature of the policies themselves which repeat and reflect the interaction of the trade norm and the environmental interest discussed above. Of course each individual policy is subject to general requirements as to necessity and proportionality as well as the operation of general principles of law recognised by the Community as embodying fundamental rights, but in addition, the interaction and formal integration of principles governing these policies also present possible limitations on their scope and effect. The Court of Justice in refining its approach to Article 30 and establishing a caselaw on the choice of legal basis has fluctuated in its approach to all of these relationships.[125]

The Legal Bases Available

The key legal bases relevant to environmental policy can, in summary, be seen to fall into three groups:

The Trade Bases

These are divided into two bases of general application dedicated to external and internal trade respectively and several internal bases covering sectoral markets.

---

[124] Case 155/91 *Commission v Council* [Waste Framework Directive Case] 1991 ECR 2867.
[125] Han Somsen on C155/91 1993 *Common Market Law Review* 121 and 29 (1992) p 140-151, *Titanium Dioxide Commission v Council 1* 991 ECR 2867. Barents, 'The Internal Market Unlimited: Some Observations on the Legal Basis of Community Legislation' 20 *Common Market Law Review* 85 (see p 92) problems of delimitation.

- Article 113: the Common Commercial Policy dedicated to measures regulating the Community's external trade. Member States are precluded from adopting such measures unilateraterally (it is formally exclusive) and must rely on the Community to adopt measures falling within the scope of this policy. The Community may adopt these by qualified majority voting in the Council and there is only limited parliamentary involvement.

- Article 100-100c: in effect several bases dedicated to the establishment and continued functioning of the common or internal market. The Community may adopt harmonisation measures affecting the market by co-decision of parliament and the council (the later acting by qualified majority voting)

Already the system provides scope for difficulty in determining the basis applicable to measures which affect external and internal trade simultaneously.

Sectoral Markets

The market is recognised to have several components, some of which serve certain social or economic ends requiring a separate definition and set of objectives principles. Among these are Agriculture (Article 43), Transport (Article 78) and Taxation (Article 99). These sectoral bases are recognised to be *lex specialis* to Article 100-100c, incorporating measures which though dedicated to establishing a functioning market, affect or are directed at objectives prescribed in these policies. Here again there is potential ground for dispute as each basis is subject to a different procedural regime.[126]

General Non-Market Bases

Including Harmonisation of Social Policy (Article 118) and Fiscal Measures (Article 99).

The Environmental Basis

Article 130r provides an alternative focus for regulation and formally encompasses measures directed at four objectives. The distinction between the basis and some but not all of the market-oriented bases is

---

[126] Community rules on competition, state aids and free movement of services, capital and persons should not be forgotten, each of which prescribe a particular freedom or substantive rule and recognise the possibility of derogation to various extents.

that measures adopted under the policy are formally, as a requirement of the Treaty, minimum stringency measures and cannot pre-empt more stringent measures consistent with the Treaty. The policy is also subject to a subsidiarity requirement (indeed between the SEA and Maastricht it was the only policy subject to this requirement). Environmental policy specifies no less than four possible procedures for the adoption of measures. Unanimity is preserved for some ill-defined policy areas, though the Council may agree to ordinary qualified majority voting for these, co-decision is prescribed for the adoption of action programmes, co-operation for all other measures.

Finding Objective Factors for Review

The central difficulty with a system of functionally defined legal bases that are procedurally distinct is that many measures formally dedicated to one function in fact effect several. The statement that the choice of legal basis must be made according to objective factors amenable to judicial review[127], while an essential element of the rule of law, results in considerable difficulty given the way in which the scope of individual bases is defined. An approach based on ascertaining legislative intention or determining the primary objective according to the content or effects of particular provisions will only rarely provide objective factors upon which the choice of legal basis can be exercised or reviewed. A centre of gravity or primary purpose test has been applied under the fiction that in most cases a most important objective may be identified. Even if this were true, this rule remains open to legislative manipulation as legislation might be drafted not according to the needs of different situations but according to which mix of provisions might reasonably be adopted pursuant to a favourable legal basis. As a result, the Commission, the Council, the Member States, and latterly the Parliament have been provided with ample room for argument before the Court. The Court's search for a definition has resulted in controversy and uncertainty. Arguably the Court has not yet managed to define these factors with sufficient certainty, leading in particular to a rather confused division between the different environmental and unitary trade modes of regulation.

The Effect of the Integration Principle

Attempts by the Treaty draftsmen to rationalise the system have perhaps ultimately served only to muddy the waters. The integration principle[128], the legal effects of which have yet to be examined by the

---

[127] *Re Generalised Tariff Preferences EC Commission v Council* 1987 ECR 1483.

[128] Art. 130r(2) states that environmental protection requirements must be integrated into the definition and implementation of other policies.

Court, at once promotes environment protection and yet has undermined at least initially the separate legal basis for environment of which it forms a part.[129] The general requirement that environmental protection requirements be integrated into the definition and implementation of other policies has allowed other bases to be used for this purpose. Article 100a (the basis for internal market harmonisation) expressly refers to environmental objectives and preserves the ability of Member States to maintain more stringent measures even after harmonisation.[130] On the other hand the environment policy is not entirely removed from taking economic factors into account. General integration can work both ways, as Article 130r(3) suggests[131] and the broad freedom granted to Member States to adopt more stringent measures under Article 130 t is more specifically limited by the words 'not incompatible with this Treaty', generally accepted to refer to trade requirements.

The Meandering Balance of Interpretations

Three distinct phases or approaches can be discerned in the Court's approach to striking the balance between legal bases, each of which displays not only the difficulties arising from an attempt to impose rational grounds for review on a system of functional bases but a degree of political activism on the part of the Court in the Community's interest.

An Expansive Interpretation of Trade Objectives

There are two factors driving an inclusive interpretation of the legal basis governing trade. Firstly the Court has always been reluctant to find particular measures ultra vires the Community and has consequently adopted a broad interpretation of Community powers generally. Secondly, the imperative to preserve a unity of conditions in the market and particularly external trade relations has supported an expansive interpretation of the scope of the trade bases in particular, the consequences of which have been to preclude unilateral action by the Member States externally.

---

[129] *Titanium Dioxide Commission v Council* 1991 E.C.R. 2867 *infra*.

[130] Art. 100a(4) and Case 41/93 *French Republic v Commission* 17 May 1994 Commission decision confirming provisions annulled. See Hans Somsen 'Applying More National Environmental Laws after Harmonisation' *European Environmental Law Review* Aug./Sept. 1994 238.

[131] In preparing its policy on the environment, the Community shall take account of; ' - environmental conditions in the various regions of the Community; - the economic and social development of the Community as a whole and the balanced development of its regions'.

Article 113 and the Inclusive Interpretation[132]

There are several statements by the Court that the legal basis for international commercial policy incorporates the power to adopt measures regulating international trade in other interests.[133] The definition of the common commercial policy established to regulate external trade expressly includes the qualification that it should be 'harmoniously achieved'. One might ask harmonious with what? Though the phrase may be adequately explained in terms of preserving some internal harmony in the move towards a liberalisation of external trade, the fact that the conditions of trade are to be regulated expressly recognises that the external trade policy at least has a regulatory as well as a deregulatory focus.[134]

In any event the Court of Justice has ruled that while pursuing the objectives of external trade the Community might also pursue objectives not simply promoting the deregulation of world trade. The *International Rubber* opinion confirmed that the establishment of a regulatory system for commodities trading under UNCTAD fell within the Community's Common Commercial Policy even though the instruments adopted did not form part of the traditional armoury of trade instruments.[135] In effect the instrumental theory of legal basis was displaced in favour of a teleological theory of legal basis.[136]

In the Generalised Tariff Preferences (Preferential Treatment itself is not GATT compatible but nonetheless agreed to by the parties) the Court confirmed that development objectives might indeed fall

---

[132] See generally Bourgeois 'The EC in the WTO and Advisory Opinion 1 /94: An Echternach Procession' 1994 *Common Market Law Review* 736.

[133] Demeret in Maresceu (ed) *The European Community's Commercial Policy After 1992: The Legal Dimension* 313-319 p355 and the instrumental character of Art. 113.

[134] Article 110: By establishing a customs union between themselves. Member States aim to contribute, in the common interest, to the harmonious development of world trade, the progressive abolition of restrictions on international trade and the lowering of customs barriers.

[135] Opinion 1/78 *International Rubber*: [45] Art. 113 empowers the Community to formulate a commercial policy based on uniform principles, thus showing that the question of external trade must be governed from a wide point of view and not only having regard to the administration of precise systems such as customs and quantitative restrictions. The same conclusion may be deduced from the fact that the enumeration in Art. 113 of the subjects covered by commercial policy . . . is conceived as a non-exhaustive enumeration which must not, as such, close the door to the application in the Community context of any other process intended to regulate external trade. And at p 2917 a measure . . . 'Must be assessed having regard to its essential objective rather than in terms of individual clauses of an altogether subsidiary or ancillary nature'.

[136] See Advocate General Lenz (1987 ECR 1493) para 57 and 58 objective and subjective tests: is it a measure which aims to influence and at the same time alter the form of world trade? Is trade objectively influenced?

within the CCP. In this case the Council argued that the aims of the measure were developmental and as such went beyond the aims of the Commercial Policy.[137] The Court, expressly noting that the Community's aims included the harmonious development of world trade[138] and developments in international law[139], suggested that such objectives must be incorporated into trade objectives. If this were not the case the CCP would become nugatory over time as trade instruments developed.[140] It must be noted that development co-operation has since achieved an independent status with the adoption of further provisions in 1992 at Maastricht.[141]

Even after the adoption of a separate environmental basis including the competence to conclude international agreements the Court continued the trend by confirming that measures touching on aspects of environment protection may also be adopted on the basis of Article 113.[142] In the *Chernobyl* case[143] the Greek government (in a minority on a vote to adopt restrictions on the import of certain agricultural products) challenged the ability of the Community to adopt such a measure on the basis of Article 113. As the matter concerned the protection of public heath (an objective of the environment policy) the Greek government argued that such a measure should have been on the basis of 130s (which incidentally required a unanimous decision). Nonetheless the Court found the measure rightly adopted on the basis that (1) the measure was intended to regulate trade between the EC and not member countries (2) the regulation established uniform import rules (3) Article 130r(2) established that environment protection might be part of other policies; (4) and Article 130r-t left intact existing powers to adopt under other bases including this one.

---

[137] Generalised Tariff Preferences 45/86 *Commission v Council* [1987] 'reflects a new concept of international trade relations in which development aims to play a major role' [18].
[138] Para 17.
[139] Para 17. The link between trade and development has become progressively stronger in modern international relations. It has been recognised in the context of the United Nations. notably by UNCTAD and in the context of GATT in particular through the incorporation in the GATT of PArt. IV entitled trade and development.
[140] Para 20.
[141] Art. 130u. The Community policy in the sphere of development co-operation which shall be complementary to the policies pursued by the Member States, shall foster the sustainable economic and social development of developing countries, and more particularly the most disadvantaged of them; the smooth and gradual integration of developing countries into the world economy; the Community and the Member States shall comply with the Commitments and take account of the objectives they have approved in the context of the United Nations and other competent international organisations. Art. 130v The Community shall take into account the objectives referred to in 130u in the policies that it implements which are likely to affect developing countries.
[142] 62/88 *Chernobyl* case 1990 ECR I 3743.
[143] n 141 above

In the environmental sphere there has been a marked reluctance to accept that environmentally related trade measures fall within the Common Commercial Policy. Member States have feared recognition that essential elements of an environmental policy should fall within the ambit of an exclusive policy precluding Member State action. Equally trade policy specialists within the Commission have feared that in recognising an exception the unity of the trade policy has been undermined. Though there have been no cases expressly covering the point, all international environmental agreements have been adopted on a basis other than Article 113.[144]

In addition the Community has adopted unilateral trade restrictions despite concerns as to the legality of some provisions under GATT. Trade measures unilaterally adopted by the Community include; measures to protect whale and cetacean products[145], seal pups[146], animals trapped by inhumane methods.[147] In each case there was some argument over the appropriate legal basis and in each, save the last, it was concluded that Article 113 was inappropriate. The Whales and Cetacean Products Directive was proposed using 113 as a basis, but German and Danish arguments that the restrictions were moral rather than environmental prevailed[148]. The Directive was adopted under Article 235 in the days before Article 130s.[149] Britain had pressed for the introduction of the ban partly on the ground of the uncertain legality of its earlier unilateral ban. The Seals Directive was also proposed using Article 113 as a basis but eventually was adopted on the basis of Article 235. The Leghold Trap Directive is the latest in this series of measures and was again proposed on the basis of 113 but interestingly was finally adopted on a dual legal basis thus preserving a non-exclusive element.[150]

---

[144] International Agreements with a trade character adopted under Art. 130s: - 88/540 OJ 1297 31.10.88 Vienna Convention for the Protection of the Ozone Laver and the Montreal Protocol Adopted under Art. 130s - 81/69 OJ 1252 5.9.81 Washington Convention on International Trade in Endangered Species (note the preamble) Art. 235 - 82/461 EEC OJ L210 18.7.82 Convention on the Conservation of Migratory Species of Wild animals: with Art.235 as a basis. - 93/98/EEC OJ L39 16.12.93 Basle Convention on Transboundary Movements of Waste, with Art. 130s as a basis - only one has been adopted on the basis of Art. 113 - International Tropical Timber Agreement L313 22.11.85 p9 85 424 OJ L236 3.9.85 p8.

[145] 348/81 OJ L39 12.2.81 Council regulations on common rules for imports of whales or other cetacean products, and, 3786/81 OJ 137731.12.81 Commission regulation laying down provisions for the implementation of common rules. These rules were subsumed in CITES Regulation 3626/82.

[146] Directives 83/129. 85/444, 89/370 Directives concerning the importation into Member States of Skins of certain seal pups and products derived therefrom.

[147] Leghold Traps 3254/91 OJ 1308. 9.11.91 adopted on a dual basis Art. 113 and 130s.

[148] See Haigh *Manual of European Environmental Policy* (Longman/IEEP. 1992) Looseleaf Service at p 9.3-3.

[149] See Haigh 9.4-3.

[150] 3254/91 OJ L. 308 9/11/91 p 1.

Article 100 and 100a - An Inclusive Interpretation of the Market

Internally, in the absence of an express power to regulate for environmental protection, those provisions designed to authorise harmonisation regulations affecting trade in the Member States became the subject of an expansive interpretation so as to include the power to regulate trade in pursuit of a rather broader range of objectives. In a sense the shift in emphasis (or more properly definition) was inevitable as the process of replacing national measures with Community harmonisation measures inevitably involved the implicit adoption by the Community through its harmonisation measures of the policy underlying the national regulations it sought to replace. Arguably it was legally justifiable in the treaty's requirement that the essentially economic objectives of the Treaty be harmoniously achieved.[151]

Of particular relevance to the current discussion, in the absence of an express basis for environmental measures, such measures were adopted under Article 100 and under Article 235. Arguably certain environmental measures 'directly affect the establishment or functioning of the common market' therefore satisfying the objectives prescribed in the former, and in so far as this was not so they were 'measures necessary to attain one of the objectives' where a power did not already exist. This latter proposition is based on a development of language in Article 2 defining the core task of the Community to include the promotion of a 'harmonious development of economic activities' and to achieve 'a better standard of living'.

In a sense the recognition of the environmental interest as one of the elements required in such a harmonious development was also reflected in the recognition of additional mandatory requirements authorising trade restrictive measures following a broader interpretation of Article 30. The objective of the general interest authorising a modification to the operation of Article 30 in ABHU both legitimised Community environmental policy and led inevitably to recognition of the interest at national level through a mandatory requirement.

Again by analogy with external trade, even after the adoption of an express basis for environmental regulation, the Court took the view that environmental measures adopted at least partially with the aim of harmonising competitive distinctions in the Member States, ought in

---

[151] Art. 2 before Maastricht amendments 'the harmonious development of economic activities throughout the Community, a continuous and balanced expansion, an increase in stability, an accelerated raising of the standard of living, and closer relations between the states belonging to the Community'.

preference to be adopted under Article 100a.[152] In *Titanium Dioxide*[153] the Commission argued that the Directive concerned was more properly adopted under Article 130s than under 100a. The Court, while it agreed that the Directive pursued two interests simultaneously decided that where two relevant bases were available, though a measure ordinarily should be adopted pursuant to all relevant bases[154], where the procedures were different and mutually incompatible, one basis had to be chosen. The Court settled on Article 100a and the co-operation procedure, as to adopt the measure under 130s alone would undermine the very substance of the guarantees afforded to Parliament in Article 100a under 100a. The Court took express comfort in the integration requirement which recognised that measures with an environmental component might be adopted pursuant to other bases.[155] The decision was much criticised as it appears to undermine the operation of 130s.

Recognising the place of a separate basis

Nonetheless in *151/91 Commission v Council*[156] the Waste Framework Directive was confirmed to fall under Article 130s rather than 100a and the internal market. The Court based its finding on the reasoning that the Directive restricted rather than promoted free movement and while it affected the operation of the market, these effects were ancillary to the main objective.

In common with the recent tendency to recognise that trade restrictive measures may be adopted under Article 130s where environmental protection is the primary purpose of the measure it appears to be accepted that 130s is also the basis for external environmentally motivated trade restrictions In *European Parliament v Council.*[157] While Parliament's right to challenge a waste regulation was denied on procedural grounds the Court confirmed the regulatory/facilitatory approach.

The place of the sectoral markets and the relationship between internal and external regulation

The recognition of particular interests or objectives pertaining to particular sectoral markets has also raised questions as to legal basis.

---

[152] A burden on undertakings justifies harmonisation of national provisions - *Re Detergents: EC Commission v Italy* 9 79 1980 E.C.R 1089. *Re Fuel Directive: EC Commission v Italy* 92 79 1980 ECR 1115

[153] *Commission* v *Council* (Titanium Dioxide) 1993 CMLR 359 Vol. 68.

[154] Paras [17]-[18].

[155] At para 22.

[156] 155/91 *Commission v Council* (Waste Framework) [1993] ECR 939. noted Nicolas de Sadeleer in *Journal of Environmental Law* 1992.

[157] Case 187/93 *E.P, v Council* Regulation of Waste Shipments 1994 ECR 2857.

The scope of operation of these policies has been determined on the basis that they form exceptions to the generality of the trade provisions. In the *Hormones* Case[158] a prohibition on growth promoters for fattening purposes was ruled to fall within Article 43, which could be interpreted to include aspects of the public interest as *lex specialis* to Article 100.[159] If a measure contributes to the objectives of Article 43 then this basis is sufficient.

As a result, so an argument goes, not only do these bases form a derogation to Article 100-100c (the general provisions) but also to Article 113. This is controversial not least because an assumption had arisen that the Common Commercial Policy represented the external face of all the community's economic competences at least. The ERTA confirmed that implied external competence was available with respect to all internal competences where this was necessary to fulfil the objectives of individual policies. In the *Veterinary Inspection* Case[160] the question whether Article 43, Article 100 or Article 113 was the appropriate basis was resolved in favour of Article 43.[161] It appears that Article 43 can be used for external trade rules as well as harmonisation of production and marketing agricultural products. In essence these measures served a dual purpose both the removal of distortions and public health.[162]

Trade-related environmental measures and the Uruguay Round opinion

Demeret has argued that in consequence of *Chernobyl* and the *Titanium Dioxide* judgments. Trade Related Environmental Measures (TREMS) ought to be adopted on the basis of 113.[163] On the other hand Volker[164] suggests that *Chernobyl was* a special case. Here the fact that there are two bases for the adoption of trade measures – one dealing with the internal the other with its external face – created a particular problem. He argues that in *Chernobyl* internal measures had been adopted under Article 31 of the Euratom Treaty which had no external equivalent requiring that Article 113 be chosen as a basis. Otherwise where measures govern internal and external trade simultaneously these are not matters falling

---

[158] 68/86 *United Kingdom v Council* 1988 ECR p 855 and see Rene Barents 'Some Reflections on the Hormones Judgement' 1988 Legal Issues of European Integration 1-19.
[159] P855.896 of Völker *infra* n 164.
[160] 131 /87 *Untied Kingdom v Quinal Health and Veterinary Inspections* 1989 ECR 3743.
[161] Sec- also 11/88 *Commission v Council* 1989 ECR 3799.
[162] Sec paras 26, 27 and 28 of the judgment.
[163] Demeret in Maresceu (ed) *The European Community's Commercial Policy After 1992: The Legal Dimension* 315-319 at 356-357. Nevertheless he does recognise that the direct regulation of trade was not an element of *Titanium Dioxide* which reduces its significance for the trade policy.
[164] Volker *Barriers to External and Internal Community Trade* (Europa Institute 1993) at 187-189.

within the ambit of Article 113 but fall to be adopted according to the internal basis.

However the recent Opinion 1/94 concerning the Uruguay Round of GATT seems to contradict even this. Here the EEC Court rejected Article 43 as the appropriate bass for provisions on phytosanitary measures. It ruled that such measures should be adopted under Article 113 on the grounds that in the case of this particular agreement the objectives it fulfilled were not of the Community's agriculture policy but that of the trade policy, namely a liberalisation in trade in Agricultural products.

Despite this the general approach of adopting an inclusive interpretation to Article 113 suffers a general reverse, if not in principle then in practice.[165] Given the concentration on a teleological rather than an instrumental method of ascertaining the legal basis the classic problem looks set to continue. The practise of adopting trade measures with an environmental object pursuant to an environmental basis seems to remain legitimate, as does the adoption of measures intended to liberalise trade which have environmental consequences on the basis of Article 113. While the integration requirement formally requires that environmental protection requirements be incorporated into Article 113 as much as any other basis, the practical effect of the requirement to date must be doubted.

Conclusion

The growing jurisprudence of the Court of Justice concerning the choice of legal basis for environmentally related instruments can hardly be said to have brought clarity to the analysis, and, as we have argued, is unlikely to do so in that it is rooted in a classical functional model of separate policies in competition which fails to reflect current and future environmental reality. The concept of sustainable development, if it is to move beyond a mere political commitment, implies in the longer term a far more fundamental integration of an environmental perspective into economic and resource policies than has hitherto been proposed or imagined. We question whether the current constitutional and legal structure of the Treaty adequately reflects these challenges.

It might be argued – and no doubt will be at the forthcoming Inter-Governmental Conference – that if the procedures for adopting Community legislation were harmonised, the political arguments concerning the correct legal basis of instruments would be largely removed. Yet. as we have tried to demonstrate, this in itself will not

---

[165] *e.g.* paras 40 and 41 concerning GATS and para 54 et seq. On TRIPs and generally Bourgeois *op at supra.*

provide the answer. There remain substantive distinctions between exclusive and non-exclusive policies, which reflect differing principles and hierarchies of norms, and which will continue to give rise to tension. Nor does the mere expression of an overall goal of sustainable development (as, post Maastricht already appears in the Treaty, albeit in rather garbled form) or the legal requirement to integrate environmental dimensions into other policy areas (as appears in Article 130R) satisfactorily deal with the problem, but glosses over underlying and more insidious distinctions in philosophy.

We have shown how certain aspects of trade-related principles within the Treaty, and especially Article 30, have been given pre-emptive legal status. One way forward would be to attribute to environmental protection requirements an enhanced status quite independent of specific Community environmental legislation and based on the development of principles of environmental protection and sustainable development.

Ultimately, these principles would provide a basis for the legal review of Community action, but also support the legal justification of national measures where these fall within the scope of Article 30. This process is not perhaps as controversial as might first appear, and can be said to have already begun in the recognition of the proximity and precautionary principles in recent caselaw on trade-restrictive measures.

This sort of development, however, still implies tensions and balancing acts. A more fundamental restructuring would recognise that the 'rational and prudent use of natural resources', one of the principles of Community environmental policy and inherent in the concept of sustainable development, is also or should be one of the aims of the market system which an economist would support. If such a principle were fully locked into the goals of the market one could envisage a situation where, say, both Community and national restrictions or measures which interfere with the attainment by the market of these objectives, could be legally challenged, both by individuals and governments. The true power of the Community legal structure would then be harnessed towards sustainable development. Such a vision may be too much to stomach for many involved in the process of Treaty development and change. Yet the fundamental philosophical differences between those promoting free trade and those promoting political union (who at the 1992 Intergovernmental Conference operated as separate committees) cannot be disguised by the fact that their handiwork appears in a single document. The compromise between the philosophy of market freedom and that of sustainable development fails to disguise a fault line in the Community structure between the centralist and the federalist, free marketeers and environmentalists, exclusive and non-exclusive competences, absolute and minimum standards, majority and unanimous decision making. Ultimately, tinkering at the edges may produce only confusion and a misplaced reassurance.

Some legal Bases relevant to the Environment

Co-decision	Article 130r(3) ENVIRONMENT	General Action Programmes setting out priority objectives to be attained
	Article 100a Approximation of Laws (by way of derogation from Article 100)	Harmonisation with the aim of establishing functioning of the internal market
Co-operation	Article 130s(l) ENVIRONMENT as a contribution to preserving, protecting and improving the quality of the environment; protecting human health: the prudent and rational utilisation of natural resources and promoting measures at an international level to deal with worldwide environmental problems	Action to achieve the objectives referred to in Article 130r
	Article 75 TRANSPORT the objectives of the Treaty in matters governed by the transport title	Common rules on international transport across the territory of one or more Member States etc
Qualified Majority Voting	Article 130r(2) ENVIRONMENT	
	Article 113 COMMON COMMERCIAL POLICY to contribute in the common interest to the harmonious development of world	Measures to implement the Common Commercial Policy

	trade, the progressive abolition of restrictions on international trade and the lowering of customs barriers	
	Article 43 AGRICULTURAL increased agricultural productivity, a fair standard of living for the agricultural community, the stabilisation of markets, the availability of suppliers and that supplies reach consumers at reasonable prices	Measures for the Common Organisation of the market in Agriculture
Unanimous Voting	Article 130s(2) ENVIRONMENT	- provisions primarily of a fiscal nature - measures concerning town and country planning, land use with the exception of waste management and measures of a general nature, and management of water - measures significantly affecting a member states choice between different energy sources and the general structure of its energy supply
	Article 100 Approximation of Laws the approximation of laws which directly affect the establishment or functioning of the common market	directives for the approximation of laws which directly affect the establishment or functioning of the common market
	Article 75(3) TRANSPORT (by way of derogation from Article 75(2)	Transport policy: where would have a serious effect on the standard of living and on employment in certain areas

	Article 99 HARMONISATION OF INDIRECT TAXATION as article 100a	Provisions for the harmonisation of legislation concerning turnover taxes.
		excise duties and other forms of indirect taxation necessary to ensure the establishment and functioning of the internal market.
Budgetary Procedure	Article 130d STRUCTURAL FUNDS to promote overall harmonious development ... leading to the strengthening of ... economic and social cohesion	The tasks priority objectives and organisation and general rules to ensure the effectiveness of the Structural and Cohesion funds

CHAPTER 21

SUBSIDIARITY AND EUROPEAN COMMUNITY ENVIRONMENTAL LAW*

The notion of subsidiarity produces conflicting resonances in different audiences. It has yet to touch the political nerves to the degree that federalism can in some European countries, although the two are clearly connected concepts, and in many ways mutually reinforcing ideas. Some writers have gone so far as to describe subsidiarity as one of the basic conditions of federalism.[1] When the principle was formally inserted into the European Treaty following Maastricht, many in the environmental field observed that this was no more an expression of what had been a long standing and express principle of Community environmental policy which can be traced back to the First Action Programme on the Environment in 1973[2]. Among the eleven principles of Community activity, it was stated that In each different category of pollution, it is necessary to establish the level of action (local, regional, national, Community, international) that befits the type of pollution and the geographical zone to be protected. Actions which are likely to be the most effective at Community level should be concentrated at that level. Given this background the new Article 3b suggested it was business as usual in the environmental field. In contrast, more Euro-sceptic policy-makers appeared to hope that the new Article 3b would force a reigning back of Community environmental law - no more conservation based legislation, no more Commission interference with national projects[3], and a retreat to purely trade-related measures.[4] Some lawyers predicted that the expression of the principle in law would give rise to a new era of judicial review and intervention – and at the very least a great deal of work trying to interpret the precise meaning of the words. Lord MacKenzie-Stuart, former president of the European Court of Justice,

* R Macrory (1999) 'Subsidiarity and European Community Environmental Law', *Revues des Affaires Eurpoeennes*, pp 363 - 369
[1] Brugmans & Duclos (1963) 'Le Federalisme contemporain: criteres, institutions, perspectives' quoted in Emiliou N (l994) Subsidiarity: Paneacea or Fig Leaf, op.cit. note 7)
[2] O.J 1973 Cl12/7.
[3] In the United Kingdom the threat of Commission Article 169 proceedings in the late 1980s in connection with a major motorway project causing environmental damage (Twyford Down) gave rise to great political concern in governmental circles. reaching the Prime Minister.
[4] According to *The Times* (7 August 1992) the then British Foreign Secretary instructed Cabinet colleagues to draw up a list of Community laws that 'interfere unnecessarily with British sovereignty' which would include laws concerning the environment, workers' protection, food hygiene, and animal welfare.

regarded the clause as 'legal gobbledegook' and observed that it was capable of no less than 30 different meanings[5]. Whether the principle is truly justiciable is again a matter of conflicting views. In the same legal volume concerning Maastricht, one writer concludes that it is inevitable that the European Court will be asked to interpret the principle, and that the Court is the institution best placed to undertake that task.[6] Another distinguished writer in the same volume concludes that while the existence of the Article in the Treaty makes legal action based on it possible, the European Court will not, and cannot, become the ultimate arbiter as to whether the principle of subsidiarity has been properly applied in a particular case.[7] Yet a third writer in the same volume urges the Court to restrict itself to what is described as a marginal review of subsidiarity questions, yet concludes that the authoritative interpretation and application of the principles of subsidiarity by the Court will further enhance its function as the Community's constitutional tribunal.[8]

The subsidiarity principle of course since Maastricht applies to all areas of Community policy, but this analysis is confined to the environmental context. What I first want to do is to consider what effect if any the principle has had in the development of environmental policy. Then I will consider some of the more significant legal issues that arise though without trying to unscramble Lord Mackenzie-Stewart's thirty different meanings. Finally, I want to inject some perspectives on the importance of the principle in the area of enforcement of legislation.

Subsidiarity as both a concept of both political philosophy and administrative theory predates the existence of the Community by many years. Its philosophical origins are generally ascribed to the enclycical letter of Pope Pius XI in 1931: It is an injustice, a grave evil, and disturbance of right order for a larger and higher association to arrogate to itself functions which can be performed efficiently by smaller and local societies.[9] Yet this expression was hardly new. A British Royal Commission in 1869 noted that the theory of the division of powers between local and central government was that all that can be done by local authorities should be done by them. . . .whatever concerns the whole nation should be dealt with nationally, while whatever concerns the district must be dealt with by the district.[10] This statement, in common with the principle stated in the Community's First Action Programme, begs the critical questions of what does concern the various levels, and

[5] Subsidiarity and the Challenge of Change, Proceedings of the Jaques Delors Colloqium. 1991.
[6] J Steiner 'Subsidiarity under the Maastricht Treaty' (1994) in O'Keefe and Twomey (eds) *Legal Issues of the Maastricht Treaty* Wiley Chancery. London
[7] A. G. Toth (1994)A legal Analysis of Subsidiarity, ibid
[8] N. Emiliou (1994) 'Subsidiarity : Panacea or Fig Leaf', ibid
[9] Encyclical Letter. Quadragesimo Anno 1931
[10] Royal Commission on Local Government 1869

both are essentially neutral as to division of powers. De Tocqueville, however, in his study on Democracy in America emphasises the benefits of decentralisation by noting that administrative centralisation brings triumph on the day of battle but in the long run diminishes a nation's power[11]

So these are not new ideas, nor peculiar to the European Community. Even before its current widespread use in discussion of European political circles, the concept of subsidiarity, in that it recognises the strength of employing differing levels of government and administration, permeated many of the fundamental legal structures of the European Community. The lack of a clear divisions of competencies between the Community and Member States, the mark of traditional federal structures, means that the Community has developed other, more subtle mechanisms for sharing responsibilities. For example, the large measure of discretion given to Member States in the choice of national instruments and mechanisms implementing Community policy objectives as defined in Directives, that legal instrument peculiar to the Community and described by the Commission as an 'instrument hybride et de statut ambigu'[12]. As Prêchai notes, the particiular characterises of the instruments means that the directive seems to go hand-in-glove with the principle of subsidiarity[13]. Despite the more recent jurisprudence of the European Court of Justice constraining a Member State's choice of methods of transposition[14] a large measure of discretion remains. Similarly, the fundamental relationship between national courts and the European Court of Justice under Article 177 References where there is a firm division of responsibilities, where the European Court does not act as a final court of appeal but confines itself to providing authoritative guidance to national courts on the interpretation and application of Community law. As the European Court itself described the system, it establishes a special field of judicial cooperation which requires the national court and the Court of Justice, both keeping within their respective jurisdiction and with the aim of ensuring that Community law is applied in a unified manner, to make direct and complementary contributions to the working out of a decision.[15] These are examples where the structure of the Community recognizes the value of decentralised powers albeit within constrained boundaries.

[11] Dc Tocqueville (1848) Democracy in America.

[12] quoted in F Snyder (1993) 'Effectiveness of European Community Law : Institutions. Processes' *Tools and Techniques Modern Law Review* p 19.

[13] Prechal S (1995) *Directives in European Community Law* p 5 Oxford University Press, Oxford

[14] Decisions requiring the use of legal as opposed to administrative measures include *Commission v Netherlands* [1987] ECR 3483, *Commission v Germany* [1991] ECR 1-2567

[15] Case 16/65 *Schwarze v Einfuhr- und Vorratsstelle fur Getreide und Futtermittel* [1965] ECR 877

The environmental sector provides a good laboratory for understanding the operation and effect of the subsidiarity principles, not least because it has been operating there longer than any other sector of Community policy. The principle contained in the First Action Programme and quoted above is, perhaps, more a statement of common sense rather than a formal principle as such, and is neutral as to the allocation of responsibilities. But it predated by some two years the first explicit Community reference to subsidiarity, contained in the Commission's submission to the Tindeman's Report on European Union in 1975. There the Commission stated that the European Union is not to give way to a centralising superstate. Consequently and in accordance with the principle *de subsidiarité* the Union will be given responsibility only for those matters which the Member States are no longer capable of dealing with efficiently.[16] The amendments to the Treaty of Rome in 1987 which first expressly introduced a legal basis for environmental policy also first introduced a legal principle of subsidiarity. This was confined to the environmental field though based on earlier draft versions of the Treaty which would have contained a general provision concerning the division of competencies between the Community and member states[17]. The wording was rather simpler than Article 3b:

> The Community shall take action relating to the environment to the extent to which the objectives [referred to in paragraph 1] can be attained better at Community level than at the level of the individual Member States.

The new Article uses both the terms 'better' and 'sufficiently achieved' as key criteria. But I tend to agree with Dr Kramer who in considering the 1987 amendments noted that 'better implies a value judgment which is unquantifiable and defines legal definition.' In other words not even the most penetrating interpretation can extract from the term any abstract guidelines in the division of competencies.[18]

Nevertheless, the procedural changes that have taken place over the last 25 years in relation to Community environmental legislation have clearly raised the possibility of Member States invoking the doctrine of subsidiarity to challenge the validity of laws. In the early years of the development of Community environmental policy, all legislation was agreed by unanimity at Council level. Concerns over the scope

---

[16] European Commission (1975) Report on European Union Bull EC Supp 5/75

[17] see the Spinelli draft Treaty (1984): 'The Union shall only act to carry out those tasks which may be undertaken more effectively in common than by the Member States acting separately, in particular those whose execution requires action by the Union because their dimension or effects extend beyond national frontiers' European Parliament OJ 1984C77/33

[18] L Kramer (1990) *EEC Treaty and Environmental Protection* Sweet & Maxwell. London

and content of proposed legislation could be expressed through the ability and political nerve of individual countries to block agreement. Since 1987 and subsequent amendments to the Treaty we have seen the growing extension of qualified majority voting in the environmental field. Minority countries, no longer able to secure compromise or the blocking of unpalatable measures by their power of veto may therefore be tempted to secure their policy goals by legal rather than political challenge.

A legal challenge concerning the competence of the Community on grounds of subsidiarity has not yet, to my knowledge, happened in the environmental field. But an example of a similar process was the United Kingdom's challenge to the Working Time Directive (Case C-84/94) decided by the European Court of Justice in 1996[19]. The United Kingdom, which had of course opted out of the Social Chapter, argued that the Directive had wrongly been based on Article 118a dealing with the safety and health of workers, and that this article should be restrictively interpreted. Furthermore the proposed provisions were disproportionate in that they went beyond what was necessary to achieve the objectives pursued. During the written procedure, the United Kingdom did not expressly argue that disregard of the subsidiarity principle was grounds for annulment, but according to Advocate General Leger created some confusion by regularly invoking the principle of subsidiarity in the course of the proceedings.[20]

The Advocate General noted that Article 3b contains both a principle of subsidiarity and a principle of proportionality but criticised the United Kingdom for equating the two. He was clear that the two principles operate in turn at two different levels. The principle of subsidiarity determines whether Community action should be set in motion at all, while proportionality defines the scope of action that can be taken. Reliance on subsidiarity implies that as a matter of principle one is contesting the possibility of the Community taking action in the area covered by the proposed measure. Article 118a of the Treaty expressly gave power to the Community to adopt legislation laying down minimum requirements in order to achieve harmonisation of working conditions. According to Advocate General Leger, in so far as harmonisation is an objective, it is difficult to criticise the measures adopted by the Council on the ground that they are in breach of the principle of subsidiarity. It would be illusory to expect the Member States alone to achieve the harmonisation envisaged since it necessarily involves supranational action.[21]

---

[19] *United Kingdom v E.U.Council* [1996] CMLR 671
[20] para 124 of his Opinion
[21] para 129 ibid

The Court itself was equally dismissive of the subsidiarity argument, and equated the arguments as formulated with questioning the need for Community action. Invoking the wording of Article 118a, it held that once the Council had decided it was necessary to improve the existing levels of worker protection and to harmonise conditions, achievement of that objective necessarily presupposes Community-wide action. The Court went on to note that the concept of minimum requirements in Article 113 did not, as the UK had argued, limit Community action to the lowest common denominator. Member States were free to provide a level of protection more stringent than that resulting from Community law, high as that may be. The principle of the capacity to adopt more stringent environmental measures, subject to some procedural limitations, is now expressly contained in both Article 100a(4) and Article 130t.

Furthermore, the Court showed itself reluctant to provide a hard look at that questions. The Council must be allowed a wide discretion in an area which as here involves the legislature in making social policy choices and requires it to carry out complex assessments[22] Judicial review must be limited to questions of manifest error or misuse of powers, or manifest exceedence of powers.

Although it is unlikely that we have seen the last of legal challenges based on the subsidiarity principle, the approach of the Court in the Working Time Directive case suggests it will be a tough hurdle to mount. The structure of the Treaty has never been based on a clear division of competencies between the Community and Member States, and in the environmental field the system has been described as following the idea of a shared competence or as Laurence Brinkhorst has put it, not so much a separation of powers but rather an intermingling of powers.[23] My own view is that the subsidiarity principle reflects what can be described as a gravitational rule rather than strict rule of competence, but this does not mean that it is deprived it of influence.

The Maastrict Treaty moved the principle from one tucked away in the environment section to a general rule at the head of the Treaty, and this action in itself caused considerable political attention. Four months after the signing of the Maastricht Treaty, the Lisbon Summit meeting of the European Council called upon the principle to be expressly considered for all proposed Community legislation and for a reexamination of existing legislation. The 1992 Edinburgh Summit approved a Commission paper considering operational principles of subsidiarity.[24] Reflecting

---

[22] Judgment of the European Court para 58

[23] L Brinkhorst (1991) 'Subsidiarity and European Community Environmental Policy - A Pandora's Box?' *European Environmental Law Review* 16, p 20

[24] Conclusions of the Presidency Bull EC 12-1992. 12

the criticisms of the British arguments in the Workers' Directive, some scholars have accused the Commission of confusing subsidiarity with proportionality in this document.[25] The paper contained three general principles which should be applied to proposed action:

- did the matter raise cross-border problems which could not be dealt with satisfactorily at Member State level?

- would existing actions or initiatives by Member State or inaction by the Community infringe other provisions of the Treaty such as competition, trade restrictions or the need to strengthen cohesion?

- would action by the Community rather than national action produce clear benefits by reason of scale or effects?

These are pretty generous guidelines and as Jan Jans concluded, if all the existing environmental legislation of the Community were reviewed against those guidelines, it seems highly unlikely whether a single environmental Directive would fail to pass the test.[26] Despite the initial political excitement in some Member States (with talk of the repeal of the Environmental Assessment Directive amongst others) this essentially is what has happened. In 1993 the Commission submitted a report on the adaptation of existing Community laws to the subsidiarity principle which made clear that while it sought reform of a raft of water and air pollution Directives, none would be repealed as such until replaced by others. No formal proposals appear to have been withdrawn on the basis of subsidiarity, though within the Commission early policy sparks may have been extinguished as potentially breaching subsidiarity, and Kramer has noted in 1997 that the most striking feature of EC environmental legislation over the last five years is the significant decrease of the legislative activity at EC level.[27] Even within proposed legislation, it seems clear that substantive principles within proposed areas of action have shown a greater sensitivity to the need for shared action by the Community and Member States, with a shift in favour of Member States. Under the proposed Directive to replace the existing Drinking Water Directive[28], certain standards such as those related to colour and taste are clearly left for determination by Member States. Greater derogations are provided. The proposed amendments to the

[25] eg see Toth A (1994) op.cit., p44
[26] J Jans (1995) *European Environmental Law* Kluwer. London
[27] L Kramer (1997) *Focus of European Environment Law*. 2nd edition Sweet & Maxwell. London.
[28] (1995 OJ C131/95

Bathing Water Directive[29] amends technical aspects of the Directive but there has been no question raised about repealing the Directive. The proposed directive on the Ecological Quality of Water gave a far greater degree of discretion to Member States than would have been seen under earlier Directives[30]. And the recently agreed Directive on Integrated Pollution Prevention and Control[31] contains more than a nod towards subsidiarity. Article 9, for example, requires that permits are based on best available techniques but taking into account the installations, geographical location and the local environmental conditions. This last provisions caused considerable unease with the German government but was very much promoted by the British, and the final drafting of the provisions suggests that the principle of subsidiarity was in the minds of negotiators. In this sense we are seeing the influence of subsidiarity as determining not so much legal competence as administrative responsibility.[32]

It is clear from the wording of the principle in Article 3b that it does not apply to areas of so-called exclusive competence of the Community. Determining what is or is not exclusive raises difficult conceptual questions, but a number of areas of policy with environmental significance are encompassed by exclusivity. The narrowest view of exclusive competence confines it to those areas based on the interpretation of the Treaty where the Community is the only authority with competence to act. According the European Court of Justice marine fisheries conservation[33] and the Common Commercial Policy[34] fall within the exclusive competence of the Community and the subsidiarity test cannot apply there. A more generous view would go onto to encompass areas which are not declared exclusive on the basis of Treaty interpretation, but where the Community has potential power, and has exercised to the extent that it preempts actions by Member States. Agricultural policies would be such an example. Toth goes further to argue that exclusivity covers any matter governed by the original EEC Treaty, and that therefore subsidiarity cannot apply to those areas.[35]

Pure environmental policies represent a concurrent area of power where the subsidiarity test applies. As I have already indicated the actual

---

[29] (1994) OJ Cl 12/3

[30] (1991) OJ C222/6

[31] Directive 96/61 OJ L257/26

[32] The notion of 'administrative subsidiarity' has been promoted by the Commission - see SEC 92 (1990). See also M Hession and R Macrory (1994) Maastricht and the Environmental Policy of the Community - Legal Issues of a New Environmental Policy in D O'Keefe and P Twomey, n 6 above.

[33] Cases 3, 4, 6/76 *Kramer et al* [1976] ECR 1279

[34] Case 41/76 *Donckerwolcke v Procureur de la Republique et al* [1976] ECR 1921

[35] A Toth (1994) n 7 above. The analysis, in my view, takes far too generous a view of exclusivity.

wording of the test involves the application of value judgments which suggests it is unlikely to be wholly justiciable. This seems particularly so in the environmental field which contain a complex web of local, regional, and global problems – and one where the sum of apparently local degradation can have significant regional or global impact[36]. The British Royal Commission on Environmental Pollution recently conducted a major study of soil quality in the United Kingdom which demonstrated the extent to which a different analytical perspective on what had previously be regarded as largely an issue of local significance could raise the level of appropriate policy response – the report concluded that by and large soil quality in the country was in good state but, set against global trends, emphasises the national and international significance of the resource[37]. With that in mind, it is possible to identify three broad types of environmental problem which may be said to pass the subsidiarity test.[38]

1) Global or regional issues which have transboundary affects with respect to other countries or the global commons.

2) Apparently localised problems whose accumulative sum or future trends imply regional or global environmental effects. In effect this amounts to a redrawing of the boundaries of (1) in the light of developing environmental scientific knowledge.

3) Problems which affect what might be described the common heritage of Europe or mankind, a far more subjective though still very real concept.[39]

Even with those areas that may be described as truly of international importance, it may be argued that the Community per se is not necessarily the most appropriate level at which to deal with them – sometimes called the supersidiarity test. Member States may argue that they rather then the Community may still be the most effective players on the international stage. There must be some real doubt whether this is the case given the combined economic and political muscle of the Community.

The Maastricht Treaty contained an explicit reference to an objective of Community environmental policy being the promotion of international

---

[36] M Hession and R Macrory (1994) n 32 above.

[37] Royal Commission on Environmental Pollution (1996) Sustainable Use of Soil 19th Report Cm 3165 HMSO, London

[38] M Hession and R Macrory (1994) n 32 above.

[39] see, in particular, W Wils (1994) 'Subsidiarity and EC Environmental : Taking People's Concerns Seriously' *Journal of Environmental Law* 85-91

measures to deal with regional or worldwide environmental problems. This did not expressly make such areas the exclusive competence of the Community, but certainly tempers the effect of the subsidiarity doctrine in those area.

Finally, the possible effect of the subsidiarity principle to the question of the enforcement and implementation of Community environmental law should be addressed. The procedures contained in the Treaty, the role of the Commission, the citizens' complaint procedure and the ultimate powers of the European Court represent a developed and unique form of supranational supervision[40]. In the Commission's 1996 communication on implementation and enforcement[41], what might be described as the administrative form of subsidiarity is strongly reflected. The Communication emphasises the role of national courts and national procedures in ensuring that Member States comply with their Community obligations. There is a distinct shift away from Community involvement in individual cases of poor implementation in practice. I have some sympathy with the approach outlined, but also recognise the dangers involved: It requires that Member States consider carefully the effectiveness and availability of national legal and administrative remedies, many of which are woefully inadequate in many countries. Similarly it has to be recognized that the more that Community legislation contains provisions that give discretion to Member States and their national authorities the less will conventional legal enforcement at Community level prove effective. Far greater open monitoring, harmonisation and consistency between national environmental indicators, and systematic exchange of information will be needed if the protection of the environment is to be maintained.

The original Commission Action Programme on the environment, produced almost 25 years ago, explicitly mentioned local and regional action as well as national and Community. It is perhaps unfortunate that the subsidiarity principle now contained in the Treaty contains no mention of levels of action 'below' the Member State, although the Preamble to the Maastricht Treaty talks of the need to create an ever closer union among the peoples of Europe in which decisions are taken as closely as possible to the citizen. To date the subsidiarity concept as developed in the Treaty has been largely considered, at least from the Anglo-Saxon perspective, in the context of the relationship between the powers of the Community and those of Member States. But in future it may be more pertinent to consider its application to the notion of regional or devolved responsibility at the expense of central government. This

---

[40] R Macrory (1992) 'Enforcement of Community Environmental Laws : Some Critical issues' *Common Market Law Review* 347-369. See also chap. 26 below,
[41] Com (96) 500 final

reflects a broader concept of federalism which moves away from the notion of a contractual arrangements between nation states and in which subsidiarity establishes a presumption that the primary responsibility and decision-making competence should rest with the lowest possible level of authority of the political hierarchy[42] More fluid relationships between the Community and levels of government beyond the nation state would result, and the subsidiarity approach, therefore, may allow the Community to deal directly with subnational governments, interest groups, and citizens without too much concern for the rights and views of the Member States.[43][44] Yet when it comes to enforcement actions under Article 169 we still retain a model of the central government being held responsible for ensuring the implementation of Community obligations, even where internally those powers have been devolved to sub-regional levels of government. The conventional response is to ensure that where European Community obligations are involved, central government always possesses powers to implement and if necessary to direct local and sub-regional governments to conform[45] The more imaginative solution – though one that may be resisted by many national governments – would be to embrace the more fluid concept of federalism and allow Article 169 proceedings to be brought directly against regional or sub-regional governments where the relevant powers were clearly within their devolved competence. We are some way from such a model, but at least can note that the legal conceptions and structures in this area are not yet in tune with more flexible visions promoted in political circles. What is, however, increasingly clear is that the concept of subsidiarity in the environmental context, far from representing a lessening of the burden on Member States, in fact strengthens the needs and obligations of each country to look critically at the adequacy of its own systems in delivering effective environmental policies.

---

[42] Emiliou N (1994) op.cit.p66

[43] Emiliou N, ibid, p 67

[44] Biancarelli (1988) La Communauté et les collectives locales. 48 Revu Française d'Administration Publique 41-55

[45] Essentially the model adopted in the United Kingdom. Even under Scottish Devolution arrangements which adopts, the principle that all matters are devolved unless reserved by national government, European Community matters are to be reserved.

CHAPTER 22

PARTICIPATORY RIGHTS, TRANSBOUNDARY ENVIRONMENTAL GOVERNANCE AND EC LAW*

1.   Introduction

During the course of the past ten years a new generation of Community environmental Directives has developed whose hallmarks are the repatriation of considerable substantive discretion to Member States but counterbalanced with the imposition of greater procedural constraints. An emerging trend within this process is the requirement that Member States must take the potential transboundary impact of environmental decision making into account at national level, and consult both potentially affected Member States as well as their citizens and environmental organisations within those States. Although cross-border rights of public participation were first introduced into EC environmental law by the 1985 Environmental Impact Assessment Directive,[1] the past decade has witnessed not only a considerable upgrading of these rights in the context of environmental assessment, but also their incorporation into the Integrated Pollution Prevention and Control Directive 96/61,[2] the Water Framework Directive[3] and most recently the Strategic Environmental Assessment Directive adopted in June 2001.[4] So pronounced is this pattern, it could be argued that transboundary participatory rights are fast emerging under Community law as a minimum procedural requirement of good environmental governance.

The purpose of this paper is to examine the nature and significance of these transboundary participatory rights under EC environmental law. In doing so, it will begin by tracing the legal and political factors that have stimulated the conferral of these rights within Community environmental law (section 2). Next, the paper examines the nature and scope of the transboundary participatory rights conferred thus far together with the Commission's proposals to expand these rights as part of its programme of reform to ensure Community ratification of the UN/ECE Aarhus Convention on Access to Information, Public Participation

---

* R Macrory and S Turner (2002) 'Participatory Rights, Transboundary Environmental Governance and EC Law', *Common Market Law Review* 39, pp 489-522

[1] O.J. 1985,L 175/40.

[2] O.J. 1996, L 257/26.

[3] O.J. 2000, L 327/1.

[4] O.J. 2001, L 197/30.

in Decision-Making and Access to Justice in Environmental Matters[5] (section 3). The enforceability of participatory rights will heavily influence the extent to which they are taken seriously by Member States, and the paper concludes with an analysis of the extent to which transboundary participatory rights are capable of effective enforcement by citizens and non-governmental organisations before national courts (section 4).

2. Legal and political factors stimulating the emergence of transboundary rights of public participation within Community environmental law

The emergence of transboundary participatory rights in the context of EC law on the environment has been stimulated by two separate but related shifts in the Community's legal and political landscape during the past decade. EC environmental law has entered an era of more intense focus on the nature of the rights conferred on individuals in the context of environmental protection. This shift in focus is due in part to the application by the European Court of Justice of its jurisprudence concerning the protection of individual rights in the context of Community environmental law, but it also reflects an emerging global consensus that effective public participation in environmental governance is fundamental to the sustainable management of national and shared natural resources. At the same time a growing political appreciation of the complexities of contemporary environmental challenges, combined with the adoption of subsidiarity as a fundamental principle of Community constitutional law, has forced a rethink of the nature and substance of Community environmental legislation.

2.1. An increasing emphasis on the nature of individual rights in Community environmental law

The issue of individual rights in the field of environmental protection has emerged as one of the most important but controversial issues in contemporary environmental law at national, European and international levels. In contrast to many other fields of Community law which are directly focused on the protection of individual interests – such as employment, health and safety, consumer protection, taxation – EC law on the environment has traditionally provided a more diffuse protection for individuals. In effect, Community legislation on the environment has been principally designed to protect the internal market, human health

---

[5] The Convention was negotiated under the auspices of the United Nations Economic Commission for Europe and was signed at Aarhus, Denmark in June 1988; ECE/CEP/43. All Member States have now signed the Convention. The full text of the Convention is available at www.eel.nl/treaties/CEP43E.htm.

and the environment and therefore is concerned with the common good.[6] Hence, while citizens were beneficiaries of the enhanced environmental protection brought about by such legislation, they were not explicitly conferred with individual rights under Community environmental law. During the 1990s, however, individuals within the field of Community environmental law were gradually transformed from being the objects of this legislation to being subjects vested with legal rights to participate in the process of environmental protection. As has been the pattern in many areas of Community law, the European Court of Justice made the greatest initial strides in this process of change. Largely as a result of the highly innovative approach taken by the Court, the development of the Community legal order has been characterised by an enduring concern to ensure effective protection for the rights of individuals conferred under EC law. In particular, the principles of direct and indirect effect, and more recently the concept of State liability, have provided individual citizens with effective mechanisms for enforcing their Community law rights before national courts.[7] However, because these principles were developed by the Court largely in the context of the traditional sectors of Community law which focus very considerably on the conferral of individual rights, their application was linked strongly to the enforcement of legislation that was concerned with individual rights. Indeed, the principle of state liability explicitly requires the conferral of individual rights as a condition of its application. Hence many commentators and national courts took the view that these mechanisms would only rarely apply to Community environmental legislation on the grounds that it was unusual for individual rights as opposed to the common good to be the focus of such legislation.[8]

However, the Court delivered a series of judgments during the past decade in which Community legislation on the environment was deemed capable of direct enforcement by private parties despite the fact that the provisions in question did not confer individual rights. Two landmark

[6] Krämer, *EC Environmental Law*, 4th ed. (Sweet & Maxwell, 2000); Jans, *European Environmental Law*, 2nd ed. (Europa, 2000); Boch, 'The enforcement of the Environmental Impact Assessment Directive in the national courts: A breach in the dyke', 9 *Journal of Environmental Law* (1997), 133.

[7] The Court's case law in this respect has been the subject of considerable analysis over a number of decades: for a detailed discussion of the Court's jurisprudence in the context of EC law on the environment, see Jans, 'Legal protection in European environmental law: An overview', in Somsen (Ed.), *Protecting the European Environment: Enforcing EC Environmental Law* (Blackstone Press, 1996); Jans, op. cit. *supra* note 6; Ward, 'Judicial review of environmental misconduct in the European Community: Problems; prospects and strategies', 1 *Yearbook of European Environmental Law* (hereafter YEEL) (2000), 137.

[8] Jans. op. cit. *supra* note 6; Jans, op. cit. *supra* note 7; Hilson, 'Community rights in environmental law: Rhetoric or reality?' in Holder (Ed.), *The Impact of EC Environmental Law in the United Kingdom* (Wiley, 1997); Hilson and Downes, 'Making sense of rights: Community rights in EC law', 24 *EL Rev.* (1999), 121.

decisions in this jurisprudence were delivered in Case C-131/88, *Commission v. Germany*[9] and Case C-361/88, *Commission v. Germany*[10] in which the Court ruled that environmental legislation that is designed to protect human health and the environment should be interpreted as creating rights and obligations for individuals. Thus measures that impose limit values, emission standards and quality objectives, which still comprise the bulk of Community legislation on the environment, were deemed to confer enforceable rights on citizens. In addition, the Court ruled that private parties could rely on the principle of direct effect in order to challenge the implementation of Community measures aimed at the protection of wildlife, despite the absence of provisions conferring rights on individuals.[11]

Five years later the Court delivered perhaps its most far-reaching ruling in this context in *Kraaijeveld*.[12] The Court held that national courts are under a duty to ensure that Member States do not exceed the limits of their discretion under Community Directives on the environment – in this case the Environmental Impact Assessment Directive. Where a State is found to have exceeded its discretionary powers, the Court ruled that national courts must set aside these national provisions. Furthermore, where the parties to the action have not questioned the Member State's exercise of its discretion – as was the case in *Kraaijeveld* – national courts may still be required to raise the issue on their own initiative. The Court in *Kraaijeveld* appeared studiously to avoid use of the direct effect doctrine, insofar as no assessment was carried out as to whether the provisions of the Directive conferred individual rights. Nor did the Court test for compliance with the most traditional requirements for direct effect; namely that the measure be sufficiently precise and unconditional. Nevertheless, the legality review required by the Court in *Kraaijeveld* effectively enabled the claimant to rely on the terms of the Directive before his national court.

Not surprisingly, *Kraaijeveld* stimulated renewed discussion amongst commentators as to the concept of direct effect.[13] One view is that

[9] [1991] ECR 1-825.
[10] [1991] ECR 1-2567.
[11] See, e.g. in relation to the requirement to designate Special Protection Areas under Art. 4(1) of the Wild Birds Directive in Case C-355/90, *Commission v Spain*. [1993] ECR 1-4221: Case C-44/95, *R v. Secretary of State for the Environment, ex parte Royal Society for the Protection of Birds*, [1996] ECR 1-3805 and Case C-3/96, *Commission v Netherlands*, [1998] ECR 1-3031.
[12] Case C-72/95. *Aannemersbedriff PK Kraaijeveld BV and others v Gedeputeerde Staten van Zuid-Holland*, [1996] ECR 1-5403.
[13] See e.g. Boch, op. cit. *supra* note 6; Jans, op. cit. *supra* note 6, pp. 188-192; Prechai, 'Does direct effect still matter?', 37 CML Rev. (2000), 1047; Edward, 'Direct Effect, the Separation of Powers and the Judicial Enforcement of Obligations', in *Scritti in onore de Giuseppe Frederico Mancini* (Giuffrè, 1998), Vol II, p. 423; Hilson and Downes, op. cit. *supra* note 8.

where the national judge is simply asked to review the legality of the Member State's exercise of discretion under Community legislation, the traditional tests for direct effect will be irrelevant, and the later decision of the Court in *Linster*[14] would appear to further support this position. In that case, the claimant sought to rely on the Member State's failure to comply with the requirements of the EIA Directive in order to challenge the State's expropriation of his land for the purposes of constructing a motorway link. The national court sought clarification from the Court concerning the relationship between the principle of direct effect and the principle laid down in *Kraaijeveld*. In particular the national court asked whether it was possible to ensure compliance with the Directive by verifying compliance with the requirements of the Directive, irrespective of whether the Directive has direct effect, or whether such verification required an appraisal of the direct effect of the Directive. Despite the specific invitation to do so, the Court avoided any discussion of the traditional concept of direct effect or indeed its relationship with the concept in *Kraaijeveld*. Instead it simply reiterated its ruling in *Kraaijeveld*. It is therefore arguable that rather than being an alternative to direct effect, the Court regards the legality review underpinning the *Kraaijeveld* principle as synonymous with direct effect. Indeed, the Court's invocation in both *Kraaijeveld* and *Linster* of its *effet utile* rationale for direct effect as the basis for legality review further supports this view. It is also clear from both cases that legality review is not dependent on the conferral of individual rights, or indeed on whether the measure in question is sufficiently precise and unconditional to be capable of judicial application.

At a policy level, the 1990s also witnessed fundamental shifts in attitudes by governments at global, European and national levels towards the issue of public rights to participate in environmental decision making. Within the context of Community policy on the environment, the question of public participation was first explicitly highlighted as a policy issue in the EC's Fourth Action Programme on the Environment in 1987.[15] However, by the time its Fifth Programme on the Environment, *Towards Sustainability*, was published in 1993,[16] an international political consensus had emerged that democratic accountability was fundamental to effective environmental governance. This drew the question of public participation from the margins to the heart of Community environmental policy in the 1990s. The high point in the expression of this new consensus was undoubtedly the seminal United Nations Conference on Environment and Development (UNCED) held in Rio de Janeiro in 1992. Attended by

---

[14] Case C-287/98, *Grand Duchy of Luxembourg v Linster*, [2000] ECR 1-6917.
[15] O.J. 1987, C 328/1, paras. 2.2 and 2.6.
[16] O.J. 1993, C 138/5.

more than 176 States, the UNCED identified sustainable development as the fundamental goal of international environmental governance.[17] More specifically, the Conference highlighted public participation in environmental protection as fundamental to the achievement of sustainability.[18] The Rio Declaration, adopted by the Conference as a non-binding instrument, codified twenty-seven principles designed to provide a framework for the development of international environmental law in light of this objective. A second instrument, Agenda 21, set out a blueprint for implementing the goal of sustainable development. The crucial importance of public participation in environmental governance was explicitly enshrined in both instruments.[19]

Almost a year after UNCED the European Community adopted its Fifth Action Programme on the Environment, *Towards Sustainability*,[20] which set out the Community's policies and priorities in relation to the environment until the turn of the century. As a signatory of the Rio instruments, the Community embraced the principle of sustainable development in the Fifth Action Programme as the principal goal for Community policy on the environment.[21] Consistent with the obligations under the Rio Declaration and Agenda 21, the Action Programme placed the participatory dimension of environmental governance at the heart of Community's strategy for achieving sustainability.[22] 'Shared responsibility' is the term used by the programme to encapsulate the Community's vision of public participation.[23] The programme explains that whereas previous action programmes on the environment had been based largely on legislation and controls involving government and manufacturing industry, the concept of shared responsibility requires a much more broadly based and active involvement of all actors, including government, enterprise and the public.[24] More specifically, the following practical measures are highlighted as being crucial to effective citizen participation in environmental governance: access to environmental information, a right to involvement in the process of assessing the environmental impact of major projects, participation in the process of environmental regulation, access to an efficient complaints facility at local, regional and national levels, and practicable access to courts

---

[17] Sands, *Principles of International Environmental Law* (Manchester University Press, 1995), p. 48.
[18] Cameron, Werksman and Roderick. *Improving Compliance with International Environmental Law* (Earthscan, 1996), p. 29.
[19] Principle 10 of the Rio Declaration specifically addresses the issue of public participation in environmental protection. The text of Agenda 21 is replete with references to public participation, in particular Chapt. 23 on strengthening the role of major groups.
[20] Cited *supra* n 16.
[21] Chap. 2.
[22] Chaps. 2 and 3.
[23] Chap. 3.
[24] Chap. 3.

for individuals and public interest groups to ensure the enforcement of environmental measures and the protection of their legitimate interests.[25] The Community's recently adopted Sixth Action Programme on the Environment, *Environment 2010: Our Future, Our Choice*, essentially proposes that this focus be maintained by the Community.[26]

2.2. The impact of subsidiarity and flexibility on the Community's approach to environmental regulation

The second key stimulus for the development of participatory rights in the field of EC environmental law – and particularly rights to cross-border participation – was provided by another major shift in the Community's political climate during the early 1990s.

Transboundary externalities or spillovers – both physical and economic – were traditionally asserted as the factors that justified the first period of Community intervention in the field of environmental governance.[27] From the point of view of physical externalities, it had long been evident that activities within one State had the capacity to have a negative impact on the environmental quality within neighbouring and more distant States. In addition, the danger of a regulatory 'race to the bottom' between Member States, and the threat to the level competitive playing field underpinning the common market project, provided a powerful economic rationale for centralising legislative action on the environment at Community level.[28] The compelling nature of these arguments enabled Community environmental law to develop rapidly during the 1970s and 1980s, but the legislation that emerged tended to be based on conventional approaches towards regulation, and was better suited towards controlling point sources of pollution rather than dealing with diffuse sources or influencing longer-term resource and consumption trends. Community legislation on the environment favoured the imposition of specific minimum emission standards or quality objectives for the Community as a whole, leaving Member States with little substantive discretion when implementing these standards. In particular, Member States had very little flexibility in terms of taking local environmental conditions into account when implementing EC environmental Directives; similarly, they retained little discretion in terms of the policy instruments that could be used to achieve

---

[25] Chaps. 7 and 9.

[26] COM (2001) 31 final. The text is available at: europa.eu.int/comm/environment/newprg/index.htm.

[27] Scott, 'Flexibility in the Implementation of EC Environmental Law', 1 *YEEL* (2000), p. 56.

[28] Revesz, 'Environmental. Regulation in Federal Systems', 1 *YEEL* (2000), 1.

implementation.[29] By the early 1990s there were growing concerns that the Community's apparently inflexible approach to regulation across several spheres – including the environment – posed a threat to the achievement of competitiveness and employment goals.[30] The Fifth Environmental Action Programme responded to the pressure for deregulation by supporting a more flexible approach to environmental regulation.[31]

At the same time a second, more fundamental wave of political change swept the Community during the early 1990s, which further intensified pressure for a repatriation of power to the Member States. Although the EC's democratic deficit had been the subject of sustained criticism for decades, successive increases in the degree of legislative power centralized in the Community's institutions ultimately culminated in a crisis of legitimacy which dominated the negotiations leading to the Maastricht Treaty in 1992.[32] Subsidiarity was identified as the principle for resolving these tensions and thus was duly enshrined in the new Treaty as a fundamental precept of EC law.[33] A detailed discussion of the nature and scope of this principle is beyond the scope of this paper;[34] however, the Protocol annexed to the Amsterdam Treaty in 1997 concerning the application of subsidiarity and the related concept of proportionality, emphasises democratic legitimacy and flexibility as the two key elements inherent in these concepts.[35] In essence, these concepts are concerned to ensure that 'decisions are taken as closely as possible to the citizens of the Union'[36] and that greater discretion is repatriated to Member States in terms of the substantive implementation of Community law. The Protocol emphasises that while the principles of subsidiarity and proportionality can only be applied in so far as they do not threaten the *acquis communautaire* or the effective enforcement of

---

[29] Knill, *The Impact of National Administrative Traditions on the Implementation of EU Environmental Policies* (EUI, 1997); Freestone and Somsen, 'The Impact of Subsidiarity', in Holder (Ed.), op. cit. *supra* note 8.

[30] *Report of the Group of Independent Experts on Legislative and Administrative Simplification*, COM (95) 288 final.

[31] Chap. 7 of the Action Programme linked this new approach to the concept of shared responsibility and emphasised that the involvement of all levels of society in a spirit of shared responsibility required a broadening of the range of instruments to complement normative legislation, including, where appropriate, market-based instruments, voluntary agreements and other forms of self-regulation.

[32] De Burca. 'The Quest for Legitimacy in the European Union', 56 *MLR* (1996), 349.

[33] Via Art. 5 (ex 3b) EC.

[34] See e.g. Macrory, 'Subsidiarity and European environmental law', *Revue des Affaires Europeennes* (1999) , 363; see also chap. 21 above; Toth, 'The principle of subsidiarity in the Maastricht Treaty', 29 CML Rev. (1992), 239.

[35] *Protocol on the Application of the Principles of Subsidiarity and Proportionality*, O.J. 1997, C 340/105.

[36] Ibid. Second Recital.

Community law, their application requires that framework Directives should be used in preference to regulations, Community measures should leave as much scope for national decision as possible and should provide Member States with alternative ways to achieve the objectives required by such measures.[37]

The discussion concerning the impact of subsidiarity in the context of EC environmental law has been going on for many years.[38] Recent legislative developments suggest that this principle, together with the pressure for deregulation in the environmental context, have stimulated the development of a new generation of Community legislation on the environment, which avoids setting detailed emission standards and limit values, and instead establishes a framework of objectives that confers considerable substantive discretion on Member States in implementing these goals. But while these measures anticipate a potentially wide variation in approach between Member States in terms of substantive implementation, this new flexibility is combined with the tightening of constraints on the procedures and processes associated with their implementation.[39]

One example of these procedural constraints is the emergence within EC environmental directives of requirements on Member States to consult with other affected Member States concerning the transboundary environmental effects of activities taking place within their territory. By ensuring that trans-boundary impacts are still taken into account during decision making on the environment, albeit at a national level, these procedural requirements address the threat to effective environmental protection that is latent in a departure from the Community's traditional approach to environmental regulation, namely, that transboundary externalities or spillovers will not properly be taken into account.[40] However, such procedural requirements also satisfy the principle of subsidiarity in two ways. Greater control over substantive environmental decision making is repatriated to the Member States, and this cross-border consultation process will also require, though to varying degrees, the involvement of citizens and non-governmental organisations. Consequently the requirement to consider transboundary environmental impacts will satisfy the principle of subsidiarity because the conferral of cross-border participatory rights

---

[37] Ibid, paras. 6 and 7.
[38] See e.g. Brinkhorst, 'Subsidiarity and European Community Environmental Policy: A Panacea or a Pandora's Box?', 2 *European Environmental Law Review* (1993), 8; Freestone and Somsen, op. cit. *supra* note 29; Macrory, op. cit. *supra* note 34; Krämer, op. cit. *supra* note 6: Jans. op. cit. *supra* note 6.
[39] Scott, op. cit. *supra* note 27.
[40] Ibid., p. 57.

will ensure that decisions are made 'as closely to the people as possible', thus contributing to that aspect of subsidiarity that requires democratic legitimacy in the exercise of power. In effect, Community environmental legislation is entering an era in which the cross-border dimension of environmental governance and the processes that this entails may be more significant than ever before.

3.   **The Nature and Scope of the Cross-Border Participatory Rights Conferred Thus Far Under EC Directives on the Environment**

       3.1.   Environmental Impact Assessment Directive 1985 and 1997

Community legislation concerning environmental impact assessment (EIA) is perhaps the area that most strongly reflects the growing emphasis within EC environmental law on the obligations of transboundary notification and consultation between states, combined with the vesting of public rights to participate in the process of cross-border environmental decision making. The initial Directive in this field (the 1985 EIA Directive[41]) was the first piece of Community environmental legislation to focus almost exclusively on the imposition of processes and procedures – a pattern that has been continued by subsequent directives in this field.[42] Community Directives on environmental assessment do not require Member States to reach a particular environmental goal, nor do they require Member States and their own competent bodies to take environmentally sound decisions concerning project authorisation. In that sense, the Directives rest on an act of faith which assumes that authorities will act in an environmentally more sensitive way if they have the information before them. The procedural emphasis of the Directives is underlined by the fact that, in contrast to United States legislation in the subject, the focus is not simply on a written environmental impact assessment or statement – instead 'assessment' in the Community context is treated as a whole process of decision making including that of consultation.

The 1985 EIA Directive required Member States to consider the potential transboundary impacts of proposed development. Article 7 of the 1985 Directive provided:

> Where a Member State is aware that a project is likely to have significant effects on the environment in another Member State or where a Member State likely to be

---

[41] Directive 85/337, OJ. 1985, L 175/40.
[42] In particular, Directive 97/11, O.J. 1996, L 73/5 (discussed below) and the Strategic Environmental Assessment Directive, O.J. 2001, L 197/30.

significantly affected so requests, the Member State in whose territory the project is intended to be carried out shall forward the information gathered pursuant to Article 5 [the information gathered by the developer] to the other Member State at the same time as it makes it available to its own nationals. Such information shall serve as a basis for consultations necessary in the framework of the bilateral relationship between the two Member States on a reciprocal and equivalent basis.

In addition, Article 8 provides that information gathered in pursuance of Article 7 must be taken into account in the development consent procedure for the project in question.

The structure of Article 7 is revealing. Either Member State concerned may initiate the process, but the consultative process is one very much in the hands of the two Member States as opposed to external interests. There is no obligation imposed on the receiving Member State to consult its own nationals, nor is it entitled to very much information - simply that supplied by the developer to the competent authority of the Member State. The views of specialised bodies within the Member State where the project is to be located do not have to be made available to the other Member State. However, while the provisions are essentially a basis for intergovernmental discussion, the European Court of Justice adopted the stance that Member States were required to transpose these obligations into national law.[43] Three years later, in *Commission v Belgium*[44] the Court of Justice ruled that the consultation obligation contained in Article 7 was not confined to projects located in regions with frontiers with other countries. Consequently the Court ruled that Belgium was obliged to transpose these provisions in relation to the Region of the capital city of Brussels even though it had no international borders. The obligation to undertake transboundary consultation was considered more recently in *Commission v Ireland*[45] in which the Court ruled that Ireland had failed to implement properly the requirements of Article 7. Although the Irish implementing legislation[46] required 'local authorities'[47] to notify the Irish Minister for the Environment of any proposed development likely

---

[43] Case C-186/91, *Commission v Belgium,* [1993] ECR 1-851.

[44] Case 133/94. [1996] ECR 1-2323.

[45] Case C-392/96, [1999] ECR 1-5901.

[46] European Communities (Environmental Impact Assessment) Regulations 1989 (SI No. 349) and Local Government (Planning and Development) Regulations 1990 (SI No. 25). For a discussion of Ireland's experience in implementing the 1985 EIA Directive, see Fitzsimons, 'Recent Developments in Environmental Impact Assessment in Ireland', 6 *Irish Planning and Environmental Law Journal* (2000), 147.

[47] The national authorities responsible for implementing the EIA Directive in Ireland.

to have significant effects on the environment of another Member State, and empowered the Minister to request that they provide him with any necessary information, he was not expressly obliged to transmit the information to the other Member State. Nor did the Minister have the power to require information from local authorities in the event that an affected Member State asked to be consulted.

The signing of the Convention on Environmental Impact Assessment in a Transboundary Context[48] (the so-called 'ESPOO Convention') by the Community in 1991 stimulated a fundamental overhaul of the obligations laid down in Article 7 of the 1985 EIA Directive. Although opened for signature a year before the UN Conference on Environment and Development, the preamble to the ESPOO Convention explicitly affirms the principle of sustainable development, which was central to the conclusions reached at UNCED the following year. Consistent with the principle of sustainability, the ESPOO Convention strengthened the requirements for international co-operation in the case of proposed activities having transboundary environmental impacts and required signatory states to afford members of the public in affected transboundary areas an opportunity to participate in the assessment process.

Directive 97/11[49] was adopted by the Community in March 1997 to introduce a series of amendments to the 1985 EIA Directive - including a completely reformulated set of provisions designed to implement the requirements of the ESPOO Convention within the Community legal order. The key impacts of the changes to Article 7 of the EIA Directive are:

- The affected Member State must be sent information 'as soon as possible' and in any event no later than when the public is informed in the original Member State.

- Rules governing the nature of the information to be sent are not only more explicit, they place Member States under an obligation to make more information available to the affected State. At the point of initial notification the affected Member State must be sent 'a description of the project, together with any available information on

---

[48] The ESPOO Convention was negotiated under the auspices of the United Nations Economic Commission for Europe, E/ECE/1250. The text of the Convention is available at: www.unece.org/env/eia/. For further discussion of the ESPOO Convention, see Sands, op. cit. *supra* n 17, p. 588.
[49] O.J. 1996, L 73/5.

its possible transboundary impact'. Furthermore, the State must receive information concerning the nature of the decision to be taken. If the affected State wishes to engage with the assessment process, it must also be sent the information provided by the developer under Article 5, relevant information regarding the assessment procedure, including the request for development consent.

- The rights of the public and competent authorities within the affected Member State are also strengthened. If the affected State wishes to participate in the assessment process, it must arrange for the above information to be made available to 'authorities likely to be concerned by the project by reason of their specific environmental responsibilities' and to the 'public concerned in the territory of the Member State likely to be significantly affected'. Both the authorities and the public concerned must be given the opportunity of sending their opinion (within a reasonable time) to the competent authority within the Member State in whose territory the project is to be carried out before development consent for the project is carried out. Article 8 requires the notifying Member State to take the results of transboundary consultations into consideration in the development consent procedure. Although Article 9 of the Directive requires the final decision (whether to grant or refuse development consent) to be conveyed to any Member State consulted under Article 7, there is no obligation to similarly inform the public living in the affected Member States of the final outcome – even members of the public who engaged in the transboundary assessment process.

3.2. Strategic Environmental Assessment Directive 2001

The most recent legislation to be adopted by the Community in the field of environmental assessment repeats and strengthens this growing emphasis on public participation in the process of transboundary environmental governance: namely, the Strategic Environmental Assessment (SEA) Directive.[50] While the EIA process is designed to assess the impact of proposals for specific projects, SEA will assess environmental impact at an earlier stage in the development process;

---

[50] Directive 2001/42 O.J. 2001, L 197/30.

specifically when 'plans and programmes' likely to have a significant environmental impact are being drawn up.[51] In particular, Article 3 requires Member States to subject draft plans and programmes prepared for a wide range of contexts; specifically: agriculture, forestry, fisheries, energy, industry, transport, waste management, water management, telecommunications, tourism, town and country planning or land use and which set the framework for future development consent of projects listed in Annexes I and II of the EIA Directive. Furthermore plans and programmes deemed to require an assessment under the Habitats Directive due to their likely impact on sites must also be subject to SEA.

Like the EIA Directive, the SEA Directive confers rights on the public and specialised agencies within the affected Member State to be informed and express their opinions on the proposed plans or programmes.[52] Similarly, the SEA Directive requires decision makers within the proposing Member State to take the results of transboundary consultations into account 'during the preparation of the plan or programme and before its adoption or submission to the legislative procedure.'[53] However, the SEA Directive also attempts to consolidate the deliberative element of the transboundary participatory obligations which is not currently[54] incorporated into the EIA or IPPC Directives (discussed below) either in the context of participation by the State's own nationals or those of other affected States. Article 9 provides that when a plan or programme is adopted, competent authorities must provide the public and any Member State consulted under Article 7 with both the plan or programme as adopted, and a statement as to how environmental considerations have been integrated into the plan and programme, and how the results of consultations have been taken into account.[55]

---

[51] The preamble to the SEA Directive also points out that the assessment of plans and programmes under the Directive is consistent with the ESPOO Convention which encourages signatories to extend its provisions to the preparation of plans and programmes on the environment. In addition, the preamble notes that the SEA Directive will ensure compliance with amendments likely to be adopted at the meeting of the Parties to the ESPOO Convention scheduled for May 2003, which will impose a binding requirement to subject plans and programmes to environmental assessment.

[52] Art. 7.

[53] Art. 8.

[54] The Commission has however submitted proposals recently to incorporate equivalent provisions into the EIA Directive. They are discussed below.

[55] Specifically, Art. 9 requires: '... a statement summarising how environmental considerations have been integrated into the plan or programme and how the environmental report prepared pursuant to Article 5, the opinions expressed pursuant to Article 6 [by the Member State's own nationals and specialised agencies] and the results of consultations entered into pursuant to Article 7 have been taken into account in accordance in Article 8 and the reasons for choosing the plan or programme as adopted, in the light of the other reasonable alternatives dealt with.'

3.3. Integrated Pollution Prevention and Control Directive 1996

Directive 96/61 concerning Integrated Pollution Prevention and Control (IPPC) is one of the most important pieces of Community legislation adopted pursuant to the policies set out in the Fifth Environmental Action Programme.[56] The IPPC Directive is a clear manifestation of the emerging generation of Community legislation on the environment which reflects the ethics of decentralisation and deregulation that are inherent in both the principles of subsidiarity and proportionality and the Community's more flexible approach to environmental regulation.[57] To this end the IPPC Directive was presented by the Commission as a framework Directive which sets out the general principles of integrated pollution prevention and control, but leaves 'as much freedom as possible to the Member States in its implementation.'[58] In essence the Directive requires Member States to operate an integrated permitting system for many types of industrial installations which must be implemented over the next decade. However, while Member States are given considerable flexibility in terms of achieving substantive implementation, the Directive imposes important controls on the processes and procedures surrounding implementation. Although the Commission's original proposal for the Directive – published in 1993[59] – contained no specific provisions concerning transboundary consultation, Article 17 of the Directive as finally adopted requires permit applications to be sent to other Member States that might suffer negative environmental effects. In addition, the affected Member State must give its own public an opportunity to comment on the application. However, although the drafting and discussion of the IPPC Directive was done in parallel with the EIA Directive 97/11,[60] the provisions concerning cross-border public consultation are rather less explicit than under the Directive 97/11. In addition, other specialized agencies within the affected Member States concerned have no right to be informed.

Article 17(1) of the IPPC Directive provides:

> Where a Member State is aware that the operation of an installation is likely to have significant negative effects

---

[56] OJ. 1996, L 257/26. Member States were required to achieve implementation by 30 Oct. 1999.

[57] Scott, op. cit. *supra* note 27, p. 37; Krämer, op. cit. *supra* note 6, p. 115.

[58] COM(93) 423 final. For further background on the amendments to the original proposal, see COM(95) 88 final and COM(96) 306 final.

[59] COM(93) 423 final.

[60] *Interrelationship between IPPC, EIA, SEVESO Directives and EMAS Regulation,* IMPEL Network, Final Report: December 1998. The Report is available at europa.eu.int/ comm/ environment/impel/interrel.htm.

on the environment of another Member State or where a
Member State likely to be significantly affected so requests,
the Member State in whose territory the application for
a permit pursuant to [the IPPC Directive – Article 4 or
Article 12(2)] was submitted shall forward the information
provided pursuant to Article 6 to the other Member
State at the same time as it makes it available to its own
nationals. Such information shall serve as the basis for any
consultations necessary in the framework of the bilateral
relations between the two Member States on a reciprocal
and equivalent basis.'

Article 17(2) then goes on to mirror the requirements under ESPOO
that the public within the Member States affected have a right to be
consulted.[61]

3.4. Water Framework Directive 2000

As the oldest sector of Community environmental law, EC Directives
concerning the aquatic environment have been characterised, perhaps
more than most other areas, by the use of detailed emission standards,
limit values and quality objectives, typical of the first generation of
EC environmental law.[62] In September 2000 the Community adopted
the Water Framework Directive which is designed to provide a single,
integrated and coherent legislative framework for the protection of
freshwater throughout the Community, and will gradually replace many
of the rigid and fragmented rules that currently exist in this sector. Like
the IPPC Directive, the Water Framework Directive avoids prescribing
precise emission or quality goals. Instead, it sets out a framework for
action in the field of water policy which, although affording considerable
discretion to Member States in terms of substantive implementation,
imposes procedures and processes which control the implementation
process.

'River basin management' is the central concept employed by the
Directive. Instead of approaching water protection from the perspective

---

[61] Specifically, Art. 17(2) provides- that: 'Within the framework of their bilateral relations,
Member States shall see to it that in the cases referred to in paragraph 1 the applications
are also made available for an appropriate period of time to the public of the Member State
likely to be affected so that it will have the right to comment on them before a competent
authority reaches its decision.'

[62] For a discussion of the EC's approach to the regulation of water pollution, see Freestone
and Somsen, op. cit. *supra* note 29, p. 92; Bache and McGillivray, 'Testing the extended
gatekeeper: The law, practice and politics of implementing the Drinking Water Directive
in the United Kingdom' in Holder (Ed.), op. cit. *supra* note 8; European Commission,
'Report to the European Council on the Adaptation of Community Legislation to the
Subsidiarity Principle', COM(93) 545 final.

of administrative and political boundaries – which underpinned previous Community legislation in this field – river basin management requires Member States to adopt a model of control which reflects the natural geographical and hydrological unit. Member States are required to identify individual river basins lying within their national territory and each must be assigned to a River Basin District (RBD). Member States are then required to draw up a River Basin Management Plan (RBMP) for each river basin that will provide the context for co-ordinating the implementation of the Directive's key objectives.[63] Wherea river basin covers the territory of more than one Member State, it must be assigned to an 'International River Basin District' (IRBD), and Member States are then required under Article 13(2) to 'ensure co-ordination with the aim of producing a single International River Basin Management Plan' (IRB-MP). In effect, the transboundary dimension to environmental governance is more deeply ingrained in the WFD than other environmental directives, potentially requiring Member States to move beyond intergovernmental consultation towards a process of close co-operation in the management of shared river basins.

However, the procedural obligations imposed on Member States to actually achieve transboundary management are weak. The Directive provides that where Member States sharing a river basin do not produce an IRBMP, each must produce RBMPs covering at least those parts of the IRBD falling within their territory. In effect, while a transboundary approach to environmental protection would appear to be fundamental to the implementation of the Water Framework Directive, the Directive also legitimises failure in this respect.

Similarly, ambivalence underlies the provisions of the WFD concerning rights of public participation. The WFD, more than any other Community directive on the environment, appears to require that the public are actively engaged in the implementation of its provisions. The preamble to the WFD emphasises that the success of the Directive relies 'on information, consultation and involvement of the public'.[64] Article 14(1) then provides that, 'Member States shall encourage the active involvement of all interested parties in the implementation of this Directive, in particular in the production, review and updating of the River Basin Management Plans.'

Article 14(2) imposes detailed obligations on Member States to provide information and ensure public consultation in relation to each stage in

---

[63] Art. 13.
[64] Recital 14.

the development of river basin management plans. It goes on to require that Member States ensure a consultation period of at least six months at each stage in this process in order 'to allow active involvement and consultation'. In this respect, the WFD appears to shift public participation from the familiar terrain of providing information and consultation – which do not concede a share in decision making power – towards a model of active citizenship in which power is shared between a wide range of stakeholders. However, while the WFD represents the most important effort on the part of the Community to deepen the level of public participation in environmental governance, the specific participatory rights conferred under the Directive may to be limited to the provision of information and consultation. Article 14(1) only obliges Member States to 'encourage' the active involvement of all interested parties in the implementation of the Directive thereby suggesting that the Directive does not actually confer more sophisticated participatory rights to share power in river basin management. Similarly, Article 14(2) does not actually require Member States to ensure active involvement, simply that an appropriate consultation period is given 'to allow' for such involvement.

There is also an unfortunate lack of clarity concerning the exact nature of the transboundary participatory rights conferred. Article 14 does not appear to make a distinction between national and transboundary participatory rights. The participatory requirements contained in Article 14(1) are expressed in relation to the 'production, review and updating of the River Basin Management Plans'. The information and consultation requirements contained in Article 14(2) are expressed in relation to 'each River Basin District'. Article 14 makes no reference to public participation in relation to 'International River Basin Management Plans' (referred to in Art. 13(2)), or to 'International River Basin Districts' (referred to in Article 3(3)). A number of interpretations concerning the conferral of cross-border participatory rights are possible. On the one hand, the use of the terms 'River Basin District' and 'River Basin Management Plans' in Article 14 would suggest that the public's legal right to participate in river basin management planning is limited to that part of the river basin within the territory of their own Member State. Both of these terms are used in the Directive in relation to river basins lying within national boundaries. Thus taking a strict interpretation of Article 14, the WFD does not appear to confer any transboundary participatory rights. This view is to some extent supported by the wording of Article 13(2), which does not actually require Member States to produce International River Basin Management Plans for shared river basins in contrast to the EIA, IPPC and SEA Directives which all require transboundary intergovernmental consultation in the event that activity within one State is likely to have a significant environmental impact in another. If this is indeed the correct interpretation of Article 14, then public participation in the management of International River Basin Districts would depend entirely on the Member States' willingness to engage in transboundary river basin management and to permit public participation in that process. In effect, the WFD would represent a marked reversal of the trend within Community environmental law towards the conferral of transboundary participatory rights.

However, a purposive interpretation of the Directive would arguably support the conclusion that cross-border rights of participation are implicit in Article 14. It is clear from the preamble to the Directive and the wide-ranging provisions concerning public participation laid down in Article 14 that such participation is a central element of the strategy adopted by the Directive. It is clear that integrated transboundary river basin management is similarly central to the successful implementation of the Directive. Thus, taking the overall spirit of the WFD into account, Article 14 could be interpreted as conferring cross-border participatory rights. Indeed, the fact that the WFD does not make separate provision for national and transboundary participatory rights, as is the case in the EIA, IPPC and SEA Directives, could support the view that cross-border rights of public participation are implicit in Article 14. However, even in the event that Article 14 is deemed to confer trans-boundary participatory rights, two important questions still remain. First, if the WFD can be interpreted to confer transboundary participatory rights, are those rights limited to the provision of information and consultation, or does it also confer enforceable rights to active citizenship in the process of cross-border river basin management? Second, are the transboundary participatory rights triggered only where Member States sharing a river basin actually exercise their discretion to engage in international River Basin Management Planning or, are they free-standing rights that may be enforced irrespective of intergovernmental action? The Court's extensive jurisprudence concerning the enforcement of Community law before national courts indicates that both questions are likely to be answered in the affirmative (discussed in section 4 *infra*).

> 3.5. The Aarhus Convention and the Development of Transboundary Participatory Rights Within Community Environmental Law

A new phase in the development of transboundary participatory rights under Community environmental law began with the Community's signature of the UN/ECE Aarhus Convention on Access to Information, Public Participation in Decision-Making and Access to Justice in Environmental Matters in June 1998.[65] The Aarhus Convention

---

[65] *Supra* note 5.

represents the most important international attempt to date to realize the objectives concerning public participation set out the Rio Declaration and Agenda 21 at UNCED in 1992. In essence, the Convention reflects the so-called 'three pillars' of rights of access to information, rights to participate in decision-making and rights of access to justice identified at UNCED as underpinning participatory rights in the context of environmental governance. Although its provisions do not explicitly address transboundary issues, the core rights of participation laid down in Article 6 extend to 'the public concerned' which is defined to mean 'the public affected or likely to be affected by, or having an interest in the environmental decision making'.[66] This definition is not expressly confined to nationals residing within the country concerned and could therefore be interpreted as extending to nationals within other countries who might be affected. In January 2001 the Commission published proposals to align a range of EC Directives on the environment with the requirements of the Aarhus Convention concerning rights of public participation in environmental decision making.[67] The proposals indicate that the Commission has interpreted the Aarhus Convention as applying to rights of public participation at both national and transboundary levels. In particular the Commission stated that:

> ...action is required to ensure that the basic procedures for public participation in environmental decision making are consistent in all Member States so that the benefits of such participation are available across the Community as well as in cases with a transboundary dimension.[68]

The Commission considers that the SEA and Water Framework Directive are already in compliance with the Convention; thus proposals were only made in relation to the EIA and IPPC Directives. Three key proposals are made in relation to transboundary participatory rights conferred under the EIA Directive, namely:

- Article 7(2) should be amended to require notifying Member States to provide a greater range of information concerning the proposed project to potentially affected Member States.[69] In the event that the affected Member State decided to engage in the development consent procedure, it would be obliged to make this information available to members of the public concerned;

---

[66] Art. 2(5).
[67] COM(2000) 839 final and COM(2000) 402 final.
[68] COM(2000) 839 final, p. 4.
[69] Draft Art. 2(3)(b).

- Although Member States would remain free to determine the practical arrangements for transboundary public participation in compliance with the principle of subsidiarity, it is proposed that Article 7(5) of the Directive be amended to explicitly require that those arrangements 'shall be such as to enable the public concerned in the territory of the affected Member State to participate effectively in the development consent procedure';[70]

- Article 9(2) should be amended to require affected Member States to ensure that all the information concerning the final outcome of the development consent procedure (the content and reasons for the decision and mitigating action) that has been received from the notifying Member State, must be made available to the public living in the affected State.

The overall effect of these proposals is undoubtedly to enhance the transboundary participatory rights conferred under the EIA Directive and ensure greater consistency between rights of public participation in the process of EIA at national and cross-border levels. However, the Commission does not propose that similar legislative strides should be taken in the context of public participation in cross-border decision-making under the IPPC Directive. In this regard, only two proposals are made. First, notifying Member States should be obliged to take the results of transboundary consultation into consideration when making a decision concerning an IPPC permit application.[71] Second, the notifying Member State should provide the potentially affected State with the content of the final decision concerning the permit, together with a copy of the permit, any conditions attached (including subsequent updates) and the reasons and considerations on which the decision is based. It is proposed that the affected Member State would be required to make this information available to members of the public in its own territory.

The process of implementing the Aarhus Convention into Community environmental law will undoubtedly ensure a more secure integration of the public's right to participate in environmental governance at national and transboundary levels. However, despite the changes proposed by the Commission, several significant inconsistencies would remain between the transboundary participatory rights conferred by the EIA, IPPC, SEA and Water Framework Directives.

---

[70] Draft Art. 2(3)(c).
[71] Draft Art. 3(5)(b).

As already stated, the drafting and discussion of the IPPC Directive was conducted in parallel with, the EIA Directive 97/11,[72] but the existing requirements concerning cross-border public consultation are rather less explicit than under the EIA Directive. While the Commission's proposals to bring the provisions of the IPPC Directive concerning transboundary participation into line with the Convention would strengthen the public's right to participate in cross-border decision making concerning IPPC permits, they would still not ensure parity with the more explicit rights conferred under the EIA Directive. In particular, while the Commission's proposals concerning the EIA Directive would entitle the public in both the notifying and affected Member States to the same information, this would not be the case under the amended IPPC Directive. Although the Commission's proposals would require notifying Member States to provide a greater range of information concerning the permit application to their own nationals and to potentially affected Member States, the nationals of the affected State would remain entitled only to the IPPC application itself. Given that the Commission's proposals emphasize the importance of public participation in environmental governance – including transboundary participation – it is unfortunate that this opportunity was not taken to implement the extensive requirements contained in Article 6 of the Convention concerning the range of information that must be afforded to members of the public concerned in order to ensure effective cross-border public participation – not least the requirement that a non-technical summary of the application be made available.

In addition, only the SEA Directive would require Member States to provide a statement explaining how the results of public consultation (including transboundary consultation) have been taken into account by decision-makers. Such a requirement forces decision-makers to engage in a meaningful process of consultation with the public and potentially provides individuals and non-governmental organisations with the transparency necessary to challenge any failure to engage in effective public consultation.

Subtle differences would also remain in the language used in the EIA, IPPC, SEA and Water Framework Directives to describe the general obligation to ensure transboundary public participation which suggest differences in the weight to be attached to the participatory process. The Commission has proposed that a general obligation should be imposed on Member States in the context of EIA to ensure 'effective' transboundary public participation, but there is no equivalent proposal made for the

---

[72] *Supra* n 60.

IPPC Directive. It is only proposed that the IPPC Directive be amended to require Member States to ensure 'early and effective' opportunities for participation for their own nationals. In contrast, Member States would only be required to ensure that permit applications are made available to the public in potentially affected Member States for 'an appropriate period of time' so that 'it will have the right to comment on them' before a final decision is reached.

A similar approach is taken in the SEA Directive[73] which only requires Member States engaging in transboundary consultation to ensure that the public in the affected Member State is 'informed and given an opportunity to forward their opinion within a reasonable time-frame.' In contrast, the SEA Directive imposes a general obligation on Member States to provide their own public with an 'early and effective' opportunity for consultation. The obligation imposed under Article 14 of the Water Framework Directive to 'encourage the active involvement of all interested parties in the implementation of this Directive' is arguably the highpoint in terms of seeking to engage Member States in a process of effective consultation verging on power-sharing with the public. However, as already stated, Article 14 does not formally require Member States actually to achieve this outcome and it remains unclear whether this provision will also apply to transboundary public participation.

4. Access to justice: The enforcement of transboundary participatory rights

Transboundary participatory rights are undoubtedly emerging as an important component in a new generation of Community environmental laws, but it is equally clear that their full impact will be considerably blunted if members of the public and environmental organisations do not have the legal means to enforce these rights. Governments and public bodies are likely to offer considerable resistance to the full implementation of these transboundary rights, especially as they have clearly moved considerably beyond the more familiar diplomatic consultations between governments.[74]

At present two principal avenues of redress are available to individuals and environmental organisations seeking to enforce cross-border participatory rights. The first, and most popular, is to report Member

---

[73] Art. 7(2).

[74] E.g. despite the decision of the ECJ in Case C-392/96, *supra* note 45, and the introduction of new legislation, the Irish Government has still failed to implement fully the transboundary participatory obligations relating to environmental assessment, and further enforcement proceedings have been announced by the Commission.

States' failures to comply with their Community obligations to the European Commission. Making a complaint to the Commission incurs not only minimal costs, it is also free of the usual time limits governing national and Community law remedies. It is also possible for an individual or organisation in one Member State to complain about alleged non-compliance in another; thus the procedure can be used to deal with failures to comply with cross-border rights. However, as has already been documented in many other contexts, Article 226 provides individuals and NGOs with only a weak form of access to justice.[75] The Commission lacks direct powers of inspection within Member States in the environmental field, and there are few, if any, procedural constraints imposed on the Commission concerning its response to complaints.[76] Following criticism by the European Ombudsman in 1996, the Commission now informs complainants of its key decisions concerning enforcement. However, despite the conferral of European citizenship, the individual's role in the context of Article 226 proceedings remains that of the 'whistle blower'[77] or 'information fodder'[78] but not a participant as of right in the enforcement of Community law.

The second avenue of redress available to individuals and NGOs is to seek to enforce their transboundary participatory rights before national courts. The Commission's most recent statement concerning the application of its own enforcement powers suggests that individuals and organisations may increasingly be forced to take proceedings before national courts to ensure compliance with cross-border participatory rights. In essence the Commission signalled its wish to concentrate its efforts under Article 226 on ensuring the formal implementation of Community obligations, and largely leave cases of non-implementation in practice for national courts to handle.[79]

However, in pursuing legal action before national courts, individuals and NGOs face two important hurdles. First, they must ensure that the case law of the Court of Justice concerning the enforcement of Community law provides a legal basis on which to rely on the requirements contained in the EIA, IPPC, SEA and Water Framework Directives concerning

---

[75] Macrory, 'The Enforcement of Community Environmental Laws: Some Critical Issues', 29 *CML Rev.* (1992). p. 367 see also chap. 26 below; Macrory, 'Environmental Citizenship and the Law: Repairing the European Road' 8/2 *Journal of Environmental Law* (1996), 219 see also chap. 19 above; Rawlings, 'Engaged elites, citizen action and institutional attitudes in Commission enforcement' 6/1 *European Law Journal* (2000), 4.

[76] Moloney, Annotation of Case C-107/95, *Bundesverband der Bilanzbuchhalter eV v Commission*, 35 CML Rev. (1998), 731.

[77] Ward, op. cit. *supra* note 7.

[78] Rawlings, op. cit. *supra* note 75, p. 13

[79] *Fifteenth Annual Report on Monitoring the Application of Community Law*, COM(98) 317 final; *Sixteenth Annual Report on Monitoring the Application of Community Law*, COM(99) 301 final.

transboundary public participation. Secondly, such parties face potential barriers posed by national procedural rules governing access to national courts. It has long been recognised that Member States could considerably reduce the individual's capacity to enforce Community law in practice by establishing procedural rules that render access to justice at national level excessively difficult or impossible.[80] However, individuals and NGOs seeking to enforce transboundary participatory rights will be required to embark on cross-border litigation and therefore may encounter additional barriers, especially with procedural rules that discriminate on the grounds of nationality or residence.

Although the importance of public participation in environmental governance has been acknowledged by the Community for many years, subsidiarity and respect for the diversity of the national legal systems[81] have, until recently, militated against the development of legislation harmonising Member States' rules on access to justice in relation to the enforcement of participatory rights conferred under EC law. Indeed, prior to the Community's signing of the UN/ECE Aarhus Convention on Access to Information, Public Participation in Decision Making and Access to Justice in Environmental Matters in June 1998, the Commission had only supported the development of 'soft law' on this issue.[82] In January 2001 the Commission published its proposals to align existing Community directives on the environment with the requirements laid down in the Aarhus Convention concerning access to justice to enforce participatory rights. While marking a seminal moment in the development of Community environmental rights, these proposals (discussed below) will not ensure a uniform access to law at national level in this context, and individuals and environmental organisations will therefore remain largely reliant on the case law of the Court of Justice concerning national procedural rules. Fortunately for such parties, the Court, in contrast to the Community legislature, has not shied from taking a highly interventionist approach to ensuring that Community law on the environment is capable of effective enforcement at national level.

---

[80] E.g. Snyder, 'The effectiveness of European Community law' 56 MLR (1993), 19; Prechai, *Directives in European Community Law* (OUR 1995); Van Gerven, 'Bridging the gap Between Community and national laws: Towards a principle of homogeneity in the field of legal remedies?' 32 CML Rev. (1995), 679; De Burca, 'National procedural rules and remedies: The changing approach of the Court of Justice' in Lonbay and Biondi (Eds.), *Remedies for Breach of EC Law* (Wiley, 1997); Himsworth, 'Things fall apart: The harmonisation of Community judicial procedural protection revisited' 22 EL Rev. (1997), 291; Ruffert, 'Rights and remedies in European Community law: A comparative view' 34 CML Rev. (1997), 307; Smith, 'Remedies for breaches of EU Law in national courts: Legal variation and selection' in Craig and De Burca (Eds.), *The Evolution of EU Law* (Oxford University Press, 1999).

[81] *Implementing Community Environmental Law*, COM(1996) 500 final, pp. 11-13.

[82] COM(1996) 500 final.

4.1. The Legal Basis for Enforcing Transbounday Participatory Rights Before National Courts

Although the EIA, SEA and IPPC Directives leave Member States with discretion to determine the practical arrangements as to the public to be consulted and the nature of the consultation required,[83] the provisions concerning transboundary participation contained in these Directives are unlikely to fail the traditional tests for direct effect. They are sufficiently precise and unconditional when taken as a whole, and they create individual rights. However, it is not sufficient to establish simply the direct effectiveness of the participatory rights. The cross-border rights of public participation conferred under these directives are not free-standing in their operation but depend first on notification by the Member State in whose territory the activity is taking place and second on a decision on the part of the notified State to engage in a cross-border consultation process. Only then is the obligation to ensure cross-border public participation triggered. Community law obligations between Member States are not normally enforceable by individuals on the grounds that they do not give rise to rights which might be affected by the breach of the obligation,[84] but the Court's decision in *CIA Securities*[85] suggests that such obligations may be directly effective where they have an impact on the rights of individuals. Clearly therefore, it could be argued that the obligation to inform an affected Member State of potentially negative cross-border environmental impacts under the EIA, SEA and IPPC Directives is capable of direct enforcement by individuals.

What then of the discretion afforded to the notified Member State to engage in the transboundary consultation process? Using the precedent established by the Court's decision in *Kraaijeveld* it could be argued that the discretion conferred on the notified Member State is limited. If the activity proposed by the notifying Member State would have a significant negative transboundary environmental impact, then arguably the affected State is obliged to engage in the cross-border decision-making process. Consequently, if a notified Member State decides not to participate in the cross-border consultation process despite the possibility of significant negative transboundary environmental impacts, individuals could rely on *Kraaijeveld* to invoke the national courts' duty to ensure that the State has not exceeded the limits of its

---

[83] The scope of this discretion in relation to the EIA and IPPC Directives is discussed *supra* note 60, pp. 8-9. The position concerning the IPPC Directive is further discussed by Scott, op. cit. *supra* note 27, pp. 54-55.

[84] Case 380/87, *Cinsello Balsamo*, [1989] ECR 2491.

[85] Case C-194/94, *CIA Security International v Signalsom SA and Securitel SPRL*, [1995] ECR 1-2201.

discretion under the directive. Where a State is found to have exceeded its discretionary powers, the national court is obliged to provide an effective remedy.

However, while the traditional principle of direct effect provides a potent tool for enforcing the cross-border participatory rights contained in the EIA, SEA and IPPC Directives, it is unclear whether the same can be said of the Water Framework Directive (WFD). Although public participation is clearly central to the process of river basin management planning under the Directive, its provisions are unclear as to whether directly effective cross-border rights of participation are vested in the case of international river basin management. The WFD is by nature a 'framework' directive and in *Comitato di Coordinamento*[86] the Court held that such provisions are neither unconditional nor sufficiently precise to be capable of conferring rights which may be relied on by individuals against the State.[87] It is certainly arguable that the requirement imposed on Member States under Article 14 of the WFD to 'encourage' rather than 'ensure' the active involvement of interested parties in the implementation of the Directive will be construed by the Court as a framework provision.

However, while the terms of Article 14 may be incapable of satisfying the traditional conditions for direct effect, the Court's decision in *Commission v Italy*[88] suggests that the exercise of Member States' discretion under Article 14 will not be immune from review. In this case the Commission sought a declaration under Article 226 that Italy had failed to comply with the obligation laid down in Article 4 of the Waste Framework Directive 75/442. The Court ruled that although Article 4 did not 'specify the actual content of the measures which must be taken' to ensure compliance with its requirements, it was nevertheless binding on the Member States as to the objectives to be achieved. Consequently, while Member States retained a margin of discretion in assessing the need for such measures, the Court concluded that 'if a situation persists and leads in particular to a significant deterioration in the environment over a protracted period without any action being taken by the competent authorities, it may be an indication that the Member States have exceeded the discretion conferred on them by that provision.'[89]

---

[86] Case C-236/92, *Comitato di Difesa v Lombardia*, [1994] ECR 1-483.
[87] According to the European Court 'framework provisions' are those 'defining the framework for the action to be taken by the Member States . . . and not requiring, in itself, the adoption of specific measures'. Ibid. para. 14.
[88] Case C-365/97, *Commission v Italian Republic (San Rocco valley)*, [1999] ECR1-7773, annotated by van Haersholte in 39 CML Rev., 407-416.
[89] Ibid. para. 68.

Even if Article 14 of the WFD is deemed insufficiently precise and unconditional to confer directly enforceable transboundary participatory
rights, the Court's decisions in *Commission v Italy* and *Kraaijeveld*
strongly suggest that national judges will still be required to ensure that
Member States do not exceed the limits on their discretion under this
provision. Thus individuals and NGOs are provided with a powerful
basis on which to challenge not only a wilful refusal on the part of
Member States sharing a river basin to 'ensure co-ordination' of the
river basin management, but also persistent failures to adhere to basic
transboundary public consultation processes required by Article 14.
However, more importantly, they will also be provided with the means
to challenge persistent failures to respond to the provisions in Article 14
requiring Member States to 'encourage' and 'allow' active citizenship and
participatory methods that go beyond standard consultation processes.
Although difficulties might arise in terms of the standard against which
such efforts are to be judged, if a national court is persuaded that a
Member State has exceeded the limits on its discretion under a directive,
it is then required to provide an effective remedy.

4.2. The Potential Impact of National Procedural Rules

The most potent procedural barriers likely to be encountered by
individuals and NGOs seeking to enforce transboundary participatory
rights conferred under Community environmental law are rules on
standing and legal aid. In May 2000, the Community's IMPEL Network[90]
published a detailed report on *Complaint Procedures and Access to Justice
for citizens and NGOs in the field of the environment within the European
Union*.[91] The report noted that while many Member States used concepts
such as 'interested parties' and persons with 'a sufficient interest' to
describe those with standing to enforce environmental law before
national courts, most national systems are not very explicit as to the
meaning of these terms.[92] Ireland was identified as one of three Member
States who appeared to grant standing to any person – even to parties
who wish to protect purely diffuse environmental and natural values.
In addition, the report noted that 'no foreigner' had ever been denied
standing in an environmental case in the Irish courts.[93] However, while
its neighbouring common law jurisdiction has also embraced a liberal
approach to standing for NGOs, several leading United Kingdom cases
emphasize the importance of a geographical link between the claimants

---

[90] European Union Network for the Implementation and Enforcement of Environmental
Law.
[91] Final Report, May 2000. Available at europa.eu.int/comm./environment/impel/access_
to_justice.htm.
[92] ibid. p. 15.
[93] ibid. Annex I, National Reports, p. 84.

and the locus of the environmental damage in order to establish a sufficient interest to enforce a diffuse interest in the environment.[94] The island of Ireland is a classic example of an instance in which the transboundary participatory rights conferred under Community environmental law are likely to be exercised actively. But the United Kingdom's approach to standing in the field of environmental litigation may present an insuperable barrier to citizens and NGOs seeking to enforce transboundary participatory rights except those living on or near the Irish border and in close proximity to the proposed activity. Consequently, the enforcement of such rights under the Strategic Environmental Assessment Directive in relation to the potential cross-border impact of, for example, national plans or programmes on agriculture, which may profoundly affect migratory species of flora and fauna, would be prevented.

In relation to national procedural rules on legal aid, the Commission's Green Paper on *Legal Aid in Civil Matters: The Problems Confronting the Cross-Border Litigant*[95] points out that 'in general Member States' legal aid systems are territorial in the sense that legal aid is granted only in respect to proceedings in that State'.[96] Consequently, individuals or NGOs seeking to enforce transboundary participatory rights in the national courts of another Member State will have to look to the legal aid system of the State in which the litigation will take place. However, the Green Paper goes on to point out that 'not all the Member States ensure equal treatment of legal aid applicants irrespective of their nationality, their residences, or their presence in the State of litigation.'[97]

Despite the absence of Community legislation harmonising national procedural rules, the case law of the Court of Justice and the provisions of the EC Treaty would strongly suggest that excessively strict *and* discriminatory rules are incompatible with Community law. Although initially reluctant to interfere with the Member States' autonomy to determine the procedural rules governing the enforcement of directly effective Community law before national courts,[98] the Court has come

---

[94] e.g. *R. v Secretary of State for the Environment, ex parte Friends of the Earth Ltd and Another* [1994] 2 CMLR 760; *R. v Inspectorate of Pollution, ex parte Greenpeace Ltd (No. 2)* [1994] 4 All ER 329; *R. v Somerset County Council, ex parte Dixon*, (1997) *Journal of Planning Law*, 1030. See also Hilson, 'Greening citizenship: Boundaries of membership and the environment'', 13/3 *Journal of Environmental Law* (2001), pp. 343-346.

[95] COM(2000) 51 final.

[96] Ibid. p. 6.

[97] Ibid, p. 7.

[98] This reticence, manifested in Case 33/76, *Rewe-Zentral Finanz eG and Rewe-Zentral AG v Landwirtschaftskammer für das Saarland*, [1976] ECR 1989 and Case 47/76, *Comet v Produktschap voor Siergewassen*, [1976] ECR 2043, has been well documented. See e.g.

Continued

to subject such rules to increasingly close scrutiny.[99] Its case law on this issue is well documented. Suffice it to say, that drawing on the co-operation clause contained in Article 10 EC and Articles 6 and 13 of the European Convention on Human Rights, the Court has made it clear that Member States are required to provide individuals with real and effective access to a judicial process in order to enforce directly effective Community rights and, if necessary to create new remedies.[100] When reviewing the legality of procedural rules in relation to the principle of effectiveness, the crucial issue for the Court is whether the domestic rule makes it excessively difficult in practice to enforce the Community right in question.[101]

In addition to the principle of effectiveness, individuals and NGOs could arguably rely on the prohibition on discrimination on the grounds of nationality and the principle of equal treatment – both of which are fundamental principles of Community law and now enshrined in the EU's Charter of Fundamental Rights[102] – as the basis for challenging procedural rules limiting standing or legal aid to citizens or inhabitants of the State. The Commission's Green Paper on legal aid[103] points out that while the Court has not addressed the application of these principles in relation to national rules on legal aid (or indeed standing), the Court's extensive case law on the application of these principles in analogous contexts suggests that:

> ... any beneficiary of a Community law right... is entitled to equal treatment with nationals of the host country, as regards both formal entitlement to bring actions and also the practical conditions in which such actions can be brought, irrespective of whether he is, or ever has been,

---

...Green and Barav, "Damages in the national courts for breach of Community law', 6 YBEL (1986), 55; Legrand. 'European legal systems are not converging', 45 ICLQ (1996), 52; Dubinsky, 'The essential function of federal courts: The European Union and the United States Compared', 42 AJCL (1994), 295; Smith, op. cit. *supra* note 80, pp. 293-300.

[99] The case law of the European Court in this regard is discussed in detail by Smith, op. cit. *supra* note 80, pp. 300-316.

[100] E.g. Case 14/83, *Von Colson and Kamann v Land Nordrhein-Westfalen*, [1984] ECR 1891; Case 222/84, *Johnston v Chief Constable of the RUC*, [1986] ECR 1651; Case 222/86, *UNECTEF v. Heylens*, [1987] ECR 4097; Case C-213/89, *R. v Secretary of State for Transport ex parte Factortame Ltd and Others*, [1990] ECR 1-2433; Case C-377/89, *Cotter and McDer-mott v Minister for Social Welfare and Attorney General* [1991] ECR 1-1155; Case C-271/91, *Marshall v Southampton and South West Area Health Authority (No. 2)*, [1993] ECR 1-4367. The Court's case law in this regard has been addressed by a wide range of commentators; e.g. *supra* note 80.

[101] ibid.

[102] Art. 21(2) contains the principle of non-discrimination on the grounds of nationality, while Art. 20 contains the principle of equality.

[103] *Supra* note 95.

resident or even physically present in that country. It is only logical that the right to bring actions comprises the effective right of access to courts, and hence entitlement to legal aid, when a national of the State would, mutatis mutandis, be so entitled... Even a condition which was not formally discriminatory (such as a residence or presence condition applicable to nationals and foreigners alike) could constitute disguised discrimination (since nationals are far more likely to satisfy it than foreigners are) and would hence be impermissible unless it could be justified [by the Member State] on objective grounds.[104]

4.3.   Commission proposals to implement Aarhus requirements concerning access to justice to enforce rights to participate in environmental decision making

The final issue to be addressed in the context of enforcing transboundary participatory rights conferred under Community environmental law concerns the likely impact of the Commission's recent proposals to implement the rights of access to justice laid down in the Aarhus Convention. Compared to the rights conferred under the other two 'pillars', the rights of access to justice guaranteed by Article 9(2) of the Convention in relation to the enforcement of the participatory rights conferred under Article 6, are less explicit. In addition, these rights do not extend to the enforcement of participatory rights guaranteed by the Convention in relation to the preparation of plans and programmes. Consequently, only the EIA and IPPC Directives required amendment to comply with the Convention in this regard. Article 9(2) of the Convention provides that:

> ... each Party shall, within the framework of its national legislation, ensure that members of the public concerned (a) having a sufficient interest or, alternatively, (b) maintaining impairment of a right, where the administrative procedural law of a Party requires this as a precondition, have access to a review procedure before a court of law and/or another independent and impartial body established by law, to challenge the substantive and procedural legality of any decision, act or omission subject to the provisions of Article 6.

Article 9(2) goes on to provide that what constitutes a sufficient interest and impairment of a right shall be determined in accordance with the

---

[104] ibid. pp. 8-9.

requirements of national law and consistently with the objective of giving the public concerned wide access to justice. For the purposes of Article 9, the interest of NGOs shall be deemed sufficient for these purposes and such organisations shall be deemed to have rights capable of being impaired. Article 9(4) also requires that access to justice procedures must provide 'adequate and effective remedies, including injunctive relief as appropriate'. In addition such procedures must also be 'fair'.

For present purposes, two features should be emphasized about the rights conferred under Article 9. First, although the Convention specifically requires that rules on standing must be consistent with the objective of giving the public wide access to justice, it is clear that signatories still retain considerable control over the procedural conditions under which such access is provided. Second, whereas Article 9(1) of the Convention guarantees a right of access to justice to 'any person' who considers that their right to information has been violated, the equivalent provisions for public participation in decisionmaking are limited to the 'public concerned'. The Implementation Guide prepared by the United Nations[105] concerning Article 9(1) points out that the term 'any person' requires that signatories allow access to justice to enforce information rights 'even to citizens or residents of other countries and requires organisations to be provided with this access even if their centre of activities is in another country.'[106] Although the concept of the 'public concerned' could be similarly interpreted to include foreign nationals seeking to enforce cross-border rights of public participation, the Implementation Guide is silent in this regard.

In seeking to implement the Aarhus requirements concerning the enforcement of participatory rights, the Commission has proposed that the EIA and IPPC Directives be amended to include provisions requiring Member States to:

> ...ensure that, in accordance with the relevant national legal system, the public concerned has access to a review procedure before a court of law or another body established by law to challenge the substantive or procedural legality of decisions, acts or omissions subject to the public participation provisions of this Directive. Any such procedure shall be expeditious and shall not be prohibitively expensive.[107]

---

[105] ECE/CEP/72. United Nations, 2000.

[106] ibid. p. 140.

[107] COM(2000) 839 final, para. 6.2.5. Draft Art. 2(5) proposes inserting this provision into a new Article 10a of the EIA Directive. Art. 3(4) proposes the insertion of an identical provision into a new Art. 15a of the IPPC Directive.

Although these proposals undoubtedly represent a seminal departure from the Commission's previous reluctance to support the adoption of Community legislation harmonising national rules on access to justice in the context of participatory rights conferred under EC environmental law, the proposed formulation of the right of access to justice leaves two important questions unanswered. First, the proposed amendment does not implement the specific caveat contained in Article 9(2) that rules on standing should be consistent with the provision of 'wide access to justice'. Thus is it unclear whether Member States retain discretion in terms of their approach to standing, thereby perpetuating the diversity in national rules in this regard, or whether it is implicit in the simple instruction to ensure 'access to a review procedure' that a wide approach to standing must be taken. Second, although this proposed formulation applies the right of access to justice to members of the public seeking to enforce participatory rights conferred under the EIA and IPPC Directives, it is unclear whether the right also extends to the enforcement of the transboundary participatory rights conferred therein. In this regard, it is noteworthy that the access to justice provision for the EIA Directive is to be inserted into Article 10, which comes after the transboundary provisions. Whereas the equivalent provisions for the IPPC Directive will be inserted into Article 15, which deals only with public consultation at a national level. The placement of these proposed amendments suggests that Member States would be under an obligation to amend national procedural rules to ensure equal access to justice for claimants living within and beyond national territory only when the litigation involves the enforcement of the participatory rights under the EIA Directive.

5. Conclusion

Legislative developments since the adoption of the Fifth Action Programme on the Environment indicate that as the principle of subsidiarity and the policy of deregulation have begun to infuse Community law on the environment, Member States are being increasingly required to consider the transboundary impact of environmental decision making within their own territory. In addition, as the imperative to achieve democratic accountability in environmental governance has moved to the heart of Community policy on the environment, EC legislation in this field has increasingly vested individuals with rights to participate in the process environmental decision-making. This process is now extending to include cross-border decision-making concerning transboundary environmental impacts. So pronounced is this trend, that consultation between Member States concerning transboundary environmental impacts and public rights to participate in that process are arguably emerging within Community environmental law as minimum procedural requirements for good environmental governance at national level. However, three tensions remain in the development of transboundary participatory rights under Community environmental law.

First, although Community law on the environment has sought to embrace a broad notion of environmental citizenship in which the right to participate in environmental governance is not linked to territory, it has yet to develop a consistent approach to the conferral of transboundary participatory rights. Once amended to reflect the requirements of the Aarhus Convention, only the Environmental Impact Assessment Directive (EIA) will ensure consistency between the participatory rights conferred on nationals within the notifying Member State and citizens from potentially affected Member States. The Integrated Pollution Prevention and Control Directive (IPPC) confers significantly weaker transboundary participatory rights compared to the other three Directives conferring such rights; whereas the Water Framework Directive is alone in seeking to embrace a form of public participation that includes not only standard consultation but also power sharing. Second, the Community remains ambivalent about developing legislative rights of access to justice to ensure the effective enforcement of the participatory rights conferred under EC environmental law. The Commission's proposals to insert access to justice requirements into the EIA and IPPC Directives, while important, are modest when compared to powerful jurisprudence being developed by the European Court of Justice on this issue. In effect, individuals and NGOs will remain dependent on the principles developed by the Court to enforce many of the transboundary participatory rights conferred thus far under Community environmental law. And third, while the Commission has been prepared to bring enforcement proceedings in respect of non-transposition of transboundary participation obligations, even successful action before the Court is no guarantee that a Member State will introduce the necessary implementing legislation, as the Irish experience demonstrates.[108] Given the fundamental weakness in the Community's enforcement mechanisms, the conferral of European citizenship surely militates in favour of conferring rights to citizens to participate in the process of enforcing Community law.

The EU's new Charter of Fundamental Rights does not guarantee a substantive right to environmental quality, or indeed procedural rights of public participation in environmental governance, but Article 37 does reaffirm the Union's commitment to ensuring a high level of

---

[108] *Supra* n 74.

environmental protection in accordance with the principle of sustainable development. Sustainability is fundamentally premised on a concept of environmental citizenship that guarantees rights of access to information, participation in decision making and access to justice. Thus, although the Charter remains non-binding, it is arguable that in the future Article 37 will work in synergy with the requirements of the Aarhus Convention and jurisprudence of the Court of Justice to stimulate a rather more

CHAPTER 23

UNDERLYING THEMES IN THE POLICY PROCESS*

Policy makers and analysts know only too well the breadth and complexities of the issues involved in the development of environmental policy, whether at national or Community level. The previous contributions in this collection give some striking illustrations of the distinctive strands of scientific, administrative and legal thinking involved.

In his Opening Address to the Conference, Lord Flowers indicated that a rigorous and dispassionate handling and integration of these various approaches is a task of no mean difficulty. Any such analysis of environmental policy must be handled with sensitivity so as to identify and integrate the contributions made by each distinctive approach, without loss of authenticity to the various disciplines and interests involved.

Our attention is drawn more to the process of policy making rather than to the substance of policy development. By 'process' we mean the constitutional style, administrative traditions, and national dispositions which shape, accommodate or even reject the content of policy proposals. The strong reliance on procedure and cross-sectoral co-operation in the environmental field lends a further dimensions to this study of process.

In analytical terms, the European Community can be seen either as a simple set of intergovernmental institutions, or as the same plus the sum of the Member States, or as a transcending dimension of European governance. All three pictures are no doubt useful. The wider impact of Community powers has already been discussed in previous contributions. But in the practical handling of specific issues, Member States may see the Community in the more straightforward intergovernmental terms, and strive to confine attention by the Community to those issues and initiatives which by their nature, scale, and timing are the most suitable for Community action. It is natural for such matters to be treated on a 'them' and 'us' basis, and to this extent – and notwithstanding the wider and longer-term vision –

* R. Macrory and J.Peachey (1983) 'Underlying Themes in the Policy Process' in Macrory (ed) *Britain, Europe and the Environment,* Imperial College Centre for Technology, London

the Community and Member States can be regarded as things apart. This should help focus analysis on the ensuing boundaries and interfaces as these take the strain of the new requirements.

We belong to a research team which looks for stabilising influences in the processes encountered in resource systems under heavy and conflicting demands - the notion of stability in this context includes both sustainability and adaptability, as well as the more usual preoccupations of productivity and equitability.

We are seeking a methodology for the review of policy process and of its influence on substantive policy development. The ultimate aim is to produce criteria to help develop the review of existing policy instruments, choose the style and manner of newly proposed policy intervention, improve the administrative design in draft policy proposals, and increase the understanding of the dynamics and functions of procedural style.

In the remainder of this paper, and as an initial step in this analytical direction, we trace certain themes which, in this country, seem to underly much of the discussion and analysis of national and Community environmental policy. These themes may only rarely be mentioned explicitly. But it is clear that they each raise a number of central questions relating to the functioning of policy process and the design, installation, and operation of new Community-based procedures. We describe these themes under the following headings:

- Handling the status quo;

- International ramifications;

- Intergovernmental effectiveness;

- Priorities and feasibility;

- Alignment and harmonisation;

- Member States as neighbours.

Handling the Status Quo

Negotiations within the Community have to reckon with widely differing circumstances, attitudes and practices as between Member States. Community Institutions also have their own distinctive style and approach. Sometimes these differences can be seen in largely technical terms where (as in the present context) varying environmental situations, development pressures, conservation needs, and technical capabilities may clearly indicate differing professional treatment. But the position is often further complicated because some differences are more telling of the national approach to getting things done than of the particular problems at issue.

All too often, the seemingly intractable nature of these differences and difficulties puts governments more firmly on the defensive than is usual for the protection of the national interest. The ensuing inhibition of response to Community initiatives can spread through the inevitable 'linkage' of one policy issue with another.

This hardening of attitude and freezing of policy advance has two effects of central importance to our analysis. Firstly, there is a somewhat exaggerated support for the status quo, and, secondly, there is the inevitable slowing and narrowing of procedural development. These difficulties have to be resolved one way or another. There may be a need to return to the design stage so as to produce more measured intervention. But it is often too late to do more than try to soften the proposals already on the table, sometimes by recourse to an uneasy plurality of approach.

It is hardly surprising that the attitudes encouraged by defensive briefing, and the upheavals caused by aggressive Community intervention, may in turn inhibit the domestic search for improved procedures at a national level. This inhibition may continue longer than would often be the case, in order not to risk disturbing the validity of past compromises or attracting fresh attention from 'the Community.

Community environmental policy provides some good examples of these difficulties – not least insofar as the United Kingdom is concerned. The Community's advocacy of fixed pollution standards in certain areas (as discussed elsewhere in this collection) is somewhat at odds with the UK preference for achieving similar levels of pollution control through the deployment, in each particular case, of the 'best practicable means' available. The technical arguments have included considerations as to how far the absorptive capacity of the receiving environment should influence the suitability and extent of the operationally feasible controls required.

In the Directive of 4 May 1976, concerning dangerous substances discharged into the aquatic environment, the UK was, in essence, allowed to retain its 'emphasis on pollution concentrations in the receiving environment. This is an example of where the uneasy plurality of approach to which we have already referred was chosen as the way forward.

The draft Directive concerning the environmental assessment of certain projects (COM (80) 313 final) has already run into difficulties reminiscent of those experienced with pollution standards. The UK has again sought to defend traditionally informal, and flexible procedures for planning assessment against more formalised approaches to the identification and assessment of environmental factors in development.

These kinds of differences in approach can indeed be often explained and treated as fundamental differences of administrative style and procedural approach, peculiar to their respective constitutional settings. These 'processes' are evolutionary in nature and, paradoxically, delicate but hard to change. It is common for joint policy agreements to paper over such differences, and the Community has no such monopoly of this device. This means, however, that even the initial and purely technical discussions of new policy proposals, at Community level, must bear the full weight of procedural dissent to be found within the Community and Member States.

The handling of the draft Directive concerning environmental assessment illustrates the kinds of administrative and policy losses that may now have to be endured. The Community is deprived of the signal contribution which the UK could bring to the design of assessment procedures through its own particular experience of adaptive planning. Britain itself loses because the argument has all but stopped a fundamental debate on national requirements for strengthening the domestic assessment of environmental factors in strategic and land-use planning. Moreover, the apparent clumsiness of the proposed intervention has further alienated industrial developers who might otherwise have accepted more rigorous forms of environmental assessment.

It is clear that reckoning with the status quo must figure large in the design of Community intervention. One step forward would be to see how the apparently contradictory procedures and practice in Member States stand up to careful monitoring and analysis, in comparative terms and as part of the working compromises of the Community. Mere assertions that one practice or procedure is better than another will not do, given the complexity of the policy issues and the scale and magnitude of the judgement involved.

International ramifications

In the inevitable calculations as to the benefits, disbenefits and untapped opportunities in Community action, it is important to consider the extent to which such action can complement other environmental programmes such as those of the Organization for Economic Cooperation and Development, the United Nations Environment Programme, the Economic Commission for Europe, and other more specialised and regional bodies.

It is also necessary to consider the implications of Community concepts of self-sufficiency and external responsibility in terms of regional environmental strategy and global resource management. These international implications of Community action raise a number of questions: can the Community act more powerfully than individual Member States to revitalise international environmental programmes? Can the Community's own resource management strategies be presented and adjusted so as to hinder the collapse of other environmentally-dependent resource systems, especially in the developing world? Can the Community do more than any other state to mobilise the protection of precious environmental treasures? Given the Community's economic power and influence in world markets, what kinds of issues would be best suited to adoption as global cause celebres?

The dovetailing of wider Community action to wider international initiatives repeats in essence – though perforce not so much in requisite sensitivity – the same process as the Member States experience in dealing with the Community. But in addition, Community states in the international scene are freer to act 'independently, being less limited in the exercise of their sovereignty. The challenge is to steer a middle way between the potentially unbalancing effect of a single Community input to international programmes, and the unnecessarily complicated consequence of unco-ordinated responses to such programmes from separate Community states. There are a number of arrangements on the environmental side which fall between these extremes, such as those concerning the development of environmental monitoring and data systems.

Intergovernmental Effectiveness

Mention has been made of the need to look at the Community in ie intergovernmental terms; this may be extended to see how well its institutions compare with other intergovernmental agencies. All these bodies should attract as much critical review and independent evaluation as that taken for granted in their national equivalents.

Apart from the more specific concerns of institutional and programmatic efficiency, there is also the question of those who have fundamental doubts about the value of the Community in any case. Because of the dominance and exclusivity of the Community ideal, such doubts can only presently be entertained in terms of conventional political alignment – at least in the UK. This is not satisfactory. A way forward, in the analysis of such doubts, would be to see how well the Community stands in comparison with other kinds of intergovernmental environmental action, in terms of design, implementation, and appropriateness. A considerable injection of policy analysis skills would be needed in such studies, if the geopolitical significance of the Community is to be properly assessed. These comparisons would have to include analysis of underlying attributes which govern Community arrangements and their nearest non-Community, equivalents. For instance, the absence of the rules and discipline of a common market, in non-Community arrangements, may weaken the individual and collective governmental will to shoulder consistent levels of responsibility. The economic intimacy implicit in the common market, let alone its wider social and political implications, can be expected to permit a greater degree of mutualism by Member States than may be available in other frameworks for intergovernmental action.

The economic emphasis in the Community concept allows environmental resources to be treated as economic resources, as a basis for mutual action, even though such considerations may not yet have fully reached the market place. This readiness to see environmental issues in economic terms enables common action to be considered for a range of environmental protection measures, which might not otherwise have a basis for consensus. The way in which the Community finally deals with the acid rain issue will be exceptionally interesting in this respect.

The Community cannot rest content in the expectation that regionalism will provide a ready answer. We have already alluded to some of the external factors, in terms of relationships with international environmental programmes. But internally, within the Community, there are huge variations in regional environment and development, conflicting policies for natural resources and agriculture, and the unevenness of the environment – economic connection.

The Sixth Amendment of the Directive of 27 June 1967 concerning dangerous substances provides a new example of a procedure which, if carried out in one Member State, is automatically valid, for the case in question, throughout the Community. It would help the intergovernmental understanding of the impact of Community policy process in national affairs to know the detailed effects that the implementation of this policy is having on the relevant administrative procedures of Member States throughout for the environmental, industrial, health and safety, and trade sectors.

Priorities and Feasibility

However ambitious Community policy making, there is no doubt that attention must be given to the extent to which proposed actions can be implemented, given present professional and administrative capabilities and intervention techniques. The style of the policy maker and the nature of his or her policy planning machine affects the content and scope of any proposal, and it can be argued that environmental policies are best advanced by bold initiatives. But policy gains are all too quickly lost if policy concept and policy device are not rigorously defined. This is where priority gives way to feasibility and principle to practice

The more distant nature of Community intervention – and the sheer comprehensiveness of Community actions – impose extra burdens in this reckoning with feasibility. This is because these actions are often dismissed as inflexible, or profligate at national or local level. The fact that intervention may be legal will not in itself remove the difficulties of its enforcement or the antagonism it may provoke. It is not fair, however, to blame the Community for those disturbances and adjustments which any Western state has to face in pursuit of acceptable environmental policies, and in the making of a responsible contribution to the integrated management of its own region. But whatever the volume of Community legislation, it is unsafe and unsound to plead the urgency and priority of the cause – or indeed the novelty of the problem – as a licence for taking liberties with administrative process.

Some recognition of these considerations is to be found in the present climate of Community thinking. More generally, in the developed world, there has been a movement away from the 'grand design' in the emphasis of national and international policy. In the UK, in particular, there has been a shift towards a more opportunistic and even minimalist approach to public sector intervention and resource allocation. The Community's Third Action Programme on the environment is indeed more strategic in emphasis than its predecessors. It might even be argued that constancy of national purposes and congruency of national style, especially within an enlarged Community, could prove insufficient to support fundamental harmonisation of the kind once assumed essential for Community intervention and development.

These changes of policy appreciation will have profound effects for the design of policy proposals and for the conduct of negotiations. Priorities may depend far more on a real but highly selective meeting of minds; feasibility will figure larger in the determination of priorities. More limited initiatives may be the order of the day.
Or, perhaps, greater emphasis on policy components other than the harmonisation of procedure would form a more effective basis for Community action. There may be, for example, potential for advance in the design and setting of criteria and guidelines, in which emphasis centres on strategic policy frameworks rather than on the detail of executive action.

Alignment and Harmonisation

In order to appraise, design, and measure performance, it is important to be clear as to the particular objectives on which specific proposals for harmonisation are based. One purpose may be to bring recalcitrant Member States into line with a prevailing status quo. But more positively, harmonisation may be seen as a precondition for reaching new levels of policy coordination or for installing new policies or practices on a Community-wide basis. The most familiar justification for harmonisation, whether in the general or the particular, rests on the need to avoid direct or indirect distortion of the common market.

Although the economic dimension dominates the present remit of Community action, the limitations that would follow from this economic preoccupation are not accepted by all of those involved in the development of Community policy. Some would claim that the Treaty of Rome provides a mandate to explore every policy opportunity for extending the harmonising and uniting influence of the Community. The environmental sector, however, raises formidable challenges to this approach, because of its peculiar heterogeneity and uncertainty. The emphasis in environmental management on designing for adaptability rails against the more singular approach. These contrasts have already been seen as they affect such issues as pollution control, conservation priorities, and environmental assessment. However, the more intensively developed the environmental setting, the easier it may be to take a simpler line and see the extension of the concept of the common market as a means of meeting the required common standards throughout the Community but with an equality of the burdens thus inflicted. The need to avoid pollution havens would be the simplest example of how the equality of the environmental burden on industries is required directly in order to help sustain the common market in which those industries may compete on a Community-wide basis. This approach poses a fundamental question – how 'natural' or underdeveloped does an environment have to be before it gains legitimate administrative exemption from the harmonising influence of the Treaty of Rome?

In lowlier vein, opportunities for harmonisation of technical or management procedures are often seen as providing new areas of agreement which would not be possible at higher policy levels. The commitment is thought to be comparatively modest, and such exercises may even be seen as paving the way to a longer-term meeting of minds. Indeed, some adaptive convergence of approach is a common feature of the influence of the Community in all walks of life, even when brought about by seemingly nebulous compromise or quite low levels of harmonisation. In the environmental sector, the British attitude to pollution control has moved sufficiently for environmental quality objectives to be regarded at least in terms of some fixed target for pollution levels. Conversely, the continental view has taken in a greater awareness of considerations of resilience in the receiving environment.

There are a number of valuable lessons to be learnt from carefully measuring the performance of Directives that have been in operation for some time. For example, are there unintended industrial havens in one part of the Community and unnecessary environmental burdens elsewhere, as a result of Community action? Have steps been taken in consequence – and within the spirit of the various compromises – to adjust the emphasis in both the Member States and in the Community in favour of the superior approach? What conclusions may be drawn for the future as to required levels and styles of harmonisation?

It would not, however, be wise to assume that harmonisation automatically becomes easier at lower levels of policy. What is gained by avoiding the irreconcilable is to some extent lost to the irreducible. As we have noted with environmental Directives, some of the difficulties are also in part due to subtle but fundamental differences of administrative or technical detail. This illustrates how important it is for the analyst and designer to achieve the finest and earliest possible calibration of similar practices in Member States – before, any attempt is made to adjust such practices for the purposes of Community harmonisation or intervention.

The importance of detail in the design of harmonisation and intervention suggests that it may not always be prudent to set aside procedural and methodological objections even though these delay major policy advances. The detail cannot always be easily disposed of after the broader agreement especially when inevitably lower levels of decision may prove too limited to cope with the design challenges of the technical, administrative, let alone constitutional, factors involved.

Member States as Neighbours

The interrelationships inherent in the concept of a European Community and fundamental to the operation of a common market require a high degree of mutual interest between Member States. There are a number of obstacles to be faced. Member States fear that other Community partners may be less observant of Community requirements, or that these requirements may favour one part of the Community rather than another. There is resistance from Member States to upheaval of their own national procedures, especially when these are seen domestically to be working well, or where intervention has been largely dictated by the needs of less advanced neighbours.

All of these factors, in one way or another, may be seen to have contributed to the frosty reception given in the UK to the current proposals for environmental assessment procedures. But, as argued earlier, defensive briefing, often sound enough in purpose, should not obscure the obligation to question and study, even in purely domestic terms, the appropriateness of national procedures. The changing needs in environmental assessment arising from the new technology industries, energy supply, agricultural expansion, and shared land-use provide good examples of where much procedural work has now to be concentrated

The treatment of the Community as a single planning unit or resource conservation region, which inevitably transcends national boundaries an(priorities, introduces a new order of sensitivity into the relationships of the Member States as neighbours. The consequences may be seen in terms of planning zones and locational incentives. These last devices may affect the extent to which the importance of a particular set of national environments assets might be downgraded as a result of a Community-wide strategy under which similar assets are more conveniently conserved or protected in some other part of the Community. It would be good to be able to predict at what stages in the development of the Community Member States might be prepared to sacrifice certain national environmental assets, resting content in the knowledge of their protection elsewhere in the Community.

Conclusions

We have sought to draw some critical attention to the procedural themes and administrative issues that have surfaced in the first ten years of Community action on the environment. This means dwelling more on the conflicts as between the new, Community ways and the older, national approaches, rather than concentrating on the considerable advances that have been made in terms of policy content. A concern for the process rather than the substance of policy is sometimes seen to be fastidious, 'legalistic', or possibly obstructive of change. But we have seen that the more subtle aspects of administrative process cannot be neglected or ignored simply because they cannot compete with the excitement and speed with which the substantive aspects of policy are generally handled and analysed.

Policy gains, however good the substance, can all too readily be lost if their operational demands are even just subtly and perhaps unwittingly discordant with administrative process. This is not to suggest that the underlying policy process may not, in turn, have to adapt and change as new policy arrangements come into force. But the essentially more evolutionary and stabilising nature of such processes may require a more delicate adjustment than the sudden shifts which may be taken for granted in substantive policy.

The experience with environmental policy suggests that quite modest Community initiatives have become key issues – not so much because of their policy substance but because of the procedural and administrative implications of the measures in question for Member States. Indeed, some of the subsequent adaptations in national administrative process have been quite startling.

We conclude that a number of important analytical opportunities are to be found in the environmental sector of the Community, for the design and definition of policy concepts, assessment procedures, control functions, intervention strategies, and administrative mechanisms, on which the substantive aims of the Community and its Member States all have to depend. Many policy concepts do not always do full justice to the wealth of experience on which they are based. Their meaning should be more precise so as to remove some of the familiar ambiguities and looseness which hinders the design and discussion of environmental policy. Environmental assessment procedure requires considerable methodological development and administrative testing. Control functions need to be seen as designed components of the administrative, environmental, and economic systems which they serve. In the environmental sector, it is necessary to choose levels, scales, and types of intervention and harmonisation that can accommodate regional environmental objectives, ensure consistency of purpose, and yet preserve the flexibility essential to cope with the varied and local nature of the environment and its management.

Administrative mechanisms, as we have indicated, are the key to all these other components and activities. They need a sympathetic but rigorous analytical perception, if they are to be fully harnessed and carefully adapted in the interests of Member States, through the development of the Community and the protection of the European environment.

SUPRA-NATIONAL ENFORCEMENT OF ENVIRONMENTAL LAW

PART 6

SUPRA-NATIONAL ENFORCEMENT OF ENVIRONMENTAL LAW

Without effective enforcement, environmental law drifts into mere symbolic reassurance. The articles in part I were concerned with new ways of thinking about regulatory enforcement and sanctions but mainly at a national level. The enforcement of supra-national obligations raises a distinct set of challenges, not least because one is generally dealing with nation states that may subscribe to the principles of compliance with international obligations but in reality are likely to resist undue interference with national sovereignty. The Achilles heel of many international environmental treaties used to be the lack of attention given their enforcement, though more recent international agreements such as the 1987 Montreal Protocol on Ozone Substances and the 1997 Kyoto Protocol on Climate Change contain more sophisticated supervisory mechanisms designed to bring pressure on non-compliant parties. Nevertheless, they largely work 'through collective decision making and co-operation rather than through formal processes of law enforcement and sanctions.'[1] A power of inspection by international enforcement bodies remains very much the exception rather than the rule. International courts have no direct power to impose sanctions on a non-compliant party.

In this context, the machinery of the European Union designed to ensure compliance by Member States of their obligations under Community law offers an intriguing example of a developed supra-national enforcement system, and as so often with Europe one that charts a distinctive course between international and national ways of doing things. Over many years, the European Court of Justice has developed principles designed to assist individuals to invoke Community law before their national courts, and this is an important tool for enforcement. This chapter, though, focuses on the powers and practice of the European Commission to ensure compliance by Member States. The machinery is common to all areas of Community law, but over the last twenty years its use in the environmental field has been particularly striking.

Distinctive features of the Community system include a dedicated legal unit with the Commission DG Environment concerned with the enforcement of all Community environmental legislation, a far broader remit possessed by any specialised secretariat under particular international environmental treaties;

---

[1] Birnie and Boye (2001) *International Law and the Environment* 2nd ed p 220, Oxford University Press, Oxford

a citizen's complaint system allowing any individual or organisation to notify the Commission of suspected breaches of Community law by their own Member State or indeed by any other Member State; and, not least, the power of the European Court of Justice to impose financial sanctions on Member States who fail to comply with its judgments concerning non-compliance (see for example, Commission v Spain v Greece (2000) in part 4 above).

Compliance Mechanisms in the European Community – A Global Model *(2006) is a broad overview of the system, taking into account the recent trends on the types of actions being taken by the Commission, and the responses of the European Court of Justice. It considers the extent to which the Community system might offer a model for the supra-national enforcement of environmental obligations in other parts of the world.*

Despite its innovative features, the system is by no means perfect. **The Enforcement of EU Environmental Law: Some Proposals for Reform** *(2005) is concerned with ways of improving current procedures, designed to make them less bureaucratic and more strategically focussed on environmental outcomes. Many Member States are uncomfortable with the prospect of enforcement actions by the Commission especially when they are concerned with particular instances of non-compliance in practice rather than merely ensuring than the national law formally reflects Community obligations. The Commission itself is under pressure, and the Secretariat General in 2007 published a policy paper that will re-orientate its general approach towards enforcement. The system can undoubtedly be improved but not, I hope, in a way that emasculates its distinctive power to bring home the legally binding implications of Community law.*

Finally, **The Enforcement of Community Environmental Law: Some Critical Issues** *(1992) considers the system against underlying legal principles. Despite developments that have taken place in the intervening fifteen years (including a renumbering of the relevant Treaty provisions), the fundamental structures and challenges inherent in the system remain today. In particular, the critical importance of the way that legislation is drafted and how that affects its enforceability is raised. In the light of current trends in the style of legislation and the greater discretion being given to Member States within common legislative frameworks, as identified in Part 5, this now has even more contemporary relevance.*

CHAPTER 24

COMPLIANCE MECHANISMS IN THE EUROPEAN UNION –A GLOBAL MODEL*

The Importance of Environmental Enforcement at EU Level

The European Commission's role in ensuring that EU environmental legislation is properly implemented within Member States is arguably the most distinctive feature of the legal system that has been created within the Union. It is by no means the only mechanism for ensuring effective implementation. Over the past two decades the European Court of Justice has itself developed important principles of law designed to assist improved implementation of EU law which has been agreed by Member States but not properly transposed into national law; the 'direct effect' doctrine, for example, which holds that precise and unconditional provisions of Directives may be invoked against state bodies, whatever the content of national law; or the principle that courts should, as far as possible interpret national legal provisions in the light of their underlying EU legislation. New networks of national environmental agencies and regulators have been developed to improve the exchange of information between those bodies responsible for enforcement at the sharp end, and perhaps indirectly to encourage a degree of peer pressure on the more recalcitrant.

Despite these developments, the Commission's powers in bringing legal pressure on Member States remains a vital part of the system. National judges are not necessarily sympathetic or indeed experienced in ensuring a European dimension to their decision-making, and in any event tend to be reactive rather than strategic in that they can only deal with particular cases before them. One cannot necessarily rely upon national environment agencies and regulators to enforce EU law-they may often been constrained within their own structures, or indeed be the source of complaint themselves. Only the European Commission can provide a systematic and strategic approach towards implementation throughout the Union. There is a growing recognition throughout the world that many contemporary environmental challenges cannot be realistically met by action at national level alone. As the most developed system of enforcement of supra-national legal obligations, the EU provides something of a global model for other regions of the world, through it

---

* R Macrory (2006) Compliance Mechanisms in the European Community – A Global Model in *International Comparative Legal Guide to Environment Law 2005*, Global Legal Group, London, 1 - 4

does not follow that the system should necessarily be slavishly copied. It is by no means perfect, and faces considerable challenges, especially in coping with the greatly increased size of the Union. Nevertheless it is one that should be carefully studied.

The core provisions in the Treaty concerning supervision and enforcement have remained remarkably constant over the years, and are common to all areas of Community law. The European Commission is given the supervisory duty to ensure that European law is applied, and each Directorate has dedicated units responsible for this task. But it is the environmental field that the Commission has taken a leading role, with almost one quarter of current infringement dossiers against Member States falling within the environmental sector. This may not be so surprising. In many areas of private and public law, such as social welfare or competition, there will be interested parties who will have a direct legal concern should a Member State fail to implement its Community obligations properly. They may often bring cases before their national courts, or notify relevant national enforcement bodies. The same is not necessarily true of the natural environment, which may be seriously harmed or destroyed with no private party having a sufficient legal interest to protect any legal rights to prevent this happening. Non-governmental organisations can fulfil a custodian role for the environment, but do not necessarily have the stamina or resources to bring cases before the courts, and, despite the Aarhus Convention on Access to Justice, standing and costs provisions still vary considerably between Member States. In this context, the enforcement activities of the Commission are all the more significant.

Verifying Formal Implementation by Member States

The Directive remains the favoured form of Community legal instrument in the environmental field. As such, it is an obligation of a Member State to introduce whatever legal or administrative measures are needed at national level to ensure that the objectives of the Directive are secured. In the interests of transparency and legal certainty, the European Court almost twenty years ago developed principles that insisted that most provisions of a Directive were transposed at national level by means of national laws or regulations, rather than less formal administrative measures which are difficult to enforce legally and could all too easily be changed. The Commission's first concern, therefore, is to ensure that Member States do introduce national legislation within the time limit specified in the relevant Directive, normally two or three years. Case law of the European Court has essentially treated this initial step of complying with time limits as a simple 'yes-no' question – excuses raised by Member States such as those relating to internal constitutional difficulties in passing national laws within the time limits have received short shrift from the Court. Given this intransigence it is surprising that deadlines are still missed by Member States. Yet the latest published annual report of the Commission (Commission Staff Working Paper Seventh Annual Survey on the implementation and enforcement of Community environmental law, Brussels, 8.9.2006 SEC (2006) 1143) covering 2005 reveals 124 cases outstanding by the end of the year that were concerned solely with non-communication, a drop of almost one third compared with the previous year, but still almost a quarter of all current dossiers. Most cases related to the air and waste sectors. This may reflect the number of recent Directives in those fields. One might have predicted that it would be countries with the strongest federal structures such as Spain, Germany, or Belgium which would find it most difficult to secure internal agreement within the time limits, but there seems to be no particular correlation between lateness of making measures and the intensity of federal structures – France heads the list followed closely by Italy, Greece, Portugal and Finland, and amongst the new accession States the Czech Republic, were the worst offenders for late transposition in 2004. Many of these cases are unlikely to reach the European Court of Justice, since they are initiated to bring pressure on the Member State concerned, and a late submission by a Member State will generally result in a case being dropped.

The second task for the Commission is to verify whether the national laws that have been submitted by Member States are in conformity with the Community legislation, and this is one that is clearly far more legally demanding than simply checking dates for submission. There is no requirement that implementation of a Directive must be by a single piece of national law. For countries with regional or devolved structures, there may therefore be numerous pieces of legislation implementing a single Directive, and failure to implement in some areas of a Member State will count as non-conformity. Other Directives such as those relating to access to information or environmental assessment can be described as horizontal in that they tend to cut across traditional sectoral divisions of national laws. Implementing these types of requirements into a national system may also require many different laws. In some instances, existing national legislation may be sufficient to reflect the obligations of a Directive, and transposition does not necessarily require a word for word reproduction of the Directive into national legislation. Indeed, the underlying rationale for the Directive as a form of legal instrument is precisely that it should allow for and accommodate different styles of administrative and legal traditions across the Member States. The use of the word, say, 'practicable' in national legislation may be a permissible translation of the term 'available' used in a Directive if in the national context it reflects the sense of the Directive's terminology. Nevertheless there is a fine balance to be drawn in allowing for a degree of national leeway and discretion, and ensuring that the national legislation faithfully transposes the Directive's obligations.

The Commission's report for 2005 shows some 86 cases outstanding concerning non-conformity, a slight reduction on the year before, with the majority in the field of nature (25.6%) and waste (23.3%), followed closely by environmental assessment (17.4%). To a large extent the problems of waste reflected the admittedly challenging task of transposing definitions and concepts of waste in Community law into national provisions. With nature protection, we are faced with the epitome of the under-protected environment. Community nature protection obligations expressed in legislation such as the Birds or Habitats Directives are potentially demanding and restrictive of economic development, and national administrations may be tempted to adopt a minimal approach to transposition. Similarly, the environmental assessment legislation potentially has extensive reach into many areas of internal administrative decision making, requiring complex changes of national laws. Italy and France continue to be the leaders in nonconformity cases, but followed closely by the United Kingdom (which has long had particular problems in ensuring full and timely transposition in Northern Ireland and Gibraltar).

Ensuring effective formal transposition is therefore a challenging task of the Commission, and one that requires officials to have an understanding of both the requirements of the Community legislation and the nature of the national legal system with which they are dealing. The Commission has for many years placed a high priority on trying to ensure that national law fully reflects European obligations, and some improvements in the way they carry out this task have been made. Increasingly, the Commission has commissioned external national consultants such as University academics to carry out an initial analysis of the national legislation as against Community legislation, a sensible use of resources provided it does not distract from the Commission's ultimate responsibility to monitor and enforce. Rather than focus on particular countries, these exercises are often conducted simultaneously across a number of Member States, and can lead to horizontal infringement actions against one or more Member States. Community Directives require Member States to transmit the texts of national legislation to the Commission but no more. It may be too unrealistic to expect Member States to alert the Commission to potential deficiencies in their national implementing legislation, but at a minimum there should be detailed tables of concordance, which identify Article by Article in their Directive their corresponding national transposing provisions. An increasing number of Member States submit such tables as a matter of good practice, but it would assist all parties if this were a standard requirement. Once national legislation (whether in the form of primary laws or subordinate regulation) has been passed at national level, a Member State is likely to resist an assertion by the Commission that it does not fully reflect Community obligations. The fear of political embarrassment in repealing and amending recently passed legislation at national level remains a powerful driver to face down the Commission rather than compromise. A more sensible approach would be to require Member States to submit draft texts of national legislation or regulations before these are finally agreed at national level. At least then there is an opportunity for sensible negotiation between Member States and the Commission at a time when changes to drafts are still feasible-and if a Member State remains unconvinced of the Commission's view, it can still retain its national legislation and risk formal infringement proceedings at a later stage. In certain areas of Community activity, such as chemicals, this sort of advanced negotiation and discussion appears to happen as a matter of course, but overall the present procedure seems to be a recipe for legal conflict, and there should be a more systematic adoption of prior consultation across the board. The additional requirement to submit proposed national legislation could be made an explicit requirement in Directives.

Failure to Implement Environmental Obligations in Practice

The Commission has rightly devoted considerable effort to ensuring formal transposition of Community measures into national systems, on the assumption that if the national law fully reflects the Community obligations, there is clearly a greater chance that the obligations will be met. The full power of the national legal system will then be brought into play behind the Community Directive – whether it is internal traditions of national administrations to comply with the rule of law, an active and critical citizenship, or accessible remedies before national courts and tribunals where failures occur. Nevertheless, the European Court of Justice has held that whatever the state of national law, the actual failure to implement in practice is as a much a breach of the Member State's obligations as the failure to communicate or transpose formal legislation. The Commission is therefore equally exercised in handling poor implementation in practice, and the report for the year 2005 shows that the majority of the Commission's current cases – some 279 are concerned with the failure of Member States to implement their obligations on the ground. Over a third of these are in the nature protection field, where, as the Commission delicately puts it, in some Member States the designation of protection areas under the key Directive 'still remains problematic'. Waste and Water follow as the next more common area for proceedings with around 20% each.

Italy, followed closely by Spain, heads the current lists, with Ireland, Portugal, Greece, and France following in the next tranche. But comparative country by country tables have to be treated with some care, and they may not reflect an objective state of poor environmental application. In the environmental field, Member States have to date been unwilling to give the Commission any power of national inspection within countries to determine or investigate potential breaches of Community law. Nor do they even possess any power to work alongside national enforcement bodies. This contrasts with a number of other areas of Community law where independent inspection powers have been granted – competition, fisheries, nuclear energy, and veterinary policy are important examples. With respect to poor application in practice, the Commission has therefore been peculiarly dependent on sources of external information. It has developed and promoted a citizen's complaint system – originally devised as an administrative tool in the field of single market legislation – and at times has positively encouraged individuals and environmental organisations to send the Commission warnings of potential infringement cases. It follows that countries with, say, under-developed non-governmental organisations, or those where access to local legal remedies is relatively straightforward and inexpensive, are less likely to give rise to large sources of complaint at European level, though their level of non-compliance in practice may be as high or higher than countries higher up the league table.

The Commission's continued willingness to pursue cases of non-implementation in practice is in many ways commendable. Such cases by their very nature are likely to be politically more sensitive than the rather more abstract and esoteric ask of matching national laws to Community legislation. The press, the public and politicians will be more engaged in what are often local or even national causes célèbres. Yet with limited resources at its disposal, the Commission cannot possibly handle all cases of non-implementation notified to it. In a general Communication in 2002, the Commission indicated that in respect of non-implementation in practice, it would focus on infringements that were considered to undermine the rule of law and infringements that undermined the smooth functioning of the Community legal system. Such generalised principles do not really assist priority selection (arguably, any failure to implement agreed Community law is really a threat to the rule of law), but in the environmental field threats to human health and violation of Community law in relation to EU financed projects were singled out. These priorities are gradually being reflected in the types of infringement proceedings being initiated by the Commission.

Systematic Failure of National Systems

Until 2005, infringement proceedings concerning failure to implement in practice were focussed on single instances. A typical example was the 1992 case brought against Greece in respect of an illegal landfill in Crete. The failure of Greece to comply with the Court's judgment and rectify the situation led to a further case against Greece and the first ever penalty imposed by the European Court in 1997. No doubt the case had been pursued by the Commission not simply to protect human health and the environment of a village in Crete, but also for its emblematic value in improving the state of compliance through Greece. Yet the fact remains that the case and the penalty related to a single site. Once Greece had rectified the legal situation concerning that site, the case would have been over, leaving the Commission to consider new legal proceedings in respect of other sites.

2005 saw perhaps the most significant development for a decade in case-law before the European Court of Justice dealing with infringement proceedings and non-implementation in practice. In *Commission v Ireland* (Case C-494/01) the Commission had been handling various complaints concerning the application of waste law in Ireland, including instances of unlicensed or under-enforced landfill sites, and unauthorised dumping of waste. Each example of non-compliance could in theory have been subject to a separate infringement proceedings, following the Greek example. But instead, and for the first time in an environmental case, the Commission argued that the examples of non-compliance reflected and represented an underlying failure of the administration to implement the law properly, and that it was this systematic failure that was the breach of the Community obligation.

The Court of Justice agreed. It accepted that the examples raised were being presented as representative of a far wider problem in Ireland, and that it was not a good defence for the Member State simply to rectify the individual problems raised by the Commission, since these could be treated as mere examples. The wider administrative failures had to be addressed. The Court also acknowledged for the first time the difficulties that the Commission faced in investigating cases of actual failure to implement when it had no independent inspectorate. It followed, according to the Court, that Member States therefore had a special duty, once allegations had been raised, to assist the Commission in investigations and fact finding; simply denying the allegations and calling on the Commission to prove their case was insufficient in the context of their respective duties and powers.

Quite what Ireland will have to do to convince the Commission that it has rectified its underlying systematic failings in enforcement in order to avoid further proceedings and a possible penalty payment from the Court remains an intriguing question. Quite clearly evidence of dealing with a single illegal site will not be sufficient. The judgment shows the Court to be consciously expanding the scope of concern of such proceedings, and has signalled that Member States must introduce effective and systematic administrative systems to ensure full application of Community law in practice. This must inevitably involve questions such as the training and numbers of enforcement officers at national level, the overall financial resources giving to national environment agencies and other bodies responsible for implementation, the size and nature of national penalties – typically areas that many Member States would argue fell wholly within their national discretion, but now appear to be part and parcel of their Community obligations.

Improving the System

There is little doubt that other improvements could be made to the current system. For example, it is not often clear why the Commission determines to pursue particular cases. Any regulator with limited resources can ill afford to be largely reactive to complaints, but needs to adopt a more systematic and proactive approach. The generalised principles of selection that have been announced by the Commission are really too vague to be of real value. The Commission should consider identifying those areas of potential breaches which pose the greatest immediate threat of serious or irreversible risk to human health and the environment, and focus effort on these areas. There are important principles of Community law such as the direct effect doctrine and those requiring national courts to interpret national laws in the light of underlying Community legislation, which are designed to make national remedies more effective. Individuals cannot bring cases before the European Court of Human Rights unless they have shown that they exhausted the national remedies available to them, and an equivalent filter system for actions by the European Commission responding to individual complaints should be considered. This would allow the Commission to concentrate on cases where national systems are weak to deal with individual complainants, or where the complaints – as in the Irish waste case – are symptomatic of deeper failings, which an individual national case is unlikely to reflect. The length of time taken to pursue cases is a scandal of near Dickensian proportions. Ludwig Kramer, formerly head of the enforcement unit in DG Environment, has recently analysed published data concerning cases, and has noted that the average length duration of court proceedings for Article 226 infringement cases is 20 months, a figure that has remained remarkably stable over the last decade. But if one adds the length of time for pre-court procedure, from the service of the initial formal letter by the Commission, the figures become disturbing. Where national or local economic interests benefit from non-compliance, these time scales are hardly likely to act as any sort of deterrent, and irreparable damage may be done to the environment in the meantime.

Here, the Commission in particular is bound up in what appear to be excessively bureaucratic internal procedures. Fact-finding in cases of non-implementation can in practice be a lengthy and time-consuming business, usually involving correspondence between the Commission in Brussels and national administrations. It would be far preferable if the initial preparation of dossiers were conducted by Commission officials based in their national offices in Member States. A more radical approach would be to draw on the analogy of the major reforms to the enforcement of competition law and policy introduced in the Community in 2003. The reforms gave greater responsibility for national bodies and courts for the direct enforcement of Community competition obligations, while strengthening the Commission's powers in inspection.

It is arguable that the Commission's dual roles as policy maker – which requires it to seek a co-operative approach with national administrations to secure the passing of legislation – and as law enforcer are institutionally incompatible with each other, and that it would therefore be preferable if the enforcement function were transferred to a more independent and discrete body such as the European Environment Agency. Many in the European Parliament would favour such a shift, but such a transformation appears politically unrealistic in the near future, and in any event may not be wholly desirable. Effective enforcement often requires policy sensitivity and the capacity to provide advice as well as the power to impose sanctions. Nevertheless, there are undoubtedly instances – though almost by definition largely unreported and difficult to substantiate – where enforcement action by the Commission is effectively blocked internally for what appear to be wholly political reasons.

The enforcement unit in DG Environment has achieved much over the last decade or so, and its efforts have been largely supported by the European Court of Justice which has proved highly sympathetic to the need for effective implementation of environmental law, even where this causes difficulties and embarrassment at national level. In the context of the enforcement of supra-national environmental obligations, the Community system provides many pointers that could be developed in other regional and supra-national systems. But it is also in need of reform if it is to cope effectively with a greatly expanded number of Member States and increasingly demanding environmental challenges. Some of these changes could be effected by the Commission itself without the need for legislative change, but others will require agreement by Member States themselves. Politicians, used to creating new laws, often resist involvement in the often mundane task of their enforcement – as a Member of the European Parliament once noted in respect of environmental legislation, 'We are good midwives, but bad mothers'. It is a sobering thought that the Council of Ministers has never systematically reviewed implementation and enforcement issues concerning the environmental legislation it has helped to pass. Voting for changes that would increase the effectiveness of the Commission in ensuring that Member States implement their obligations may not appear to be in the short-term interest of many national governments. But at the end of the day it must surely be in the interests of all citizens and their governments that environment laws agreed at supra-national level are not simply politically reassuring symbols, but represent obligations that are fully implemented throughout the Union.

CHAPTER 25

THE ENFORCEMENT OF EU ENVIRONMENTAL LAW – SOME PROPOSALS FOR REFORM*

1   The Context

My concern is mainly with the procedures available to the European Commission to ensure that Member States fully comply with their obligations under EC environmental laws. As is well known, the Commission has a duty under the Treaty to ensure that Community measures 'are applied', but in the environmental field it was a duty that was largely ignored until the mid 1980's. So while the overall title of this collection is *Reflections on 30 Years of EU Environmental Law*, in reality we are talking of twenty years of Community enforcement of environmental law. Indeed, it was during the period of Ludwig Kramer's headship of the legal unit within DG Environment that the enforcement procedures, available in all sectors of Community law, were significantly re-invigorated and applied in the field of the environment. Currently roughly a third of all complaints and infringements procedures fall within the environment sector.

Effective enforcement of national environmental laws is fraught with difficulties. Bodies responsible for detection and enforcement may be insufficiently resourced, and national courts often lack the specialised knowledge to handle the complexities of contemporary environmental law. The enforcement of many international environmental treaties is even more a challenge, largely due to sensitivities concerning national sovereignty. It is true that in recent years much greater efforts have been made in recent environmental treaties such as the Montreal Protocol to move away from a system that largely relied upon conventional and often ineffective methods of international dispute resolution towards what has been described as a more 'managerial approach' involving more sophisticated methods to encourage compliance including greater transparency, improved reporting procedures, and dedicated secretariats[1]. In the context of supra-national obligations, though, the powers and procedures available under the Treaty, including the

* R Macrory (2005) The Enforcement of EU Environmental Law: Some Proposals for Reform in Macrory (ed) *Reflections on 30 years of EU Environmental Law – A High Level of Protection?* Europa Law Publishing, Netherlands, pp 385 - 395
[1] Michael Faure and Jürgen Lefevere: 'Compliance with international environmental agreements', p. 138 in: Norman Vig–Regina Axelrod (eds.), *The Global Environment–Institutions, Law and Policy,* (1999) Washington DC: CQ Press.

possibility of the imposition of financial penalties by the European Court of Justice and the encouragement of citizens and non-governmental organisations to lodge formal complaints concerning instances of non-compliance, remain unrivalled in contemporary supra-national arrangements. Whatever the shortcomings of the systems – and there are many – this fact should not be forgotten. This does not necessarily mean that the European Union offers an ideal model for other regional systems of environmental law to follow, though there are certainly important lessons to be learnt.[2] The key question for those working in Europe today is the extent to which, particularly in the context of the enlarged Union, we can continue rely upon the existing system, and what improvements might be sought in the light of future challenges.

2   The Present Picture

The most recent report of the Commission on the implementation of EU environmental law, published in 2004, hardly paints a reassuring picture.[3] In 2003, the Commission brought 58 cases against Member States before the ECJ, with a further 112 reasoned opinions issued. Given the very strict case law of the ECJ concerning the failure of Member States to even communicate national legislation within time limits, it remains surprising that failures still occur. As Somsen has noted, 'The European Court of Justice has always remained unpersuaded by the range of often imaginative justifications that have been forward.'[4] Yet the position at the end of 2003 indicates 88 outstanding cases for non-communication, and spread (with the exception of Denmark and Sweden) almost equally among Member States. Over 50 per cent of these fell with the field of air pollution, probably reflecting a large number of Directives in this field that had been agreed in previous years. In the area of perhaps the most pressing contemporary environmental issue, climate change, only one country had submitted a greenhouse gas emissions trading scheme within the deadline required.[5] Chemicals and Waste form the next highest sectors for non-communication.

There are 118 cases concerning non-conformity of national legislation, clearly a more complex and contestable area of legal interpretation.

[2] See Ludwig Krämer (2003), 'Dispute resolution in environmental law–can the European Union be a model?', in Alexandre Kiss – Dinah Shelton – Kanami Ishibashi (eds.), *Economic Globalization and Compliance with International Environmental Agreements*, (2003) The Hague-London-New York: Kluwer Law International, p. 271.
[3] European Commission (2003) 5th Annual Survey on the Implementation and Enforcement of Community Environmental Law 2003 SEC (2004) 1025.
[4] Han Somsen: 'Discretion in European Community environmental law–an analysis of ECJ case law' (2003) *Common Market Law Review* 40, p. 1413.
[5] The position had improved by mid 2004, though proceedings have been started against Greece and Italy for non-transposition, and a further written warnings to 11 Member States for failing to fully transpose Directive 2003/87 on emission trading.

Cases are open against all Member States, though France and Italy stand out as the current worst offenders. Waste, Water and Nature Protection form the key sectors, accounting for nearly 70 per cent of all cases. As to bad application in practice,[6] there were 93 outstanding cases at the end of 2003, with around a third in the water sector, followed by waste, nature, and air. Surprisingly, perhaps, given the large amount of case law that has been generated by the legislation, there was only one case concerning environmental impact assessment. There are cases against all Member States, though spread unevenly, with the Scandinavian countries and Germany at the lower end, and Ireland, Italy and France into double figures.

It is, of course, not easy to tell whether this represents in any way an objective picture of compliance, though one can be pretty confident that, if anything, it will underestimate what goes on in practice. Differences across individual Member States may well reflect the experience and confidence of individual case-officers within the Commission, as well as the availability of national remedies. In terms of non-application in practice, the Commission is still heavily reliant on complaints being made,[7] and the numbers received from Member States reflect the campaigning tactics of national environmental organisations, national views of the environmental credentials of the Commission and a host of other factors as well as any comparative objective picture of compliance. Nevertheless, in the straightforward words of the then Commissioner Wallstrom, 'Implementation of EU environmental law is bad'.[8]

It is not the purpose of this contribution to review the history of enforcement by the Commission, or to consider in any detail the underlying legal and administrative procedures. There are other sources for this type of analysis.[9] A radical approach for reform would argue for wholesale reliance on the national authorities and national courts to ensure effective enforcement of Community obligations. Even

---

[6] This is now defined in the Commission report as to encompass the 'failure to implement certain derived or secondary obligation contained in Community acts, such as setting out plans, classifying sites and designating areas, adopting programmes, submitting monitoring data, reporting, etc.' It is not clear, whether this implies that the failure, say, to reach a required environmental standard in a particular case is excluded.

[7] The total number received during 2003 in the environmental sector was 505, representing a slight decrease from the previous two years. The report does not contain figures for individual countries

[8] Commission Press Release of 19 August 2004.

[9] See, for example, Richard Macrory and Ray Purdy: 'The enforcement of EC environmental law', p. 9 in Jane Holder (ed.), *The Impact Of EC Environmental Law in the United Kingdom* (1997) Chichester: Wiley and Sons; Ludwig Krämer, *EC Environmental Law* 5th ed.(2003) London: Sweet & Maxwell, esp. chapter 12; Richard Macrory: 'Community supervision in the field of the environment', p. 27 in Han Somsen (ed.), *Protecting the European Environment* (1996) London: Blackstone Press.

where there have been inadequate or a lack of national implementing measures, it is arguable that the combined effect of doctrines developed by the European Court of Justice such as those concerning sympathetic interpretation, direct effect, *Francovich* damage claims, and duties of national courts to ensure implementation,[10] is now sufficiently powerful to avoid the need for a supra-national enforcement mechanism. That might be true in an ideal world. But there remain significant disparities within Member States as to the powers and effectiveness of national enforcement bodies. Equally there remain major differences in the costs of litigation by third parties, and the remedies available to them to prevent abuse or lacklustre performance by local enforcement agencies. The *Aarhus* Convention, if and when fully implemented through out the Community, may go some way to meet these concerns. Nevertheless, I start from the proposition that in the foreseeable future there remains an important role for the Commission in the supervision and enforcement of Community environmental law. What follows are a number of suggestions for change which are intended to improve its effectiveness and focus.

3   Suggestions for Improvement

3.1   Conformity of National Transposition Measures

Any enforcement body is likely to have limited resources, and the Commission is no exception. Certainly there is a strong argument that the focus of the Commission should be to ensure that national legislation fully reflects obligations under Community law. Of course, perfect transposition does not guarantee effective enforcement at national level, for some of the reasons indicated above, but it is good starting place. The Commission's 1996 paper on implementation[11] indeed indicated that this would be its priority area in future, though the subsequent figures on types of enforcement action do not bear out this policy. But there are real problems with current procedures, and useful changes could be made.

There should be a general legal requirement that Member States supply annotated versions of national transposition measures, clearly indicating which provisions of their national legislation are meant to reflect which provisions of the Directive in question. Some Member States appear to do this as a matter of practice, and recently the United Kingdom has begun to adopt this as a policy, but there seems no good reason where

---

[10] As developed in case C-72/95 *Kraaijeveld* (1996) ECR I-5403.
[11] European Commission (1996) Implementing Community Environment Law, COM (96) 500 of 22 October 1996.

the provision of a compliance table should not be a general Community legal requirement.[12] Equally such tables should be made available publicly. This will assist national courts and enforcement bodies, as well as the general public, to understand the connection between the Community law and its national implementing measures. In recent years, the Commission has (rightly, in my view) made greater use of independent national legal experts to carry out initial compliance reports, but from personal experience, without a systematic annotation table provided by the Member State, it is often extraordinarily difficult to analyse the detailed rationale for all of the transposition measures taken. Directives are intended to allow a degree of latitude in how they are transposed within a national system, and simple 'copy out' of Directives word for word into national law does not necessarily meet the challenge that is required, or the spirit of legislative mechanism. Nevertheless, it is important that Member States resist producing bland annotation tables. Where, for example, there are significant changes in the words used between a Directive and national measures, the table should explain the rationale for doing so. Presumably a national draftsperson has made a conscious decision in interpreting the Directive and formulating a national provision, and there is no good reason where the explanation should not be given.

Once a Member State has enacted legislation, whether in the form of primary national laws or secondary regulations, it is inherently likely to be defensive as to its validity in terms of transposition. Being required to amend legislation once passed at national level at a later date is both time-consuming and represents a certain loss of face for national administrations. Although the Commission has in recent years made greater use of anticipatory meetings and discussions with Member States in some sectors, a far more systematic approach could be adopted. Draft legislation should be regularly provided by Member States, providing a more realistic opportunity for changes where differences of view arise. If this cannot be achieved by agreement, I would prefer to extend the time limit for implementation, with Directives in future including a requirement that *draft* implementation measures are provided to the Commission within, say, two years of agreement of the Directive, with a further six months or twelve months for provision of final measures. Similarly, the Commission should be prepared to give greater advance guidance as to its own view on the meaning of Directives, thus anticipating possible conflict areas. Such guidance cannot be taken as legally binding, since at the end of the day only the European Court

---

[12] Since 1991, the Commission has required Member States to identify the provisions of national legislation which correspond with the provisions of the Directive concerned: See (1991) OJ C 338, p. 1, Annex C, s 8. But this is not a legal requirement, and practice by Member States as to the detail provided appears to vary.

can give a definitive ruling as to the legal meaning of Community legislation, but it would surely assist Member States in considering the design of their own transposition measures. Similarly, the introduction of the submission of draft national legislation for consideration by the Commission cannot inhibit the Commission from taking enforcement action at a later date, should it come to change its view on the meaning of the Directive. And this sort of procedure will not necessarily resolve all conflicts between the Commission and Member States. At the end of the day, there may still be legitimate differences of opinion as to the meaning of a Directive and the adequacy of the national measure concerned, which may eventually only be resolved by enforcement proceedings before the European Court of Justice. My concern is that current practice does not assist in identifying the real areas of dispute, and often allows for defective implementation and the need for subsequent infringement proceedings by default.

Transposition issues are mainly associated with the implementation of Directives[13], and it is arguable that the more wholesale use of Regulations would remove the problem of transposition. There has been very little detailed analysis on the underlying principles that should determine the use of Directives or Regulations, nor is it an issue yet subject of judicial intervention by the ECJ. Despite the superficial attraction of greater use of Regulations, I suspect that, especially in the context of enlargement and an even greater range of administrative and legal traditions across the Union, the Directive, or its equivalent under the proposed Constitution, will remain a preferred choice of instrument for many areas of environmental policy.

3.2   Non-application in Practice

As mentioned above, the ECJ has developed a range of what I have described as 'internalising' doctrines which are designed to ensure that non-transposed provisions of Directives nevertheless still have legal impact within national systems. Nevertheless, each doctrine has limitations, and, even if effectively applied by national courts, cannot provide a comprehensive solution to 'gap-filling'. More liberal national standing rules, less deterrent costs rules, greater use of specialist national environmental tribunals and similar measures may all assist to ensure better enforcement at national level, thereby reducing the burden on the Commission. Nevertheless, realistically there is always likely to be areas where the enforcement of non-application in practice is best suited for the Commission.

---

[13] I deliberately use the terminology of legislative acts under the existing Treaty rather than the proposed Constitution.

This is clearly the most controversial area for involvement by the Commission, since it can threaten real-life projects involving national pride and serious economic commitment. Within my own country, for example, news of the Commission's decision in the early 1990s to consider infringement proceedings concerning environmental impact assessment and a controversial national motorway scheme (Twyford Down) was known to have reached the Prime Minister personally.[14] The decision to initiate enforcement proceedings remains one of discretion by the Commission, and Williams, amongst others, has presented a fairly jaundiced view of the political pressures that can brought to bear on the Commission to refrain from proceedings, particularly those involving non-application in practice,[15] and an equally scathing account of the lack of legal accountability of the Commission.[16]

Nevertheless, it is clear from case-law of the European Court that the failure to implement in practice is as much of a breach of obligations by Member States as is the failure to transpose provisions of Directives into national law.[17] There seems little doubt that well-chosen, high profile cases can bring home to Member States the reality of the commitments made in Community environmental legislation, and are consistent with contemporary policy approaches that emphasise the need to focus on environmental outcomes rather than simply the formality of legislation. But equally there are significant improvements in current procedures could be developed.

The current mechanisms for the Commission to investigate allegations of non-application in practice are often extraordinary cumbersome, and usually very reactive. Officers in Brussels learn of allegations of non-compliance mainly through complaints sent by individuals or non-governmental organisations, or through Members of the European Parliament. Lengthy correspondence is conducted with the Member State to try to establish further facts, normally working through the national representation office in Brussels, who in turn must liaise

---

[14] According to the *Independent* (22 October 1991) Prime Minister John Major was so incensed that he threatened to block the signing of the Maastricht Treaty, quoted in Philip Lowe and Stephen Ward: *British Environmental Policy and Europe* (1998) London: Routledge. Tromans and Fuller note that intervention by the Commission in the early 1990's concerning EIA on a number of major UK projects 'became tied up with general popular anti-EC sentiment and the perception of undue interference by Brussels in domestic decision-making': Stephen Tromans and Karl Fuller: *Environmental Impact Assessment–Law and Practice* (2003) London: Butterworths, chapter 2.15.

[15] Rhiannon Williams: 'The European Commission and the enforcement of environmental law: an invidious position' (1994) *Yearbook of European Law* 14, p. 351.

[16] Rhiannon Williams: 'Enforcing European environmental law: can the European Commission be held to account?' (2002) *Yearbook of European Environmental Law* 2, p. 271.

[17] ECJ cases C-431/92 *Commission v Germany* (1995) ECR I-7657, C-365/97 *Commission v Italy* (1999) ECR I-7773.

with national government departments, who often themselves have to established facts from local authorities or other bodies. Ideally, one might seek equivalent powers of direct inspection by the Commission equivalent to those in the competition field, and fisheries field, but this seems politically unlikely. A more modest reform would be to ensure that initial fact finding and dossier preparation were undertaken by Commission officials based in the Commission offices of Member States rather than conducted at long distance from Brussels. Rather more radical would be to draw from the major reforms introduced to the enforcement of competition law and policy introduced in 2003.[18] These give much greater responsibility to national bodies and courts for the direct enforcement of Community competition, while both strengthening the Commission's own powers of inspection, and establishing a European Competition Network of competition authorities to ensure exchange of experience and a consistent approach. The analogy may not be perfect, since the scope of environmental law is much broader than competition law, and the national bodies responsible for its enforcement are generally far more diffuse that those concerned with competition law. Nevertheless, one could envisage, as Krämer has argued[19], the establishment of national centres charged not with direct enforcement, but with monitoring the application of Community environmental law within the country concerned. Such centres would prepare dossiers, and make recommendations to the Commission concerning infringement proceedings.

The Commission should be more systematic in choosing priorities for investigation. This means making judgments (in conjunction, perhaps, with the European Environment Agency) on what areas are posing the greatest risks to the environment at any particular time. The complaint system has provided the Commission with significant information on failures in practice – as well as being an important political tool for connecting the Commission with citizens throughout the Community. Nevertheless, it can lead to a highly reactive rather than proactive system, and one that may often reflect the campaigning priorities of national environmental organisations rather than a considered assessment by the Commission of the threats posed to the environment from a European perspective. All enforcement authorities have limited resources, and many national authorities are now developing risk-based approaches to regulation – a policy that concentrates effort on those areas presenting the most significant problems, and adopting a lighter touch in others where appropriate. I accept that deciding, say,

---

[18] Regulation 1/2003, (2003) OJ L 1, p. 1.
[19] Ludwig Krämer: 'The future role of the ECJ in the development of European environmental law', in: Jan Jans (ed.), *The European Convention and the Future of European Environmental Law* (2003) Groningen: Europa Law Publishing, p. 85.

whether chronic air pollution in Athens is a greater priority than the immediate destruction of a habitat in Portugal places the Commission in an invidious position, but the reality for any enforcement body is that difficult choices often have to be made. Criteria could be developed to help identify priorities – Is the likely damage irreversible? Could a complainant make use of national legal remedies? Is the situation one replicated in other countries, meaning that an infringement action that will resonate more widely? Does the infringement reflect a hierarchy of priority environmental risks identified by the European Environment Agency? The reality is that these sorts of questions are probably in the mind of Commission officials, even if only sub-consciously, when they decide on pursuing particular cases. But in a contemporary system we should expect to see a more transparent and developed set of principles which underpin the exercise of administrative discretion in such an important area.

IMPEL (European Union Network for the Implementation and Enforcement of Environment Law) has, since 1992, provided an important focal point for national regulatory bodies to exchange information on actual enforcement in practice, and feedback to the better design of legislation from lessons learnt. But although it has expanded its scope of concerns, it remains largely pollution and waste orientated.[20] We have yet to see equivalent development of the intensity of effort in, say, nature conservation or environmental assessment. Again, the number and range of national bodies involved in enforcement in these areas pose a particular challenge, but it remains a significant lacuna in present network arrangements. Clearly, if one were to see the development of the type of national centres for monitoring the enforcement of Community environmental law advocated by Krämer, they would form the natural basis for an exchange network.

The Commission has often commissioned reports from independent national experts on the state of actual application of environmental legislation, mirroring those concerning formal transposition measures. They can provide valuable independent critiques on the state of compliance in practice within a Member State, but too often, in my view, there have been insufficient procedures for effectively evaluating

---

[20] This can be illustrated by looking at its 2004 work programme which covers: 1.IMPEL Review Working Group (IRI) 2. Electronic reporting in IPPC implementation 3. Waste-related conditions in environmental permits 4. EMAS project 5. Transfrontier shipment of Waste – Threat assessment 6. TFS network in the accession countries 7. Consideration of human health through the IPPC Directive 8. Identification of good practice in the implementation of the EU emissions trading scheme 9. Implementation and use of BREFs 10. Informal resolution of environmental conflicts by dialogue 11. IMPEL Review Initiative (IRI) Sweden 12. Inspection – environmental inspection guidelines for the tanning industry 13. TFS seaport project 14. TFS project – Verification of the destination of notified waste.

such reports. All too often, in common with other research reports, they can enter a 'black hole' on completion.

4   The European Court of Justice

The power of the European Court of Justice to fine Member State for failure to comply with its judgments is unique amongst international courts, and the first two such actions took place in the environmental field. According to the Commission, in 2003, 17 letters of formal notice and 11 reasoned opinions were issued in the environmental field against Member States under Article 228 EC Treaty. My personal view at the time these powers were being proposed, was that they were undesirable – resorting to having to threaten a Member State with a financial payment to ensure compliance with a judgment of the European Court appeared to devalue the notion of the rule of law. But I have changed my view. In practice, even the threat of the powers appear to have had considerable effect in focusing the attention of Member States on resolving issues which hitherto had been presented as largely insummountable. At national level it has meant that Finance or Treasury Departments now have a direct interest in ensuring that EU environmental legislation is effectively implemented, a positive development that heightens the internal status given to environmental protection.

Although any resort to Court action implies a failure in the regulatory system whether at national or European level, the European Court of Justice will clearly continue to play a significant role in this area. But the current lengthy time in procedures is reaching unacceptable levels. Ludwig Krämer has recently carried out a systematic analysis of periods involved that makes for uncomfortable reading.[21] The average length of proceedings from the initial issue of a formal notice by the Commission to judgment was 45 months, rising to 52 months (over 4 years) in the case of non-application in practice. seven cases during 2002/3 took more than 80 months. As he rightly notes, the blame does not wholly rest on the Court, and much of the delay occurs during pre-litigation stages. Certainly, the large variation in periods suggests, there is room for substantial improvements that could be made. The system of environmental enforcement developed within the European Union may be distinctive, but this scale of delay in bringing cases before a court would be unacceptable in most European national systems. It needs to be addressed with urgency, if confidence is to be retained in a legal system, let alone the environment effectively protected. Infringement proceedings could, for example, be assigned to the Court of First

---

[21] Ludwig Krämer: 'Data on environmental judgments by the EC Court of Justice' (2004) *Journal of European Environmental and Planning Law* 2, p. 127.

Instance, unless raising significant issues of principle. In preparation for the Nice Treaty amendments, the Ole Due Working Group on the Community Court System recommended that the Commission's claim of infringement by a Member State should be binding on the State concerned unless challenged within a specified time limit, a proposal that would also have speeded up the system.[22] The recommendation was never pursued.

5   Conclusions

The system of supra-national enforcement within the European Union remains unique amongst contemporary systems of governance, and European environmental lawyers need not be unduly defensive for what has been developed. It is almost trite to repeat that the environment does not respect national boundaries, but this will remain the reality, and we should be looking to ways of developing and strengthening rather than weakening the current system. My contribution has deliberately avoided examining the actual substance of Community environmental law but focussed on the process of enforcement. Legal substance, of course, vitally influences enforceability, and poorly drafted legislation makes enforcement nearly impossible. The central responsibility of the European Commission in supervising implementation of Community obligations by Member States remains unchallenged in the foreseeable future. The core procedures concerning infringement actions and the powers of the European Court of Justice have remained intact and unchanged in the proposed European Constitution. This may have been something of a lost opportunity, and should not be taken to imply that all is well with the current system. Many of my proposals for reform, though, require no Treaty change, but a recognition that much could be done to improve current procedures, with an approach that is both more systematic and transparent. Member States as well as the Commission need to recognise that effective and consistent enforcement of Community environmental legislation throughout the Union, though uncomfortable at times, is in their long-term interests. In this context, it is salutary to note that the Council of Ministers has never regularly reviewed on a systematic basis the actual implementation of existing Community environmental laws. It should do so. But the first responsibility lies with the Commission. The Commission's last major communication of the implementation of Community environmental law was published in 1996. Against the background of the expanded Union and the proposed Constitution, it should, for a start, mark the tenth anniversary in 2006 with a fresh examination, and the publication of

---

[22] Quoted in Dryberg (2001), 'What should the Court of Justice be doing?' (2001) *European Law Review*, p. 291 (p. 299).

a new paper that grapples effectively with the contemporary challenges of environmental enforcement.

CHAPTER 26

THE ENFORCEMENT OF COMMUNITY ENVIRONMENTAL LAWS: SOME CRITICAL ISSUES*

1. Introduction

Community environmental legislation will only be effective
if it is fully implemented and enforced by Member State.[1]

In recent years both the European Parliament[2] and the Council of
Ministers have stressed the importance of ensuring that Community
law is fully implemented within Member States.[3] New mechanisms and
procedures are under discussion at a political level, while traditional
tools are employed in the meantime. Yet it is a sensitive area. Member
States may subscribe to the concept of the supremacy of Community
law and the need for better implementation, but are reluctant to
accept interference with national administrative arrangements for
enforcement.

The field of environmental policy is particularly striking in this
context. Since the Community began development of Community
environmental policies in 1972 a large body of Directives, regulations,
and decisions has been agreed, and in terms of the sheer amount of
legislation that now exists the programme must be considered one
of the success stories of the Community.[4] The aim of this article is
to consider the mechanisms associated with the implementation
and enforcement of Community environmental legislation, with
'implementation' denoting the process by which legal obligations
under Community law are fulfilled, while 'enforcement' implies the
methods available to ensure that implementation takes place. The vast
majority of Community environmental laws have been in the form of

---

* R Macrory, (1992) The Enforcement of Community Environmental Law: Some Critical
Issues. *Common Market Law Review*. Vol. 29: 347-369
[1] Statement of European Council, Bull. EC 6-1990, 18-21, note 4.
[2] See European Parliament Resolutions of 11 Apr. 1984, O.J. 1984, C 127/67; of 19 March
1990, O.J. 1990, C 68/172; and most recently, of 7 Nov 1991.
[3] At an informal meeting of the Council of Ministers on 11-13 Oct. 1991, it was agreed
that there is a need both for the 'further development and enforcement of environmental
legislation' within the Community and to 'improve the compliance and enforcement
structures concerning environmental legislation and the implementation within the
Member States'.
[4] Around 200 regulations, Directives, and decisions have been agreed in the environmental
field.

Directives, with the consequence that attention to date has been largely with ensuring that Member States rather than private interests comply with their obligations under these laws. In that context, my particular concern will be with the use of the Article 169 enforcement procedures by the European Commission. I make no excuse for this focus. Although the process has been subject to criticism for reasons that will become apparent, and while new methods of ensuring improved compliance are being considered,[5] the Article 169 procedure will remain a central and critical *legal* tool for enforcement at Community level, whatever the nature of other initiatives agreed upon.

One of the underlying difficulties associated with the implementation and enforcement of Community environmental law is the differing structural character of the legislation that has been agreed. Some directives prescribe explicit and precise goals that must be achieved in a given sector which in theory should be reasonably straightforward to monitor and enforce.[6] Another class contains similarly precise goals within specified sectors or areas but leaves a large element of discretion to Member States in determining where they are to apply.[7] Examples of more recent legislation cut across conventional administrative boundaries and sectors, and impose obligations that reach deep into national decision making at many levels. This type of 'horizontal' directive, exemplified by the 1985 Environmental Assessment Directive,[8] raises acute difficulties for both Member States and the Community institutions when it comes to ensuring full implementation.

2.   The Role of the Commission

A key function of the European Commission under the Treaty of Rome is to ensure the effective application of Community law.[9] The Commission's role in enforcement is therefore one of its institutional duties, yet it was not until the early 1980s, a decade after the initiation of

---

[5] e.g. at an informal meeting of the Council of Ministers in Oct. 1991, it was agreed that Member States should establish an informal network of national enforcement officers concerned with environmental law.

[6] e.g. Directive 80/779 on air quality limit values and guide values for sulphur dioxide and suspended particulates O.J. 1980, L 229/30, Directive 80/778 relating to the quality of water intended for human consumption O.J. 1980, L 229/11.

[7] e.g. Directive 78/659 on the quality of fresh waters needing protection or improvement in order to support fish life O.J. 1978, L 229/11; Directive 76/160 concerning the quality of bathing water O.J. 1976, L 229/11; Directive 79/409 on the conservation of wild birds O.J. 1979, L 79/409.

[8] Directive 85/337 on the assessment of the effects of certain public and private projects on the environment, O.J. 1985, L 175/40. Another notable example of such a horizontal directive is Directive 90/313 on access to environmental information, O.J. 1990, L 158/56.

[9] Art. 155 EEC provides that the Commission shall, '... ensure that the provisions of this Treaty and the measures taken by the institutions pursuant thereof are applied; ...'

explicit Community environmental policies, that it began to take its role seriously in this field. The European Parliament played an important part in the process of galvanising concern. The disappearance of toxic waste being transported from Seveso in 1983 revealed the extent of defective implementation of existing environmental directives governing toxic and dangerous wastes, and the Parliament's subsequent inquiry and Resolution criticised both the Commission and Member States over their failure to ensure effective implementation of Community environmental legislation.[10] Since that date, the Commission, largely through its legal unit within Directorate-General XI, has concentrated on improving its enforcement efforts, using both conventional legal processes available under Community law, and less formal methods. Before examining the machinery that is employed, it is worth asking whether there are particular features of the Community's programme of environmental legislation which have fostered problems of poor implementation by Member States.

Dr. Ludwig Krämer, head of the legal unit within D.G. XI, has argued that a fundamental characteristic of environmental law, both at Community and national level, is the lack of readily identifiable vested interests willing and able to secure enforcement.[11] The same is not true of, say, Competition, Employment or Agricultural Law where the failure by Member States to implement Community law can directly effect economic interests. There is undoubtedly considerable truth in this assertion. Many aspects of the environment are not susceptible to conventional concepts of legal property rights which are capable of enforcement by private interests. Amenity and environmental groups who *would* lay claim to having an interest in general environmental protection may lack the necessary *locus* to commence legal proceedings, or prefer to devote limited resources to creating political rather than legal pressure on defaulting administrations.

There are other aspects, though, of the Community's environmental policies which have contributed to the problems of implementation. The programme is comparatively young, and before the passing of the Single European Act 1987 lacked explicit legal basis under the Treaty.[12] In that climate, the attraction for policy makers initiating Community activity in this field to concentrate on the creation of an ambitious body of environmental laws, even if this implied legislation at the expense of implementation, would have been understandable. Directorate-General XI still remains comparatively small in staff numbers compared

---

[10] European Parliament Resolution of 11 April 1984 O.J. 1984, C 127/67.
[11] Krämer, *EEC Treaty and Environmental Protection* (1990), p. 26.
[12] See Art. 130r-t and Art. 100a EEC. Before the amendments to the Treaty, environmental legislation was generally based on either Art. 100 or Art. 235 or both.

to the rest of the Commission, but its purchase power and influence is considerable given the scope of the legislation now in place.

A further reason relates to the form of legislation adopted. The vast majority of Community laws have taken the form of Directives, and many of those now giving rise to serious tensions over interpretation and implementation were passed during the 1970s and early 1980s. The drafting and precise meaning of many of the requirements are open to differing interpretations, and were agreed by Member States at a time when they probably failed to appreciate the extent to which the Directives represented more than a commitment of policy intention but a genuine legal obligation. Since that period, the developing jurisprudence of the European Court of Justice, both in relation to the direct effect doctrine[13] the so-called doctrine of sympathetic interpretation,[14] and its strict approach towards the transposition of directives into national laws and procedures, has transformed the legal nature of Directives.[15] One can only speculate whether Member States would have readily agreed the terms of some the earlier environmental directives had they appreciated their full legal significance, or had the development in the European Court's jurisprudence occurred at earlier date. Certainly, it might have been predicted that these legal developments, coupled with the Commission's own more intensive efforts at enforcement, would have made Member States more reluctant to agree new Directives in the environmental field.[16] This does not appear to have happened - or if it did, has been more than counterbalanced by a growing political imperative given to environmental issues within Europe. Environmental directives with significant resource, legal, and administrative implications have continued to be proposed and agreed.

3.   Formal Enforcement Procedures

The formal legal procedures available to the Commission in persuading a Member State to comply with Community obligations, derive from Article 169 EEC, and as such are common to all areas of Community

[13] See, e.g. Case 41/74, *van Duyn v Home Office*, [1974] ECR 1337; Case 8/81, *Becker v Finanzamt Munster-Innenstadt*, [1982] ECR 53; Case 148/78, *Pubblico Ministero v Tullio Ratti*, [1979] ECR 1629. There is as yet no decision of the Court of Justice dealing with the direct effect of environmental directives as such, although the *Ratti* case was concerned with the packaging and labelling of solvents and toxic substances.

[14] Case 14/83, *von Colson and Kamann v Land Nordrhein-Westfalen*, [1984] ECR 1891. Again there is no decision of the Court of Justice applying this doctrine to environmental Directives.

[15] See, e.g. Case 300/81, *Commission v Italy*, [1983] ECR 449; Case 102/79, *Commission v Belgium*, [1980] ECR 1473, and Case 361/88 and 59/89, *Commission v Germany* 30 May 1991, n.y.r.

[16] Rehbinder and Stewart, *Integration through Law: Environmental Protection Policy* (1985) argue to this effect: pp. 316 et seq.

policy. The terms of Article 169 are interpreted to divide into three separate stages; (i) the sending of a formal Article 169 letter to the Member State (ii) the sending of a reasoned opinion and finally (iii) referral to the European Court. The first two stages may, and often do, end in a settlement in that either the Member State complies with the Commission's requirements, or a mutually acceptable agreement is reached without the need for intervention by the Court. As might be expected of any complex process of legal enforcement, these formal stages, and particularly the service of an Article 169 letter are not normally initiated without some considerable forewarning and correspondence between the Member State and the Commission.

The Commission's concern is with a Member State's failure to implement Community agreed obligations, but what is actually implied by the concept of 'implementation' is by no means cut and dried. For administrative purposes, the Commission itself has broken down the subject into three main areas: (i) a failure by a Member State to communicate to the Commission national laws and other national measures implementing the Community instruments in question; (ii) incomplete or incorrect transposition of Community obligations into national law and (iii) the failure to apply the Community obligations in practice, whatever the state of the national law.

4. Black Letter Implementation

The first two categories are, by their nature, confined to the implementation of directives, and are concerned with what might be described as the formal aspect of implementation, ensuring at the very least that the 'black letter' national law is in place. Monitoring the failure to communicate national measures within the time-scale specified in the Directive is a reasonably straight forward, and quasi-mechanical process; either communication has been made by the specified date or it has not.

In the early 1980s, the Commission standardised the enforcement machinery relating to non-communication across all sectors of Community law.[17] Member States are notified within two months of the Directive being adopted, that they are required to notify the Commission of the texts of national implementing measures, with a further reminder letter generally sent six months before the deadline specified in the directive. If no notification has been made by the date required, the Commission will generally move straight into Article 169 proceedings without further warning, starting with a formal letter and

---

[17] See, e.g. Commission *Manual of Procedures* Fifth Updating, March 1982.

moving to a reasoned opinion without referring back to Commissioners for approval.

Table 1. Art. 169 Infringement Proceedings 1982-1990

	Non-communication	Non- conformity	Poor application
Environment			
1982	15	1	—
1983	23	10	2
1984	48	15	2
1985	58	10	1
1986	84	32	9
1987	68	30	58
1988	36	24	30
1989	46	17	37
1990	131	24	62
All sectors			
1982	206	10	37
1983	140	19	27
1984	222	46	17
1985	257	30	14
1986	268	51	54
1987	260	42	125
1988	282	33	117
1989	327	25	169
1990	616	37	162

Source: 8th Report of the Commission to the European Parliament on the enforcement of Community law, 1991.

The rise in the volume of legal proceedings for non-communication has been dramatic, with in 1982 just 15 proceedings begun for non-communication in the environmental sector rising to 131 in 1990 (see Table 1). Indeed in 1990, proceedings for non-communication represented almost 60% of the total commenced in the environmental sector, a figure matched on the overall picture. This represents a higher proportion of the three classes of actions than for the previous three years, and could in part simply be attributable to a higher volume of legislation agreed in previous years. At the same time, the Commission has become more confident on legal grounds that the transposition of directives in most cases is required to be in the form of national legislation rather than administrative means, and in this respect has been bolstered by recent decisions of the European Court of Justice.[18] More disturbingly, though,

[18] See especially Cases 361/88 and 59/89, cited n 15 *supra,* concerning implementation of Directive 80/779 on air quality limits values and guide values for sulphur dioxide and suspended particulates O.J. 1980, L 222/30, and Directive 82/884 on limit values for lead in air O.J. 1982, L 378/15.

it could suggest that Member States are more complacent on the issue, especially as they must be aware that the European Court of Justice has in its decisions on non-communication showed little sympathy for any excuses made by Member States on internal political or constitutional grounds.[19] In this respect, the Commission's policy of a more aggressive and regularised approach in respect of non-communication may have diluted the shock value of Article 169 proceedings, though in the absence of more effective legal sanctions their tactics are understandable if only to bring to the light the current state of noncompliance with the most basic of obligations.

Determining an infringement of the second type, incomplete or incorrect transposition, is a task that is intellectually much more demanding. Communication of national laws has taken place with the required time limits but it is argued that they fail to reflect the obligations under the directive in question. This requires both an understanding of the legal meaning of the provisions of the Directive, itself not always an easy matter, together with the ability to interpret the meaning of national legislation in the light of the Member State's own legal and administrative practice. The position is made more complex because Member States may have relied upon pre-existing legislation to meet the aims of the Directive, in which case its detailed terminology is unlikely to be closely aligned with that of the Directive.[20]

Furthermore, some of the more recent environmental Directives, which cut across conventionally drawn boundaries of administrative and legal responsibility, may as a result prevent the Member State from relying upon a single item of legislation as its means of implementation. The Environmental Assessment Directive[21] offers the prime example, with some countries needing to pass twenty or so individual laws in different sectoral and jurisdictional areas;[22] in communicating the text of these measures to the Commission, only the most selfless of Member States is likely to draw attention to detailed deficiencies that may exist.

Examples have existed where Member States have discussed the draft text of environmental legislation with the Commission well before the

[19] e.g. Case 77/69, *Commission v Belgium*, [1970] ECR 237; Case 79/72, *Commission v Italy*, [1973] ECR 667; Case 52/75, *Commission v Italy*, [1986] ECR 1359.

[20] For recent examples where a Member State relied upon pre-existing national law to implement environmental Directives see Case 360/87, *Commission v Italy*, judgment of the Court of Justice 28 Feb. 1991, n.y.r. and Case 131/88, *Commission v Germany*, judgment 29 Feb. 1991, n.y.r. Both cases involved Directive 80/68 on the protection of groundwater against pollution by certain dangerous substances O.J. 1980, L 103/1, and in both the Commission was successful in claiming that the Member State had failed to transpose adequately the Directive into national law.

[21] Note 8 *supra*.

[22] This has been the case for the United Kingdom and for Germany.

implementation date, and common sense suggests that at this stage a Member State faced with criticism may be more ready to modify the final version. In contrast, once national law has been passed, whether by way of primary or secondary legislation, there must be an understandable tendency on the part of the Member State to defend the status quo. Despite this, there appears to be no regular procedure, either as a legal requirement or as a matter of administrative practice, by which Member States and the Commission discuss draft texts of national laws during the period following agreement of a directive and the state for its implementation.[23]

5.   Implementation in Practice - Conceptual and Practical Difficulties

The third category, non-implementation in practice, is perhaps the most difficult area of enforcement for the Commission, and certainly one that can touch a raw nerve of the sensibilities of Member States. Examples of this category include the failure of local drinking water supplies or particular stretches of bathing waters to meet prescribed Community standards, the failure of a waste disposal licence to meet the prohibitions contained in the Groundwater Directive, failure to carry out an environmental assessment for a project falling within mandatory classes of the Environmental Assessment, and, in the future, no doubt the failure by public authorities to provide members of the public with information as required under the Access to Environmental Information Directive.[24]

The need to ensure effective implementation in practice has been endorsed by Member States, yet clearly there exist tensions and controversy when the Commission takes steps to pursue this task. To start with, it is not always clear whether a particular example of apparent breaches of Community law should be classified as incomplete or incorrect transposition of the Directive or a failure to implement in practice. One can again take the case of the Environmental Assessment Directive where a Member State has failed to introduce the necessary implementing legislation covering all the project classes specified in the Directive. A particular project in that Member State is proposed and no environmental assessment is undertaken. Is that a failure to implement the Directive in practice, or simply an example of the results of failing to correctly transpose the Directive into national law?

---

[23] During oral proceedings in Case 252/89, *Commission v Luxembourg* and Case 330/89, *Commission v Belgium* on 7 Nov 1990, both concerning the failure to implement the Environmental Assessment Directive, the Court expressed concern that the Commission had failed to give any response when Luxembourg had sent to the Commission the text of a proposed new law implementing the Directive.

[24] Directive 90/313 O.J. 1990, L 158/56.

At first sight, the distinction seems unimportant. The Article 169 legal procedures are the same whatever category of breach is alleged by the Commission. Yet compared with more general proceedings taken against a Member State for incomplete transposition, action initiated in respect of a particular project may have considerable local political impact, possibly even bringing pressure to suspend or bring to the halt construction of the project in question.[25] Furthermore, injunctive remedies from the European Court may be available to stop continuing work on an individual project, though the Commission's only experience to date with such proceedings in the environmental sector was unsuccessful.[26] Yet in reality in such cases it is the underlying failure of the Member State to introduce appropriate legislation which has given rise to the problem – indeed the national authorities dealing with such a project may themselves possess no power to require environmental assessment procedures.

The above illustrates a further difficulty with this type of infringement proceedings. Assuming that the national legislation is in place, failure to implement in practice may well be due to the action or inaction of a local or regional public authority, or even a local court. All such bodies fall within the overarching concept of the 'Member State', yet in practice it is the central governments of Member State who assume the responsibility for being at the receiving end of infringement proceedings. It is they who will be expected to take appropriate remedial steps against internal authorities who fail to implement Community obligations, be it by the use of default powers or the promotion of new legislation. In an era of greater regionalisation and where federalism is explained by its proponents to imply a real devolvement of powers as much as their centralisation, it must be questioned whether the current focus of infringement proceedings against Member States through the medium of central governments is still appropriate. There may well be a case for adopting a practice of permitting proceedings to be taken directly against the particular authority responsible for the failure in practice, at whatever level of government it is placed. Where a local authority makes an illegal planning decision in the United Kingdom, we expect to see judicial review proceedings taken against that body, not against the Secretary of State for the Environment even though he may have overall political responsibility for the planning system. The same should be true of infringement procedures if one is to view Community environmental

---

[25] It is interesting to note the application of the Environmental Assessment Directive in a procedure in the Netherlands, *Texaco v Minister van Economische Zaken*, where the president of the Court suspended, in summary proceedings, the approval of a plan involving construction of a conventional power station. See annotation by H. Sevenster, (1991) *Utilities Law Review*, 65-66.

[26] Case 57/89 *Commission v Germany*, [1989] ECR 2849.

law as a mature legal system integral to the national systems within Member States, and a stage removed from more straight-forward international agreements between individual States represented by their central governments.

We can identify further areas of tension that arise from dealing with the failure to apply directives in practice. The economic cost of complying with the requirements of Directives may often be the root cause of the failure to implement, and while some environmental Directives expressly incorporate an economic criterion such as 'best available technology not entailing excessive costs',[27] others do not.

An important case before the European Court of Justice in 1990 concerned the failure to implement the standards contained in the Drinking Water Directive[28] in local supplies, and suggests that in such cases the Court will take a strict attitude. Although the directive contained provisions allowing Member States to obtain derogations in exceptional cases, mainly due to particular geographical problems, financial and technical difficulties were not expressly mentioned. The Belgian Government had argued that the costs and complexities of constructing suitable treatment works in the localities specified had caused the delay in compliance. The Court rejected this as an excuse:

> . . . il y a lieu de rappeler que, selon la jurisprudence de la Cour, un État membre ne saurait exciper des difficultés pratiques ou administratives pour justifier le non-respect des obligations et délais prescrits par les directives communautaires. *Il en va de même pour les difficultés financiéres qu'il appartient aux États membres de surmonter en prenant les mesures appropriées.*
>
> (para 24) (author's emphasis)[29]

Many provisions in environmental directives involve various types of discretionary powers to be exercised by Member States or competent bodies, and the issue here concerns the principles on which the exercise of such discretionary powers should amount to a failure to implement a Directive in practice, giving rise to infringement proceedings. There

---

[27] See Directive 84/360 on combatting of air pollution from large industrial plants, O.J. 1984, L 336/1.

[28] Directive 80/778 relating to the quality of water intended for human consumption.

[29] Case 42/89, *Commission v Belgium,* judgment of the Court of Justice 5 July 1990, n.y.r. '... according to the Court's case law, a Member State may not rely on practical or administrative difficulties for the justification of failure to respect the obligations and time limits laid down by Community Directives. The same holds for financial difficulties, which it is for Member States to overcome by taking appropriate measures.' (Editors' translation).

is some emerging case law, though little in the way of developed principle.

A common provision of a number of environmental directives, particularly those concerning water pollution, is a power given to Member State to designate areas falling within the requirements of the directive. In the Bathing Water Directive, for example, Member States must designate areas of water to be subject to the standards contained in the directive, but the definition of bathing water is expressed in quasi-objective terms: all fresh water or sea water in which 'bathing is either explicitly authorised by the Member States, or is not prohibited and is traditionally practised by a large number of bathers' (Article 1.2). This has given the Commission clear leverage to question the determinations made by a Member State on the basis that water falling outside the definition had not been designated. Other Directives, though, contain no such objective definitions, but are expressed in a way that appears to given a clear discretion to Member States. But the failure by a Member State even to address the question of designation may render the aims of the directive ineffective, and here the European Court has held that in such cases there may be an infringement by the Member State.[30]

A similar issue has arisen in the case of the Environmental Assessment Directive which requires assessment procedures to be carried out in respect of proposals for projects falling within classes specified in the directive. For those falling within Annex I, assessment is mandatory, while for those falling within the much larger list in Annex II, assessment is required only where such projects may give rise to significant environmental effects; Member States are given discretion to determine appropriate criteria and thresholds to decide which particular projects falling within Annex II should be subject to assessment. Some Member States, initially at any rate, considered that this was an unfettered discretion giving them the right to exclude totally whole classes of projects from their national provisions on assessment. It is an interpretation that the Commission has firmly resisted; in order to achieve the aims of the Directive, Member States are obliged to address the problem of criteria and thresholds for *all* classes of projects specified within the Directive.

The European Court is likely to support this approach. That the failure by a Member State to address the exercise of a discretionary power may amount to an infringement of the directive is hardly contentious. A more difficult question, though, arises when it is sought to question the actual

---

[30] Case 322/86, *Commission v Italy*, [1988] ECR 3995 concerning the failure by Italy to designate waters under Directive 78/659 on the quality of fresh waters needing protection or improvement in order to support fish life O.J. 1978, L 222/1 and under Directive 79/923 on the quality required for shellfish waters O.J. 1979, L 281/47.

judgments made by Member States in the exercise of such powers. On what principles should both the Commission and the European Court approach to the issue? The Environmental Assessment Directive again provides good examples of the type of issue that increasingly is likely to arise. To what extent is the determination of specific thresholds for Annex II projects by a Member State a reviewable decision? Is the actual scope and content of assessment information provided in a particular case grounds for infringement proceedings? Should the decision by a local authority to grant permission for the proposed project to proceed, in the face of overwhelming evidence of adverse environmental effects, be questionable as a matter of Community law?

Leaving aside the particular wording of provisions of the Directive in question, one can assume that the exercise of discretionary power would be subject to such general principles as proportionally and non-discrimination. Thresholds for Annex II classes of projects, for example, which made a distinction between projects involving national interests and those of other Member States would therefore be contrary to Community law. Beyond that, principles of review are underdeveloped. But some suggestion of an appropriate approach is found in the 1990 decision of the European Court in *Commission v France*[31] concerning Council Regulation 3626/82 of 3 December 1982 on the implementation in the Community of the Convention on international trade in endangered species (the CITES convention). Under the Regulation, Member States are required to issue permits for the importation from third countries of certain specified animals or plants, and Article 10(b) provides that the import permit may only be issued where, *inter alia,* ' . . . it is clear or where the applicant presents trustworthy evidence, that the capture or collection of the specimen in the wild will not have a harmful effect on the conservation of species or on the extent of the territory occupied by the population in question of the species.'

The proceedings arose out of the decision by the French authorities in 1986 to grant permits for the importation of some 6000 wild cat skins from Bolivia. It was this decision that the Commission questioned. The decision of the French authorities had been taken against a background of international concern over illicit trade in wild animals from Bolivia, with a meeting of the contracting parties to the CITES Convention calling for a suspension of imports from the country until the Bolivian Government had demonstrated that it had adopted all practical measures to implement the Convention. The Commission had notified Member States of the terms of this Resolution, and in effect argued that in the light of these concerns, the French decision to grant import

---

[31] Case 182/89, judgment of the Court of Justice 29 Nov 1990 n.y.r.

permits must have been contrary to the terms of Article 10(b) of the Council Regulation. The French argued that the CITES Resolution had no legal effect, and that the decision whether or not to grant import permits was one for national authorities; indeed Article 9 specifically states that Member States shall recognise the decisions of competent authorities of other Member States, and that import permits granted by one country should be valid throughout the Community. The European Court held that there had been a breach of the Directive. In the light of the factual background and the terms of Article 10(b) the French authorities, according to A.G. Mischo,

> '...n'ont pas raisonnablement pu aboutir a la constation qu'il etait evident que la capture des chats sauvages en question n'aurait pas d'influence notive sur leur conservation ni sur l'entension de l'aire de leur distribution.'
> (Opinion, 18 October 1990, para 13)[32]

This appears to be very close to *Wednesbury* principles of judicial review of administrative decisions, familiar to British courts.[33] Certainly the very particular nature of the decisions that were the subject of the proceedings illustrates just how deep into the decision making of national authorities the process of enforcement of Community environmental law has reached. British courts have long subscribed to the principle that it is not for them to substitute their own judgment for those in administration entrusted with the task of decision-making. Yet the Bolivian import case comes perilously close to just that. How far the European Court and the Commission will elaborate principles of review which forbear from second judging administrative decisions is likely to prove a challenging area of law over the next decade, especially when set against the political pressures that emphasise the importance of ensuring implementation of Community law in practice.

---

[32] '... could not reasonably have come to the conclusion that it was obvious that the capture of the wild cats in question would not have a harmful effect on their conservation or on the extent of the territory occupied by their population.' (Editors' translation).

[33] *Wednesbury Corporation v Ministry of Housing and Local Government*, [1965] 1 WLR 261. In Case 42/84, *Remia BV v Commission*, [1985] ECR 2545 the Court of Justice reviewed the discretion of the Commission to determine the permitted duration of a non-competition clause under Art. 85(3) of the EEC Treaty. The Court recognised that the Commission's decision was based on a complex economic appraisal, and that its grounds for review should be limited, 'to verifying whether the relevant procedural rules had been complied with, whether the statement of the reasons for the decision is adequate, whether the facts have been accurately stated, and whether there had been any manifest error of appraisal or misuse of powers'. These principles were concerned with the Commission's decision-making functions, but it is suggested they might be use fully adapted to those of national authorities in the sorts of examples given in the text.

6.   Information Gaps and the Complaint Procedure

In the environmental sector, the Commission has no express powers to assist its investigations of the kind it has been granted in the competition field.[34] There are as yet no Community environmental inspectors, working alongside national enforcement officers, although the idea has been mooted in the past, and may yet surface again.[35] In 1990, the Council of Ministers adopted a Regulation establishing a European Environmental Agency, though as yet no location for the Agency has been agreed.[36] In any event, the title of the body is rather misleading, since its terms of reference are clearly restricted to data collection and analysis, largely in cooperation with national authorities. During discussions of the draft proposal, the European Parliament pressed hard for the Agency to have more explicit enforcement functions, but in the event managed only to secure a commitment in the Regulation to review the role of the Agency in this respect two years after it comes into existence.

Against this background, the Commission has been peculiarly dependent on its own complaint system to enable it to be alerted to possible infringements in practice. The procedures, governed by the Commission's internal rules of administration,[37] permit any member of the public, including environmental groups and industries, to notify the Commission of alleged infringements. The system is common to all areas of Community law, and was first developed in the 1960s in the context of the internal market. But it is environmental issues that have given rise to a spectacular growth in the numbers of complaints received, and they now represent almost half of all total number received annually by the Commission (Table 2).

A number of criticisms can be made about the current system. It means that the Commission is, initially at any rate, playing a largely reactive

---

[34] See Council Regulation No. 17 of 6 Feb. 1962, O.J. Special Edition 1959-62,87.

[35] In Nov 1991 the UK government called for the creation of a small Community 'Audit Inspectorate' to work alongside national enforcement bodies to monitor and report on compliance with EEC environmental legislation. Department of the Environment Press Release 25 Nov 1991.

[36] Regulation 1210/90 O.J. 1990, L 120/1. Despite pressure from the European Parliament to give the agency a more explicit inspection and enforcement function, the Regulation restricts its activities broadly to the gathering and assessment of environmental data, though even this limited role is likely to assist the Commission in its enforcement activities. Art. 20, however, provides that two years after the entry into force of the Regulation (which takes place when its location has been agreed) the Council, having consulted the Parliament and on the basis of a report from the Commission, must decide on further tasks for the Agency including, '... associating in the monitoring of the implementation of Community environmental legislation, in cooperation with the Commission and existing competent bodies in the Member States.'

[37] See note 17 *supra*.

role to the type of issues and subject matter raised; its stated commitment to investigate every complaint received, while a laudable goal of an administration exercising enforcement powers, leaves little room for strategic decision making, especially given the current limited manpower involved.[38] When the numbers of complaints are broken down on a country by country basis, it is clear that there are considerable disparities, which reveal as much about a country's tradition of environmental activism and political protest as they do about the state of implementation of Community law (see Table 3).

Table 2. Complaints registered by Commission 1982-90

	Environment	All sectors
1982	10	352
1983	8	399
1984	9	476
1985	37	585
1986	165	791
1987	150	850
1988	216	1137
1989	465	1195
1990	480	1252

Source: As Table 1 above

Table 3. Complaints registered in environmental sector 1990

Belgium	17
Denmark	3
France	47
Germany	56
Greece	40
Ireland	19
Italy	33
Luxembourg	3
Netherlands	7
Portugal	19
Spain	111
United Kingdom	125

Source: Commission

---

[38] According to Dr. Ludwig Krämer, the unit in October 1991 had a staff of 10 lawyers, six of whom were on secondment; evidence taken before House of Lords Select., Committee on the European Communities (Sub-Committee F) 13 Oct. 1991.

In the Commission's favour it should be stressed that these realities are recognized, and in the end there is a more balanced approach towards Member States than might be apparent at first glance. Complaints on a particular issue from one Member State may sometimes lead to an investigation of the state of compliance within all Member States, and the figures on the number of reasoned opinions and referrals to the Court indicate that action against Member States is not eventually dictated by the number of complaints received from each (Table 4).

Table 4. Reasoned opinions and referrals to Court of Justice in environmental sector 1989

	Reasoned opinion	Referral to ECJ
Belgium	8	11
Denmark	0	0
France	6	7
Germany	8	8
Greece	5	3
Ireland	5	0
Italy	16	7
Luxembourg	2	1
Netherlands	5	2
Portugal	4	0
Spain	9	3
United Kingdom	8	5

Source: Commission Report on Enforcement of Community Environmental Law 8/2/1990.

In 1990, the Commission took the bold step of releasing publicly figures on a country by country basis of the numbers of Article 169 letters that had been issued in the environmental sector, a deliberate political move to highlight the issue of implementation and one that caused considerable disquiet among some Member States at the time. One of the benefits of this unprecedented exercise in public administration was that, as with the reasoned opinions and Court referrals, it confirmed that enforcement action against Member States was not driven by complaint numbers, but probably reflected a reasonable approximation of the relative levels of compliance (Table 5). Nevertheless, when broken down on a sector by sector basis, the figures suggest that the current procedures are vulnerable to the focus of attention of national environmental interests (Table 6). The high number of infringements in the field of water pollution in the United Kingdom, for example, has been largely driven by highly directed campaigns by amenity bodies, while equivalent groups in France appear to have paid particular attention to hunting activities and the protection of wild animals.

Table 5. Article 169 formal letters in environmental sector 1989

Belgium	27
Denmark	5
France	28
Germany	13
Greece	37
Ireland	16
Italy	17
Luxembourg	9
Netherlands	18
Portugal	10
Spain	45
United Kingdom	18

Source: Commission Report on Enforcement of Community environmental law 8/21/90.

Note a number of Member States disputed the accuracy of these figures when they were released, though any errors appeared to have been marginal.

Table 6. Infringement proceedings sector by sector at 31.12.89

	Water	Air	Waste	Chemicals	Noise	Nature*
Belgium	11	3	18	5	2	7
Denmark	2	-	-	-	1	-
France	15	3	2	1	-	20
Germany	9	4	2	3	-	11
Greece	10	4	6	2	3	20
Ireland	7	2	3	2	-	7
Italy	9	4	10	2	3	12
Luxembourg	5	2	2	-	1	2
Netherlands	6	2	2	3	3	8
Portugal	2	1	4	-	-	7
Spain	12	2	10	4	-	29
U.K.	16	5	3	3	-	4

* includes environmental assessment

Source: As Table 5 above.

A further concern of present procedures is the extent to which the Commission may be dependent on a Member State's co-operation in complying with the Commission's initial requests for information following the lodging of a complaint. An absolute refusal to respond may result in the Member State being threatened with infringement proceedings for failure to comply with its duty to assist the Commission in its tasks under Article 5 of the EEC Treaty.[39] But the provision of poor or incomplete information by Member States poses peculiar difficulties for the Commission, and while in some cases site visits have been undertaken or consultants' reports commissioned, the current system is hardly geared to this type of intensive investigatory work, although it may be required.

Defective implementation in practice is likely to be a continuing focus of attention, and while in formal terms the dispute is between the Member State and the Commission it is clear that in practice private parties may find themselves heavily involved in the process. The complainant himself may dispute a decision of the Commission not to initiate infringement proceedings, particularly where his own private interests are being threatened by alleged illegal action, and given the limitations of the direct effect doctrine it may not be possible to raise such issues before national courts. But parties, other than the complainant, may also find their interests at stake. For example, the legality of an authorisation given under national law to a private project may be thrown into doubt should the Commission decided to commence proceedings against the Member State for failure to apply the Environmental Assessment Directive; similarly, a permit given to a private operator of a waste disposal facility may be questioned because of its incompatibility with the Groundwater Directive.

Current principles of Community law need development to recognise the reality of these relationships. Private interests which are indirectly involved in this way currently have no rights *vis-à-vis* the Commission to ensure that their point of view is heard during the investigatory procedures. The Court of Justice has continued to confirm that the decision to commence Article 169 procedures is a matter of discretion for the Commission, and that a third party, whether a complainant or, one must presume, another party directly effected by this decision, has no locus before the Court in such cases to question the legality of its action.[40]

---

[39] 'Member States shall take all appropriate measures, whether general or particular, to ensure fulfilment of the obligations arising out of the Treaty or resulting from action taken by the institutions of the Community. They shall facilitate the achievement of the Community's tasks.' See also the annotation of Case C-374/89, *Commission v Belgium* in this issue by

[40] Case 246/81, *Bethell v Commission*, [1982] ECR 2277; Case 87/89, *Societe National Interprofessionelle de la Tomate (SONITO) v Commission*, [1991] 3 CMLR 439.

The initiation of infringement proceedings concerning failure to implement in practice, is subject to no period of limitation of the type familiar to national systems of administrative law, and designed to provide legal certainty to private and public interests. The extent to which these types of issues are currently addressed is largely left to the discretion and sense of propriety of the Commission; if the enforcement process is to be strengthened and extended in future, the time may now have come to develop more considered legal principles governing the procedures.

7.   Some Concluding Remarks

The Commission's own achievements to date in revealing the extent to which deficiencies of implementation exist within most Member States underlines the continuing importance of the issue. New institutional arrangements such as the European Environment Agency,[41] the proposed network of national environmental bodies,[42] and the proposed environmental audit inspectorate[43] should all assist in improving the information flow on implementation gaps. But for the foreseeable future the Commission's enforcement role as legal guardian of the Treaty is likely to remain of central importance, and this article has identified a number of areas where current procedures and principles appear to require reassessment to improve both their efficacy and their acceptability. Full implementation of Community law, though, may always be an impossible goal, and in any event is unlikely ever to be achieved solely by the 'top-down' mechanisms implicit in the Article 169 procedure.[44] In the long run, it requires a genuine *internal* political will by Member States of the need to implement Community environmental policies, and this in turn demands both the dynamic participation of citizens and amenity groups, and an active recognition by national courts and authorities of their own role in giving effect to Community obligations. Until this occurs, the gap between the law in theory and in practice can be expected to remain intact.

---

[41] See n 35 *supra.*

[42] See n 5 *supra.*

[43] See n 34 *supra.*

[44] Notwithstanding the proposed provisions giving power to the European Court to impose financial penalties on Member States which failed to comply with its judgments; see new Art. 171(2) of Draft Treaty on European Union, following the 1991 Maastricht Summit.

INDEX

Aarhus Convention
    Access to Justice   216, 233-234, 239-243, 542-544, 679-681, 691-695
    Transboundary rights of public participation   679-683

Accommodatory model of decision-making   379-380

Administrative Penalties
    Appeal mechanisms   31-32, 93-99
    Current use   67-80
    Fixed penalties   82-85
    Income streams   91
    Private prosecution, relationship to   92
    Regulatory sanction, justification as   80-81, 257-259
    Variable penalties   29-31, 85-91

Aggregates Tax, whether a State Aid   473-476

Amsterdam Treaty
    Environmental integration duty   555-560
    Higher national environmental standards   561-564
    Legislative Procedures   560-561
    Sustainable Development as goal of EU   553-555

Ashby, Lord and concept of ignition events   17-18

Bathing Water Directive
    Non-compliance by Member States   289, 385, 745

Best Available Techniques   160, 232, 535, 537-541, 656

Best practicable environmental option   18-19, 422,

Bicycles and the law   433- 438

Biodiversity and free trade   444-447

Burke, Tom   188, 399

Cambridge Water Company case   373-375

Carnwath Report   213

CCTV, enforcement and privacy issues   414-418

Centralization, tendencies in
   environmental governance   191-193, 385-386

Codification of environmental laws   423-424

Command and control,see Regulation

Competition law
   Market abuse and environmental exemptions   431
   Greening public procurement   453-456
   State Aids and aggregate tax   473-476

Constitutional change and the environment   189-207

Contaminated land
   Contaminated soil a waste   463-466
   Liability of successor companies   498-501
   Liability for nuclear contamination   503-505

Corporate Rehabilitation Orders   124-129

Criminal Law
   Financial penalties, limitations of   28-29, 52-56, 99-101
   Heavy reliance on criminal sanctions in
     UK regulatory enforcement   47-51, 357-359
   Strict Liability Offences
     'Act or default' and   533
     Use of in regulatory sanctions   26-28
     Meaning of 'causes'   477-482
     Development in UK   367-369 , 372-374, 533
     Sentencing Guidelines   Council 41, 46

Cross-border participation under EC environmental law
   Enforcement of cross-border rights   683-691
   Environmental assessment   670-673
   Strategic environmental assessment   673-674
   Integrated Pollution and Prevention Control   675-676
   Water Framework Directive   676-679

Devolution
   impact on UK environmental policy   194-196, 200, 205-206

implications for enforcement action by
    European Commission   385-387, 658

Directive, see Subsidiarity

Drinking Water Directive
    Enforcement action against United Kingdom   385
    Financial difficulties not a defence by Member State   744
    Pesticide standards   378,
    Subsidiarity   655

Eco-labelling   382-384

Economic instruments
    Not a substitute for regulation   161-162, 165-166, 399

Elephant,
    Liability for escaping circus elephant   372-373
    Difficulties of estimating effective LSD dose   397

Energy Policy
    Judicial Review of Government Energy Policy   541-544

Enforceable undertakings as regulatory sanction   106-115

Enforcement
    Enforcement notices as enforcement tool   103-106
    Enforcement discretion   27, 143, 359, 372
    Penalty principles   26, 60-73
    Satellites   178
    Technological equipment   178
    Transparency   178-179, 369-372

English Nature
    Structure and functions   305-308

Environment Agency England and Wales
    Structure and functions   299-305

Environment Agencies in Europe, see Environmental Governance

Environment and Heritage Service, see Northern Ireland

Environmental Appeals
    Incoherence under UK law   217-226

Number of appeals 227-230
Concerns about appeal mechanisms 230-233
Role of Environmental Tribunal in handling appeals 250-256

Environmental assessment
 Cross-border participation 670-673
 Discretionary projects and judicial review 508-511
 Procedural requirements of EC Directive 488-492
 Transposition difficulties 741
 UK planning procedures incompatible with EC Directive 470-473
 UK difficult negotiations on draft directive 700

Environmental Court , Proposals in UK 22-23, 213, 209-262,
 see also Environmental Tribunal

Environmental externalities, problems of quantifying 158-159

Environmental Governance
 English Nature 305-308
 Environment Agency England and Wales 299-305
 Environment Agencies in Europe 317-321
 European Environment Agency 170, 200, 721, 730
 Executive Agencies 291-292, 294-295
 Environment and Heritage Service, Northern Ireland 281-286
 IMPEL (European Union Network for the
  Implementation and Enforcement of Environment Law) 688, 731
 Irish Environmental Protection Agency 311-316
 Non-departmental public bodies 292-296
 Non-ministerial Government Departments 296
 Northern Ireland 263-348
 Scottish Environment Protection Agency 308-311
 Swedish Environment Protection Agency 316-317

Environmental integration
 Duty under EC Treaty 424- 426, 555-560, 567-583
 Codification as form of integration 423-424
 Conceptual challenges involved 387-387
 Legal techniques 427-432
 Integrating with other areas of law 453-455

Environmental Law
 Codification 423-434
 Distinctive Character 233-235
 Formalism 169, 353-365
 Scope of 421-432

Environment rights , see also Human Rights
    European Community environmental law   201-203, 587-590,
                       662-665

Environmental Standards
    Expansion in UK pollution law   359-361, 376-381
    Opportunities to challenge   364-365
    And Legitimacy   393-401
    Development in European law   394-396

Environmental Tribunal, potential role in UK   22-23, 209-262

European Commission
    Enforcement Role against Member States   286-289, 384-386,
                       713-722, 735-753
    Chain of Regulation as enforcement concept   177
    Complaint system   287-288, 718-720, 729-730, 748-750
    Formal transposition   715-717, 726-728, 741-742
    Failure to implement in practice   717-718, 728-732, 742-748
    Notification of national law   714-715, 739-741
    Penalty payments by European Court of Justice   450-453, 489
    Proposals to improve system   590-595, 720-722, 723-734
    Systematic failure of national administration   719-720
    Rule of Law   595-598
    Subsidiarity and implications   658-659
European Convention on Human Rights
    Access to independent tribunal   245-246
    Environment   202-203, 587
    Nature conservation and designation of Sites of
       Special Scientific Interest   511-515
    Planning law and access to independent review   492-495
    Privacy and monitoring by satellite   412-415
    Self-incrimination and investigation by
       environmental regulators   482-485
    Sewerage flooding and human rights   495-498

European Environmental Advisory Bodies   336-338

European Union
    Cross-border rights of participation   661-695
    Development of environmental policies   196-198
    Environmental integration principle   424-428, 555-560, 567-583
    Environmental rights under EC
       environmental law   587-590, -665
    Global Player   700-701

Harmonizing influences   704-706
Member States ability to impose higher
  environmental standards   459-462, 468-470, 561-564
Need to define new goals for the market   603-5
Pre-emptive nature of economic freedoms   599-603
Subsidiarity   198-200, 667-670

Executive Agencies   291-292, 294-295

Food Standards Agency   296

German Council of Environmental Advisors   343-345

Genetically Modified Organisms
  Regional ban unlawful under EC law   468-479

Grant M 21,   213

GATT
  EU Trade restrictions   639
  Free trade provisions compared with EU   608, 616, 629
  Influence on EC Treaty   395, 601
  Scientific uncertainty   175

Grove-White, Robin   387

Habitats Directive, see Nature Conservation

Haigh, Nigel   169, 192, 385

Hampton Review on Reducing
  Administrative Burdens   13-14, 24, 44-45

Human rights, see also European Convention on Human Rights
  Access to review by independent
    court or tribunal   245-247, 492-498
  Environmental rights   201-203, 586-587

Integrated Pollution and Prevention Control
  Best Available Techniques and judicial review   537-541
  Cross-border participation rights under EU law   675-676
  Development of Integrated pollution control in UK   18-20
  Form of integration   421-423

Integration of environmental policies into other areas, see
Environmental Integration

Irish 5th Century law, extended liability concepts of   391-392

Irish Environment Protection Agency   311-316

Johannesburg Principles on the Role of Law and
Sustainable Development   213

Judicial review
    Number and type of environmental judicial reviews in UK 235-239
    Standing issues   534-537

Land fill tax   161-163

Leaded petrol
    Common law action against oil companies   390-391
    Differential taxes   161

Leggatt Review on Tribunals   31, 216-217, 238-239, 253-254

Local Government
    Delivery of environmental policy   192-194, 296-298

Macrory Review on Regulatory Sanctions   24-34, 35-154,

Monkey, liability for escaping and relationship to
    environmental law   367

Nature Conservation
    Biodiversity and free trade   444-447
    Designation under Habitats Directive, economic and social
    interests not relevant   440-450
    English Nature, role and structure   305-308
    Human rights and designation of Sites of Special
Scientific Interest   511-515
    Marine Waters and Habitats Directive   519-525
    Strategic environmental assessment and Habitats Directive   674

Nitrates Directive and polluter pays principle   442-444

Noise nuisance
    Defence of Public Interest   528-532

Damages in lieu of injunction	530-532
Non-departmental public bodies	292-296
Non-Ministerial Government Department	296
Northern Ireland	
Advisory bodies	335-336, 345-346
Departmental structures	276-281
Environmental Governance	263-348
Environment and Heritage Service	
Accountability mechanisms	329-334
Options for reform	321-329
Structure and functions	281-286
Northern Ireland Audit Office	333-334
Nuclear	
Judicial Review of Government Energy Policy	541-544
Liability for nuclear contamination	503-505
Nuisance	
Liability in public nuisance	505-508
Packaging Directive and Garden Centres	525-528
Parliamentary Select Committees	
Environmental policy, significance for	204-205
European Parliament , difficult relationship with	381-382
Regulators, need for Select Committee	145-146
Penalty principles	26, 60-73
Pesticide Controls	168-
Polluter pays principle	
Nitrates Directive	442-444
Pollution laws	
Development of	353-357
Environmental standards in	376-379
Precautionary Principle	174-176, 400, 516, 563, 614, 628-629

Public participation and access to information   362-365, 398
(and standards)

Regulation, see also Enforcement and Sanctions
    Chain of Regulation as enforcement concept   177
    Command and Control   159-161, 180 , 398-399
    Direct and Determine as new paradigm   179-180
    Economic instruments, limitations of   161-166
    Market failure as justification   157- 158
    Meaning of   155
    Voluntary agreements   166-171

Regulatory Enforcement and Sanctions Bill 2007,   34

Regulatory Governance, see also Environmental Governance
    Accountability and Transparency   132-147, 177-179
    Compliance deficit   57
    Enforcement policy   33, 67, 135-137
    Outcome measurements   33-34, 67, 137-139
    Output measurements   33, 139-140
    Penalty Principles   26, 60-73
    Perverse incentives need to avoid

Regulatory Sanctions, principles   26, 60-67

Regulatory Tribunal, role of   31-32, 94-99

Responsibility, need for extended notions of   389-392

Restorative Justice   32-33, 115-119

Risk assessment   172-176 , 397-398

Royal Commission on Environmental Pollution
    Structure and role   338-343
    5th Report (Air Pollution)   18-19, 360
    10th Report (Tackling Pollution)   19
    18th Report (Transport)   158, 164-166
    21st Report (Environmental Standards)   233
    22nd Report (Energy)   166
    23rd Report (Environmental Planning)   21-22, 209, 214-215, 254, 541

Sanctions
    Corporate Rehabilitation Orders   124-129
    Enforceable undertaking   106-115

Financial penalties, limitations of   28-29, 52-56, 99-101
Penalty Principles   26, 60-73
Profits orders   120-124
Publicity Orders   29, 129-131

Satellites and remote sensing
Digital images and evidential value   406-410
Data protection   416-419
Enforcement tool   404-406
Privacy issues   412-416

Science
Higher national standards under EC law   563-564
Scientific Uncertainty   396-397, 399-400
Sound Science, meaning of   173-74
Standards in legislation   380

Scottish Environment Protection Agency   308-311

Sentencing for regulatory offences
Corporate Rehabilitation Order   28
Criticisms of fines   52-56
Profits Order   28

State aid and aggregates tax   473-476

Statutory Nuisance   485-488

Strategic environmental assessment
Cross-border rights of participation   673-674

Strict Liability Offences , see Criminal Law

Subsidiarity
Access to Justice   685
Directives   651-652
Enforcement of EC law   658-659
General   649-659
Impact on EU environmental law   198-200, 566, 604, 667-670
Legal and policy implications   571-572, 654-657

Sustainable Development
Competing visions   190-191

Goal of EU Treaty   553-555
Johannesburg Principles on the Role of Law and
     Sustainable Development   213
Relationship to environmental standards   399

Swedish Environment Protection Agency   316-317

Third party rights of appeal   243-245

Toxicology and environmental standards   378, 396-397

Trade and environment
     Biodiversity and free trade   444-447
     EC and GATT compared   608, 616, 629
     EC law , free trade and environment   607-609, 616-629
     Significance for legal basis of EC laws   560-561, 629-643
     Pre-emptive norms of EC Trade freedoms   599-603, 612-613

Transport
     Bicycles and the law   433- 438
     Calculating externalities   158-159
     Fuel tax escalator   164-66

Voluntary Agreements   166-171

Waste
     Agricultural slurry not a waste   466-468
     Contaminated soil as waste   463-466
     Hazardous waste offences, European survey of   369-371
     Landfill Tax   161-162
     Recycling of waste and when ceases to be a waste   515-518
     Waste and by-products   456-459

Water
     Common law liability   373-375
     EU Water framework directive and cross
       border participation   676-679
     Sewerage flooding and human rights   495-498
     Strict liability for water pollution offences   477-482, 532-534

Winter. Gerd   397, 403, 418-419, 438

Woolf, Lord   21, 213

ABOUT THE AUTHOR

Richard Macrory is a barrister with Brick Court Chambers and Professor of Environmental Law at University College London where he is director of the Centre for Law and the Environment. After qualifying as a barrister, he was legal adviser at Friends of the Earth between 1975 and 1978, and then joined Imperial College, where in 1991 he became the first Professor of Environmental Law in the United Kingdom. Richard Macrory was the first chairman of the UK Environmental Law Association and founding editor of the *Journal of Environmental Law*. He has been Standing Counsel to the Council for the Protection of Rural England, was a member of the Royal Commission on Environmental Pollution for eleven years, and was chair of the steering board of European Environmental Advisory Councils in 2001-2. Professor Macrory has also been a specialist adviser to select committees in both the House of Commons and the House of Lords. Between 1999 and 2004 he was a board member of the Environment Agency, England and Wales, and was Hon. President of the National Council for Clean Air and Environmental Protection in 2004-5. In 2005-6 he was appointed by the Cabinet Office to conduct the Review on Regulatory Sanctions. He was hon. chairman of Merchant Ivory film productions for almost twenty years. Richard Macrory is the author of over 100 published articles and books on environmental law. He is currently legal correspondent to ENDS Report, and in 2006 was appointed a member of General Electric's Ecomagination Board. In 2000 he was awarded the C.B.E, for services to law and the environment and in 2008 was appointed a Q.C. (Hon Causa) for his work on the development of environmental law.